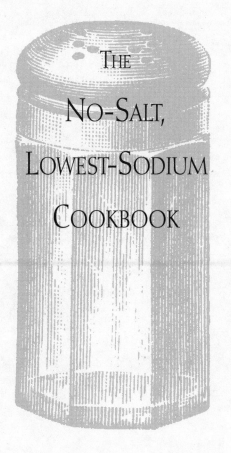

The
No-Salt,
Lowest-Sodium
Cookbook

The No-Salt, Lowest-Sodium Cookbook

❖ ▪ ❖ ▪ ❖ ▪ ❖ ▪ ❖ ▪ ❖

HUNDREDS OF FAVORITE
RECIPES CREATED TO COMBAT
CONGESTIVE HEART FAILURE AND
DANGEROUS HYPERTENSION

DONALD A. GAZZANIGA

THOMAS DUNNE BOOKS

ST. MARTIN'S PRESS

NEW YORK

THOMAS DUNNE BOOKS.
An imprint of St. Martin's Press.

THE NO-SALT, LOWEST-SOLDIUM COOKBOOK. Copyright © 2001 by
Donald A. Gazzaniga. All rights reserved. Printed in the
United States of America. No part of this book may be used
or reproduced in any manner whatsoever without written permission except in the case of brief quotations embodied in
critical articles or reviews. For information, address
St. Martin's Press, 175 Fifth Avenue, New York, N.Y. 10010.

www.stmartins.com

Book design by Carol Malcolm Russo/Signet M Design, Inc.

ISBN 0-312-25252-8

First Edition: January 2001
10 9 8 7 6 5 4 3 2 1

A Note to Readers

This book is for informational purposes only. Readers are advised to consult a physician before making any major change in diet.

CONTENTS

ACKNOWLEDGMENTS

I extend my heartiest thank-you to the following people who contributed to this book and helped test each and every recipe. When developing any recipe, often it must be prepared many times and by different people to ensure that it is correct. We did our best to make that happen here. The most difficult element in this testing was getting the testers to remember that flavors were going to change a bit here and there because of the extraction of salt, baking powder, baking soda, soy sauce, and other high-sodium foods. They performed wonderfully and I thank each and every one of them from the bottom of my heart.

The testers and contributors who participated were:

My wife, Maureen
Home Economist Marlene Winger
Michael Fowler, M.B., F.R.C.P., Stanford University School of
    Medicine
Sandra Barbour, M.D., Kaiser Permanente
Rebecca A. Gazzaniga, M.D.
Nasir Moloo, M.D.
Jeannie M. Gazzaniga, Ph.D., R.D.
Mary Waldman, R.N., Stanford Cardiovascular Clinic
Lisa Prikazsky, R.N., Stanford Cardiovascular Clinic
Valerie Cannon, Stanford Cardiovascular Clinic
Suzanne Domeny
Scott Domeny
Maria Lubamersky
Kim Craig
Susan Sundell
Nancy Vanberg (World's Greatest Cookie Maker)
Scott Leysath, The Sporting Chef
Kathleen Gazzaniga, M.S.

Shae Gazzaniga
Charlotte Gazzaniga, M.S.
Leon Silverman
Ken Chung (Hong Kong)
Michael McCay (Zarautz, Spain)
Mae DiMarco (Palermo, Sicily)
Picha Srisansansee (Bangkok, Thailand)
Sakar Moloo (Pakistan)

Contributions in this book are from:

Michael B. Fowler, M.B., F.R.C.P., Associate Professor of Medicine, Stanford University School of Medicine
Sandra Barbour, M.D., Cardiologist, Kaiser Permanente Group
Jeannie M. Gazzaniga, Ph.D., R.D., Research Scientist, Institute for Health and Aging, University of California, San Francisco
Rebecca A. Gazzaniga, M.D.
Marlene Winger, Home Economist, Southern Counties Gas Company
Scott Leysath, Master Chef, Silver Sage Caterers, Inc., The Sporting Chef, Inc.

This book would not have made it into your hands without the incredibly talented help of those at Thomas Dunne Books (St. Martin's Press), who worked diligently to make it happen. This book is not "just another cookbook," but instead a specially designed recipe book with a meal planning guide that required some rather intense parsing, typesetting, editing, reediting, and organizing. I owe all this to Ruth Cavin, without whom this book may not ever have been published. I also owe much to her assistant, Julie Sullivan, and to all the editors who worked so hard to get it here.
    Thank you.

                                        Donald A. Gazzaniga

INTRODUCTION

Congestive heart failure is a term used to describe a number of disease processes in which the heart fails to adequately perform its pump function. There are many causes of congestive heart failure in the United States, but the most common are atherosclerosis (narrowing of the arteries due to plaque buildup), heart attack (complete blockage of an artery to the heart causing death of the muscle supplied by that artery), and hypertension (high blood pressure).

In order to better understand "heart failure," it helps to visualize the circulatory system as simply another hydraulic system with the heart as its pump. The left side of the heart, specifically the left ventricle, pumps oxygenated blood to the various organs of the body. After nourishing the organs with oxygen and nutrients, the blood returns to the right side of the heart. The blood is then pumped by the right ventricle to the lungs where it is oxygenated. This blood then returns to the left side of the heart where the process begins anew.

If the muscle of the left ventricle is damaged by a heart attack, or weakened by high blood pressure, it cannot pump efficiently. Failure of the pump causes pooling of blood and buildup of pressure in various places, including your lungs and other organs. This causes "congestion," because the lungs are now congested with fluid and blood that would normally be pumped out to the tissues needing oxygenated blood. Imagine the failure of a pump that keeps a flood-prone basement dry: Water backs up, pressure increases, and eventually the pressure of the accumulated water causes it to seep through the basement walls. So, too, with the circulatory system.

Your doctor can prescribe medications to help your heart pump better, but there are two very important things you can do for yourself to help your heart, reduce congestion, and decrease symptoms of congestive heart failure: Reduce fluid intake and reduce your sodium intake.

Sodium comes in many foods and condiments, but the highest content is found in salt. The term "salt" refers to a number of chemical compounds that include sodium and potassium chloride. Salts in general, and sodium in particular, attract water and cause fluid retention. Thus, in people with heart failure and congestion, reducing sodium intake necessarily results in less fluid retention and therefore less congestion.

Sources of salt include not only what you add from the salt shaker, but from hidden sources as well. Examples of hidden sodium include baking powder, baking soda, soy sauce, most commercial tomato sauces, steak sauces, and other similar products that are excessively high in sodium. Often, a few slices of commercial breads have enough sodium for your total daily intake. (See the "Eating Out" section.) In evaluating the "salt" content of foods, you must pay close attention to the sodium content that is calculated in milligrams (mg) and is listed under the nutrition facts on the labels.

A general recommendation for those with congestive heart failure is to consume no more than 1,500 mg of sodium per day; lower is even better. Compare this with the average American diet that contains up to 8,000 mg a day.

Keeping track of one's sodium intake can be tedious and time-consuming, but it is very important. This cookbook helps you plan and prepare low-sodium meals in keeping with your doctor's recommendations. Each recipe in this book lists the sodium content per item, the total sodium per serving, and the total sodium per recipe.

Remember, even spices and condiments contain sodium. Even though a slice of tomato may have only 2 to 4 mg of sodium, the total amount of sodium consumed in a twenty-four-hour period should not exceed your doctor's recommendation.

You'll be able to enjoy delicious recipes for breakfast, lunch, and dinner. You can make your favorite breads, eat your favorite entrées, and enjoy many snacks and desserts without excessive sodium. With the help of this book, you can often get through most days with no more than 500 mg of sodium.

Remember, low-sodium means less congestion and improved quality of life. A low-sodium diet may also help reduce high blood pressure. If your doctor recommends a low-salt diet, this cookbook will permit you to enjoy great-tasting food and still comply with your doctor's recommendations.

SANDRA BARBOUR, M.D.
CARDIOLOGIST
KAISER PERMANENTE FOUNDATION

STRAIGHT TALK FROM A CARDIOLOGIST

❖ ❖ ❖ ❖ ❖ ❖ ❖ ❖

Dr. Michael B. Fowler, Fellow, Royal College of Physicians
Stanford Heart Transplant Clinic, Stanford Medical School

Few patients with heart failure fully appreciate the pivotal role that sodium plays in the severity of their symptoms, and their ability to be free of alarming sensations and avoid hospitalization. Conversely, those individuals who do understand the role of sodium and who adjust their diets to control their sodium intake at consistently low levels frequently experience a dramatic improvement in their general well-being. I have known many patients whose heart failure symptoms were recurrent and so severe that they were advised to undergo heart transplantation, yet these same patients improved so much with sodium restriction that they no longer required a heart transplant. *The author of this book is one of those. The diet he himself designed and followed brought his daily sodium intake to under 500 mg and had a profound impact on his ability to live without overt heart failure symptoms and thereby remove his need for a heart transplant.*

Heart failure from any cause is characterized by symptoms that result from retention of sodium (salt is the biggest culprit). Sodium is used by the body to regulate fluid status. In all circumstances that lead to heart failure sodium (and with it water) tends to be retained. In some individuals this may only be apparent at times of additional stress to the heart such as lack of blood-carrying oxygen (leading to angina), change in heart rhythm, intercurrent illnesses such as flu, or when the dietary intake of sodium is especially high (as with pizza). The majority of individuals with heart failure (and many with hypertension) have to combat a constant tendency to retain sodium. Those individuals are generally treated with diuretic drugs.

All diuretics ("water pills") work by increasing the amount of sodium removed from the bloodstream by the kidneys and from the body by elimination. Most diuretics also cause potassium to be lost, an undesirable side effect often requiring potassium supplementation and/or the use of special potassium-retaining diuretics.

The amount of sodium loss achieved by a diuretic is largely dependent on the dose of the drug and how often it is taken. The required dose of diuretics is strongly influenced by the dietary sodium intake, although an individual's diuretic requirement in heart failure also varies widely depending on other factors, including the tendency to retain sodium and the individual's sensitivity to the actual diuretics being given.

It follows that restricting sodium to a constant low level of ingestion is a crucial component to finding and maintaining the correct dose and type of diuretic. Too high a dose will cause a patient to be susceptible to dehydration and lightheadedness, particularly when the dietary sodium intake falls. A more common problem is that even high-dose diuretics may be incapable of removing all the sodium ingested by an individual who does not keep to a carefully regulated and restricted sodium intake. This will result in recurrent episodes of salt and water retention accompanied by breathlessness or abdominal bloating and possible swelling of the ankles. By using this book and sticking to a diet you design, you will achieve a constant level, one that should not alter your lowered level of sodium to the point where your diuretics react in a way you would not desire.

Individuals who remove all added sodium from their diet, whether that added by the manufacturer or in the patient's own kitchen, will provide the best environment to achieve the maximum improvement in symptoms and a reduced risk of hospitalization. These individuals will also create the clinical stability to achieve the correct doses of other drugs, especially ACE inhibitors and beta blockers necessary for the control of the patient's heart failure.

Here are some of the symptoms and adverse effects of sodium in heart failure:

· Difficulty in breathing, especially when lying flat. Waking at night short of breath. The need to sleep with additional pillows.
· Weight gain due to extra fluid. Bloating, especially of the abdomen. Swelling of the ankles.
· Thirst; an excessive desire to drink water.
· Increased diuretic requirements. "Refractory" sodium retention. Low concentration of sodium in the blood. Loss of potassium.
· Hospitalization; emergency room visits.

The benefits of low sodium achieved by a careful fresh food diet are:

- Allows stability of the diuretic dose.
- Allows stability of potassium replacement measures.
- Increases the possibility of optimizing the doses of other drugs that lessen the risk of major adverse events.

Such a regime usually also results in reduced fat intake (important especially in coronary artery disease or when the patient is overweight).

Patients with heart failure, especially those who are treated with diuretics or who take diuretics every day, will benefit from restricting their sodium to the few milligrams per day they find in food consisting of, or prepared from, fresh ingredients. The recipes in this book make it clear that there is little hardship when following this important aspect of living well and as long as possible with heart failure.

Patients who had previously had their dose of diuretics increased to deal with recurrent episodes of decompensated heart failure may become dehydrated and run the risk of reduced kidney function or spells of lightheadedness (or even blackouts) if they abruptly reduce their sodium intake from previously high levels. *Patients should discuss these issues with their physicians before making substantial changes in their sodium intake and ensure that they report these changes to their doctor.*

In general, be creative with your cooking ideas and have fun. If you have a "salt tooth," you can learn to prefer low-sodium food just by eating it. Within two months your tastes should adjust to the point where you won't miss the salt. Removing salt can bring out flavors that have been hidden by the salt.

Dr. Michael B. Fowler is a leading researcher in the medical field of congestive heart failure (CHF). Since 1982, he has been with the Stanford Heart Transplant Clinic, where he has been involved in research leading to the use of new beta-blockers such as carvedilol (Coreg) and low-sodium diets to help improve the quality of patients' lives as well as the survival rate for those who develop congestive heart failure.

The Importance of Good Nutrition for a Healthier Heart

Jeannie M. Gazzaniga, Ph.D., R.D.
INSTITUTE FOR HEALTH AND AGING, UNIVERSITY OF CALIFORNIA
SAN FRANCISCO

The keys to good nutrition are balance, variety, and moderation. High-fat foods must be balanced with high-fiber, low-fat foods, and calorie intake must be offset by enough activity to maintain a healthy weight. Variety is critical when choosing foods to ensure we get the optimum balance of nutrients. While some foods are more nutrient rich than others, no single food or food group has it all—so eating a variety of food is essential. Moderation means eating neither too little nor too much of any food or nutrient. Too much food can lead to excess weight, while too little of certain nutrients can lead to numerous nutritional deficiencies.

A healthy diet can help prevent—and even reverse—some forms of heart disease. But how can you achieve a heart-healthy diet? For starters, become familiar with the nutrients that make up a healthy diet. In general, there are seven categories of nutrients: fats, cholesterol, protein, carbohydrates and fiber, vitamins, minerals, and sodium.

Fats. Fats provide energy and help the body absorb and use fat-soluble vitamins. You need a certain amount of fat in your diet for good health. There are three major types of dietary fats: saturated, polyunsaturated, and monounsaturated. Foods that contain fats generally have a mix of all three types, just in differing proportion. Ideally, you should keep your fat intake to at or below 30 percent of your total calories, and limit your intake of saturated fats—which contribute to high blood cholesterol levels—to no more than 10 percent of your total calories. Saturated fat is found in foods from animal sources, such as meats and dairy products, and tropical oils, such as palm kernel and coconut.

Cholesterol. Cholesterol is a fat-like substance found in foods from animal sources, such as meat, poultry, fish, egg yolks, milk, and milk products. Cholesterol is not found naturally in fruits, vegetables, breads and cereals, nuts, seeds, or dry beans and peas. Your body needs some cholesterol for good health, but it actually manufactures all the cholesterol it needs. So, if the foods you eat contain too much saturated fat and cholesterol, you could raise your blood cholesterol levels and increase your risk of heart disease. Unless you are instructed otherwise by your physician, the American Heart Association recommends limiting dietary cholesterol to no more than 300 milligrams per day. This is roughly equivalent to the amount of cholesterol in one large whole egg. You will find in the twenty-eight days of menus provided in this book that we have tried to keep fat calories to less than 30 percent of total calories and cholesterol to fewer than 300 milligrams per day.

Protein. Protein is needed by the body to build and repair body tissues. Proteins are made of amino acids, of which the body requires twenty-two different amino acids to work properly. A food that supplies all the amino acids in the right amount is a complete protein. Foods from animal sources, such as milk, eggs, cheese, and meat, are complete proteins. Plant foods are incomplete proteins; however, they can be combined with other foods to provide the right amount of amino acids. Nevertheless, protein should make up only 12 to 15 percent of your daily calories—and the protein should come from low-fat sources such as lean cuts of **beef, fish, poultry,** and low-fat **dairy products.**

Carbohydrates and Fiber. Carbohydrates provide energy. Simple carbohydrates, such as sugars, are found in fruits, juices, and refined sugars. Complex carbohydrates, such as starches and fiber, are found in whole-grain breads, cereals, potatoes, pasta, and beans. Experts agree that we should eat at least 55 percent of our daily calories from carbohydrates, preferably complex carbohydrates, and avoid too much sugar. Increasing the amount of fiber in your diet is also a heart-smart move. Fiber-rich foods can help you lose or maintain weight because compared to other foods they tend to be low in calories, take longer to chew, and make you feel full. In addition, soluble fiber (includes pectins and gums) helps lower blood cholesterol levels by eliminating bile acids in the stools before they are absorbed into the bloodstream.

Vitamins. Vitamins are organic substances produced by plants or animals. Research has shown that vitamins do play an important role in disease prevention. Taken alone, certain vitamins will not prevent heart disease; but when used as part of an overall healthy lifestyle, they may have a beneficial effect. For example, antioxidants, primarily vitamins C and E and beta-carotene, may protect against cancer by stopping the damaging effects of "free radicals." Free radicals are created by normal functions of the body's cells and by environmental factors such as tobacco smoke. If left to do their dirty work, free radicals can damage the healthy cells in your body. In the long run the damage can be irreparable and lead to disease.

Antioxidant vitamins, especially vitamin E, may lower the risk of heart disease by reducing the buildup of fatty plaque on artery walls. Vitamin E is found in vegetable oil, margarine, eggs, fish, whole-grain cereals, dried beans, and wheat germ. Good sources of vitamin C are citrus fruits, berries, tomatoes, peppers, and leafy green vegetables. Beta-carotene, which is converted to vitamin A in the body, is found in orange, yellow, and green fruits and vegetables such as squash, carrots, sweet potatoes, peaches, spinach, and mangoes.

Another important vitamin is folic acid. Researchers believe there is a new risk for heart disease: elevated blood levels of homocysteine and folic acid may help lower this risk. Homocysteine is thought to be involved in the clogging of arteries. In Harvard's ongoing Physicians' Health Study, for example, men with high homocysteine levels had a three times greater risk of a heart attack than men with lower levels, even when other risk factors were taken into account. Researchers think elevated homocysteine levels may be linked to a genetic defect, but folic acid has been shown to lower homocysteine levels in the blood. Good food sources of folic acid include beans, peas, enriched whole-grain cereals, nuts, seeds, orange juice, and green leafy vegetables.

Minerals. Minerals also play a critical role in making a healthy diet. Minerals are important in bone structure, muscle contraction, blood formation, and many other body processes. Some minerals that are important for a healthy heart include calcium, potassium, and magnesium.

Eating foods rich in potassium will help protect people from developing high blood pressure. But do not take potassium supplements unless directed by your physician. Good food sources of potassium include many fruits (apricots, peaches, bananas, prunes, orange juice), vegetables (sweet potatoes, spinach, pumpkin, potatoes), dairy products, and fish.

Research has shown that populations with low dietary calcium intakes have high rates of high blood pressure. However, it has not been proven that taking calcium tablets will prevent high blood pressure. Rather, emphasis should be placed on calcium-rich foods such as low-fat dairy products, sardines and other fish, and green leafy vegetables.

A diet low in magnesium may make your blood pressure rise, but doctors do not recommend taking extra magnesium to help prevent high blood pressure. Rather, focus on foods rich in magnesium, including whole grains, green leafy vegetables, nuts, seeds, and legumes.

As with any major change in your diet, check with your physician first. And, remember, the keys to a healthy diet are balance, variety, and moderation.

Author's Note

This book may have been recommended by your physician. The recipes included here are to help you respond to your doctor's request that you substantially lower your sodium and salt intake. You'll find that they do not require any out-of-the ordinary foods or supplements. They are not intended to replace the advice of a physician. If you believe that a recipe may contain vitamins, supplements, or other ingredients that might affect your condition, please check with your physician first.

Be cautious about what you "hear" and even about what you read about your heart disease. Educate yourself and be wary about accepting anyone's guesses about your food, whether you read it in a newspaper or magazine, or see it on the Internet or on TV, or hear it in a restaurant. It's just too important to you now to let yourself absorb the wrong information. You can find out all you want to know about sodium in foods in this book or from reference materials and books listed at the end of this section.

The down and dirty truth is if you really want to lower your sodium intake (and you acknowledge that it is necessary and important to do so), you're going to have to adapt your tastes and food desires to new flavors and textures. Table salt, creams, cream cheeses, soy sauce, bottled sauces, ketchup, baking soda, baking powder all must be altered, dismissed from active duty, or just plain thrown out of our lives.

But all is far from lost. There are acceptable substitutes and more genuinely low-sodium foods on the market all the time. We use a baking powder called Featherweight, made by Hain, that unlike other baking powders has inconsequential amounts of sodium. It is available in health food stores. We use some no-salt-added canned goods, where they become necessary, such as tomato sauce and tomato paste. These new products are a boon for us, and we hope food processors figure it out and see that they have a huge market out here for such goods. Del Monte and Hunt's also make a no-salt, low-sodium ketchup. You'll find that most of the foods made our way are just as tasty and good as what you may be used to.

Speak with your physician and ask what kind of sodium regime you should be on. Some medical doctors feel it's impossible to get below 1,500 mg of sodium a day, even though it might be desirable. That's because before this book, creative low-sodium recipes were difficult to find. Using this book makes it possible and easy to lower your sodium count to as little as 500 mg a day.

You or someone in your household will have to prepare your meals—no more running out to the fast-food joint or ordering in takeout; not if you want your life to extend beyond what might have been an awakening prognosis. But you *can* eat out; it just takes a bit of forethought. . . .

Many restaurants have become more cooperative in preparing meals to conform to special dietary restrictions. However, even these restaurants may not understand what your requirements are when you ask for a low-sodium meal. They still believe that salt is sodium and exclusively so. These restaurants will assume that by leaving salt out of the preparation, they have cut out all sodium, but salt isn't the sole source of sodium. You'll have to ask them how they prepare everything you plan on ordering. Ask them if they use MSG, preservatives, sulfites on the salad, baking soda or baking powder, and whether or not the "griddle" or frying pan or grill has been brushed off from the previous use, which more than likely was sprayed with salt or some other such substance. Some restaurants also tend to use baking powder on steamed or cooked vegetables to preserve their color. Ask them, they'll leave it out if you request. Waiters and restaurant owners today are generally more amenable to these requests. You are the one who must make them, however. Progress is being made. It may surprise you to learn that Denney's Restaurants actually lists a low-sodium breakfast. It's still a bit high in sodium, but in a pinch it will serve.

I take my own sandwich bun with me when my family visits fast-food places. I order the burger cooked without salt, and "dry," that is, only the meat, lettuce, onion, and tomato. When it comes, I put the burger and its trimmings into my homemade bun, which has only 2 mg of sodium. That cuts about 600 mg from the fast-food bun and all the milligrams from the ketchup, salt, mustard, and any mayonnaise. They also usually accommodate my order of French fries without salt, although I am quick to let them know when they slip up on that. Considering the weight of the usual meat patty, I figure I'm eating about 40 mg of sodium, or cutting about 1,000 mg from the meal.

Restaurants with "precooked" meals, however, will present an almost impossible situation for you. My own fear has always been that I would become a big pain for those I ate out with. So I or my wife often call the restaurant in advance and tell them my needs. They have always accommodated me without any problems or any stress for my fellow diners. Choices on restaurant menus can often be juggled around to make an acceptable meal for you.

Airlines however, do not yet provide low-sodium meals. And if you ever have to spend the night at a hospital, ask your physician to order a low-sodium meal for you.

When you have become familiar with the kind of recipes in this book, you may want to adjust them or compose your own favorite dishes from scratch, *always keeping the sodium count at a level that ensures you are not eating more sodium a day than your doctor has recommended.* It's not difficult to do this, because each recipe has the sodium levels listed next to each ingredient. Complete nutrition data is also provided. Assuming you are as interested in nutrients as you are in eating low-sodium foods, these recipes will fill the bill. We use mostly fresh vegetables (although no-salt-added canned and frozen foods are acceptable since the sodium in these is all natural).

If you want less fat in the finished dish, you can adjust the amount given in the recipes. As an example, see the recipe for **Danny Boy's Chocolate Chip Cookies.** These delicious chocolate chip cookies are made for the general marketplace with butter, salt, and baking soda. We came up with a no-salt-added version low in fat and sodium and with no baking soda or baking powder. In place of butter, we used homemade applesauce, which makes an excellent substitute for butter or other fat in most baked goods. The changed version has almost 9 fewer grams of fat than the ordinary one, and we added some fiber and other nutrients. You'll find the recipe on page 346.

By keeping track of what you eat every day for a period of time, you'll soon figure out how to get to your sodium target. Even if it's as low as 500 mg a day, you can do it easily with the recipes in this book and the four-week meal planner at the end of the book (as a *guide, not* a bible). You may want to write down your own month's diet and add up the sodium (and fat) for yourself.

If you would like a reference book or software for your personal use, try *Food Values of Portions Commonly Used,* also known as

"Bowes & Church's," 17th edition, from Lippincott. Jean A. T. Pennington is the author. This is one of the most respected non-USDA nutrient-data publications in the United States. Another book that is readily available is *The Corinne T. Netzer Encyclopedia of Food Values,* from Dell, ISBN 0-44050367-1. Our software was from the Nutrition Company and is called Foodworks, ISBN 1-892219-00-X, copyright © 1998. You can contact them at:

The Nutrition Company
P.O. Box 477
Long Valley, NJ 07853
908/876-5580

For other sources of information we recommend:

FDA—www.fda.gov
American Cancer Society—www.cancer.org
American Dietetic Association—www.eatright.org
American Diabetes Association—www.diabetes.org
American Heart Association—www.amhrt.org
American Lung Association—www.lungusa.org
National Heart, Lung, & Blood Institute—www.nhlbi.nih.gov
National Stroke Association—www.stroke.org
Healthy Heart Market—www.healthyheartmarket.com

For recipe and book updates, log onto www.megaheart.com

If you have difficulty with any of these recipes, we'd like to hear from you. Please let us know what the problem was, or if you found any of the recipes inadequate. We'll do everything possible to fix it in future editions (and, with your permission, add your name to the list of testers).

If you have developed any low-sodium recipes and would like us to consider adding them in future editions of this book, E-mail it directly to the author at don@megaheart.org.

Thank you, everyone, for helping to make this a great guide for all of us who have had to change our diets in order to maintain and improve our health.

SOURCE OF SODIUM DATA USED IN THIS BOOK

◈ ◈ ◈ ◈ ◈ ◈ ◈ ◈

The sodium values in this cookbook are based on the most recent data supplied by the Food and Drug Administration (FDA) and the United States Department of Agriculture (USDA) and by manufacturers of many of the food products we use. We used a USDA-based software program called Foodworks, from The Nutrition Company, to list calories and all nutrients, including fats, cholesterol, protein, fiber, calcium, and sodium.

Nutrition labels, however, do not often list actual sodium per unit. For instance, if ⅛ teaspoon is the serving size and the package says 0 mg sodium, it may well be any amount up to 5 mg. This is because the FDA permits manufacturers to round to the nearest increment of 5. Thus, should your recipe call for 1 tablespoon, you could actually be adding up to 75 mg sodium, not a zero amount. Therefore, when the sodium count next to our ingredients doesn't match the package nutrition label you are using, you may assume that the package amount is rounded off.

Most sodium and other nutrient data listed by the USDA and manufacturers are averages. Foods are grown and treated differently in various parts of the world and can thereby acquire or lose sodium. Baking powder for instance can range from 290 mg per teaspoon (Tone's) to 480 mg per teaspoon (Calumet), depending upon the brand and where it was manufactured. The same goes for frozen foods, no-salt-added foods, and meats. Use this book as a guideline. If we err, we err on the high side.

Where we have listed specific manufacturer brands for use in no-salt recipes, we have checked with the manufacturer and obtained the exact sodium and other nutrient levels. We specify olive oil for oil cooking except where you may not care for the flavor. We suggest olive oil since it is the lowest in polyunsaturated fats. If, as we recommend, you use nonstick cooking utensils, the oil is only used for flavor. Values do not compensate for crop growing conditions, and your own method of cooking may also affect the nutrient contents.

A few canned or packaged products list numbers that may differ from USDA figures. Sometimes they are higher, sometimes lower. For instance, Sun Maid Raisins lists their golden seedless raisins at 10 mg for a ¼ cup. USDA figures for ½ cup of the same raisins is also 10 mg. A ¼ cup difference but nevertheless an error in one or the other. A good rule of thumb is that if anything is listed in fractions of a teaspoon you may want to look up the USDA figures unless you know the accurate count from experience.

When purchasing goods that publish nutrition labels, get used to reading them for sodium, fats, calories, and other nutrients. Make sure you know what you are eating. Also, when you read these labels, you will discover that manufacturers often use different serving sizes. Salt packages, for instance, often use ⅛ teaspoon as the serving size, although salted foods usually have more per serving, so sodium levels appear lower than they really are. Be sure to check these numbers so you will know what you are adding to your foods.

WHERE TO BUY THE LOW-SODIUM PRODUCTS FEATURED IN THIS BOOK

❖ ❖ ❖ ❖ ❖ ❖ ❖ ❖

A few low-sodium products may be purchased in the "natural food" section of many supermarkets. However, be aware that most "natural food" sections emphasize low-fat items, many of which are high in sodium. You can probably find "no-salt-added" foods from Del Monte, Hunt's, S&W, and other national brands at your local supermarket. Health Valley soups and stews are often found in the natural food section as well, but are also easily available from Healthy Heart Market (HHM) on the Web. HHM carries a variety of no-sodium or low-sodium food products, including spices, salt replacements, seasonings for all recipes, sauces, ketchup and other condiments. They can be reached at www.healthyheartmarket.com or by calling 1-800/753-0310 or by fax at 1-612/428-3926.

You can find a plethora of low-sodium foods at the chain called Trader Joe's. To locate a Trader Joe's nearest you, call 1-800/SHOPTJS and punch in your zip code. If there isn't a Trader Joe's in your area, go to www.traderjoes.com. At this writing they indicate they intend to sell via the Internet, although they are not yet set up for it. If you still find it difficult to obtain their products, call Healthy Heart Market and ask them to order the items for you.

Featherweight Baking Powder, a replacement for off-the-shelf baking powder, has approximately 500 mg less sodium per teaspoon. At this writing, the company that manufactures Featherweight, Estee, was purchased by Hain. Hain is a popular food and marketing company that may get Featherweight into local super-markets. Meanwhile, the product is generally available in health food stores and at HHM.

Unsalted beans, grains, butter, and other cooking items are generally available at your local market. Items like unsalted dips, chips, and other goodies are also usually available. If not, once again we recommend you call Healthy Heart Market. If you have trouble determining how much sodium or other nutrient is in a food you want to purchase, you can visit the Web site for the FDA (http://www.fda.gov/). This site will guide you easily through the maze and help you with nearly anything you need to learn about a food.

HIDDEN SODIUM

❖ ❖ ❖ ❖ ❖ ❖ ❖ ❖

Contrary to what many people think, table salt is far from the only source of sodium in our diet. It is present in almost everything we eat, least so in fresh fruit, herbs, and grains, but often these foods are processed in various ways that add sodium. It is important for you to read labels on the food you buy, or the nutrient listings on recipes you may want to try, and to understand what they mean. (See also the Source of Sodium Data, page 14.)

Unfortunately for us, there are many hidden sources of sodium in packaged, canned, frozen, and prepared foods. The most prevalent of these are:

SALT

(commercially produced salt is 99.9 percent pure sodium chloride; 2,350 mg sodium per teaspoon). The old "salt mines" no longer provide us our table salt. Sea salt is mined from the sea, but its sodium count is nearly as high with 2,132 mg per teaspoon.

BAKING SODA OR SODIUM BICARBONATE

(821 mg to 980 mg per teaspoon). Generally used to leaven breads and cake, added to vegetables in cooking (especially at restaurants), and often included in antacids. Thus far, there is no replacement on the market for baking soda.

BAKING POWDER

(320 to 480 mg per teaspoon, depending upon manufacturer). Used mostly to leaven quick breads and cakes. A brand called Feather-

weight makes a baking powder with only 2 mg sodium per teaspoon. You can find it in health food stores.

MSG, Monosodium Glutamate

A dangerous sodium for those who may suffer from asthma or migraine headaches. It is used as a seasoning in home, restaurant, and hotel cooking. It is present in packaged, canned, and frozen foods. Used extensively in Chinese restaurants and often is the flavor enhancer in foods that advertise "Natural Flavorings."

Low-fat foods often have a higher sodium count than the "standard" or higher-fat products. Some have as much as ten times more. Check your next purchase of sour cream and compare the labels. Do this with all products when considering the lower-fat option. This doesn't mean you should purchase the higher saturated fat products, only that you will want to be aware of the increased sodium while using the low-fat products.

Products marked "no salt added" may still contain sodium, so keep an eye out for the count and adapt it to any of your recipes.

Substitutes for Salt when Seasoning

We are all in luck. Several national companies have heard our plea and come up with herb and spice blends that are more than adequate substitutes for salt, but with no sodium. McCormick's, Lawry's, Spice Island, and Mrs. Dash are some of the brands. We specifically recommend the following mixes.

Frontier

"dash o' dill"
"oriental seasoning"
"cajun seasoning"
"mexican seasoning"
"pasta sprinkle"
"all-purpose seasoning"
"barbecue seasoning"
"salad sprinkle"
"pizza seasoning"

Fortner's numbers their blends, then in small type they suggest what to use them for. Although this can be an inconvenient system for remembering which is which, you only have to deal with these four:

#37 (complements poultry, pork, and vegetable dishes)
#55 (complements barbecue, broiling, oven roasting, and microwave dishes)
#75 (complements hamburger, meat loaf, ground meat, stew, and casserole dishes)
#89 (complements fish, salad, egg, seafood dishes, and sauces)

These are excellent flavorings to add to your no-salt cooking. If we don't specifically mention them with a recipe, that doesn't mean you shouldn't sprinkle one of them on your food. They are the best mix of herbs and spices we have found so far, but they will not help to preserve breads or other baked goods, as salt itself will.

Other spice blends available via the Internet (healthyheartmarket. com), or at your local health food store and sometimes your regular supermarket are:

SPICE ISLAND

Salt Free Herb Season
Salt Free Original Seasoning
Salt Free Spicy Pepper

MRS. DASH

Lemon & Herb Salt Free
Low Pepper–No Garlic–Salt Free
Garlic & Herb Salt Free
Original Blend Salt Free
Table Blend Salt Free

McCormick

Salt Free All-Purpose Seasoning
Parsley Patch Salt Free Garlic Saltless
Parsley Patch Salt Free Lemon-Pepper
Seasoned Pepper

Other Flavor Enhancers

Use the following spices and ingredients to replace salt in your recipes. Herbs and spices often do a better job. If you haven't been using these, you will acquire a taste for them, just as you once did for salt. These flavor enhancers have very little, if any, sodium in them.

ALLSPICE. Use with lean meats, tomatoes, peaches, stews, pies, applesauce, and gravies.

BASIL. Fish, lamb, lean ground meats, stews, pasta, salads, soups, and sauces.

BAY LEAVES. Excellent with lean meats, stews, poultry, soups, pasta, tomatoes, and sauces.

CARAWAY SEEDS. Lean meats, stews, soups, salads, breads, cabbage, asparagus, and pasta.

CHIVES. Salads, sauces, soups, potatoes, peas, beans, corn, and lean meat dishes.

CIDER VINEGAR. Salads, vegetables.

CINNAMON. Applesauce, oatmeal, fruit, breads, pie crusts, decaffeinated tea, cranberries, and fat-free cookies.

CORIANDER. Soups, meats.

CUMIN. Vegetables, beef, and lamb.

CURRY POWDER. Lamb, veal, chicken, fish, tomatoes, and soup.

DILL. Tomatoes, cabbages, carrots, cauliflower, soups, green beans, pasta, potatoes, salads, lean beef, chicken, and fish.

GARLIC POWDER (*not* garlic salt). Meats, fish, poultry, salads, vegetables, and garlic bread.

MUSTARD. There are currently many low-sodium mustard products available. Look for mustard with sodium levels below 15 mg per tablespoon.

MUSTARD SAUCE (see page 182). Lean meats, salads, asparagus, broccoli, Brussels sprouts, cabbage, and sauces.

NUTMEG Fruits, pie crust, lemonade, potatoes, lean meats, pies, toast, and pudding.

ONION POWDER (*not* onion salt). Lean meats, stews, fresh vegetables, hamburgers, salads, and soups.

PAPRIKA. Chicken pot pies, fish, lean meats, soups, salads, sauces, and fresh vegetables.

PARSLEY. Lean meats, soups, salads, sauces, and vegetables. Great with white-fleshed fish.

PINE NUTS. Salads, lean meats, green beans, salmon.

ROSEMARY. Chicken, lean meats, sauces, stuffings, potatoes, lima beans, and some bread mixes.

SAGE. Lean meats, stews, biscuits (substitute for salt in like quantity), tomatoes, green beans, fish, lima beans, onions, and lean pork.

SAVORY. Salads, lean pork, lean ground meats, soups, green beans, squash, lima beans, and peas.

THYME. Sauces, soups, onions, peas, tomatoes, salads, and lean veal and pork.

"SALT"

There are some "salt substitutes" on the market, but salt substitutes aren't always the solution. Most have enough sodium in them to render them useless for heart patients. Such salt substitutes are made by Morton, Lawry's Salt-Free, Estee, Featherweight, and Health Valley. These are difficult and sometimes almost impossible to find. Although they taste the same, they don't seem to provide the same "leavening" action needed in breads and, more important, are high in potassium chloride, which you may want to avoid. *Please check with your physician before adding these to your diet.*

GARLIC

Garlic was first mentioned in 5000 B.C. It has been praised in the Bible and in the writings of the Romans, Greeks, Hebrews, and ancient Egyptians. It was used as a cure by the ancients for many ailments and successfully by World War I doctors for treating typhus, dysentery, infections, and gangrene in battle wounds. Some Europeans, especially some Slavic people, continue to eat a raw clove of garlic daily to stave off colds and influenza left over from the worldwide flu epidemic in 1918 that killed 20 million people. And in Gilroy, California, the garlic capital of the world, thousands of people flock to the annual Garlic Festival. These visitors are treated to garlic in so many different recipes, meals, and desserts that it would take more than one volume to contain them.

It has been shown in epidemiological studies that garlic can lower serum cholesterol levels. Many researchers believe that garlic reduces serum cholesterol by somehow inhibiting its biosynthesis. They believe that eating garlic regularly could have dramatic effects on atherosclerotic heart disease. Along with these benefits, garlic has also been shown to lower high blood pressure. According to researchers, garlic expands (dilates) vessel walls. These same researchers have learned that garlic also thins the blood by inhibiting platelet aggregation. This reduces the risk of blood clots and helps prevent heart attacks.

You'll find that many of our recipes are *loaded* with garlic, which is not in our recipes for the purpose of curing or healing, but instead because we just happen to like the culinary addition of garlic for flavor. A heavier dose of garlic in most recipes where salt is called for tends to make up for salt's otherwise ubiquitous presence. Consequently, to gain health benefits with garlic and be able to lower sodium intake is a plus that few expect.

SUBSTITUTIONS

❖ ❖ ❖ ❖ ❖ ❖ ❖ ❖

There are some kitchen staples you feel you can't do without—and then you find that they are prohibitively high in sodium and you cannot eat them. What are you to do?

Help is on the way, if moving a bit slowly. Not only are there low-sodium substitutes for several common ingredients available in health food stores and over the Internet, but some long-established packagers of regular-count sodium foods have put out low-sodium, no-salt-added versions of their wares.

Hunt's, S&W, Contadina, and Del Monte are some of the familiar brands who have made no-salt-added tomato products available in supermarkets: canned tomatoes, tomato sauce, tomato paste, and tomato juice; even the high-sodium ketchup has a no-salt ketchup sibling. Estee also makes a low-sodium tomato ketchup. And, of course, especially in season, there are fresh tomatoes, which lend themselves beautifully to all sorts of recipes.

Healthy Heart has East Shore Mustard. The familiar Grey Poupon offers a honey mustard low in sodium. Mendocino Mustard, only available at this writing in the western U.S., is also relatively low in sodium.

Cheese is a no-no to heart patients in its usual form, but Tilla-mook makes a very low-sodium cheddar available everywhere a market will carry it. If a market carries Tillamook, the cheese can be ordered for customers. Probably easier for you to find is the some-what sodium-higher, but still acceptable Alpine Lace, which pro-vides a Cheddar, a Jack, and a "Swiss" cheese, the last being the lowest of the low-sodium cheeses.

Relishes and pickles can be a problem but you can make your own; try whipping up our **Dill Pickle and Red Pepper Relish.** We also provide a **Soy Sauce Replacement** that works, and a Texas firm called Southwest Seasoning makes a hot sauce called Chipotle del Sol that is both tasty and allowable. You can find it at Healthy Heart.

Check the labels on breakfast cereals; shredded wheat, for instance, has 0 mg sodium. Canned food tends to be much higher in sodium than fresh frozen—and usually fresh produce is best of all. But keep alert; you will certainly find, I believe, that as time goes on more and more manufacturers will wake up to the very large and active market that exists for low- and no-sodium packaged foods.

STAPLES

❖ ❖ ❖ ❖ ❖ ❖ ❖ ❖

MEATS AND SODIUM

All meats, including wild game, have an appreciable amount of sodium. Although wild game has relatively the same sodium levels as domestic meat, it is much lower in fat and cholesterol, and is therefore an excellent replacement for commercial meats. The following list shows the sodium and saturated fat content for domestic meat and domestically raised wild game or, if you hunt, the real thing. It has been recommended that people should lower their intake of animal meat because of its saturated fat content.

This list is provided as a guide only. Various meat grades will have different levels of sodium. This cookbook uses choice grade ¼-inch trim for all recipes except where noted.* Recipes in this book are more specific with each cut and grade of meat recommended.

BEEF (RETAIL TRIM ONLY; 4 OUNCES) Average sodium.

brisket, whole, all grades (69 mg ¼-inch fat; 74 mg 0-inch trimmed
    fat), chuck (67 mg ¼-fat; 70 mg 0-inch trimmed fat)
flank (0-inch trim, 79 mg)
ground, raw, extra lean (56 mg)
ground, extra lean baked, well done (73 mg)
ground, extra lean, pan-fried (79 mg)
ground, raw, lean (64 mg)
ground, lean, baked (81 mg)
ground, lean, broiled (101 mg)
ground, lean, pan-fried (87 mg)

*Meat trimmed to 0-inch or ¼-inch fat refers to the amount of fat present during cooking. For "lean only" listings, all visible fat is trimmed before cooking. (Bear in mind that a small amount of fat is always present, even in meat trimmed to 0-inch fat before cooking.)

porterhouse steak (69 mg)
ribs, whole (70 mg)
ribeye (73 mg)
round, full cut (69 mg)
shank crosscuts (69 mg)
short loin (T-bone, top loin, sirloin, top), broiled (70 mg)
tenderloin (71 mg)
corned beef (1,286 mg)
beef jerky, Hickory Farms (1,360 mg, 1 ounce)

LUNCHEON MEATS Generally not usable in low-sodium diets

WILD GAME (DOMESTICALLY RAISED OR HUNTED; 4 OUNCES)
Today you can purchase wild game meats at many butcher shops,
specialty markets, and in some areas at your local supermarket.

rabbit (48 mg sodium, saturated fat .5 g)
venison (deer, elk, antelope) (60 mg sodium, saturated fat 1.4 g)
quail, chukker, grouse (58 mg sodium, saturated fat 3.7 g)
wild bear (67 mg sodium, saturated fat 1.2 g)
wild turkey (80 mg sodium)

FOWL (BONE-IN, SKINNED; 4 OUNCES)

Chicken, broiler or fryer:
   Light meat (76 mg)
   Dark meat (96 mg)
Turkey, young hen
   Light meat (68 mg)
   Dark meat (84 mg)

PORK (4 OUNCES)

back rib, braised (74 mg)
loin, whole, braised (85 mg)
loin, blade, braised (78 mg)
loin, center, braised (58 mg)
loin, center rib, braised (59 mg)
loin, sirloin, braised (61 mg)
shoulder, whole, roasted (77 mg)
shoulder, arm, braised (116 mg)
shoulder cut, boneless (66.4 mg)

spareribs, braised (105 mg)
tenderloin, roasted (76 mg)

WATER

The recipes that use water require that you purchase bottled no-sodium water. I strongly recommend this when making soups, stews, and bread recipes. The water you use in your home has sodium in it. I elected when I started to work on this book to list water with 0 mg sodium simply because to use a national average would be misleading. If you live in Aberdeen, South Dakota (48 mg per 8 oz), for instance, 8 glasses of water a day would pretty much fill up your day's sodium requirements. If you live in an area with the national average listed by the USDA (7.11 mg per cup), 8 glasses of water would not harm you or add so much as to push you over the top.

But many of us live in areas where the sodium is even lower than 7.11 mg. I didn't want to present recipes with false figures, so I recommend the sodium-free bottled water.

To learn what your water has in it, you can call your water agency. Most of them have these figures on file and will send you a copy right away.

If you live, as I do, in the country or where you use ground water, you can get a local lab to test your water for all nutrients, sodium included, and even check to see if your water may have toxins.

If you don't want to purchase bottled water for your cooking and drinking use, then please add in the sodium levels of your water to each recipe calling for water. You can figure the serving amount by dividing the number of servings into the figure.

COOKING OILS

Right from the top, let me suggest that you get rid of all foods in your house where the ingredients include cottonseed, palm, and palm kernel oils. These foods can include processed cookies, crackers, cereals, coconut, margarine, and solid vegetable shortenings. The culprit here is the hydrogenation of these oils. To replace hydrogenated margarine, use unsalted butter or extra-virgin olive oil, expeller-pressed canola oil, or dark-roasted sesame oil when you want the sesame oil flavor. Buy your oil by the small bottle, not by the large can. Oils can turn rancid quickly after opening. When that happens, they become just as harmful to your heart and general health as hydrogenated oils.

If you use, as we suggest, good nonstick cookware, you need not use any oil or butter, but you may want it simply for the flavor.

You can find extra-virgin olive oil in your supermarket. Expeller-pressed canola oil can be found in some supermarkets or at your local health food store. Dark-roasted sesame oil can be found in a Chinese or Japanese grocery store or in your supermarket's Asian food section. You may want to avoid the canola oil available in your local supermarket, since it has been extracted using chemicals. If you cannot find expeller-pressed canola oil, then use the supermarket brands sparingly. We use mostly olive oil in this book except where the olive oil flavor may interfere with the cooked item. In those cases we suggest canola oil or unsalted butter. If any of the recipes in this book turn out to have too much olive oil flavoring for your taste, then switch to the canola oil or unsalted butter. In all baked goods calling for butter, we suggest replacing the butter with **Homemade Applesauce.**

SUGAR

If sugar is a problem, then in most of our bread recipes where sugar is used, you can leave it out. Where we use juices like orange juice, apple juice, etc., you may replace them with like amounts of water. Entrées using brown sugar or even white sugar can be cooked without the sugar but in some cases a replacement flavoring will be needed. Pies, cakes, and cinnamon rolls generally cannot be made without sugar. If you have any questions about a recipe's content and suggested replacement for sugar, and have Internet access, visit www.megaheart.com and click on the "Ask the Chef" icon.

IODINE REPLACEMENT

A salt-free diet can deplete your normal iodine intake and that in turn could bring about an iodine deficiency problem. The sodium level of iodized salt averages 2,350 mg per teaspoon; noniodized salt comes in at around 2,132 mg. Both are too high for hypertensive or heart disease patients.

However, iodine is needed by everyone, in uncountable trace amounts. It's needed for a healthy thyroid gland and the prevention of goiter.

Good food sources of iodine besides iodized salt include asparagus, garlic, mushrooms, sesame seeds, seafood, saltwater fish, kelp, and lima beans. You can also obtain iodine from spinach, summer squash, soy beans, and turnip greens. Another way to add iodine to your diet is with a daily vitamin tablet supplement that contains iodine. Check the label to make sure you are getting 100 percent RDA for iodine.

MISCELLANEOUS

Salt is used as a preservative in many foods. When we take out the salt, we find we have to be more strict about refrigerating the foods we make. Our low-salt brownies will be a bit heavier, but oh, my, just as tasty.

When we take out heavy cream, we discover the consistency of the food we make changes, but the flavors are for the most part retained.

The eggs we use are "medium," about 55.5 mg of sodium unless otherwise noted. "Large" eggs have about 63 mg.

EATING OUT

BY MARLENE WINGER, HOME ECONOMIST

CAN WE EAT OUT SAFELY?

Many restaurants have become more cooperative in preparing meals for special dietary restrictions. However, even these restaurants may not understand what your requirements are when you ask for a *low-sodium* meal. They may still believe that salt is the only sodium in their menu. Salt has sodium in it, but it isn't the sole source of sodium. These restaurants often assume that by leaving salt out of the preparation, they have cut out all sodium. Unfortunately, many restaurants use other ingredients to enhance some of their servings. Baking powder, MSG, sulfites are used for salads, fresh and steamed vegetables, and even some meats and fish. Packaged sauces are used for meats, salads, desserts, and of course, any cheese items or spreads are very high in sodium.

You'll have to ask them how they prepare everything you plan on eating. Ask them to brush off the griddle or pan which more than likely was sprayed with salt or some other such substance. Some restaurants also tend to use baking powder on steamed or cooked vegetables at the beginning of the day, to keep them appearing fresh when they "prepare" them. Ask them to use vegetables that haven't been through an early day preparation. (You'll often get: "Oh, we don't do that here." But many do.)

Waiters and restaurant owners today are generally more amenable to these discussions. You may even discover that others have "taught" them before you arrived. So many Americans are on a no-salt, low-sodium diet that the waiter's experience with our request for a low-sodium meal often precedes our first visit. Just a few weeks ago I visited a popular restaurant in Ft. Bragg, California. I was ready. But right after I'd explained that I needed a very low-sodium meal, the waitress put her hands up and said, "Can do. But you can't have our bread, because each slice has over 200 milligrams of sodium." I could only smile. Someone had already "trained" this waitress.

You, however, are the one who must initiate the conversation and, if necessary, the cooking instructions.

Progress for low-sodium eating-out is being made. It may surprise you to learn that Denny's Restaurants actually list a low-sodium breakfast. It's still a bit higher in sodium than I like, but in a pinch it will serve.

The author of this book takes his own sandwich bun with him when his family visits fast-food places such as In-N-Out Burgers. (He has grandkids, and you know where they like to eat.) He orders the burger cooked without salt and "dry," that is, only the meat, lettuce, onion, and tomato. When it comes, he places the contents of the burger into his homemade bun with its 2 mg of sodium. That cuts about 600 mg from the fast-food bun and all the mg from the ketchup, salt, mustard, and any mayonnaise. He also orders French fries without salt and they usually accommodate, although he is quick to caution that many fast-food companies don't always succeed with that effort since their potatoes arrive already salted. With the weight of the usual meat patty, he figures he's eating about 40 mg of sodium per burger, or cutting about 1,000 mg from the meal.

THE
RECIPES

❖ ❖ ❖ ❖

NOTE: WHEN A RECIPE MENTIONS ANOTHER RECIPE
IN THIS BOOK, THE NAME OF THE OTHER RECIPE APPEARS
IN **BOLDFACE TYPE**. YOU WILL BE ABLE TO FIND
ITS PAGE NUMBER BY CONSULTING THE INDEX.

APPETIZERS

❖ ❖ ❖ ❖ ❖ ❖ ❖ ❖

❖ ROASTED GARLIC TOAST ❖

MAKES 16 SERVINGS   SODIUM PER RECIPE: 42.6 MG
SODIUM PER SERVING: 2.662 MG

While in Milan a few years ago, I ate dinner at the Michelangelo Hotel. They served a great garlic bread, so I had to ask what their recipe was. The spread had no salt, but the bread did. Use your own freshly made bread for this one. With very low sodium this is a great treat with spaghetti, linguine, or any other Italian pasta dish. It's also terrific by itself.

6 **whole heads garlic* (23.1 mg)**
3 **tablespoons olive oil† (trace)**
2 **tablespoons unsalted butter (3.124 mg)**
1 **or 2 homemade Crusty French Bread Baguettes, page 248**
   (11.7 mg)

1. Preheat the oven to 375°F.
2. Cut off the papery tips at the stem end of the garlic heads. Brush generously with 2 tablespoons of the oil and place in a garlic roaster and bake for about 1 hour, or until garlic is soft but not browned. Once roasted, the garlic will spread like soft butter.
3. While the garlic is roasting, slice the baguette loaves lengthwise into two pieces. Combine the butter with the remaining tablespoon of olive oil and lightly coat the baguette slices.
4. When the garlic is ready, toast the buttered baguette slices on a baking sheet under the broiler until golden brown, or bake in the oven at 375°F for about 8 to 10 minutes. Spread the roasted garlic on the toasted baguette slices. Serve hot.
5. Can be dipped into our **Homemade Marinara Sauce** (page 146)‡.

Calories: 141. Sodium: 2.66 mg. Fiber: 0.89 g. Protein: 2.863 g. Carbohydrate: 18.3 g. Cholesterol: 9.71 mg. Calcium: 19.9 mg. Iron: 1.679 mg. Potassium: 69.9 mg. Total Fat: 6.4 g; Saturated fat: 2.6 g, Monounsaturated fat: 2.9 g, Polyunsaturated fat: 0.5 g.

*It is best to use the whitest heads you can find.
†Use slightly more if needed.
‡Be sure if you use the Marinara as a dip that you count the sodium intake for the Marinara, too.

Cajun Chicken Wings with Honey
❖ and Cayenne Pepper ❖

MAKES 15 CHICKEN WINGS   SODIUM PER RECIPE: 402.3 MG
SODIUM PER CHICKEN WING: 26.8 MG

A great party appetizer. The original version of this appetizer calls for deep-fat frying, and in California, restaurants serve it with blue cheese dressing. I like to bake these instead and eliminate the blue cheese entirely. For flavor enhancement I use cayenne pepper, which is considered by many to be a strong antioxidant. This is due to the presence of capsaicin, which is the hot element in the fruits of cayenne. Whether its antioxidant properties help you or not, cayenne does turn these chicken wings into an exciting snack or meal.

15 **skinless chicken wings (285 mg)**
¼ **cup unbleached flour (.625 mg)**
 4 **teaspoons cayenne pepper (2 mg)**
⅛ **teaspoon black or white pepper (.1 mg)**
¼ **teaspoon sage (trace)**
 2 **medium egg whites, well beaten (109.6 mg)**
⅓ **cup honey (4.75 mg)**
 2 **tablespoons distilled or red wine vinegar (.3 mg)**
 2 **teaspoons arrowroot powder (2 mg)**

1. Preheat the oven to 450°F.
2. Wash and dry the skinless chicken wings. Combine the flour, 1 teaspoon of the cayenne, the black or white pepper, and the sage. Dredge the chicken in this mixture, coating each wing well. Dip the wings into the egg white mixture and transfer the pieces to a lightly oiled baking sheet. Bake in a 450°F oven, turning once, until crisp and brown but not blackened. While chicken is cooking, mix well the honey, the remaining cayenne pepper, the vinegar, and the arrowroot in a nonstick saucepan. Heat to boiling while stirring with a whisk until the mixture is thick. When ready, pour it over the chicken wings.

Calories: 77. Sodium: 26.26 mg. Fiber: 0.16 g. Protein: 7.165 g. Carbohydrate: 8.488 g. Cholesterol: 18 mg. Calcium: 2.239 mg. Iron: .187 mg. Potassium: 24.1 mg. Total Fat: 1.8 g: Saturated fat: 0.5 g, Monounsaturated fat: 0 g, Polyunsaturated fat: 0 g.

❄ MARINATED BEEF STRIPS ❄

MAKES 12 SLICES   SODIUM PER RECIPE: 201 MG   SODIUM PER SLICE: 16.8 MG

This recipe originally came to us as elk carpaccio, or raw elk marinated and eaten without cooking. We played with it and came up with the following cooked meat appetizer. You can use leftover meat or cook it for the purpose. It's best if the cooked meat is medium rare.

12 ounces cooked beef, pork, or lamb (198.2 mg)
 2 tablespoons freshly squeezed lemon juice (.3 mg)
 2 tablespoons extra-virgin olive oil (trace)
 1 tablespoon red wine vinegar (.15 mg)
 1 clove garlic (.51 mg)
 1 tablespoon cayenne pepper or freshly ground black pepper
    (1.59 mg)
 2 tablespoons fresh minced basil (.212 mg)

1. Place the cooked meat in the freezer until very cold but not frozen. Slice it as thinly as possible. You should be able get at least 12 slices from a 12-ounce tenderloin or other full piece of meat.

2. Arrange equal portions of sliced meat on six plates. Combine the lemon juice, olive oil, vinegar, garlic, pepper, and basil and drizzle it over the meat. Let stand 3 to 4 minutes before serving.

Calories: 85. Sodium: 16.75 mg. Fiber: 0.15 g. Protein: 5.219 g. Carbohydrate: .641 g. Cholesterol: 2.46 mg. Calcium: 4 mg. Iron: .648 mg. Potassium: 101.1 mg. Total Fat: 6.7 g; Saturated fat: 0.4 g, Monounsaturated fat: 0.8 g, Polyunsaturated fat: 0.1 g.

❄ DEVILED EGG APPETIZER ❄

MAKES 12 HALVES   SODIUM PER RECIPE: 379.2 MG
SODIUM PER EGG HALF: 31.6 MG

 6 large hard-cooked eggs (378 mg), shells removed
 1 clove garlic, minced (.5 mg)
½ teaspoon dry mustard (0 mg)
½ teaspoon pepper (.462 mg)
 3 tablespoons vinegar (.45 mg)
    Dash paprika (.178 mg)

1. Halve the eggs lengthwise. Slip out the yolks and mash them with a fork. Mix in the garlic, mustard, pepper, and vinegar. Fill the egg halves with egg-yolk mixture. Heap it up lightly to make a mound. Sprinkle with paprika.

Calories: 39. Sodium: 31.63 mg. Fiber: 0.04 g. Protein: 3.175 g. Carbohydrate: .703 g. Cholesterol: 106.25 mg. Calcium: 13.6 mg. Iron: .427 mg. Potassium: 37.6 mg. Total Fat: 2.5 g; Saturated fat: 0.8 g, Monounsaturated fat: 1 g, Polyunsaturated fat: 0.4 g.

❈ BABA GANOUJ ❈

SERVES 6   SODIUM PER RECIPE: 36.2 MG   SODIUM PER SERVING: 6.04 MG

*Everyone has heard about the benefits of the Mediterranean diet.
This tasty preparation makes a wonderful sandwich spread or a
dip for vegetables or salad.*

2 eggplants (6 mg)
   Juice of 1 lemon (.47 mg)
½ cup fresh sesame butter or tahini (15.4 mg)
6 cloves garlic, minced (3 mg)
½ cup chopped scallions or green onions (8 mg)
   Dash black pepper (trace)
1 red onion, chopped (optional) (3.3 mg)
1 tablespoon extra-virgin olive oil (trace)

1. Preheat the oven to 400°F.
2. Pierce the eggplants all over with a fork. Place them directly on the
oven rack. Bake for 45 minutes, or until soft. Scoop out the centers and
mash them well. Add the lemon juice, sesame butter, garlic, scallions,
black pepper, and onion. Chill thoroughly. Drizzle the olive oil across the
top before serving either as a dip, sandwich spread, or pita filler.

*Calories: 174. Sodium: 6.04 mg. Fiber: 1.8 g. Protein: 4.745 g. Carbohydrate: 11.8 g. Cho-
lesterol: 0 mg. Calcium: 220.5 mg. Iron: 4.326 mg. Potassium: 197.9 mg. Total Fat: 13.3 g;
Saturated fat: 1.9 g, Monounsaturated fat: 5.8 g, Polyunsaturated fat: 5 g.*

❈ VEGETABLE PLATTER WITH HERB DIP ❈

SERVES 12   SODIUM PER RECIPE: 252 MG   SODIUM PER SERVING: 21 MG

   Romaine lettuce leaves
1 cup whole cherry tomatoes (16.2 mg)
1 cup broccoli florets (19.2 mg)
1 cup snow peas, trimmed (2.5 mg)
2 small zucchini, cleaned and sliced (7 mg)
1 pound crookneck squash, sliced (7.8 mg)
½ pound mushrooms, halved (7.36 mg)

DIPPING SAUCE
1 cup nonfat plain yogurt (187.4 mg)
2 teaspoons tarragon, minced (2 mg)
¼ teaspoon dry mustard mixed with 1 teaspoon extra-virgin
      olive oil (trace)
1 green pepper, top and seeds removed (2.38 mg)

1. Arrange the vegetables on a romaine-lined platter. Mix the dipping sauce ingredients in a small bowl. An added touch is to remove the top of a bell pepper, clean out the ribs, and use it as a bowl for the sauce.

Calories: 38. Sodium: 20.99 mg. Fiber: 1.71 g. Protein: 2.634 g. Carbohydrate: 6.345 g. Cholesterol: 0.37 mg. Calcium: 61.1 mg. Iron: .812 mg. Potassium: 315.3 mg. Total Fat: 0.7 g; Saturated fat: 0.1 g, Monounsaturated fat: 0.3 g, Polyunsaturated fat: 0.2 g.

❈ PIZZA SNACKS ❈

MAKES ABOUT 36 BITE-SIZE SQUARES   SODIUM PER RECIPE: 17.5 MG
SODIUM PER BITE-SIZE SQUARE: .487 MG WITHOUT CHEESE
When my nephew Zach was eight he decided these should be called "Pizza Snacks," and that's what we have called them ever since.

THE DOUGH
   1 cup water (0 mg)
3½ tablespoons extra-virgin olive oil (trace)
   2 teaspoons basil (.958 mg)
   1 tablespoon sugar (.126 mg)
4½ cups best for bread flour (11.2 mg)
   2 teaspoons bread machine yeast (3.96 mg)

1. Combine the above ingredients in your bread machine and select the Dough cycle. While this is happening, prepare the topping or sauce. (You can substitute the **Marinara** recipe for pizzas in this book if you like.) Once the dough is ready, spread it out on a lightly greased pizza sheet or cookie pan. Cover and let rise.

THE TOPPING
   2 cloves garlic, crushed (1.02 mg)
   ¼ cup extra-virgin olive oil (trace)
1½ tablespoons sweet basil (.159 mg)

1. Preheat the oven to 375°F.
2. Spread the garlic, olive oil, and basil on the dough and bake it for up to 30 minutes. (You may later want to add some marinara and mushrooms or other vegetables to give it more punch, but the "cracker" style of the pizza crust makes a great appetizer.)
3. Cut the pizza into bite-size squares and serve.

Per bite-size square. Calories: 84. Sodium: 0.49 mg. Fiber: 0.51 g. Protein: 1.724 g. Carbohydrate: 12.5 g. Cholesterol: 0 mg. Calcium: 4.61 mg. Iron: 1.034 mg. Potassium: 25 mg. Total Fat: 3 g; Saturated fat: 0.4 g, Monounsaturated fat: 2.1 g, Polyunsaturated fat: 0.3 g.

❖ FRANK LLOYD WRIGHT MUSHROOMS ❖

SERVES 8   SODIUM PER RECIPE: 17.3 MG   SODIUM PER SERVING: 2.168 MG

I call these Frank Lloyd Wright Mushrooms because of my first experience with mushrooms as a complete entree. As a brand-new Marine Second Lieutenant infantry officer, I had just reported to Japan for staging to my outfit. I ran into a childhood friend in Tokyo, and he took me to dinner at the Imperial Hotel, designed by Frank Lloyd Wright and built before World War II. We were served a huge platter of steaming hot (cooked in oil) mushrooms. That was the total course, except for the ubiquitous sake. I was amazed and at first disappointed. But the meal turned out to be delicious and ample. Later, I developed this recipe for serving appetizers. It's as close to what we were served as I can remember.

1 **pound button mushrooms (15.4 mg)**
2 **tablespoons extra-virgin olive oil (trace)**
3 **teaspoons minced garlic (1 mg)**
¼ **teaspoon thyme (.191 mg)**
¼ **teaspoon marjoram (.116 mg)**
¼ **teaspoon ground coriander (.159 mg)**
   Pinch ground cloves (.5 mg) (optional)
   Pepper to taste (trace)

1. Combine all the ingredients and marinate for an hour or more in the refrigerator. Place the mushrooms on a grill or in a lightly oiled pan and roll around until lightly browned. Serve hot.

2. If using the barbecue or a broiler, use the cooling rack for the grill or skewers to keep the mushrooms from "falling through."

Calories: 43. Sodium: 2.17 mg. Fiber: 0.65 g. Protein: 1.064 g. Carbohydrate: 2.558 g. Cholesterol: 0 mg. Calcium: 5.495 mg. Iron: .705 mg. Potassium: 182.2 mg. Total Fat: 3.6 g; Saturated fat: 0.5 g, Monounsaturated fat: 2.5 g, Polyunsaturated fat: 0.4 g.

❧ BECKY'S STUFFED MUSHROOMS ❧

MAKES 12 APPETIZERS   SODIUM PER RECIPE: 160.2 MG
SODIUM PER SERVING: 13.4 MG

My sister Becky is a committed vegetarian with a large book of her own recipes. She grows much of her own food. This appetizer actually serves her as a complete meal after a long day in her garden.

12 large fresh mushrooms (11 mg)
 6 tablespoons extra-virgin olive oil (trace)
 2 cloves garlic, crushed (1 mg)
¼ teaspoon thyme (.191 mg)
 1 tablespoon parsley (5.874 mg)
⅛ teaspoon marjoram (trace)
⅛ teaspoon oregano (trace)
 1 medium onion, chopped (3.3 mg)
 3 medium-size celery stalks, chopped (104.4 mg)
 1 tart green apple, cored, peeled, and chopped (0 mg)
   Pepper to taste (trace)
 1 quart cubed homemade bread (8.676 mg)
 1 cup Scott's Vegetable Broth, page 43 (25.6 mg) or use Herb-Ox Low Sodium instead (5 mg)

1. Preheat the oven to 350°F.
2. Wash the mushrooms and remove the stems. Warm 2 tablespoons of the olive oil over medium-high heat in a large skillet. Add 1 clove crushed garlic and the thyme, and stir for 2 minutes. Add the whole mushroom caps and sauté them for a few minutes, moving them around occasionally so that they brown evenly. Remove the mushrooms and set them aside. Add the remaining olive oil to the skillet along with the second clove of garlic, the herbs, the chopped onion, the celery, and the apple. Chop the mushroom stems and add them to the skillet, stirring often. Sauté the mixture until the onions are transparent. Add the bread cubes, and toss well with the other ingredients. Pepper to taste.
3. Continue cooking the mixture until the bread cubes have absorbed the butter. If it seems too dry, moisten with a little **Vegetable Broth.** Stuff the mushroom caps, pressing several spoons of the mixture into each one and forming a small mound on top. In a large nonstick baking dish with a tight-fitting lid, arrange the stuffed mushrooms in a single layer. Pour the remaining broth into the dish and cover it tightly.
4. Bake the mushrooms for 45 to 50 minutes. Serve hot.

Calories: 157. Sodium: 13.35 mg. Fiber: 1.85 g. Protein: 2.61 g. Carbohydrate: 17.5 g. Cholesterol: 0 mg. Calcium: 18.3 mg. Iron: 2.176 mg. Potassium: 205.6 mg. Total Fat: 7.9 g; Saturated fat: 1.1 g, Monounsaturated fat: 5.6 g, Polyunsaturated fat: 0.8 g.

❈ MUSHROOM KABOBS ❈

SERVES 6   SODIUM PER RECIPE: 31.5 MG   SODIUM PER SERVING: 5.25 MG

From Russia with love. Simple appetizers, easy to make.

½ **pound large button mushrooms (7.36 mg)**
2 **tablespoons olive oil (trace)**
2 **tablespoons plain nonfat yogurt (23.4 mg)**
1 **teaspoon minced garlic (.5 mg)**
¼ **teaspoon thyme (.191 mg)**
⅛ **teaspoon cayenne pepper (0 mg)**

1. Combine all the ingredients in a large bowl and marinate for 1 to 3 hours. Arrange the marinated mushrooms on skewers and grill until lightly browned. Serve with the basting sauce for dipping or as cooked.

Calories: 51. Sodium: 5.26 mg. Fiber: 0.41 g. Protein: .973 g. Carbohydrate: 2.031 g. Cholesterol: 0.09 mg. Calcium: 13.7 mg. Iron: .485 mg. Potassium: 129.6 mg. Total Fat: 4.7 g; Saturated fat: 0.6 g, Monounsaturated fat: 3.3 g, Polyunsaturated fat: 0.4 g.

❈ QUICK NACHOS ❈

**MAKES 15 PORTION SERVINGS   SODIUM PER RECIPE: 423.6 MG
SODIUM PER SERVING: 28.2 MG**

1 **bag of unsalted tortilla chips* (43.6 mg)**
8 **ounces Ortega canned hot jalapeno peppers or fresh Anaheim chilis (160 mg)**
4 **ounces shredded Tillamook Low Sodium Cheddar Cheese (210 mg)**

1. Spread chips on a large lightly oiled cookie sheet. On top of the chips lay diced fresh jalapeno, Anaheim or chili peppers.
2. Cover this with grated Tillamook Low Sodium Cheddar and broil in the oven until the cheese melts. Serve hot.

Calories: 43. Sodium: 28.24 mg. Fiber: 0.08 g. Protein: 1.962 g. Carbohydrate: 2.081 g. Cholesterol: 6.67 mg. Calcium: 7.181 mg. Iron: .018 mg. Potassium: 2.256 mg. Total Fat: 3 g; Saturated fat: 1.6 g, Monounsaturated fat: 0.1 g, Polyunsaturated fat: 0.1 g.

*Available nationally under various brand names. Most bags are 16-ounce or one-pound. If you can't find it in your area, write to Mexi-Snax Inc. T., 2035 W. Winton Ave., Hayward, CA 94545-1207, or phone (510) 786-2751, and ask them where you can find their unsalted tortilla chips. Also available at Trader Joe's, and specialty stores elsewhere. Also available on the web at www.healthyheartmarket.com, or call Healthy Heart Market at 1-800/753-0310.

Soups

❖ ❖ ❖ ❖ ❖ ❖ ❖ ❖

Those of us whose sodium intake must remain low must not eat canned soups. Not even the newer "low salt" soups. You can make your own soups without salt, but you'll probably want more spices, garlic, and other taste enhancers in each batch. Although most of the tomato bases for many soups come in cans with high sodium levels, a few companies are now producing tomato paste and other tomato products with no added salt. Del Monte, Hunt's, Estee (now Hain—under the Featherweight brand name), and S&W are four that I know of who put out "no-salt-added" stewing tomatoes and peeled tomatoes. These are okay to use if you calculate the sodium from each recipe you create.

❖ BASIC CHICKEN BROTH ❖

MAKES 6 CUPS   SODIUM PER RECIPE: 58.2 MG   SODIUM PER CUP: 9.704 MG
*This is a basic low-sodium chicken broth you can make in a few hours. Store it in the freezer for up to six months or refrigerate for use within three days. For another chicken broth recipe, see **Chef Scott's Chicken Broth** (page 42).*

 8 cups water (0 mg)
   Giblets and bones of 1 chicken (57.8 mg)
 2 thin slices peeled ginger root (.5 mg)

1. In a large pan, cover the giblets, bones, and ginger root with water and bring to a boil. Reduce heat, cover, and simmer for about 2 hours. Strain the broth through a strainer or cheesecloth and use it immediately for cooking or soup. You may store it in the refrigerator for up to three days or in the freezer for up to six months.

Calories: 16. Sodium: 9.7 mg. Fiber: 0.01 g. Protein: 2.246 g. Carbohydrate: .316 g. Cholesterol: 32.75 mg. Calcium: 1.35 mg. Iron: 11.4 mg. Potassium: 31 mg. Total Fat: 0.6 g; Saturated fat: 0.2 g, Monounsaturated fat: 0.1 g, Polyunsaturated fat: 0.1 g.

❧ MOTHER'S CHICKEN BROTH ❧

MAKES 10 CUPS SODIUM PER RECIPE: 198.2 MG. SODIUM PER CUP: 19.8 MG
A real home-style broth.

1 chicken carcass, wing bones, leg bones, backbones, totaling 5
    pounds*
3 medium onions, cut into chunks (9.9 mg)
1 large celery stalk (55.7 mg)
½ cup chopped fresh parsley (16.8 mg)
3½ quarts water (0 mg)

1. In a large 8-quart soup pot combine all the ingredients. Bring the mixture to a boil, then cover and simmer for 3 hours. Strain the broth into a bowl and chill it in the refrigerator. When the fat has congealed on top, scoop it off and store the broth in the freezer to use as needed.

Calories: 60. Sodium: 19.81 mg. Fiber: 0.8 g. Protein: 3.65 g. Carbohydrate: 3.271 g. Cholesterol: 23.61 mg. Calcium: 41.2 mg. Iron: 3.477 mg. Potassium: 115.9 mg. Total Fat: 3.6 g; Saturated fat: 1.1 g, Monounsaturated fat: 1.7 g, Polyunsaturated fat: 0.5 g.

❧ CHEF SCOTT'S CHICKEN BROTH ❧

MAKES UP TO 10 CUPS SODIUM PER RECIPE: 972.6 MG
SODIUM PER CUP: 97.3 MG

Scott Leysath has taught me more than I thought I wanted to know about cooking. One of his passions is that good cooking demands the use of "homemade" everything, including broth. This chicken broth serves beautifully for many of the recipes in this book that call for broth instead of low-sodium bouillon. (Make a batch and freeze some in small Mason jars for future use.)

3 pounds skinless chicken parts (20 chicken wings, 6 necks, and
    8 sets of fat-trimmed giblets) (871.6 mg)
3 to 4 quarts water (0 mg)
2 stalks of celery, cut into 1- or 2-inch pieces (69.6 mg)
1 large yellow onion, quartered (4.5 mg)
1 clove garlic (.5 mg)
2 bay leaves (.273 mg)
1 large carrot, cut into 2-inch pieces (25.2 mg)
8 black peppercorns (.924 mg)

1. Clean the chicken parts and put them into a pot and cover with water. Bring to a boil over moderate heat. Skim the fat and scum that rises to the

*You can use chicken, turkey, or other fowl wing bones, leg bones, or backbones.

top of the water. Add the rest of the ingredients and return to a boil. Partially cover the pot and occasionally skim the fat from the water during this period. Let it cook for about 1½ to 2 hours. When ready, remove and strain the ingredients through cheesecloth; a sieve with a fine mesh will also work. Discard the chicken and vegetables. Cool, chill, and remove the rest of the fat from the broth. Save in canning jars in your refrigerator for future use. If you want to preserve the stock for a longer time, place it in vacuum-seal bags or ½-quart jars (filled only ½ full) and store it in the freezer.

Calories: 182. Sodium: 97.26 mg. Fiber: 0.72 g. Protein: 21.5 g. Carbohydrate: 4.022 g. Cholesterol: 184.86 mg. Calcium 24.7 mg. Iron: 17.4 mg. Potassium: 307.7 mg. Total Fat: 8.3 g; Saturated fat: 2.3 g, Monounsaturated fat: 2.4 g, Polyunsaturated fat: 1.9 g.

SCOTT'S VEGETABLE BROTH

MAKES 8 CUPS   SODIUM PER RECIPE: 204.8 MG   SODIUM PER CUP: 25.6 MG
Scott Domeny is a trained chef but also works as a river guide and high school home economics teacher. He developed this vegetable broth.

- **3 medium celery stalks with leaves (105 mg)**
- **2 large carrots (50.4 mg)**
- **3 yellow Spanish onions (9.9 mg)**
- **2 medium green peppers, skin on (4.76 mg)**
- **2 cups shredded cabbage (25.2 mg)**
- **1 teaspoon thyme (.7 mg)**
- **1 bay leaf, shredded (.3 mg)**
- **1 teaspoon sweet basil (1 mg)**
- **8 black peppercorns (8 mg)**
- **3 quarts water (0 mg)**

1. Slice celery and carrots into ½-inch pieces. Cut the onions and peppers into 1-inch chunks. Place all the ingredients into a stockpot and simmer, partially covered, for 8 hours or overnight. Stir occasionally. Skim off any scum that appears. Cook it this way for 45 minutes. (If you use a Crock-Pot, cook at low heat for 8 to 12 hours. Skim scum when done.) Remove the ingredients from the pot and strain the stock through cheesecloth or a cheesecloth-lined vegetable strainer or sieve. Throw out the solids, then simmer the strained stock until it reduces to about 8 cups.

Calories: 40. Sodium: 25.57 mg. Fiber: 2.7 g. Protein: 1.365 g. Carbohydrate: 9.177 g. Cholesterol: 0 mg. Calcium: 41.3 mg. Iron: 3.877 mg. Potassium: 275.5 mg. Total Fat: 0.3 g; Saturated fat: 0 g, Monounsaturated fat: 0 g, Polyunsaturated fat: 0.1 g.

❧ BROCCOLI SOUP ❧

SERVES 6   SODIUM PER RECIPE: 442.7 MG   SODIUM PER SERVING: 73.8 MG
*Here's a popular soup usually made with cream and adapted to a
low-sodium, low-fat recipe. Not only is this tasty, it's loaded with
vitamins A and C.*

  3 **cups finely chopped broccoli florets and peeled stems***
     (57.5 mg)
1½ **cups water (0 mg)**
  1 **tablespoon unsalted butter (1.56 mg)**
 ½ **cup chopped onions (2.4 mg)**
  1 **tablespoon flour (1.56 mg)**
  3 **cups nonfat milk (378.5 mg)**
  2 **garlic cloves, crushed (1 mg)**
 ½ **teaspoon pepper (.462 mg)**
 ⅓ **teaspoon paprika (.235 mg)**
 ¼ **teaspoon celery seed (.8 mg)**

1. In a 3-quart saucepan, add the broccoli to the water and bring it to a
boil. Simmer, covered, for 10 minutes. Drain, and reserve the liquid. Melt
the butter in a larger saucepan. Sauté the onions until soft. Blend in the
flour and cook until thickened. Add the milk, broccoli, and the garlic, pepper, paprika, and celery seed. Blend together and heat slowly. Serve the
soup hot.

*Calories: 82. Sodium: 73.78 mg. Fiber: 1.44 g. Protein: 5.659 g. Carbohydrate: 10.5 g. Cho-
lesterol: 7.39 mg. Calcium: 175.9 mg. Iron: 2.587 mg. Potassium 351.3 mg. Total Fat: 2.3 g;
Saturated fat: 1.4 g, Monounsaturated fat: 0.6 g, Polyunsaturated fat: 0.2 g.*

❧ SPANISH BROTH / COCIDO ❧

MAKES 6 CUPS   SODIUM PER RECIPE: 705 MG   SODIUM PER CUP: 117.5 MG
*This tasty broth can also be served as a stew or soup. For soup,
simply cut the meat from the bones and into bite-size pieces and
chop the vegetables into smaller pieces.*

  1 **medium carrot (21.4 mg)**
 ½ **large leek (7 mg)**
 ½ **turnip (41 mg)**
   A 3-pound stewing chicken (459.8 mg)
 ½ **pound meaty pork ribs (172 mg)**
 ½ **teaspoon saffron (.5 mg)**
  2 **cloves garlic, minced (1 mg)**

*Peeled broccoli stems are great for salads, too.

1. Clean the carrot and halve it lengthwise. Split the leek and wash it thoroughly, then trim and quarter it, and also quarter the turnip. In 4 quarts of unsalted water in a large pot, simmer the chicken, pork, carrots, leek, and turnip for 1 hour. Stir in the saffron and simmer for another 2 to 3 hours. Skim when necessary. When done, let the broth cool for 30 minutes. Strain it through a strainer or cheesecloth into a large bowl and let it cool to room temperature. Skim any fat from the surface, cover, and refrigerate overnight. When removing from refrigerator, skim any fat from the surface.

TIP: You can refrigerate this broth for about 3 days or freeze it for a month or two.

Calories: 265. Sodium: 117.47 mg. Fiber: 0.64 g. Protein: 27.5 g. Carbohydrate: 3.083 g. Cholesterol: 90.59 mg. Calcium: 33.5 mg. Iron: .692 mg. Potassium: 412 g. Total Fat: 15.1 g; Saturated fat: 4.9 g, Monounsaturated fat: 5.7 g, Polyunsaturated fat: 2.4 g.

❖ SQUASH SOUP ❖

SERVES 8   SODIUM PER RECIPE: 46.5 MG   SODIUM PER SERVING: 5.8 MG
This easy-to-make soup has vitamins, extremely little fat, and is as low sodium as you can get for a tasty soup.

1 **large queen or acorn squash, or 1 to 2 pounds banana squash (any winter squash will do) (13 mg)**
4 **medium potatoes, peeled, cut into 1-inch squares (28 mg)**
1 **tablespoon olive oil (trace)**
1 **large onion, finely chopped (4.5 mg)**
2 **cloves garlic, minced (1 mg)**
· **Frontier all-purpose seasoning blend to taste (0 mg)**
· **Pepper to taste (trace)**

1. Preheat the oven to 400°F.
2. For queen or acorn squash, cut the squash in half. Scrape out the seeds, place face- or cut-side down on a shallow baking bag or dish filled with a quarter inch or so of water. If using banana squash, place it facedown on the same dish but make sure you have a sharply curved piece of squash. If not, place a piece of outer-layer skin under the edges of the squash so that the piece is just off the surface of the pan. Bake for 45 to 60 minutes.
3. While the squash is baking, bring 3 cups of water to a boil in a large pan or pot. Add the potatoes, reduce the heat, and simmer for 20 minutes. Now, heat the olive oil in a small frying pan. Add the onion and garlic and sauté until the onion is translucent. When the squash is done, dig or cut out the meat and add it to the potatoes and water. Mash this mixture together until chunky (don't use beaters), then add the rest of the ingredients. Now you may add the spices to taste. Let this simmer for another 20 to 30 minutes. If you want a thinner soup, add a little more water.

Calories: 89. Sodium: 5.81 mg. Fiber: 2.06 g. Protein: 1.848 g. Carbohydrate: 17.7 g. Cholesterol: 0 mg. Calcium: 22.9 mg. Iron: .441 mg. Potassium: 219.5 mg. Total Fat: 1.8 g; Saturated fat: 0.3 g, Monounsaturated fat: 1.3 g, Polyunsaturated fat: 0.2 g.

❈ GARLIC SOUP ❈

SERVES 4   SODIUM PER RECIPE: 95.6 MG   SODIUM PER SERVING: 23.9 MG

*This soup replaces chicken soup, especially when you're feeling down and need a light soup to cheer you up. (See **Important Ingredients: Garlic,** page 23.)*

  4 **cups chicken broth made by combining 4 teaspoons Herb-ox Low Sodium Chicken Broth (20 mg) and 4 cups water (0 mg)**
 ½ **cup white wine (5.5 mg)**
 14 **whole cloves garlic (7.14 mg)**
  2 **onions, quartered (3.3 mg)**
  1 **large carrot, sliced into 1-inch pieces (25.2 mg)**
  1 **medium celery stalk, sliced into 1-inch pieces (34.8 mg)**

1. Combine all the ingredients in a Crock-Pot or large soup pot. Cook this one slowly at low or medium heat for several hours to "steep" the garlic. If you cook with too high a heat, the garlic will turn bitter.

2. If you use a Crock-Pot, set it on low heat and cook for 10 to 12 hours. If you use a large soup pot, bring the mixture to a boil, reduce the heat, and let the soup bubble gently, uncovered, for 2 to 3 hours. Add more water if needed. When done, strain out the vegetables. If you prefer to puree the vegetables, you can add them back in. If you remove them, the sodium count for the soup drops about 5 mg per serving. Serve with toasted homemade **Crusty French Bread (Baguette)** (page 248).

Calories: 63. Sodium: 23.9 mg. Fiber: 1.43 g. Protein: 1.273 g. Carbohydrate: 10.2 g. Cholesterol: 0 mg. Calcium: 35.7 mg. Iron: .451 mg. Potassium: 192.7 mg. Total Fat: 0.1 g; Saturated fat: 0 g, Monounsaturated fat: 0 g, Polyunsaturated fat: 0.1 g.

❈ GARLIC SOUP WITH GRAPES /AJO CON UVAS ❈

SERVES 6   SODIUM PER RECIPE: 24.3 MG   SODIUM PER SERVING: 4 MG

This recipe comes from Michael McCay, who lives in Barcelona, Spain. He claims it is one of the best soups he's ever tasted. Garlic is good for the heart and the grapes add a nice flavor.

  7 **ounces stale homemade Crusty French Bread (Baguettes), page 248, crusts removed (5.826 mg)**
 3¼ **cups water (0 mg)**
 3½ **ounces unsalted almonds, blanched and skinned (10.9 mg)**
  6 **cloves garlic, minced (3 mg)**
 ½ **cup extra-virgin olive oil (trace)**
  5 **tablespoons white or red wine vinegar (.75 mg)**
 ½ **pound or 2 cups muscatel grapes, seeded (3.68 mg)**

1. Soak the bread in 1 cup of the water until softened. Use a bit more if necessary. Squeeze the water out and blend the bread in a food processor along with the almonds and minced garlic. Blend until it becomes a paste, adding a little water a tablespoon at a time if necessary. While the processor continues to run, add the oil in a slow stream, followed by the vinegar. Beat in half of the remaining water, then pour the mixture into a wooden bowl or pitcher and add the remaining water. Taste for seasoning, adding more vinegar if needed. You may also add spices you like or pepper to zip it up if you think it needs it. The soup should be tangy. Chill. Stir before serving. Garnish with the grapes.

Calories: 381. Sodium: 4.05 g. Fiber: 3.5 g. Protein: 6.067 g. Carbohydrate: 31.3 g. Cholesterol: 0 g. Calcium: 61.8. Iron: 7.27 mg. Potassium: 256.7 mg. Total Fat: 27 g; Saturated fat: 3.3 g, Monounsaturated fat: 18.9 g, Polyunsaturated fat: 3.5 g.

❖ FRENCH ONION SOUP WITH GARLIC ❖

SERVES 6   SODIUM PER RECIPE: 45.48 MG   SODIUM PER SERVING: 7.58 MG

Low in fat and low in sodium, this soup is a low-sodium translation of the popular French onion soup. Because cheese is so high in sodium, we recommend you try it without. However, if you must have cheese, use a light sprinkle of low-sodium Parmesan, generally available at most supermarket deli departments.

- 3 **medium onions, sliced (9.9 mg)**
- 1 **tablespoon olive oil (trace)**
- ¼ **cup dry Italian Swiss Colony sherry* (2 mg)**
- 5 **large cloves garlic, minced (2.5 mg)**
- 4 **cups (4 teaspoons seasoning dissolved in water) Herb-ox Low Sodium Chicken Broth (20 mg)**
- 2 **rounds (slices) homemade Crusty French Bread (1.5 mg)**
- 3 **tablespoons grated low-sodium Parmesan cheese (9.45 mg)— ½ tablespoon per serving**

1. Sauté the onions in the oil in a 2-quart saucepan set over medium heat for 5 minutes. Stir frequently. Add the sherry and garlic, then cover and cook over low heat for 25 minutes. Stir occasionally. Add the stock and bring to a boil over high heat. Reduce heat, cover, let simmer for 10 minutes. Serve in soup bowls. Place a toast round in each bowl before serving. If using low-sodium Parmesan, sprinkle over the soup and broil until the cheese browns lightly.

*Do not use "cooking" sherry. Use Italian Swiss Colony drinking sherry. You may substitute ¼ cup Welch's white grape juice (1.25 mg) or leave this ingredient out of the recipe all together. The sherry replaces the standard Worcestershire sauce, which is usually high in sodium, unless you can find a product called All Natural Lifer. You could also substitute white wine vinegar (1.287 mg) for the sherry.

2 Before using any alcoholic beverage in cooking, check with your doctor about the interaction it may have with your medications.

Calories: 115. Sodium: 7.58 mg. Fiber: 1.35 g. Protein: 2.852 g. Carbohydrate: 15.3 g. Cholesterol: 1.98 mg. Calcium: 52.1 mg. Iron: .844 mg. Potassium: 119.1 mg. Total Fat: 3.5 g; Saturated fat; 0.9 g, Monounsaturated fat: 2.1 g, Polyunsaturated fat: 0.3 g.

◈ CORN AND CHILI CHOWDER ◈

SERVES 6   SODIUM PER RECIPE: 663.90 MG   SODIUM PER SERVING: 110.7 MG
This recipe calls for Anaheim chilies, but if you can't find them, substitute mild green chilies, bell peppers, or some other pepper that is available. If you can't get fresh corn, make sure you use the no-salt-added frozen corn. Most of the sodium in this recipe comes from the nonfat milk that constitutes most of the stock.

3½ cups nonfat milk (420.2 mg)
1 medium yellow onion, diced (3.3 mg)
1 bay leaf (.137 mg)
1½ teaspoons fresh thyme (.108 mg)
2 teaspoons dried marjoram (.924 mg)
2 teaspoons chopped fresh parsley (1.404 mg)
3 cloves garlic (1.53 mg)
7 peppercorns (2.84 mg)
3 Anaheim chilies (or 1 large bell pepper) (.42 mg)
½ pound fresh Roma or Italian tomatoes (22.1 mg) or equivalent
     amount of no-salt canned tomatoes (22.1 mg)
6 medium ears white (or yellow) corn (65.7 mg) or no-salt-
     added frozen corn (14.2 mg)
4 cups water (0 mg)
2 tablespoons unsalted butter (3.124 mg)
4 ounces low-sodium Swiss cheese (140 mg)
   Garnish: chopped cilantro leaves (2.5 mg) or additional
     chopped parsley (2.128 mg)

1. Slowly heat the milk with half of the diced onion and the whole bay leaf, marjoram, thyme, parsley, garlic, and peppercorns. Before it comes to a boil, turn off the heat and cover the pot. This permits the herbs to steep and flavor the milk.
2. Roast the chilies (or pepper) over a flame (you can set them down on a hot stove burner; turn them over quickly when they begin to blacken). Transfer them immediately to a bowl and cover it so that the chilies are allowed to steam. After a few minutes, pour ice water over and then peel the chilies. Remove all the seeds and veins. Cut the chilies into strips or squares.
3. Bring 3 cups of the water to a boil. Lower the heat to a simmer and drop in the fresh Roma or Italian tomatoes. Cook them slowly for 10 min-

utes. Puree the tomatoes in a blender, food processor, or with a masher. If using canned tomatoes, simply drain them and then puree them. If using fresh corn, cut the kernels off the cobs. Make sure that you press hard when cutting the kernels off so that you draw out the corn's milky liquid. Add the liquid to the corn in a bowl. Set aside 1 cup of the corn and blend the rest at high speed with the remaining cup of water. Next, press the blended corn through cheesecloth or a fine-mesh sieve, pressing out all liquid.

4. Melt the butter in a pot with a little water; add the remaining onion and cook over low to medium heat until it is soft. Add the pureed tomatoes, peppers, and corn kernels and cook for 3 minutes. Stir in the corn kernels and strained milk and continue to cook over low heat for about ½ hour. Stir frequently. If using cheese, cut it into small squares, and put a portion into each soup bowl, and pour the soup over. Garnish with either cilantro or parsley.

Calories: 226. Sodium: 110.66 mg. Fiber: 3.24 g. Protein: 13.2 g. Carbohydrate: 25.59 g. Cholesterol: 26.14 mg. Calcium: 206.9 mg. Iron: 2.283 mg. Potassium: 573.9 mg. Total Fat: 9.2 g; Saturated fat: 5.4 g, Monounsaturated fat: 1.5 g, Polyunsaturated fat: 0.7 g.

❊ CREAM OF SPINACH SOUP ❊

SERVES 6   SODIUM PER RECIPE: 658.9 MG   SODIUM PER SERVING: 109.8 MG
During World War II, we ate tomato and spinach soup more than anything else for dinner. They still taste good to us now.

    1 **carrot, thinly sliced (25.2 mg)**
    1 **yellow onion, diced (3.3 mg)**
    2 **cloves garlic, mashed (1 mg)**
    1 **large red potato (7 mg)**
    1 **pound fresh trimmed spinach (359 mg)**
 ⅓ **cup unbleached white flour (.825 mg)**
 ⅓ **cup unsalted butter, melted (8.24 mg)**
    2 **cups nonfat milk (252.4 mg)**
 ½ **teaspoon basil (.24 mg)**
 ¼ **teaspoon nutmeg (trace)**
 ¼ **teaspoon thyme (.191 mg)**
 ¼ **teaspoon marjoram (.116 mg)**
    1 **teaspoon parsley flakes (1.356 mg)**

1. Cover the carrot, onion, garlic, and potato with water and lightly boil or steam items until tender. When done, puree the vegetables, using some of the same water, as needed, and set it aside. Steam spinach until wilted and then puree it also. Make a roux by whisking together the flour, butter, and milk. Cook it over the lowest heat, stirring until thick. Add the pureed spinach to the roux, along with the basil, nutmeg, thyme, marjoram, and parsley. Next add the pureed vegetables to the spinach mixture. Taste and adjust the seasoning. If the soup has become too thick, add a touch of milk. Heat over very low heat and stir until smooth and creamy. It will take on a nice green color and give off a wonderful aroma.

Calories: 189. Sodium: 109.82 mg. Fiber: 3.35 g. Protein: 6.592 g. Carbohydrate: 18.5 g. Cholesterol: 28.8 mg. Calcium: 193.4 mg. Iron: 2.735 mg. Potassium: 647.1 mg. Total Fat: 10.7 g; Saturated fat: 6.5 g, Monounsaturated fat: 3 g, Polyunsaturated fat: 0.5 g.

❋ MUSHROOM SOUP ❋

MAKES 4 CUPS   SODIUM PER RECIPE: 93 MG   SODIUM PER SERVING: 23.3 MG

  1 **tablespoon olive oil (trace)**
  1 **medium onion, chopped (3.3 mg)**
  1 **medium celery stalk, coarsely chopped (35 mg)**
 10 **ounces mushrooms, sliced (9.2 mg)**
  5 **cups Scott's Vegetable Broth,* page 43 (25.6 mg)**
  1 **tablespoon chopped chives (trace)**
    Dash pepper (trace)
  2 **tablespoon low-fat, light, or nonfat sour cream (20 mg)**

1. Using a 4-quart or larger saucepan, heat the olive oil over medium heat. Add the onion and celery and cook for about 5 minutes, until softened. Stir in the mushrooms. Cook for an additional 5 minutes. Add the broth and simmer, partially covered, for about 10 minutes, or until the mushrooms are soft. Stir in the chives and pepper and simmer for another few minutes. Top each serving with a dollop of sour cream.

Calories: 77. Sodium: 23.25 mg. Fiber: 2.06 g. Protein: 2.214 g. Carbohydrate: 8.255 g. Cholesterol: 2.5 mg. Calcium: 23.5 mg. Iron: 1.817 mg. Potassium: 356 mg. Total Fat: 4.5; Saturated fat: 1 g, Monounsaturated fat: 2.5 g, Polyunsaturated fat: 8.4 g.

❋ CHICKEN AND TURKEY CHOWDER ❋

SERVES 8   SODIUM PER RECIPE: 1,124 MG   SODIUM PER SERVING: 140.5 MG
*Reminiscent of New England clam chowder, this dish is exceptional with a mixture of fowl—turkey, chicken, Cornish game hen, goose, or domestically raised quail and pheasant. Serve with warm **Sourdough Bread** (page 243). This provides a lot of calcium.*

  ½ **cup cooked pork loin or chops, coarsely chopped (43.9 mg)**
  2 **tablespoons extra-virgin olive oil (trace)**
  1 **clove garlic, minced (.5 mg)**

*Or substitute 5 cups broth made by combining 5 teaspoons Herb-ox Low Sodium Chicken Broth with 5 cups water.

1 medium yellow onion, finely chopped (3.3 mg)
½ cup coarsely chopped green bell pepper, (1.49 mg)
1 cup coarsely chopped celery (104.4 mg)
1½ pounds red new potatoes, skin on and quartered (28 mg)
3 cups chicken and other fowl, boned and cut into bite-sized
    pieces (230.1 mg)*
1 cup chicken broth made by combining 1 teaspoon Herb-ox
    Low Sodium Chicken Broth mix (5 mg) and 1 cup water
3 cups nonfat milk (378.5 mg)
2½ cups whole milk (298.9 mg)
1 tablespoon Life All Natural Worcestershire sauce (4 mg)†
1 teaspoon Tabasco sauce or other similar hot sauce (29.8 mg)
    Mrs. Dash or Frontier seasoning blend and white pepper to
    taste (trace)

1. In a large nonstick saucepan over medium heat, cook the pork in the olive oil until it is almost as crisp as fried bacon. Drain on paper towels. Sauté the garlic, onion, bell pepper, celery, and potatoes in the olive oil for 3 to 4 minutes. If the pan has gone dry, add another tablespoon of olive oil. Add the fowl pieces and continue to cook until the onions are translucent and the meat is lightly browned. Add the chicken broth, all the milk, and the Worcestershire sauce and bring the mixture to a boil. Reduce the heat to a simmer, add hot sauce. Stir occasionally and cook until the potatoes are tender. Add pork and season with Mrs. Dash or Frontier seasoning blend plus white pepper to taste. This will not be as thick and creamy as regular chowder. To make it thicker, cook it down a little longer, uncovered. Serve hot.

Calories: 237. Sodium: 140.48 mg. Fiber: 1.6 g. Protein: 20 g. Carbohydrate: 20.9 g. Cholesterol: 45.08 mg. Calcium: 222.2 mg. Iron: .644 mg. Potassium: 514.1 mg. Total Fat: 8.1 g; Saturated fat: 2.8 g, Monounsaturated fat: 4 g, Polyunsaturated fat: 0.7 g.

*You can also use just one kind of poultry.
†Lea & Perrins Worcestershire Sauce has 165 mg per tablespoon.

❈ Dante's Lentil Soup with Spinach ❈

SERVES 6   SODIUM PER RECIPE: 134.1 MG   SODIUM PER SERVING: 22.4 MG
Two soups sustained my father when he was in college during the Depression—lentil soup and okra soup. I like lentil soup, but I never got the hang of okra. This is his recipe but with a great deal of the sodium removed.

4 cups chicken broth made by combining 4 teaspoons Herb-ox
    Low Sodium Chicken Broth (20 mg) and 4 cups water (0 mg)
1½ cups fresh chopped spinach (35.5 mg)
½ cup dry bulgur (11.9 mg)
½ cup dry lentils (9.6 mg)
2 cloves garlic, minced (1 mg)
2 large fresh tomatoes (about 2 pounds), chopped (32.8 mg)
2 tablespoons no-salt-added tomato paste (20 mg)
1 teaspoon tarragon (1 mg)
1 teaspoon thyme (.776 mg)
2 tablespoons dried basil (1.54 mg)

1. Bring the Herb-ox broth to a boil. Add the spinach, bulgur, and lentils and bring back to a boil. Simmer for 20 minutes, uncovered. Add the garlic, chopped tomatoes, tomato paste, and tarragon and thyme. Cook for 30 minutes, or until the lentils are soft. Add the basil during the final 5 minutes.
2. Serve with **Crusty French Bread** (page 248). If you're up to it, you can make a batch of **Scott's Vegetable Broth** (page 45) and use that instead of the Herb-ox.

Calories: 125. Sodium: 22.36 mg. Fiber: 8.48 g. Protein: 7.24 g. Carbohydrate: 24.5 g. Cholesterol: 0 mg. Calcium: 47.8 mg. Iron: 3.58 mg. Potassium: 408.9 mg. Total Fat: 0.6 g. Saturated fat: 0.1 g, Monounsaturated fat: 0.1 g, Polyunsaturated fat: 0.3 g.

❈ Garbanzo and Lentil Soup ❈

SERVES 4   SODIUM PER RECIPE: 61.3 MG   SODIUM PER SERVING: 15.3 MG
Really a hearty stew.

1¾ cups dry pink lentils (23.5 mg after cooking)
4½ cups water (0 mg)
¾ medium onion, finely chopped (2.54 mg)
¾ tablespoon extra-virgin olive oil (trace)
2 tablespoons chopped fresh cilantro (5.14 mg)
2 red potatoes, finely chopped (14 mg)
1⅓ cups fresh garbanzo beans (chickpeas), cooked (15.3 mg after
    cooking)
1 clove garlic, minced (.51 mg)
2 tablespoons lemon juice (0 mg)
    Dash of cayenne pepper (trace)

1. Boil the lentils in 3½ cups of the water in a covered pot over medium heat for about 20 minutes. Sauté the onion with the oil in a large pot over medium heat for about 3 to 4 minutes. Add the cilantro and potatoes and stir-fry for about 5 minutes. Add the chickpeas and the remaining cup of water. Cover and simmer for approximately another 15 minutes, stirring occasionally. Combine the chickpea mixture with the cooked lentils and add the garlic, lemon juice, and cayenne pepper. Simmer for an additional 5 minutes. Serve hot or warm.

Calories: 458. Sodium: 15.33 mg. Fiber: 14.61 g. Protein: 27.3 g. Carbohydrate: 77.5 g. Cholesterol: 0 mg. Calcium: 68.8 mg. Iron: 16 mg. Potassium: 702 mg. Total Fat: 5.9 g; Saturated fat: 0.9 g, Monounsaturated fat: 2.6 g, Polyunsaturated fat: 1.8 g.

❖ LENTIL AND MORE SOUP ❖

SERVES 4*   SODIUM PER RECIPE: 107.3 MG   SODIUM PER SERVING: 26.8 MG
If you have beans left over from a previous meal, you can use them in this recipe to make a hearty full-meal soup. I like it with chickpeas (garbanzos) or black-eyed peas. It's a variation of our
Garbanzo and Lentil Soup.

　1　**stalk celery (34.8 mg)**
　1　**medium onion, chopped (3.3 mg)**
　1　**teaspoon extra-virgin olive oil (trace)**
　1　**cup lentils (19.2 mg after cooking)**
　7　**cups water (0 mg)**
　½　**teaspoon cinnamon (.3 mg)**
　¼　**teaspoon ginger (.146 mg)**
　¼　**teaspoon turmeric (.208 mg)**
　1　**clove garlic, minced (.5 mg)**
　1　**cup chickpeas (11.5 mg after cooking)**
　½　**cup chopped fresh cilantro (coriander) (12.8 mg)**
　1½　**large ripe tomatoes, chopped (24.6 mg)**
　2　**tablespoons lemon juice (.3 mg)**
　　Dash of pepper (trace)

1. In a large soup pot, sauté the onion with the oil for approximately 3 minutes over medium-high heat. Add the lentils, celery, and the water. With the pot covered, cook over medium heat for approximately 35 to 45 minutes. Add the cinnamon, ginger, turmeric, garlic, chickpeas, and cilantro. Continue cooking, covered, for approximately 10 minutes, at which time add the tomatoes and lemon juice and continue cooking for another 10 minutes.

Calories: 272. Sodium: 26.82 mg. Fiber: 19.58 g. Protein: 18.3 g. Carbohydrate: 46.1 g. Cholesterol: 0 mg. Calcium: 67.2 mg. Iron: 20.2 mg. Potassium: 825.5 mg. Total Fat: 3 g; Saturated fat: 0.4 g, Monounsaturated fat: 1.2 g, Polyunsaturated fat: 0.9 g.

*Double or triple the recipe for added servings.

❖ OKRA SOUP WITH WILD RICE ❖

SERVES 4   SODIUM PER RECIPE: 243.1 MG   SODIUM PER SERVING: 60.8 MG
*I mention in the **Dante's Lentil Soup with Spinach** recipe that my father survived the Depression and his college years by eating that soup and okra soup. Well, here's the okra soup recipe he used.*

- 1 **cup wild rice mix (11.2 mg)***
- 1 **¾-pound chuck, sirloin, or stew meat, cut into bite-size pieces (171.4 mg)**
- 2 **teaspoons extra-virgin olive oil (trace)**
- 1 **large onion, chopped (4.5 mg)**
- 1 **pound okra, chopped (32 mg)**
- 2 **tomatoes, chopped (22.1 mg)**
- 2 **cloves garlic, peeled and chopped (1 mg)**
- 2 **tablespoons red wine vinegar (.3 mg)**
- 2 **tablespoons lemon juice (.3 mg)**
- ½ **teaspoon coriander (.318 mg)**

1. Cook the wild rice mix per the package instructions and set aside.
2. In a nonstick fry pan set over medium heat sauté the meat with the oil for 5 to 8 minutes, then add the onions and stir-fry for an additional 3 to 5 minutes. Add the okra, and tomatoes, garlic, vinegar, lemon juice, and coriander. Stir-fry for an additional 10 minutes. Serve hot over the cooked wild rice or substitute cooked brown rice.

Calories: 450. Sodium: 60.79 mg. Fiber: 7.19 g. Protein: 24.3 g. Carbohydrate: 45.4 g. Cholesterol: 58.8 mg. Calcium 112 mg. Iron: 3.943 mg. Potassium: 940.2 mg. Total Fat: 20.4 g: Saturated fat: 7.9 g, Monounsaturated fat: 9.6 g, Polyunsaturated fat: 1.3 g.

❖ PEA SOUP ❖

MAKES 8 CUPS   SODIUM PER RECIPE: 228.2 MG   SODIUM PER CUP: 28.5 MG
Ham has so much sodium that a few bites could make up your monthly allowance. This recipe is for pea soup without ham or ham hocks. It's just as tasty and very nourishing.

- 1 **tablespoon olive oil (trace)**
- ¼ **pound shallots or 1 large white onion, finely chopped (12 mg)**
- 2 **stalks celery, coarsely chopped (55.7 mg)**
- 2 **carrots, diced (50.4 mg)**
- 2 **cloves garlic, minced (1 mg)**
- ¼ **teaspoon caraway seeds (trace)**
- 7 **cups broth made by combining 7 teaspoons Herb-ox Low Sodium Chicken Broth (35 mg) and 7 cups water**
- 1 **tablespoon chopped fresh basil* (.1 mg)**
- ⅛ **teaspoon pepper (trace)**

*Wild rice mix consists of wild rice (a grain) and white rice.

1. In a 4-quart or larger saucepan, heat the oil over medium heat. Add the finely chopped white onions or shallots, the celery, the carrots, the garlic, and the caraway seeds. Add approximately 3 tablespoons of the broth and sauté, stirring frequently for about 5 minutes, or until mixture has softened and slightly browned. Stir the split peas into the saucepan and add the remaining broth. Bring the mixture to a boil, then simmer, partially covered, for approximately 1 hour to 1 hour 15 minutes, or until the split peas are tender enough to eat. Stir occasionally while the split peas are simmering. When done, add the basil and pepper and let sit, covered, for approximately 5 minutes.

2. Note: If you have access to fresh ham—that is, a ham not cured with salt—you can use it in this soup. Cook the ham without using salt first, then add to soup while simmering. The amount of sodium is 4 to 8 oz at 19 mg an ounce.

Calories: 253. Sodium: 28.53 g. Fiber: 16.43 g. Protein: 15.7 g. Carbohydrate: 43.4 g. Cholesterol: 0 mg. Calcium: 48.9 mg. Iron: 3.043 mg. Potassium: 732.4 mg. Total Fat: 2.5; Saturated fat: 0.3 g, Monounsaturated fat: 1.4 g, Polyunsaturated fat: 0.5 g.

❖ WHITE BEAN SOUP ❖

MAKES APPROXIMATELY 8 CUPS   SODIUM PER RECIPE: 102.3 MG
SODIUM PER CUP: 12.8 MG

Variations of this soup can be made, guided by your own taste. However, always use dried beans to keep the sodium count low.

2 cups dried white beans† (21.5 mg)
1 tablespoon olive oil (trace)
1 large onion, thinly sliced (4.5 mg)
7 cloves garlic, minced (3.57 mg)
6 cups broth made by combining 6 teaspoons Herb-ox Low
Sodium Chicken Broth (30 mg) and 6 cups water (0 mg)
2 medium carrots, thinly sliced (42.7 mg)
Dash of pepper (trace)
½ teaspoon dried sage (trace)

1. Follow the package directions for soaking the beans or place them in a large saucepan and cover with water. Bring the water to a boil and boil it for approximately 2 minutes. Remove the pan from the heat and let the beans soak for at least 1 hour or overnight. Drain the beans, rinse thoroughly under cold water, and then drain them again.

*You may substitute parsley for the basil.
†You may use no-salt-added canned white beans; the sodium count remains the same.

2. Using a 4-quart or larger saucepan, heat the oil over medium heat. Add the onion, garlic, 4 tablespoons of the broth, and sauté the mixture for approximately 5 minutes until softened (but not browned). Add the carrots and sage and sauté for another 2 minutes, stirring constantly. Add the soaked beans and the remaining stock, then bring the mixture to a boil. Simmer the soup, partially covered, for about 1½ hours, stirring occasionally, or until the beans are fork-tender. Remove the soup from the heat. Using a slotted spoon, put approximately 1½ cups of the beans and vegetables into a blender and puree until smooth. Add approximately ½ cup of the liquid and process to combine. Return this puree to the soup and season with pepper. Simmer for approximately 3 more minutes. Serve in bowls with a sprinkle of sage on top.

Calories: 102. Sodium: 12.79 mg. Fiber: 3.69 g. Protein: 4.902 g. Carbohydrate: 16.8 g. Cholesterol: 0 mg. Calcium: 53.7 mg. Iron: 1.84 mg. Potassium: 340.9 mg. Total Fat: 1.9 g; Saturated fat: 0.3 g, Monounsaturated fat: 1.3 g, Polyunsaturated fat: 0.2 g.

◈ MINESTRONE ◈

SERVES 4   SODIUM PER RECIPE: 237.7 MG   SODIUM PER SERVING: 59.4 MG
In Italy, minestrone is often served daily. This is an adaptation of a recipe I discovered in Milan while filming there.

 1 **pound white kidney beans (17.7 mg after boiling)**
 2 **ounces uncooked pasta shells (3.99 mg)**
 1 **tablespoon olive oil (trace)**
 3 **cloves garlic, chopped (1.5 mg)**
 1 **large red or yellow onion, chopped (4.5 mg)**
 2 **carrots, sliced (50.4 mg)**
 2 **large red potatoes (14 mg)**
 1 **medium celery stalk, chopped (34.8 mg)**
1½ **cups beef broth made by combining 1½ teaspoons Herb-ox**
      Low Sodium Beef Broth (15 mg) and 1½ cups water (0 mg)
 1 **cup Del Monte No Salt Added Tomato Sauce (80 mg)***
 2 **tablespoons Contadina No Salt Added Tomato Paste† (20 mg)**
 2 **teaspoons oregano (.4 mg)**
 ¾ **cup fresh green peas (2.82 mg)**

1. Prepare the white beans the day before. Follow the directions for soaking beans on the package or put the beans in a large saucepan, cover with water, and bring to a boil. Continue to boil for approximately 2 minutes. Remove the pan from the heat and let the beans soak for at least 1 hour or overnight. Drain the beans, rinse thoroughly under cold water, and then

---

*Hunt's No Salt Added Tomato Sauce is lower in sodium and is also recommended.
†Or another no-salt-added brand.

drain again. Cook the pasta shells according to instructions on the package, then drain and set aside.

2. In a large saucepan, heat the oil over low heat. Add the garlic, onion, carrots, potatoes, and celery. Cover and sauté, stirring occasionally for approximately 20 minutes. Add the beef broth, tomato sauce, tomato paste, and oregano. Increase the heat to medium and cook, stirring occasionally, until the potatoes and carrots are tender. Stir the pasta shells and peas into soup and cook until the Minestrone is hot throughout.

Calories: 340. Sodium: 59.42 mg. Fiber: 15.07 g. Protein: 15.3 g. Carbohydrate: 61.9 g. Cholesterol: 0 mg. Calcium 124.2 mg. Iron: 5.706 mg. Potassium: 749.9 mg. Total Fat: 4 g; Saturated fat: 0.6 g, Monounsaturated fat: 2.5 g, Polyunsaturated fat: 0.6 g.

❧ POTATO VEGETABLE SOUP ❧

SERVES 6   SODIUM PER RECIPE: 248.8 MG   SODIUM PER SERVING: 41.5 MG
Try to find very white garlic.

- **3 large red potatoes, diced (21 mg)**
- **2 cups water (0 mg)**
- **3 tablespoons extra-virgin olive oil (0 mg)**
- **1 onion, diced (3.3 mg)**
- **1 medium carrot, diced (21.4 mg)**
- **1 spear broccoli (40.8 mg)**
- **1 green pepper (2.38 mg)**
- **2 zucchini, sliced (11.8 mg)**
- **1 cup unsalted fresh peas (7.2 mg)**
- **1 quart soy milk,* warmed (115.2 mg)**
- **1 cup corn kernels from 2 ears corn (23.1 mg) or use unsalted frozen kernels (8.2 mg)**
- **2 cloves garlic, minced (1 mg)**
- **½ teaspoon thyme (trace)**
- **½ teaspoon dill weed (1 mg)**
- **½ teaspoon sweet basil (.479 mg)**
- **Dash of nutmeg (trace)**
- **Pepper to taste (trace)**

1. Cook the diced potatoes in the water. When soft, remove and reserve all but about ½ cup water, mash the potatoes in water, adding more if necessary. Discard the extra water. Heat the oil in a nonstick skillet or cooking pan. Sauté the chopped onion and carrot pieces until soft. Skin the stem of the broccoli spear and dice it along with the floweret to make at least 1 cup chopped. Add the broccoli to the sautéed onions and carrots.

*Or use nonfat milk. If using nonfat milk, add 400 mg of sodium to the total recipe.

Cook for an additional 5 minutes. Add the green pepper, zucchini, and fresh peas in the pod if you can find them. Add these to the soup pan. Cook until the vegetables are just tender. Add the potatoes, then slowly add the warmed milk. Next add the garlic, thyme, dill weed, basil, peas, and corn. Heat slowly over medium to low-medium heat, stirring often. Add pepper to taste.

Calories: 234. Sodium: 41.46 mg. Fiber: 6.83 g. Protein: 9.809 g. Carbohydrate: 29 g. Cholesterol: 0 mg. Calcium: 51.7 mg. Iron: 2.294 mg. Potassium: 709.9 mg. Total Fat: 10.6 g; Saturated fat: 1.4 g, Monounsaturated fat: 5.6 g, Polyunsaturated fat: 2.2g.

❖ TURKEY VEGETABLE SOUP ❖

MAKES 18 SOUP-BOWL-SIZE SERVINGS   SODIUM PER RECIPE: 687.5 MG
SODIUM PER SERVING: 38.2 MG

When she was eighty-seven years old, Mae DiMarco wrote down her family's recipes for her grandchildren. She assumed they already knew how to cook, needing only the recipes for specific dishes. This one is an adaptation of her original recipe, changed only to reduce the sodium.

1 (21-pound) turkey carcass, pieces, and parts (435.8 mg)
  Water as needed (0 mg)
3 medium onions, chopped (9.9 mg)
3 medium carrots, chopped (64.1 mg)
3 celery stalks, chopped (104.4 mg)
2 sprigs parsley, chopped (1.12 mg)
2 bay leaves, broken (.409 mg)
12 ounces egg noodles (71.8 mg)

1. In a large stockpot place the turkey carcass in water to cover. Bring to a boil, then reduce to a simmer and simmer, covered, for about ½ hour. Take the turkey from the water (saving water), remove the bones and return the meat to the water. Add 2 of the chopped onions, 2 of the chopped carrots, and 2 of the celery stalks to the pot. Simmer for approximately 1 hour. Add the remaining chopped onion, carrot, and celery and the noodles. Let cook for an additional ½ hour. Remove from the heat and cool for an hour with the lid on. Chill in the refrigerator overnight. Next morning scrape off all fat that has congealed on the surface. Reheat to serve. Store in the refrigerator, covered, for up to 5 days.

Calories: 187. Sodium: 38.2 mg. Fiber: 1.29 g. Protein: 9.246 g. Carbohydrate: 16.5 g. Cholesterol: 65.97 mg. Calcium: 89.1 mg. Iron: 1.842 mg. Potassium: 213.6 mg. Total Fat: 8.9 g; Saturated fat: 2.9 g, Monounsaturated fat: 2.8 g, Polyunsaturated fat: 2.5 g.

❧ CREAM OF MUSHROOM SOUP ❧

SERVES 4   SODIUM PER RECIPE: 118.4 MG   SODIUM PER SERVING: 29.6 MG

*Boy, do I remember hating this dish as a child. Yuk. But upon
maturity I discovered mushrooms. And now you can't stop
me from adding these fungi to nearly every supper
recipe I make—or eat.*

  1 **medium celery stalk, chopped (34.8 mg)**
  2 **cloves garlic, minced (1 mg)**
 ½ **pound mushrooms, chopped (7.36 mg)**
1½ **teaspoons extra-virgin olive oil (trace)**
  1 **small onion, chopped (2.1 mg)**
1½ **cups water (0 mg)**
1½ **cups soy milk (43.2 mg)**
  3 **tablespoons cornstarch (2.16 mg)**
1½ **tablespoons whole wheat flour (.562 mg)**
  3 **tablespoons finely chopped fresh parsley (6.384 mg)**
  2 **tablespoons celery seed (20.8 mg)**
     Dash of pepper (trace)

1. In a large soup pot sauté the celery, garlic, onion, and mushrooms in
the oil over medium-high heat for 5 to 7 minutes, or until the onion has
softened. Add the water, soy milk, cornstarch, flour, parsley, celery seed,
pepper to taste, and continue to cook over medium heat. Stir often so that
the soup doesn't burn. When it begins to thicken, serve.

2. *Note:* You may use nonfat or regular milk instead of soy milk. If you do,
add 194.8 mg sodium to the total recipe, or 48.7 mg per serving.

*Calories: 113. Sodium: 29.61 mg. Fiber: 3.12 g. Protein: 4.885 g. Carbohydrate: 15.2 g.
Cholesterol: 0 mg. Calcium: 78.7 mg. Iron: 5.984 mg. Potassium: 432.5 mg. Total Fat: 4.5 g;
Saturated fat: 0.5 g, Monounsaturated fat: 2.1 g, Polyunsaturated fat: 1.1 g.*

❧ CREAM OF CELERY SOUP ❧

SERVES 4   SODIUM PER RECIPE: 315.7 MG   SODIUM PER SERVING: 78.9 MG
*The soy milk helps lower the sodium, much of which is accounted for by the celery. Substitute **Scott's Vegetable Broth** for the Herb-ox Low Sodium Bouillon and you cut another 80 mg of sodium. Serve with low-sodium homemade **Dinner Rolls** or **Crusty French Bread (Baguette)**, if desired.*

- **4 celery stalks, chopped (139.2 mg)**
- **1 carrot, chopped (21.4 mg)**
- **½ onion, chopped (1.65 mg)**
- **1 clove garlic, minced (.5 mg)**
- **1 white or red potato, chopped (7 mg)**
- **1½ teaspoons extra-virgin olive oil (trace)**
- **1½ cups low-fat soy milk (43.2 mg)**
- **4 cups vegetable broth made by combining 4 teaspoons Herb-Ox Low Sodium Vegetable Bouillon (20 mg) with 4 cups water (0 mg)**
- **¼ teaspoon dried dill weed (.5 mg)**
- **Pepper to taste (trace)**

1. Sauté the celery, carrot, onion, garlic, and potato in the olive oil in a large soup pot set over medium-high heat for approximately 3 to 5 minutes. Transfer half of the vegetable mixture to a blender and pulse. Add the soy milk and blend for an additional 2 minutes or so. Return this liquid to the pot. Fill the pot with the vegetable broth and add the dill weed and pepper. Simmer over medium heat for 10 to 12 minutes. Serve this one hot.

Calories: 126. Sodium: 78.93 mg. Fiber: 5.74 g. Protein: 5.094 g. Carbohydrate: 20.3 g. Cholesterol: 0 mg. Calcium: 70.4 mg. Iron: 4.721 mg. Potassium: 593.4 mg. Total Fat: 3.8 g; Saturated fat: 0.5 g, Monounsaturated fat: 1.6 g, Polyunsaturated fat: 1.1g.

❧ TOMATO SOUP WITH CORN ❧

SERVES 4   SODIUM PER RECIPE: 191.4 MG   SODIUM PER SERVING: 47.8 MG
Canned tomato soup, an American staple, is out of the question on a low-sodium diet. This homemade soup, created by my sister Rebecca Gazzaniga, replaces the canned variety with so much more flavor that you may want to eat more than one serving per sitting.

- **1 medium onion, chopped (3.3 mg)**
- **2 cloves garlic, chopped (1 mg)**
- **1 medium celery stalk, chopped (34.8 mg)**
- **½ teaspoon red pepper flakes (.27 mg)**
- **2 tablespoons extra-virgin olive oil (trace)**

4 large ears fresh white corn, cut from the cob (85.8 mg), or use
   unsalted frozen corn (17.04 mg for 20 oz, 8.56 mg for 10 oz)
   when fresh is out of season
4 large tomatoes, cut into bite-size chunks (65.5 mg)
¾ cup water* (0 mg)
1 teaspoon chopped cilantro or coriander (.636 mg)

1. Sauté the onion, garlic, celery, and red pepper flakes together in the oil.
Add the corn, tomatoes, and water and bring to a boil. Simmer for ap-
proximately ½ hour. Puree the mixture in the blender or food processor.
Serve with chopped cilantro (coriander) on top.

*Calories: 237. Sodium: 47.84 mg. Fiber: 6.81 g. Protein: 6.724 g. Carbohydrate: 39.3 g.
Cholesterol: 0 mg. Calcium: 27.7 mg. Iron: 3.305 mg. Potassium: 878.3 mg. Total Fat: 9.2 g;
Saturated fat: 1.3 g, Monounsaturated fat; 5.6 g, Polyunsaturated fat: 1.7 g.*

BARLEY SOUP /
❖ PREPARE A DAY AHEAD OF SERVING ❖

MAKES 16 CUPS   SODIUM PER RECIPE: 831.4 MG   SODIUM PER CUP: 52 MG
*This Crock-Pot soup is easy to make and can be refrigerated to last
for a few weeks. Store what you don't use the first night in quart
Mason jars with lids. A really good winter evening dinner. I like to
add mushrooms and other vegetables if I have them available.*

1½-pound boneless chuck roast† (455.9 mg)‡
   Black pepper to taste (trace)
2 (14-ounce) cans S&W Ready-Cut Peeled, No Salt Added
   Tomatoes, with liquid (210 mg)
4 medium carrots, peeled and sliced (85.4 mg)
1 cup celery, chopped (35 mg)
1 cup onion, chopped (3.3 mg)
1 cup uncooked barley (makes 4 cups cooked) (18 mg)
2 cups vegetable bouillon made by combining 4 teaspoons
   Herb-ox Low Sodium Vegetable bouillon (10 mg) with 4 cups
   water (0 mg)
2 cups apple juice (13.9 mg)
1 teaspoon Lawry's garlic powder with parsley (0 mg)

*The quantity can vary from ½ cup to 1 full cup, depending on the consistency you
like.
†A two-pound bone-in roast is preferred for flavor. The weight of the bone does
not change the sodium count.
‡If you use a heavier roast, add 18 mg of sodium per pound of meat.

1. Pepper your chuck and put it into your Crock-Pot on top of the tomatoes, carrots, celery, and onion. Cook at low temperature overnight or for just 6 hours on a high setting. In the morning, or at the end of the 6-hour session, should you choose that method, separate the meat from the fat and place meat in separate dish. Store in refrigerator. Chill the soup mixture in the refrigerator overnight. After chilling, skim off the jelled fat.

2. Next put the broth and vegetables in a large cooking pot along with the meat, which you have defatted as much as possible and broken into small chunks. Add all the Herb-ox Low Sodium bouillon, one cup of the apple juice and the garlic powder, and bring the soup to a medium boil.

3. In the meantime, cook the barley according to package directions. When done, pour off the water, rinse with cold water, and add the barley kernels along with the apple juice to the soup, which is still cooking. Bring it to a boil and turn down the heat and simmer at the lowest possible setting. It's ready now. Serve it hot. Store the remainder in the refrigerator in Mason jars or in tightly sealed plastic containers.

Calories: 137. Sodium: 51.96 mg. Fiber: 3.02 g. Protein: 11 g. Carbohydrate: 18 g. Cholesterol: 25.51 mg. Calcium: 13.7 mg. Iron: 3.497 mg. Potassium: 339.8 mg. Total Fat: 2.1 g; Saturated fat: 0.7 g, Monounsaturated fat: 0.7 g, Polyunsaturated fat: 0.2 g.

❄ YAM AND PEAR SOUP ❄

SERVES 8   SODIUM PER RECIPE: 98.6 MG   SODIUM PER SERVING: 12.3 MG
A river rafter recipe. It's a great source of beta-carotene.

1 **large onion, chopped (4.5 mg)**
1 **tablespoon unsalted butter (0 mg)**
2 **large yams, peeled and cut into small chunks (33.8 mg)**
2 **fresh pears, peeled, cored, and quartered (0 mg) or equivalent canned pears (18 mg)**
1½ **quarts Basic Chicken Broth,* page 41 (58.2 mg)**
1 **teaspoon fresh thyme leaves or ½ teaspoon dry (trace)**
3 **tablespoons lime juice (.45 mg)**
  Black pepper to taste (trace)

1. In a large saucepan, sauté the onions in the butter until translucent. Add the yams, pears, and broth to the onion. Bring the mixture to a boil and let it simmer until the yams are very soft. Pour the soup through a strainer set over a bowl. Next puree the yam mixture in a blender or food processor until it is smooth. Meanwhile, return the broth to pan and continue to simmer for approximately 25 minutes. Pour the puree into the broth and add the thyme, lime juice, and pepper and simmer for another 5 minutes. Serve hot.

Calories: 98. Sodium: 12.33 mg. Fiber: 2.62 g. Protein: 2.687 g. Carbohydrate: 18.2 g. Cholesterol: 28.45 mg. Calcium: 19.1 mg. Iron: 8.941 mg. Potassium: 191.7 mg. Total Fat: 2.2 g; Saturated fat: 1.1 g, Monounsaturated fat: 0.6 g, Polyunsaturated fat: 0.3 g.

*You may also use **Mother's Chicken Broth,** page 42.

❧ VEGETARIAN SOUP ❧

SERVES 6   SODIUM PER RECIPE: 188.7 MG   SODIUM PER SERVING: 31.5 MG
You'll swear this has meat in it, but it doesn't. Its whole body flavor
and healthy vegetables make it a perfect winter meal.
A perfect Crock-Pot soup.

BROTH
- 4 **heads (1 cup) garlic (23.1 mg)**
- 6 **cups water (0 mg)**
- 1 **cup chopped broccoli (23.8 mg)**
- ½ **zucchini, sliced (2.94 mg)**
- ½ **celery stalk, diced (27.8 mg)**
- 1 **bay leaf, crushed (.137 mg)**
- 3 **sprigs parsley (1.68 mg)**

VEGETABLES
- 1 **large carrot, diced (25.2 mg)**
- 1 **large red or white potato, diced (7 mg)**
- ½ **cup radishes, diced (13.9 mg)**
- 1 **parsnip, diced (13.3 mg)**
- 1 **cup peeled, cubed winter squash (4.64 mg)**
- ½ **cup chopped spinach (11.9 mg)**
- ½ **cup chopped parsley (16.8 mg)**
- ½ **cup chopped mustard greens (7 mg)**
- ½ **cup chopped fresh string beans (3.3 mg)**
- ½ **cup chopped zucchini (2.94 mg)**
- ½ **cup sliced mushrooms (1.4 mg)**

1. Break the garlic into cloves; leave them unpeeled. Put the garlic, water, broccoli, zucchini, celery, bay leaf, and parsley in a stockpot or Crock-Pot and bring it to a boil, then let simmer for 2 hours. Using a sieve or strainer, strain out all the solid ingredients. Return the broth to the pot or Crock-Pot. **2.** Add the vegetables and cook for an additional 2 hours. Serve hot.

Calories: 99. Sodium: 31.46 mg. Fiber: 3.94 g. Protein: 4.189 g. Carbohydrate: 22 g. Cholesterol: 0 mg. Calcium: 95.3 mg. Iron: 9.737 mg. Potassium: 575.3 mg. Total Fat: 0.5 g; Saturated fat: 0.1 g, Monounsaturated fat: 0.1 g, Polyunsaturated fat: 0.2 g.

❖ "Gazzy-Pacho" (Gazpacho) ❖

SERVES 4   SODIUM PER RECIPE: 138.1 MG   SODIUM PER SERVING: 34.5 MG

Originally a Spanish dish, this uncooked vegetable dish has made its way around the world. We first discovered its flavors in Italy, of all places, in a small town northeast of Turin. The small town is named "Gazzaniga." Thus the "gazzy-pacho" name. Make sure you use only no-salt tomato juice.

6 ounces mushrooms (5.52 mg)
2 cloves minced garlic (1 mg)
2 tablespoons olive oil (trace)
1 fresh red tomato (11.1 mg)
½ green pepper (119 mg)
1 medium celery stalk (34.8 mg)
½ medium cucumber, peeled (2.1 mg)
½ medium onion (1.65 mg)
1 green onion, finely chopped (2.4 mg)
1 tablespoon chopped parsley (2.13 mg)
⅓ cup red wine vinegar (.75 mg)
⅛ teaspoon Tabasco sauce (2.75 mg)
24 ounces any low-sodium no-salt-added tomato juice (72.8 mg)

1. Finely chop all the vegetables very thin—the smaller the better. Sauté the mushrooms and minced garlic lightly in the olive oil. Combine all the ingredients in a large bowl and cover and chill before serving. This soup is served ice cold.

Calories: 126. Sodium: 34.52 mg. Fiber: 3.22 g. Protein: 3.071 g. Carbohydrate: 15.8 g. Cholesterol: 0 mg. Calcium: 39.1 mg. Iron: 2.079 mg. Potassium: 750.6 mg. Total Fat: 7.2 g; Saturated fat: 1 g, Monounsaturated fat: 5 g, Polyunsaturated fat: 0.8 g.

❖ RAFTER'S WILD BLACKBERRY SOUP ❖

SERVES 4 SODIUM PER RECIPE: 531.2 MG SODIUM PER SERVING: 66.4 MG

If you don't have access to wild blackberries, use unsalted frozen blackberries.

1 **quart orange juice with calcium (9.95 mg)**
4 **cups of any combination of strawberry yogurt, low-fat buttermilk* or sour cream (520 mg)†**
1 **tablespoon honey (.84 mg)**
2 **tablespoons fresh lemon juice (.3 mg)**
  Dash of cinnamon (trace)
  Dash of nutmeg (trace)
3 **cups fresh wild blackberries (0 mg) or unsalted frozen blackberries sprigs of fresh wild mint for garnish.‡**

1. Mix and chill all the ingredients except the blackberries. Wash and drain the berries. When you are ready to serve, divide the berries into individual serving bowls. Ladle the soup on top. Garnish with sprigs of fresh wild mint.

Calories: 124. Sodium: 66.4 mg. Fiber: 3.15 g. Protein: 11.5 g. Carbohydrate: 55.6 g. Cholesterol: 12.5 mg. Calcium: 169.1 mg. Iron: 17.6 mg. Potassium: 344.7 mg. Total Fat: 2.8 g; Saturated fat: 1.5 g, Monounsaturated fat: 0 g, Polyunsaturated fat: 0.1 g.

*Buttermilk by definition is nonfat—it is the milk that is left after the butter fat is taken out.
†All listed average 130 mg per cup. Low-fat has more sodium, but it's minimal, so if desired use that instead.
‡If you use other berries, leave them whole, except for strawberries.

RED MEATS

❖ ❖ ❖ ❖ ❖ ❖ ❖ ❖

◈ ROAST BEEF WITH THYME POTATOES ◈

SERVES 10   SODIUM PER RECIPE: 753 MG   SODIUM PER SERVING: 75.3 MG*
This is a quick but delicious meal. Serve with **Steamed Vegetables**
(page 297) and **Chopped Vegetable** *(page 185).*

> 1 (3-pound) rolled beef roast (695 mg)
> 16 to 24 creamer small red potatoes (56 mg)
> 1 tablespoon ground thyme (2.3 mg)†
> ¼ cup extra-virgin olive oil (trace)
> Pepper to taste (trace)

1. Preheat oven to 325°F. Rub the roast with pepper to taste. Put the roast on a rack in the center of a deep baking dish. In a small pan, stir together the thyme and olive oil. Roll the cleaned, unskinned creamer potatoes in this mixture and put the potatoes around the roast in the baking dish. Bake the meat and potatoes together in a 325°F oven ½ hour for each pound of roast, or until your meat thermometer reads rare, medium rare, or medium, whichever you like best. Do not overcook the roast, as that will toughen it.

TIP: When cooking roasts, prepare enough meat for sandwiches or another dinner later in the week. Use a slicer to cut the cold cooked meat. To maintain freshness, store in zip-lock bags or vacuum-sealed packages in the freezer or meat compartment of your refrigerator.

Calories: 516. Sodium: 75.3 mg. Fiber: 1.6 g. Protein: 26.2 g. Carbohydrate: 16.4 g. Cholesterol: 96.7 mg. Calcium: 19.1 mg. Iron: 3.524 mg. Potassium: 390.4 mg. Total Fat: 37.9 g; Saturated fat: 14.6 g, Monounsaturated fat: 18.5 g, Polyunsaturated fat: 1.7 g.

---

*Based on an individual serving of 4 ounces meat, which will leave enough meat left over for sandwiches during the week.
†If you have fresh thyme, finely chop it and use 2 to 3 tablespoons. You may also substitute fresh or dried rosemary.

MOM'S OLD-FASHIONED
❖ ITALIAN MEATBALLS ❖

SERVES 8   SODIUM PER RECIPE: 618.8 MG   SODIUM PER SERVING: 77.3 MG

If you enjoy meatballs with your pasta, then you can eat these and feel comfortable that the sodium is as low as possible. You can use any mixture of meat you like. You can even replace the turkey with ground pork, but keep it lean. Ground turkey averages about 27 mg of sodium per ounce, while lean ground beef averages about 20 mg. If you substitute, it's easy to adjust the sodium counts so that you know what you're eating.

1½   teaspoons extra-virgin olive oil (trace)
 3   cloves garlic, finely chopped (1.53 mg)
 2   celery stalks, finely chopped (69.6 mg)
 ¾   pound lean ground beef (223.7 mg)
 ¼   pound lean ground turkey (107.2 mg)
 ½   homemade (unsalted) bread crumbs (2.169 mg)
 1   medium egg white (54.8 mg)
 ¼   teaspoon oregano (trace)
 ¼   teaspoon basil (1.12 mg)
     Nonstick vegetable oil spray
     A 28-ounce can of any no-salt-added stewed tomatoes (133 mg)
 2   onions, chopped finely (6.6 mg)
 2   tablespoons Contadina Natural Tomato Paste (20 mg)
 1   tablespoon dried parsley (6 mg)
     Pepper to taste (trace)

1. Preheat the oven to 350°F.

2. In a small to medium sauté pan, heat the oil over medium heat. Add the garlic and celery and sauté for 5 minutes, until softened and lightly browned. Remove the pan from the heat and let it cool while continuing the preparations.

3. In a bowl, mix the ground beef, ground turkey, and bread crumbs, egg white, oregano, and basil. Stir in the celery mixture until lightly combined. With your hands, shape the meat mixture into 12 to 16 meatballs. Using a vegetable oil spray, prepare a cookie rack or other rack. Put the meatballs on the prepared rack over a baking sheet (perhaps a cookie sheet). Bake for 10 to 20 minutes, or until well browned on all sides. Turn the meatballs three or four times during the baking. When done, transfer the meatballs to a plate or a server and hold. I prefer baking to frying just to help keep the fat content down. While the meatballs are cooking, combine the tomatoes, onions, and tomato paste in a nonstick skillet or roaster pan. Cover and simmer for approximately 12 to 15 minutes, or until slightly thickened. Next mix in the sautéed garlic and celery. Add the meatballs to the tomato sauce in the skillet, then cover and cook for approximately 20 minutes, or until cooked through. Stir the parsley into the tomato sauce and add pepper to taste.

Calories: 208. Sodium: 77.35 mg. Fiber: 2.76 g. Protein: 13.9 g. Carbohydrate: 16.6 g. Cholesterol: 40.5 mg. Calcium: 69.5 mg. Iron: 3.072 mg. Potassium: 628.7 mg. Total Fat: 9.9 g: Saturated fat: 3.4 g: Monounsaturated fat: 4.5 g, Polyunsaturated fat: 0.8 g.

✸ PAPPY'S BEEF KABOBS WITH PEPPERS ✸

SERVES 4   SODIUM PER RECIPE: 295.9 MG   SODIUM PER SERVING: 74 MG

When my father returned from Guadalcanal and other South Pacific islands after World War II, he brought with him many new recipes. Apparently, the mouth-watering recipes of better food than K rations were traded among the starved Marines and the other services. It was a time when the cultures and tastes from different parts of America came together as never before. A renowned pilot from Fresno, California, a close friend of my father's named Pappy Boyington, contributed his personal Beef Kabobs. Although there are many variations, this one is best for its low sodium content.

1 **pound lean steak (263.1 mg)—top sirloin, tri-tip, chuck, or other steak of choice**
2 **tablespoons extra-virgin olive oil (trace)**
1 **tablespoon fresh squeezed lemon juice (1.15 mg)**
1 **tablespoon water (0 mg)**
2 **teaspoons of any brand no-salt honey mustard (20 mg)**
1 **teaspoon honey (1 mg)**
1 **medium-size fresh red pepper (2.38 mg)**
1 **teaspoon oregano (.22 mg)**
   Black pepper to taste (trace)
1 **medium green bell pepper, cut into 1-inch pieces (2.38 mg) (see Anaheim Chilies, page 308)**
8 **large mushrooms or 1 portabella mushroom, cut into large pieces (7.36 mg)**
4 **(10- to 12-inch) skewers**

1. Cut the meat into 1-inch strips or pieces. Mix the oil, lemon juice, water, mustard, honey, and oregano in a large bowl (you may add black pepper to your own taste). Next add the beef, bell pepper, and sliced mushrooms. Coat the meat with this marinade. Alternately thread meat, pepper, and mushrooms onto the skewers. Put the kabobs on a broiler rack or pan so that the meat is approximately 3 to 4 inches from the heat. Turn the kabobs occasionally while broiling and broil to taste. You may also grill these, but the flavor from the broiler or barbecue is much better. If you do not have skewers, you can stir-fry this mixture in a medium-hot nonstick pan, using water as the stir-fry base instead of oil. Serve hot.

Calories: 249. Sodium: 73.97 mg. Fiber: 1.86 g Protein: 26.1 g. Carbohydrate: 8.458 g. Cholesterol: 69.17 mg. Calcium: 21.9 mg. Iron: 4.219 mg. Potassium: 696.7 mg. Total Fat: 12.6 g: Saturated fat: 2.7 g, Monounsaturated fat: 7 g, Polyunsaturated fat: 1 g.

◈ PEPPERCORN KABOBS ◈

SERVES 4   SODIUM PER RECIPE: 234.8 MG   SODIUM PER SERVING: 58.7 MG

I've gone through so many skewers that you'd think I only cooked with them over the barbecue. Not true. I cook on grills and grates, over open pits, and in broilers and roasting pans. It's just that cooking with skewers seems the purest non-oil way to prepare a dinner like this one. I think you'll enjoy it as much as we have.

  1 **pound lean sirloin, 1 inch thick (222.5 mg)**
1½ **teaspoons crushed peppercorns (1.4 mg)**
  ½ **teaspoon paprika (.33 mg)**
  1 **garlic clove, crushed (.5 mg)**
  1 **medium onion, cut into quarters (3.3 mg)**
  4 **Anaheim peppers, peeled, from the Anaheim Chili recipe,**
      page 308 (.5 mg)
  4 **(12-inch) skewers**
  4 **small cherry tomatoes (6.1 mg)**

1. Cut the 1-inch-thick beef steak into kabob-size slices (about 1 inch). (You may also use a very good chuck, or pork tenderloin, or even chicken breast chunks with this recipe.)

2. Combine the peppercorns, paprika, and garlic. Add the meat and toss to coat. String an equal number of meat pieces on each of the four skewers, along with three sturdy onion wedges and the peeled Anaheim peppers. Put the kabobs on a rack in the broiler pan, so that the surface of meat is 3 to 4 inches from the heat. Broil the kabobs for 9 to 12 minutes for rare to medium, turning occasionally. Beef kabobs may also be barbecued. Place them on a grill over medium coals—8 to 11 minutes for beef; 15 minutes for chicken breasts. Cool and slice the chicken into chunks. Then put with vegetables on skewers and cook them for another 10 to 15 minutes, making sure to turn them every 2 or 3 minutes. Serve hot. Add cherry tomatoes for garnish.

"This one is a beefeater's delight. Try it on a George Foreman Grill."
—William Price, Kissimmee, Florida

Calories: 301. Sodium: 58.67 mg. Protein: 21.8 g. Carbohydrate: 4.894 g. Fiber: 1.39 g. Cholesterol: 9.22 mg. Calcium: 21 mg. Iron: 3.261 mg. Potassium: 484.2 mg. Total Fat: 21.2 g. Saturated fat: 0.9 g. Monounsaturated fat: 0 g. Polyunsaturated fat: 0.1 g.

❖ TOP LOIN WITH EGGPLANT RELISH ❖

SERVES 4   SODIUM PER RECIPE: 266.8 MG   SODIUM PER SERVING: 66.7 MG

*We live in a small town in northern California called Loomis.
Loomis is the site of the Eggplant Festival. Many eggplant recipes
abound and each year we can taste new dishes. After one such
event, I came home and experimented to adapt this recipe for the
low-sodium diet. I admit I love a good piece of beef, even
with its share of sodium. But if you eat only 3 to 4 ounces
per day, you'll be okay.*

1 **eggplant (16.4 mg)**
1 **medium red pepper (2.38 mg)**
1 **garlic clove, minced (.5 mg)**
1 **tablespoon chopped cilantro (2.5 mg)**
2 **teaspoons balsamic vinegar (trace)**
¼ **teaspoon 0-mg sodium or no-salt lemon pepper, not "lemon
     pepper seasoning" (trace)**
1 **pound lean tenderloin steak (244.9 mg)**

1. To make the eggplant relish, place the eggplant and the red pepper on
a rack in a broiler pan about 2 to 3 inches from the heat. Broil for approximately 8 minutes, or until the skins blister, turning occasionally. Place
the vegetables on paper on a plate, cover with paper toweling or waxed
paper, and then let cool. Remove and discard the skins from the eggplant
and chop it into fine dice. Remove the seeds and veins from the pepper,
then finely dice the pepper. Combine the eggplant, pepper, garlic, cilantro,
vinegar, and lemon pepper. Preheat a nonstick heavy skillet or pan (a 10-
or 12-inch pan works best) over medium heat for about 5 minutes. Pan-
broil steaks for 9 to 11 minutes, or until the meat reads between 140°F and
160°F on the meat thermometer and suits your taste. Turn the steak at least
once. (You may also oven-broil this meat.) Carve the steak into thin slices,
as you would with a London broil. Spoon the eggplant relish over steak
slices and serve.

*Calories: 234. Sodium: 66.75 mg. Protein: 25.3 g. Carbohydrate 10.8 g. Fiber: 4.11 g. Cholesterol: 70.31 mg. Calcium: 21.8 mg. Iron: 3.716 mg. Potassium: 777.6 mg. Total Fat:
10.1 g; Saturated fat: 3.7 g, Monounsaturated fat: 3.7 g, Polyunsaturated fat: 0.5 g.*

❧ BEEF GOULASH ❧

SERVES 6   SODIUM PER RECIPE: 540.9 MG   SODIUM PER SERVING: 90.1 MG

My mother, Alice, who made as many casserole dishes and stews as anyone, handed down this recipe to our family.

  1 **pound boned beef sirloin (263.1 mg)**
1½ **pound mushrooms, thinly sliced (7.63 mg)**
1½ **large Spanish onions, thinly sliced (6.75 mg)**
1¾ **tablespoons paprika (4 mg)**
  3 **quarts water for cooking noodles (0 mg)**
 10 **ounces dried egg noodles (59.8 mg)**
1¼ **cups beef bouillon made by combining 1¼ teaspoons Herb-ox**
     Low Sodium Beef Broth (6.25 mg) with 1¼ cups water (0 mg)
  1 **tablespoon cornstarch (.72 mg)**
  1 **cup light sour cream (160 mg)**
2¼ **tablespoons fresh chopped parsley (4.78 mg)**
  4 **red potatoes, quartered (28 mg)**
  3 **quarts water (0 mg)**
     Dash Frontier pasta sprinkle seasoning to taste
     Pepper to taste (optional) (trace)

1. Trim the fat from the beef. Cut the meat into slices about ⅛ inch thick or thinner to taste. Heat a nonstick roaster pan until hot. Add the beef and stir while frying until lightly browned. When done (about 3 minutes), transfer the meat to a large warm or heated pan and set aside. Put the mushrooms in the hot roaster pan and stir until they are browned (about 3 minutes). Add these to the meat. Add the onions to the pan and stir until they are lightly browned (about 2 to 3 minutes). Lower the heat to medium and after a few moments add the paprika with the onions and continue to stir.

2. While preparing the above, bring to a boil 3 quarts water. Cook the noodles according to package directions. Drain the noodles when done (tender but not soft or hard) and place them on a large heated serving platter to keep them warm.

3. Combine the Herb-ox Broth and the cornstarch. Add this to the onion mixture and stir until it comes to a boil. Pour the beef and mushrooms into the pan and stir until hot (no more than 2 minutes). Add in the sour cream and stir just until hot (no more than 1 minute).

4. Ladle the meat mixture over the hot noodles and serve. You may pepper to taste but not salt.

Calories: 427. Sodium: 90.15 mg. Protein: 27 g. Carbohydrate 57.5 g. Fiber: 4.01 g. Cholesterol: 104.57 mg. Calcium: 34.6 mg. Iron: 17.2 mg. Potassium: 611.5 mg. Total Fat: 9.9 g; Saturated fat: 4.4 g, Monounsaturated fat: 1.9 g, Polyunsaturated fat: 1 g.

SERVES 6 SODIUM PER RECIPE: 813.60 MG SODIUM PER SERVING: 135.6 MG

Turn an otherwise tough piece of meat into this delicious fare. Works with beef or pork tenderloin and venison, too. Cook in **Sweet-and-Sour Zinfandel Sauce.**

> **2-pound flank steak* (607 mg)**
> **4 ounces Alpine Lace low-sodium Swiss or Jack cheese, grated (140 mg)**
> **1 bunch fresh basil (.5 mg)**
> **5 cloves garlic, mashed into paste (2.55 mg)**
> **1 tablespoon fresh ground pepper (2.8 mg)**
> **2 tablespoons extra-virgin olive oil (trace)**
> **Butcher string**
> **Sweet-and-Sour Zinfandel Sauce, page 176 (60 mg)**

1. Lay the flank steak out and push it down to flatten. If the steak is thicker than ¾ inch, butterfly it until it is within ½ to ¾ inch. Pick whole basil leaves and lay them flat on the flank steak, covering the entire inside surface. Distribute the grated cheese evenly over the basil. Brush on half of the mashed garlic. Sprinkle on half of the pepper. Cut a piece of string 3 feet long. Begin rolling steak lengthwise. Roll tightly. Tuck in the stuffing as the steak is rolled. Use both hands to insure that the steak is rolled as snugly as possible. Loop the string over one end and make a knot. Continue looping the string around the roast, pulling the long end of the string through each loop tightly until you reach the end of the roast. Tie off the string and cut off any excess. Rub the remaining garlic over the roast and coat with pepper.

2. Preheat the oven to 375°F.

3. In an ovenproof skillet set over medium-high heat, add the oil. Place the rolled steak in the skillet and sear it until it is browned on all sides. Place the skillet in the oven for 12 to 15 minutes, or until meat is cooked to medium-rare. Remove the roast from the oven and let it sit for 5 minutes (it will continue cooking during this period, browning a bit more). Remove the string and slice into 6 sections. Spoon **Sweet-and-Sour Zinfandel Sauce** onto each plate and place a roast section on the sauce.

BUTTERFLYING YOUR BONE-IN ROAST

1. Trim any excess fat, gristle, and silver skin from the roast. Be careful not to make any deep knife cuts into the roast while trimming; keep the butterflied roast intact. Lay the roast on a cutting surface and begin butterflying by making a knife cut through the bottom third of the roast along the

*You may also use beef roast, pork roast, or venison roast. Butterfly these roasts per the instructions that follow and continue with the balance of recipe as described.

side, stopping about ¾ of an inch before you slice through the roast. Open the roast at the "hinge" and make a second cut through the larger section, starting at the hinge, stopping the cut again ¾ inch before slicing through the roast, following the path of the first cut. Flatten the roast with the palm of your hand. Continue until entire roast is butterflied. The meat should be no more than ½ to ¾ inches thick before stuffing.

THE EASIER WAY

1. Ask your butcher to butterfly the roast and tell him what you want to do with it. Most butchers are accommodating and will do it quickly and neatly.

Calories: 407. Sodium: 135.61 mg. Fiber: 0.77 g. Protein: 38.3 g. Carbohydrate: 11.7 g. Cholesterol: 104.05 mg. Calcium: 53.5 mg. Iron: 4.701 mg. Potassium: 749.8 mg. Total Fat: 22.6 g; Saturated fat: 6.2 g, Monounsaturated fat: 8.3 g, Polyunsaturated fat: 1 g.

❖ CHILI CON CARNE /CHILI WITH MEAT ❖

MAKES 12 CUPS   SODIUM PER RECIPE: 342.1 MG
SODIUM PER SERVING: 28.5 MG

This recipe was created by my wife just for my no-salt diet. You can adjust the picantismo by using more or less hot pepper.

> 3 **cups dried red kidney beans,* boiled without salt (26.5 mg)**
> ½ **pound "7% fat" ground beef (149.2 mg)**
> 1 **tablespoon extra-virgin olive oil (trace)**
> 1 **onion, diced (3.3 mg)**
> 1 **red pepper, diced (2.38 mg)**
> ¼ **pound mushrooms, diced (3.68 mg)**
> ½ **cup bean cooking liquid† (accounted for)**
> 1 **(14-ounce) can no-salt-added diced tomatoes (120 mg)‡**
> 1 **teaspoon or more chili powder to taste (26.3 mg)**
> 1 **tablespoon fresh oregano, chopped (.662 mg)**
> 1 **tablespoon cumin (10.1 mg)**
>   **Pepper to taste (trace)**

1. Soak the beans overnight. Boil per the instructions on the package. (You can cook twice as much as the recipe calls for and use the rest to make **Refried Beans** later.) Do not discard the cooking liquid.
2. Sauté the meat in a nonstick pan until nearly cooked. Add the oil, onions, peppers, and mushrooms and continue to sauté. In a large pot, combine the tomatoes, sautéed vegetables, ½ cup of the bean cooking liq-

*You may use more if you want to. Add 4 mg per cup to the sodium count.
†You can add more if you like a more liquid chili or if you add more beans.
‡Varies from supplier to supplier. It can be as low as 70 mg or as high as 150 mg; check the nutrition label before buying.

uid, and the chili powder, oregano, cumin, and pepper and bring to a light boil. Simmer for ½ hour, uncovered. Serve hot. At this point, it can be frozen or refrigerated and reheated.

Calories: 129. Sodium: 28.51 mg. Fiber: 5.19 g. Protein: 8.567 g. Carbohydrate: 13.4 g. Cholesterol: 12.99 mg. Calcium: 35.1 mg. Iron: 2.28 mg. Potassium: 353.8 mg. Total Fat: 4.7 g; Saturated fat: 1.5 g, Monounsaturated fat: 2.3 g, Polyunsaturated fat: 0.4 g.

Note: The total fat is probably lower than stated. Neither the USDA nor the FDA have analyzed (for public dissemination, anyway) this new 7% fat ground beef.

QUICK CHILI CON CARNE
❖ LOW-SODIUM STYLE ❖

SERVES 4   SODIUM PER RECIPE: 348.6 MG   SODIUM PER SERVING: 87.2 MG

   1 **cup Chili Sauce, page 173* (36.5 mg)**
   1 **pound lean ground beef or lamb (304 mg)**
   2 **cups S&W Nutradiet Kidney Beans† (8 mg)**
   ½ **bay leaf, dried, crumbled (trace)**
   2 **tablespoons extra-virgin olive oil (trace)**

1. Prepare the **Chili Sauce,** if used. Sauté the meat, stirring it around in the pan so that it won't stick together in clumps. Cook it well. When done, pour in the **Chili Sauce,** beans, and bay leaf and heat, cooking slowly, for about 1 hour, covered. Makes a great addition to tacos, barbecue meats, and is also excellent as a dip.

Calories: 545. Sodium: 87.16 mg. Fiber: 1.41 g. Protein: 36.2 g. Carbohydrate: 41.9 g. Cholesterol: 76 mg. Calcium: 15 mg. Iron: .702 mg. Potassium: 236.6 mg. Total Fat: 28.3 g; Saturated fat: 8.6 g, Monounsaturated fat: 5.1 g, Polyunsaturated fat: 0.7 g.

*Or use Featherweight Chili Sauce.
†Fresh cooked beans are better tasting, but not always available. If using dried kidney or pinto beans, cook according to package instructions, except do not add any salt. (You'll like your freshly cooked beans better.)

❖ "BEEF WELLINGTON" ❖

SERVES 8   SODIUM PER RECIPE: 943 MG   SODIUM PER SERVING: 117.9 MG

*I was on a working trip to St. Louis in the mid-1970s when the advertising account exec for my client invited me to dinner. We went to a basement restaurant that served Beef Wellington. My first. It was probably loaded with sodium and fat, but it sure did taste good. I wanted to come up with something similar, and here it is. The salt flavors are gone, but the combination of spices and the proper roasting of the meat make this delicious. The real Beef Wellington has Yorkshire pudding wrapped around it. When serving this one, cut the **Pancake à la Popover** (call it "Yorkshire pudding"), into 8 sections and top each one with carved meat slices and a dash of the au jus pan gravy.*

1 (3-pound) boneless prime rib or crossrib roast (428.7 mg)
1 teaspoon rosemary (.594 mg)
1 teaspoon coriander (.636 mg)
1 teaspoon thyme (.766 mg)
1 teaspoon ground cloves (5.099 mg)
   Pancake à la Popover (page 216) (507.3 mg)

1. Preheat the oven to 325°F.

2. Trim the fat off the roast. Set the roast on a baking rack. Combine the rosemary, coriander, thyme, and cloves and rub the mixture into the meat, especially on the side that will face up during baking.

3. If using an automatic thermometer probe, set for 160°F and bake at 325°F. Otherwise bake at 325°F for about 1½ hours.

4. About ½ hour before the roast is finished, in another oven bake the **Pancake à la Popover**. If you have only one oven, remove the roast after 1¼ hours and wrap it in heavy-duty aluminum foil; it will continue to bake slowly this way. While it rests, bake the Yorkshire pudding (the **Pancake à la Popover**). When it is done, cut it into 8 sections and serve each with carved meat set on top. Ladle a dash of the meat juice (au jus) on the pudding first. Serve hot.

Calories: 363. Sodium: 110.5 mg. Fiber: 1.54 g. Protein: 23 g. Carbohydrate 29.8 g. Cholesterol: 87.2 mg. Calcium: 118.1 mg. Iron: 2.908 mg. Potassium: 443.2 mg. Total Fat: 16.5 g; Saturated fat: 1.4 g, Monounsaturated fat: 1.4 g, Polyunsaturated fat: 0.4 g.

❋ CROCK-POT STEW ❋

***SERVES 8   SERVING SIZE: 1½ CUPS   SODIUM PER RECIPE: 973.6 MG
SODIUM PER SERVING: 121.7 MG***

*First, there was the black kettle that hung over the fireplace—at
least that's the image we've conjured up for our historical past.
Then came the pressure cooker, and, now, more convenient than
any of its predecessors, we have the Crock-Pot.*

*This basic stew recipe tastes so good that it's a shame we don't keep
it in that old-fashioned black kettle on the fire all winter. My wife,
Maureen, came up with it. You can use it as presented or adapt it
to your own tastes. Just remember, the goal is to get it tasty while
keeping the sodium as low as possible.*

1 **(2½-pound) chuck pot roast (681 mg)**
  Water to cover meat (0 mg)
3 **large carrots, peeled and cut into 1-inch lengths (75.6 mg)**
3 **stalks celery, cut into 1-inch bite-size lengths, including the
    leaves (104.4 mg)**
4 **large potatoes, peeled, quartered, and cut into 1-inch cubes
    (28 mg)**
¼ **cup water (0 mg)**
1 **medium onion, cut into 1-inch dice (3.3 mg)**
1 **recipe Sweet-and-Sour Zinfandel Sauce (page 176) (80.1 mg)**

1. Trim all the fat from the meat. Add water to the Crock-Pot first. Then
put in all the prepared vegetables, finishing with the meat on the top. Set
Crock-Pot on high for 6 hours, or low for 8 to 10 hours.

2. To prepare the **Zinfandel Sauce**, wait until the stew has about an hour
to go. Ladle or pour out 1 cup of the pot juices and substitute it for the
Herb-ox Low Sodium Broth in the recipe. Let the stew continue to cook
while you prepare the sauce. When you have combined all the sauce ingredients, let it simmer.

3. When the stew is done, ladle it into a large casserole and pour sauce
over it. Serve hot.

*Calories: 507. Sodium: 121.7 mg. Fiber: 2.66 g. Protein: 28.8 g. Carbohydrate 25.6 g.
Cholesterol: 11.01 mg. Calcium: 46.3 mg. Iron: 4.757 mg. Potassium: 1,080 mg. Total Fat:
32.3 g; Saturated fat: 1.5 g, Monounsaturated fat: 2.5 g, Polyunsaturated fat: 0.4 g.*

◆ BEEF AND BEAN STEW ◆

2 cups kidney beans (44.2 mg)
½ pound chuck roast, cut to 1-inch chunks (152 mg)
1 onion (3.3 mg)
1 green pepper, chopped (.5 mg)
1 celery stalk, chopped (35 mg)
1 medium carrot, chopped (21.4 mg)
1 teaspoon chili powder (26.3 mg)
  Pinch of cloves (1 mg)
  Pinch of ginger (trace)
  Pinch of dry mustard (trace)
  Pinch of coriander (trace)
1 cup cider vinegar (0 mg)
1 tablespoon brown sugar (5 mg)
  14-ounce can stewed no-salt-added tomatoes (105 mg)
  6-ounce can Contadina Natural Tomato Paste to thicken
    (50 mg)

1. Prepare the beans by soaking overnight. The next day boil for 2 hours, reserving the cooking liquid. In a large stew or soup pot combine all the ingredients, including the reserved bean cooking liquid, and simmer for approximately 2 hours. Serve hot.

Calories: 309. Sodium: 74.11 mg. Fiber: 11.36 g. Protein: 23.8 g. Carbohydrate: 48.8 g. Cholesterol: 22.68 mg. Calcium: 67.6 mg. Iron: 7.037 mg. Potassium: 1,186 mg. Total Fat: 2.5 g; Saturated fat: 0.7 g, Monounsaturated fat: 0.7 g, Polyunsaturated fat: 0.5 g.

❈ VEAL OSSO BUCO ❈

SERVES 6   SODIUM PER RECIPE: 396.9 MG   SODIUM PER SERVING: 66.1 MG

*Osso buco means "bone with a hole through the center." While in Milan I watched an Italian master chef draw the marrow out of the bones for use in the "sauce." He then cooked the veal shanks. He served this with **Risotto Milanese** (page 137).*

4 **veal shanks, cut into 2-inch pieces with marrow intact (289.2 mg)**
1 **large onion, finely chopped (4.5 mg)**
2 **medium celery stalks, finely chopped (34.8 mg)**
1 **carrot, finely chopped (21.4 mg)**
3 **tablespoons extra-virgin olive oil (trace)**
2 **tablespoon unsalted butter (3.1 mg)**
½ **cup white wine* (5.15 mg)**
8 **dried mushrooms (7.36 mg)**
¾ **cup no-salt-added tomato sauce or no-salt-added canned tomatoes (20.1 mg)**
1 **cup beef broth made by combining 1 teaspoon Herb-ox Low Sodium Beef Broth (5 mg) and 1 cup water (0 mg)**
   Dash of freshly ground white pepper (trace)
½ **teaspoon marjoram (.2 mg)**
1 **tablespoon finely chopped parsley (5.8 mg)**
1½ **teaspoons grated lemon peel (trace)**

1. In a Dutch oven or heavy pot sauté the shanks, onion, celery, and carrot in the oil and butter until deeply browned. Add the wine, then cover and cook over medium heat for about 5 minutes. Add the mushrooms, unsalted tomato sauce (or tomatoes), broth, marjoram, and pepper to taste. Cover and cook over medium heat until tender. Remove the shanks from the pan. Strain the sauce and put it back into the pan with the shanks. Add the parsley and lemon peel. Simmer for an additional 5 minutes and then serve.

Calories: 201. Sodium: 66.15 mg. Protein: 12.5 g. Carbohydrate 7.777 g. Fiber: 1.84 g. Cholesterol: 52.89 mg. Calcium: 35.2 mg. Iron: 1.53 mg. Potassium: 521.8 mg. Total Fat: 12.5 g; Saturated fat: 3.8 g, Monounsaturated fat: 6.7 g, Polyunsaturated fat: 1 g.

*You may substitute ¼ cup white grape juice or ½ cup nonalcoholic wine, but don't use cooking wine.

◙ MEAT AND RICE CASSEROLE ◙

SERVES 4   SODIUM PER RECIPE: 256.6 MG   SODIUM PER SERVING: 64.1 MG
A great-tasting, healthy dish. Make it in individual serving dishes or in a larger casserole. Use chicken, beef, turkey, or pork. The data for this recipe was compiled using beef sirloin. If using turkey, the sodium content will increase by approximately 5 mg per serving.

½ **pound beef sirloin (or chicken, turkey, or pork) (131.5 mg)**
2 **tablespoons olive oil (trace)**
1 **large onion, chopped (4.5 mg)**
¼ **cup chopped red pepper (.745 mg)**
¼ **cup canned (no-salt) pimientos (6.72 mg)**
4 **ounces Ortega diced chilies (100 mg)**
1 **cup uncooked rice (white, arborio, or basmati) (2 mg)**
2 **cups chicken broth made by combining 2 teaspoons Herb-ox Low Sodium Chicken Broth (10 mg) and 2 cups water (0 g)**
¼ **teaspoon ground coriander (trace)**
¼ **teaspoon cumin* (.8 mg)**
¼ **teaspoon Fortner's 375 seasoning blend† (trace)**

1. Preheat oven to 375°F. Slice the meat into bite-size pieces. Sauté them in oil with the chopped onion, the pepper, the pimientos, and the chilies. If using individual serving dishes, add ¼ cup rice to each. If using a larger casserole, place all the rice in bottom of the dish. Add the chicken broth. Next add the sautéed mixture to the casserole dish (or dishes), and add the coriander, cumin, and seasoning blend. Bake in the preheated oven for 20 minutes for individual dishes or 25 minutes for a large casserole. The cooking time may vary depending upon your oven or altitude. Keep an eye on it and check for rice softness and absorption of broth. Don't let it get too dry. Serve with a dollop of light sour cream on the side.

Calories: 350. Sodium: 64.14 mg. Protein: 16 g. Carbohydrate 47.6 g. Fiber: 2.55 g. Cholesterol: 34.59 mg. Calcium: 16.6 mg. Iron: 4.098 mg. Potassium: 340.8 mg. Total Fat: 9.7 g; Saturated fat: 1.9 g, Monounsaturated fat: 6.1 g, Polyunsaturated fat: 0.8 g.

*If you like cumin, add up to 1 teaspoon. If you don't like cumin, leave out and replace with white pepper.
†Fortner's seasonings can be purchased mail order by calling 1-800/753-0310.

❈ APPLESAUCE PORK CHOPS ❈

SERVES 4   SODIUM PER RECIPE: 157.5 MG   SODIUM PER SERVING: 39.4 MG

*Quick and easy, these chops are tasty and go well with a baked
potato, applesauce, and a green vegetable such as asparagus,
broccoli, or peas.**

**4 (3-ounce edible meat weight) lean, center loin rib pork chops
with bone (154.8 mg)**
½ **cup water (0 mg)**
**1 cup Homemade Applesauce (page 360) or unsalted
commercial applesauce (.9 mg)**
2 tablespoons honey (1.68 mg)
¼ **teaspoon cinnamon (.151 mg)**

1. In a nonstick roaster or frypan, add the chops to the water. Spread ½
cup of the applesauce over the chops. Cook at medium to medium-high
heat, uncovered, for about 10 minutes. Turn the chops, mixing the applesauce, and adding a touch of water if needed. Cook for another 10 minutes.
Near the end of the cooking, ladle the honey on chops and then sprinkle
with cinnamon. Serve hot with remaining ½ cup applesauce, warmed, and
baked potato or creamer potatoes with either asparagus, broccoli, or peas.

*Calories: 252. Sodium: 39.37 mg. Fiber: 2.59 g. Protein: 19.2 g. Carbohydrate: 32.6 g. Cho-
lesterol: 47.3 mg. Calcium: 31 mg. Iron: 2.048 mg. Potassium: 469 mg. Total Fat: 5.5 g; Saturated fat: 1.8 g, Monounsaturated fat: 2.3 g, Polyunsaturated fat: 0.7 g.*

PORK ROAST BARBECUE WITH
❈ DON'S BARBECUE SAUCE ❈

SERVES 12   SODIUM PER RECIPE: 1,291 MG   SODIUM PER SERVING: 107.6 MG

*I love to barbecue in the summer and will cook anything on my
charcoal-burning barbecue. I use one of those old-fashioned
round top units. I am not a fan of gas or propane barbecues. For
me, that's a lot like cooking the meal in the kitchen oven. I will
barbecue lamb, turkey (for Thanksgiving especially), beef, chicken,
fish, and vegetables, including potatoes. I use mostly convection
heat, setting the coals to the side and bringing the lid down. The
meat stays tender that way and doesn't get so "burned." The real
magic however is in the sauce. Over the years I've created a
number of sauces but the one I like for this recipe is*
Don's Barbecue Sauce.

*"The Applesauce Pork Chops were delicious and easy to prepare. My wife, who
is not always thrilled about my low sodium cooking, even loved them. The thing
I really like about Don's recipes is they are quick and easy to prepare, and use
common, easy to find ingredients. Many cookbooks fail in that regard."—Pete
Eiden, healhtyheartmarket.com

4-pound pork tenderloin roast (907.2 mg)
1 complete recipe Don's Barbecue Sauce, page 169 (383.4 mg)

1. Prepare **Don's Barbecue Sauce** a few hours before cooking time.
2. In a large dish or pan add the roast and half the sauce, then put it in the refrigerator to marinate. Don't throw this marinade away, but save the balance, storing it in the refrigerator.
3. After the coals are ready, set the roast off the heat on the grill. Brush the reserved marinade over the roast and close the lid of the barbecue. If you use a hot barbecue, the roast should cook in about 1 hour. Use a meat thermometer to determine the doneness you like. Turn the roast every 30 minutes, brushing fresh sauce on it while cooking. When ready to serve, slice the roast and reheat the remaining sauce. Once hot, ladle a spoonful on each plate and top with the meat slices. Serve with your favorite vegetable(s) or other side dish.

Calories: 331. Sodium: 107.55 mg. Fiber: 2.13 g. Protein: 33.8 g. Carbohydrate 32.2 g. Cholesterol: 98.28 mg. Calcium: 50.2 mg. Iron: 3.572 mg. Potassium: 1,079 mg. Total Fat: 16.9 g; Saturated fat: 2.1 g, Monounsaturated fat: 4 g, Polyunsaturated fat: 0.9 g.

❖ PORK TENDERLOIN CHILI VERDE ❖

SERVES 8   SODIUM PER RECIPE: 882.4 MG   SODIUM PER SERVING: 110.3 MG
Here's a dish from The Sporting Chef, Scott Leysath. Originally a wild boar recipe, this adaptation brings a whole new flavor to pork tenderloin, and with low sodium to boot.

3 pounds pork tenderloin, cut into 1-inch pieces (680.4 mg)
3 tablespoons extra-virgin olive oil (trace)
2 cups chopped yellow onion (9.6 mg)
8 cloves garlic, chopped (4 mg)
1 cup chopped green bell pepper (2.98 mg)
1 cup chopped red bell pepper (1 mg)
1 cup chopped Anaheim pepper (1 mg)
3 Ortega jalapeño peppers,* seeds, removed and diced fine (40 mg)
1 tablespoon dried oregano (.66 mg)
1 tablespoon chili powder (75 mg)
2 tablespoons cumin (20 mg)
1 teaspoon cayenne pepper (.5 mg)
2 cups fresh tomatillos, quartered (or canned, juice removed) (2.6 mg)
4 cups chicken broth made by combining 4 teaspoons Herb-ox Low Sodium Chicken Broth (25 mg) and 4 cups water (0 mg)†
1 cup fresh cilantro, chopped (24.8 mg)

---

*Fresh are better; use them if they are readily available in your area. Only the Ortega brands seem to have the canned variety with very low sodium.
†Featherweight or Life Line Low Sodium Broths are also available.

1. In a large stockpot, cook the oil over medium-high heat. Add the pork and lightly brown on all sides. Add the onion, garlic, and peppers and sauté until the onion is translucent. Add the oregano, chili powder, cumin, cayenne pepper, tomatillos, and enough chicken broth to cover to just below the top of the other ingredients. Lower the heat and simmer for 1 hour, adding more chicken broth as needed to keep the mixture moist. Check the meat to see if it has softened and begun to shred. If not, simmer for a while longer. Add the cilantro and simmer for another 10 minutes. Serve hot.

CAUTION: When preparing hot peppers such as jalapeños, be sure to wear rubber gloves and wash your hands thoroughly afterward. If you cut a jalapeño and then touch your eyes, you will appreciate this word of caution.

Calories: 307. Sodium: 110.32 mg. Fiber: 3.04 g. Protein: 37.6 g. Carbohydrate: 11.6 g. Cholesterol: 110.56 mg. Calcium: 56.7 mg. Iron: 4.11 mg. Potassium: 931 mg. Total Fat: 12 g; Saturated fat: 2.8 g, Monounsaturated fat: 6.7 g, Polyunsaturated fat: 1.4 g.

❧ HOT BARBECUED COUNTRY PORK RIBS ❧

SERVES 4   SODIUM PER RECIPE: 422.7 MG   SODIUM PER SERVING: 105.7 MG
Pick the leanest pork ribs, bone-in or country-style, and follow the recipe below. This dish can be cooked either in the oven or over the barbecue.

1 **pound boneless country pork ribs (303.9 mg)**
1 **small, 6-oz can Contadina no-salt-added tomato paste (100 mg)**
3 **tablespoons light brown sugar (16 mg)**
1 **tablespoon lemon juice (trace)**
2 **cloves garlic, minced (1 mg)**
1 **tablespoon vinegar (trace)**
¼ **teaspoon sage (trace)**
¼ **teaspoon thyme (trace)**
¼ **teaspoon coriander (trace)**
¼ **teaspoon marjoram (trace)**
½ **cup water (0 mg)**

1. Trim all fat from the ribs. Place ribs into a deep dish or pan. In a skillet or pan mix together all the other ingredients and heat over medium heat, stirring once. Cook for about 10 minutes, stirring often. Pour this mixture over the ribs and turn the ribs once in the mixture. Let the ribs sit in the refrigerator, covered, for 2 to 18 hours, no longer.
2. If using the oven, heat to 400°F, unless the ribs are thin, then bake at 375°F. Place ribs in a single layer on a rack in the roasting pan. Brush with sauce and bake, uncovered, for about 30 minutes. Turn the ribs and brush again, then bake for an additional 30 minutes.

3. If using a barbecue, put the ribs on a rack in the center of the grill away from direct heat, and cook covered, turning once halfway through. It might take only 45 minutes to cook the ribs on a charcoal barbecue. Brush with sauce every 15 minutes.

4. Serve with corn-on-the-cob and broccoli or asparagus.

Calories: 260. Sodium: 105.68 mg. Fiber: 1.45 g. Protein: 24.6 g. Carbohydrate: 19.1 g. Cholesterol: 72.58 mg. Calcium: 42.5 mg. Iron: 7.609 mg. Potassium: 449.2 mg. Total Fat: 9.4 g; Saturated fat: 3.2 g, Monounsaturated fat: 4.2 g, Polyunsaturated fat: 1 g.

A note to barbecued pork aficionados: A tastier sauce can be made by using the above spices plus 1½ cups brown sugar (84.8 mg), 2 cans tomato sauce (16 ounces, 146.4 mg), and 1 can Contadina tomato paste (6 ounces, 100 mg). Leave the water out. Cook the sauce down in the pan over low heat after bringing it to a boil. The sodium is higher for this, but if you barbecue over hot coals (about ½ hour total), half the sauce will burn off. The remaining sodium will reduce to about half, or fairly close to 153 mg per serving.

◼ PORK CASSEROLE ◼

SERVES 4   SODIUM PER RECIPE: 268 MG   SODIUM PER SERVING: 67 MG
My wife's Irish parents hailed from Leadville, Colorado, where, with the rustic roads leading in and out of town, food was a valuable commodity during the Depression years—and continues to be today. So, using their resources sparingly and still providing interesting and exciting meals, the residents came up with many recipes that have served well through more than a few generations. This is one of those. You'll find it one of the easiest meals to put together, as well as one of the most tasteful for a low-sodium diet.

1 **tablespoon extra-virgin olive oil (trace)**
3 **russet potatoes (22 mg)**
1 **large yellow onion, sliced (4.5 mg)**
4 **lean boneless pork chops, 4 ounces meat each (113.8 mg)**
1 **cup nonfat milk (126.2 mg)**
2 **teaspoons fresh tarragon, chopped or dried (2 mg)**
2 **garlic cloves, minced (1 mg)**

1. Preheat the oven to 375°F. Rub the oil around a 9x12-inch Pyrex casserole dish until used up. Peel and cut potatoes into ⅛-inch or slightly thicker slices. Layer the potato slices over the bottom of the casserole dish. Put the onion slices on top of the potatoes. Next, put the pork chops on top of the onions, spreading them from end to end. Pour the milk over this and sprinkle with the tarragon and minced garlic. Bake in the preheated oven for 1 hour. A perfect accompaniment is steamed broccoli and a dab of sour cream (10 mg).

2. This recipe may be doubled. If doubling, spread one layer of potatoes across the bottom, then one layer of onions, then the second layer of potatoes and the second layer of onions, and finally the pork chops. Serve hot.

Calories: 274. Sodium: 67 mg. Fiber: 2.19 g. Protein: 19.6 g. Carbohydrate: 23.3 g. Cholesterol: 41.47 mg. Calcium: 105.4 mg. Iron: 1.324 mg. Potassium: 917.1 mg. Total Fat: 11.3 g; Saturated fat: 3.3 g, Monounsaturated fat: 5.9 g, Polyunsaturated fat: 1.2 g.

✺ MOCK PORK SAUSAGE ✺

SERVES 6   SODIUM PER RECIPE: 364.3 MG   SODIUM PER SERVING: 60.7 MG
You can make pork-less sausages from this recipe if you want low fat. Substitute 4 fresh minced garlic cloves and ⅓ cup finely diced yellow onion for the onion and garlic powders.

12 ounces ground lean turkey (319.8 mg)
 3 ounces ground pork (40.8 mg)
 1 teaspoon dried sage (trace)
 ¼ teaspoon dried tarragon (.249 mg)
 ¼ teaspoon dried oregano (trace)
 ¼ teaspoon red pepper flakes (.135 mg)
 ½ teaspoon cumin seed, lightly toasted in a skillet (1.762 mg)
 ½ teaspoon garlic powder (.369 mg)
 ½ teaspoon onion powder (.369 mg)
 ½ teaspoon freshly ground black pepper (.462 mg)
    Nonstick olive oil pan spray (trace)

1. Combine all the ingredients except the olive oil spray. Form the mixture into 3-to-4-inch diameter patties. Lightly coat a nonstick skillet with pan spray and put the pan over medium heat. Brown the patties on both sides, about 3 to 4 minutes per side, or until cooked through. Serve hot.

Calories: 111. Sodium: 60.71 mg. Fiber: 0.2 g. Protein: 13.3 g. Carbohydrate: .689 g. Cholesterol: 53.11 mg. Calcium: 17.5 mg. Iron: 1.09 mg. Potassium: 211.1 mg. Total Fat: 5.8 g; Saturated fat: 1.6 g, Monounsaturated fat: 2.3 g, Polyunsaturated fat: 1.3 g.

✺ EASY PORK CHOP CASSEROLE ✺

SERVES 4   SODIUM PER RECIPE: 468 MG   SODIUM PER SERVING: 117 MG
Quick, simple, delicious.

1 tablespoon olive oil or nonstick olive oil spray (trace)
4 lean top loin pork chops (167.4 mg)
1 large onion, thinly sliced (4.5 mg)
6 medium russet potatoes, peeled and sliced ⅛ inch or less thick
   (42 mg)

2 cups thin white sauce* (254 mg)
   Pepper or other spices to taste (trace)
   Dash Fortner's #37 seasoning blend† (trace)

1. Preheat the oven to 375°F.
2. Spray or spread the oil around a 9x12-inch Pyrex casserole dish. Next layer half the sliced potatoes on the bottom. Now add a layer of sliced onions. Put the pork chops on top of the onions and follow with the remaining potatoes and then the remaining onions, spreading everything out evenly. Top with the white sauce and the seasonings and bake in a 375°F oven for 45 minutes. Serve hot.

Calories: 383. Sodium: 117 mg. Fiber: 3.43 g. Protein: 28.6 g. Carbohydrate: 40.8 g. Cholesterol: 61.13 mg. Calcium: 179.4 mg. Iron: .954 mg. Potassium: 656.6 mg. Total Fat: 11.6 g; Saturated fat: 4.3 g, Monounsaturated fat: 5.6 g, Polyunsaturated fat: 1 g.

❖ GINGERED WONTON TREATS ❖

SERVES 4   SODIUM PER RECIPE: 454.9 MG   SODIUM PER SERVING: 113.7 MG
This recipe is from our Sporting Chef, Scott Leysath. It is an adaptation of his Duck Ravioli and Vegetable Wonton recipes. You can use fresh meats, shrimp, or vegetables to make these marvelous side-dish treats. If you order a dish like this in a restaurant, however, the sodium count can be as high as 600 to 1,000 mg per wonton, but these are just as tasty and a lot healthier.

   2 medium egg whites (93.1 mg)
 ½ pound fresh ground lean pork tenderloin (113.4 mg)
 ⅓ cup finely chopped onion (1.584 mg)
   1 clove garlic, minced (.5 mg)
   2 teaspoons finely minced fresh ginger (.52 mg)
   1 teaspoon sesame seed oil (0 mg)
 ½ tablespoon lemon juice (trace)
   Pepper to taste
 12 wonton skins (205.7 mg)
   8 cups chicken broth made by combining 8 teaspoons Herb-ox
      Low Sodium Chicken Broth (40 mg) and 8 cups water (0 mg)
   Olive oil or olive oil spray for coating baking sheets

1. Separate egg yolks from whites. Keep whites. In a blender or food processor, process the pork (or substitute shrimp or oysters or lean ground

*You can use a broth sauce instead and cut the calories and fat by half. Don't use a commercial white sauce or a recipe calling for salt.
†If you can't find Fortner's seasonings in a local store, you can mail-order it from Healthy Heart Market at 1-800/753-0310 or www.healthyheartmarket.com.

beef), onion, garlic, ginger, sesame seed oil, lemon juice, and pepper until well blended. While machine is still running, add the egg whites, a little at a time, and process until the mixture is well pureed. Place a tablespoon of this filling in the center of each wonton square. Moisten the edges of each wonton with water and fold it into a triangle, pressing the edges together to make sure there are no air bubbles. Fold one corner of the wonton skin over the filling; moisten and overlap the two opposite corners to form a square shape. The wontons now may be frozen for future use by placing them in a single layer on a baking sheet and flash-freezing them. As soon as they freeze remove the baking sheet and transfer the wontons to Ziplock-type bags and return them to the freezer.

2. To cook, heat the broth to boiling and add half of the wontons. When the broth returns to a boil, cook the wontons until they float to the top, about 2 minutes for fresh wontons, about 3 to 4 minutes for frozen wontons. Lift them out of the water when done and drain gently but well. Cook the second batch in the same way.

3. Put the drained wontons on two baking sheets that have been lightly greased (or sprayed) with olive oil. Press the wontons gently onto the pan to coat the bottom with the oil, then turn the wontons over and press again. If you want to hold off the final step until close to serving time, you may set the pieces in the refrigerator (covered with plastic wrap) for a few hours. When ready to serve, preheat the oven to 400°F and bake the wontons for 3 minutes on one side, then turn and bake for another 3 minutes on the other side. The wontons may be served with **Plum Sauce, Ginger and Orange Sauce, Raspberry Sauce,** or **Sweet-and-Sour Dipping Sauce.**

Calories: 140. Sodium: 113.73 mg. Fiber: 0.41 g. Protein: 14.1 g. Carbohydrate: 9.924 g. Cholesterol: 36.86 mg. Calcium: 10 mg. Iron: .994 mg. Potassium: 271.4 mg. Total Fat: 4.2 g; Saturated fat: 1.2 g, Monounsaturated fat: 1.7 g, Polyunsaturated fat: 1 g.

❋ RASPBERRY LAMB ❋

SERVES 4   SODIUM PER RECIPE: 281.3 MG   SODIUM PER SERVING: 70.3 MG
Fresh raspberries may make this taste a bit better, but not enough to wait for raspberry season. Frozen berries are generally just as tasty as fresh berries. Also works as a base for roasted elk, venison, lamb, and lean pork.

4 (4-ounce) servings of lean roasted lamb, either tenderloin or leg (276.72 mg)
   10-ounce package frozen raspberries (2.84 mg)
2 teaspoons fresh lemon juice (trace)
2 tablespoons honey (1.68 mg)
   Low Sugar Mint Jelly (trace)

1. After the lamb is cooked, thinly slice it. Using a food processor or blender, puree all but a handful of raspberries until smooth. Strain this through a fine sieve or through cheesecloth. Add in the lemon juice and honey and mix together. Spread a quarter of the puree onto each of four individual serving dishes. Place lamb slices in tiers on each dish. Suggested accompaniments are baked red potatoes and peas. Garnish with mint jelly. Place the remaining raspberries on top of the meat.

Calories: 247. Sodium: 70.32 mg. Fiber: 3.15 g. Protein: 23.8 g. Carbohydrate: 27.3 g. Cholesterol: 72.58 mg. Calcium: 18.2 mg. Iron: 2.57 mg. Potassium: 416.7 mg. Total Fat: 4.9 g; Saturated fat: 1.7 g, Monounsaturated fat: 1.9 g, Polyunsaturated fat: 0.5 g.

❖ BARBECUED BUTTERFLIED LEG OF LAMB ❖

SERVES 12*   SODIUM PER RECIPE: 1,113.6 MG
SODIUM PER SERVING: 92.8 MG

4-pound† boneless leg of lamb, butterflied (1,107 mg)
1 tablespoon dried oregano (.6 mg)
12 cloves garlic (6.12 mg)

1. Cut a dozen 1-inch-deep slits in the lamb and stuff each with oregano and a clove of garlic. Barbecue the lamb on a hot charcoal grill for about 10 to 15 minutes on each side. The lamb should be served medium rare to medium. When done, slice and serve. (If using a gas grill, crank up the flame.) Serve with red potatoes with rosemary spinach and dinner rolls.

Calories: 195. Sodium: 92.8 mg. Fiber: 0.22 g. Protein: 31.3 g. Carbohydrate: 1.234 g. Cholesterol: 96.77 mg. Calcium: 20.4 mg. Iron: 2.968 mg. Potassium: 456.8 mg. Total Fat: 6.4 g; Saturated fat: 2.3 g, Monounsaturated fat: 2.6 g, Polyunsaturated fat: 0.6 g.

*Serving size is 4 ounces.
†Weight after boning.

✳ BABY BACK RIBS/WITH APRICOT MARINADE ✳

SERVES 6   SODIUM PER RECIPE: 563.4 MG   SODIUM PER SERVING: 93.9 MG
Great for baby back ribs, country ribs, and leg of lamb.

  2 **cloves garlic, diced or minced (1.02 mg)**
24 **ounces lean country ribs (455.9 mg)**
⅔ **cup apricot syrup (66 mg)**
⅓ **cup mild molasses (40 mg)**
  2 **tablespoon apple cider vinegar (.15)**

1. Dice, chop, or mince garlic. Simmer all ingredients until just boiling. Pour over lean meat for marinade. Let stand in refrigerator for about 4 or more hours. Bake or barbecue meat. Pour heated marinade sauce over each piece of meat before serving.

The marinade only:

Calories: 139. Sodium: 17.92 mg. Protein: .125 g. Carbohydrate: 36.3 g. Dietary Fiber: .371 g. Total sugars: 32.4 g. Cholesterol: 0 mg. Total Fat: .1 g; Saturated fat: 0 g, Monounsaturated fat: 0 g, Polyunsaturated fat: 0 g. Vitamin K: 0 mcg.

Country ribs with marinade:

Calories: 317. Sodium: 93.9 mg. Protein 22 g. Carbohydrate: 36.3 g. Dietary Fiber: .371 g. Total sugars: 32.4 g. Cholesterol: 72.58 mg. Calcium: 73.4 mg. Potassium: 705.6 mg. Total Fat: 9.4 g; Saturated fat: 3.2 g, Monounsaturated fat: 4.2 g, Polyunsaturated fat: 1 g. Vitamin K: 0 mcg.

CHOICE OF MEAT

Choose either lean, boneless country ribs, or baby back ribs, leg of lamb, or boneless chicken thighs. Barbecue, roast, grill, or oven bake.

Sodium per serving figured into above with marinade based on lean country ribs:

24 ounces precooked choice of meat: Lean country ribs: 455.9 mg. Baby back ribs: 517.1 mg. Boneless leg of lamb: 442.3 mg. 6 skinless, boneless chicken thighs: 356 mg.

❦ LAMB STEW WITH BASMATI RICE ❦

SERVES 6   SODIUM PER RECIPE: 415.8 MG   SODIUM PER SERVING: 69.3 MG

A great way to use leftover lamb. You can also make it with freshly cooked lamb.

1½ **pounds cooked lamb (334.5 mg)**
  1 **tablespoon extra-virgin olive oil (optional) (trace)**
  3 **large tomatoes, diced* (49.1 mg)**
 ½ **cup water (0 mg)**
 ½ **teaspoon coriander (.3 mg)**
 ¼ **teaspoon thyme (trace)**
 ¼ **teaspoon basil (trace)**
 ¼ **teaspoon bay leaf, crumbled (trace)**
 ½ **teaspoon minced fresh parsley (.7 mg)**
 ¼ **cup uncooked basmati rice (.4 mg)**
 ½ **celery stalk (27.8 mg)**
 ½ **onion, chopped (1.65 mg)**
  2 **cloves garlic, minced (2 mg)**

1. If the meat is not cooked, brown it in the oil. Otherwise, place the leftover meat into a stew pot, add the tomatoes, water, and the coriander, thyme, basil, bay leaf, and parsley and cook for about 1 hour. If using fresh, uncooked lamb, cook it longer, or until meat is tender. When meat is ready, remove fat from surface and add the rice, celery, onion, and garlic and cook for ½ hour more. You may also cook this one in a Crock-Pot. Just follow your Crock-Pot's instructions.

Calories: 316. Sodium: 69.33 mg. Fiber: 1.51 g. Protein: 15.7 g. Carbohydrate: 12.2 g. Cholesterol: 201.28 mg. Calcium: 168.1 mg. Iron: 7.221 mg. Potassium: 520.3 mg. Total Fat: 22.7 g; Saturated fat: 11.2 g, Monounsaturated fat: 8.1 g, Polyunsaturated fat: 0.9 g.

*If you prefer to use a cup of canned unsalted tomatoes, add the difference in sodium that is listed on the side of the can and leave out the water. Pathmark, S&W, and a few others produce unsalted cooking tomatoes in cans.

❧ Herb Patties with Vegetable Kabobs ❧

SERVES 2   SODIUM PER RECIPE: (BEEF/CHICKEN = 156.1 MG)
(TURKEY = 218.4 MG)   SODIUM PER SERVING: (BEEF/CHICKEN = 78 MG)
(TURKEY = 109.2 MG)

Everyone gets into the act with this one. Originally a vegetarian delight that used tofu and black-eyed beans, this recipe came to us from our vegetarian friends in Santa Barbara, California.

½ **pound ground turkey, chicken, or beef (152 mg to 213.2 mg)**
¼ **teaspoon rosemary dried (.1 mg)**
¼ **teaspoon sage (trace)**
½ **small pepper red (1.1 mg)**
1 **small zucchini, raw, sliced (3.5 mg)**
⅛ **teaspoon pepper (trace)**
¼ **teaspoon thyme, ground (1.1 mg)**
½ **small Anaheim chili pepper, raw (skinned) trace)**
2 **teaspoons olive oil (trace)**

1. Shape ground meat into two patties about 4 to 5 inches in diameter. Combine pepper, rosemary, and thyme; sprinkle onto both sides of patties. Thread vegetable pieces alternatively on two skewers. Brush lightly with oil; sprinkle with pepper. Place patties and kabobs on rack in broiler pan so surface of meat is 3 to 4 inches from heat. Broil 5 minutes on first side; roll skewers and turn meat. Broil vegetables 5 additional minutes and meat from 5 to 7 minutes.

Beef: Calories: 316. Sodium: 78.04 mg. Protein 22 g. Carbohydrate 2.264 g. Fiber: 1 g. Cholesterol: 76 mg. Calcium 16.5 mg. Iron .612 mg. Potassium 159.3 mg. Total Fat: 24 g: Saturated fat: 8 g, Monosaturated fat: 2.7 g, Polyunsaturated fat: 1.4g.

Turkey: Calories: 300. Sodium: 109.21 mg. Fiber: 1 g. Protein: 20.7 g. Carbohydrate: 2.264 g. Cholesterol: 90.06 mg. Calcium: 31.3 mg. Iron: 2.07 mg. Potassium: 424.9 mg. Total Fat: 23.1 g: Saturated fat: 4.4 g, Monounsaturated fat: 13.5 g, Polyunsaturated fat: 3.5 g.

POULTRY

❖ ❖ ❖ ❖ ❖ ❖ ❖ ❖

DON'S QUICK AND EASY
❖ CHICKEN CASSEROLE ❖

SERVES 4   SODIUM PER RECIPE: 382 MG   SODIUM PER SERVING: 95.5 MG
Slice a few potatoes, open a can of Health Valley Potato Leek Soup,
add a skinless, boneless chicken breast on top and bake for about
50 minutes and you've got a very, very tasty dinner.
Cleanup is easy, too.

4 **medium red or russet potatoes (22.1 mg)**
   15-ounce can Health Valley Potato Leek Soup* (70 mg)
2 **boneless, skinless chicken breast halves† (about 1 pound)**
   (288 mg)
1 **teaspoon coriander (.636 mg)**
1 **teaspoon tarragon (.997 mg)**
   Dash of cloves (.255 mg)
   Pepper to taste (trace)

1. Preheat oven to 350°F.
2. Clean and slice potatoes. Layer half the potatoes at the bottom of a 9x9-inch baking pan (glass is best with this recipe). Pour ½ can of the soup on the potatoes. Layer the remaining potatoes on top and cover with the remaining soup over that.
3. Next put the chicken breasts on top. Combine the coriander, tarragon, and cloves, and "pinch" over chicken breasts once set into the pan. Add pepper after cooking. Cover with foil and bake at 350°F for 30 minutes. Remove the foil and continue to bake for another 30 to 40 minutes. Test the potatoes. When they are done, the chicken will be done. Serve with broccoli, green beans, or banana squash.

Calories: 234. Sodium: 95.5 mg. Fiber: 3.2 g. Protein: 30.1g. Carbohydrate: 24.5 g. Cholesterol: 64 mg. Calcium: 14.3 mg. Iron: .909 mg. Potassium: 517.7 mg. Total Fat: 1.8 g; Saturated fat: 0.4 g, Monounsaturated fat: 0.1 g, Polyunsaturated fat: 0.1 g.

*Available from your local grocery store or www.healthymarket.com.
†You can substitute thin, lean pork chops for the chicken breast.

❖ CHICKEN POT PIE ❖

SERVES 6   SODIUM PER RECIPE: 582 MG   SODIUM PER SERVING: 97 MG
*This is one of the tastiest chicken pot pies we've tested and we prepare it at least once a month during the winter. You can use some of **Chef Scott's Chicken Broth** you prepared and stored in your freezer or refrigerator. I use a pastry dough very similar to a great pie dough. It has no salt and is basically a zero-sodium crust. It's definitely worth the effort.*

THE CRUST
1½ cups Stone Buhr unbleached white flour (3.75 mg)
½ cup extra-virgin olive oil (trace)
1 to 2 tablespoons lukewarm water (0 mg)

THE FILLING
1 cup frozen unsalted peas or fresh peas (7.25 mg)
3 tablespoons extra-virgin olive oil (trace)
6 tablespoons unsalted butter (9.3 mg)
2 medium carrots, thinly sliced (42.7 mg)
½ pound mushrooms—dark or portabella types—sliced (7.36 mg)
½ cup thinly sliced onions (2.4 mg)
1 leek—white and pale green parts only; washed, thinly sliced (2.4 mg)
8 skinless chicken thighs, boned (474.7 mg)
Pepper to taste (optional)
3 tablespoons unbleached white flour (1.6 mg)
1½ cups chicken broth made by combining 1½ teaspoons Herb-Ox Low Sodium Chicken Broth (7.5 mg) and 1½ cups water (0 mg)—or substitute Chef Scott's Chicken Broth
½ cup half-and-half or whole milk, low sodium (3.5 mg)
2 tablespoons chopped fresh parsley (4.25 mg)
1½ teaspoons dried tarragon (1.5 mg)
1 large egg yolk (7 mg)

1. For the crust, mix together the flour and oil with a fork, adding water as needed. When done, roll it into a ball, wrap it in waxed paper, and store it in the refrigerator for at least ½ hour while you prepare the pie filling. When ready to use, remove the dough from the refrigerator and let it stand for about 10 to 15 minutes before rolling it out.

2. Place the fresh or unsalted thawed peas into a large baking dish. Heat 2 tablespoons of the oil and 4 tablespoons of the butter in a large skillet. Sauté the mushrooms over medium-high heat for about 5 minutes; stir frequently to prevent burning. Remove the mushrooms with a slotted spoon and add to the peas in the baking dish. Heat the remaining oil in the same skillet, add the carrots, onions, and leeks and cover. Cook for 10 minutes over low heat, stirring occasionally to prevent burning. When done, remove the vegetables with a slotted spoon and add them to the baking dish.

3. Cut chicken into 1-inch cubes, then pat with a paper towel until dry. Season with pepper to taste, but do not add salt. In the same skillet sauté the chicken in the remaining butter and oil for about 15 minutes over medium-high heat. When done, remove the other ingredients in the baking dish with a slotted spoon and add them to the chicken pieces. The skillet should still have some fat in it. If not, add additional butter and olive oil. Stir the flour into the fat and cook over high heat, stirring continuously with a wooden spoon for about 12 minutes. Stir in the chicken broth and the half-and-half and simmer. Stir, scraping up any brown bits on the bottom of the skillet and mixing it into the sauce. Cook for about 5 minutes this way until the sauce is smooth and thick—the thicker the better. Add the sauce to the baking dish and stir gently to blend. Add the fresh parsley and tarragon. Season with additional pepper if you like, but no salt. You can use any Mrs. Dash, Lawry's, or Spice Island for salt-free herb mix (0 mg sodium). If you want to make individual servings now is the time to do it. Ladle one-sixth of the mixture into each dish. Your pastry mix can be made to cover the individual serving dishes or a single large baking dish.

PLACING THE CRUST ON TOP OF THE PIE AND BAKING

Preheat the oven to 425°F.

Roll the pastry out to a 12-to-14-inch round or whatever size your baking dish is—or cut individual rounds to fit the smaller serving dishes. When laying pastry over a dish, fold the edges to sit up as a ridge on the dish's rim. Cut slashes in the top of crust to let steam escape. In a small bowl beat the egg yolk with 2 teaspoons water and brush this glaze over the top and sides of the pie crust.

If using a large baking dish, place it in the center of the oven and reduce the heat to 375°F and bake for about 40 to 50 minutes. If using individual servers, place them on a rack close to the center of the oven and bake for 30 to 40 minutes. Pot pie is best served hot.

Calories: 625. Sodium: 97.03 mg. Fiber: 3.74 g. Protein: 25.1 g. Carbohydrate: 38.8 g. Cholesterol: 110.21 mg. Calcium: 69.1 mg. Iron: 4.267 mg. Potassium: 610.1 mg. Total Fat: 41.3 g. Saturated fat: 12 g, Monounsaturated fat: 22.9 g, Polyunsaturated fat: 3.7 g.

Cajun Seasoned Chicken with
✸ Mustard and Lemon ✸

SERVES 2   SODIUM PER RECIPE: 154.9 MG   SODIUM PER SERVING: 77.4 MG

2 boneless, skinless chicken breast halves (153.4 mg)
2 to 4 teaspoons Frontier cajun seasoning* (trace)
2 cloves garlic, minced (1 mg)
1 teaspoon olive oil (trace)
  Juice of 1 lemon (.5 mg)
1 teaspoon dry mustard (trace)

1. Coat the chicken breasts with the Frontier cajun seasoning combined with the minced garlic. In a nonstick pan heat the oil and sauté the chicken. When done, remove the chicken to a platter. Combine the lemon juice and dry mustard in the hot pan. Mix with the chicken coating spices remaining in the pan. Return the chicken to the pan and cook for an additional minute or so, rolling the chicken around in the sauce. Serve, spooning the remaining sauce over the chicken.

Calories: 164. Sodium: 77.45 mg. Fiber: 0.16 g. Protein: 27.8 g. Carbohydrate: 7.17 g. Cholesterol: 68.44 mg. Calcium: 22.6 mg. Iron: .976 mg. Potassium: 347.6 mg. Total Fat: 4 g; Saturated fat: 0.7 g, Monounsaturated fat: 2.1 g, Polyunsaturated fat: 0.6 g.

Roasted Chicken with
✸ Grilled Red Bell Pepper Sauce ✸

SERVES 4   SODIUM PER RECIPE: 324.7 MG   SODIUM PER SERVING: 81.2 MG

4 chicken breasts halves, boned and skinned† (306.8 mg)
3 garlic cloves, minced (1.5 mg)
1 tablespoon lemon pepper‡ blend (2 mg)
1 cup Grilled Red Bell Pepper Sauce, page 183 (13.6 mg)

1. Preheat the oven to 475°F.
2. Rub the chicken with the garlic and season with lemon pepper. Place the breasts in a roasting pan and roast in a preheated 475°F oven for 8 to 10 minutes. Reduce the heat to 425°F and continue roasting for approximately another 20 minutes. Since oven temperatures vary greatly, be careful not

*Obtainable at some health food stores or mail-order from www.healthyheartmarket.com or 1-800/753-0310.
†About 5 ounces each. Add or subtract 18 mg sodium for each ounce over or under.
‡Do not use lemon pepper seasoning unless it's "salt-free."

to undercook or overcook the chicken—cooked breast meat should be tender when pressed with a finger. Remove the breasts from the oven, place on plates, and drizzle **Grilled Red Bell Pepper Sauce** over each.

3. Serve with **Polenta** (pages 136–7).

Calories: 192. Sodium: 81.18 mg. Fiber: 1.87 g. Protein: 28.4 g. Carbohydrate: 7.449 g. Cholesterol: 68.44 mg. Calcium: 36 mg. Iron: 1.734 mg. Potassium: 479.7 mg. Total Fat: 5.2 g; Saturated fat: 0.7 g, Monounsaturated fat: 2.5 g, Polyunsaturated fat: 1.5 g.

SOUTHERN FRIED CHICKEN/
❖ THE LOW-FAT, LOW-SODIUM WAY ❖

SERVES 4   SODIUM PER RECIPE: 304.1 MG   SODIUM PER SERVING: 76 MG

Surprisingly delicious, these baked pieces will remind you of your favorite deep-fat–fried chicken.

**4 boneless, skinless chicken thighs or 6 chicken legs totaling
    ¾ pound (237.4 mg)**
½ cups enriched cornmeal (0 mg)
¼ cup Best for Bread unbleached flour (.625 mg)
½ teaspoon ground coriander (.3 mg)
½ teaspoon thyme (.4 mg)
¼ teaspoon ground cloves (1.2 mg)
2 garlic cloves, minced (1 mg)
Pepper to taste (trace)
½ cup nonfat milk (63.1 mg) or 1 well-beaten egg white (53 mg)
3 tablespoons extra-virgin olive oil (trace)
**Unsalted butter (trace) or additional olive oil (trace) for
    dabbing chicken**

1. If you are using a standard oven, preheat it to 400°F; for a convection oven, preheat 375°F. Combine the cornmeal, flour, coriander, thyme, cloves, garlic, and pepper to taste. Dip the chicken pieces into the milk or egg white, then coat with the cornmeal mixture. Bake the chicken on a nonstick rack or in a pan lightly coated with extra-virgin olive oil. Dab the chicken with unsalted butter or olive oil before baking. Bake for 40 minutes in a standard oven, or for about 30 to 35 minutes in a convection oven. Serve hot.

Calories: 242. Sodium: 76.03 mg. Fiber: 1.05 g. Protein: 16.2 g. Carbohydrate: 14.6 g. Cholesterol: 57.82 mg. Calcium: 54.5 mg. Iron: 2.628 mg. Potassium: 230.5 mg. Total Fat: 13.2 g; Saturated fat: 2.1 g, Monounsaturated fat: 8.4 g, Polyunsaturated fat: 1.6 g.

SERVES 6   SODIUM PER RECIPE: 550.2 MG   SODIUM PER SERVING: 91.7 MG

You'll have this dish more than once. As a matter of fact, you might have it again tomorrow night. The leftovers are just as tasty as the meal itself.

<pre>
  2 tablespoons finely crumbled dried rosemary (3.2 mg)
  2 tablespoons finely crumbled dried sage (.44 mg)
  3 garlic cloves, minced (1.5 mg)
 ½ cup olive oil (trace)
  6 (4-ounce) boneless chicken breast halves or thighs or a mix of
       both (460.2 mg)
1½ tablespoons paprika (1 mg)
  3 pounds small red new potatoes, peeled, cut in half, and sub-
       merged in water in a large pan (70 mg)
  2 large yellow onions, peeled and cut into quarters (9 mg)
  8 whole garlic cloves, peeled (4.08 mg)
  3 tablespoons red wine vinegar (.45 mg)
</pre>

1. Preheat the oven to 450°F.

2. With a wooden spoon, mix together the rosemary, sage, minced garlic, and olive oil in a small bowl. Add the chicken after rinsing under cold water and patting it dry. Immerse the chicken pieces one at a time in the mixture and roll. Sprinkle paprika over the coated chicken parts. Let stand in the refrigerator for 1 to 2 hours.

3. After potatoes have soaked for ½ hour, pat them dry. Add them along with the onions and garlic to the bowl with the chicken, then mix well.

4. Place all the ingredients, including all the marinade, into a preheated roasting pan in the 450°F oven. Spread the mixture evenly in the pan. Cook for 25 minutes, then reduce the heat to 400°F, and cook for an additional 30 to 45 minutes (or less if the chicken appears cooked and the potatoes are browned). Baste the chicken occasionally during the cooking time. When done, transfer the chicken to a serving dish and stir in the vinegar.

Calories: 471. Sodium: 91.68 mg. Protein: 32.2 g. Carbohydrate: 41.5 g. Fiber: 4.8 g. Cholesterol: 68.44 mg. Calcium: 59.4 mg. Iron: 1.8 mg. Potassium: 438.9 mg. Total Fat: 20.1 g; Saturated fat: 3.2 g, Monounsaturated fat: 13.7 g, Polyunsaturated fat: 1.9 g.

EASY BARBECUED CHICKEN WITH

❖ ORANGE AND ROSEMARY ❖

SERVES 6   SODIUM PER RECIPE: 479.9 MG   SODIUM PER SERVING: 80 MG

For a complete outdoor repast, add seasoned vegetables and boiled red potatoes to the grill as well. This preparation also works well with turkey, duck, and wild fowl.

1 cup white wine—not cooking wine (11.8 mg)
¼ cup genuine brewed rice vinegar (.6 mg)
¼ teaspoon sugar (.5 mg)
1 teaspoon dill (.415 mg)
6 chicken breast halves without skin (totaling about 1½ pounds) (460.2 mg)
3 tablespoons olive oil (trace)
3 cloves garlic, minced (1.5 mg)
1½ cups Smucker's Low Sugar Orange Marmalade (4.335 mg)
1 tablespoon fresh minced rosemary (.44 mg)
   Pinch white pepper (trace)
   Dash Frontier barbecue seasoning* (trace)

1. In a large bowl, mix the wine, vinegar, sugar, and dill. Place the breasts in the marinade, cover, and refrigerate for 24 hours.† Preheat the barbecue coals or gas charbroiler to medium-hot. Combine the remaining ingredients. Place the breasts on the grill, skin-side down (or meat-side down if skinless). Turn after 6 to 8 minutes. Baste frequently with the marinade. Grill the chicken for about 8 to 10 minutes, or until the breast meat is just firm to the touch.‡ Top with any leftover sauce (not marinade) and serve immediately.

Calories: 358. Sodium: 79.98 mg. Fiber: 1.47g. Protein: 27.8 g. Carbohydrate: 35.9 g. Cholesterol: 68.44 mg. Calcium: 33.3 mg. Iron: 1.362 mg. Potassium: 429.6 mg. Total Fat: 8.7 g; Saturated fat: 0.9 g, Monounsaturated fat: 4.5 g, Polyunsaturated fat: 2.5 g.

> *William Prince, of Kissimmee, Florida, writes, "After having bypass surgery, the doctors told me to lose as much sodium as possible. I could no longer have fried foods either. So, with this recipe I sort of kill two birds with one stone. I grill the chicken plain because most bottle sauces are too high in sodium. With this recipe I can put some flavor in an otherwise bland diet."*

*Available by mail order from Healthy Heart Market at 1-800/753-0310.
†Or, if you have one, use the FoodSaver vacuum sealer unit for marinating and marinate for only 20 minutes.
‡Your barbecue may require shorter or longer cooking time.

❈ SPICY CHICKEN ❈

SERVES 4   SODIUM PER RECIPE: 370.5 MG   SODIUM PER SERVING: 92.6 MG

This recipe uses nutritional herbs and a tomato base. Essentially a Middle Eastern dish, we've modified it greatly to fit with a low-sodium diet.

> 4 chicken breast halves or 1 whole chicken cut into serving pieces (306.8 mg)
> 1 level tablespoon curry powder (3.2 mg)
> 1 hot green chili, diced (3 mg), or 1 Ortega brand canned chili, diced (10 mg)
> 3 tablespoons extra-virgin olive oil (trace)
> ¼ cup ginger root, grated (3 mg)
> 6 cloves garlic, minced or crushed (3 mg)
> 3 medium onions, chopped (3.3 mg)
> 2 medium tomatoes, chopped (22 mg)
> 3 tablespoons chopped fresh coriander* (5.2 mg)
> 2 tablespoons Contadina Natural Tomato Paste (20 mg)
> 1 teaspoon oregano (trace)
> 1 teaspoon chopped fresh basil (trace)
> Pepper to taste (trace)
> Mrs. Dash or Frontier seasoning blend to taste (trace)

1. Sauté the curry and the chili in the oil for about 1 minute. While stirring constantly, add the ginger and garlic and continue to cook for an additional minute or two. Next add the onions and cook until they begin to color. Add the tomatoes, coriander, tomato paste, oregano, basil, pepper and seasoning to taste, and cook for another 3 minutes, or until oil begins to show on the surface. Add the chicken,† cover, and simmer over low heat for 40 minutes, or until the chicken is tender to the touch. The sauce will have thickened.

Calories: 283. Sodium: 96.62 mg. Protein: 29.9 g. Carbohydrate 13.4 g. Fiber: 4.08 g. Cholesterol: 68.44 mg. Calcium: 73.3 mg. Iron: 3.725 mg. Potassium: 641.3 mg. Total Fat: 12.8 g; Saturated fat: 1.9 g, Monounsaturated fat: 8.5 g, Polyunsaturated fat: 1.4 g.

*If coriander is not available, substitute fresh cilantro. If neither is available, use level tablespoons of dried coriander or cilantro.
†Other versions of this recipe include 2 large sliced potatoes that are added at the same time as the chicken. If you use potatoes, select white or new potatoes, red potatoes, or peeled russets and add 14 mg of sodium to the total.

❧ BAKED CHICKEN LEGS ❧

MAKES 10 LEGS   SODIUM PER RECIPE: 557.1 MG
SODIUM PER SERVING: 55.7 MG

Rich in vitamins A, C, and E, this is also a delicious way to make chicken snacks. I like to bake them, put them into the refrigerator in resealable bags, and have them available during the week for lunch or afternoon snacks. The paprika, chili flakes, safflower oil, and rice vinegar serve as good plant antioxidants.

10 skinless chicken drumsticks (545.6 mg)
 1 teaspoon extra-virgin olive oil for oiling the baking pan
   (trace)
1½ teaspoons dry mustard* (0 mg)
 ¾ teaspoon paprika (.5 mg)
 ¼ teaspoon chili flakes (6.5 mg)
 2 teaspoons red wine or balsamic vinegar† (trace)
 ¼ teaspoon sugar (trace)
 1 cup soft homemade bread crumbs‡ (4.33 mg)

1. Preheat the oven to 400°F.
2. Brush the baking pan with the oil. Mix the mustard, paprika, and chili flakes with the vinegar and sugar and spread the mixture over the chicken legs. Roll the chicken legs in the crumb mixture and transfer them to the baking pan. Bake, covered, at 400°F until tender, approximately 25 minutes. For more antioxidant help, sprinkle fresh basil over legs when done.

Calories: 125. Sodium: 55.71 mg. Fiber: 0.44 g. Protein: 14.1 g. Carbohydrate: 8.985 g. Cholesterol: 47.74 mg. Calcium: 10.2 mg. Iron: 1.488 mg. Potassium: 168.4 mg. Total Fat: 3.3 g; Saturated fat: 0.7 g, Monounsaturated fat: 1.4 g, Polyunsaturated fat: 0.7 g.

*Or use Hain or Featherweight Low Sodium Mustard. You may alter the flavor slightly by using Grey Poupon Honey Mustard (15 mg).
†Or a vinegar of your choice from white to natural rice wine. The vinegar will dominate the flavors here, so pick one you really enjoy.
‡Use any homemade bread recipe in this book.

❧ PAELLA ❧

SERVES 6   SODIUM PER RECIPE: 931.4 MG   SODIUM PER SERVING: 155.2 MG

Michael McCay, who lives in a town in Spain called Zarautz in the province of Guipúzcoa, just down the road from San Sebastián-Donostia, sent this along with the added info that Paella has so many different variations that it is impossible to keep up with them. The reason? Paella is one of those "throw all the leftovers into the pot" meals. This version is his favorite.

1 small onion, minced (2.1 mg)
4 tablespoons minced fresh parsley (8.5 mg)
3 cloves garlic, minced (1.53 mg)
⅓ cup extra-virgin olive oil (trace)
  Generous pinch of saffron (.3 mg)
6 cups chicken broth made by combining 2 tablespoons Herb-ox Low Sodium Chicken Broth (30 mg) and 6 cups water (0 mg)
6 skinless, boneless chicken breast halves, cut into large chunks (432 mg)
2 medium green peppers, seeded and sliced (4.76 mg)
1 sweet red pepper, seeded and sliced (2.38 mg)
  8-ounce can Del Monte No-Salt-Added Tomato Sauce (73.2 mg)
1 teaspoon sugar (trace)
4 cups arborio or regular rice (37 mg)
7 cups water (0 mg)
  Pinch of Frontier all-purpose blend seasoning (trace)
½ pound shrimp, shells on (339.7 mg)

1. Sauté the onion, parsley, and garlic in the oil until the onion becomes translucent. Add the saffron, chicken broth, chicken, and peppers and sauté until the chicken turns white. Add the tomato sauce and sugar and stir. Next add the rice and water and bring to a boil. Season to taste. Boil for 5 minutes, stirring occasionally. Add the shrimp, boil for an additional 5 minutes, stirring frequently. Simmer for 10 minutes, covered, stirring occasionally. If the rice appears to be getting too dry during the last 10 minutes, add more water. If the rice is too wet at the end of the 10 minutes, uncover and cook away the unwanted liquid.

Calories: 768. Sodium: 155.24 mg. Fiber: 3.65 g. Protein: 43.9 g. Carbohydrate: 110.1 g. Cholesterol: 122.14 mg. Calcium: 74.1 mg. Potassium: 507.6 mg. Total Fat: 15.2 g; Saturated fat: 2.4 g, Monounsaturated fat: 9.1 g, Polyunsaturated fat: 1.6 g.

❧ CHICKEN IN ALMOND SAUCE ❧

SERVES 6   SODIUM PER RECIPE: 420.4 MG   SODIUM PER SERVING: 70.1 MG
Pollo *is the Spanish word for chicken. Delicious is the word for this recipe from Mike McCay, who lives near Madrid, Spain.*

1½ **pounds skinless, boneless chicken, a mix of breast halves, thighs, and legs (356 mg)**
   Pepper to taste (trace)
   Unbleached flour to coat chicken pieces (.15 mg)
 3 **tablespoons extra-virgin olive oil (trace)**
20 **unsalted almonds, blanched and skinned (2 mg)**
 6 **cloves garlic (3 mg)**
 1 **thick slice unsalted homemade Crusty French Bread, page 248, crust removed (.8 mg)**
 1 **onion, chopped (3.3 mg)**
 1 **tablespoon chopped fresh parsley (2 mg)**
 ¼ **teaspoon ground cinnamon (.15 mg)**
   Pinch of grated fresh nutmeg (trace)
   Pinch of ground cloves (1 mg)
 8 **peppercorns or ground black pepper (1 mg)**
 ⅓ **teaspoon saffron (.5 mg)**
 ¼ **cup white wine (5.9 mg)**
 ½ **cup chicken broth made by combining ½ teaspoon Herb-ox Low Sodium Chicken Broth (2.5 mg) with ½ cup water (0 mg)**
 2 **bay leaves, broken (.4 mg)**
 1 **hard-cooked egg, yolk only (7 mg)**
 1 **tablespoon toasted sesame seed (11 mg)**

1. Rub the chicken with pepper and roll in flour. Heat the olive oil in a large nonstick roaster pan and brown the chicken on both sides. Set the chicken aside. Add the almonds, garlic, and bread to the same pan and "stir-fry" them until the bread is golden brown. Set them aside. Add the onion to the oil and sauté slowly. (If no oil is left, add another tablespoon.) Blend the almonds, garlic, and bread in a food processor along with the parsley, cinnamon, nutmeg, cloves, peppercorns, and saffron. Pour in the wine. Combine the spice mixture with the sautéed onion and pour it over the browned chicken pieces. Add enough broth to partially cover the chicken. Add the bay leaves. Simmer, covered, in the pan for about 1 hour, or until the chicken is tender. Or you may bake the chicken in a large casserole dish in the oven at 325°F for about 45 minutes. Just before serving, mash the egg yolk and stir it into the sauce to help thicken it. Serve sprinkled with the toasted sesame seeds.

Calories: 256. Sodium: 70.06 mg. Fiber: 2 g. Protein: 17.9 g. Carbohydrate: 10.1 g. Cholesterol: 96.1 mg. Calcium: 41.8 mg. Iron: 2.268 mg. Potassium: 293.2 mg. Total Fat: 14.7 g: Saturated fat: 2.4 g, Monounsaturated fat: 8.2 g, Polyunsaturated fat: 2.8 g.

SERVES 4   SODIUM PER RECIPE: 369.7 MG   SODIUM PER SERVING: 92.4 MG

*A terrific recipe to serve an important vegetable. Sprinkle with
unsalted cashews for a taste treat.*

**4 skinless, boneless chicken breast halves—about 1 to 1¼
pounds (306.8 mg)**
1 tablespoon cornstarch (.72 mg)
¼ teaspoon black pepper (.23 mg)
2 cups broccoli—about 1 pound (47.5 mg)
4 green onions (9.6 mg)
1 hot chili pepper* (3.15 mg)
1 teaspoon vinegar (trace)
1 teaspoon lemon juice (trace)
1 teaspoon hot sesame seed oil (0 mg)
4 cloves garlic, minced (2 mg)
1 teaspoon sugar (trace)
1 teaspoon finely chopped ginger root (.26 mg)
2 tablespoons extra-virgin olive oil (trace)

1. Cut the chicken into bite-size pieces. Mix the chicken with the dissolved cornstarch and pepper in a medium-size bowl. Cover tightly with plastic wrap and refrigerate for about 20 to 30 minutes while preparing the balance of the recipe.

2. Cut off the flowerets and peel broccoli stems. Slice the stem lengthwise into 3 or 4 strips. Slice these strips into bite-size pieces. Break up the flowerets. Steam the broccoli until just tender. When done, rinse in cold water and drain. Cut the green onions diagonally into bite-size lengths (about 1 inch or less). Remove the seeds from the chili pepper and cut it into thin slices.

3. Mix together the vinegar, lemon juice, sesame oil, garlic, sugar, ginger root, and garlic. Set the skillet or wok over high heat until hot. Add the olive oil and roll the pan to coat the bottom and sides. Add vinegar/sesame oil mix and stir-fry for about 10 seconds. Add the chicken and stir-fry for another 2 minutes, or until chicken turns white. Add the broccoli and onions and stir-fry for another minute, or until the broccoli is hot.[†]

*Calories: 201. Sodium: 92.44 mg. Fiber: 0.64 g. Protein: 29.3 g. Carbohydrate: 6.852 g.
Cholesterol: 68.44 mg. Calcium: 53.2 mg. Iron: 1.706 mg. Potassium: 542.1 mg. Total Fat:
6.2 g; Saturated fat: 1 g, Monounsaturated fat: 3.3 g, Polyunsaturated fat: 1.2 g.*

*Or ½ teaspoon cayenne pepper or 1 teaspoon chili pepper flakes. You can use canned chilies, but then you need to add 30 mg of sodium per chili.
[†]If you feel the chicken is not cooked through, cook for an additional minute, stirring constantly.

❖ LEMON CHICKEN ❖

SERVES 4   SODIUM PER RECIPE: 348.7 MG   SODIUM PER SERVING: 87.2 MG

For years we prepared this dish in our Crock-Pot. It worked just fine but took too much time, so, now we make it on top of the stove in a pot, cooking it over low heat for 1 hour.

　4　boneless chicken breast halves (306.8 mg)*
　¼　cup flour (2.5 mg)
　2　tablespoons extra-virgin olive oil (trace)
　　　6-ounce can frozen lemonade, thawed and undiluted (8.76 mg)
　3　tablespoons brown sugar (10.5 mg)
　1　tablespoon vinegar (red wine) (.15 mg)
　¼　cup Hunt's No Salt Added Tomato Sauce (20 mg)

1. Remove all the skin and fat from the chicken. Coat the chicken with flour and brown on all sides in hot olive oil. Remove the chicken from the pan. Stir in the lemonade concentrate, brown sugar, vinegar, and tomato sauce and mix well. Transfer the chicken either to a sauté pan or a Crock-Pot. For stovetop preparation, cook over low heat for 1 hour. If using a Crock-Pot, cover and cook on high for 3 to 4 hours or on low for 6 to 8 hours.

Calories: 403. Sodium: 87.19 mg. Fiber: 1.31 g. Protein: 30.6 g. Carbohydrate: 57.4 g. Cholesterol: 68.44 mg. Calcium: 109 mg. Iron: 11.3 mg. Potassium: 1,578 mg. Total Fat: 5.3 g. Saturated fat: 0.9 g. Monounsaturated fat: 2.9 g. Polyunsaturated fat: 0.8 g.

❖ BARBECUED LEMON CHICKEN ❖

SERVES 4   SODIUM PER RECIPE: 314.4 MG   SODIUM PER SERVING: 78.6 MG

　4　(5-ounce) boneless, skinless chicken breasts, washed and fat
　　　removed (306.8 mg)
　1　lemon, juiced, the rind grated (.5 mg)
　2　cloves garlic, minced (1 mg)
　½　cup red wine vinegar (1.2 mg)
　4　basil leaves, chopped (trace)
　1　teaspoon sage (trace)
　1　teaspoon coriander (.6 mg)
　¼　cup extra-virgin olive oil (trace)

1. Combine all the marinade ingredients in a large bowl and stir well. Add the chicken in the marinade and either draw it using a vacuum sealer such

*Or substitute just thighs (4 large) or boneless, skinless breast halves. If you choose to use a whole chicken, add another 350 mg sodium and double the fat to the recipe count.

as the FoodSaver Unit (for only 20 minutes), or put it in the refrigerator to marinate for at least 2 hours. Grill the chicken over barbecue coals, turning often and ladling on marinade each time, or grill on the stove over medium heat turning the pieces until they are cooked through.

Optional: If you're a mustard lover, you can use any of the unsalted mustards, such as the Featherweight prepared mustard or the Grey Poupon, Hain Stone Ground, or Mendocino Honey Mustards at an average 15 mg sodium per tablespoon.

Calories: 261. Sodium: 78.65 mg. Fiber: 0.42 g. Protein: 27.5 g. Carbohydrate: 3.781 g. Cholesterol: 68.44 mg. Calcium: 28 mg. Iron: 1.37 mg. Potassium: 372.5 mg. Total Fat: 15.1 g; Saturated fat: 2.2 g. Monounsaturated fat: 0.4 g. Polyunsaturated fat: 1.5 g.

❖ CRISPY CHICKEN WITHOUT THE FRYING ❖

SERVES 4   SODIUM PER RECIPE: 503.6 MG   SODIUM PER SERVING: 125.9 MG
An alternative to deep-fried chicken, these crunchy chicken pieces have plenty of character. Serve with sweet white summer corn-on-the-cob, coleslaw, and a glass of freshly brewed iced tea. This method also works great with pheasant breasts.

- 1 **cup unbleached white bread flour (2.5 mg)**
- 1 **tablespoon garlic powder (2 mg)**
- 1 **tablespoon Spice Island onion (3.4 mg)***
- 1 **tablespoon dried basil flakes (1.54 mg)**
- 4 **chicken breast halves,† boned, skinless washed, and fat removed, each cut into 6 pieces (306.8 mg)**
- 3 **medium eggs, lightly beaten (166.3 mg)**
- 3 **tablespoon unsalted mustard (0 mg)‡**
- 2 **cups homemade bread crumbs§ (2.8 mg)**
- 1 **tablespoon cracked black pepper (2.8 mg)**
- 3 **tablespoons mustard seeds (1.6 mg)**
- 3 **tablespoons sesame seeds (2.97 mg)**
- 2 **tablespoons celery seeds (10.4 mg)**
- ½ **teaspoon Mrs. Dash Lemon & Herb Salt Free blend (trace)**

*Brand like McCormack Onion Flakes recommended, since others can have as much as 1,000 mg sodium per teaspoon.
†You may substitute boned thighs or legs.
‡Hain unsalted has 10 mg sodium per tablespoon. Featherweight has 0 mg. If you use Hain instead of Featherweight, add to the sodium count.
§Use bread from the **Homemade Bread** or **Sandwich Buns** recipe. Dry either by toasting or leaving out overnight. Break up into crumbs.

1. Preheat the oven to 375°F.

2. Sift together the flour, garlic powder, onion powder, and basil flakes. Dredge the chicken pieces in seasoned flour to coat evenly. Dip each floured piece into the egg mixture. Combine the remaining ingredients in a medium-size bowl and mix well. Roll each chicken piece in the coating mixture and then refrigerate for 30 minutes. Transfer the chicken pieces to a lightly greased baking dish and bake, uncovered, until golden brown, about 35 to 40 minutes.

Calories: 472. Sodium: 125.87 mg. Fiber: 4.9 g. Protein: 41.1 g. Carbohydrate: 50.7 g. Cholesterol: 208.7 mg. Calcium 214 mg. Iron: 7.654 mg. Potassium: 617.6 mg. Total Fat: 12.3 g; Saturated fat: 2.2 g, Monounsaturated fat: 5.4 g, Polyunsaturated fat: 3.1 g.

❖ CHICKEN WITH ORANGE-HONEY GLAZE ❖

SERVES 4   SODIUM PER RECIPE: 318.8 MG   SODIUM PER SERVING: 79.7 MG

1 teaspoon dried coriander (.6 mg)
1 teaspoon thyme (.766 mg)
1 teaspoon ground cloves (5.099 mg)
4 chicken breast halves, boned and skinned* (306.8 mg)
  Pepper to taste (trace)
6 tablespoons honey (3.36 mg)
¾ cup freshly squeezed orange juice (1.8 mg)
4 tablespoons freshly granted orange rind (.2 mg)

1. Preheat the oven to 375°F.

2. Combine the thyme, coriander, and cloves in a small bowl so that you can add it later on. Rinse the chicken and pat it dry with paper towels. Season lightly with pepper.

3. Place chicken meat-side down in a 9x9-inch baking dish. Pour the orange juice into the dish. Brush the chicken with half of the honey and sprinkle on half of the spice mixture. Bake in the preheated oven for about 20 minutes. Turn the chicken over, so that it is meat-side up. Brush the remaining honey on the meat and sprinkle on the remaining spice mix. Lower the oven temperature to 325°F and continue baking for 20 to 25 minutes. Remove the chicken and arrange it on a platter on individual serving plates. Season with additional pepper to taste. Pour some sauce over each chicken breast half. Top with grated orange rind. Serve hot.

Calories: 221. Sodium: 79.7 mg. Fiber: 0.85 g. Protein: 27.8 g. Carbohydrate: 23.4 g. Cholesterol: 68.44 mg. Calcium: 35.9 mg. Iron: 1.606 mg. Potassium: 423.7 mg. Total Fat: 1.8 g; Saturated fat: 0.4 g, Monounsaturated fat: 0.4 g, Polyunsaturated fat: 0.4 g.

*About 5 ounces each. Add or subtract 18 mg sodium for each ounce over or under.

❖ QUICK CHICKEN DINNER FOR ONE ❖

SERVES 1   SODIUM PER RECIPE: 98.2 MG

Of course you can make more. But when I'm home alone, this recipe makes a great meal, and it goes from oven to table in the same dish. Tasty, nutritious, and very satisfying, I think you'll like it, too.

1 **large skinless chicken thigh (59.3 mg)**
1 **medium or large red potato (7.32 mg)**
³/₈ **teaspoon olive oil (trace)**
½ **Spanish or sweet white onion (1.65 mg)**
6 **baby carrots or ½ medium carrot (21 mg)**
4 **tablespoons natural maple syrup* (7.2 mg)**
2 **pinches Don's Herb Chicken Spices (page 184) (.863 mg)†**
   Pinch rosemary (trace)

1. Preheat the oven to 325°F.
2. You may also use a boneless thigh in this recipe. Clean the potato and cut it in half. Lightly rub the potato with some of the olive oil. Skin and thinly slice the onion. If you are using the ½ medium carrot, skin it and cut it into slices. Rub a single-serving oblong baking dish with the remaining olive oil. Place the sliced onions on bottom, spreading them out. Ladle the maple syrup over the onions. Lay the carrots on top of the onions or to the side. Set a potato half at either end and add a pinch of rosemary to each. Put the chicken in the center of the dish. Ladle the honey over the chicken. Spread pinches of herb mixture on the chicken. Bake in the 325°F preheated oven for 20 minutes. Turn the chicken over and raise the heat to 350°F and bake for another 15 to 20 minutes. Serve hot.

Calories: 513. Sodium: 98.23 mg. Fiber: 4.3 g. Protein: 17.4 g. Carbohydrate: 103.1 g. Cholesterol: 57.27 mg. Calcium: 102.4 mg. Iron: 3.662 mg. Potassium: 1,260 mg. Total Fat: 5.2 g; Saturated fat: 1.1 g, Monounsaturated fat: 2.2 g, Polyunsaturated fat: 1.2 g.

*Use only pure maple syrup. Others are high in sodium.
†Make a bunch of this and store it in an old spice bottle.

❧ CHICKEN AND VEGETABLES ❧

SERVES 4   SODIUM PER RECIPE: 490.7 MG   SODIUM PER SERVING: 122.7 MG

3 medium carrots, peeled and cut into 1-inch pieces (64.1 mg)
3 yams, peeled and cut into ½-inch dice (54 mg)
4 large red potatoes, cut into halves (44.2 mg)
3 medium yellow onions, cut into quarters (6 mg)
4 boneless, skinless chicken breast halves (306.8 mg)
  lemon juice, spritz (0 mg)
1 cup white wine or white grape juice (11.8 mg)
  Rosemary sprigs (trace)

1. Preheat the oven to 350°F.
2. Put the veggies on the bottom of a nonstick roasting pan. Put chicken into the pan—either directly on the bottom or on top of the veggies. Squirt lemon juice on the chicken and cover with 1 cup white wine or grape juice. Throw in some sprigs of rosemary. Bake, uncovered, in the pre-heated 350°F oven for 2 hours. Serve hot.

Calories: 543. Sodium: 122.68 mg. Protein: 34.8 g. Carbohydrate: 87.1 g. Fiber: 11.95 g. Cholesterol: 68.44 mg. Calcium: 85.5 mg. Iron: 365 mg. Potassium: 2,,849 mg. Total Fat: 2.1 g; Saturated fat: 0.5 g, Monounsaturated fat: 0.4 g, Polyunsaturated fat: 0.6 g.

❧ CHICKEN SUPREME ❧

SERVES 4   SODIUM PER RECIPE: 312.7 MG   SODIUM PER SERVING: 78.2 MG

This tasty, quick and easy dish is just what you may want on a cold wintry night. Serve it with brown or wild rice and freshly steamed green beans.

5 cloves garlic, minced (2.5 mg)
1 onion, finely chopped (3.3 mg)
2 tablespoons extra-virgin olive oil (trace)
4 boneless, skinless chicken breast halves (306.8 mg)

1. In a shallow roaster pan, sauté the garlic and onions in olive oil over medium or lower heat. Add the chicken breasts, cover, and heat on low until the chicken is cooked through, about 30 to 40 minutes. Serve with **Mustard Sauce** (page 182).

Calories: 206. Sodium: 78.17 mg. Protein: 27.8 g. Carbohydrate: 3.613 g. Fiber: 0.57 g. Cholesterol: 68.44 mg. Calcium: 25.3 mg. Iron: 1 mg. Potassium: 359.1 mg. Total Fat: 8.3 g; Saturated fat: 1.3 g, Monounsaturated fat: 5.3 g, Polyunsaturated fat: 0.9 g.

❄ CHICKEN CURRY ❄

SERVES 4   SODIUM PER RECIPE: 339.7 MG   SODIUM PER SERVING: 84.9 MG
*Great served with **Sakar Spinach**.*

1 **large onion, minced (4.5 mg)**
2 **large cloves garlic, minced (1 mg)**
2 **pounds chicken breast halves, skinless, with bones, cut into**
   serving-size pieces (306.8 mg)
3 **tablespoons extra-virgin olive oil (trace)**
3 **teaspoons ground coriander (1.9 mg)**
1 **teaspoon ground cloves (.5 mg)**
1 **teaspoon ground ginger (.5 mg)**
1 **teaspoon ground cumin (3.5 mg)**
1 **teaspoon dry mustard seeds (0 mg)**
½ **teaspoon ground chili—or less or more according to taste**
   (13.1 mg)

1. Sauté the onion and garlic in the oil in a deep skillet or roasting pan. Combine the coriander, cloves, ginger, cumin, mustard seeds, and the ground chili. Add the spices to the onion mixture. Sauté over low heat for about 3 to 4 minutes. This cooks the spices and is an important step in the recipe. Stir the mixture frequently to prevent sticking. Add the chicken pieces and combine with the seasoning. Cook, covered, slowly for about 1 hour, or until the chicken is tender. Add water if needed, checking frequently if necessary. Drain the fat.

Calories: 253. Sodium: 84.9 mg. Protein: 28.5 g. Carbohydrate: 6.664 g. Fiber: 1.84 g. Cholesterol: 8.44 mg. Calcium: 45.8 mg. Iron: 1.87 mg. Potassium: 451.3 mg. Total Fat: 2.4 g; Saturated fat: 1.9 g, Monounsaturated fat: 8.2 g, Polyunsaturated fat: 1.4 g.

HERB ROASTED WILD TURKERY
❄ WITH CHERRY CHUTNEY ❄

SERVES 8   SODIUM PER RECIPE WILD TURKEY: 595.3 MG
SODIUM PER SERVING: 74.4 MG

If fresh herbs are not available, substitute with half-quantities of dry herbs even though the finished dish will have a less aromatic flavor. The turkey must be cleaned and plucked carefully so that the skin is intact. May also be used for domestic turkey, but should cook longer until domestic bird reaches at least 170°F.

1 **large wild tom turkey, skin intact (about 3 pounds yield[1])**
   (585.9 mg)

[1]About 4 ounces per serving.

½ cup fresh basil, chopped (.8 mg)
1 tablespoon fresh rosemary, minced (.4 mg)
2 tablespoons fresh tarragon, finely chopped (5.9 mg)
4 garlic cloves, minced (2 mg)
    pepper to taste (trace)

1. Preheat oven to 350°F.
2. Starting at the neck opening and working towards the small part of the breast, carefully maneuver fingers between the skin and breast of the turkey. Combine fresh herbs, garlic, and chopped bacon and spread evenly between the skin and breast. Sprinkle with pepper. Place in oven and roast 10 minutes for each pound of turkey. Remove turkey from oven when internal temperature reaches 145°F. Let turkey sit for 10 minutes. Carve and serve with chutney.

Serve with Cherry Chutney (Locate in Index). Total Sodium after adding chutney will be 103.8 mg per serving.

Calories: 182. Sodium: 74.41 mg. Fiber: 0.26 g. Cholesterol: 77.89 mg. Calcium: 36.3 mg. Iron: 1.724 mg. Potassium: 383.9 mg. Total Fat: 7.5 g; Saturated fat: 2 g, Monounsaturated fat: 2.8 g, Polyunsaturated fat: 1.8 g.

◆ NASIR'S CHICKEN CURRY ◆

SERVES 8   SODIUM PER RECIPE: 767.3 MG   SODIUM PER SERVING: 95.9 MG
Curry recipes abound, but they can often take as much time to prepare as they do to cook. This tasty dish is easy, however. It came to our attention at a wedding party in Breckenridge, Colorado, where the groom's family, from Pakistan, whipped up quite a few exciting dishes. You can add more chili to this if you like, but be careful—it can overpower the rest of the spices easily.

3 pounds boneless, skinless chicken breasts (732.2 mg)
2 large onions, minced (9 mg)
2 large cloves garlic, minced (1 mg)
4 tablespoons extra-virgin olive oil (trace)
1 tablespoon ground coriander (1.76 mg)
1 teaspoon ground cloves (5 mg)
1 teaspoon ground ginger (.5 mg)
1 teaspoon ground cumin (3.5 mg)
1 teaspoon mustard seeds (trace)
¼ teaspoon ground chili (6.5 mg)—do not use chili seasoning

1. Cut the chicken into cubes. Sauté the onions and garlic slowly in the oil. Add the coriander, cloves, ginger, cumin, mustard seeds, and chili and sauté over low heat for up to 4 minutes, stirring frequently. Add the

chicken pieces, then stir. Cook slowly, covered, for approximately 1 hour, or until the chicken is tender. Add water if necessary. Serve hot with un-salted peas and steamed broccoli.

Calories: 366. Sodium: 95.91 mg. Protein: 25.2 g. Carbohydrate: 5.692 g. Fiber: 1.46 g. Cholesterol: 117.6 mg. Calcium: 35.6 mg. Iron: 2.497 mg. Potassium: 417 mg. Total Fat: 26.7 g; Saturated fat: 6.5 g, Monounsaturated fat: 13.1 g, Polyunsaturated fat: 4.9 g.

❖ CHICKEN ENCHILADAS ❖

SERVES 6   SODIUM PER RECIPE: 822 MG   SODIUM PER SERVING: 137 MG
SODIUM PER ENCHILADA: 68.5 MG

It's hard to believe we can make these without sodium overload. My wife came up with this delicious recipe. (A standard enchilada entrée for a single serving can have as much as 1,100 mg.)

4 **boneless, skinless chicken breast halves (306.8 mg)**
¼ **cup olive oil (trace)**
2 **large onions, thinly sliced (6.6 mg)**
4 **ounces Dromedary pimientos* (13.4 mg)**
3 **tablespoons low-fat low-sodium cream cheese† (133 mg)**
1 **dozen no-salt corn tortillas‡ (33 mg)**
¾ **cup nonfat milk (94.6 mg)**
4 **ounces Tillamook Low Sodium Cheddar cheese, sliced or grated (220 mg)**
2 **green onions, sliced (4.8 mg)**
½ **cup sliced radishes (14 mg)**
6 **lemon or lime wedges (9.72 mg)**

1. Sauté the chicken breast halves in a little olive oil in a nonstick pan. When done, cut the chicken into small cubes for use in the enchilada. Sauté the onions in some more of the oil. When the onions are translucent or limp, add the pimientos or roasted peppers, chicken, cream cheese, and stir until the cheese melts. Heat the tortillas one at a time. Fill each with some of the above mixture, roll up, and place them in an oiled nonstick casserole or roasting pan. With a tablespoon, spoon milk over each en-chilada, then cover with grated or sliced cheese. The dish may be refrig-erated at this point for cooking later.

*You may substitute fresh red pepper, sliced and sautéed with onions, or some other no-salt-added canned pimientos.
†You can find low-sodium cream cheese in some health food stores or at places like Trader Joe's.
‡Most no-salt brands will show 0 mg on their nutrition facts label. This is because each tortilla actually has, on the average, only 2.75 mg and the manufacturer has rounded the number to the lowest allowed.

2. Preheat oven to 350°F.

3. To complete the preparation, cover the pan with foil and bake it in the oven for 30 minutes. Remove the foil and continue cooking for another 15 minutes. Garnish with sliced green onion and radishes. Squeeze lemon or lime juice over the enchiladas. A dollop of low-sodium sour cream may be used to top each serving (add mg sodium to each serving, if you do so).

Calories: 208. Sodium: 68.52 mg. Fiber: 3.11 g. Protein: 36.1 g. Carbohydrate: 28.9 g. Cholesterol: 33.52 mg. Calcium: 100.3 mg. Iron: 1.12 mg. Potassium: 257.9 mg. Total Fat: 9.8 g; Saturated fat: 3.3 g, Monounsaturated fat: 3.8 g, Polyunsaturated fat: 0.8 g.

❈ CORNISH GAME HEN À LA GARLIC ❈

SERVES 6   SODIUM PER RECIPE: 700.2 MG   SODIUM PER SERVING: 116.7 MG

Cornish game hens were part of my "staple" repertoire many years ago. I loved them. This is a basic recipe for preparing these wonderfully flavored birds. Adapt it to your own tastes if you like— the hen won't mind at all. Add or subtract vegetables and herbs.

   1 **medium onion, chopped (2 mg)**
   1 **medium celery stalk, chopped (35 mg)**
 ½ **green pepper, chopped (1.2 mg)**
   6 **ounces mushrooms, chopped (5.5 mg)**
   2 **cloves garlic, minced (2 mg)**
   1 **tablespoon fresh minced basil (trace)**
 ¾ **teaspoon oregano (trace)**
 ½ **teaspoon tarragon (.5 mg)**
1½ **tablespoons chopped fresh parsley (3.1 mg)**
 ¼ **cup extra-virgin olive oil (trace)**
   4 **frozen whole Cornish game hens (650.1 mg)**
    Pepper to taste (trace)
    Olive oil spray for spritzing birds (trace)

1. Preheat oven to 325°F.

2. Add the chopped onion, celery, green pepper, mushrooms, garlic, and herbs to the oil and mix. Season the hens with pepper to taste. Stuff the birds with equal amounts of the vegetable mix. Place the birds in roaster pan or baking dish, breast-side up. Spritz the birds with olive oil. Cover and bake for 1½ hours at 325°F, then brown quickly at 500°F.

Calories: 284. Sodium: 116.6 mg. Protein: 32.9 g. Carbohydrate: 4.171 g. Fiber: 1.08 g. Cholesterol: 145 mg. Calcium: 36.8 mg. Iron: 1.854 mg. Potassium: 598.7 mg. Total Fat: 14.5 g; Saturated fat: 2.6 g, Monounsaturated fat: 8.4 g, Polyunsaturated fat: 2.1 g.

❋ TURKEY STUFFING ❋

MAKES 10 CUPS   SODIUM PER RECIPE: 254.5 MG
SODIUM PER SERVING: 25.4 MG

What kind of Thanksgiving could we possibly have without a great stuffing? Regular stuffing recipes are very, very high in sodium. Your guests will never know that salt and excessive sodium are missing from this replacement.

10 thick slices from a loaf of Italian Milano bread (page 247), cubed into 6 cups (8.227 mg)
½ cup unsalted butter (12.5 mg)
2 cups onion, chopped (9.6 mg)
2 cups celery, chopped (208.8 mg)
2 cups mushrooms, chopped (5.6 mg)
2 medium to large green apples, chopped (trace)
1 cup unsalted dry roasted pecans, chopped (optional)* (1.34 mg)
¼ teaspoon ground sage (.019 mg)
½ teaspoon ground thyme (.383 mg)
1 teaspoon ground pepper (.924 mg)
2 teaspoons Lawry's garlic powder with parsley (1.475 mg)
1 cup apple juice (6.997 mg)

1. Bake **Italian Milano** bread in bread machine. Slice ten ¾- to 1-inch slices from loaf. Toast each side on an ungreased baking sheet in your oven under the broiler until just golden brown. Cool and cut into small, ½-inch cubes. You'll get about 16 cubes from each slice of bread. Melt butter in large sauté pan or 6-quart pan. Sauté onion, celery, mushrooms, apples, and pecans together. When vegetables and apples are cooked through, add bread crumbs and spices. Coat with buttered mixture and add apple juice to moisten.

2. When ready to bake, put mixture into lightly oil-sprayed baking dish (9 x 13) and bake 325°F for 20 to 30 minutes. If it's been refrigerated, heating time will take longer. Serve hot.

Dried Apricots: If you like dried apricots, chop ½ cup and add to the mix prior to baking.

With pecans:

Calories: 309. Sodium: 25.5 mg. Fiber: 3.1 g. Protein: 4.866 g. Carbohydrate: 36.4 g. Cholesterol: 24.85 mg. Calcium: 31.5 g. Iron: 2.399 g. Potassium: 262.3 mg. Total Fat: 17.1 g; Saturated fat: 6.4 g, Monounsaturated fat: 2.7 g, Polyunsaturated fat: 0.5 g.

Without pecans:

Calories: 234. Sodium: 25.5 mg. Fiber: 2.9 g. Protein: 3.951 g. Carbohydrate: 33.8 g. Cholesterol: 24.85 mg. Calcium: 31.5 g. Iron: 2.399 g. Potassium: 262.3 mg. Total Fat: 9.8 g; Saturated fat: 5.8 g, Monounsaturated fat: 2.7 g, Polyunsaturated fat: .544 mg.

*Pecans are high in fat and calories. If you leave them out, the calories drop to 234 per cup and fat drops to only 9 g per cup.

FISH AND SEAFOOD

❖ ❖ ❖ ❖ ❖ ❖ ❖ ❖

❖ FISH WITH POTATOES AND GARLIC ❖

SERVES 4   SODIUM PER RECIPE: 438.4 MG   SODIUM PER SERVING: 109.6 MG
This recipe came about like many of my other recipes, accidentally.
It started as a fish-and-potato-with-broccoli dinner one night, but
turned out even better.

4 **(4-ounce) white fish steaks—swordfish, halibut, bass, cod,**
   sole, or turbot (362.9 mg)
2 **teaspoons Hain Stone Ground No Salt Added Mustard* (7.5 mg)**
3 **tablespoons lemon juice (.45 mg)**
2 **pounds red potatoes, not peeled (42 mg)**
4 **cloves garlic, crushed or finely chopped (2 mg)**
2 **tablespoons extra-virgin olive oil (trace)**
   Black pepper to taste (trace)
1 **medium tomato, sliced (11 mg)**

1. Marinate the fish in a small bowl with a mixture of mustard and lemon
juice. Cover and refrigerate until ready to cook. The potatoes may be prepared in one of two ways: cut them either in quarters or in thin slices.
Combine the garlic, oil, and pepper and spread the mixture in the roasting
pan. Add the potatoes, spreading them across the bottom.
2. Preheat the oven to 450°F and bake the potatoes for up to 30 minutes,
or until they begin to brown. Turn the potatoes at least once during cooking. When they are just brown, place the fish, mustard-side up, on top and
bake for another 15 minutes, or until the fish is slightly cooked but still
moist. Top the fish with the tomato slices and some additional lemon juice,
then bake until the fish flakes—approximately 5 to 10 minutes. Serve hot.

Calories: 314. Sodium: 109.62 mg. Fiber: 3.15 g. Protein: 25.5 g. Carbohydrate: 34.1 g.
Cholesterol: 53.76 mg. Calcium: 28 mg. Iron: 629 mg. Potassium: 489.9 mg. Total Fat: 8.9 g;
Saturated fat: 1.4 g, Monounsaturated fat: 5.3 g, Polyunsaturated fat: 1 g.

*Or use East Shore Mustard, available from Healthy Heart Market, or substitute dry
mustard mixed with 1 tablespoon water. Mustard is optional, although recommended.

◧◧ MADDJACK'S FISH FILLETS IN FOIL ◧◧

SERVES 4   SODIUM PER RECIPE: 312.4 MG   SODIUM PER SERVING: 78.1 MG

Here's a simple low-sodium fish dish contributed by cyberspace fan Jack Davis. You can use bass, orange roughy, cod, halibut, or shark.

2   whole fresh chilies or canned Ortega low-sodium jalapeño or Anaheim peppers, diced (40 mg)*
1   teaspoon dill seed (.415 mg)
2   cloves garlic (1 mg)
½   medium onion, sliced (1.65 mg)
¼   cup lemon juice (1.22 mg)
1   pound white cod fillets (307.8 mg)†

1. Prepare the chilies according to the recipe for **Anaheim Chilies** (page 308). Dice after cooking. If using Ortega chilies (20 mg per ounce), use the diced version or dice 2 whole chilies in the food processor. In the food processor combine the chilies, dill seed, and garlic and blend into a paste. Tear a piece of aluminum foil large enough to put the fish on and also form a ridge a couple of inches high all the way around. Make a foil pan tightly around the fish with no open spaces. Add the lemon juice to the paste and mix well. Pour the mixture evenly over the fish and broil on high for 10 to 15 minutes, or until the top of the fish is browned and flaky. Save the juice from the fish and pour it over split baked potatoes or boiled then broiled red or white potatoes.

Calories: 108. Sodium: 78.09 mg. Protein: 19.9 g. Carbohydrate: 5.018 g. Fiber: 0.71 g. Cholesterol: 40.1 mg. Calcium: 23.8 mg. Iron: .481 mg. Potassium: 523.5 mg. Total Fat: 0.8 g; Saturated fat: 0.1 g, Monounsaturated fat: 0.1 g, Polyunsaturated fat: 0.3 g.

*The sodium count is based on using canned jalapeño peppers. Fresh peppers only have a trace of sodium.
†The sodium count is based on using cod fillets. Whole fresh fish, bone-in, has a much higher count.

❧ FISH FILLETS ON RED PEPPER ❧

SERVES 4   SODIUM PER RECIPE: 421.6 MG   SODIUM PER SERVING: 105.4 MG

My wife found a stack of serving dishes that she thought would be great for making individual chicken pot pies, lasagna, and other such recipes, but when we got them home, our first meal to hit these "lasagna dishes" was this one. The cleanup is minimal, the compliments many.

 4 **sole or other white-fleshed fish fillets (362.9 mg)***
 1 **tablespoon extra-virgin olive oil (trace)**
 1 **tablespoon red wine vinegar (.3 mg)**
 1 **tablespoon genuine brewed rice vinegar (.3 mg)**
 ½ **teaspoon white sugar (trace)**
 1 **tablespoon bread crumbs made from the Italian Milano**
    Homemade Bread recipe (page 247) (trace)
 1 **tablespoon finely grated low-sodium Parmesan† (3.15 mg)**
 ¼ **teaspoon paprika (.178 mg)**
 1 **cup broccoli florets (19.2 mg)**
 1 **cup fresh corn kernels, uncooked (23.1 mg)**
 1 **small red onion, thinly sliced (2.1 mg)**
 2 **tablespoons chopped fresh parsley (4.26 mg)**
 1 **red pepper, cut into thin strips (2.38 mg)**
 1 **tablespoon chopped fresh basil or 1 teaspoon dried parsley**
    (.1 mg)
    Black pepper to taste (trace)
16 **fresh asparagus spears, trimmed and cleaned (3.84 mg)**

1. Marinate the fish in the refrigerator in a mix of olive oil, red wine vinegar, rice wine vinegar, and sugar. While the fish is refrigerated, in a small bowl combine the bread crumbs with the Parmesan and paprika until blended.

2. Lightly oil 4 ovenproof "lasagna earthenware dishes" or individual casseroles. Next preheat the oven to 425°F. Combine the broccoli, corn, onion, parsley, red pepper, and basil, adding pepper to taste. Divide this mixture evenly into the 4 dishes, cover with foil, and bake for about 35 minutes, or until the vegetables are barely tender. Uncover the dishes and top the vegetables with the fish fillets. Cover again and bake for another 10 minutes, or until fish is barely cooked and still moist in the thickest part. Uncover, sprinkle with bread crumb mixture, lay 4 asparagus spears on

---

*Approximately 4 ounces each. If more, add 23 mg sodium per ounce to the count. You may use fresh or frozen thawed fillets.

†Optional. Low-sodium Parmesan is available at health food stores or sometimes at Trader Joe's. If you can't locate it, use tablespoon of deli-packed grated Parmesan at 93 mg sodium per tablespoon.

top of each serving at an angle, and continue to bake, uncovered, for 2 to 4 minutes until the topping is golden. Serve at once.

Calories: 205. Sodium: 105.37 mg. Fiber: 3.61 g. Protein: 25 g. Carbohydrate: 14.8 g. Cholesterol: 54.75 mg. Calcium: 67.2 mg. Iron: 1.592 mg. Potassium: 802.6 mg. Total Fat: 5.8 g; Saturated fat: 1.1 g, Monounsaturated fat: 1 g, Polyunsaturated fat: 1 g.

❈ BAKED RED SNAPPER ❈

SERVES 4   SODIUM PER RECIPE: 439.8 MG   SODIUM PER SERVING: 109.9 MG

FOR THE FISH
- ½ **cup orange juice (1.24 mg)**
- ½ **teaspoon minced ginger (.3 mg)**
- **Dash Fortner's #89 blended seasoning (trace)**
- 4 **(6-ounce) snapper fillets (435.2* mg)**

FOR THE SAUCE
- ¾ **cups orange or mandarin juice (1.86 mg)**
- 1 **tablespoon grated orange peel (.2 mg)**
- 1 **tablespoon cornstarch (.72 mg)**
- 12 **thin slices or chunks of fresh California Valencia orange (0 mg)**
- ½ **teaspoon minced ginger (.3 g)**

1. Combine the juice, ginger, and seasoning and marinate the fish in the mixture for 1 hour.
2. Preheat the oven to 350°F. Put the fish and marinade in a baking dish and bake, uncovered, for about 30 minutes, or until the fish is tender to the touch.
3. To make the sauce, combine the juice, orange peel, and cornstarch in a small saucepan. Bring to a boil, reduce heat, and cook until the mixture has thickened, stirring constantly. When done, remove from the heat. Add the orange slices and ginger and stir. Pour the sauce over the fish and serve hot.

Calories: 238. Sodium: 109.9 mg. Fiber: 1.88 g. Protein: 36.1 g. Carbohydrate: 17.8 g. Cholesterol: 62.9 mg. Calcium: 90.1 mg. Iron: .579 mg. Potassium: 981.4 mg. Total Fat: 2.6 g; Saturated fat: 0.5 g, Monounsaturated fat: 0.5 g, Polyunsaturated fat: 0.9 g.

*This recipe is based on the fillets coming from 3 pounds raw fish. After baking, the sodium count drops to about 60 mg.

❧ STUFFED RED SNAPPER ❧

SERVES 8   SODIUM PER RECIPE: 636.6 MG   SODIUM PER SERVING: 79.58 MG

*I traveled to Atlanta, Georgia, for a few months while working on a corporate image film. One of my client's favorite ending adventures was to visit a Greek restaurant where, if you ordered ahead, a giant stuffed red snapper was served. Usually we had 10 or more people at the table, but the fish was always so huge, it was never completely eaten, and not because we didn't try. The meal was always exquisite. When I came home I developed two red snapper recipes from that experience—this one and one for **Baked Red Snapper.***

1 cup hot water (0 mg)
½ cup melted unsalted butter (12.5 mg)
4 eggs (221.8 mg)
1 cup unbleached white flour (2.5 mg)
¼ cup diced celery (26.1 mg)
¼ cup diced red onion (1 mg)
1 bay leaf (trace)
2 ounces fresh blue or Dungeness crabmeat, steamed or boiled (165.5 mg)
½ cup fresh unsalted shrimp (41.1 mg)
4 drops hot Tabasco sauce (11 mg)
1 tablespoon Hain No Salt Added Mustard (10 mg)
1 teaspoon black pepper (.9 mg)
¼ teaspoon Frontier all-purpose seasoning (0 mg)*
2 tablespoons extra-virgin olive oil (trace)
½ cup dry white wine (8 mg)
1 (3-pound) whole red snapper (136 mg)†

1. Combine the water, unsalted butter, and eggs in a heavy pan and stir. Add flour, stir over medium heat until thick (about 15 minutes). When smooth, it's done. Set aside.
2. Preheat the oven to 350°F.
3. Sauté the celery, onion, bay leaf, crabmeat, shrimp, hot sauce, mustard, pepper, and seasoning in the olive oil. Add the egg mixture and simmer for 5 minutes. Remove the bay leaf. Add the wine. Stuff the snapper with this mixture and bake in the preheated oven for 45 to 60 minutes. Serve hot.

Calories: 271. Sodium: 79.58 mg. Fiber: 0.64 g. Protein: 12.1 g. Carbohydrate: 13.3 g. Cholesterol: 143.84 mg. Calcium: 35 mg. Iron: 2.417 mg. Potassium: 220.3 mg. Total Fat: 17.9 g; Saturated fat: 8.4 g, Monounsaturated fat: 6.8 g, Polyunsaturated fat: 1.3 g.

*If not available locally, call 1-800/753-0310 to order by mail.
†The sodium count is based on using the flesh only.

❊ Baked Salmon in Parchment Paper ❊

SERVES 4   SODIUM PER RECIPE: 183.4 MG   SODIUM PER SERVING: 45.9 MG

Just like our baked trout in parchment paper, this recipe produces a highly flavorful and very tender salmon dinner. Serve over hot beans, wild rice, or fettuccine. The salmon may also be cooked in a barbecue.

4 square sheets parchment paper, plus 4 pieces aluminum foil if barbecuing
4 (3-ounce) fresh salmon fillets (159.8 mg)
2 tablespoons olive oil (trace)
2 cloves garlic, minced (1 mg)
2 tablespoons chopped fresh dill (2.6 mg)
2 tablespoons sage (.44 mg)
4 teaspoons tarragon (2 mg)
2 medium lemons, cut into 8 large slices (6.48 mg)
4 large slices, cut from 1 medium tomato (11.1 mg)

1. Preheat oven to 400°F or preheat barbecue with red-hot coals.

2. Spread the parchment paper out. Rub the fillets lightly with the oil and garlic and put one fillet in the center of each piece of parchment paper. Sprinkle the dill, sage, and tarragon on the fillets. On both sides of each fillet add 1 lemon slice, then put 1 tomato slice on top of each fillet. Wrap parchment paper around the fish, tuck it closed, and set the packet on a cooking rack or pan. If barbecuing, wrap this package in aluminum foil and seal tightly.

3. *Alternative method.* If you like pasta, cook fettuccine till al dente (just done), drain, and toss with olive oil and garlic. Put a layer of this onto each parchment square and place the salmon on top of it, along with the rest of the ingredients above. Wrap and cook for only 10 minutes in the hot oven.) Add 3 mg per serving.

4. Serve the parchment pouches unopened. When ready to eat, opening the packets at the dinner table sets off a great aroma that promises a delicious meal. This fish is delicious accompanied by asparagus, broccoli, or zucchini.

Calories: 250. Sodium: 45.86 mg. Fiber: 4.07 g. Protein: 19 g. Carbohydrate: 10.6 g. Cholesterol: 56.1 mg. Calcium: 132.8 mg. Iron: 2.279 mg. Potassium: 564.2 mg. Total Fat: 16.7 g; Saturated fat: 3.2 g, Monounsaturated fat: 9.2 g, Polyunsaturated fat: 2.6 g.

Poached Salmon Steaks with
◈ Dry Mustard Sauce or Dill Sauce ◈

SERVES 4   SODIUM PER RECIPE: 270.8 MG WITH MUSTARD SAUCE, 251.7 MG WITH DILL SAUCE   SODIUM PER SERVING: 67.7 MG WITH MUSTARD SAUCE, 62.9 MG WITH DILL SAUCE

You can poach either salmon steaks, fillets, or a whole fish cut up for this recipe. Salmon is a great addition to our diets and we should try to eat at least one or two fish dinners every week. Choose one of the sauces given below for your salmon.

THE SALMON
- 4 (5-ounce) salmon fillets (234.6 mg)
- 2 cups chicken broth prepared by combining 2 teaspoons Herb-ox Low Sodium Chicken Broth (10 mg) with 2 cups water (0 mg)
- ¼ teaspoon dried dillweed (.5 mg)
- ¼ teaspoon marjoram (trace)
- ¼ teaspoon ground nutmeg (trace)
- 1 medium onion, diced (3.3 mg)

THE MUSTARD SAUCE
- 2 tablespoons white wine vinegar (.3 mg)
- 2 tablespoons Grey Poupon, Hain, Stone Ground or Mendocino Honey Mustard (20 mg)
- 2 tablespoons honey (1.68 mg)
- 2 tablespoons extra-virgin olive oil (trace)

THE DILL SAUCE
- 1½ cloves garlic, minced (.765 mg)
- ½ medium onion, diced (1.65 mg)
- 2 tablespoons extra-virgin olive oil (trace)
- 1 tablespoon chopped fresh dill (.305 mg)
- 2½ tablespoons white wine vinegar (.375 mg)

1. To prepare the salmon, combine the broth, dillweed, marjoram, nutmeg, and onion in a large skillet. Add the salmon and cover with cold water. Turn on the heat and bring the mixture to a boil, uncovered. At the boil, turn the heat down and simmer for 5 minutes, then turn off the heat and let the salmon stand for 10 minutes. It will be perfectly cooked.

2. To make the mustard sauce combine all the ingredients and whisk them together until well blended. Heat and whisk again just before serving. Serve hot.

3. To make the dill sauce, mix all the ingredients together. Spoon the sauce on the salmon before cooking. (This can also be used as a marinade, but generally one is not necessary in such a dish.) Serve hot.

With Mustard Sauce: Calories: 302. Sodium: 67.65 mg. Fiber: 0.57 g. Protein: 28.4 g. Carbohydrate: 13.1 g. Cholesterol: 57.38 mg. Calcium: 54.6 mg. Iron: .955 mg. Potassium: 598.6 mg. Total Fat: 14.9 g; Saturated fat: 2.6 g, Monounsaturated fat: 7.7 g, Polyunsaturated fat: 3.1 g.

With Dill Sauce: Calories: 271. Sodium: 62.93 mg. Fiber: 0.82 g. Protein: 28.1 g. Carbohydrate: 5.619 g. Cholesterol: 57.38 mg. Calcium: 59.1 mg. Iron: .98 mg. Potassium: 622 mg. Total Fat: 14.4 g; Saturated fat: 2.6 g, Monounsaturated fat: 7.7 g, Polyunsaturated fat: 3.1 g.

❖ BOB'S BARBECUED SALMON ❖

SERVES 4   SODIUM PER RECIPE: 203.8 MG   SODIUM PER SERVING: 50.9 MG

*Bob Quinn catches fresh salmon off the northern California coast
from his boat Hog Heaven. He fillets his fish and barbecues
it to succulence.*

THE SALMON
   4 (4-ounce) fresh Coho salmon fillets (195.5 mg)

THE SAUCE
   3 cloves garlic, minced (1.5 mg)
   1 onion, diced (3.3 mg)
   ⅓ cup extra-virgin olive oil (trace)
   2 tablespoons chopped fresh dill (2.6 mg)
   ⅓ cup white wine vinegar (.792 mg)

1. Mix all the sauce ingredients together and spoon over the salmon before cooking. (The sauce can also be used as a marinade, but it is generally not necessary in a dish such as this.)

2. Arrange the charcoal barbecue coals at outer edge of your barbecue—this works best in a Weber or Kingsford barbecue. Once the coals are hot, put the salmon, skin-side down, directly on the grill but off the coals. Never turn the salmon. Cover the grill and begin cooking. Check in 8 minutes and spoon on more dill sauce at that time. If the salmon is only half cooked, let it cook for another 4 minutes. If still not quite done, cook in 2-minute intervals until meat is lightly done. Do not overcook—fish is not like red meat or chicken. When done, add a spoonful of sauce and serve hot.

Calories: 339. Sodium: 50.94 mg. Fiber: 1.24 g. Protein: 24 g. Carbohydrate: 6.106 g. Cholesterol: 47.81 mg. Calcium: 99.1 mg. Iron: 1.419 mg. Potassium: 560.6 mg. Total Fat: 24.7 g; Saturated fat: 3.8 g, Monounsaturated fat: 15.7 g, Polyunsaturated fat: 3.7 g.

Barbecued Salmon with
❖ Special Barbecue Sauce ❖

SERVES 4   SODIUM PER RECIPE: 220 MG   SODIUM PER SERVING: 55 MG
Clark Powers was the principal at our local elementary school. We
visited him often for his favorite barbecue of salmon and fresh
vegetables. He would make a boat out of heavy-duty aluminum,
large enough to hold the salmon he was going to cook, and put it
on the hot charcoal grill with the salmon and his sauce given here.
You can add, take away, or modify this to your own tastes.

  1 pound fresh Chinook salmon, filleted (159.8 mg)
  1 cup brown sugar (56.6 mg)
  ½ cup extra-virgin olive oil (trace)
  1 onion, diced (3.3 mg)
  3 tablespoons lemon juice (.45 mg)

1. Make a boat to hold the fish by rolling up the sides of two or three folds of aluminum foil. Crimp the corners. Mix the remaining ingredients together until smooth. Put some of the mixture on the bottom of the boat and put the salmon into the boat skin-side up. Once the barbecue is hot, put on the salmon boat. After about 7 minutes, turn the salmon and cook for another 7 minutes. While cooking, brush the remaining sauce on the salmon frequently, especially when you turn the fish. Serve hot with **Barbecued Vegetables** (page 296).

Calories: 541. Sodium: 55.04 mg. Fiber: 0.54 g. Protein: 17.4 g. Carbohydrate: 38.6 g. Cholesterol: 56.1 mg. Calcium: 55.8 mg. Iron: 1.462 mg. Potassium: 517.5 mg. Total Fat: 35.9 g: Saturated fat: 5.8 g, Monounsaturated fat: 23.7 g, Polyunsaturated fat: 4 g.

❖ Salmon—Preparing for Freezing ❖

If you fish or receive a gift of fresh salmon, halibut, cod, or other
sea fish, you'll want to freeze some for future use. To freeze fresh
salmon fillets or steaks (as well as sea fish), use the
following method.

THE FISH
  1 packet Knox Gelatin (trace)
  1 cup fresh or bottled lemon juice (trace)
  2 cups water (0 mg)

1. Dip the fish in the lemon juice, turn, and dip again. Place the fish on a sheet of plastic wrap and freeze. When frozen, take the fish out of the freezer and hermetically seal it in a FoodSaver Vacuum Sealer and return it to the freezer. If you don't have a FoodSaver, then wrap the fish tightly in aluminum foil and return it to the freezer. In a FoodSaver vacuum-sealed bag the fish will remain fresh for up to 3 months. In aluminum foil, it will remain "fresh" for about a month. The fish will still be safe to eat after that, but the "freshness" will slowly disappear.

❄ SPANISH COD / BACALAO ESPAGNOLE ❄

SERVES 4   SODIUM PER RECIPE: 278 MG   SODIUM PER SERVING: 69.5 MG
Another recipe sent to us from Zarautz, Spain, by Michael McCay.

- **1 pound fresh Atlantic cod fillets (183.6 mg)***
- **2 tablespoons extra-virgin olive oil (0 mg)**
- **1 small onion, minced (2.1 mg)**
- **4 cloves garlic, minced (2 mg)**
- **½ red bell pepper, diced (1.2 mg)**
- **½ green bell pepper, diced (1.2 mg)**
  8-ounce can unsalted (no-salt-added) tomato sauce (70 mg)†
- **½ bay leaf, crushed (trace)**
- **¼ teaspoon oregano (trace)**
- **½ cup water (0 mg)**
  Pepper to taste (trace)
- **2 lemons, quartered (trace)**
- **1 cup wild rice mix, cooked in unsalted water (11.2 mg)**

1. Cut the fillets into 4 portions of 4 ounces each. To cook the fish evenly, place thickest cuts in the pan first, followed a few minutes later by the thinner cuts. In a large nonstick pan with a cover, heat the oil over high heat until it's sizzling hot. Sauté the onion, garlic, and peppers until slightly browned but still crisp—about 3 to 4 minutes.

2. Stir in the tomato sauce, bay leaf, oregano, and water. Bring to a boil, cover, and reduce the heat and simmer for 10 to 15 minutes. Stir occasionally from the bottom up. Cook, uncovered, for a few minutes or until the sauce thickens.

3. Place the fish in the sauce skin-side up, thick cuts in first. Spoon a bit of sauce over the fish, then cover and simmer when all the pieces are in the pan. Cook for about 5 minutes per inch thickness, then turn and continue to cook. Turn carefully, since cod can break up easily. Serve the fish over the prepared wild rice. Spoon some sauce over each serving. Season with pepper to taste and garnish with lemon wedges.

Calories: 261. Sodium: 69.51 mg. Fiber: 6.92 g. Protein: 22.4 g. Carbohydrate: 43.8 g. Cholesterol: 36.55 mg. Calcium: 69.4 mg. Iron: 2.824 mg. Potassium: 695 mg. Total Fat: 1.3 g; Saturated fat: 0.2 g, Monounsaturated fat: 0.2 g, Polyunsaturated fat: 0.6 g.

*Pacific cod is 58 mg higher in sodium for the same amount (24.6 mg).
†The Finast brand No-Salt-Added Tomato Sauce has only 10 mg sodium per 8 ounces. Hunt's and Del Monte have 50 mg each. Pathmark's sauce contains 25 mg and Health Valley's has 43 mg.

❧ FISH SAUSAGE ❧

MAKES 4 SINGLE-SERVING SAUSAGES   SODIUM PER RECIPE: 434.7 MG
SODIUM PER SERVING: 108.7 MG

*When a visitor to www.megaheart.com asked for a sausage recipe
that would fit into his no-salt, low-sodium diet, Chef Scott Leysath
came up with this recipe. He also had this to say in his response to
the Web site visitor: "For your basic sausage to be cooked rather
than cured, smoked, or dried you can omit salt and use additional
dry spices to liven it up. I like dried and ground lemon peel, sage,
garlic, onion, and lots of cracked black pepper. As a rule of thumb
when making salted sausage, you combine 10 pounds of
combined meats and fat with 4 ounces of seasoning. Without salt,
I'd add additional seasoning. Meat sausages can be made even
tastier and healthier by mixing in rice or barley, about 10 to 15
percent by volume, with the mixture. Sausage is anything you
want it to be. You can mix up ground beef with a little pork
fat, add some seasonings, and call it sausage.
This is one of my favorites."*

3 **cups skinless raw fish fillets, broken into small pieces***
   (329.4 mg)
2 **green onions (scallions), diced (4.8 mg)**
2 **cloves garlic, minced (1.02 mg)**
¼ **cup chopped fresh basil (.424 mg)**
2 **medium (or large) eggs (110.9 mg)**
½ **cup heavy cream (49.2 mg)**
⅛ **teaspoon red chili pepper flakes (trace)**
⅛ **teaspoon white pepper (trace)**
3 **tablespoons freshly squeezed lemon juice (trace)**
   Hot water for poaching

1. Combine the fish, onions, garlic, and basil in a food processor and
process until blended but still a bit coarse. Add the eggs, cream, chili pepper, white pepper, and lemon juice and process into a coarse paste. Depending on the water content of the fish, you may need to add a little
more fish if the mixture is too thin.

2. Preheat the oven to 350°F.

3. Spread a piece of plastic wrap on a flat surface. Spoon about ⅔ cup of
the mixture onto the center of the plastic wrap. Roll the plastic wrap up
snugly, forming a "sausage" with the fish mixture. Twist and tie off each
end of the plastic. Continue until you have completed the sausage-making.

*Estimated amount. You can adjust the amount to make as many sausages as you
want. Just add in the other stuff in the same proportion and keep track of the
sodium count.

Put the sausages in a baking dish. Carefully pour hot water into the dish until the sausages are just floating or almost covered. Place the dish in the preheated oven and poach for 25 to 30 minutes, or until the sausages become firm.

Note: They will firm up further after their removal from the oven. Serve hot at breakfast, with waffles, eggs, etc.

Calories: 154. Sodium: 108.66 mg. Fiber: 0.39 g. Protein: 19.6 g. Carbohydrate: 3.785 g. Cholesterol: 125.91 mg. Calcium: 87.7 mg. Iron: .768 mg. Potassium: 438.7 mg. Total Fat: 6.5 g; Saturated fat: 2.9 g, Monounsaturated fat: 2.4 g, Polyunsaturated fat: 0.5 g.

❖ SCAMPI IN WINE ❖

**SERVES 4   SERVING SIZE: 3 SHRIMP   SODIUM PER RECIPE: 118 MG
SODIUM PER SERVING: 29.5 MG**

Scampi are a very large shrimp delicacy generally found in the Mediterranean waters. I first ran into true scampi while in Italy many years ago. I returned with this recipe. Fortunately, you don't have to miss out on this tasty entrée just because you're on a low-sodium diet. As long as you use fresh shrimp and not too much of it per serving, you can enjoy this recipe. Serve the scampi with zucchini, yellow squash, or baked red potatoes. The alcohol in the wine will burn off. However, you may want to check with your doctor before eating anything cooked with alcohol.

  2 **tablespoons extra-virgin olive oil (0 mg)**
  1 **tablespoon unsalted butter (1.5 mg)**
  1 **large garlic clove, finely chopped (.5 mg)**
  2 **teaspoons finely chopped parsley (1.4 mg)**
     Juice of 1 lemon (.47 mg)
  ⅓ **cup dry white wine* (7.4 mg)**
     Dash of pepper (trace)
 12 **medium raw fresh shrimp† (106.6 mg)**

1. Heat the oil and butter in a sauté pan, add the garlic and parsley, and brown lightly. Blend in the lemon juice and wine. Pepper to taste. Add shrimp and sauté quickly, stirring until tender—approximately 5 minutes. Pour the cooking sauce over the shrimps. Serve with asparagus or broccoli or zucchini over rice.

Calories: 134. Sodium: 29.48 mg. Fiber: 0.09 g. Protein: 3.837 g. Carbohydrate: 1.779 g. Cholesterol: 35.13 mg. Calcium: 16.7 mg. Iron: .645 mg. Potassium: 85.1 mg. Total Fat: 10 g; Saturated fat: 2.8 g, Monounsaturated fat: 5.9 g, Polyunsaturated fat: 0.8 g.

*You can substitute nonalcoholic wine or ¼ cup white grape juice. The alcohol will burn off during cooking, in any case.
†About 3 ounces per serving. You must use fresh shrimp—not imitation or frozen.

EGG AND CHEESE DISHES

❖ ❖ ❖ ❖ ❖ ❖ ❖ ❖

SCRAMBLED EGGS WITH
❖ PEPPERS AND MUSHROOMS ❖

SERVES 2   SODIUM PER RECIPE: 198.3 MG   SODIUM PER SERVING: 99.1 MG

Eggs are a quick and easy way to make a delicious breakfast. In this recipe, the bulk of the sodium comes from the eggs.

1 **fresh jalapeño chili* pepper, minced (.5 mg)**
1 **tablespoon olive oil (trace)**
4 **ounces fresh mushrooms, thinly sliced (4 mg)**
½ **green pepper, diced (1.5 mg)**
½ **fresh Spanish onion, diced (1.5 mg)**
3 **large eggs (189 mg)**
1 **clove garlic, minced (.5 mg)**
1 **tablespoon finely chopped fresh chives (0 mg)**
   Pepper to taste (trace)
1 **tablespoon unsalted butter (1.5 mg)†**

1. Clean and seed the chili pepper. If you are using the **Anaheim Chili** (page 308) or fresh chili pepper, you can prepare it the night before.
2. Heat the oil in a large nonstick skillet set over medium-high heat. Sauté the mushrooms, bell pepper, onion, and chili pepper for 10 minutes. Stir frequently while sautéing. When the mixture is browned lightly, remove it to a plate and drain the remaining liquid.
3. Whisk together the eggs, garlic, chives, and pepper. Wipe the skillet clean and set it over medium heat. Add the butter and heat it until it begins to sizzle, then pour in the egg mixture and stir until nearly set. Add the mushroom mixture and scramble with the eggs. Serve hot.

Calories: 260. Sodium: 99.14 mg. Protein: 11.3 g. Carbohydrate: 9.04 g. Fiber: 2.05 g. Cholesterol: 334.2 mg. Calcium: 54.7 mg. Iron: 2.035 mg. Potassium: 404 mg. Total Fat: 20.4 g; Saturated fat: 6.9 g, Monounsaturated fat: 9.5 g, Polyunsaturated fat: 2 g.

*I prefer the Anaheim pepper, but you'll have to prepare it. Make sure that if you use a canned jalapeño, that it's the low-sodium kind or Ortega. Add the sodium count of the canned chili pepper to your recipe.
†If you exchange the butter for olive oil you will cut the fat by 4 grams.

❀ MARIA'S EGG WITH COTTAGE FRIES ❀

SERVES 2   SODIUM PER RECIPE: 154.7 MG   SODIUM PER SERVING: 77.4 MG

*Our daughter returned from attending the University of
Salamanca in Spain with this Spanish recipe. Leftover baked
potatoes make this one easy to prepare.*

2 **baked potatoes (32 mg)**
1 **tablespoon chopped red pepper (trace)**
1 **tomato, sliced (11 mg)**
2 **tablespoons olive oil (trace)**
2 **eggs (110.9 mg)**
1 **clove garlic, minced—optional (.5 mg)**
1 **tablespoon chives (1 mg)**

1. If the potatoes are not leftovers, bake them in advance and chill them.
Slice the chilled potatoes into rings about ⅛ inch or slightly thicker. In a
nonstick frying pan, sauté the potatoes and red pepper in the oil. When
nearly done, scramble the eggs. Just before eggs stiffen but while they are
still a little runny, mix the potatoes with the eggs while still cooking, and
add garlic to taste. Sprinkle with chives when done. Decorate with sliced
tomato. Serve hot accompanied by orange juice.

*Calories: 422. Sodium: 77.37 mg. Fiber: 2.14 g. Protein: 10.9 g. Carbohydrate: 55.3 g. Cho-
lesterol: 187 mg. Calcium: 29.2 mg. Iron: 1.033 mg. Potassium: 208.5 mg. Total Fat: 18.3 g;
Saturated fat: 3.3 g, Monounsaturated fat: 11.7 g, Polyunsaturated fat: 1.8 g.*

❀ APPLE OMELET ❀

SERVES 2   SODIUM PER RECIPE: 202.2 MG   SODIUM PER SERVING: 101.1 MG

*You won't need much filling for these omelets. Tasty, they are also
a great breakfast that will "stick" with you through the morning.*

3 **medium eggs (166 mg)**
   Pepper to taste (trace)
½ **tablespoon olive oil (trace)**
¼ **cup Quick Applesauce (page 359)* (.1 mg)**
1 **ounce Alpine Lace Low-Sodium Swiss (35 mg)**
1 **teaspoon fresh chopped thyme (.7 mg)**

1. Whisk together the eggs and pepper in a small bowl. In a nonstick skillet set over medium heat, heat the olive oil. When hot, pour in the egg

---

*Or use a no-salt-added commercial variety. You may substitute **Caramelized Apples** (page 361) or pears for the **Applesauce.**

mixture. Within 5 to 10 seconds, begin to pull the cooked edges toward the center and allow the liquid in the center to spill onto the hot pan. Cook for 20 to 30 seconds more, then spread the applesauce down the center line of the forming omelet; lay the cheese on top of this along the same line. By tilting the pan and using a scraper or spatula, fold a third of the omelet over the filling. Cover pan with a lid and cook for 2 minutes. Now fold the other third over and allow it to finish cooking. When done, sprinkle with thyme and additional pepper if wanted. Slice the omelet onto the plate and cut in half for 2 servings.

Calories: 201. Sodium: 101.12 mg. Protein: 12.4 g. Carbohydrate: 8.02 g. Fiber: 0.96 g. Cholesterol: 290.5 mg. Calcium: 61.5 mg. Iron: 1.926 mg. Potassium: 113.2 mg. Total Fat: 13.1 g; Saturated fat: 4.5 g, Monounsaturated fat: 5 g, Polyunsaturated fat: 1.2 g.

❖ DON'S OMELET ❖

SERVES 3   SODIUM PER RECIPE: 217.4 MG   SODIUM PER SERVING: 72.5 MG
Twice a year I make this omelet for the whole family.
This recipe serves 3.

¼ **onion, diced (trace)**
¼ **green pepper, diced (.5)**
1 **clove garlic, minced (.5 mg)**
4 **ounces mushrooms, thinly sliced (4 mg)**
½ **medium avocado (11 mg)**
1 **medium tomato (11 mg)**
3 **medium eggs (166.3 mg)**
2 **tablespoons olive oil (trace)**
1 **ounce Alpine Lace Low Sodium Swiss, thinly sliced (35 mg)**

1. Combine the onion, pepper, garlic, and mushrooms, and set aside. Slice the avocado lengthwise into thin slices. Cut the tomato into quarters, dicing 2 of these quarters and cutting the remaining 2 in half lengthwise. Set them aside. Beat the eggs.
2. In a large nonstick skillet or fry pan, heat the oil over medium heat. When hot, pour the eggs into the pan. After cooking for about 2 to 3 minutes—or when egg appears to be hardening at bottom—spread the vegetable mixture across one half of the omelet. You'll be folding the other half over the vegetables soon. Lay the cheese slices across the vegetables. Cover the pan and cook for another 3 to 5 minutes over medium heat. Uncover and fold the omelet in half. Cover again and cook for another 2 to 3 minutes.
3. When done, cut the omelet into 3 sections and slide them onto serving plates. Garnish with avocado and tomato slices. Serve hot. You may garnish with low-fat, low-sodium sour cream (6.396 mg) if you wish. A bread

for this meal could be a **Baguette** (page 248) you've already made and frozen or toasted **Sandwich Bun** bread (page 258).

Calories: 156. Sodium: 72.47 mg. Protein: 9.341 g. Carbohydrate: 4.96 g. Fiber: 1.05 g. Cholesterol: 193.67 mg. Calcium: 36.4 mg. Iron: 1.296 mg. Potassium: 285.5 mg. Total Fat: 11.2 g; Saturated fat: 3.3 g, Monounsaturated fat: 5 g, Polyunsaturated fat: 1.1 g.

❖ EGG-WHITE OMELET ❖

SERVES 4 SODIUM PER RECIPE: 366.1 MG SODIUM PER SERVING: 91.5 MG

This omelet recipe came to us from a river rafter who lives in Sonora, California.

> 6 **whites or medium eggs (300.6 mg)—2 yolks = 14 mg**
> 2 **tablespoons extra-virgin olive oil (trace)**
> 2 **green onions (scallions), chopped (4.8 mg)**
> 4 **ounces fresh mushrooms, sliced (4 mg)**
> 2 **cloves garlic, minced (1 mg)**
> 4 **tablespoons fresh Homemade Tomato Salsa, page 307, warmed (3.3 mg)**
> ½ **avocado, sliced (10.4 mg) or ½ tomato, sliced (5.5 mg)**
> **Pepper to taste (trace)**

1. Separate the eggs. Put 2 of the yolks in a bowl and save the rest for another recipe. Add the 6 whites in the same bowl and beat the yolks and whites together very slightly. Pour the oil on a griddle or pan and heat to medium heat. Add the egg batter to the griddle or pan and let cook, covered, for about 4 minutes, or until the bottom of the eggs show some stiffness. When omelet appears close to "turning," sprinkle the onions, mushrooms, and garlic over half of the eggs. Fold the other half over this and let cook, covered, for another 3 to 4 minutes. When done, slice the omelet into 4 servings and spread a tablespoon of warmed (not hot) salsa on top of each. Add pepper to taste. Serve with avocado slices or tomato slices.

Calories: 166. Sodium: 91.52 mg. Protein: 7.95 g. Carbohydrate: 5.06 g. Fiber: 1.7 g. Cholesterol: 106.3 mg. Calcium: 27.6 mg. Iron: 1.066 mg. Potassium: 352.7 mg. Total Fat: 13.2 g; Saturated fat: 2.3 g, Monounsaturated fat: 8.4 g, Polyunsaturated fat: 1.4 g.

❧ FAVORITE FRITTERS ❧

SERVES 4   SODIUM PER RECIPE: 35.7 MG   SODIUM PER SERVING: 8.916 MG

My mother used to make these from leftover mashed potatoes.

1 fresh jalapeño or Anaheim chili pepper (.14 mg)—do not use canned variety
1 large egg yolk (7.2 mg)
2 tablespoons cilantro leaves, roughly chopped (5.8 mg)
1 small onion, finely diced (2.1 mg)
  Dash of paprika (trace)
  Dash of oregano (trace)
3 baked potatoes, chilled (21 mg)
2 tablespoons olive oil (trace)

1. Prepare the chili pepper (see page 308). Beat the egg yolk. Add the cilantro, onion, paprika, oregano, and chili pepper. Cut the baked potatoes into edible slices. Heat the oil in a heavy nonstick skillet. Mix the potatoes and egg batter together and sauté in the skillet until hot or browned. Serve with fresh fruit or as accompaniment with dinner.

Calories: 149. Sodium: 8.92 mg. Fiber: 1.86 g. Protein: 2.731 g. Carbohydrate: 17 g. Cholesterol: 53.16 mg. Calcium: 11.8 mg. Iron: .304 mg. Potassium: 53 mg. Total Fat: 8.2 g; Saturated fat: 1.4 g, Monounsaturated fat: 5.5 g, Polyunsaturated fat: 0.8 g.

❧ POTATO AND EGG FRITTATA ❧

SERVES 4   SODIUM PER RECIPE: 290 MG   SODIUM PER SERVING: 72.5 MG

Mae DiMarco has simplified this early-morning breakfast, popular in Spain as well as Italy. We have adjusted it only for the sodium count. Frittata *is the Italian word for "omelet."*

2 medium potatoes, sliced* (14 mg)
1 teaspoon olive oil (trace)
4 medium eggs (221.8 mg)
  Dash black pepper (trace)
1 clove garlic, minced (.5 mg)
1 sprig parsley or 1 teaspoon parsley flakes (.5 mg)
1½ ounces grated Alpine Lace Low Sodium Swiss† (52.5 mg)

*You may use russets or red or white potatoes, which you previously cooked and are leftover, or fresh potatoes that you will fry in olive oil.
†Use Alpine Lace, or substitute Monterey jack or Tillamook Low-Sodium Cheddar instead if you can find it. The sodium count per ounce is 70 mg for the jack.

1. Slice and cook raw potatoes first or slice already cooked potatoes.
2. Lightly coat a large nonstick frying pan with oil and warm over medium heat. Add the potatoes to the warmed pan. Mix the eggs in a separate bowl with the pepper, garlic, and parsley. Pour the egg mixture over the potatoes and cover the pan. Cook until the eggs are done, turning once or twice as you would a large pancake. Toward end of cooking, sprinkle the Swiss Cheese over the cooked mixture.

Calories: 149. Sodium: 72.5 mg. Protein: 9.816 g. Carbohydrate: 11.8 g. Fiber: 1.01 g. Cholesterol: 194.5 mg. Calcium: 37 mg. Iron: 1.133 mg. Potassium: 389.2 mg. Total Fat: 6.7 g; Saturated fat: 2.9 g, Monounsaturated fat: 1.7 g, Polyunsaturated fat: 0.6 g.

❈ VERY-LOW-SODIUM PIZZA ❈

**MAKES 1 EXTRA LARGE PIZZA—10 SLICES   SODIUM PER RECIPE: 219.2 MG
SODIUM PER SERVING: 21.9 MG**

Pizza is one item that you can no longer eat in a restaurant if you have a sodium restriction. The sodium count in a standard-size pizza with mozzarella or Cheddar cheese and any of the meats used can exceed 4,000 mg. And who ever sat down and ate just once slice of a pizza? After a few years of testing and trying, I came up with this sauce for a low-sodium pizza. The pizza dough has zero sodium and a great history behind it.

  1 **large white onion, minced (4.5 mg)**
  3 **cloves garlic, minced (1.53 mg)**
  2 **tablespoons olive oil (trace)**
  1 **(14.5-ounce can) S&W (or other) No Salt Added, peeled or
     stewed tomatoes (105 mg)**
  1 **cup (8-ounce can) Del Monte natural No Salt Added Tomato
     Sauce (80 mg)**
 ⅛ **teaspoon sugar (trace)**
  1 **tablespoon (heaping) fresh basil, finely chopped (trace) or
     1 teaspoon dry basil (trace)**
  1 **pinch of pepper (trace)**
  1 **Pizza Dough, Thin Crust (page 261) (6.9 mg)**
  1 **zucchini, thinly sliced (9.69 mg)**
  8 **large mushrooms, thinly sliced (7.36 mg)**
 ¼ **sweet red pepper, thinly sliced (.5 mg)**
  1 **ounce Low Sodium Alpine Lace Swiss cheese, grated (35 mg)***
  1 **medium onion, thinly sliced (3.45 mg)**
    Juice of 1 small lime or lemon (trace)

*Or Tillamook Low Sodium Cheddar, grated (55 mg). Simply add 20 mg to the total of the recipe or 2 mg per slice if using Tillamook instead of Swiss.

1. Using a large sauté pan set over medium heat, sauté the onion and garlic in the oil for about 5 minutes, stirring occasionally. Drain the liquid from the tomatoes and combine the tomatoes, tomato sauce, sugar, basil, and pepper, and simmer for 45 minutes, uncovered, stirring occasionally. You should end up with about 2 cups of sauce when finished. The sauce can be made the day before and stored in the refrigerator or freezer in an airtight bag.

2. Preheat oven to 500°F. To assemble the pizza, spread the thinly sliced zucchini, mushrooms, and red pepper over the sauce, then spread the grated cheese of choice on top. Lay the thinly sliced onion on top of this. If you want to add unsalted meat, such as ground meat, add in 18.7 mg sodium per ounce to your count (see nutrient data below). A pizza this size would hold about 8 ounces of stir-fried lean ground beef or turkey. Of course, cook the meat before putting on pizza.

3. Bake at 500°F for 10 to 13 minutes. Ovens will vary. When fluted edges turn golden brown, your pizza should be done. You can freeze slices of this pizza successfully. Use a microwave to defrost and reheat. Spritz pizza slices with lime juice and serve piping hot.

Per serving, without meat: Calories: 152. Sodium: 21.92 mg. Fiber: 2.63 g. Protein: 4.016 g. Carbohydrate: 25 g. Cholesterol: 0 mg. Calcium: 17.1 mg. Iron: 2.079 mg. Potassium: 289.7 mg. Total Fat: 3.8 g; Saturated fat: 0.5 g, Monounsaturated fat: 2.6 g, Polyunsaturated fat: 0.5 g.

Per serving, with lean ground beef: Calories: 205. Sodium: 36.84 mg. Fiber: 2.63 g. Protein: 8.242 g. Carbohydrate: 25 g. Cholesterol: 15.59 mg. Calcium: 18.7 mg. Iron: 2.52 mg. Potassium: 353.9 mg. Total Fat: 7.7 g; Saturated fat: 2.1 g, Monounsaturated fat: 4.2 g, Polyunsaturated fat: 0.6 g.

BEANS, PASTA AND
PASTA SAUCES, RICE,
AND OTHER GRAINS

❖ ❖ ❖ ❖ ❖ ❖ ❖ ❖

❖ RICE PILAF ❖

SERVES 5   SODIUM PER RECIPE: 58.6 MG   SODIUM PER SERVING: 11.7 MG
*This is actually a two-rice pilaf. It's served around our house often
and tastes great with any entrée but especially with chicken
or pot roast of beef.*

1 **cup white and wild rice packaged mix (6.6 mg)**
4 **ounces mushrooms, sliced (3.68 mg)**
1 **onion, coarsely chopped (3.3 mg)**
1 **celery stalk (34.8 mg)**
1 **tablespoon extra-virgin olive oil (trace)**
2 **cups chicken broth made by combining 2 teaspoons Herb-ox**
  Low Sodium Chicken Broth (10 mg) and 2 cups water (0 mg)
2 **tablespoons chopped chives (.18 mg)**
  Pinch of black pepper (trace)

1. Rinse the rice mixture in a sieve and drain. In a large nonstick skillet
sauté the mushrooms, onion, and celery in the oil for about 10 minutes.
Add the rice and sauté for another minute. Add the broth, cover, and simmer according to the directions of the package until all the liquid is absorbed (about 22 to 23 minutes). Remove the skillet from the heat and stir
in the chives and a pinch of black pepper. Serve with your favorite entrée.

*Calories: 171. Sodium: 11.72 mg. Fiber: 2.34 g. Protein: 4.398 g. Carbohydrate: 31.7 g.
Cholesterol: 0 mg. Calcium: 13.7 mg. Iron: 1.503 mg. Potassium: 212.9 mg. Total Fat: 3.1 g.
Saturated fat: 0.4 g. Monounsaturated fat: 2.1 g. Polyunsaturated fat: 0.4 g.*

❧ BASMATI PILAF ❧

SERVES 6   SODIUM PER RECIPE: 12.3 MG   SODIUM PER SERVING: 2.049 MG

This recipe comes to us from Sakar Moloo, who lives and teaches in Pakistan. Basmati rice has its own exciting flavors and texture. Generally from the foothills area of the Himalayas, basmati rice can be found in specialty stores and sometimes in the supermarket.

    2   cups basmati rice (3.9 mg)
    5   seeds from cardamom pods (1.063 mg)
    ¼   teaspoon ground cloves (1.275 mg)
    2   bay leaves, crushed (.409 mg)
    ½   teaspoon cinnamon (.303 mg)
    1   medium onion, thinly sliced (3.3 mg)
    4   cloves garlic, minced (2.04 mg)
    1   tablespoon extra-virgin olive oil (trace)
    5   cups water (0 mg)
        Unsalted blended seasoning to taste (trace)

1. Rinse and drain the rice three times, then soak rice for 20 minutes. Combine the rest of the ingredients in a large nonstick pan and bring to a boil. Cover the pan and simmer for about 10 minutes, or until the rice is three-quarters cooked.

2. Preheat the oven to 400°F. Drain the rice mixture and put it in a large casserole dish. Cover the casserole with a lid or aluminum foil, reduce the oven heat to 300°F, and cook for 6 to 9 minutes. Turn the oven off and let the casserole remain inside for another 5 minutes. Serve hot.

Calories: 269. Sodium: 2.05 mg. Fiber: 1.77 g. Protein: 4.776 g. Carbohydrate: 55.1 g. Cholesterol: 0 mg. Calcium: 22.3 mg. Iron: 9.929 mg. Potassium: 107 mg. Total Fat: 2.8 g. Saturated fat: 0.4 g. Monounsaturated fat: 1.8 g. Polyunsaturated fat: 0.3 g.

❀ FRIED BASMATI RICE ❀

SERVES 4   SODIUM PER RECIPE: 292.2 MG   SODIUM PER SERVING: 73 MG
Use this recipe for leftovers, including basmati rice, meats,
vegetables, etc.

1 **cup raw basmati rice, cooked** (3.9 mg)
1 **onion, thinly sliced** (3.3 mg)
¼ **teaspoon cumin seeds** (.9 mg)
¼ **teaspoon ground cumin** (.9 mg)
¼ **unpacked cup raisins** (4.35 mg)
¼ **cup blanched unsalted almonds** (4.26 mg)
2 **tablespoons extra-virgin olive oil** (trace)
½ **pound lean ground round*** (149.2 mg)
1 **onion, diced** (3.3 mg)
  1-inch ginger root, grated (trace)
4 **cloves garlic, minced** (2 mg)
1 **tomato, diced†** (11 mg)
  Frontier Oriental Seasoning (trace)
2 **medium eggs** (110.9 mg)
  Pepper to taste (trace)

1. Cook basmati with 1½ cups of water. This will yield 3 cups of cooked rice. When rice is done, stir in the onion, cumin seeds, ground cumin, raisins, and almonds. Set aside. Heat the oil in a regular or nonstick pan; begin cooking the ground round. Stir it around loosely. Add the cooked rice just before meat is done and continue to stir. Next add the ginger root, garlic, tomatoes, and seasonings, stirring constantly. When nearly done, crack the eggs at one side of the mixture and scramble them until they are nearly done. Finally, combine the cooked eggs with the rest of the mixture and stir for about 1 minute or until fully cooked. Serve hot.

Calories: 515. Sodium: 73.05 mg. Fiber: 3.47 g. Protein: 19.7 g. Carbohydrate: 55.1 g. Cholesterol: 132.49 mg. Calcium: 61.7 mg. Iron: 4.695 mg. Potassium: 530.3 mg. Total Fat: 4.2 g; Saturated fat: 6 g, Monounsaturated fat: 13.4 g, Polyunsaturated fat: 2.5 g.

*You can use leftover pork, chicken, lamb, or beef in this recipe instead of ground round—just omit the precooking step.
†You may add green or red peppers or other leftover vegetables, diced.

RISOTTO MILANESE /FROM MILAN, ITALY

SERVES 6   SODIUM PER RECIPE: 48.8 MG   SODIUM PER SERVING: 8.139 MG

While filming in Italy during the 1970s for a show I was directing, I was lucky enough to capture on film an Italian chef whipping up a batch of risotto and Veal Osso Buco. I have adapted his recipes to what you find here. You won't find the bone marrow he meticulously dug out of the veal shanks, but you will need saffron. In Italy, saffron is a delicacy and very expensive, but you can find it in your local supermarket in various forms, although it is a bit expensive.

1 cup minced onions (4.8 mg)
3 tablespoons extra-virgin olive oil (trace)
2 cups short-grain Italian arborio rice (0 mg)—none other will work as well; arborio will absorb water without getting mushy
½ cup dry white wine (5.9 mg)
5 cups chicken broth made by combining 5 teaspoons Herb-ox Low Sodium Chicken Broth (25 mg) and 5 cups water (0 mg), heated
½ teaspoon saffron threads, crumbled (.5 mg)
4 tablespoons low-sodium Parmesan cheese (12 mg)

1. In a heavy nonstick saucepan set over medium heat, sauté the onions in 1 tablespoon of oil for 3 minutes, stirring occasionally. Add the rice and stir to make sure it gets coated with the oil. Add the wine (or, if you don't want wine, substitute Welch's white grape juice—10 mg) and simmer, stirring, until it is reduced by half. Add ½ cup of the heated broth and simmer the rice. Cook until most of the broth is absorbed. Stir constantly and add all but ¼ cup of the balance of the broth ½ cup at a time, waiting between half-cups for the rice to absorb the broth. This will take about 25 minutes. You want risotto creamy, yet *al dente*.

2. In a medium or smaller bowl, combine the saffron with the remaining ¼ cup of broth stock and stir the mixture into the hot rice. Add the remaining oil. Stir gently to combine.

Note: Why not make extra rice and keep it in the fridge for lunch tomorrow or the next day?

Calories: 551. Sodium: 8.14 mg. Fiber: 9.37 g. Protein: 10.6 g. Carbohydrate: 102.1 g. Cholesterol: 2.63 mg. Calcium: 53 mg. Iron: 19.2 mg. Potassium: 62.2 mg. Total Fat: 9.3 g; Saturated fat: 25.4 g, Monounsaturated fat: 5.3 g, Polyunsaturated fat: 0.6 g.

❊ FRIED RICE ❊

SERVES 4   SODIUM PER RECIPE: 148.7 MG   SODIUM PER SERVING: 37.2 MG

In the late fifties, traveling in Japan, we would be "hawked" through the open train window at each stop by men selling fried rice. It was usually cooked with small fish heads. You can make it with leftover or freshly cooked meat of any kind and vegetables.

2 tablespoons extra-virgin olive oil (trace)
2 cups cooked and chilled short-grain white rice (4 mg)
1 clove garlic, minced (.5 mg)
¾ cup mixed chopped vegetables* (15 mg)
½ chicken breast—optional (76.7 mg)
1 egg (55.4 mg)
Pepper to taste (trace)

1. In a nonstick sauté pan, skillet, or wok, heat the oil over medium-high heat. When hot, combine the rice, garlic vegetables, and chicken if used, then stir-fry for about 3 minutes. Push the mixture to one side and drop in a single egg. Stir it around to scramble it. When it is close to hardening, stir it into the rice mixture and continue to stir-fry for another 2 minutes. Pepper to taste. Serve hot.

Calories: 445. Sodium: 37.91 mg. Fiber: 2.92 g. Protein: 14.9 g. Carbohydrate: 81.2 g. Cholesterol: 63.86 mg. Calcium: 13 mg. Iron: 4.626 mg. Potassium: 167.5 mg. Total Fat: 5.4 g; Saturated fat: 1 g, Monounsaturated fat: 3.2 g, Polyunsaturated fat: 0.7 g.

❊ SPANISH RICE ❊

SERVES 8   SODIUM PER RECIPE: 114.4 MG   SODIUM PER SERVING: 14.3 MG

Not the spiciest Cajun meal around, this one at least fits into your low-sodium diet with very little sodium and lots of flavors. You can add cayenne pepper and black peppers to heat it up if you like, but first try it this way.

1 teaspoon extra-virgin olive oil (trace)
1 tablespoon whole wheat flour (.375 mg)
3 large yellow onions, chopped (13.5 mg)
1 large stalk celery, chopped (55.7 mg)
4 cloves garlic, minced (2 mg)
3 cups uncooked short-grain brown rice (22.8 mg)
4 cups chicken broth made by combining 4 teaspoons Herb-ox
   Low Sodium Chicken Broth (20 mg) and 4 cups water (0 mg)
Pepper to taste (trace)

*You may use any cooked vegetable leftover from the previous evening's meal. Or you can substitute canned mixed vegetables, such as A&P No Salt Added vegetables.

1. Heat the oil in a large nonstick saucepan and add the flour, stirring with a whisk for 2 minutes over medium heat. Do not brown the roux too much or it will taste bitter. Add the onions and cook slowly over medium heat, stirring constantly. The onions will become soft and brown after about 5 to 8 minutes. At this point add the celery along with the garlic and uncooked rice. Sauté until the celery is soft, then add the chicken broth and bring to a boil. Let it boil, uncovered, for 20 minutes. If the liquid doesn't cover the rice, add more broth or water. Cover the pan, lower the heat, and cook for another 25 minutes, or until all the liquid is absorbed by the rice and the rice is tender. Season to taste with the Frontier spices. Serve hot.

Calories: 296. Sodium: 14.3 mg. Fiber: 3.72 g. Protein: 6.28 g. Carbohydrate: 61.6 g. Cholesterol: 0 mg. Calcium: 41 mg. Iron: 1.502 mg. Potassium: 312 mg. Total Fat: 2.6 g; Saturated fat: 0.5 g, Monounsaturated fat: 1.1 g, Polyunsaturated fat: 0.8 g.

❖ POLENTA ❖

SERVES 6   SODIUM PER RECIPE: 262.2 MG   SODIUM PER SERVING: 43.7 MG

Polenta is a popular Italian dish made from cornmeal and sometimes served as the main course. It also serves as a base under other meat or poultry. Polenta with herbs is a popular side dish with stews, while mushroom-sauced polenta works great with duck, beef, or by itself. We have included two polenta recipes for your use. Most polenta recipes also call for cheeses such as Parmesan, gorgonzola, or feta. We have left those out because they are high in sodium. If you add them, make sure you account for the extra sodium.

½ **cup pine nuts (pignolias) (2.72 mg)**
1 **cup polenta or yellow cornmeal (5.85 mg after cooking)**
2 **cups water (0 mg)**
2 **cups nonfat milk (252.4 mg)**
  Dash pepper (trace)
2 **cloves garlic, crushed (1 mg)**
2 **tablespoons chopped basil or parsley (.212 mg)**

1. Bake pine nuts in a preheated 325°F oven until lightly browned. In a small bowl, combine the cornmeal with 1 cup of the water. Bring the milk and remaining water to a boil in a nonstick saucepan. Season with a dash of pepper. Reduce the heat slightly and stir the cornmeal into the milk mixture. Add the garlic and cook, stirring constantly, for about 5 minutes, or until the mixture boils and thickens slightly. Reduce the heat to low and simmer the polenta gently. Stir often for about 10 minutes, or until the mixture is smooth and thick. Remove the pan from the heat. Add the chopped basil and stir to mix thoroughly. Place the polenta in a nonstick baking pan and spread to a depth of about a quarter of an inch. Chill for

2 hours to set. When ready, use a cookie cutter or the top of a small drinking glass to cut rounds from the polenta; use the trimmings and reform to make more. Or cut the polenta into wedges. Broil these for about 5 minutes, until golden. Serve warm or hot.

Calories: 185. Sodium: 43.7 mg. Fiber: 4.18 g. Protein: 6.944 g. Carbohydrate: 20.9 g. Cholesterol: 1.47 mg. Calcium: 108.3 mg. Iron: 4.265 mg. Potassium: 272.9 mg. Total Fat: 8.9 g; Saturated fat: 1.4 g, Monounsaturated fat: 4.1 g, Polyunsaturated fat: 3 g.

❈ MUSHROOM SAUCE POLENTA ❈

SERVES 6 SODIUM PER RECIPE: 91.5 MG SODIUM PER SERVING: 15.3 MG
A hybrid sauce, gleaned from family recipes but excluding the high-sodium ingredients. If you like mushrooms, you'll like this sauce. Serve it with meats or stews.
Note: *When buying polenta, do not buy a "mix." The sodium content in these mixes is too high. Either buy pure polenta or a brand-name cornmeal such as Albers or Quaker yellow cornmeal.*

1 **cup yellow cornmeal* (5.85 mg)**
1 **cup water (0 mg)**
3 **cups chicken broth made by combining 3 teaspoons Herb-ox**
  Low Sodium Chicken Broth (15 mg) with 3 cups water (0 mg)
  Dash of pepper (trace)
2 **tablespoons extra-virgin olive oil (trace)**
1 **leek, white part only, chopped (17.8 mg)**
1 **stalk celery, chopped (34.8 mg)**
2 **cloves garlic, finely chopped (1 mg)**
¾ **pound mushrooms, sliced (11 mg)**
¼ **cup red wine (5.9 mg)**
½ **teaspoon thyme (trace)**

FIRST STEP FOR THE POLENTA
1. In a small bowl, combine the cornmeal with the water. Put the broth in a nonstick saucepan and add a dash of pepper. Bring it to a boil over high heat and pour in the cornmeal slowly, stirring constantly. Simmer the mix gently, stirring constantly, for about 10 minutes. Remove this from the heat and let stand for about 5 minutes. Grease a pie pan with 1 teaspoon of the olive oil. Pour the polenta in and spread it out with a wooden spoon. Cover with plastic wrap and chill for about 2 hours, or until set.

MUSHROOM SAUCE
1. Heat the remaining oil in a nonstick skillet set over medium heat. Sauté the leeks, celery, and garlic until softened. Add the mushrooms and sauté

*The Albers brand works well, or use degermed cornmeal with no more than 5 mg sodium per cup.

for about 5 minutes, or until softened. Add the wine and thyme and simmer for about 8 to 10 minutes, or until a thick sauce has formed.

FINAL STEP FOR THE POLENTA

1. Cut polenta into 4 or 6 wedges. Place these on a broiler rack and broil for about 5 minutes, or until they are golden brown. Bring the cooked polenta wedges to a serving dish and spoon the mushroom sauce over them.

Calories: 153. Sodium: 15.25 mg. Fiber: 3.58 g. Protein: 2.694 g. Carbohydrate: 21.2 g. Cholesterol: 0 mg. Calcium: 18.8 mg. Iron: 2.841 mg. Potassium: 304.1 mg. Total Fat: 5.5 g; Saturated fat: 0.7 g, Monounsaturated fat: 3.5 g, Polyunsaturated fat: 0.8 g.

❧ COUSCOUS ❧

SERVES 4   SODIUM PER RECIPE: 103.9 MG   SODIUM PER SERVING: 26 MG

Becoming more popular as times goes by, couscous tastes a bit like pasta and works well with vegetables, chops, beans, and salads. Couscous is made from hulled durum wheat. Although the original couscous had to be steamed for a half hour or more, the variety you will find in your market needs only 5 minutes' cooking time.

1 tablespoon extra-virgin olive oil (trace)
1 celery stalk, diced (34.8 mg)
½ onion, diced (2.25 mg)
1½ large carrots, diced (37.8 mg)
1 zucchini, sliced (5.88 mg)
1 medium crookneck squash, sliced (1.3 mg)
4 large mushrooms, sliced (3.68 mg)
2 tablespoons fresh shredded basil or ½ tablespoon dried basil (.212 mg)
¾ cup couscous (13 mg)
1 cup chicken broth made by combining 1 teaspoon Herb-ox Low Sodium Chicken Broth (5 mg) with 1 cup water (0 mg)
Dash of pepper and spices to taste (trace)

1. Heat the oil in a large nonstick saucepan. Add the celery, onion, and carrots and sauté for about 7 minutes, or until soft but not browned. Add the zucchini, squash, and mushrooms, sautéing for about 3 minutes, or until slightly soft. Add the basil and the pepper and spices to taste and toss to mix. Add the couscous to the saucepan and stir with a wooden spoon, combining it with the vegetables. This will help coat the couscous grains. Pour the broth into the saucepan and mix. Bring the broth to a boil, then cover the saucepan and remove it from the heat. Let it stand for 5 minutes, or until the couscous grains are tender and the liquid is absorbed. Lightly separate the grains by fluffing with a fork. Serve with vegetables, pork chops, chicken, or beans. You may also serve this with a hot salad.

2. After cooking, couscous is also good as a stuffing for squash, or served with stew, toasted with almonds and raisins, and as a spicy pepper sauce made with fresh jalapeño or Anaheim chili peppers.

Calories: 191. Sodium: 25.99 mg. Fiber: 4.17 g. Protein: 5.948 g. Carbohydrate: 33.6 g. Cholesterol: 0 mg. Calcium: 36.9 mg. Iron: 1.198 mg. Potassium: 446.7 mg. Total Fat: 3.9 g; Saturated fat: 0.5 g, Monounsaturated fat: 2.5 g, Polyunsaturated fat: 0.5 g.

❄ HUMMUS ❄

MAKES ABOUT 50 TABLESPOONS (OR 5 CUPS)   SODIUM PER RECIPE: 184.3 MG
SODIUM PER TABLESPOON: 3.686 MG

Hummus is a chickpea (garbanzo) pâté with a spicy, rich flavor that also has a great deal of natural protein. Hummus is also excellent as a dip eaten with unsalted chips.

2½ **cups dried chickpeas (garbanzo beans) (16-ounce package) (120 mg boiled)**
  6 **cloves garlic, minced (3 mg)**
  1 **tablespoon grated lemon peel (.36 mg)**
     Juice of 3 medium-size fresh lemons (1.41 mg)
 ¾ **cup fresh sesame butter (tahini) (40 mg)**
 ⅓ **cup (packed) finely minced parsley (11.1 mg)**
 ½ **cup minced scallions, including green stems (8 mg)**
     Pepper to taste (trace)
     Paprika to taste (trace)

1. Soak the chickpeas overnight or per package instructions. After soaking, boil them in water to cover until soft, about 1½ to 2 hours. Use a food processor with a metal blade or a masher or a food grinder to mash them to a thick paste. Use a tablespoon or more of the cooking water as needed to make the hummus the consistency of frosting. When ready, add the garlic, lemon peel and lemon juice, the tahini, parsley and scallions. Combine thoroughly and then chill for about 2 to 3 hours. You can make this hummus and store in refrigerator for many later uses (it will last for about 2 weeks in a sealed container). Taste and adjust the seasonings to your taste. Make it without pepper and then add pepper to taste. Sprinkle with paprika. Spread the hummus on a homemade **Sandwich Bun** with onions, tomatoes, cilantro, and avocado, on homemade **Whole Wheat Bread** (add an additional 1.4 mg sodium to the count), or stuff it into a homemade **Pita Bread.**

Calories: 78. Sodium: 3.69 mg. Fiber: 2.18 g. Protein: 3.211 g. Carbohydrate: 8.26 g. Cholesterol: 0 mg. Calcium: 77.3 mg. Iron: 1.962 mg. Potassium: 136.7 mg. Total Fat: 4 g: Saturated fat: 0.5 g, Monounsaturated fat: 1.4 g, Polyunsaturated fat: 1.8 g.

❁ COOKING SPAGHETTI ❁

SERVES 6   SODIUM PER RECIPE: 44.4 MG   SODIUM PER SERVING: 7.4 MG
A basic spaghetti recipe.

1 **pound spaghetti or spaghettini (31.8 mg)**
2 **tablespoons plus ½ teaspoon extra-virgin olive oil (trace)**
4 **tablespoons grated low-sodium Parmesan (12.6 mg)**

1. Cook 1 pound spaghetti or spaghettini (6 average servings) in boiling unsalted water with a ½ teaspoon of the oil. Cook until *al dente* (when it can be chewed without being mushy).
2. Remove it immediately and pour it into a colander. Drain. Do not rinse the paste after cooking. Put the drained spaghetti in a large serving bowl and mix well with the remaining oil and 4 tablespoons grated low-sodium Parmesan cheese.
3. Top with **Basic Tomato Sauce** (below). Serve hot. Pass any remaining sauce around.

Calories: 339. Sodium: 7.4 mg. Fiber: 1.82 g. Protein: 11.1 g. Carbohydrate: 56.6. Choles-terol: 2.63 mg. Calcium: 59.5 mg. Iron: 2.971 mg. Potassium: 126.1 mg. Total Fat: 7.1 g; Sat-urated fat: 1.5 g, Monounsaturated fat: 4 g, Polyunsaturated fat: 0.9 g.

❁ BASIC TOMATO SAUCE FOR SPAGHETTI ❁

SERVES 8   SODIUM PER RECIPE: 148.4 MG   SODIUM PER SERVING: 18.6 MG
Another Mae DiMarco recipe "from the old country." Add a bit
more garlic for a tangier sauce if you want. If during the cooking
the sauces seem a bit tart to you, add some sugar.

½ **medium onion, diced (1.65 mg)**
4 **cloves garlic, minced (2.04 mg)**
2 **tablespoons extra-virgin olive oil (trace)**
   8-ounce can any no-salt-added tomato puree (42.5 mg)
   6-ounce can Contadina Natural Tomato Paste (102 mg) or
   Hunt's No Salt Added Tomato Paste (100 mg)
2 **cups water (0 mg)**
½ **teaspoon dried sweet basil or 4 fresh leaves (trace)**
   Dash of cinnamon (trace)
   Dash of oregano (trace)
   Pepper and sugar to taste (trace)

1. In a medium pan, sauté the onion and garlic in oil until golden brown. Add the tomato puree and paste and stir until all is combined. Add the water and stir well, then add the seasonings. Cook for about 1 hour or until the sauce is reduced to a somewhat thickened consistency. Add cooked ground meat (account for added sodium) or serve alone with pasta.

Calories: 59. Sodium: 18.55 mg. Fiber: 1.38 g. Protein: 1.232 g. Carbohydrate: 6.80 g. Cholesterol: 0 mg. Calcium: 15.6 mg. Iron: 2.699 mg. Potassium: 284.6 mg. Total Fat: 17.2 g; Saturated fat: 0.5 g, Monounsaturated fat: 2.5 g, Polyunsaturated fat: 0.4 g.

❖ BASIC PESTO ❖

MAKES APPROXIMATELY 1 CUP (GENERALLY 6 SERVINGS)
SODIUM PER RECIPE: 8.679 MG   SODIUM PER SERVING: 1.446 MG
Use this recipe to top linguine, fettuccine, or spaghetti noodles. It also goes well with some meats, including chicken.

⅓ **cup pine nuts (pignolias), lightly toasted in a 350°F oven (1.795 mg)**
1 **cup fresh basil leaves (1.696 mg)**
2 **garlic cloves, chopped (1.02 mg)**
4 **teaspoons low-sodium Parmesan* (4.095 mg)**
⅓ **cup extra-virgin olive oil (trace)**
⅓ **tablespoon pepper to taste (trace)**
  Pinch of tarragon (optional) (trace)

1. Put the pine nuts, basil, garlic, Parmesan, and oil in a food processor and blend to a coarse paste. Season with pepper; add a pinch of tarragon if you're having a chicken-based pasta. To store, cover the pesto with a little additional olive oil, press plastic wrap down over the top, cover, and store in freezer. Serve hot.

Calories: 156. Sodium: 1.45 mg. Fiber: 0.64 g. Protein: 2.491 g. Carbohydrate: 1.752 g. Cholesterol: 0.86 mg. Calcium: 29.6 mg. Iron: .989 mg. Potassium: 82.8 mg. Total Fat: 16 g; Saturated fat: 2.4 g, Monounsaturated fat: 10.3, Polyunsaturated fat: 2.6 g.

*If you use this low-sodium cheese, you may add more Parmesan. Using regular Parmesan would add 335.105 mg sodium to recipe total. Check with Trader Joe's or other specialty and health food stores or call Healthy Heart Market at 1-800/753-0310 for low-sodium Parmesan.

❧ SUN-DRIED TOMATO PESTO ❧

MAKES APPROXIMATELY 1 CUP (GENERALLY 6 SERVINGS)
SODIUM PER RECIPE: 39.6 MG   SODIUM PER SERVING: 6.6 MG

This recipe, popular around the world, comes directly to us from Scott Leysath. He uses it with upland game birds such as pheasant, grouse, and dove, but you can use it with chicken, turkey, and even no-meat pasta. You may also use this effectively as a pizza topping.

⅓ **cup pine nuts (pignolias), lightly toasted in a 350°F oven (1.75 mg)**
1 **cup basil leaves (1.6 mg)**
2 **cloves garlic, chopped (1 mg)**
½ **cup sun-dried tomatoes, drained and softened (35 mg)**
⅓ **cup extra-virgin olive oil (0 mg)**
   Pepper to taste (0 mg)
   Pinch of sage (optional) (trace)

1. Put the pine nuts, basil, garlic, tomatoes, and oil in a food processor and blend to make a coarse paste. Season with pepper and add a pinch of sage if you're having a chicken-based pasta dish. To store, top the paste with a little additional olive oil, then cover the container and refrigerate.

Calories: 222.4. Sodium: 6.6 mg. Fiber: 1.8 g. Protein: 3.207 g. Carbohydrate: 5.212 g. Cholesterol: 0 mg. Calcium: 14.7 mg. Iron: 1.002 mg. Potassium: 81.7 mg. Total Fat: 21.8 g; Saturated fat: 3 g, Monounsaturated fat: 14.7 g, Polyunsaturated fat: 3.1 g.

❖ HOMEMADE MARINARA SAUCE ❖

MAKES 1 CUP   SODIUM PER RECIPE: 90.9 MG   SODIUM PER PASTA SERVING:
22.7 MG   SODIUM PER TABLESPOON (DIPPING SAUCE): 5.679 MG

*Serve on vegetables, pasta, or with **Roasted Garlic Toast**. Use as a*
dipping sauce for shrimp, vegetables, unsalted chips,
and fried pork.

2 tablespoons extra-virgin olive oil (trace)
1 medium onion, chopped (3.3 mg)
4 cloves garlic, chopped (2.04 mg)
½ pound mushrooms, chopped (7.36 mg)
1 14.5-ounce can No Salt Added Tomatoes (Hunt's, S&W,
  Pathmark, others) (76 mg)
¼ cup water (0 mg)
1 teaspoon oregano (.22 mg)
1 teaspoon basil (.479 mg)
¼ teaspoon cloves (1.275 mg)
1 bay leaf, crumbled (.137 mg)
  Pepper to taste (trace)

1. Heat the oil in large sauté or frying pan. Add chopped onion, garlic, and mushrooms and sauté for only a few minutes. Next add the tomatoes, the water, and the spices. When thoroughly cooked, this dish may be served with steamed vegetables, ground beef round, or ground turkey over any 8-ounce bag of boiled pasta. The best way to add ground meat is to dry-fry it in a nonstick pan, crumbled, then add it to the sauce toward the end of the cooking period; be sure to account for the increased sodium total. The sauce alone is a good accompaniment to **Roasted Garlic Toast** (page 33) as a dipping sauce.

Per pasta serving, based on 4 servings. Calories: 125. Sodium: 22.72 mg. Fiber: 3.4 g. Protein: 3.333 g. Carbohydrate: 14.5 g. Cholesterol: 0 mg. Calcium: 85.8 mg. Iron: 2.648 mg. Potassium: 677.5 mg. Total Fat: 7.3 g; Saturated fat: 1 g, Monounsaturated fat: 5 g, Polyunsaturated fat: 0.8 g.

Per tablespoon as dipping sauce: Calories: 31. Sodium: 5.68 mg. Fiber: 0.85 g. Protein: .833 g. Carbohydrate: 3.618 g. Cholesterol: 0 mg. Calcium: 21.4 mg. Iron: .662 mg. Potassium: 169.4 mg. Total Fat: 1.8 g; Saturated fat: 0.3 g, Monounsaturated fat: 1.3 g, Polyunsaturated fat: 0.2 g.

ALICE'S OLD COUNTRY SPAGHETTI SAUCE /
❖ CIRCA 1930S ❖

SERVES 8   SODIUM PER RECIPE: 488.1 MG   SODIUM PER SERVING: 61 MG
For the best Italian food, shop at an Italian-American import store.
Imported or high-grade extra-virgin olive oil should always be used
in making a true Italian sauce. Use Hunt's or other no-salt-added
tomato paste to complete the recipe.

½ **pound lean ground round (149.2 mg)**
¼ **cup extra-virgin olive oil (trace)**
5 **cloves garlic, finely chopped (2.55 mg)**
2½ **onions, chopped (8.25 mg)**
2 **(14½-ounce) cans S&W No-Salt-Added Ready-Cut Peeled**
  Tomatoes (liquid) (218.4 mg)*
  6-ounce can Contadina Natural Tomato Paste (102 mg)†
¾ **cup water (0 mg)**
5 **ounces fresh mushrooms, sliced (4.6 mg)**
¼ **teaspoon black pepper (.231 mg)**
3 **dried bay leaves, crumbled (1.228 mg)**
½ **teaspoon dried oregano (.11 mg)**
½ **teaspoon sweet dried basil (.24 mg)**
¼ **teaspoon powdered cloves (1.275 mg)**
  Pinch of thyme (trace)

1. Brown the meat in a nonstick pan, stirring to keep from clumping. Use
a little olive oil to help but not much. Set aside. For vegetarians, simply
omit the meat.
2. In a large, heavy pot, brown the garlic and onions together in the oil.
Do not burn. Add the canned tomatoes and the tomato paste plus an
amount of water equal to the paste. Simmer for ½ hour on medium-low.
Add the sliced mushrooms.
3. After the sauce has simmered, add the beef and the seasonings and stir
until the ingredients are well distributed. (For vegetarians, leave out the
meat.) Simmer for another 3 hours, stirring occasionally. Serve hot on
spaghetti or other preferred noodles.

Calories: 208. Sodium: 61.02 mg. Fiber: 5.78 g. Protein: 9.391 g. Carbohydrate: 17.7 g.
Cholesterol: 19.49 mg. Calcium: 1000 mg. Iron: 3.72 mg. Potassium: 867.9 mg. Total Fat:
26.1 g; Saturated fat: 3 g, Monounsaturated fat: 7.2 g, Polyunsaturated fat: 1.1 g.

*Other brands may have higher or lower sodium counts.
†Contadina sodium levels are lower than those for other pastes, per FDA figures.

❖ Maddjack's Spaghetti Sauce ❖

SERVES 6   SODIUM PER RECIPE: 127.6 MG   SODIUM PER SERVING: 21.3 MG

Use this sauce with or without meat. Also check out the recipe for
Basic Tomato Sauce *(page 143).*

> 2 tablespoons extra-virgin olive oil (trace)
> 1 tablespoon fresh grated garlic (1.53 mg)
> 1 tablespoon sweet dried basil (.106 mg)
>   6-ounce can Contadina Natural Tomato Paste (102 mg)
> ½ cup any good no-salt-added tomato sauce (20.1 mg)
> 4 ounces mushrooms, sliced (3.68 mg)
> 1 tablespoon fresh lemon or lime juice (.15 mg)
>   Water as needed
>   Juice of 1 lime, cut into quarters (.15 mg)

1. Set a wok over two burners of your stove (if an electric stove, set one at high and the other on low). Or use an electric wok instead. Heat the oil rapidly until it just starts to smoke, then add the garlic and basil and stir until it just starts to brown. Stir in the tomato paste and tomato sauce, and simmer. Add the sliced mushrooms. Next add the lemon juice and enough water to thin the paste to the desired consistency. The sauce has to cook down. Simmer for 1 to 2 hours and serve over pasta. Squeeze fresh lime juice over each serving. This adds a flavor similar to salt.

Calories: 73. Sodium: 21.27 mg. Fiber: 1.56 g. Protein: 1.609 g. Carbohydrate: 7.644 g. Cholesterol: 0 mg. Calcium: 15.7 mg. Iron: .875 mg. Potassium: 371.1 mg. Total Fat: 23 g; Saturated fat: 0.6 g, Monounsaturated fat: 3.3 g, Polyunsaturated fat: 0.5 g.

Pasta with Balsamic Onion
❖ and Sun-Dried Tomatoes ❖

SERVES 4   SODIUM PER RECIPE: 109.7 MG   SODIUM PER SERVING: 27.4 MG

This recipe came to us from our son-in-law, who is a chef. He uses it on river trips in the summer when he trades his chef's toque for a guide's cap. It's mouth-watering delicious and very low in sodium.

> 2 large red onions (9 mg)
> 2 tablespoons extra-virgin olive oil (trace)
> ½ cup brown sugar (28.3 mg)
> 2 tablespoons lemon juice (.3 mg)
> ⅛ cup balsamic vinegar (.3 mg)
> ½ cup sun-dried tomatoes, chopped or diced,* reconstituted in
>   water (40 mg)
> 1 pound fettuccine, cooked and kept hot (31.8 mg)

*Sun-dried tomatoes vary in sodium count from producer to producer. Check the nutrition label before buying.

1. Slice the onions into thin half-rounds. Sauté the onions in the oil until translucent. Add the brown sugar and caramelize the onions over medium heat, stirring continuously. Add the lemon juice and balsamic vinegar. Let this mix simmer for about 1 minute. Add the sun-dried tomatoes and continue to simmer until they are hot. Immediately toss with cooked pasta.

2. You may also use this same sauce to top turkey burgers, hamburgers, **Soyburgers** (page 266), and barbecue ribs.

Calories: 610. Sodium: 27.42 mg. Fiber: 6.1 g. Protein: 17.4 g. Carbohydrate: 116 g. Cholesterol: 0 mg. Calcium: 51.8 mg. Iron: 4.965 mg. Potassium: 381.1 mg. Total Fat: 8.7 g; Saturated fat: 1.2 g, Monounsaturated fat: 5.2 g, Polyunsaturated fat: 1.3 g.

❧ PASTA SUPREME ❧

SERVES 4   SODIUM PER RECIPE: 324.7 MG   SODIUM PER SERVING: 81.2 MG

This one will help your weight, your low-sodium needs, and will appeal to your taste buds. Similar versions of this recipe can be found in restaurants, but not with the low sodium count. Many restaurant chefs add soy sauce, which is a killer for low-sodium diets, so we replaced that with garlic and chilies. Remember, this is no-salt, low-sodium, so those flavors will be absent and this whole new flavor will be your treat instead.

  4 **boned, skinned chicken breast halves (306.8 mg)—or replace with fish fillets (329.4 mg) or 226.8 pork (298.3) mg ground beef lean**

  3 **tablespoons lemon juice (.45 mg)**

  3 **teaspoons fresh jalapeño chili, chopped (trace)**

  2 **cloves garlic, minced (1 mg)**

  1 **tablespoon cornstarch, diluted in 4 tablespoons water (.72 mg)**

⅓ **cup chopped fresh chives (.45 mg)**

¼ **cup chopped fresh cilantro (6.21 mg)**

  1 **cup chicken broth made by combining 1 teaspoon Herb-ox Low Sodium Chicken Broth (5 mg) with 1 cup water (0 mg) Dash of Frontier pasta seasoning (trace)**

10 **ounces spaghetti—use your favorite pasta (3.99 mg)**

1. Preheat oven to 450°F.

2. Arrange the chicken in a single layer in a large baking dish and add lemon juice. Cover the dish tightly with foil. Bake in the preheated oven until the chicken is cooked through but not dry—about 30 minutes (fish may take about 12 minutes, pork about 30 minutes).

3. While the chicken is baking, in a blender or food processor puree the chilies and garlic with the cornstarch. Add the cilantro, chives, and the broth, then blend. Transfer the mixture to a 12-inch frying pan and stir over high heat until it comes to a boil. When done keep it warm while you prepare the pasta per instructions on package until tender to the bite. Drain and return the pasta to the pan.

4. Stir the juices from the baked chicken (or fish or pork) into the pepper sauce. Season with the Frontier blend. Combine 1½ cups of this sauce with the pasta, then transfer the pasta to a serving dish and top with the chicken. You may serve it hot, or chill it for next-day use. To reheat, simply microwave under waxed paper or with microwave-safe plastic wrap.

Calories: 200. Sodium: 81.17 mg. Fiber: 0.64 g. Protein: 46.8 g. Carbohydrate: 130.8 g. Cholesterol: 68.44 mg. Calcium: 24.6 mg. Iron: 1.554 mg. Potassium: 372 mg. Total Fat: 1.7 g; Saturated fat: 0.4 g, Monounsaturated fat: 0.4 g, Polyunsaturated fat: 0.4 g.

❖ CHICKEN MUSHROOM PASTA ❖

SERVES 4   SODIUM PER RECIPE: 352.4 MG   SODIUM PER SERVING: 88 MG
Another tasty recipe from Maddjack (Jack Davis) in cyberspace.

¼ **cup extra-virgin olive oil (trace)**
2 **tablespoons dried basil (3 mg)**
2 **tablespoons finely chopped garlic (2 mg)**
1 **teaspoon dried oregano (.22 mg)**
1 **teaspoon powdered rosemary (.6 mg)**
1 **jalapeño pepper, finely chopped (optional) (.14 mg)**
1 **pound skinless, boneless chicken breast, cut into 1-inch pieces (306.8 mg)**
½ **pound mushrooms, finely chopped (8 mg)**
1 **pound spaghetti (31.8 mg)**

1. Heat the oil until it just smokes, then stir in the basil, garlic, oregano, and rosemary and the jalapeño if you are using it. Add the chicken and reduce the heat to medium and cook, stirring continuously. When the chicken is done (no blood shows), add the mushrooms. Reduce the heat and cover and cook for 5 minutes. Serve over hot pasta of choice.

Calories: 695. Sodium: 88.01 mg. Fiber: 4.64 g. Protein: 43.3 g. Carbohydrate: 89.9 g. Cholesterol: 68.44 mg. Calcium: 98.8 mg. Iron: 7.126 mg. Potassium: 760.9 mg. Total Fat: 17.2 g; Saturated fat: 2.5 g, Monounsaturated fat: 10.5 g, Polyunsaturated fat: 2.4 g.

⬥ CHICKEN FETTUCCINE ⬥

SERVES 4   SODIUM PER RECIPE: 299.6 MG   SODIUM PER SERVING: 74.9 MG
Fettuccine is just too delicious not to include it in this cookbook.
The low sodium per serving here gives you a great meal with plenty
of nutrients and protein.

> 2 **boneless, skinless chicken breast halves, cut into bite-size**
>   **pieces (153.4 mg)**
> 2 **cloves garlic, minced (1 mg)**
> 1 **tablespoon plus 1 teaspoon extra-virgin olive oil (trace)**
> 2 **quarts water (0 mg)**
> ½ **pound Ronzoni fettuccine noodles (or pasta of your choice)**
>   **(12 mg)**
> ½ **cup nonfat milk* (63.1 mg)**
> 2 **ounces Alpine Lace Low Sodium Swiss† (70 mg)**
>   **Ground nutmeg, ginger, or cloves to taste (trace)**

1. In a nonstick pan add 1 tablespoon of the oil and sauté the chicken with the garlic. When done, pat the pieces dry with paper towels to absorb any oil or chicken fat.

2. Bring the water and the remaining teaspoon of oil to a boil. Add the fettuccine noodles slowly. Cook for about 9 minutes, or until tender to the bite (*al dente*). Drain. Return the pasta to the saucepan and reheat over low heat with the milk, cheese, and chicken pieces. When warm enough to eat, transfer to a dish and sprinkle with nutmeg. You may adjust the amount of cheese to taste.

Calories: 373. Sodium: 74.91 mg. Fiber: 0.07 g. Protein: 25.8 g. Carbohydrate: 43.1 g. Cholesterol: 44.77 mg. Calcium: 59.8 mg. Iron: 16.5 mg. Potassium: 207.8 mg. Total Fat: 9.1 g; Saturated fat: 2.9 g, Monounsaturated fat: 3.5 g, Polyunsaturated fat: 0.5 g.

*Or, if your diet permits, use full-fat milk or even heavy cream. The sodium count remains the same; only the fat count changes.
†The sodium count varies from the deli-sliced to the prepackaged version—the former is 35 mg, the latter is 25 mg.

❖ FETTUCCINE ALFREDO ❖

SERVES 4   SODIUM PER RECIPE: 145.2 MG   SODIUM PER SERVING: 36.3 MG
So close you'll swear it's the real thing. The difference is that this version has a whole lot fewer milligrams of sodium.

  2 quarts water* (0 mg)
  1 tablespoon extra-virgin olive oil (trace)
 ½ pound fettuccine noodles (12 mg)
 ½ cup nonfat milk (63.1 mg)
  2 ounces Alpine Lace Low Sodium Swiss† (70 mg)
    Nutmeg to taste (trace)

1. Cook the fettuccine as directed in the recipe for **Chicken Fettuccine** (page 151). Drain. Return the pasta to the saucepan and reheat over low heat with the milk and cheese. When warm enough to eat, transfer the fettuccine to a serving dish and sprinkle with nutmeg. Adjust the amount of cheese and nutmeg to taste.

Calories: 296. Sodium: 36.29 mg. Fiber: 0.02 g. Protein: 12.1 g. Carbohydrate: 42.5 g. Cholesterol: 10.55 mg. Calcium: 50.5 mg. Iron: 16 mg. Potassium: 51.1 mg. Total Fat: 7.3 g; Saturated fat: 2.5 g, Monounsaturated fat: 2.5 g, Polyunsaturated fat: 0.3 g.

❖ MACARONI AND CHEDDAR CHEESE ❖

SERVES 4 TO 6   SODIUM PER RECIPE: 100.6 MG
SODIUM PER SERVING: 25.2 MG (BASED ON 4 SERVINGS)
You can find Cheddar cheese with less sodium than Tillamook, but not as easily. You may also use low-sodium Colby cheese. Use friendly spices to enhance the flavor—nutmeg, ground cloves, or cinnamon work well. This basic recipe may be adjusted to your tastes by adding mushrooms, broccoli or zucchini or other vegetables, either mixed into the macaroni or sprinkled on top just before baking. If you have children, you know what they like, so adjust for that and they'll love this version, too.

  2 quarts water (0 mg)
  1 cup chicken broth made by combining 1 teaspoon Herb-ox
    Low Sodium Chicken Broth (5 mg) with 1 cup water (0 mg)
 ½ pound macaroni (0 mg)
 ½ cup nonfat milk‡ (65 mg)

*Or, if your diet permits, use full-fat milk or even heavy cream. The sodium count remains the same; only the fat count changes.
†The sodium count varies from the deli-sliced to the prepackaged version—the former is 35 mg, the latter is 25 mg.
‡If your diet permits, use full-fat milk or even heavy cream. The sodium count remains the same; only the fat count changes.

1 tablespoon flour (trace)
2 ounces Tillamook low-sodium Cheddar (15.8 mg)*
2 tablespoons grated onion (trace)
Pepper to taste (0 mg)
(*Note:* Some children do not like pepper or onions; both may
be omitted)

1. Bring the water and chicken broth to a boil. Add the macaroni slowly. Cook for about 10 minutes, or until tender to the bite (*al dente*). Drain. Return the pasta to the saucepan and reheat over low heat with the milk and flour (making a rue). When warm enough to eat, transfer the macaroni to a dish and sprinkle with the grated low-sodium or Tillamook Cheddar and the onion. Sprinkle with a dash of nutmeg.
2. Preheat the oven to 375°F. Transfer the pasta to a baking dish and bake, covered, for 30 minutes, then uncovered for an additional 15 minutes.
3. This dish may also be served with our **Homemade Marinara Sauce** (page 146).

Per serving: Calories: 365. Sodium: 25.15 mg. Fiber: 1.51 g. Protein: 22.5 g. Carbohydrate: 48.4 g. Cholesterol: 20.33 mg. Calcium: 435.8 mg. Iron: 17.1 mg. Potassium: 254.2 mg. Total Fat: 8.3 g: Saturated fat: 3.1 g, Monounsaturated fat: 3.7 g, Polyunsaturated fat: 0.8 g.

*If you can't find low-sodium cheddar, replace with Tillamook Cheddar, but add 100 mg to the sodium count for the 2 ounces, or 25 mg per serving.

LASAGNA /

❖ WITH OR WITHOUT MEAT ❖

SERVES 12   SODIUM PER RECIPE: 909.3 MG
SODIUM PER SERVING: 75.8 MG

Based on an old family recipe (created in Italy), this lasagna can be easily converted to a vegetarian dish. Simply leave out the meat and deduct the sodium level listed with the meat. Replace with a layer of steamed spinach, zucchini, and mushrooms with some low-sodium Swiss. We have included the alternate ingredients of sodium levels for you in the listing at the end of this recipe. You may halve this recipe except for the water in the marinara sauce. That remains at ½ cup.

LASAGNA SAUCE
- ½ pound lean (10% or less) ground beef (149.2 mg)
- 1 large onion (4.8 mg)
- 6 cloves garlic, minced (1.53 mg)
- 1 tablespoon fresh parsley, chopped (2.128 mg)
- 2 14.5-ounce cans S & W (or other) no-salt-added peeled tomatoes (210 mg)
- 1 can Contadina tomato paste (100 mg)
- 2 bay leaves (remove after cooking) (.409 mg)
  dash pepper (.044 mg)
- ½ cup bottled no-sodium water (0 mg)
- ½ teaspoon oregano (.11 mg)
- ¼ teaspoon ground cloves (1.275 mg)

BÉCHAMEL (ROUX) SAUCE
- 6 tablespoons unsalted butter (12.5 mg)
- 6 tablespoons white unbleached flour (1.248 mg)
- 1½ cups nonfat milk (252.4 mg)
- 3 tablespoons fresh lemon juice (.45 mg)
- 2 tablespoons parsley, chopped (4.256 mg)
- 3 cloves garlic, minced (1.53 mg)
- 2 tablespoons cinnamon (.06 mg)

LASAGNA LAYERS
- 12 ounces lasagna noodles (16 noodles) (23.9 mg)
- 6 ounces Alpine Lace Swiss Cheese, grated (210 mg)
- 1 Italian béchamel sauce (included)

1. Cook meat lightly, and brown onion and garlic in the same nonstick pan.

2. While that is sautéing, combine balance of ingredients in a medium-size stock pot. Add in the sautéed ingredients when the meat is close to being cooked. Bring sauce to boil, then turn down to simmer for an hour, stirring occasionally. When sauce is done, throw out the bay leaves.

3. While the sauce has 30 minutes remaining to simmer, heat noodle water in a large pan so that it's ready when you are close to putting the lasagna together.

4. While the water is heating and the sauce is simmering, make the bechemel sauce in a smaller saucepan. Set aside when done. Cook the lasagna noodles per package instructions in unsalted water. When noodles are done, drain and layer on wax paper to cool for a few moments before working with them.

TO PREPARE THE BÉCHAMEL SAUCE

Melt butter in medium-sized pan on low heat, stirring as it does. Don't let it burn. Add in flour, stirring constantly, until fully dissolved and smooth. When it bubbles, remove from heat and add in the nonfat milk, stirring constantly. Return to medium heat and stir in the lemon juice, parsley, garlic, and dash of cinnamon. Stir until it's smooth and slightly bubbles. It will thicken.

TO MAKE THE LASAGNA

1. Preheat oven to 350° F.

2. Slightly grease a 9x13-inch glass baking dish with a light spray of olive oil. This will not add any sodium or traceable fat. Arrange noodles in a single rectangular layer to form a "noodle box," lining the sides of the dish and layering the bottom. The noodles will be sticky to sit up against the dish sides. Layer the bottom with ⅓ of the marinara, ¼ of the cheese, and ⅓ of the béchamel sauce. Repeat another layer of noodles. Cover this layer with ⅓ of the sauce, ¼ of the cheese, and ⅓ of the béchamel sauce. Repeat another layer of noodles. Spread the rest of the marinara and béchamel over the noodles, but not the cheese. One more layer of the noodles (this is the top), and spread the balance of the cheese evenly over the noodles.

3. Seal the dish with aluminum foil, making sure to create a slight "tent" effect to prevent the cheese from melting to the foil.

4. Bake at 350°F for 30 minutes. Remove foil and bake for another 10 minutes. Lasagna may be prepared ahead of time and refrigerated until you want to cook it. This is also an excellent dish to freeze cooked serving sizes for use later, or store in refrigerator after cooking for serving the next day. Wrap well in foil and freeze after it has thoroughly cooled.

5. Thaw and reheat to serve. Serve hot with steamed zucchini and a salad.

Note: Béchamel will go down in "chunks" since it becomes very thick. Best to lay it in where you believe you'll be forming servings.

FOR VEGETARIAN, exchange the 149.2 mg for the meat with the following:
1 large zucchini (.48 mg)
1 cup steamed spinach (23.7 mg)
When making the vegetarian version this way, subtract 125.02 mg from recipe total or 10.418 mg from each serving.

Calories: 307. Sodium: 75.77 mg. Fiber: 2.19 g. Cholesterol: 39.09 mg. Calcium: 68.7 mg. Potassium: 289.5 mg. Protein: 14.4 g. Carbohydrate: 32.8 g. Total Fat: 11.6 g; Saturated fat: 6 g, Monounsaturated fat: 3.1 g, Polyunsaturated fat: 0.6 g.

❖ Fresh Garlic Noodles ❖

SERVES 6   SODIUM PER RECIPE: 82.9 MG   SODIUM PER SERVING: 13.8 MG
Fine as a side dish or a main-course entrée.

2 cups unbleached Best for Bread flour (5 mg)
3 egg yolks (21.4 mg) plus 1 medium egg (55.4 mg)
2 cloves garlic, minced (1 mg)
4 to 6 tablespoons water (0 mg)

1. In a medium to large mixing bowl, make a well in the center of the flour and place the 3 egg yolks, the whole egg, and the garlic in the well. Using a wooden spoon, slowly mix the egg into the flour. Add water 1 tablespoon at a time. Mix thoroughly before adding each tablespoon. When the dough reaches the right consistency, do not add more water.
2. Turn the dough onto a well-floured board and knead until smooth and elastic. This might take 10 or more minutes. Cover and let rest for about 10 minutes before rolling out the dough.
3. Divide the dough into 4 parts, cover the dough you aren't working with while you roll out one part at a time into paper-thin rectangles. If you have a pasta rack, this is when you'll need it. Otherwise have a floured cloth nearby. Cut the dough crosswise into ⅛-inch strips for narrow noodles and ¼-inch for wider noodles. Shake out the strips and put them on the cloth or the rack and let dry for about 2 hours.
4. Break dry strips into smaller pieces or cook as is in 3 to 4 quarts of boiling water for about 8 to 12 minutes, or until tender. Drain thoroughly. Serve with Marinara sauce or other pasta sauce.

Calories: 194. Sodium: 13.81 mg. Fiber: 1.15 g. Protein: 6.675 g. Carbohydrate: 32.4 g. Cholesterol: 137.49 mg. Calcium: 23 mg. Iron: 2.682 mg. Potassium: 65.3 mg. Total Fat: 3.7 g; Saturated fat: 1.1 g, Monounsaturated fat: 1.3 g, Polyunsaturated fat: 0.6 g.

❧ LENTIL CROQUETTES ❧

MAKES 8 CROQUETTES SERVES 4 SODIUM PER RECIPE: 63.7 MG
SODIUM PER SERVING: 15.9 MG

This Greek recipe came to us from friends who hailed from Athens.
They swear it's the tastiest way to prepare lentils without adding
salt or other high-sodium ingredients.

  1 cup lentils (13.4 mg)
  3 cups water (0 mg)
  1 onion, finely chopped (3.3 mg)
  1 cup bulgur (23.8 mg)
  ½ cup chopped fresh parsley (16.8 mg)
  ¼ finely chopped fresh mint (1.984 mg)
  1 teaspoon cumin (3.524 mg)
  ¼ teaspoon coriander (.159 mg)
  1 clove garlic, minced (.5 mg)
  1 tablespoon lemon juice (.15 mg)
  1 tablespoon extra-virgin olive oil (trace)
  Pepper to taste (trace)

1. Boil the lentils in water with the onion over medium-high heat for 30 minutes. Add the bulgur, parsley, mint, cumin, coriander, and garlic. Continue to cook for an additional 10 to 15 minutes, stirring occasionally. Remove from the heat. Stir in the lemon juice and let the mixture cool. When cool, form 8 croquettes and fry in oil in a nonstick pan set over medium-high heat for about 5 minutes, then flip the croquettes over gently and fry for another 5 minutes.

Calories: 334. Sodium: 15.92 mg. Fiber: 12.59 g. Protein: 17 g. Carbohydrate: 58.9 g. Cholesterol: 0 mg. Calcium: 59 mg. Iron: 11.5 mg. Potassium: 533.2 mg. Total Fat: 5.1 g; Saturated fat: 0.7 g, Monounsaturated fat: 2.9 g, Polyunsaturated fat: 1.1 g.

❧ REFRIED BEANS ❧

SERVES 6   SODIUM PER RECIPE: 111.2 MG   SODIUM PER SERVING: 18.5 MG
Spice this one up anyway you like. For hotter or tangier refried beans, add Tabasco sauce (30 mg sodium per teaspoon), minced onion, hot chili peppers, and additional garlic.

   2 **cups raw pinto beans (38.6 mg)**
      Water to soak beans (0 mg)
   3 **tablespoons extra-virgin olive oil (0 mg)**
   2 **cups minced red onion (9.6 mg)**
   4 **cloves garlic, minced (2.04 mg)**
   2 **teaspoons ground cumin (7.049 mg)**
   2 **teaspoons chili powder (52.5 mg)**
   ½ **green pepper, minced (1.19 mg)**
   ¼ **teaspoon ground pepper (.231 mg)**

1. Cover the pinto beans with water and let soak for about 2 to 3 hours. Drain the water and cover with fresh water and bring to boil. Lower the temperature to medium and cook for about 2 hours, or until well-done. Keep water level over the beans while cooking—you may have to add water as they cook. When the beans are soft, drain off the water and mash them well.

2. Heat the olive oil in a nonstick roaster pan or skillet. Add the onions, garlic, cumin, and chili powder and cook over low heat until the onions are translucent. Add the green pepper, cover, and simmer for 5 to 8 minutes. Add this mixture to the beans and sprinkle in the black pepper. Mix well. Serve immediately or keep hot in the oven until serving. Can be chilled and reheated.

Calories: 310. Sodium: 18.54 mg. Fiber: 17.27 g. Protein: 14.5 g. Carbohydrate: 47.5 g. Cholesterol: 0 mg. Calcium: 102.3 mg. Iron: 4.619 mg. Potassium: 993.9 mg. Total Fat: 7.9 g; Saturated fat: 1.1 g, Monounsaturated fat: 5.3 g, Polyunsaturated fat: 1 g.

❧ PESTO BEANS AND NOODLES ❧

SERVES 4   SODIUM PER RECIPE: 102.3 MG   SODIUM PER SERVING: 25.6 MG
We grew up with this staple. Beans and noodles and pesto. We've seen similar recipes in many cookbooks, but none are as low in sodium as this one. A satisfying meal with plenty of great flavors, this can also serve as a side dish for 8 to 10. Eden beans are available at Healthy Heart Market, toll-free at 1-888/685-5998.

   1 **cup dry white kidney beans (44.2 mg)—or substitute the un-**
      salted canned variety (15 mg) and omit the broth
   2 **cups chicken broth made by combining 2 teaspoons Herb-ox**
      Low Sodium Chicken Broth (10 mg) with 2 cups water (0 mg)

1   **medium to large carrot, diced (29.2 mg)**
8   **ounces penne pasta (or pasta of your choice) (15.9 mg)**
1   **sprig parsley (.56 mg)**
1   **cup fresh chopped basil (1.7 mg)**
¼   **cup toasted pine nuts (pignolias) (1.36 mg)**
4   **teaspoons fresh grated low-sodium Parmesan (4 mg)**
3   **tablespoons extra-virgin olive oil (trace)**
    Dash of pepper (trace)

1. In a large bowl add the beans and plenty of cold water, then cover the bowl (lid, plastic wrap, dish) and let stand overnight, or up to 8 hours. (For quicker soaking, bring the beans to a boil, remove the pan from the heat and let stand for 2 hours. Drain and rinse beans, then cook in fresh water until tender.) (If you use no-salt-added canned white beans, the above step is unnecessary.) Bring the broth to a boil, add the diced carrot, reduce the heat, and simmer until tender. Using a slotted spoon, remove the carrots to a small bowl and set aside. Return the broth to a boil, add the white beans, and once again bring it to a boil and reduce the heat to moderately low. Partially cover and simmer for up to 1 hour, or until the beans are tender to the fork and the liquid is absorbed, remembering to stir occasionally while cooking. If the beans are too liquidy, remove the pan from the heat and cover for between 10 to 15 minutes.
2. Bring a pot of water to a boil and cook the pasta according to the directions on the package. Drain and refresh the pasta under cold water.
3. While pasta is cooking, make the pesto in a blender by combining parsley, basil, pine nuts, Parmesan, and oil.
4. When ready, toss the cooked beans and carrots with the pasta, then toss with pesto to coat thoroughly. Add pepper to taste.

Calories: 524. Sodium: 25.56 mg. Fiber: 14.15 g. Protein: 21.2 g. Carbohydrate: 74.5 g. Cholesterol: 1.23 mg. Calcium: 120.9 mg. Iron: 11.2 mg. Potassium: 898.4 mg. Total Fat: 16.3 g; Saturated fat: 2.5 g, Monounsaturated fat: 9.4 g, Polyunsaturated fat: 3.3 g.

✦ FRIED TOFU ✦

SERVES 2   SODIUM PER RECIPE: 77.4 MG   SODIUM PER SERVING: 38.7 MG
A crispy dish from a friend in Hong Kong. It is served in some of the finest Hong Kong restaurants as well as in homes.

- 8 ounces firm organic tofu (13.3 mg)
- 2 tablespoons extra-virgin olive oil (trace)
- ¼ cup unbleached flour (6.35 mg)
- 2 cloves garlic, minced (1 mg)
- 1 teaspoon sesame seed oil (0 mg)
- ½ cup chicken broth made by combining ½ teaspoon Herb-ox Low Sodium Chicken Broth (2.5 mg) and ½ cup water (0 mg)
- 1 egg (55.4 mg)
- 1 green onion, finely chopped (2.4 mg)
- 2 ounces sliced mushrooms (1.8 mg)
- 1 teaspoon minced ginger root (.26 mg)

1. When cutting the tofu, slice it lengthwise down the middle, then slice it from side to side sideways to make thinner strips. Pat the tofu dry.

2. Heat the olive oil over medium heat in a nonstick skillet or a wok, if you have one. Mix together the garlic, sesame seed oil, and broth and set aside. Beat the egg. Coat the tofu pieces with flour and then dip them into the egg. Add the tofu to the pan and fry for about 1 minute. Turn and fry until both sides are golden brown. Add the onion, mushrooms, ginger, and the prepared sesame sauce. Pierce the tofu with a knife or fork to allow the liquid to evaporate. When all the liquid is gone, the tofu is done. Serve with your favorite sauce from this book, or bean paste or sliced avocado with plain yogurt on top. Many of our sauces work great with this—but I particularly like the wild blackberry.

Calories: 351. Sodium: 38.7 mg. Fiber: 4.95 g. Protein: 21.1 g. Carbohydrate: 22.1 g. Cholesterol: 93.5 mg. Calcium: 25.3 mg. Iron: 1.545 mg. Potassium: 165.3 mg. Total Fat: 20.2 g. Saturated fat: 2.9 g, Monounsaturated fat: 12.4 g, Polyunsaturated fat: 3.8 g.

❖ TOFU STIR-FRY ❖

SERVES 2   SODIUM PER RECIPE: 84.4 MG   SODIUM PER SERVING: 42.2 MG
A complete meal, this recipe is not only delicious, it's totally healthful, with protein, nutrients, and the cancer-fighting genistein that comes with the tofu.

1 **cup raw white and wild rice mix, cooked* (12 mg)**
2 **tablespoons extra-virgin olive oil (trace)**
1 **medium carrot, sliced (21.4 mg)**
1 **small onion, finely chopped (2 mg)**
6 **garlic cloves, minced (3 mg)**
4 **asparagus spears, sliced (1.28 mg)**
½ **broccoli head, broken into florets (15.4 mg)**
1 **teaspoon sesame seed oil (0 mg)**
1 **crookneck yellow squash, sliced (1 mg)**
16 **whole snow pea pods (2.1 mg)**
4 **ounces mushrooms, sliced (3.68 mg)**
7 **ounces firm Nigari organic tofu, diced (10.5 mg)**
½ **cup dry-roasted unsalted cashews (11 mg)**

1. Cook the rice first per package instructions. Set it aside with lid on to keep warm.
2. Prepare the vegetables. Heat the olive oil in a large nonstick pan set over medium heat. Stir-fry the carrot first. After a few minutes add the onion, garlic, asparagus, broccoli, and sesame seed oil. Turn the heat up to medium-high and stir-fry for 3 minutes. Add the ginger, squash, snow peas, mushrooms, and tofu. Stir-fry for another 4 to 5 minutes, turning continuously. Serve hot and accompany with a small bowl of sesame seed oil to dip food into when desired. Sprinkle the cashews over top.

Calories: 793. Sodium: 42.22 mg. Fiber: 13.48 g. Protein: 34.6 g. Carbohydrate: 94.7 g. Cholesterol: 0 mg. Calcium: 105.4 mg. Iron: 5.893 mg. Potassium: 1,216 mg. Total Fat: 34.7 g: Saturated fat: 5.5 g, Monounsaturated fat: 20.9 g, Polyunsaturated fat: 6.6 g.

*Optional. Hinode packages an excellent white and wild rice mixture. Stir-fried tofu generally makes a complete meal by itself. However, if you want to stretch this recipe to serve 4, add the rice or a similar amount of cooked pasta. Serve the stir-fry over the rice, or over the cooked pasta, mixed with a smattering of garlic and oil.

❧ KUNG PAO TOFU ❧

SERVES 2   SODIUM PER RECIPE: 52 MG   SODIUM PER SERVING: 26 MG

Another delicious recipe substituting tofu for animal meat. If you haven't tried tofu yet, please do. It's not only an effective cancer fighter, it's also a great source for low-calorie and low-sodium protein. This dish makes a great dinner entrée. Serve it with fresh steamed vegetables.

THE MAKINGS

    2 tablespoons extra-virgin olive oil (trace)
    2 chilies, dried and diced (1 mg)
    2 cloves garlic, minced (1 mg)
    8 ounces tofu* (32 mg)
    1 tablespoon toasted sesame seeds (11 mg)
    6 mushrooms, cut in half (5 mg)

THE KUNG PAO

    ½ teaspoon sugar (trace)
    ½ teaspoon red wine vinegar (trace)
    2 garlic cloves, minced (1 mg)
    1 teaspoon cornstarch (.216 mg)
    2 teaspoons sesame oil (0 mg)
    1 teaspoon lemon juice (trace)
    6 tablespoons water (0 mg)

1. Heat the oil in a nonstick skillet, wok, or frying pan. Stir-fry the chilies and garlic. Add the mushrooms and stir-fry for about another minute. Add the Kung Pao ingredients and continue stirring until the sauce thickens. Now add the tofu and stir-fry to heat well—about 1 minute. Sprinkle with sesame seeds and serve hot. A perfect accompaniment is **Mom's Mango Chutney** (page 302). Spoon a tablespoon or two on each serving.

Calories: 400. Sodium: 25.99 mg. Fiber: 1.85 g. Protein: 21.2 g. Carbohydrate: 14.8 g. Cholesterol: 0 mg. Calcium: 46.4 mg. Iron: 2.75 mg. Potassium: 325.9 mg. Total Fat: 31.5 g; Saturated fat: 4.6 g, Monounsaturated fat: 12.9 g, Polyunsaturated fat: 4.6 g.

*There are some tofu cakes with zero sodium. Check the nutrition label before buying.

❖ SWEET-AND-SOUR TOFU MIX ❖

SERVES 2   SODIUM PER RECIPE: 65 MG   SODIUM PER SERVING: 32.5 MG
This recipe comes to you from my friend in Hong Kong; I have made a few changes to adapt it for low-sodium diets. Using low-sodium tofu as your protein and cancer fighter, this proves to be one of the lowest-sodium dinner recipes in the book.

THE MAKINGS
3 tablespoons extra-virgin olive oil (trace)
8 ounces firm organic low-sodium tofu, diced (13.4 mg)
1 cup canned pineapple chunks in juice (drained) (4.9 mg)
½ cup diced green pepper (1.5 mg)
½ cup diced red pepper (1.5 mg)

THE SWEET-AND-SOUR
2 tablespoons lemon juice (.3 mg)
1 clove garlic, minced (.5 mg)
½ cup sugar (0 mg)
1 tablespoon cornstarch, mixed with water (.72 mg)
⅓ cup white vinegar (.792 mg)
¼ no-salt-added tomato paste (40 mg)
½ cup water (0 mg)

1. Mix together the sweet-and-sour ingredients and set them aside. Heat 1 tablespoon of the oil in a nonstick pan set over medium-high heat and stir-fry the tofu chunks until golden brown. Remove from the heat and set aside, covered, to keep warm. Heat the remaining 2 tablespoons oil in same skillet and stir-fry the pineapple and diced peppers quickly. Add the sweet-and-sour mixture and stir until it thickens. Add the tofu, cook for another minute, and serve hot.

Calories: 664. Sodium: 32.48 mg. Fiber: 8.01 g. Protein: 19.8 g. Carbohydrate: 102.6 g. Cholesterol: 0 mg. Calcium: 24.5 mg. Iron: 7.226 mg. Potassium: 319.7 mg. Total Fat: 22.6 g; Saturated fat: 2.8 g, Monounsaturated fat: 15.6 g, Polyunsaturated fat: 3.2 g.

✦ GREEN CHILI TACOS ✦

SERVES 4   SODIUM PER RECIPE: 60.8 MG   SODIUM PER SERVING: 15.2 MG

4 Anaheim or Pasilla chilies (.56 mg)
8 corn tortillas (zero-sodium variety) (55 mg)*
2 yellow onions (6.6 mg)
1 tablespoon olive oil (trace)
2 medium uncooked ears of corn (21.9 mg)
  Frontier mexican seasoning to taste† (0 mg)
1 California (Haas) avocado, sliced (20.8 mg)
1 tomato, diced (11 mg)
1 tablespoon low-sodium sour cream (optional) (15–20 mg)

1. Roast the Anaheim or Pasilla chilies in your oven broiler or over a gas flame, until the skins bubble or appear to bubble off the chilies. Plunge the chilies into a bowl of ice water and then peel off the skins. (As an alternative, you may also cook the chilies over a hot barbecue grill or directly on your stovetop burners until they turn black; then dip them into ice water and peel off the skins.)

2. While preparing this recipe, heat the tortillas in a tortilla steamer. To use the steamer correctly, soak the inside of the lid with water, then place the tortillas in the bowl and set in a preheated 350°F oven for 10 to 12 minutes.

3. Peel and slice the onions into rings and cut in half. Sauté onions in oil until transparent, then add the prepared chilies. Steam the corn lightly, cut it off the cob, and add the kernels to the chili and onion mixture. Sauté until hot, then add the seasoning and fill the tortillas with the mixture. Top with the sliced avocados and diced tomatoes. You may garnish with sour cream if you wish. Roll and enjoy.

Calories: 300. Sodium: 15.22 mg. Protein: 4.853 g. Carbohydrate: 30 g. Fiber: 6.83 g. Cholesterol: 0 mg. Calcium: 19.4 mg. Iron: 1.07 mg. Potassium: 557.5 mg. Total Fat: 11.6 g; Saturated fat: 1.7 g, Monounsaturated fat: 7.5 g, Polyunsaturated fat: 1.5 g.

*The package will state 0 mg, but in fact the tortillas may have as much as 5 to 7 mg (and still be legally listed). Some corn tortillas use salt, some don't. Those that don't list the 0 mg, but corn itself does have sodium.
†Available by mail order from www.healthymarket.com, or phone 1-800/753-0310.

▩ ENCHILADA SAUCE ▩

MAKES 1 QUART   SODIUM PER RECIPE: 159.8 MG
SODIUM PER SERVING: 39.9 MG

*Here's a low-sodium, great-flavored enchilada sauce that can be
used with your own enchilada recipe or **Chicken Enchiladas.**
This recipe doesn't include cheese.*

   6-ounce can Contadina Natural Tomato Paste (102 mg)
3 **cups water (0 mg)**
   Pinch of cayenne pepper (trace)
½ **teaspoon garlic powder (.369 mg)**
1 **tablespoon Spice Islands onion powder (3.482 mg)**
⅛ **teaspoon cumin (.441 mg)**
⅛ **teaspoon pepper (.115 mg)**
⅛ **teaspoon coriander (trace)**
2 **teaspoons chili powder (52.5 mg)**
1 **tablespoon cornstarch (.72 mg)**
   Additional 2 tablespoons water (0 mg)

1. In a large saucepan set over medium heat, combine and cook the
tomato paste, water, cayenne, garlic powder, onion powder, cumin, coriander, pepper, and chili powder until the sauce boils. Reduce the heat
and simmer for 10 to 12 minutes. In a small bowl, dissolve cornstarch in
the additional water and gradually add it to the sauce, stirring continuously, until the sauce thickens.

*Calories: 54. Sodium: 39.95 mg. Fiber: 2.39 g. Protein: 1.979 g. Carbohydrate: 12.4 g. Cho-
lesterol: 0 mg. Calcium: 26.1 mg. Iron: 7.396 mg. Potassium: 446 mg. Total Fat: 27.9 g; Saturated fat: 0.1 g, Monounsaturated fat: 0.1 g, Polyunsaturated fat: 0.2 g.*

▩ APPLESAUCE OATMEAL ▩

SERVES 2   SODIUM PER RECIPE: 16.4 MG   SODIUM PER SERVING: 8.185 MG*
*Our favorite winter breakfast. On a cold morning, nothing
surpasses this for low sodium and high satisfaction.*

2 **cups of water (0 mg)**
1 **cup of unsalted Quick Quaker Oats (3.24 mg)**
½ **cup golden raisins (10 mg)**
½ **cup unsalted applesauce†**
½ **teaspoon cinnamon (.6 mg)**

*If using milk, please add 32.5 mg per ¼ mg per cup.
†If using commercially canned applesauce, make sure you use "no salt added."
Find Quick or Homemade Applesauce recipe in Index.

1. Over high heat, boil 2 cups of water in a small or medium-size saucepan. Before reaching boil, add in raisins, applesauce, and cinnamon. When water boils, add in fast-cooking, zero-sodium oatmeal. You may add more cinnamon if you want to. Reduce heat to medium and stir for one minute. Remove from heat and cover. Set aside for about 3 to 5 minutes. Serve hot.

If using raw oats instead of ground or instant, cook oats over medium heat for about 5 to 7 minutes. Exchange raisins for dried cranberries for a very special flavor.

You can add a flavorful bite to your oatmeal by using ½ cup of orange juice in place of ½ cup of water. Also, you can replace raisins with cranberry raisins.

TIP: To create your own flavored oatmeal, exchange the applesauce and raisins for diced drived apricots, dates, cranberries, prunes, or a jam such as marmalade. Add in a touch of brown sugar or honey or maple syrup.

Calories: 316. Sodium: 8.19 mg. Total sugars: 0 mg. Fiber: 7.13 g. Protein: 7.868 g. Carbohydrate: 69.6 g. Cholesterol: 0 mg. Calcium: 56.9 mg. Iron: 11 mg. Potassium: 456.8 mg. Total Fat: 2.9 g; Saturated fat: 0.5 g, Monounsaturated fat: 0.8 g, Polyunsaturated fat: 1 g.

SAUCES

❋ ❋ ❋ ❋ ❋ ❋ ❋ ❋

❋ THIN WHITE SAUCE ❋

MAKES 2 CUPS   SODIUM PER RECIPE: 254 MG   SODIUM PER CUP: 127 MG

Chances are this basic recipe already exists in your repertoire. Everyone I know makes a white sauce by mixing flour, butter, and milk or cream. The recipes that follow show you the exact nutrients of the ingredients you are using.

- **1 tablespoon unsalted butter (1.5 mg)**
- **1 tablespoon flour (.156 mg)**
- **2 cups nonfat milk (252.4 mg)**

1. In a saucepan melt the butter and stir in the flour. Bring the mixture to a medium boil, then remove it from the heat. Add the milk and return the pan to the stove and stir and cook over medium heat until thick.

Calories: 151. Sodium: 127.03 mg. Fiber: 0.11 g. Protein: 8.818 g. Carbohydrate: 14.9 g. Cholesterol: 19.95 mg. Calcium: 304.6 mg. Iron: .29 mg. Potassium: 411.7 mg. Total Fat: 6.2 g; Saturated fat: 3.9, Monounsaturated fat: 1.8 g, Polyunsaturated fat: 0.2 g.

❋ MEDIUM WHITE SAUCE ❋

MAKES 2 CUPS   SODIUM PER RECIPE: 255.8 MG   SODIUM PER CUP: 127.9 MG

Basic medium white sauce is used for casseroles and easy-to-prepare meat dishes.

- **2 tablespoons unsalted butter (3.124 mg)**
- **2 tablespoons flour (.312 mg)**
- **2 cups nonfat milk (252.4 mg)**

1. In a saucepan melt the butter and stir in the flour. Bring the mixture to a medium boil, then remove from the heat. Add the milk and return the pan to the stove and stir and cook over medium heat until thick.

Calories: 216. Sodium: 127.89 mg. Fiber: 0.21 g. Protein: 9.281 g. Carbohydrate: 17.8 g. Cholesterol: 35.49 mg. Calcium: 306.8 mg. Iron: .483 mg. Potassium: 417.8 mg. Total Fat: 12 g; Saturated fat: 7.5 g, Monounsaturated fat: 3.4 g, Polyunsaturated fat: 0.5 g.

❈ HEAVY WHITE SAUCE ❈

MAKES 2 CUPS   SODIUM PER RECIPE: 257.5 MG   SODIUM PER CUP: 128.8 MG

3 tablespoons unsalted butter (4.686 mg)
3 tablespoons flour (.468 mg)
2 cups nonfat milk (252.4 mg)

1. In a saucepan melt the butter and stir in the flour. Bring the mixture to a medium boil, then remove from the heat. Add the milk and return the pan to the stove and stir and cook over medium heat until thick.

Calories: 281. Sodium: 128.75 mg. Fiber: 0.32 g. Protein: 9.744 g. Carbohydrate: 20.8 g. Cholesterol: 51.04 mg. Calcium: 309.1 mg. Iron: .675 mg. Potassium: 423.8 mg. Total Fat: 17.8 g; Saturated fat: 11.1 g, Monounsaturated fat: 5.1 g, Polyunsaturated fat: 0.7 g.

❈ CHICKEN BAKING SAUCE ❈

SERVES 6   SODIUM PER RECIPE: 47.7 MG   SODIUM PER SERVING: 7.947 MG
To add a tangy flavor to your skinless chicken, try this sauce.

1 cup freshly squeezed lemon juice (2.44 mg)
½ cup packed brown sugar (42.9 mg)
3 tablespoons fresh grated ginger root (2.34 mg)

1. Combine the ingredients and mix well. To use, pour the sauce over skinless chicken breasts, thighs, or legs in a baking dish. Bake at 350°F for 45 to 60 minutes and serve hot. This sauce goes well with pork also.

Calories: 81. Sodium: 7.95 mg. Fiber: 0.22 g. Protein: .207 g. Carbohydrate: 21.8. Cholesterol: 0 mg. Calcium: 19 mg. Iron: .377 mg. Potassium: 126.3 mg. Total Fat: 0 g; Saturated fat: 0 g, Monounsaturated fat: 0 g, Polyunsaturated fat: 0 g.

❈ DIPPING MUSTARD ❈

MAKES ¼ CUP   SODIUM PER RECIPE: .585 MG
SODIUM PER SERVING: TRACE
This sauce can be made hotter with a touch more of minced garlic.
Use it for dipping appetizers or over chicken or pork.

¼ cup dry mustard (Coleman's or other) (0 mg)
3 tablespoons water (0 mg)
1½ teaspoons lemon juice (trace)
1 clove garlic, minced (.51 mg)

1. Mix the mustard, water, and lemon juice until smooth. Add the minced garlic if you want it hotter. Allow the sauce to sit for about 10 minutes before serving. Cover and refrigerate for use later or even the next day.

Calories: 114. Sodium: 0.58 mg. Fiber: 0.09 g. Protein: 6.219 g. Carbohydrate: 5.24 g. Cholesterol: 0 mg. Calcium: 66 mg. Iron: 25.5 mg. Potassium: 153.3 mg. Total Fat: 7.2 g; Saturated fat: 1.2 g, Monounsaturated fat: 3.6 g, Polyunsaturated fat: 2.4 g.

❄ SWEET-AND-SOUR DIPPING SAUCE ❄

MAKES 1¼ CUPS   SODIUM PER RECIPE: 41.9 MG
SODIUM PER TABLESPOON: 2.094 MG
Hot to the touch, this one is for hearty diners.

¼ cup Contadina All Natural Tomato Paste (39.3 mg)
1 teaspoon lemon juice (trace)
½ cup red wine vinegar (1.2 mg)
⅓ cup sugar plus 1 tablespoon (.792 mg)
12 drops hot Tabasco red pepper sauce (.54 mg) or 1 teaspoon
  cayenne pepper (.54 mg)

1. Mix the tomato paste and lemon juice until it becomes the consistency
of ketchup. Mix this with the vinegar, sugar, and pepper sauce. Cover and
refrigerate before serving. Serve with appetizers or stir-fry chicken or pork
as a dipping sauce.

*Calories: 19. Sodium: 2.09 mg. Fiber: 0.16 g. Protein: .132 g. Carbohydrate: 4.984 g. Cho-
lesterol: 0 mg. Calcium: 1.696 mg. Iron: .109 mg. Potassium: 38.9 mg. Total Fat: 2.1 g; Saturated fat: 0 g, Monounsaturated fat: 0 g, Polyunsaturated fat: 0 g.*

❄ DON'S BARBECUE SAUCE ❄

SERVES 12*   SODIUM PER RECIPE: 383.4 MG   SODIUM PER SERVING: 32 MG
*While working in the state of Washington during the seventies, I
developed a barbecue sauce that became so popular it was used
commercially by a restaurant in Olympia, Washington. They
actually listed "Oysters Gazzaniga" on their menu.*

2 tablespoons extra virgin-olive oil (trace)
6-ounce can Contadina All Natural Tomato Paste (102 mg)
2 (8-ounce) cans Del Monte No Salt Added Tomato Sauce
  (146.4 mg)
⅛ teaspoon ground cloves (.637 mg)
1 teaspoon sage (trace)
1 teaspoon marjoram (.462 mg)
1 teaspoon thyme (.766 mg)
¼ teaspoon cayenne pepper (.135 mg) (optional)
3 tablespoons balsamic vinegar (.45 mg)
3 cloves garlic, minced (1.53 mg)
2 large onions, chopped (9 mg)
1¼ cups packed brown sugar (107.2 mg)

*The serving size is based on the amount that would be used by brushing the
sauce on servings of barbecued chicken, ribs, steak, roasts, or other cooked meats.
Also try **Don's Quick Barbecue Sauce** (page 171).

1. Combine all the ingredients except the brown sugar in a medium to large saucepan set over medium-high heat. Bring to a slow boil, stirring frequently, then reduce the heat and simmer, uncovered, for up to 1 hour, stirring occasionally. Incorporate the brown sugar halfway through the simmering period and continue to simmer, uncovered, until sauce slightly thickens.

Calories: 150. Sodium: 31.95 mg. Fiber: 2.13 g. Protein: 2.056 g. Carbohydrate: 32.2 g. Cholesterol: 0 mg. Calcium: 42.6 mg. Iron: 1.712 mg. Potassium: 525.7 mg. Total Fat: 11.7 g; Saturated fat: 0.4 g, Monounsaturated fat: 1.7 g, Polyunsaturated fat: 0.3 g.

❖ SWEET-HOT BARBECUE SAUCE ❖

MAKES APPROXIMATELY 3½ CUPS   SODIUM PER RECIPE: 274.8 MG
SODIUM PER CUP: 78.5 MG
Great for all meats.

1 tablespoon extra-virgin olive oil (trace)
1 medium onion, finely diced (3.3 mg)
2 cloves garlic, minced (2 mg)
2 tablespoons lemon zest, finely diced (.72 mg)
1 cup packed brown sugar (85.8 mg)
½ teaspoon chili flakes (0 mg)
½ teaspoon cayenne pepper (13.1 mg)
¼ teaspoon freshly ground black pepper (.231 mg)
¼ cup Contadina tomato paste (39.3 mg)
2 (8-ounce) cans any no-salt-added tomato sauce (128.1 mg)
½ cup cider vinegar (1.2 mg)
½ tablespoon Life All Natural Worcestershire sauce (2 mg)*

1. In a medium saucepan set over medium heat, heat the oil and sauté the onions, garlic, and lemon peel until the onions become translucent but not brown. Add the sugar and cook for another 3 minutes, stirring often. Add the chili flakes, cayenne, pepper, tomato paste and sauce, vinegar, and Worcestershire, then bring to a boil, reduce the heat to low, and cook for 30 minutes. Serve hot.

Nutrient Values based on 1 Cup. Calories: 346. Sodium: 78.52 mg. Fiber: 3.73 g. Protein: 2.86 g. Carbohydrate: 80 g. Cholesterol: 0 mg. Calcium: 94.8 mg. Iron: 2.945 mg. Potassium: 950.4 mg. Total Fat: 16.4 g; Saturated fat: 0.6 g, Monounsaturated fat: 2.9 g, Polyunsaturated fat: 0.5 g.

*Do not use Lea & Perrins unless you can afford to add 110 mg sodium.

❧ Don's Quick Barbecue Sauce ❧

MAKES 2 CUPS   SERVES 8   SODIUM PER RECIPE: 120.7 MG
SODIUM PER SERVING: 15.1 MG

Surprise guests dropping by? Need to barbecue meat in a hurry? Try this quick sauce that I developed years ago and still use on a regular basis. Works well with chicken and pork ribs, and with any of these broiled in your oven.

8-ounce can no-salt-added tomato sauce (73.2 mg)*
½ cup packed brown sugar (42.9 mg)
2 tablespoons extra-virgin olive oil (trace)
1 medium onion, diced (3.3 mg)
¼ teaspoon tarragon (.249 mg)
  Pinch of ground cloves (.51 mg)
¼ teaspoon ground coriander (.159 mg)
¼ teaspoon cilantro (.216 mg)
¼ teaspoon thyme (.191 mg)

1. Combine all ingredients and bring to a boil, stirring constantly until well mixed. When a light boil is reached, reduce the heat and simmer over low heat for about 5 minutes, uncovered. Spread the sauce on barbecued ribs, chicken, steaks, or burgers while cooking. Save some to spread on the hot meat just before serving.

Calories: 96. Sodium: 15.09 mg, Fiber: 0.76 g, Protein: .581 g. Carbohydrate: 16.9 g. Cholesterol: 0 mg. Calcium: 20.7 mg. Iron: .623 mg. Potassium: 185.4 mg. Total Fat: 3.5 g; Saturated fat: 0.5 g, Monounsaturated fat: 2.5 g, Polyunsaturated fat: 0.3 g.

❧ Balsamic Cherry Sauce ❧

MAKES APPROXIMATELY 1 CUP   SODIUM PER RECIPE: 64.8 MG
Great with all fowl.

2 tablespoons balsamic vinegar (.3 mg)
1½ cups dry red wine† (48 mg)
2 tablespoons brown sugar (10.8 mg)
2 teaspoons minced fresh rosemary (.364 mg)
1 cup dried cherries (4.65 mg)
1 tablespoon cornstarch mixed with 1 tablespoon cold water
  (.72 mg)
  Pepper to taste (trace)

*You may substitute 1 cup red grape juice for the wine.
†This sodium count is based on the Del Monte brand.

1. In a medium saucepan set over high heat, add vinegar, wine, sugar, rosemary and half of the dried cherries. Reduce the liquid by half, then transfer the mixture to a blender or food processor and process for 15 seconds. Return the sauce to the pan and add the remaining cherries, lower the heat, and simmer for 3 to 4 minutes. Add the cornstarch mixture, stirring it in a little at a time until the sauce thickens. Season with pepper. Serve with pork, lamb, fowl, or all game meats.

Calories: 638. Sodium: 64.84 mg. Fiber: 2.78 g. Protein: 2.828 g. Carbohydrate: 63.6 g. Cholesterol: 0 mg. Calcium: 103.1 mg. Iron: 3.823 mg. Potassium: 938.5 mg. Total Fat: 0.6 g; Saturated fat: 0.1 g, Monounsaturated fat: 0.1 g, Polyunsaturated fat: 0.2 g.

❄ CRANBERRY-TANGERINE SAUCE

MAKES APPROXIMATELY 1½ CUPS   SODIUM PER RECIPE: 9.99 MG
Best with vegetables, lamb, wild game, and salads.

  2 **medium to large tangerines (1.96 mg)**
12 **ounces fresh cranberries (2.85 mg)**
  2 **medium tart green apples (1.1 mg)**
  2 **cups water (0 mg)**
1½ **cups sugar (3 mg)**
  1 **cup unsalted pecans (1.08 mg)**

1. Coarsely chop the unpeeled tangerines (seeds removed). Rinse the cranberries and chop the apples into small pieces. Combine the tangerines and the water in a saucepan. Cook rapidly until the peel is tender—about 15 to 20 minutes. Add the cranberries, apples, and sugar and bring to a boil over medium-low heat, stirring occasionally, until the sugar is dissolved. Increase the heat and boil gently for about 30 minutes. As the mixture thickens, stir frequently. Add the pecans during the last 5 minutes of cooking. Cool and refrigerate or freeze.

Calories: 2,191. Sodium: 9.99 mg. Fiber: 24.69 g. Protein: 11.2 g. Carbohydrate: 399.4 g. Cholesterol: 0 mg. Calcium: 109.1 mg. Iron: 19.6 mg. Potassium: 1,153 mg. Total Fat: 74.3 g; Saturated fat: 6 g, Monounsaturated fat: 45.7 g, Polyunsaturated fat: 18.5 g.

◈ CHILI SAUCE ◈

MAKES 2½ QUARTS SODIUM PER RECIPE: 365 MG
SODIUM PER CUP: 36.5 MG SODIUM PER TABLESPOON: 2.2 MG

Make it hotter or cooler by adjusting the pepper, cayenne powder, or cloves. Use with tacos, burgers, dip, or chili con carne. Make a batch and freeze, or can it for future use.

6 quarts fresh medium tomatoes, washed, peeled, and cut into quarters (265.7 mg)
4 green peppers, seeds removed (9.52 mg)
4 large white onions (skinned) (18 mg)
2 teaspoons dried hot pepper pods (1.6 mg)
1 teaspoon cayenne pepper (.5 mg)
½ teaspoon coriander (.6 mg)
½ teaspoon cinnamon (.3 mg)
½ teaspoon nutmeg (trace)
½ teaspoon ginger (.3 mg)
½ teaspoon ground cloves (2.5 mg)
½ teaspoon ground cumin (1.7 mg)
½ teaspoon celery seed (1.6 mg)
1 cup unpacked brown sugar (56.6 mg)
1½ cups cider vinegar (3.6 mg)
4 cloves garlic, minced (4 mg)
1 tablespoon dry mustard (0 mg)

1. Grind the peppers, hot pepper pods, and onions in a food processor. Pour into 3 quart pan, mix together, and simmer until sauce is thick. This may take up to 2 hours or more. Stir frequently so sauce won't scorch. Add more minced garlic if needed. When done, bottle sauce in airtight and sterile jars. Store in cool dark place or refrigerator.

Calories: 165. Sodium: 36.49 mg. Fiber: 5.47 g. Protein: 3.965 g. Carbohydrate: 39.3 g. Total Sugars: 14.1 g. Cholesterol: 0 mg. Calcium: 55.1 mg. Potassium: 943.1 mg. Total Fat: 1.5 g. Saturated fat: 0.2 g. Monounsaturated fat: 0.3 g. Polyunsaturated fat: 0.6 g.

◈ PISTACHIO PESTO CREAM SAUCE ◈

MAKES APPROXIMATELY 2 CUPS   SERVES 4 WITH PASTA   SODIUM PER RECIPE:
107.2 MG*   SODIUM PER SERVING WITH 4 PORTIONS: 26.8 MG
For use with poultry, pasta, and pork.

1 **cup unsalted California pistachios (7.68 mg)**
6 **cloves garlic (3.06 mg)**
2 **tablespoons low-sodium grated Parmesan† (6.3 mg)**
1 **cup chopped fresh basil (1.696 mg)**
¼ **cup extra-virgin olive oil (trace)**
1 **cup light (25% fat) cream‡ (88.4 mg)**
White pepper to taste (trace)

1. Shell the pistachios and roast them in 400°F oven until lightly browned. Roast the garlic until golden brown but not burned. In a blender or food processor, blend ½ cup of pistachios with the Parmesan, garlic, basil, and olive oil. Transfer to a medium saucepan set over medium-high heat and add the cream and the remaining pistachios. Reduce the liquid by half and season with pepper. Serve with fowl or game birds.

Calories: 471. Sodium: 26.8 mg. Fiber: 3.98 g. Protein: 9.663 g. Carbohydrate: 12.1 g. Cholesterol: 6.29 mg. Calcium: 156.1 mg. Iron: 2.69 mg. Potassium: 487.9 mg. Total Fat: 44.8 g; Saturated fat: 4.8 g, Monounsaturated fat: 20.6 g, Polyunsaturated fat: 3.5 g.

◈ LEMON CREAM SAUCE ◈

MAKES APPROXIMATELY 1 CUP   SODIUM PER RECIPE: 183.5 MG
SODIUM PER TABLESPOON: 11.47 MG
Try with chicken ravioli; it goes well with all poultry.

2 **cups dry white wine (32 mg)**
1 **shallot, finely diced (1.2 mg)**
2 **cloves garlic, minced (1.02 mg)**

*The same amount of regular Parmesan instead of low-sodium would add 163.3 mg to the recipe total. Check with Trader Joe's or other specialty shops including health food stores or call Healthy Heart Market at 1-800/753-0310 to order low-sodium Parmesan.

†The same amount of regular Parmesan instead of low-sodium would add 163.3 mg to the recipe total. Check with Trader Joe's or other specialty shops including health food stores or call Healthy Heart Market at 1-800/753-0310 to order low-sodium Parmesan.

‡You may use lighter cream if it is available. The sauce also works with light sour cream.

1½ cups light cream* (147.7 mg)
¼ cup fresh lemon juice (.61 mg)
2 tablespoons sugar (.252 mg)
White pepper to taste (.71 mg)

1. In a medium saucepan set over high heat, add first the wine, shallots, and garlic. Cook and reduce the liquid to ½ cup. Strain out the shallots and garlic. Add the cream, lemon juice, and sugar and reduce to 1 cup liquid. Season with white pepper.

Calories: 58. Sodium: 11.47 mg. Protein: .868 g. Carbohydrate: 4.066 g. Fiber: 0.26 g. Cholesterol: 8.37 mg. Calcium: 29.3 mg. Iron: .261 mg. Potassium: 60.6 mg. Total Fat: 2.6 g; Saturated fat: 1.6 g, Monounsaturated fat: 0.8 g, Polyunsaturated fat: 0.1 g.

❧ WILD BLACKBERRY SAUCE ❧

MAKES APPROXIMATELY 2 CUPS   SODIUM PER RECIPE: 10.2 MG
SODIUM PER TABLESPOON: .319 MG

This sauce goes great with soufflés, meats, wild game. If you are lucky enough to live in wild blackberry country, this is a wonderful sauce to make with freshly picked berries. Otherwise, use frozen blackberries.

1 pound (4 cups) frozen or fresh wild blackberries (6.04 mg)
3 tablespoons sugar (.378 mg)
1½ teaspoons vanilla extract (.567 mg)
3 tablespoons orange juice with calcium (.929 mg)
3 tablespoons brandy (.84 mg)
2 tablespoons cornstarch (1.44 mg)
2 tablespoons water (0 mg)

1. If you're using frozen berries, defrost them. Put the berries (fresh or defrosted) in a saucepan with the sugar, vanilla, brandy, and orange juice. Combine the cornstarch and water and add it to the berry mixture. Bring the mixture to a boil. Immediately reduce the heat and cook the sauce over the lowest heat for 10 minutes. Cool. You can store this for a few days in the refrigerator. Gently reheat to serve. Serve with meats or tofu.

Per 2 cups. Calories: 848. Sodium: 10.19 mg. Protein: 7.804 g. Carbohydrate: 57.8 g. Fiber: 30.53 g. Cholesterol: 0 mg. Calcium: 289.1 mg. Iron: 6.064 mg. Potassium: 1,034 mg. Total Fat: 2.7 g; Saturated fat: 0.1 g, Monounsaturated fat: 0.3 g, Polyunsaturated fat: 1.5 g.

Per Tablespoon. Calories: 26. Sodium: 0.32 mg. Fiber: 0.95 g. Protein: .244 g. Carbohydrate: 4.932 g. Cholesterol: 0 mg. Calcium: 9.033 mg. Iron: .19 mg. Potassium: 32.3 mg. Total Fat: 0.1 g; Saturated fat: 0 g, Monounsaturated fat: 0 g, Polyunsaturated fat: 0 g.

*Use 2% milk to lower the fat content. Add 46 mg sodium to the total recipe if you substitute milk.

❀ SWEET-AND-SOUR ZINFANDEL SAUCE ❀

SERVES 8   SODIUM PER RECIPE: 97 MG   SODIUM PER SERVING 12.1 MG

This sauce is one of The Sporting Chef's favorites. It was created by him while he managed a large restaurant chain. I have altered it slightly to lower the sodium.

   4 **cloves garlic, minced (2.04 mg)**
   ⅓ **cup finely diced yellow onion (1.089 mg)**
   2 **tablespoons extra-virgin olive oil (trace)**
   ¼ **cup brown sugar (21.5 mg)**
   2 **cups zinfandel (20.6 mg)***
   2 **tablespoons balsamic vinegar (.3 mg)**
   1 **cup chicken broth made by combining 1 teaspoon Herb-ox**
      Low Sodium Chicken Broth (5 mg) and 1 cup water (0 mg)
   3 **tablespoons any no-salt-added tomato paste (43.3 mg)**
   2 **tablespoons unsalted butter (3.124 mg)**
      Pepper to taste (trace)

1. In a medium saucepan set over medium-high heat, sauté the garlic and onion in the oil for 2 to 3 minutes. Add the brown sugar and cook until the sugar liquefies and caramelizes the onion and garlic. Add the zinfandel, vinegar, broth, and tomato paste and combine. Cook over high heat, uncovered, until the contents are reduced to approximately 1½ cups liquid. Remove the pan from the heat and whisk in the butter pieces, one at a time, until the sauce is thickened. Season sparingly with pepper. If you need to heat the sauce at a later time, do so over low heat. Do not boil or the sauce will separate.

With Zinfandel: Calories: 129. Sodium: 12.1 mg. Fiber: 0.37 g. Protein: .508 g. Carbohydrate: 10.1 g. Cholesterol: 7.77 mg. Calcium: 16.9 mg. Iron: .552 mg. Potassium: 157.1 mg. Total Fat: 10.3 g; Saturated fat: 2.3 g, Monounsaturated fat: 3.3 g, Polyunsaturated fat: 0.4 g. Alcohol: 21%.

With grape juice: Calories: 108. Sodium: 10.2 mg. Fiber: 0.4 g. Protein: .465 g. Carbohydrate: 13.2 g. Cholesterol: 7.77 mg. Calcium: 14 mg. Iron: .362 mg. Potassium: 105.9 mg. Total Fat: 10.3 g; Saturated fat: 2.3 g, Monounsaturated fat: 3.3 g, Polyunsaturated fat: 0.4 g.

❀ PLUM SAUCE ❀

MAKES APPROXIMATELY 2 CUPS   SODIUM PER RECIPE: 124.7 MG
SODIUM PER TABLESPOON: 3.9 MG

This sauce goes well with poultry, fresh pork, and
Gingered Wonton Treats.

*You may substitute 1 cup Welch's concord grape juice (5 mg) for the wine.

1½ cups plum preserves (115.6 mg)
¾ cup Homemade Applesauce, (page 360) (5.738 mg)
½ teaspoon ground ginger (.292 mg)
3 cloves garlic, minced (1.53 mg)
1 teaspoon chili flakes (.54 mg)
1 tablespoon cornstarch (.72 mg)
2 tablespoons cider vinegar (.3 mg)

1. In a saucepan set over medium heat, combine the preserves and applesauce and cook until the mixture boils. Add the ginger, garlic, chili flakes, cornstarch, and vinegar and reduce heat and cook until the sauce thickens. Serve with chicken, turkey dark meat, or wild game birds.

For 2 cups. Calories: 1,073. Sodium: 124.67 mg. Protein: 6.213 g. Carbohydrate: 265.2 g. Fiber: 16.49 g. Cholesterol: 0 mg. Calcium: 173.2 mg. Iron: 7.015 mg. Potassium: 2,687 mg. Total Fat: 4 g; Saturated fat: 0.5 g, Monounsaturated fat: 0.4 g, Polyunsaturated fat: 1.6 g.

Per tablespoon. Calories: 34. Sodium: 3.9 mg. Fiber: 0.52 g. Protein: .194 g. Carbohydrate: 8.288 g. Cholesterol: 0 mg. Calcium: 5.412 mg. Iron: .219 mg. Potassium: 84 mg. Total Fat: 0.1 g; Saturated fat: 0 g, Monounsaturated fat: 0 g, Polyunsaturated fat: 0 g.

❖ SWEET-AND-SOUR ORANGE SAUCE ❖

MAKES ABOUT 3 CUPS   SODIUM PER RECIPE: 25 MG
SODIUM PER CUP: 8.34 MG   SODIUM PER TABLESPOON: .521 MG
*A bit different than our **Plum Sauce** (page 176), this one works well as a dipping sauce or with chicken and pork.*

2 cups crushed pineapple in heavy syrup (5.08 mg)*
½ cup sugar (1 mg)
½ cup water (0 mg)
½ cup white vinegar (1.2 mg)
1 tablespoon cornstarch (.72 mg)
2 cloves garlic, minced (1.02 mg)
1 cup orange marmalade (16 mg)†

1. In a medium pan, heat the pineapple with syrup, with the sugar, water, vinegar, cornstarch, and garlic. Bring the mixture to a boil, stirring constantly. When done, cool to room temperature and then add the marmalade and stir. Cover the mixture and refrigerate before serving with appetizers as a dipping sauce or with chicken, pork, or lamb.

Per tablespoon. Calories: 26. Sodium: 0.52 mg. Fiber: 0.09 g. Protein: .045 g. Carbohydrate: 6.56 g. Cholesterol: 0 mg. Calcium: 1.882 mg. Iron: .143 mg. Potassium: 14.1 mg. Total Fat: 0 g; Saturated fat: 0 g, Monounsaturated fat: 0 g, Polyunsaturated fat: 0 g.

*The sodium count varies from company to company. Check the can before you buy a particular brand.
†Look for Smucker's Low Sugar to find the one that contains the lowest sodium count.

❈ DILL SAUCE ❈

SERVES 8   SODIUM PER RECIPE: 6.329 MG   SODIUM PER SERVING: .791 MG

From Marge Quinn, of Fort Bragg, California, comes this sauce, which she has used for years on the fresh salmon her husband catches off the northern California coast. The salmon there is some of the best cold-water fish in the world, with a deep reddish-pink color and a rich, succulent flavor.

3 **cloves garlic, minced (1.53 mg)**
1 **medium onion, diced (3.3 mg)**
⅓ **cup extra-virgin olive oil (trace)**
2 **tablespoons fresh chopped dill (.679 mg)**
⅓ **cup white wine vinegar (.792 mg)**

1. Put all the ingredients in a bowl and whisk to combine. Spoon the sauce on the salmon before cooking. (This sauce can also be used as a marinade, but generally salmon does not need marination. This sauce is good with **Bob's Barbecued Salmon** (page 122) or salmon baked in the oven.

Calories: 87. Sodium: 0.79 mg. Fiber: 0.27 g. Protein: .236 g. Carbohydrate: 2.153 g. Cholesterol: 0 mg. Calcium: 5.686 mg. Iron: .152 mg. Potassium: 37 mg. Total Fat: 8.9 g: Saturated fat: 1.2 g, Monounsaturated fat: 6.6 g, Polyunsaturated fat: 0.8 g.

❈ BARBECUE RIB SAUCE ❈

MAKES 1 CUP   SODIUM PER RECIPE: 252.4 MG
SODIUM PER TABLESPOON: 15.8 MG

Our daughter, Suzanne, created this low-sodium, very tasty sauce for the barbecued ribs she loves.

   8-ounce can Del Monte No Salt Added Tomato Sauce (80 mg)
   6-ounce can Contadina All Natural Tomato Paste (100 mg)
¾ **cup packed brown sugar (64.3 mg)**
3 **cloves garlic, minced (1.53 mg)**
1 **medium onion, diced (3.3 mg)**
½ **teaspoon ground cloves (2.55 mg)**
½ **teaspoon dried or fresh thyme (.383 mg)**
½ **teaspoon ground coriander (.318 mg)**

1. Combine all the ingredients in a medium saucepan and bring it to a low boil, stirring well. Turn the heat off. If you are barbecuing ribs, brush the sauce on during cooking. If you are cooking ribs in the oven, brush the bottom of the baking dish, then put the ribs in and brush each layer of ribs. When the baking dish is full, pour the rest of sauce over the ribs and distribute evenly. Bake the ribs for 1 hour at 325°F.

Calories: 57. Sodium: 15.78 mg. Protein: .954 g. Carbohydrate: 13.9 g. Fiber: 0.74 g. Cholesterol: 0 mg. Calcium: 14.9 mg. Iron: 1.658 mg. Potassium: 107.1 mg. Total Fat: 0.1 g: Saturated fat: 0 g, Monounsaturated fat: 0 g, Polyunsaturated fat: 0 g.

❧ SOY SAUCE REPLACEMENT ❧

MAKES 1 CUP   SODIUM PER RECIPE: 27.4 MG
SODIUM PER TABLESPOON: 1.711 MG

This recipe came to us from a friend in Thailand who has had to develop his own recipes because of his heart disease. This is a very good soy replacement and it goes well with tofu, Asian dishes, and wherever you might want soy sauce. Store it in a glass bottle in the refrigerator.

¾ **cup garlic vinegar* (1.8 mg)**
3 **tablespoons Br'er Rabbit dark molasses (22.2 mg)**
3 **teaspoons Spice Islands onion powder (3.375 mg)**

1. Combine all the ingredients and pour the mixture into a glass jar. Refrigerate and use as needed (lasts about 1 month). Warm and shake well before using.

Calories: 13. Sodium: 1.71 mg. Fiber: 0.02 g. Protein: .04 g. Carbohydrate: 3.561 g. Cholesterol: 0 mg. Calcium: 9.792 mg. Iron: .255 mg. Potassium: 69.9 mg. Total Fat: 0 g; Saturated fat: 0 g, Monounsaturated fat: 0 g, Polyunsaturated fat: 0 g.

GAME SAUCES

A flavorful sauce is almost as important as proper game preparation. An unfortunately common practice among game cooks is to match wild game with a can of prepared soup or a dry soup mix and stew for several hours until the meat is moist and tender. While one cannot argue that the dish is indeed edible, it hardly does justice to that animal that we worked so hard for and dreamed about during the off-season.

By following the handling and cooking techniques below, virtually all "gamey-ness" is eliminated. Several recipes specify utilizing only parts of an animal—the breasts of game birds and waterfowl, for example. The best way to make use of the leftover parts is to wrap, label, and freeze them until there is sufficient inventory to make a large quantity of game stock, which has a more pronounced and less salty flavor than commercially prepared broth.

Pour the prepared stock through a strainer, cool, and skim off and discard any fat that forms on the top. The stock can then be

---

*You can easily make your own garlic vinegar by heating vinegar slightly; pour over peeled and sliced garlic cloves to taste, let stand overnight, strain and discard the garlic.

frozen in small quantities. I prefer to freeze my stocks in ice cube trays. Once they are frozen, I store the cubes in plastic zip-lock-type bags and thaw them as needed.

Don't drown game dishes in sauce. Instead, when serving, put a small quantity of sauce on the plate, arrange the game artistically over the sauce, and drizzle a little sauce over the meat. Offer additional sauce in a serving bowl. Garnish with a sprig or two of fresh herbs or some celery leaves.

❧ GAME STOCK ❧

MAKES ABOUT 1 QUART   SODIUM PER RECIPE: 329.4 MG*
SODIUM PER CUP: 82.36 MG
*Make good use of frequently discarded bones
to create a marvelous game stock.*

1½ to 2 pounds neck, back, and/or rib bones from a large game
    animal and bird carcasses (231 mg)
2 tablespoons extra-virgin olive oil (trace)
1 medium onion, unpeeled and quartered (3.3 mg)
1 large carrot, unpeeled and sliced into 1-inch pieces (25.2 mg)
2 medium celery stalks, cut in half (69.6 mg)
2 quarts cold water (0 mg)

1. Combine all the ingredients in a large stockpot, bring to a medium boil, and cook until the stock is reduced to about 1 quart. When finished, drain the liquid and remove all the bones and meat. Refrigerate in mason jar.

Per cup: Calories: 217. Sodium: 82.36 mg. Fiber: 1.38 g. Protein: 26.7 g. Carbohydrate: 4.928 g. Cholesterol: 96.39 mg. Calcium: 24 mg. Iron: 20.1 mg. Potassium: 519.3 mg. Total Fat: 9.6 g. Saturated fat: 2 g. Monounsaturated fat: 5.7 g. Polyunsaturated fat: 1.1 g.

❧ RASPBERRY SAUCE ❧

MAKES ABOUT 1 CUP   SODIUM PER RECIPE: 58.818 MG
*Great for chicken, pork, barbecued beef. This sauce came to us
from The Sporting Chef, Scott Leysath.*

1 cup dry red wine (not cooking wine) (16 mg)
1 teaspoon chicken broth made by combining Herb-ox Low
    Sodium Chicken Broth (5 mg) and 1 cup water (0 mg)

*Includes venison and bird stock.

1 **shallot, diced (2.4 mg)**
3 **fresh rosemary sprigs (6 tablespoons, chopped) (2.6 mg)**
½ **cup frozen sweetened raspberries (1 mg)**
¼ **cup raspberry preserves (32 mg)**
1 **tablespoon cornstarch mixed with 1 tablespoon cold water (.7 mg)**
Black pepper to taste

1. In a medium saucepan over medium-high heat, bring the wine, broth, shallot, and rosemary to a boil. Reduce the heat to medium and cook until the liquid is reduced to about 1 cup. Stir in the raspberries and preserves and simmer for 12 to 15 minutes. Pour the mixture through a strainer and return the sauce to the pan. When there is approximately 1 cup sauce, increase the heat to medium-high. Add the cornstarch mixture, a little at a time while stirring, until the sauce thickens. Season with pepper to taste. Store in refrigerator.

Calories: 402. Sodium: 58.77 mg. Fiber: 2.39 g. Protein: 1.818 g. Carbohydrate: 69.1 g. Cholesterol: 0 mg. Calcium: 71.9 mg. Iron: 2.168 mg. Potassium: 374.8 mg. Sodium: 58.8 mg. Total Fat: .785 g; Saturated fat: 0.3 g, Monounsaturated fat: 0.2 g, Polyunsaturated fat: 0.1 g.

◈ GINGER AND ORANGE SAUCE ◈

SERVES 6   SODIUM PER RECIPE: 136.5 MG   SODIUM PER SERVING: 22.7 MG
I use this sauce over salmon and sometimes over steamed fresh vegetables. If you do a parchment paper–wrapped salmon or halibut in your oven or on your barbecue, this sauce is especially wonderful on it.

2⅓ **tablespoons unsalted butter (3.4 mg)**
3 **tablespoons extra-virgin olive oil (trace)**
1½ **tablespoons freshly grated ginger (1 mg)**
2 **large cloves garlic (1 mg)**
⅓ **cup white or whole wheat flour (2 mg)**
1 **cup nonfat milk (126.2 mg)**
1 **cup fresh orange juice (2.48 mg)**
2 **teaspoons freshly grated orange zest (.12 mg)**
Black pepper to taste (trace)

1. Melt butter in a medium saucepan and combine with oil. Add the ginger and garlic and sauté for 1 or 2 minutes. Stir or whisk in the flour and cook for about 3 to 4 minutes. Slowly add the milk, still whisking. Cook over lowest heat for 5 minutes. Add the orange juice, zest, and pepper to taste. Cook for another 10 minutes, stirring occasionally.

Calories: 157. Sodium: 22.75 mg. Fiber: 1.02 g. Protein: 2.739 g. Carbohydrate: 11.8 g. Cholesterol: 12.65 mg. Calcium: 61.7 mg. Iron: .426 mg. Potassium: 189.8 mg. Total Fat: 11.5 g; Saturated fat: 3.7 g, Monounsaturated fat: 6.3 g, Polyunsaturated fat: 0.8 g.

❧ ONION MARMALADE ❧

MAKES ½ CUP SAUCE   SODIUM PER RECIPE: 5.82 MG
Goes great with fish, chicken, and white rice.

1   **medium red onion, cut into 6 to 10 wedges (3.3 mg)**
1   **teaspoon extra-virgin olive oil (trace)**
¾   **cup fresh orange juice (1.9 mg)**
1   **teaspoon freshly grated orange rind (.06 mg)**
¼   **cup balsamic vinegar (.6 mg)**

1. Sauté the onion wedges in the oil until light brown, turning once or twice. Combine the orange juice, orange rind, and vinegar and bring to a boil over high heat. Reduce the heat, cover, and let simmer until the onion is tender—this might take anywhere from 30 to 45 minutes.

Calories: 175. Sodium: 5.82 mg. Fiber: 2.56 g. Protein: 2.608 g. Carbohydrate: 32.9 g. Cholesterol: 0 mg. Calcium: 49.3 mg. Iron: 1.007 mg. Potassium: 608.9 mg. Total Fat: 5 g; Saturated fat: 0.7 g, Monounsaturated fat: 3.4 g, Polyunsaturated fat: 0.5 g.

❧ MUSTARD SAUCE ❧

MAKES 1¼ CUPS   SODIUM PER RECIPE: 161.3 MG
SODIUM PER LEVEL TABLESPOON: 8 MG
This sauce works well with rice, meats, goulash.

½   **cup water (0 mg)**
¼   **cup sugar (.5 mg)**
4   **teaspoons any dry mustard (.6 mg)**
1   **cup any light sour cream (160 mg)**
1   **tablespoon unbleached white flour (.156 mg)**

1. Mix the water, sugar, flour and mustard together in a saucepan set over low heat and cook until the sugar dissolves. Mix in the sour cream. Serve hot or warm.

Calories: 30. Sodium: 8.06 mg. Fiber: 0.11 g. Protein: .605 g. Carbohydrate: 3.826 g. Cholesterol: 4 mg. Calcium: 3.523 mg. Iron: .285 mg. Potassium: 4.97 mg. Total Fat: 1.4 g; Saturated fat: 0.8 g, Monounsaturated fat: 0.1 g, Polyunsaturated fat: 0 g.

◆ GRILLED RED BELL PEPPER SAUCE ◆

MAKES ABOUT 2 CUPS   SERVES 8 TO 12   SODIUM PER CUP: 6.78 MG
SODIUM PER SERVING BASED ON 8 SERVINGS: 1.65 MG

The Sporting Chef, Scott Leysath, uses this sauce for many of his upland game recipes. You can use it for any fowl or pork roast or in barbecued turkey burgers.

½ **medium red onion, sliced into 2 rings (2.2 mg)**
1 **clove garlic, minced (.5 mg)**
1 **medium tomato, cut in half (5.5 mg)**
2 **tablespoons olive oil (trace)**
1 **large or 2 small red bell peppers (3.28 mg)**
⅓ **teaspoon dried red pepper flakes (trace)**
   tablespoon red wine vinegar (.15 mg)
⅓ **cup chicken or beef broth made by combining ⅓ teaspoon**
   Herb-ox Low Sodium Chicken or Beef Broth (2 mg) and
   ⅓ cup water (0 mg)
2 **tablespoons minced fresh basil, or 1 tablespoon dried (.2 mg)**
   Black pepper to taste (trace)

FOR BARBECUE COOKING
1. Brush onion, garlic, and tomato with 1 tablespoon of the oil. Put the bell pepper on the hottest part of a greased barbecue grill over white-hot coals. Add the onion and tomato onto the grill and cook until grill marks appear on both sides. Remove and set aside. Place the garlic on foil or in a small pan and grill until lightly browned. Grill the bell pepper until blackened on all sides, then remove it from the grill and put it in a small paper bag. Close the top of the bag and allow to steam for 10 minutes. Remove the pepper, then pull out the stem and clean out the seeds and discard the debris. Place the peppers blackened-side out on a flat surface and scrape as much skin as you can off the flesh with the edge of a knife. A few bits of skin won't hurt the finished sauce. Continue to prepare as below.

FOR STOVETOP COOKING
1. You can easily prepare this on your stovetop. Blanch the pepper and tomato in a steamer, then peel the skin from the pepper. Place the vegetables in a food processor along with the pan-grilled onion and puree. Continue to prepare as below.

FOR BOTH METHODS
1. Place all ingredients except Herb-ox, basil, and pepper with the vegetables already in the food processor, add the pepper flakes and vinegar and pulse until smooth. Transfer the mixture to a small saucepan and heat to the boiling point. Add the broth and basil and cook over medium heat

for 4 to 5 minutes. Season with pepper. Serve hot or cold on all meats. Works well with BBQ, roasted or grilled.

Note: For a heavier version of the sauce—if you aren't concerned about saturated fat—substitute heavy cream for the broth. If you do so, add 33 mg to the sodium total for the exchange. Try the broth first, however, because it will store better and it tastes simply great.

Calories: 55. Sodium: 3.39 mg. Fiber: 1.4 g. Protein: .399 g. Carbohydrate: 2.834 g. Cholesterol: 0 mg. Calcium: 12 mg. Iron: .385 mg. Potassium: 149.7 mg. Total Fat: 3.7 g; Saturated fat: 0.3 g, Monounsaturated fat: 2.1 g, Polyunsaturated fat: 1.1 g.

❧ DON'S HERB CHICKEN SPICES ❧

SODIUM PER BATCH: 8.634 MG   SODIUM PER PINCH: .432 MG

Why not make a double batch of this and store it in an old spice bottle. Simply double the ingredients to 2 tablespoons each. If curry and cloves have too much bite for you, cut the quantities in half.

1 teaspoon dried thyme (.766 mg)
1 teaspoon ground cloves (5.099 mg)
1 teaspoon dried crushed marjoram (.462 mg)
1 teaspoon dried coriander (1.266 mg)
1 teaspoon curry (1.04 mg)
Black pepper to taste (optional)

1. If the ingredients are too thick for a salt shaker, mix them together and crush or grind to a fine "dust." If you'd rather not pulverize, "pinch" the mixture onto meats. This mix can be used for "salting" fowl. Add pepper to taste if you wish.

Calories: 20. Sodium: 8.63 mg. Fiber: 2.2 g. Protein: .714 g. Carbohydrate: 4.02 g. Cholesterol: 0 mg. Calcium: 69 mg. Iron: 3.25 mg. Potassium: 101.3 mg. Total Fat: 0.9 g; Saturated fat: 0.2 g, Monounsaturated fat: 0.2 g, Polyunsaturated fat: 0.2 g.

Salads and Salad Dressings

❂ ❂ ❂ ❂ ❂ ❂ ❂ ❂

◐ Quick Mixed Green Salad ◑

SERVES 2   SODIUM PER RECIPE: 21.2 MG   SODIUM PER SERVING: 10.6 MG
In a hurry? Try this healthy combination.

1 medium tomato (11.1 mg)
1 cup shredded iceberg lettuce and 1 cup shredded romaine
   lettuce (9.43 mg)
¼ cup Oil and Vinegar Dressing (page 209) (.653 mg)
   Pepper or Frontier salad seasoning to taste (trace)

1. Dice the tomato, toss with the lettuce, and mix with dressing. Sprinkle on Frontier salad seasoning or pepper to taste.

Calories: 152. Sodium: 10.58 mg. Fiber: 1.54 g. Protein: 1.254 g. Carbohydrate: 7.96 g. Cholesterol: 0 mg. Calcium: 20.2 g. Iron: .955 g. Potassium: 291.2 g. Total Fat: 13.8 g; Saturated fat: 1.9 g, Monounsaturated fat: 10 g, Polyunsaturated fat: 1.3 g.

◐ Chopped Vegetable ◑

SERVES 4   SODIUM PER RECIPE: 45.5 MG   SODIUM PER SERVING: 11.4 MG
Home Economist Marlene Winger brought us this great salad recipe. By anyone's standard it is delicious and worthy to be served with your best meals. It's guaranteed that your guests will want this recipe, so have it ready.

THE SALAD
5 cups chopped romaine, loosely packed (22.4 mg)
1 cup red onion, sliced (3.45 mg)
1 cup jicama, julienned into 1½-inch strips (5.2 mg)
¼ cup chopped cilantro (1 mg)
2 cups fresh mandarin sections* (3.9 mg), or you may substitute
   tangerine or orange sections (trace)

*You can also find canned mandarins that have a very low sodium content.

THE DRESSING

¼ **cup fresh or "homestyle" refrigerated orange juice (2.4 mg)**
1 **teaspoon granulated sugar (trace)**
½ **teaspoon cumin (1.72 mg)**
1½ **tablespoons extra-virgin olive oil (trace)**

1. To prepare, combine the salad ingredients and set aside. Then whisk the dressing ingredients together and toss with the salad mixture and serve.

Calories: 154. Sodium: 11.36 mg. Fiber: 5.77 g. Protein: 2.855 g. Carbohydrate: 25.7 g. Cholesterol: 0 mg. Calcium: 59.7 mg. Iron: 1.492 mg. Potassium: 593.3 mg. Total Fat: 5.7 g; Saturated fat: 0.8 g, Monounsaturated fat: 3.8 g, Polyunsaturated fat: 0.6 g.

❧ TOFU SALAD GREEK-STYLE ❧

SERVES 6   SODIUM PER RECIPE: 387.4 MG   SODIUM PER SERVING: 64.6 MG
Instead of grape leaves, we use spinach.

SALAD MAKINGS

16 **ounces tofu, cubed (64 mg)**
3 **medium tomatoes, cubed (33.2 mg)**
2 **large cucumbers, cubed* (12 mg)**
1 **medium red onion, coarsely chopped (3.3 mg)**
1 **bunch spinach, well washed and torn into bite-size pieces (268.6 mg)**
½ **cup cranberry raisins† (3.9 mg)**

THE DRESSING

½ **cup extra-virgin olive oil (trace)**
⅓ **cup red wine vinegar (.7 mg)**
1 **teaspoon dried sweet basil (.5 mg)**
½ **teaspoon ground pepper (.46 mg)**
½ **teaspoon dried oregano (.1 mg)**
1 **clove garlic, minced (1 mg)**

1. Combine the tomatoes, cucumbers, onions, spinach, and cranberry raisins in a salad bowl and set aside. In another bowl whisk the dressing ingredients until well combined. Marinate the tofu cubes in the dressing in the refrigerator for about 1 hour. Next combine all the ingredients and toss. Let the salad chill in the refrigerator for another hour before serving.

Calories: 346. Sodium: 64.57 mg. Fiber: 3.99 g. Protein: 15.1 g. Carbohydrate: 20.8 g. Cholesterol: 0 mg. Calcium: 86.3 g. Iron: 2.473 mg. Potassium: 653.5 mg. Total Fat: 25.3 g; Saturated fat: 3.6 g, Monounsaturated fat: 13.3 g, Polyunsaturated fat: 1.8g.

*Use an extra cucumber if you like them.
†These are dried cranberries; sometimes found under the Ocean Spray Craisins® label. If not available use currants.

Mixed Green Salad
❖ with Balsamic Vinaigrette ❖

SERVES 2   SODIUM PER RECIPE: 47.2 MG   SODIUM PER SERVING: 11.8 MG
*Use either **Balsamic Vinaigrette** or **Oil and Vinegar Dressing***
on this salad.

4 **cups romaine lettuce, cleaned and shredded (17.9 mg)**
2 **medium tomatoes, diced (22.1 mg)**
1 **medium red onion (3.3 mg)**
3 **cloves garlic, minced (1.53 mg)**
1 **recipe Balsamic Vinaigrette Dressing, page 209 (2.322 mg)**

1. Combine all the ingredients and toss well. Serve the salad chilled.

Calories: 196. Sodium: 11.8 mg. Fiber: 2.19 g. Protein: 1.955 g. Carbohydrate: 7.889 g.
Cholesterol: 0 mg. Calcium: 33.9 mg. Iron: 1.127 mg. Potassium: 360.2 mg. Total Fat:
18.4 g; Saturated fat: 2.5 g, Monounsaturated fat: 13.3 g, Polyunsaturated fat: 1.7 g.

❖ Sesame Tofu with Avocado ❖

SERVES 2   SODIUM PER RECIPE: 79.2 MG   SODIUM PER SERVING: 39.6 MG
Tofu has been embraced as a cancer fighter for centuries. Chinese
women, who eat tofu on a daily basis, have 80 percent less breast
cancer than American women. Tofu, soy milk, soy nuts, or
flaxseed are all excellent cancer fighters. Tofu may substitute for
meat in many of our recipes.

4 **medium Napa cabbage leaves—or red cabbage if not available**
   (16.6 mg)
1½ **tablespoons sesame seed oil (0 mg)**
1½ **tablespoons red wine vinegar (.225 mg)**
1 **tablespoon honey (.84 mg)**
1½ **tablespoons water (0 mg)**
½ **teaspoon East Shore or Mendocino honey mustard (3.3 mg)**
1 **California (Hass) avocado (21 mg)**
8 **ounces firm organic tofu (32 mg)**
¼ **cup dry-roasted unsalted cashew nuts (5 mg)**

1. Shred the cabbage. Mix together the sesame seed oil, vinegar, honey, water, and mustard and set aside. Peel and pit the avocado; cut into lengthwise slices, then halve those. Cut the tofu into bite-size pieces. In two serving dishes put like amounts of tofu and avocado on top of Napa cabbage. Gently toss. Spoon the dressing over and sprinkle with cashews. It's ready to serve.

Calories: 553. Sodium: 39.5 mg. Fiber: 5.85 g. Protein: 23.3 g. Carbohydrate: 28.4 g. Cho-
lesterol: 0 mg. Calcium: 40.1 mg. Iron: 2.761 mg. Potassium: 775 mg. Total Fat: 43.4 g; Sat-
urated fat: 6.9 g, Monounsaturated fat: 18.4 g, Polyunsaturated fat: 7.4 g.

❖ Broccoli Salad ❖

SERVES 6   SODIUM PER RECIPE: 148.8 mg   SODIUM PER SERVING: 24.8 mg

Here's our friend Becky again with a wonderful vitamin-loaded salad. However, if you're taking Coumadin (blood thinner), you must consult your doctor before eating cruciferous vegetables such as broccoli, kale, spinach, and brussels sprouts. These foods are high in vitamin K, which is a beneficial blood coagulant (clotting agent), but patients on Coumadin may be advised to avoid these vegetables. By the way, broccoli was brought to the U.S. by the Italian family of Broccoli; a descendant of that family, Albert "Cubby" Broccoli, brought us the James Bond movies.

4 cups cut-up broccoli florets (76.7 mg)
1 cup diced red onions (4.8 mg)
½ cup unsalted sunflower seeds (1.92 mg)
½ cup slivered unsalted almonds (7.5 mg)
1 cup seedless raisins, plumped in warm water for 5 to 10
    minutes (17.4 mg)
2 tablespoons cider vinegar (.3 mg)
2 tablespoons granulated sugar (.25 mg)
2 tablespoons plain yogurt (39.8 mg) or sour cream (10 mg)

1. In a bowl, combine the broccoli and onion. Add the sunflower seeds, almonds, and raisins, then toss. In another bowl, mix together the vinegar, sugar, and sour cream (or plain yogurt). Chill.

Note: Broccoli stems are delicious and nutritious when prepared correctly. Skin the stems and steam them until softened. Slice them into ½-inch pieces and mix them into the salad. You'll love them.

Calories: 248. Sodium: 24.8 mg. Fiber: 5.63 g. Protein: 6.934 g. Carbohydrate: 34.4 g. Cholesterol: 0.58 mg. Calcium: 97.4 mg. Iron: 1.86 mg. Potassium: 583.6 mg. Total Fat: 11.7 g; Saturated fat: 1.3 g, Monounsaturated fat: 4.9 g, Polyunsaturated fat: 4.9 g.

❖ BEET SALAD ❖

MAKES 3 CUPS   SODIUM PER RECIPE: 195.4 MG
SODIUM PER SERVING: 65.1 MG

I love beets. Although beets are high in sodium when raw, they are low enough to enjoy after boiling or steaming to softness. Even the low-sodium canned beets are safe.

¼ cup unsalted walnuts (.312 mg)
3 fresh 2-inch beets, boiled or steamed (191.9 mg)
3 navel oranges (0 mg)
2 tablespoons shredded coconut packaged, unsalted, sweetened, flakes (1.9 mg)
1 teaspoon honey (.277 mg)
Juice of ½ lemon (0 mg)
Zest from ½ lemon, chopped
2 tablespoons currants (.28 mg)
1 teaspoon vinegar (trace)

1. Roast the walnuts for 8 to 10 minutes in a 300°F oven. Wash the beets, then boil or steam whole until tender. Let the beets cool. Next peel and then grate them. Peel and seed the oranges and then cut them into chunks. Place half the oranges in a blender with the coconut, honey, lemon juice, and lemon zest, and blend well. In a serving bowl, combine the blender mixture and the currants and vinegar. Chill for at least 2 hours. Top with the roasted walnuts when serving.

Calories: 190. Sodium: 65.12 mg. Fiber: 6.21 g. Protein: 5.328 g. Carbohydrate: 29.7 g. Cholesterol: 0 mg. Calcium: 73.6 mg. Iron: 1.26 mg. Potassium: 570.3 mg. Total Fat: 7.4 g; Saturated fat: 1.3 g, Monounsaturated fat: 1.5 g, Polyunsaturated fat: 4 g.

❖ CARROT SALAD WITH ORANGE ZEST ❖

SERVES 4   SODIUM PER RECIPE: 137.3 MG   SODIUM PER SERVING: 34.3 MG

*Carrots are an excellent antioxidant. This dish, and **Becky's Carrot Salad**, are healthy, tasty, and easy to prepare.*

3 cups finely grated carrots (134.4 mg)
½ cup currants (1.12 mg)
½ cup orange juice (1.24 mg)
1 tablespoon lemon juice (.15 mg)
1 teaspoon grated orange zest (.12 mg)
¼ cup toasted and chopped unsalted cashews or black walnuts (.32 mg)

1. Mix all the ingredients together, tossing well. Serve chilled.

Calories: 113. Sodium: 34.32 mg. Fiber: 3.4 g. Protein: 3.326 g. Carbohydrate: 16.5 g. Cholesterol: 0 mg. Calcium: 42.6 mg. Iron: 1.003 mg. Potassium: 463.8 mg. Total Fat: 4.7 g; Saturated fat: 0.3 g, Monounsaturated fat: 1 g, Polyunsaturated fat: 3 g.

❖ BECKY'S CARROT SALAD ❖

SERVES 4   SODIUM PER RECIPE: 95 MG   SODIUM PER SERVING: 23.7 MG

¼ cup walnut pieces (.31 mg)
1 tablespoon shredded coconut packaged, unsalted, sweetened flakes (1 mg)
2 cups grated carrots (89.6 mg)
1 apple, cored and grated (0 mg)
1 tablespoon grated lemon zest (.36 mg)
   Juice of ½ lemon (.235 mg)
½ cup orange juice (1.24 mg)
½ cup currants (1.12 mg)
1½ teaspoons grated ginger (.986 mg)

1. Toast the walnut pieces and coconut in a 300°F oven. Remove the walnuts after 10 minutes and the coconut after another 5. Combine the remaining ingredients, then add the walnuts and coconut. Serve chilled.

Calories: 127. Sodium: 23.74 mg. Fiber: 3.32 g. Protein: 3.181 g. Carbohydrate: 19.4 g. Cholesterol: 0 mg. Calcium: 37.6 mg. Iron: .98 mg. Potassium: 414.6 mg. Total Fat: 5.3 g; Saturated fat: 0.8 g, Monounsaturated fat: 1.1 g, Polyunsaturated fat: 3.1 g.

❖ SNAKE RIVER CARROT SALAD ❖

SERVES 4   SODIUM PER RECIPE: 272.2 MG   SODIUM PER SERVING: 68 MG
Yet another carrot salad from our healthy rafter friends who serve this as a complete lunch. It's easy to prepare and very high in antioxidants and calcium.

1 pound carrots, coarsely grated (156.8 mg)
2 medium apples, grated (0 mg)
1 cup whole firm plain yogurt (113.7 mg)
1 tablespoon honey (.84 mg)
   Pinch of celery or sunflower seeds (.32 mg)
   Juice of 1 small lemon (.47 mg)
   Pepper to taste (trace)

1. Combine the ingredients, tossing well. Serve the salad chilled.

Calories: 146. Sodium: 68.04 mg. Fiber: 5.29 g. Protein: 3.482 g. Carbohydrate: 30.1 g. Cholesterol: 7.78 mg. Calcium: 111.1 mg. Iron: 77 mg. Potassium: 554.1 mg. Total Fat: 2.5 g; Saturated fat: 1.4 g, Monounsaturated fat: 0.6 g, Polyunsaturated fat: 0.2 g.

❖ SWEET PEPPER SALAD ❖

MAKES 2 SERVINGS   SODIUM PER RECIPE: 34.4 MG
SODIUM PER SERVING: 17.2 MG

½ **yellow pepper (1.8 mg)**
½ **orange pepper (1.8 mg)**
½ **green pepper (1.1 mg)**
2 **leaves butter lettuce (.5 mg)**
2 **leaves romaine lettuce (1.6 mg)**
2 **Roma tomatoes (16.4 mg)**
½ **cucumber (3 mg)**
½ **red onion (1.65 mg)**
2 **tablespoons extra-virgin olive oil (trace)**
2 **tablespoons honey (1.68 mg)**
2 **tablespoons red wine vinegar (.3 mg)**
¼ **cup seedless golden raisins (4.35 mg)**

1. Clean the peppers, digging out all the seeds. Slice into 1-inch-long thin strips. Wash the lettuces and break by hand into bite-size or slightly larger pieces. Wash the tomatoes and slice them thinly. Peel the cucumber and cut into slices. Cut onion into 1-inch pieces. Transfer all the ingredients to a bowl. Combine the oil, honey, and vinegar and add the mixture to the bowl, tossing well. Transfer the completed salad to 2 (or 3) individual salad bowls, sprinkle the raisins on top, and serve cold with a toasted **Sandwich Bun** (page 258) half.

Calories: 315. Sodium: 17.2 mg. Fiber: 4.46 g. Protein: 3.71 g. Carbohydrate: 49.4 g. Cholesterol: 0 mg. Calcium: 50.5 mg. Iron: 1.909 mg. Potassium: 806.4 mg. Total Fat: 14.3 g; Saturated fat: 1.9 g, Monounsaturated fat: 10 g, Polyunsaturated fat: 1.4 g.

❖ VEGETABLE SALAD ❖

SERVES 4   SODIUM PER RECIPE: 125.4 MG   SODIUM PER SERVING: 31.3 MG

SALAD MAKINGS
1 **spear broccoli (40.8 mg)**
¼ **head cauliflower (43.1 mg)**
1 **small carrot (17.5 mg)**
1 **small zucchini (3.54 mg)**
¼ **green or red bell pepper (.5 mg)**
¼ **red onion (.8 mg)**
6 **ounces fresh mushrooms (5.5 mg)**
1 **large tomato (11 mg)**

DRESSING
⅓ **cup extra-virgin olive oil (trace)**
⅓ **cup red wine vinegar (.7 mg)**

1 tablespoon lemon juice (.7 mg)
½ tablespoon water (0 mg)
2 cloves garlic (1 mg)
¼ teaspoon oregano (trace)
¼ teaspoon sweet basil (.12 mg)
¼ teaspoon thyme (.19 mg)
1⅓ teaspoons sugar (trace)

1. Cut all the vegetables into bite-size pieces. Combine the dressing ingredients and pour the mixture over the vegetables. Toss everything well. Chill for about 1 hour before serving.

Calories: 281. Sodium: 31.34 mg. Fiber: 2.81 g. Protein: 3.576 g. Carbohydrate: 13.6 g. Cholesterol: 0 mg. Calcium: 48.3 mg. Iron: 1.817 mg. Potassium: 600.8 mg. Total Fat: 18.4 g; Saturated fat: 2.5 g, Monounsaturated fat: 13.2 g, Polyunsaturated fat: 1.7 g.

◈ LEON'S PITA SALAD ◈

SERVES 4   SODIUM PER RECIPE: 88.3 MG   SODIUM PER SERVING: 22.1 MG
Leon Silverman is one of my friends from the entertainment world. He claims he is not a good cook, but this is an absolutely delicious recipe for a pita salad. You can follow the recipe or simply stuff your pita with the salad ingredients.

1 cup shredded romaine lettuce (4.5 mg)
1 green onion (2.4 mg)
½ cucumber, peeled (2 mg)
1 medium tomato (11 mg)
¼ cup minced fresh parsley (8.4 mg)
1 tablespoon lemon juice (.15 mg)
2 tablespoons extra-virgin olive oil (trace)
1 clove garlic, minced (.5 mg)
1 medium avocado (20.8 mg)
1 ounce low-sodium Swiss cheese, diced (20 mg)
2 homemade Pita Bread, page 251 (3.541 mg)

1. Cut or tear the lettuce into bite-size pieces. Chop the onion into fine dice. Peel and slice the cucumber into bite-size pieces. Chop the tomato and the minced parsley. (Add other ingredients to your taste, such as chopped green or red pepper [1 mg sodium], or ½ fresh, blanched chili pepper, chopped [3 mg].) Toss all the salad ingredients together. Cut the **Pita Bread** into bite-size pieces and add to vegetables, then toss once more. (It can be made into a pita sandwich by slicing the bread in half and splitting it open, then stuffing with the ingredients.)

TIP: You may add 6 ounces of thinly sliced baked or sautéed chicken to this recipe if you want more protein. This is true of any vegetarian recipe if you are so inclined. See chicken sodium ratings (page 27) to determine added sodium.

Calories: 246. Sodium: 22.08 mg. Fiber: 4.23 g. Protein: 6.103 g. Carbohydrate: 20.3 g. Cholesterol: 5 mg. Calcium: 34.7 mg. Iron: 4.09 mg. Potassium: 508.2 mg. Total Fat: 16.8 g; Saturated fat: 3.2 g, Monounsaturated fat: 10.3 g, Polyunsaturated fat: 1.7 g.

❈ PICHA'S THAI SALAD ❈

SERVES 4   SODIUM PER RECIPE: 55.9 MG   SODIUM PER SERVING: 14 MG

I worked with a young man from Thailand named Picha Srisansansee. This was his favorite recipe for salad.

½ **small head red cabbage (31.2 mg)**
1 **bunch cilantro (6 mg)**
½ **cup seedless raisins (9.9 mg)**
½ **cup unsalted peanuts (4.38 mg)**
¼ **cup honey (3.39 mg)**
⅓ **cup red wine vinegar (1.7 mg)**
1 **tablespoon hot sesame oil (0 mg)**

1. Clean and shred the cabbage. Chop the cilantro. Soak the raisins in lukewarm water for about ½ hour, then drain and pat dry. Put the cabbage, cilantro, raisins, and peanuts in a medium-size salad bowl and toss. Combine the honey, vinegar, and sesame oil and pour it over the salad ingredients. Serve cold.

Calories: 286. Sodium: 13.96 mg. Fiber: 3.83 g. Protein: 6.093 g. Carbohydrate: 43.3 g. Cholesterol: 0 mg. Calcium: 60.5 mg. Iron: 1.445 mg. Potassium: 466.5 mg. Total Fat: 12.8 g; Saturated fat: 1.8 g, Monounsaturated fat: 5.9 g, Polyunsaturated fat: 4.4 g.

❈ Potato Salad "Old-Fashioned" ❈

SERVES 10   SODIUM PER RECIPE: 340.4 MG   SODIUM PER SERVING: 34 MG

Picnics were a big thing when we grew up. "Picnics" and "the Sunday Drive" were synonymous. It was a time when you worked all week, then renewed friendships on the weekend. One of the great things about our picnics was this potato salad. The original used a great deal of salt, so you'll have to add herb salt substitutes to your own taste. This is no problem for me.

  6 **russet potatoes in jackets* (42 mg)**
  ½ **teaspoon celery seed (1.6 mg)**
     Pepper to taste (trace)
     Frontier salad sprinkle† (0 mg)
  1 **Featherweight or low-sodium dill pickle, finely diced‡ (5 mg)**
  3 **cloves garlic, minced (1.53 mg)**
  1 **cup chopped red onion (4.8 mg)**
  1 **cup celery, thinly sliced (107.9 mg)**
  3 **hard-cooked eggs (166.3 mg)**
  1 **cup Hain Low Sodium Mayonnaise§ (trace)**
  2 **teaspoons Hain Stone Ground No Salt Added Mustard# (6.6 mg)**
  2 **to 4 tablespoons vinegar (.6 mg)**
     and
  2 **to 4 tablespoons extra-virgin olive oil (trace)****
     Iceberg or romaine lettuce leaves for serving

1. Wash and boil the potatoes until almost done, then cool in the refrigerator overnight. If using red potatoes or white potatoes, you may leave skin on (great fiber); if russets, peel when cold. Dice the potatoes while cold (don't try this when they're warm or hot or they'll fall apart), add the cel-

---

*You may use 10 large red potatoes or 8 large white potatoes instead. I prefer the red potatoes.

†You can get Frontier seasoning blends by mail order from www.healthyheart-market .com or by calling 1-800/753-0310.

‡Higher sodium (but comparatively low sodium still) kosher pickles are available at www.healthyheartmarket.com or call 1-800/753-0310. Ask for Cascadian Farms Low Sodium Kosher Dills. They will add 135 mg sodium per recipe or 13.5 mg per serving.

§Available at Healthy Heart Market. Or you can make your own by combining ½ cup light sour cream (80 mg), ⅓ cup plain yogurt (50 mg), and 1 teaspoon dill (0 mg). Chill for 10 to 20 minutes. Be sure to add in the sodium count if you do.

#Or use the sweeter Mendocino Honey Mustard or Grey Poupon Honey Mustard. Add 30 mg to the sodium count for Grey Poupon.

**To your taste. I prefer pickle vinegar from Regina, garlic or basil vinegar, or, for a zestier flavor, use 2 tablespoons balsamic vinegar. A dash of sesame oil for those who love the flavor will kick this up to another level; mix it with olive oil to make a French-type dressing and then add it to the salad.

ery seed, pepper, salad herbs, pickle, garlic, onion, celery, and 2 of the cooked eggs, diced.

2. In a bowl, combine the mayonnaise with the mustard and vinegar/oil to taste. Add this to the potatoes. Continue adding dressing until the salad is moist enough for your taste.

3. Layer your serving bowl with iceberg or Romaine lettuce and heap the salad atop them, allowing the lettuce to jut out at the edges for appearance. Lay thin slices of your last egg around the edge of the salad. Serve cold.

Calories: 286. Sodium: 34.04 mg. Fiber: 1.61 g. Protein: 3.47 g. Carbohydrate: 15.3 g. Cholesterol: 64.1 mg. Calcium: 18.4 mg. Iron: .384 mg. Potassium: 87.8 mg. Total Fat: 23.4 g; Saturated fat: 4.1 g, Monounsaturated fat: 2.5 g, Polyunsaturated fat: 0.4 g.

❈ PICNIC POTATO SALAD ❈

SERVES 8   SODIUM PER RECIPE: 157.5 MG   SODIUM PER SERVING: 19.7 MG

This recipe is based on a potato salad I came to love in a restaurant in Burbank, California, across from our office. Seems a bit tart at first, but it grows on you because of the variety of flavors.

```
10  medium red potatoes* (35 mg)
 ⅓  cup diced onion (1.58 mg)
 ½  large celery stalk, chopped (27.8 mg)
 1  teaspoon dried dill (.4 mg)
 ½  cup white wine vinegar or substitute red wine vinegar (0 mg)
 ¼  cup broth made by combining ¼ teaspoon Herb-ox Low
       Sodium Chicken or Vegetable Broth (1.25 mg)
 ¼  teaspoon dry mustard (0 mg)
 ⅓  teaspoon sugar (trace)
 ¼  teaspoon coriander (.15 mg)
       Sprinkle of fresh rosemary (trace)
 ½  cup extra-virgin olive oil (trace)
 ¼  teaspoon Frontier salad sprinkle† or Mrs. Dash Lemon & Herb
       Salt Free blend (0 mg)
 2  teaspoons Bac*Os bits (90 mg)
```

1. In a covered pan, cook the potatoes in their jackets until just tender; do not overcook them. Set them aside and let cool. Slice the potatoes (with jackets still on) into bite-size chunks and transfer them to a large bowl. Sauté the onion, celery, and dill together in a nonstick pan and then set

---

*Or white potatoes. They should be about 4 to 5 inches in diameter. Use more potatoes if you want a drier salad, fewer if you like a "wet" salad.

†Frontier seasoning blends are available by mail order from www.healthyheartmarket.com or by calling 1-800/753-0310.

aside. Bring the vinegar, broth, dry mustard, and sugar to a boil, then remove from the heat and add the coriander, rosemary, olive oil, and seasoning blend. Pour this into the pan with the vegetables and mix. Transfer the mixture to the bowl with the potatoes, sprinkle Bac*Os over the salad, and stir gently. Serve hot (warm) or chill and serve cold.

Calories: 185. Sodium: 19.69 mg. Fiber: 1.3 g. Protein: 1.859 g. Carbohydrate: 14.8 g. Cholesterol: 0 mg. Calcium: 8.435 mg. Iron: .229 mg. Potassium: 41.1 mg. Total Fat: 13.8 g; Saturated fat: 1.9 g, Monounsaturated fat: 10 g, Polyunsaturated fat: 1.2 g.

River Guide Black-Eyed Pea Salad /
❧ A Picnic Specialty ❧

SERVES 4   SODIUM PER RECIPE: 168 MG   SODIUM PER SERVING: 42 MG
Try this one, but watch the celery—celery has 35 mg sodium per stalk.

12-ounce bag dried black-eyed peas (11.6 mg)
  6 cups water (0 mg)
  3 medium celery stalks (104 mg)
  1 large purple onion (4.5 mg)
  1 sweet red pepper (3.28 mg)
  2 medium tomatoes (22.1 mg)
  1 medium avocado (20.8 mg)
  ½ cup extra-virgin olive oil (trace)
  ½ cup balsamic vinegar (1.2 mg)
  Black pepper to taste (trace)

1. Bring peas to a boil in water, and simmer for 1 hour. Check to make sure you don't run out of water. Drain water when done. Slice and dice the celery. Dice the purple onion, red pepper, tomatoes, and avocado. Combine the oil, vinegar, and pepper and add along with the vegetables to a salad bowl. Toss and let it sit in the refrigerator for a few hours, then serve.

Calories: 428. Sodium: 41.99 mg. Fiber: 8.43 g. Protein: 4.602 g. Carbohydrate: 28.3 g. Cholesterol: 0 mg. Calcium: 124.3 mg. Iron: 2.266 mg. Potassium: 971.1 mg. Total Fat: 35.1 g; Saturated fat: 4.9 g, Monounsaturated fat: 24.8 g, Polyunsaturated fat: 3.4 g.

❧ Dill Chicken Summer Salad ❧

SERVES 4   SODIUM PER RECIPE: 452.6 MG   SODIUM PER SERVING: 113.1 MG
Serve with chilled sliced cantaloupe or watermelon.

THE SALAD
  3 medium boneless chicken breast halves (230.1 mg)
  2 medium celery stalks, diced (69.6 mg)

½ red onion, diced (1.65 mg)
1½ cups washed Thompson seedless grape halves (4.8 mg)
 4 lettuce leaves (3.6 mg)
½ lemon (.58 mg)

THE DRESSING
½ cup light sour cream (80 mg)
⅓ cup plain yogurt (61.9 mg)
 1 teaspoon dried dill (.4 mg)

1. Poach the chicken for about 30 minutes. Chill (overnight or quickly by setting the chicken in a bowl over a bowl with ice). Dice the chilled chicken into 1-inch pieces or smaller. Add the celery, onion, and grapes and combine.

2. Mix together the sour cream, yogurt, and dill. Stir it into the salad mixture. Divide the salad into 4 portions and serve each on a lettuce leaf. Squeeze lemon on salad when serving. Best served immediately.

Calories: 205. Sodium: 113.15 mg. Fiber: 1.69 g. Protein: 23.6 g. Carbohydrate: 17.4 g. Cholesterol: 61.69 mg. Calcium: 84 mg. Iron: 1.91 mg. Potassium: 509.8 mg. Total Fat: 4.7 g; Saturated fat: 2.5 g, Monounsaturated fat: 0.3 g, Polyunsaturated fat: 0.4 g.

❖ ALICE'S CHICKEN SALAD ❖

SERVES 4   SODIUM PER RECIPE: 397 MG   SODIUM PER SERVING: 99.2 MG

THE SALAD
 2 large boneless chicken breast halves, cut into bite-size pieces
    (153.4 mg)
 2 medium-size (5-inch diameter) cantaloupes (99.4 mg)
 1 medium onion, diced (3.3 mg)
½ cup thinly sliced celery (52.2 mg)
1½ cups fresh seedless grapes (4.8 mg)
½ cup toasted slivered unsalted almonds (7.59 mg)

THE DRESSING
¼ cup low-fat plain yogurt (43 mg)
¼ cup regular sour cream (30.6 mg)
½ teaspoon grated lemon zest (.12 mg)
 2 tablespoons lemon juice (.3 mg)
 2 tablespoons chopped ginger root (1.56 mg)
 2 tablespoons syrup (sugar syrup) from preserved ginger* (.7 mg)

*Available in specialty stores. If you cannot find it, use fresh ginger. To make ginger syrup, take 2 tablespoons ground fresh ginger and bring to a light boil with 4 tablespoons white sugar and 1 teaspoon water. Simmer for 10 minutes, stirring constantly. Chill before using.

1. To cook the chicken, put it into a 3-quart pan and add 2 cups water and 1 onion cut into quarters. Bring to a boil and let simmer until done, about 20 minutes. Save the broth for soup making.

2. Cut the seeds and pulp out of the melon. Make small balls using a melon baller or dice into bite-size pieces. Combine with the onion, celery, grapes, and almonds. Chill. In another bowl, combine the dressing ingredients and let chill. Mix the dressing with the salad ingredients before serving.

Calories: 372. Sodium: 99.24 mg. Fiber: 6.06 g. Protein: 21 g. Carbohydrate: 46.1 g. Cholesterol: 41.54 mg. Calcium: 150.1 mg. Iron: 1.98 mg. Potassium: 1,412 mg. Total Fat: 14.1 g: Saturated fat: 3.4 g, Monounsaturated fat: 6.9 g, Polyunsaturated fat: 2.6 g.

❖ GRILLED CHICKEN SALAD ❖

SERVES 4   SODIUM PER RECIPE: 404.4 MG   SODIUM PER SERVING: 101.1 MG

This salad has every flavor a chicken salad should have. It's a complete entrée that will fill you up and leave you satisfied. Low in sodium for a complete meal, it's high in flavor and vitamins. If you want to increase the experience, try adding a dash of sesame seed oil.

½ teaspoon ground coriander (.3 mg)
½ teaspoon dried basil flakes (.24 mg)
2 tablespoons honey (1.68 mg)
½ cup orange juice (1.24 mg)
2 tablespoons Grey Poupon Honey Mustard* (30 mg)
4 boneless, skinless chicken breast halves (306.8 mg)
2 teaspoons balsamic vinegar (trace)
4 teaspoons water (0 mg)
4 tablespoons brown sugar (14.1 mg)
⅓ cup slivered unsalted almonds, blanched (5 mg)
½ medium red onion, peeled and sliced into very thin rings
    (1.65 mg)
¾ navel orange segments, skin removed (1.65 mg)
1 head butter leaf lettuce, torn into 2-inch pieces (8.15 mg)
1 head romaine lettuce, hearts only, with large leaves torn in
    half (8.96 mg)
½ cup Balsamic Vinaigrette, page 209) (2.32 mg)
2 tomatoes, sliced in triangular shapes (22 mg)

*Mendocino Honey Mustard and East Shore Honey Mustard are slightly lower in sodium. Check the nutrition label of any honey mustard you buy to adjust the recipe count.

1. Combine the coriander, basil, honey, orange juice, mustard, and vinegar in a bowl. Put the chicken breasts into the marinade, cover, and refrigerate for 3 to 4 hours, turning the breasts occasionally.

2. Grill or barbecue the breasts over medium heat until just cooked. Remove from the heat and allow to cool. Once cooled, cut the breasts into ¾-inch cubes.

3. Preheat the oven to 375°F. In a small, ovenproof nonstick skillet over medium heat, add the water, sugar, and almonds. Stir frequently while the sugar caramelizes and coats the almonds. When the caramel starts to thicken, place the skillet in the oven until the almonds are lightly browned, spreading them out to brown evenly. Remove the skillet and let cool. After the nuts are cool, break up into large pieces.

4. In a large bowl, toss the breasts, almonds, onions, oranges, lettuces, and **Balsamic Vinaigrette.** Top each portion with sliced fresh tomatoes.

Calories: 500. Sodium: 101.1 mg. Fiber: 4.63 g. Protein: 31.6 g. Carbohydrate: 337.9 g. Cholesterol: 68.44 mg. Calcium: 108.8 mg. Iron: 3.109 mg. Potassium: 925.3 mg. Total Fat: 25.9 g. Saturated fat: 3.4 g. Monounsaturated fat: 17.5 g. Polyunsaturated fat: 3.3 g.

❖ TURKEY SALAD ❖

SERVES 6   SODIUM PER RECIPE: 278.5 MG   SODIUM PER SERVING: 46.4 MG
Sandra Barbour is a highly respected cardiologist with Kaiser Permanente in Sacramento. She has collected a volume of recipes that she's adjusted for sodium and fat. Her turkey salad takes a little time to prepare, but it is excellent and worth the effort.

THE SALAD
    1 cup wild rice (11.2 mg)
       Water for boiling rice and barley (0 mg)
    1 cup barley—regular or quick-cooking (22.1 mg)
1½ breasts (2½ cups) cooked, diced skinless turkey (191.1 mg)
    2 cups cooked green beans, sliced into 1-inch pieces (13.2 mg)
    1 medium red pepper, cleaned and diced (2.38 mg)
  ¾ cup finely diced yellow onion (3.6 mg)
    2 tablespoons finely chopped parsley (4.26 mg)
       Pepper to taste (trace)

THE DRESSING
    2 tablespoons Mendocino or Grey Poupon Honey Mustard (30 mg)
  ¼ cup balsamic vinegar (.6 mg)
  ⅓ cup extra-virgin olive oil (trace)

1. To make the salad, bring the rice and 3 cups water to a boil in a heavy saucepan. Reduce the heat to low and cook, tightly covered, for 40 to 45 minutes or per package instructions. Meanwhile cook the barley in 2 cups water for about 10 minutes for the quick-cooking variety or about 40 to 45 minutes for the regular. Make sure it's cooked through but remains chewy. Drain and rinse both the barley and the rice under cold-running water. (You can cook the rice and barley a few days ahead of time and refrigerate it safely in a resealable bag.) When ready, mix the wild rice and barley in a large salad bowl with the turkey, beans, red pepper, onion, and parsley. Season to taste and toss.

2. To make the dressing, whisk together the mustard, vinegar, and oil, then toss with the salad. Serve immediately or refrigerate until serving.

Calories: 417. Sodium: 46.41 mg. Fiber: 9.01 g. Protein: 24.9 g. Carbohydrate: 50.8 g. Cholesterol: 40.3 mg. Calcium: 44 mg. Iron: 3.09 mg. Potassium: 603.3 mg. Total Fat: 13.4 g: Saturated fat: 2 g. Monounsaturated fat: 9 g, Polyunsaturated fat: 1.7 g.

✦ LEON'S TABOULI ✦

SERVES 6   SODIUM PER RECIPE: 75 MG   SODIUM PER SERVING: 12.5 MG
*Tabouli is a popular Middle Eastern salad that can be beautiful when presented well. It is quite filling. This low-sodium version is fine as a salad or as a sandwich filling, especially as a filling for low-sodium **Pita Bread.***

   1 **cup bulgur (23.8 mg)**
   2 **cups water (0 mg)**
  ½ **cup finely chopped fresh parsley (16.8 mg)**
   3 **green onions (scallions), finely chopped (7.2 mg)**
  ½ **red onion, chopped (1.65 mg)**
   1 **large tomato, chopped (16.4 mg)**
   1 **cucumber, peeled and finely chopped (4 mg)**
   2 **teaspoons dried mint (3.44 mg)**
   1 **clove garlic, minced (.5 mg)**
   1 **tablespoon extra-virgin olive oil (trace)**
  ¼ **cup lemon juice (.61 mg)**
   1 **teaspoon cinnamon (.6 mg)**

1. Soak the bulgur in water for 1 hour in a very large bowl. The bulgur will expand. Combine the parsley, scallions, onions, tomato, cucumber, mint, garlic, oil, lemon juice, and cinnamon. Add to the soaked bulgur and toss well. Chill before serving.

Calories: 123. Sodium: 12.5 mg. Fiber: 5.6 g. Protein: 3.827 g. Carbohydrate: 23 g. Cholesterol: 0 mg. Calcium: 37.3 mg. Iron: 12.2 mg. Potassium: 295 mg. Total Fat: 2.8 g: Saturated fat: 0.4 g. Monounsaturated fat: 1.7 g, Polyunsaturated fat: 0.4 g.

❧ RICE AND PEPPER SALAD ❧

SERVES 4   SODIUM PER RECIPE: 57.5 MG   SODIUM PER SERVING: 14.4 MG

3 tablespoons extra-virgin oil (trace)
3 fresh dried ancho or poblano chilies* (1.4 mg)
1 teaspoon cumin seeds (3.5 mg)
½ cup millet (5 mg)
⅔ cup converted rice (2 mg)
2 cups water (0 mg)
1 large red bell pepper (3.28 mg)
1 fresh jalapeño or Anaheim chili, skinned and blanched (.14 mg)
2 teaspoons red wine vinegar (trace)
1 cup fresh sweet white corn kernels cut from ears—not canned
    (23.1 mg)
4 green onions (scallions), thinly sliced (9.6 mg)
2 cloves garlic, crushed (1 mg)
⅓ cup chopped fresh cilantro (coriander) (8.1 mg)
    Pepper to taste (trace)

1. Heat 1 tablespoon of the oil in a large saucepan set over medium-high heat. Combine the ancho chilies and cumin and cook for 1 minute. Add the millet and continue to cook for about 4 to 5 minutes. Add the rice and water, cover, and bring to a boil. Reduce the heat and let simmer until the water is absorbed by the rice (about 12 to 15 minutes). Remove from the heat and let stand, covered, for about 5 minutes. Remove and discard the ancho chilies and put the remaining ingredients in a large mixing bowl.
2. Peel half the red pepper with a peeler. Cut this half into chunks. Put the pepper chunks in the blender with the remaining 2 tablespoons of oil, the jalapeño or Anaheim chili, and the vinegar and puree. When well blended, pour this over the rice mixture.
3. Dice the other half of the red pepper, add it to the rice mixture along with the corn, scallions, garlic, and cilantro. Toss to combine. You may add pepper to taste, but no salt. Serve immediately.

Calories: 420. Sodium: 14.36 mg. Fiber: 6.07 g. Protein: 8.24 g. Carbobydrate: 70.4 g. Cholesterol: 0 mg. Calcium: 29.6 mg. Iron: 8.019 mg. Potassium: 357 mg. Total Fat: 12.9 g: Saturated fat: 1.7 g, Monounsaturated fat: 8 g, Polyunsaturated fat: 1.8 g.

*Dried ancho chilies may be found in the imported food aisle of large supermarkets or in Hispanic markets.

❧ ASIAN RICE SALAD ❧

SERVES 6 SODIUM PER RECIPE: 93.6 MG SODIUM PER SERVING: 15.6 MG
This one takes a bit longer to prepare than your usual salad, so allow enough lead time.

THE SALAD

  2 cups cooked medium- or short-grain brown rice (15.2 mg)
  ½ cup golden raisins (10 mg)
  2 green onions (scallions), chopped (9 mg)
  ¼ cup toasted unsalted pine nuts (pignolias) (1.36 mg)
  ½ cup canned unsalted water chestnuts, sliced (3.5 mg)
  ¼ cup toasted unsalted cashews (5.48 mg)
  1 cup bean sprouts (6.24 mg)
  1 medium green pepper, chopped (2.38 mg)
  1 medium celery stalk, sliced diagonally (35 mg)
    Sprinkle of chopped fresh parsley (.4 mg)

THE DRESSING

  ¾ cup orange juice (1.86 mg)
  ½ cup extra-virgin olive oil (trace)
  2 tablespoons sesame oil (0 mg)
  2 tablespoons any white wine (1.27 mg)
  1 lemon, juice (.47 mg)
  2 cloves garlic, minced (1 mg)
  1 teaspoon ground ginger (.584 mg)
    Pepper to taste (trace)

1. Combine the above salad ingredients and chill. Next combine the dressing ingredients and chill until ready to serve. When it's time, toss the salad and dressing and serve.

Calories: 613. Sodium: 15.59 mg. Fiber: 4.3 g. Protein: 9.518 g. Carbohydrate: 78.9 g. Cholesterol: 0 mg. Calcium: 55.9 mg. Iron: 3.143 mg. Potassium: 613.2 mg. Total Fat: 30.2 g; Saturated fat: 4.5 g, Monounsaturated fat: 18.5 g, Polyunsaturated fat: 5.8 g.

❧ Black Bean Salad ❧

SERVES 4 SODIUM PER RECIPE: 48.4 MG SODIUM PER SERVING: 12.1 MG

This one takes a while to prepare because you'll have to cook the dried beans prior to making your salad. You'll need to cook enough to make 20 ounces, or what would otherwise constitute a large can of beans, 3 cups or more.

20 **ounces cooked black beans (5.16 mg)**
2 **small to medium ears sweet white corn, blanched and removed from cobs (21.9 mg)**
1 **medium green bell pepper, seeded and diced (2.38 mg)**
4 **green onions (scallions), cut into ½-inch pieces (9.6 mg)**
1 **white onion, diced (3.3 mg)**
2 **cloves garlic, crushed (1 mg)**
   Zest of 1 lime (1.34 mg)
1 **tablespoon chopped fresh cilantro (2.5 mg)**
3 **tablespoons fresh lime juice (.45 mg)**
¼ **cup cider vinegar (.6 mg)**
1 **tablespoon sesame seed oil (0 mg)**
   Pepper to taste

1. To prepare for the salad, wash black beans, drain. Put beans in 5 to 6 cups of water and bring to a boil. Turn heat down and simmer for 2 hours. Drain and chill in refrigerator for 2 hours. Follow recipe for mixing together ingredients. Combine all the ingredients in large salad bowl. Let it marinate in your refrigerator for 8 hours or more before serving.

Calories: 268. Sodium: 12.1 mg. Fiber: 14.18 g. Protein: 13.8 g. Carbohydrate: 47.1 g. Cholesterol: 0 mg. Calcium: 65.6 mg. Iron: 3.565 mg. Potassium: 750.5 mg. Total Fat: 4.7 g; Saturated fat: 0.8 g, Monounsaturated fat: 1.6 g, Polyunsaturated fat: 2 g.

❧ Pasta Salad ❧

SERVES 6 SODIUM PER RECIPE: 58.8 MG SODIUM PER SERVING: 9.8 MG

THE SALAD MAKINGS
3 **cups dry pasta shapes* (23.9 mg)**
½ **teaspoon olive oil (trace)**
½ **cup chopped zucchini (1.86 mg)**
½ **pound mushrooms, diced (7.36 mg)**
½ **cup chopped broccoli (9.5 mg)**
¼ **cup chopped carrots (11.2 mg)**
1 **tablespoon chopped bell pepper (.186 mg)**

*Use twisted or bow-tie pasta or shells or a mix of any of these.

½ cup Ocean Spray Craisins® (dried sweetened cranberries)
  (.475 mg)*
⅛ teaspoon grated lemon zest (trace)

THE DRESSING (MARINADE)
¼ cup canola oil (0 mg)
3 tablespoons lemon juice (.45 mg)
5 tablespoons red wine vinegar (.75 mg)
2 garlic cloves, minced (1 mg)
½ teaspoon thyme (.3 mg)
½ teaspoon sweet basil (.24 mg)
¼ teaspoon oregano (trace)
½ teaspoon low-sodium Worcestershire sauce (1.32 mg)†
½ teaspoon dry mustard or 1 teaspoon Grey Poupon Honey
  Mustard (2.5 mg)

1. Boil the pasta in water without salt. Add ½ teaspoon of olive oil to keep the water from boiling over the edge of pan. Cook until *al dente* (tender to your touch or bite). Drain. Transfer the pasta to a salad bowl, add the vegetables, Craisins, and lemon zest, then toss well.
2. Whisk the dressing ingredients together, add to the pasta, and toss gently. Chill before serving.

Calories: 177. Sodium: 9.81 mg. Fiber: 1.88 g. Protein: 5.869 g. Carbohydrate: 19.2 g. Cholesterol: 18.05 mg. Calcium: 23.2 mg. Iron: 1.713 mg. Potassium: 261.2 mg. Total Fat: 10.2 g; Saturated fat: 0.9 g, Monounsaturated fat: 5.6 g, Polyunsaturated fat: 3 g.

❖ FRESH FRUIT SALAD ❖

SERVES 8   SODIUM PER RECIPE: 104.9 MG   SODIUM PER SERVING: 13.1 MG
A great summer salad, especially when the weather's hot.

1 medium cantaloupe (49.7 mg)
½ watermelon (45.2 mg)
4 peaches (0 mg)
1 cup strawberries (1.66 mg)—or other favorite berries
1 cup seedless grapes (3.2 mg)
  Juice of 1 lemon (.47 mg)
4 bananas (4.72 mg)

*If dried cranberries not available, use currents or seedless raisins. Add 10 mg sodium for the exchange.
†Life All Natural Worcestershire is a low-sodium brand. Others will be available at your supermarket or health food store. Do not use Lea & Perrins, as it is loaded with sodium.

1. Cut the cantaloupe, watermelon, peaches, and strawberries into bite-size pieces and stir together in a large bowl, along with the grapes. Sprinkle the lemon juice over the fruit. Chill. Add the bananas, sliced, just before serving.

Calories: 212. Sodium: 13.11 mg. Fiber: 5.06 g. Protein: 3.59 g. Carbohydrate: 50.8 g. Cholesterol: 0 mg. Calcium: 41.7 mg. Iron: .994 mg. Potassium: 949.7 mg. Total Fat: 1.9 g; Saturated fat: 0.3 g, Monounsaturated fat: 0.4 g, Polyunsaturated fat: 0.6 g.

❖ MANDARIN-AVOCADO SALAD ❖

SERVES 4   SODIUM PER RECIPE: 37.6 MG   SODIUM PER SERVING: 9.392 MG
When pineapple is available this makes a terrific salad. But beware of the new "Golden" pineapple, which tastes like sugar water. Pineapple is always available in our markets.

> 1 **medium ripe avocado (20.8 mg)**
> 2 **large mandarins* (1.96 mg)**
> 3 **large slices fresh pineapple, peeled and cored† (1.41 mg)**
> 3 **cups shredded romaine lettuce (13.4 mg)**

1. Peel and pit the avocado and dice it. Peel the mandarins, section, and cut each section in half. Cut the pineapple slices into bite-size chunks. Toss and chill the ingredients. Serve on a bed of romaine lettuce.

Calories: 115. Sodium: 9.39 mg. Fiber: 4.24 mg. Protein: 2.053 g. Carbohydrate: 12.4 g. Cholesterol: 0 mg. Calcium: 32 mg. Iron: 1.162 mg. Potassium: 517.7 mg. Total Fat: 7.7 g; Saturated fat: 1.1 g, Monounsaturated fat: 4.9 g, Polyunsaturated fat: 1 g.

❖ AVOCADO VINAIGRETTE WITH DILL ❖

SERVES 4   SODIUM PER RECIPE: 76.3 MG   SODIUM PER SERVING: 19.1 MG
This goes well with oily fish such as salmon or tuna or with a tossed green salad.

> 1 **egg white (54.8 mg)**
> 1 **teaspoon dry mustard mixed with a little water (.15 mg)**
> 1 **tablespoon white wine vinegar (.15 mg)**
> ½ **cup extra-virgin olive oil (trace)**
> ¾ **medium ripe avocado, sliced into 1-inch chunks (15.6 mg)**

*Satsuma mandarins are available fresh during November and December. If fresh mandarins are not available, use tangerines.
†You may use canned pineapple packed in water. The sodium count remains the same. For juice-packed canned pineapple, add about 10 mg sodium per slice to your total.

2 tablespoons chopped fresh or dried dill (2.607 mg)
1 clove garlic, minced (.51 mg)
1 tablespoon chopped green onions (scallions) (2.4 mg)
  Dash of coriander (trace)

1. Combine the egg white, mustard, and vinegar. Whisk in the oil. Add the avocado, dill, garlic, and green onions. Season with salt and a dash of coriander. Serve with salmon or baked chicken, or with a tossed green salad for a delicious vegetarian meal.

Calories: 317. Sodium: 19.07 mg. Fiber: 2.53 g. Protein: 2.418 g. Carbohydrate: 5.205 g. Cholesterol: 0 mg. Calcium: 63 mg. Iron: 1.207 mg. Potassium: 280 mg. Total Fat: 33.4 g; Saturated fat: 4.5 g, Monounsaturated fat: 24 g, Polyunsaturated fat: 3 g.

Aunt Dee Dee's Favorite

❖ Persimmon Salad ❖

SERVES 8   SODIUM PER RECIPE: 12.3 MG   SODIUM PER SERVING: 1.536 MG

Aunt Dee Dee (Margaret Sundell) was born in Leadville, Colorado, at about the time Baby Doe Tabor was guarding the Matchless Mine. At 10,000 feet, with only dirt and gravel roads to connect Leadville with the outside world, salads were a luxury, so this was always a special treat around our house. It still is.

6 2- to 3-inch firm, ripe persimmons, sliced (Fuyu variety)
  (10.1 mg)
  8-ounce can pineapple, drained, packed in juice or water, cut
  into 3-inch pieces (.47 mg)
½ cup or more broken pecan pieces (1 mg)
1 teaspoon cinnamon (.6 mg)

1. Mix all the salad ingredients together and serve chilled.

Calories: 186. Sodium: 1.54 mg. Fiber: 6.06 g. Protein: 1.896 g. Carbohydrate: 27.7 g. Cholesterol: 0 mg. Calcium: 19.4 mg. Iron: .624 mg. Potassium: 263.9 mg. Total Fat: 9.4 g; Saturated fat: 0.8 g, Monounsaturated fat: 5.8 g, Polyunsaturated fat: 2.3 g.

⬧ SAN FRANCISCO FISHERMAN'S WHARF SALAD ⬧

SERVES 6   SODIUM PER RECIPE: 247.8 MG   SODIUM PER SERVING: 62 MG

A summer day on Fisherman's Wharf can be a treat when the crowds aren't too great. The usual crowd pleaser for the one-time visitors are crab salad, crab Waldorf, crab this and crab that. But this one also is served alongside the wharf, where fishing boats roll against the dock with the surge of the incoming tide.

THE SALAD

   3 large, firm apples, cut into bite-size pieces (0 mg)
      Juice of 2 lemons (.94 mg)
   1 large California orange or mandarin (0 mg)
   ¼ cup California golden raisins (4.95 mg)
   1 stalk celery (34.8 mg)
   ½ cup toasted unsalted cashews (11 mg)

THE DRESSING

   1 cup plain yogurt (172 mg)
   1 small, ripe California avocado (20.8 mg)
   ½ teaspoon freshly grated lemon zest (trace)
   4 tablespoons honey (3.36 mg)

1. Soak the apple chunks in half the lemon juice. Combine the remaining lemon juice with the yogurt, avocado, lemon zest, and honey and puree in a blender until smooth. Mix the apples, orange, celery, raisins, and cashews with the pureed dressing and chill until ready to serve.

Calories: 242. Sodium: 41.3 mg. Fiber: 3.71 g. Protein: 5.164 g. Carbohydrate: 35 g. Cholesterol: 2.49 mg. Calcium: 101.9 mg. Iron: 1.354 mg. Potassium: 516.9 mg. Total Fat: 11.2 g; Saturated fat: 2.2 g, Monounsaturated fat: 6.5 g, Polyunsaturated fat: 1.6 g.

NEW YORK, NEW YORK /
⬧ MODIFIED WALDORF SALAD ⬧

SERVES 4   SODIUM PER RECIPE: 236.2 MG   SODIUM PER SERVING: 59.1 MG

Based on the original Waldorf salad, this recipe was created by New York friends who prefer tofu over mayonnaise. So do we. Mayonnaise, by the way, is high in sodium and fats.

THE SALAD

   5 tart apples, such as McIntosh, Macoun, or Cortland (0 mg)
1½ oranges (4.77 mg)
   1 medium stalk celery (34.8 mg)
      Juice of 1 lemon (3.24 mg)
   ⅓ cup seedless golden raisins (6.5 mg)
   ½ cup unsalted roasted or toasted cashews, peanuts, or walnuts
      (11 mg)

THE DRESSING

1 cup plain yogurt (172 mg)
3 tablespoons tofu (2 mg)
Juice of 1 lemon (.47 mg)
3 teaspoons grated lemon zest (.36 mg)
4 teaspoons honey (1 mg)

1. Clean and core the apples, then slice into bite-size pieces. Soak the apples in lemon juice to keep them from turning brown and to add tang to their flavor. Peel the oranges and cut into bite-size pieces. Slice the celery into very small pieces. Put these ingredients in a salad bowl. Add the raisins. Make the lemon zest and set aside for the dressing.
2. Next mix together yogurt, tofu, lemon juice, lemon zest and honey. Pour the dressing over the salad ingredients and toss. Chill and add the nuts prior to serving.

Calories: 341. Sodium: 59.05 mg. Fiber: 10.13 g. Protein: 8.463 g. Carbohydrate: 66.5 g. Cholesterol: 3.74 mg. Calcium: 204.3 mg. Iron: 2.381 mg. Potassium: 745.1 mg. Total Fat: 10.2 g; Saturated fat: 2.4 g, Monounsaturated fat: 5 g, Polyunsaturated fat: 1.6 g.

❖ CRANBERRY RAISIN SALAD ❖

SERVES 4   SODIUM PER RECIPE: 33.6 MG   SODIUM PER SERVING: 8.404 MG
This is a refreshing and delicious salad. You can use a mixed dressing of honey, red wine vinegar, and olive oil, or the dressing recipe given below to make this tasty salad. Chill before serving.

THE SALAD

5 cups chopped romaine (22.4 mg)
¾ cup Ocean Spray Craisins® (dried cranberries) (.825 mg)
1 cup jicama, cut into 1½-inch julienne (5.2 mg)
2 cups fresh mandarin or tangerine sections (3.9 mg)

THE DRESSING

½ cup orange juice with calcium (1.244 mg)
1 teaspoon granulated sugar (trace)
1 tablespoon extra-virgin olive oil (trace)

1. Combine the salad ingredients and chill in the refrigerator for about ½ hour. Combine the dressing ingredients and toss with the salad, then serve.

Calories: 123. Sodium: 8.4 mg. Fiber: 5.95 g. Protein: 2.274 g. Carbohydrate: 22.5 g. Cholesterol: 0 mg. Calcium: 81.9 mg. Iron: 1.148 mg. Potassium: 478.6 mg. Total Fat: 3.8 g; Saturated fat: 0.5 g, Monounsaturated fat: 2.5 g, Polyunsaturated fat: 0.4 g.

❖ AFTERNOON SALAD SNACK ❖

SERVES 1   SODIUM PER RECIPE: 43.6 MG

1 **serving Ranch-Style Salad Dressing, page 211 (29.2 mg)**
1 **serving Grilled Zucchini strips, page 293 (4.845 mg)**
½ **cup broccoli flowerets (9.58 mg)**
  Season to taste with pepper (trace)

1. Prepare the **Ranch-Style Salad Dressing** according to the recipe. Clean the zucchini and grill according to its recipe. Clean the broccoli and partially steam (to very lightly soften). Dip the broccoli in the dressing and munch. You can also dip the grilled zucchini in the dressing. Season with pepper to taste.

Calories: 66. Sodium: 43.59 mg. Fiber: 2.25 g. Protein: 5.466 g. Carbohydrate: 14.4 g. Cholesterol: 3.29 mg. Calcium: 116.6 mg. Iron: 3.24 mg. Potassium: 627.9 mg. Total Fat: 1.1 g; Saturated fat: 0.5 g, Monounsaturated fat: 0.1 g, Polyunsaturated fat: 0.2 g.

❖ OIL AND VINEGAR DRESSING ❖

SERVES 4   SODIUM PER RECIPE: 1.36 MG   SODIUM PER SERVING: .326 MG
A simple dressing used for salads, sandwiches, and sometimes added to meats. Can be stored in the refrigerator for a week.

¼ **cup extra-virgin oil (trace)**
½ **cup red wine vinegar (1.2 mg)**
2 **teaspoons granulated sugar (trace)**

1. Combine the ingredients and shake vigorously before serving.

Calories: 132. Sodium: 0.33 mg. Fiber: 0 g. Cholesterol: 0 mg. Calcium: 1.84 mg. Iron: .233 mg. Potassium: 30 mg. Total Fat: 13.5 g; Saturated fat: 1.8 g, Monounsaturated fat: 9.9 g, Polyunsaturated fat: 1.1 g.

❖ BALSAMIC VINAIGRETTE ❖

MAKES ½ CUP   SODIUM PER ½ CUP: 2.322 MG
SODIUM PER TABLESPOON: .29 MG

2 **tablespoons balsamic vinegar (1.3 mg)**
⅓ **cup extra-virgin olive oil (trace)**
½ **teaspoon East Shore, Grey Poupon, or Mendocino honey mustard (1.75 mg)**
⅛ **teaspoon black pepper (.115 mg)**
  pinch of minced garlic (.127 mg)

1. In a small jar with a tight-fitting lid, combine all the ingredients and shake vigorously. The dressing can be refrigerated for up to 1 week.

Per tablespoon. Calories: 81. Sodium: 0.29 mg. Fiber: 0.01 g. Protein: .031 g. Carbohydrate: .295 g. Cholesterol: 0 mg. Calcium: .554 mg. Iron: 0.68 mg. Potassium: 4.53 mg. Total Fat: 9 g; Saturated fat: 1.2 g, Monounsaturated fat: 6.6 g, Polyunsaturated fat: 0.8 g.

❧ PEPPERCORN VINAIGRETTE ❧

SERVES 6   SODIUM PER RECIPE: 7.377 MG   SODIUM PER SERVING: 1.23 MG
Great with fish.

⅓ cup white wine vinegar (.792 mg)
1 garlic clove, minced (.51 mg)
½ teaspoon dry mustard (0 mg)
1 tablespoon pink peppercorns, crushed (2.816 mg)
1 tablespoon green peppercorns, crushed (2.816 mg)
¼ teaspoon freshly ground black pepper (.231 mg)
1 tablespoon sugar (0 mg)
1 cup extra-virgin olive oil (trace)

1. In a food processor or blender, process all the ingredients except the olive oil for 30 seconds. While the motor is running, add the oil in a very thin stream until emulsified and the vinaigrette thickens. Warm in a saucepan over very low heat to serve over white or pink fish.

Calories: 335. Sodium: 1.23 mg. Fiber: 0.6 g. Protein: .317 g. Carbohydrate: 4.506 g. Cholesterol: 0 mg. Calcium: 11.9 mg. Iron: .877 mg. Potassium: 44.1 mg. Total Fat: 36.1 g; Saturated fat: 4.9 g, Monounsaturated fat: 26.6 g, Polyunsaturated fat: 3.1 g.

❧ ROASTED GARLIC VINAIGRETTE ❧

SERVES 8   SODIUM PER RECIPE: 70.8 MG   SODIUM PER SERVING: 8.55 MG

4 cloves garlic (2 mg)
2 tablespoons finely chopped shallot (2.4 mg)—or substitute the
   white part of green onions (2.4 mg)
⅓ cup rice vinegar* (.72 mg)
1 teaspoon white sugar (trace)
1 tablespoon Hain Stone Ground No Salt Added Mustard (10 mg)
   Pinch of white pepper (trace)
1 egg white (55.4 mg)
1 cup extra-virgin olive oil (trace)

1. Roast the garlic in a 350°F oven until softened and lightly browned. In a food processor or blender, process the shallots, vinegar, sugar, mustard, pepper, and egg white until blended. While the machine is running, add oil in a thin stream until emulsified.† Use as a marinade for wild game birds, chicken, pork roast, or as salad dressing. Use for fowl or pork dishes.

Calories: 256. Sodium: 8.85 mg. Fiber: 0.06 g. Protein: .979 g. Carbohydrate: 2.278 g. Cholesterol: 23.38 mg. Calcium: 7.222 mg. Iron: .31 mg. Potassium: 31 mg. Total Fat: 27.7 g; Saturated fat: 3.8 g, Monounsaturated fat: 20.1 g, Polyunsaturated fat: 2.3 g.

*Use Genuine Brewed only. Other types have high sodium contents.
†If you do not have a processor or blender, mash the garlic in a medium bowl, add the other ingredients except the oil, and whisk in the oil a little at a time until emulsified.

❧ MUSTARD SALAD DRESSING ❧

SERVES 4 **SODIUM PER RECIPE: 3.053 MG** **SODIUM PER SERVING: .763 MG**

For mixed green salads and mixed green salads with fruit.

- 2 **tablespoons red wine vinegar (.3 mg)**
- 1 **tablespoon dry or ground mustard seed (.51 mg)**
- 1 **tablespoon honey (.84 mg)**
- ½ **cup extra-virgin olive oil (trace)**
- ¼ **cup toasted pine nuts (1.36 mg) (optional)**

1. Combine the vinegar, mustard seed, honey, and oil. Toss with salad greens and top with pine nuts (from China).

Calories: 317. Sodium: 0.7 mg. Fiber: 0.8 g. Protein: 2.754 g. Carbohydrate: 6.955 g. Cholesterol: 0 mg. Calcium: 17.6 mg. Iron: 1.231 mg. Potassium: 80.3 mg. Total Fat: 32.1 g; Saturated fat: 4.3 g, Monounsaturated fat: 22.1 g, Polyunsaturated fat: 4.2 g.

❧ HONEY AND MUSTARD DRESSING ❧

MAKES ½ CUP **SODIUM PER RECIPE: 19.2 MG** **SODIUM PER SERVING: 4.8 MG**

This is good with a variety of salad lettuce.

- 1 **large shallot, minced (2.4 mg)**
- 1 **tablespoon low-sodium East Shore, Grey Poupon, or Mendocino honey mustard (15 mg)**
- 2 **tablespoons red wine vinegar (.3 mg)**
- 1 **tablespoon honey (.84 mg)**
- 2 **tablespoons extra-virgin olive oil (trace)**
- 1 **tablespoon water (0 mg)**
- ¾ **teaspoon coarse cracked black pepper (.63 mg)**

1. Combine ingredients, mix and serve.

Calories: 89. Sodium: 4.81 mg. Fiber: 0.11 g. Protein: .127 g. Carbohydrate: 6.799 g. Cholesterol: 0 mg. Calcium: 4.346 mg. Iron: .391 mg. Potassium: 31.9 mg. Total Fat: 6.8 g; Saturated fat: 0.9 g, Monounsaturated fat: 5 g, Polyunsaturated fat: 0.6 g.

❧ RANCH-STYLE SALAD DRESSING ❧

MAKES ¾ CUP **SODIUM PER RECIPE: 116.6 MG**
SODIUM PER SERVING: 29.2 MG

You can't replace the heavy salt (sodium) flavor of commercial ranch-style dressing. Significant ingredients of these commercial varieties are salt and MSG. After a few experiments, we came up with this recipe. We call it ranch-style although it can also work, with a change of spices, as a general "creamy" salad dressing or sandwich spread.

½ (8-ounce) container plain yogurt (79.7 mg)
  Juice of 1 lemon (.47 mg)
1 tablespoon garlic powder (2.12 mg)
½ tablespoon onion powder (1.74 mg)
2 teaspoons Frontier "dash o' dill"* (0 mg)
4 tablespoons cultured buttermilk†
  Black pepper to taste (trace)

1. Combine all the ingredients, stir, and chill.

Per serving: Calories: 34. Sodium: 29.1 mg. Fiber: 0.31 g. Protein: 2.535 g. Carbohydrate: 7.835 g. Cholesterol: 3.29 mg. Calcium: 57.4 mg. Iron: 2.255 mg. Potassium: 112 mg. Total fat: 0.8 g; Saturated fat: 0.5 g, Monounsaturated fat: 0.1 g, Polyunsaturated fat: 0 g.

❈ CREATIVE SALAD DRESSING ❈

MAKES 1 CUP   SODIUM PER RECIPE: 27.9 MG
SODIUM PER TABLESPOON: 1.73 MG

This is one you can play with. Adjust the quantities of one or all of the ingredients until you get the flavor you like the best. Be sure the sodium count is within your limits. Add walnuts or raisins or onion slices to make it even more exciting.

½ cup white balsamic vinegar (1.2 mg)
½ cup extra-virgin olive oil (trace)
¼ cup packed brown sugar (21.5 mg)
1 tablespoon chopped fresh rosemary (.44 mg)
4 cloves garlic, minced (2 mg)
  Juice of 1 fresh lemon (.47 mg)
¼ cup dried cranberries (Ocean Spray Craisins®) (2.25 mg)

1. Combine all the ingredients in a food processor, blend, store in the refrigerator.

Calories: 82. Sodium: 1.74 mg. Fiber: 0.14 g. Protein: .062 g. Carbohydrate: 5.858 g. Cholesterol: 0 mg. Calcium: 5.284 mg. Iron: .157 mg. Potassium: 26.8 mg. Total Fat: 6.8 g; Saturated fat: 0.9 g, Monounsaturated fat: 5 g, Polyunsaturated fat: 0.6 g.

*Frontier products are available at your local market or at the Web site www.healthyheartmarket.com or by calling 1-800/753-0310.
†Make sure you use a low-sodium buttermilk such as Knudsen or one that lists about 130 mg sodium per cup.

QUICK BREADS

❖ ❖ ❖ ❖ ❖ ❖ ❖ ❖

❖ WHOLE WHEAT PANCAKES ❖

MAKES 12 PANCAKES   SODIUM PER RECIPE: 229 MG
SODIUM PER SERVING: 19.1 MG

These whip up very well on a camping trip. Crisp morning air, the sounds of a stream nearby, the smell of fresh ground coffee, and your Coleman stove sizzling with pancakes—it can't get much better. Bring along genuine maple syrup for a real treat.

   1 cup whole wheat flour (6 mg)
1¼ cups nonfat milk (162.5 mg)
   1 medium egg (55.4 mg)
   1 teaspoon Featherweight baking powder* (2 mg)
   1 tablespoon granulated sugar (trace)
 ½ teaspoon cinnamon (trace)
   Grated zest of 1 orange (.18 mg)
   Olive oil as needed for frying (trace)

1. Combine all the ingredients, mixing with a wooden spoon until smooth. Ladle batter onto a hot griddle or into a nonstick frying pan with a touch of olive oil set over medium-high heat. Cook until brown on both sides. Allow 2 pancakes per person. Serve with pure or "natural" maple syrup (1.8 mg per tablespoon).

Calories: 54. Sodium: 19.09 mg. Protein: 2.673 g. Carbohydrate: 9.98 g. Fiber: 1.33 g. Cholesterol: 16.1 mg. Calcium: 28.4 mg. Iron: .516 mg. Potassium: 88.6 mg. Total Fat: 0.6 g; Saturated fat: .1 g, Monounsaturated fat: .2 g, Polyunsaturated fat: .1 g.

❖ BECKY'S OATMEAL PANCAKES ❖

MAKES 14 PANCAKES   SODIUM PER RECIPE: 281.38 MG
SODIUM PER PANCAKE: 20.1 MG

Easy to make, tasty as they come, these pancakes come to us from a river-rafting guide who makes these for her guests.

1¼ cups nonfat milk (or low-fat, low-sodium buttermilk) (157.7 mg)
   1 cup rolled oats (2.34 mg)
   2 medium eggs, beaten (110.9 mg)

½ cup whole wheat flour (3 mg)
1 tablespoon brown sugar (3.51 mg)
1 tablespoon extra virgin olive oil (trace)
1 teaspoon cinnamon (.6 mg)
1 orange, grated skin only (.36 mg)
1 teaspoon Featherweight baking powder (2 mg)
1 cup Quick applesauce (.861 mg)

This recipe will make a thick pancake. If you prefer thinner or lighter pancakes, add ¼ cup or slightly more of orange juice or water.
1. Combine milk and oats in a bowl and let stand for 5 minutes. Add oil and eggs and mix well. Stir in the flour, sugar, and baking powder. Mix until the ingredients are just moistened. Bake on hot greased griddle using ¼ cup batter for each pancake.

Calories: 77. Sodium: 20.09 mg. Protein: 2.616 g. Carbohydrate: 13 g. Fiber: 1.59 g. Cholesterol: 27.11 mg. Calcium: 39.7 mg. Iron: .548 mg. Potassium: 99.1 mg. Total Fat: 2 g, Saturated fat: 0.4 g; Monounsaturated fat: 1 g, Polyunsaturated fat: 0.3 g.

❈ CORNMEAL CRÊPES ❈

MAKES 12 (8-INCH) CRÊPES   SODIUM PER RECIPE: 386.1 MG
SODIUM PER SERVING: 32.2 MG
*Crêpes are made basically the same way worldwide, with few variations. These Mexican-style crêpes make a great breakfast with toppings such as **Caramelized Apples** or fresh fruits and syrup. Use them at lunchtime as you would a tortilla.*

1½ cups nonfat or low-fat no-salt-added buttermilk (195 mg)
3 large eggs (189 mg)
½ cup best for bread flour (1.25 mg)
⅔ cup Albers yellow cornmeal (.8 mg)
1 teaspoon granulated sugar (trace)
1 tablespoon olive oil (trace)
Additional olive oil for cooking crêpes (trace)

1. Put all the ingredients into a blender or food processor and process until mixed well. Pour the mixture into a bowl. Because cornmeal will settle to the bottom of the bowl, stir before making each crêpe.
2. Brush an 8-inch nonstick skillet or crêpe pan with oil and heat over medium-high heat. Pour 2 to 4 tablespoons of batter into the pan and tilt the pan to spread the batter thinly over the surface. Drain the extra batter back into the bowl. Cook until set. Turn the crêpe with a spatula and cook for about a minute or until light brown marks appear on the bottom. Re-

move the crêpe to a plate and fold into quarters. Do the same with the rest of the batter. Serve hot with **Caramelized Apples** (page 361) or **Fruit Compote** (page 363).

Calories: 80. Sodium: 32.18 mg. Protein: 3.612 g. Carbohydrate: 11.5 g. Fiber: 0.27 g. Cholesterol: 56.25 mg. Calcium: 7.05 mg. Iron: 4.775 mg. Potassium: 26.9 mg. Total Fat: 3.1 g; Saturated fat: 0.9 g, Monounsaturated fat: 1.3 g, Polyunsaturated fat: 0.3 g.

❈ RUSSIAN BLINIS ❈

SERVES 4   SODIUM PER RECIPE: 149.2 MG   SODIUM PER SERVING: 37.3 MG
While filming in Helsinki, Finland, in 1978, my crew and I were under constant surveillance by Russian agents. At that time, Finland was a major "open door" for Russian agents to get into the free world. After about four days of the crew becoming somewhat nervous, I approached the two agents who, it turned out, spoke English very well. They had been assigned to keep an eye on the American film crew, ostensibly in case we were U.S. agents. I invited them to join us for the filming, to see that we weren't anything more than what we appeared to be. After a day with us, they invited us to dinner across the border. Only one of the crew would go with me. It turned out to be an experience I will never forget. It was my first blinis, my first and only time behind the Iron Curtain, and I had no problems or regrets. We ate in a small, austere, and extremely dark and quiet Russian restaurant. The best I can do to duplicate that meal follows.

2 teaspoons active dry yeast (3.96 mg)
1 cup lukewarm water (0 mg)
1 cup nonfat milk (126.2 mg)
2 bananas, mashed (1.2 mg)
¾ cup whole wheat bread flour (4.5 mg)
1 cup buckwheat flour (13.2 mg)
1½ teaspoons extra-virgin olive oil (trace)

1. Dissolve yeast in lukewarm water (about 100°) in a large bowl for about 5 minutes. Combine the milk, bananas, and flour with the yeast and mix well. Let the bowl sit in warm place for about 1 hour. Heat the oil on a large nonstick griddle set over medium heat. Using a cup, pour mix to make only 4 "pancakes." Don't permit them to touch each other. You might have to make only 1 or 2 at a time, depending on size of your griddle or frypan. Cook each for 5 minutes. Flip and cook for another 4 minutes. Serve warm as a main dish with **Fruit Compote** (page 363) or with chopped, steamed, or creamed vegetables. (The Russians served them to us with chopped onions, caviar, chopped garlic, and chopped zucchini, laid out to divide the top of the blini in quarters.)

Calories: 246. Sodium: 37.25 mg. Protein: 10 g. Carbohydrate: 48.1 g. Fiber: 6.87 g. Cholesterol: 1.1 mg. Calcium: 98.6 mg. Iron: 4.542 mg. Potassium: 522.1 mg. Total Fat: 3.4 g; Saturated fat: 0.6 g, Monounsaturated fat: 1.7 g, Polyunsaturated fat: 0.6 g.

❈ PANCAKE À LA POPOVER ❈

SERVES 8   SODIUM PER RECIPE: 507.3 MG   SODIUM PER SERVING: 63.4 MG*
*This is essentially the **Popover** recipe cooked differently to make a breakfast pancake. It's not your normal pancake, but it makes a great replacement since it doesn't need baking powder or baking soda. You can also use this with prime rib or cross-rib roast of beef to simulate Beef Wellington.*

THE POPOVER PANCAKE
   ½ **tablespoon extra-virgin olive oil (trace)**
   3 **large eggs (189 mg)**
2½ **cups lukewarm nonfat milk (315.4 mg)**
   ⅔ **cup best for bread flour (1.65 mg)**

SUGGESTED PANCAKE FILLING
   2 **cups fresh berries† (4 mg)**
   ½ **cup sifted confectioners' sugar (1 mg)**

1. Preheat the oven to 450°F.
2. Set a rack at the lower third of the oven. Prepare a large nonstick oven-safe skillet by heating the oil until warm.
3. Beat eggs on high speed with an electric beater or in the blender for about 1 minute. Don't overbeat. Add milk and flour and continue beating for another minute, or until blended and foamy. Pour the mixture into your prepared skillet. (I use a 12-inch roaster pan.) Put in the oven and bake for 20 minutes. Reduce the heat to 350°F and continue baking for another 10 minutes, or until golden brown and puffed up. The edges will show some dark brown after about 15 minutes of baking. This is normal. You will have to continue baking for the full length of time to make sure center is done. Sprinkle the pancake with the berry mixture, dust with powdered sugar, and serve.

Calories: 170. Sodium: 63.41 mg. Fiber: 1.23 g. Protein: 6.268 g. Carbohydrate: 29.3 g. Cholesterol: 81.07 mg. Calcium: 105.4 mg. Iron: .791 mg. Potassium: 160.8 mg. Total Fat: 3.1 g; Saturated fat: 0.8 g, Monounsaturated fat: 1.4 g, Polyunsaturated fat: 0.4 g.

*Based on 8 servings. You could get 10 servings with a slightly larger roaster pan.
†You can use strawberries, raspberries, blackberries, Logan berries, or blueberries. You can also substitute frozen, unsalted berries for the fresh.

WHOLE WHEAT WAFFLES
❖ WITH ORANGE JUICE ❖

MAKES 3 ROUND WAFFLES   SODIUM PER RECIPE: 103.6 MG
SODIUM PER SERVING: 34.5 MG

You can make these crispy or full-bodied. Note the added calcium to this recipe. If you want a fluffier, full-bodied waffle, add ½ teaspoon Featherweight Baking Powder.

½ cup best for bread flour (1.25 mg)
½ cup best for bread whole wheat flour (3 mg)
⅓ teaspoon ground cinnamon (.2 mg)
1 tablespoon granulated sugar (.12 mg)
½ teaspoon Featherweight Baking Powder (1 mg)
1 medium egg, separated (55.4 mg)
⅓ cup orange juice with calcium (.821 mg)
2 tablespoons unsalted or Homemade Applesauce, page 360
   (.954 mg)
⅓ cup nonfat milk (41.6 mg)
Nonstick cooking spray to oil wafflemaker (trace)

1. In a large mixing bowl, sift together the flours, cinnamon, and sugar. If you're going to use the Featherweight Baking Powder, then add it here. Next add the egg yolk, orange juice, applesauce, and nonfat milk and beat to make a smooth batter. In another bowl, whisk or beat the egg white until it forms stiff peaks. Fold this into the batter. When ready, lightly spray oil on the waffle grid and pour ½ cup or slightly more of the batter. Press down to spread the batter around and then cook as usual.

Calories: 214. Sodium: 34.54 mg. Protein: 7.888 g. Carbohydrate: 41.9 g. Fiber: 3.53 g. Cholesterol: 62.82 mg. Calcium: 90.3 mg. Iron: 2.144 mg. Potassium: 229.7 mg. Total Fat: 2.1 g; Saturated fat: 0.6 g, Monounsaturated fat: 0.6 g, Polyunsaturated fat: 0.5 g.

ORANGE ZEST WAFFLES
❖ WITH CINNAMON APPLESAUCE TOPPING ❖

MAKES 3 ROUND WAFFLES   SODIUM PER RECIPE: 92.3 MG
SODIUM PER SERVING: 30.8 MG

You'll get compliments galore with this recipe. You can easily double or triple it for a crowd.

THE WAFFLE
1 cup best for bread flour (2.5 mg)
1 teaspoon vanilla sugar (.378 mg)
⅓ teaspoon ground cinnamon (.2 mg)
1 medium egg, separated (55.4 mg)

1 tablespoon grated orange zest (.36 mg)
¾ cup orange juice with calcium (1.866 mg)
¼ cup nonfat milk (31.5 mg)
   Nonstick cooking spray to oil the waffle maker (trace)

THE TOPPING*
   1 cup Quick or Homemade Applesauce, page 360 (7.65 mg)
   Juice of 1 orange (.86 mg)

1. In a medium to large mixing bowl, sift together the flour, sugar, and cinnamon. Separate the egg (save the white) and add egg yolk, orange peel gratings (zest), orange juice, and nonfat milk and beat to make a smooth batter. In another bowl, whisk the egg white until it forms stiff peaks. Fold this into the batter. When ready, lightly spray oil on the waffle grid and pour ½ cup or slightly more of the batter on it. Press down to spread the batter around and then cook as usual.

2. To prepare the topping, combine the applesauce and the orange juice and heat over low heat, stirring occasionally. Serve the waffles with the topping.

Calories: 217. Sodium: 30.76 mg. Protein: 7.326 g. Carbohydrate: 41 g. Fiber: 1.81 g. Cholesterol: 62.7 mg. Calcium: 123.6 mg. Iron: 2.345 mg. Potassium: 226.1 mg. Total Fat: 2 g; Saturated fat: 0.6 g, Monounsaturated fat: 0.6 g, Polyunsaturated fat: 0.4 g.

❖ SOURDOUGH BELGIAN WAFFLES ❖

MAKES 12 (4-INCH X 4-INCH) BELGIAN WAFFLES
MAKES 6 LARGE (8-INCH DIAMETER) ROUND WAFFLES
MAKES 18 PANCAKES   SODIUM PER RECIPE: 232.9 MG
SODIUM PER SERVING: 16.3 MG

   1 cup whole wheat flour (6 mg)
   1 cup best for bread flour (2.5 mg)
   ½ cup sourdough starter, room temperature (trace)
1½ cups lukewarm 2% buttermilk[†] (195 mg)
   ½ cup orange juice fortified with calcium (1.244 mg)
   3 egg yolks (21.4 mg)
   ¼ cup Homemade Applesauce, page 360, or unsalted applesauce
      (1.912 mg)
   2 tablespoons granulated white sugar (trace)
   1 teaspoon Featherweight Baking Powder (4.5 mg)
      Nonstick olive oil spray for pancakes (trace)

*Optional. Warm natural maple syrup is also a great accompaniment. Add 1.8 mg sodium per tablespoon.
[†]Make sure you use a brand of buttermilk that has only 130 mg sodium per cup listed on the "Nutritional Facts" label. If it is not available, substitute 2¼ cups nonfat milk mixed with 2 tablespoons white vinegar or lemon juice.

1. In a large bowl, combine the wheat and white flours, sourdough starter, orange juice, and buttermilk. Beat until blended. Cover and let stand at room temperature for about 45 minutes—this is necessary.

2. Beat together the egg yolks and applesauce. Add this to the flour mixture and stir or beat until blended. Stir the sugar and baking powder into the batter, then let it stand for 5 minutes. (For crispier waffles or pancakes, leave the baking powder out or cut it in half.)

3. For standard waffles, preheat the electric waffle iron, add the batter, and bake until browned. You may let the waffles cool down and then freeze them for later use. Make between 4 and 6 round waffles or a dozen smaller square waffles. You can also use a Belgian waffle maker.

4. If making pancakes instead of waffles, replace buttermilk and orange juice with 1 cup nonfat milk when preparing the original mix. Drop the batter by large spoonfuls onto a medium-hot greased griddle. Lightly spritz with nonstick olive oil spray. Heat until browned on both sides. Makes 24 small pancakes (about 3 inches to 4 inches in diameter).

Per Belgian waffle: Calories: 110. Sodium: 19.41 mg. Protein: 4.367 g. Carbohydrate: 21.1 g. Fiber: 1.6 g. Cholesterol: 56.29 mg. Calcium: 77.5 mg. Iron: 5.389 mg. Potassium: 120.8 mg. Total Fat: 2.2 g; Saturated fat: 0.8 g, Monounsaturated fat: 0.5 g, Polyunsaturated fat: 0.3 g.

Per Standard waffle. Calories: 220. Sodium: 38.81 mg. Fiber: 3.2 g. Cholesterol: 112.57 mg. Protein: 8.734 g. Carbohydrate: 42.3 g. Calcium: 155 mg. Iron: 10.8 mg. Potassium: 241.7 mg. Total Fat: 4.4 g; Saturated fat: 1.6 g, Monounsaturated fat: 1 g, Polyunsaturated fat: 0.6 g.

Per Pancake. Calories: 74. Sodium: 16.27 mg. Fiber: 1.05 g. Cholesterol: 37.07 mg. Protein: 3.079 g. Carbohydrate: 13.7 g. Calcium: 52.1 mg. Iron: 2.639 mg. Potassium: 90 mg. Total Fat: 1.4 g; Saturated fat: 0.5 g, Monounsaturated fat: 0.4 g, Polyunsaturated fat: 0.2 g.

❖ FRENCH TOAST ❖

SERVES 6   SODIUM PER RECIPE: 179.5 MG   SODIUM PER SERVING: 29.9 MG

A standard slice of French toast can contain as much as 300 to 350 mg of sodium. Ours has only 30 mg and tastes just as great. You'll have to make your own bread first, or buy one of those salt-free, fat-free breads in the health food section of your market.

  2 **medium eggs (110.9 mg)**
 ½ **cup nonfat milk (63.1 mg)**
  6 **pieces Italian Milano bread, page 247 (4.936 mg)***
  1 **teaspoon vanilla extract (trace)**
  1 **tablespoon extra-virgin olive oil (trace)**
  2 **tablespoons confectioners' sugar (.15 mg)**
     Dash of ground cinnamon (trace)

1. Beat the eggs, milk, and vanilla together. Oil a nonstick pan or griddle and heat to medium-high. Dip the bread into the egg mixture and add the

*Bake any of our homemade white breads, cut into ¼-inch to ¾-inch slices— ¾-inch slices will produce only 3 pieces of French Toast. **Italian Milano** works incredibly well.

slices to the hot pan or griddle. If necessary, you can stretch the egg mixture by adding another ¼ cup of milk. (If you add the milk, remember it adds 32.5 mg sodium per ¼ cup.) Grill the bread slices until golden brown on both sides. Sprinkle with powdered sugar and a dash of cinnamon.

Note: If you like syrup with your French Toast, use only natural maple syrup, not syrups whose nutrition labels show sodium present. Berry syrups are generally okay.

Calories: 162. Sodium: 29.92 mg. Protein: 5.359 g. Carbohydrate: 25.2 g. Fiber: 0.83 g. Cholesterol: 62.7 mg. Calcium: 37.2 mg. Iron: 1.941 mg. Potassium: 91.3 mg. Total Fat: 4 g: Saturated fat: 0.8 g, Monounsaturated fat: 2.3 g, Polyunsaturated fat: 0.5 g.

❈ OAT BRAN AND JAM MUFFINS ❈

SERVES 12   SODIUM PER RECIPE: 249.3 MG   SODIUM PER SERVING: 20.8 MG
This recipe came from a friend of mine, a well-known writer who has had bypass surgery and must stick to a low-fat, low-sodium diet. A regular bran muffin will have between 350 and 500 mg of sodium. These have only 20 mg of sodium and are very tasty.

2¼ cups oat bran (8.46 mg)
 ¼ cup packed brown sugar (21.5 mg)
  1 tablespoon Featherweight Baking Powder (6 mg)
  1 teaspoon granulated white sugar (trace)
  2 teaspoons ground cinnamon (1 mg)
  2 medium egg whites (110.9 mg)
 ½ cup nonfat milk (63.7 mg)
 ¾ cup apple juice concentrate (25.1 mg)
  2 tablespoons no-salt applesauce* (.954 mg)
 12 heaping teaspoons all-fruit or low-sugar jam or jelly of your
      choice† (2.16 mg)

1. Preheat the oven to 425°F. Insert paper baking cups in your muffin pans. Mix together the oat bran, brown sugar, baking powder, granulated sugar, and cinnamon, then stir in the milk, egg whites, and apple juice concentrate until smooth. Half-fill the muffin cups—you will have enough batter left to cover the jam layer. To each muffin add 1 heaping teaspoon jam, then cover with more batter until topped. Bake for 15 to 16 minutes. Allow the muffins to cool in the pan for about 10 minutes, then remove and cool completely. The muffins now can be refrigerated or frozen.

Calories: 120. Sodium: 20.8 mg. Protein: 4.452 g. Carbohydrate: 28.4 g. Fiber: 3.33 g. Cholesterol: 31.37 mg. Calcium: 92.7 mg. Iron: 1.537 mg. Potassium: 327.6 mg. Total Fat: 2.1 g: Saturated fat: 0.5 g, Monounsaturated fat: 0.7 g, Polyunsaturated fat: 0.6 g.

*Use our **Quick Applesauce** or any canned or bottled no-salt applesauce.
†Blueberry or strawberry jam make the best. But any jam or jelly will do. Many jams have fewer milligrams of sodium.

My Favorite Pumpkin Muffin
❈ À la Orange ❈

MAKES 12   SODIUM PER RECIPE: 160.5 MG   SODIUM PER SERVING: 13.4 MG
Great with strawberry jam.

  2 **medium eggs (110.9 mg)**
  ¾ **cup granulated sugar (0 mg)**
  ¼ **cup extra-virgin olive oil (trace)**
  ½ **cup apple juice (8.6 mg)**
  1 **cup Libby's No Salt Added Pumpkin (12.2 mg)***
  ⅔ **cup packed golden raisins (13.3 mg)†**
  2 **tablespoons orange zest, grated (.18 mg)**
  2 **cups best for bread flour (5 mg)**
  1 **tablespoon Featherweight Baking Powder (6 mg)**
  ¼ **teaspoon ground cinnamon (trace)**
  ¼ **teaspoon ground mace (trace)**
  ¼ **teaspoon ground cloves (1.2 mg)**
  ½ **cup walnuts or pecans, chopped (.6 mg)**

1. Preheat the oven to 400°F.
2. Combine the eggs, sugar, oil, apple juice, pumpkin, raisins, and orange zest, whisking until mixed well. In a separate bowl mix together the flour, baking powder, cinnamon, cloves, and pecans. With a wooden spoon, combine all the ingredients until well mixed. Pour the batter into greased and floured muffin cups. Bake in the preheated oven for 20 to 25 minutes. Cool and serve.

Calories: 265. Sodium: 13.37 mg. Protein: 4.897 g. Carbohydrate: 44 g. Fiber: 1.89 g. Cholesterol: 31.17 mg. Calcium: 33.4 mg. Iron: 1.763 mg. Potassium: 183.5 mg. Total Fat: 8.5 g. Saturated fat: 1.1 g. Monounsaturated fat: 4.3 g. Polyunsaturated fat: 2.5 g.

*Other brands may have higher sodium levels.
†The sodium level can vary depending on the brand. Read nutrition label to find out the exact count.

❈ CRANBERRY WHOLE WHEAT MUFFINS ❈

MAKES 12   SODIUM PER RECIPE: 299.5 MG   SODIUM PER MUFFIN: 25 MG
*Another treat for the Thanksgiving holidays. It's also terrific made
with blueberries—then it's a blueberry muffin!*

2 **medium eggs (110.9 mg)**
¾ **cup loosely packed brown sugar (42.4 mg)**
½ **cup canola oil* (0 mg)**
1 **cup nonfat milk (126.2 mg)**
   Zest of 1 orange, grated (.36 mg)
2 **cups best for bread whole wheat flour (12 mg)**
1 **tablespoon Featherweight Baking Powder (6 mg)**
1½ **cups Ocean Spray cranberries chopped (1.5 mg)**
½ **cup chopped pecans (.6 mg)**

1. Preheat the oven to 400°F.
2. Whisk together the eggs, brown sugar, oil, milk, and orange zest. In a
separate bowl combine the flour, baking powder, cranberries, and pecans.
Blend together until well mixed. Pour the batter into slightly greased and
floured muffin cups. Bake in the preheated oven for 20 to 25 minutes.
Cool and serve.

*Calories: 225. Sodium: 24.96 mg. Protein: 4.602 g. Carbohydrate: 27.2 g. Fiber: 3.26 g.
Cholesterol: 31.53 mg. Calcium: 46.6 mg. Iron: 1.146 mg. Potassium: 174.3 mg. Total Fat:
11.8 g; Saturated fat: 1.1 g, Monounsaturated fat: 6.6 g, Polyunsaturated fat: 3.3 g.*

❈ ORANGE BANANA MUFFINS ❈

MAKES 12   SODIUM PER RECIPE: 21.7 MG   SODIUM PER MUFFIN: 1.8 MG

1 **orange (0 mg)**
3 **ripe bananas (4.5 mg)**
1 **teaspoon vanilla extract (0 mg)**
½ **cup granulated white sugar (1 mg)**
⅓ **cup orange juice fortified with calcium (.81 mg)**
1½ **cups best for bread flour (3.75 mg)**
4 **teaspoons Featherweight Baking Powder (8 mg)**
¾ **cup chopped walnuts or pecans (1 mg)**

1. Preheat the oven to 400°F.
2. Completely puree an entire orange (including the peel) in a blender or
food processor along with the bananas, vanilla extract, sugar, and orange
juice.

*If you really "love" cranberries, replace the oil with homemade **Ocean Spray®
Cranberry Sauce** (page 303) or Ocean Spray® cranberry sauce. This will cut your
fat-per-muffin count in half.

3. Sift together the flour and baking powder and add to the wet ingredients. Add the nuts and stir together until just mixed. Grease 12 muffin cups lightly and evenly and dust well with flour since the muffins have no shortening in them and would otherwise stick to the metal or paper cups. Pour the batter into the muffin cups and bake in the preheated oven for 20 to 25 minutes. Serve hot or reheated.

Calories: 216. Sodium: 1.81 mg. Protein: 4.888 g. Carbohydrate: 37.6 g. Fiber: 2.59 g. Cholesterol: 0 mg. Calcium: 24.6 mg. Iron: 1.245 mg. Potassium: 330.6 mg. Total Fat: 6.3 g; Saturated fat: 0.5 g, Monounsaturated fat: 1.4 g, Polyunsaturated fat: 4 g.

◈ MILDRED'S OATMEAL MACAROON MUFFINS ◈

MAKES 12   SODIUM PER RECIPE: 213.1 MG   SODIUM PER MUFFIN: 17.8 MG

  1 **cup buttermilk (130 mg)**
  1 **cup rolled oats (3.24 mg)**
  1 **cup best for bread flour (2.5 mg)**
1½ **teaspoons Featherweight Baking Powder (3 mg)**
  ½ **cup Quick Applesauce, page 359 (.431 mg)***
  1 **egg (55.4 mg)**
  ½ **cup granulated white sugar (1 mg)**
  ⅓ **cup packed currants (3.8 mg)**
  ¾ **cup shredded unsalted coconut (11.5 mg)**

1. Preheat oven to 400°F.
2. Heat the buttermilk slowly over low heat and then pour it over the oats. Let sit for 10 minutes. Sift together the flour and baking powder. In a separate bowl mix the applesauce and the egg, then the sugar, currants, and coconut. Combine all the ingredients and stir just enough to moisten. Grease 12 muffin or paper cups and dust well with flour since the muffins have no shortening and would otherwise stick to the metal or paper cups. Pour the batter into the muffin cups. *Optional:* Add a dab of preserves in the center of each muffin and cover with a dab of dough before cooking. Bake in the preheated oven for 20 minutes. Serve warm or room temperature.

Calories: 153. Sodium: 17.76 mg. Protein: 3.69 g. Carbohydrate: 30.6 g. Fiber: 1.73 g. Cholesterol: 17.67 mg. Calcium: 11.5 mg. Iron: 3.893 mg. Potassium: 99.5 mg. Total Fat: 2.9 g; Saturated fat: 1.8 g, Monounsaturated fat: 0.4 g, Polyunsaturated fat: 0.3 g.

With unsalted butter instead of Quick Applesauce. Calories: 174. Sodium: 18.24 mg. Protein: 3.705 g. Carbohydrate: 27.2 g. Fiber: 1.38 g. Cholesterol: 28.02 mg. Calcium: 34.9 mg. Iron: 3.852 mg. Potassium: 87 mg. Total Fat: 6.7 g; Saturated fat: 4.2 g, Monounsaturated fat: 1.5 g, Polyunsaturated fat: 0.4 g.

*May use ¼ cup unsalted butter instead (6.242 mg) (see nutrient data below).

❖ SOUR CREAM COFFEE CAKE ❖

SERVES 12   SODIUM PER RECIPE: 219.2 MG   SODIUM PER SERVING: 18.3 MG
A fattening treat but one low in sodium. If you are on a low-fat diet, this will be all the fat you'll want to include in your day's total. If fat is not a problem for you, enjoy the cake without guilt.

THE COFFEE CAKE

  1 teaspoon unsalted butter, softened (.515 mg)
  1 cup Quick Applesauce, page 359 (.5 mg)*
1¼ cups granulated sugar (1 mg)
  2 medium eggs, well beaten (110.9 mg)
  1 cup any reduced-fat sour cream (98 mg)
  1 teaspoon vanilla extract (.4 mg)
  2 cups unbleached white flour (5 mg)
  1 teaspoon Featherweight Baking Powder (2 mg)
  1 tablespoon confectioners' sugar (.08 mg)

THE TOPPING

½ cup finely chopped unsalted nuts (.6 mg)
½ teaspoon ground cinnamon (.3 mg)
½ cup sugar (.5 mg)

1. Preheat the oven to 350°F.

2. Cream the butter, applesauce, and sugar, then add the beaten eggs, sour cream, and vanilla and mix well. Sift together the flour and baking powder then stir them into the mixture and beat well. If the mixture becomes too thick to beat, stir with a wooden spoon until it is smooth and well combined.

3. To make the topping, combine the nuts, cinnamon, and sugar and mix well. If the quantity is not enough for layering, make a second batch.

4. Pour the batter into a lightly greased baking pan or springform pan in increments. Start with one thin layer, then some topping, then another layer, more topping, and a final layer, then cap off with topping. Bake for 1 hour. When done, sprinkle powdered sugar on top. Cool before serving.

Calories: 203. Sodium: 18.34 mg. Protein: 4.975 g. Carbohydrate: 31.3 g. Fiber: 1.4 g. Cholesterol: 39.79 mg. Calcium: 34.3 g. Iron: .489 g. Potassium: 107.8 g. Total Fat: 6.7 g. Saturated fat: 2.2 g. Monounsaturated fat: 1.8 g. Polyunsaturated fat: 2.3 g.

*You can replace the applesauce with unsalted butter or you can use ½ cup applesauce and ½ cup unsalted butter. The butter will increase the saturated fat content by 57 grams per ½ cup.

❧ Lemon and Currant Scones ❧

MAKES 12 LARGE SCONES   SODIUM PER RECIPE: 142.1 MG
SODIUM PER SERVING: 11.8 MG

From my mother's recipe book, dated 1948. The original recipe called for salt and standard baking powder. Those scones had 390 mg sodium each, while these have only 11.7 mg. They are healthier and just as tasty, although you won't taste the heavy salt and baking soda flavor you get with standard scones.

2 cups best for bread flour (5 mg)
2 teaspoons Featherweight Baking Powder (4 mg)
2 tablespoons plus 2 teaspoons granulated sugar (.35 mg)
¼ cup unsalted butter, softened (6.248 mg)
¼ cup Quick Applesauce, page 359 (.109 mg)
2 eggs, separated (123.9 mg)
1 tablespoon plus 2 teaspoons grated lemon zest (.60 mg)
⅓ cup freshly squeezed lemon juice (.8 mg)
½ cup Zante dried currants (1.12 mg)

1. Preheat the oven to 425°F.

2. Using a wooden spoon, stir together the flour, baking powder, and 4 teaspoons of the sugar. Blend in applesauce with a fork and stir until the applesauce becomes crumbly. Beat the 2 egg yolks and 1 of the whites together. Add 1 tablespoon of the lemon zest and all the lemon juice (or you can substitute nonfat milk, which adds 41.6 mg sodium to the recipe). Add this mixture to the dry ingredients, stir in the currants, and mix thoroughly. Turn the dough out on a floured board and knead for about 2 minutes. Roll to about ½-inch to ¾-inch thick. If you make ½-inch dough, cut it into triangles and roll them up, or cut the ¾-inch dough into circles—whichever you prefer. Place the scone dough pieces on an ungreased cookie sheet, brush with the remaining egg white, and sprinkle on a mixture of the remaining sugar and lemon zest. Bake in the preheated oven for about 12 to 13 minutes. Serve hot out of the oven or store overnight in the refrigerator in a zip-lock-type bag.

Calories: 145. Sodium: 11.8 mg. Protein: 3.357 g. Carbohydrate: 22 g. Fiber: 0.86 g. Cholesterol: 45.8 mg. Calcium: 49.2 mg. Iron: 1.239 mg. Potassium: 149.8 mg. Total Fat: 4.9 g; Saturated fat: 2.7 g, Monounsaturated fat: 1.5 g, Polyunsaturated fat: 0.4 g.

❧ PEAR COFFEE CAKE ❧

SERVES 16   SODIUM PER RECIPE: 286.3 MG   SODIUM PER SERVING: 17.9 MG
*Cakes of any nature are generally high in sodium due to their use
of baking soda or powder and salt. This coffee cake is an exception
with only 18.2 mg of sodium per serving. Along with a glass of
orange juice, this can become an occasional breakfast, especially
when you feel rushed. Aside from that, it's absolutely delicious.*

1¼ cups firmly packed brown sugar (107.2 mg)
⅓ cup olive or canola oil (0 mg)
½ teaspoon almond extract (0 mg)
   The whites of 2 medium eggs (109.6 mg)
1 medium whole egg (55.4 mg)
2 cups unbleached white flour (5 mg)
2 teaspoons Featherweight Baking Powder (4 mg)
1 teaspoon ground cinnamon (.6 mg)
½ teaspoon ground nutmeg (trace)
¼ teaspoon ground cloves (1.3 mg)
1¼ cups diced fresh pear (0 mg)
¼ cup Zante dried currants (3 mg)

1. Preheat the oven to 350°F and coat an 8-inch square baking pan with
nonstick spray (or use a nonstick baking pan).
2. Combine the sugar, oil, almond extract, the egg whites, and the whole
egg in a bowl and beat with an electric mixer on low speed until well
blended. Combine the flour, baking powder, cinnamon, nutmeg, and
cloves in another bowl. Stir well and gradually add the flour mixture to the
sugar mixture, beating until just blended. Stir in the pears and currants.
Pour the batter into the prepared pan and bake for 40 minutes, or until a
wooden toothpick inserted in the center comes out clean. Let cool in the
pan for 10 minutes on a wire rack, then serve.

*Calories: 182. Sodium: 17.9 mg. Protein: 2.551 g. Carbohydrate: 32.8 g. Fiber: 1 g. Choles-
terol: 11.69 mg. Calcium: 51.1 mg. Iron: 4.452 mg. Potassium: 186.1 mg. Total Fat: 5 g; Saturated fat: 0.7 g. Monounsaturated fat: 3.4 g. Polyunsaturated fat: 0.5 g.*

❧ POPOVERS OVEN-BAKED ❧

*MAKES 8 POPOVERS   SODIUM PER RECIPE: 254.7 MG
SODIUM PER SERVING: 31.81 MG*
*My experience has been that using nonfat milk actually helps the
dough rise when you don't use salt in your baking. These popovers
make a great side dish for a roast beef dinner. With a touch of the
juice from the roast you'll have the flavor of a beef Wellington.*

2 large eggs (126 mg)
1 cup best for bread flour (2.5 mg)

1 cup nonfat milk (130 mg)
1 tablespoon extra-virgin olive oil (trace)

1. Preheat the oven to 450°F.
2. Let the eggs stand at room temperature for about ½ hour. Have the flour at room temperature also. Combine the eggs, flour, and milk in a medium-size bowl and beat for 1½ minutes with an electric beater. Add the oil and beat for another ½ minute until well blended. Don't overbeat. Fill 8 well-greased and warmed Pyrex glass custard cups ½ full. Let them stand at room temperature for 20 minutes. Bake in the preheated oven for 15 minutes. Reduce heat to 350°F, and bake for another 25 to 30 minutes, or until brown and firm. *Note:* Before removing the popovers from the oven, prick each one with a fork to allow the steam to escape. Serve hot with jam.

Calories: 101. Sodium: 31.84 mg. Protein: 4.22 g. Carbohydrate: 13.6 g. Fiber: 0.42 g. Cholesterol: 3.68 mg. Calcium: 46.3 mg. Iron: .924 mg. Potassium: 82.6 mg. Total Fat: 3.1 g; Saturated fat: 0.7 g, Monounsaturated fat: 1.7 g, Polyunsaturated fat: 0.4 g.

❧ OVEN SOUFFLÉ POPOVERS ❧

SERVES 4   SODIUM PER RECIPE: 253.4 MG   SODIUM PER SERVING: 63.3 MG

You can put these into greased cups or bake them in a soufflé pan. Great for breakfast or served with roast beef à la Wellington.

3 eggs, beaten with a fork (189 mg)
½ cup best for bread flour (1.25 mg)
½ cup nonfat milk (63.1 mg)
1 tablespoon olive oil (trace)

1. Preheat the oven to 450°F.
2. Mix all the ingredients together and pour into a 2-quart Pyrex or oven-safe nonstick soufflé pan or 4 individual Pyrex cups. (The cups are my preference.) If you're using one large pan, bake it at 450°F for 18 minutes; reduce the heat to 350°F and bake for another 10 minutes. If you're using individual cups, bake them at 450°F for 12 minutes, then reduce the heat to 350°F and bake for an additional 6 to 8 minutes. Serve with pure natural maple syrup (1.8 mg sodium per tablespoon), honey (.84 mg sodium per tablespoon), jam or fruits (.8 mg per tablespoon), all-fruit jams (4.815 mg), or low-sugar jams and marmalade (.18 mg sodium per tablespoon). Also a great accompaniment to prime rib or roast beef. Serve hot.

Calories: 153. Sodium: 63.34 mg. Protein: 7.342 g. Carbohydrate: 13.9 g. Fiber: 0.42 g. Cholesterol: 159.93 mg. Calcium: 58.5 mg. Iron: 1.29 mg. Potassium: 112.8 mg. Total Fat: 7.3 g; Saturated fat: 1.7 g, Monounsaturated fat: 3.9 g, Polyunsaturated fat: 0.9 g.

Baking Powder Cornbread /
❖ Made by Hand ❖

SERVES 12   SODIUM PER RECIPE: 204.2 MG   SODIUM PER SERVING: 17 MG

This recipe had its origin on the Albers Cornmeal box. We changed the baking powder to low sodium, took out any salt and substituted applesauce for the butter. We cut the fat a great deal. You can add jalapeño peppers or dried cranberries or Zante currants. Be sure to use Featherweight Baking Powder.

1 cup yellow cornmeal (5.85 mg)
1 cup best for bread flour (2.5 mg)
¼ cup granulated sugar (.5 mg)
1 tablespoon Featherweight Baking Powder (13.5 mg)
½ cup unsalted applesauce (2.5 mg) or Quick Applesauce, page 359 (.218 mg)
1 egg, lightly beaten (55.4 mg)
1 cup nonfat milk (126.2 mg)
2 tablespoons Diced Ortega jalapeño peppers (optional)

1. Preheat the oven to 400°F.
2. Combine the corn meal, flour, sugar, and baking powder in a medium bowl. In another bowl, combine the applesauce, egg, and milk and mix well. Add the milk mixture to the flour mixture and stir just until blended. Pour the batter into a greased 8-inch square pan. Bake in the preheated oven for 25 minutes, or until a wooden pick inserted in the center comes out clean. Serve warm.

Calories: 114. Sodium: 17.02 mg. Fiber: 1.94 g. Protein: 2.931 g. Carbohydrate: 24.1 g. Cholesterol: 15.95 mg. Calcium: 84.5 mg. Iron: .911 mg. Potassium: 220.7 mg. Total Fat: 0.9 g; Saturated fat: 0.2 g, Monounsaturated fat: 0.3 g, Polyunsaturated fat: 0.3 g.

Baking Powder Cornbread
❖ with Buttermilk / Made by Hand ❖

SERVES 16   SODIUM PER RECIPE: 461.4 MG   SODIUM PER SERVING: 28.8 MG

Here's a cornbread made into a loaf. Slice it for sandwiches, French toast, or toast.

¼ cup water (105°F to 110°F) (0 mg)
1 tablespoon active or bread machine dry yeast (6 mg)
Pinch of sugar
2 cups buttermilk (260 mg)
⅓ cup honey (4 mg)

5 tablespoons olive oil (trace)
7 cups best for bread flour (17.5 mg)
1 teaspoon Featherweight Baking Powder (2 mg)
1 cup Albers, Quaker, or other yellow cornmeal (1.26 mg)
⅓ teaspoon dry mustard (0 mg)
2 medium eggs, well beaten (110.9 mg)
1 teaspoon unsalted butter (.515 mg) for greasing dough
1 egg white, slightly beaten (50.1 mg)
2 teaspoons sesame seeds (2 mg)

1. Pour warm faucet water (105°F to 110°F) into a small bowl and float the yeast with a pinch of sugar for 5 minutes. Heat the buttermilk slowly in a small saucepan with the honey and olive oil until the mixture reaches about 110°F. Set this mixture aside.

2. Using a food processor with a bread paddle or an electric beater with a bread paddle, mix together buttermilk mixture, 3 cups of the flour, and the Featherweight Baking Powder. While the mixer continues to run, add in the dissolved yeast, cornmeal, dry mustard, and the whole eggs. Continue to mix at medium speed until all ingredients are well combined. Gradually add the remaining flour until a dough is formed. (Add more flour if necessary in ¼-cup increments.) Put dough on a well-floured board and knead for about 10 minutes, or until the dough is smooth and elastic. Roll it into a ball and place it in a well-greased bowl, turning the dough to cover all surfaces with the grease. Be sure to grease the top of the dough when setting it in the bowl. Cover the bowl tightly with plastic wrap. Let it rise in a warm place until doubled in bulk (about 1 to 2 hours).

3. Preheat the oven to 375°F. You will use the center rack for this loaf.

4. Place the dough on a floured board and knead for another 2 to 3 minutes. Roll the dough and pinch the ends shut. Flatten the dough. Bring one side to the center, then do the same with the other side. Transfer the dough to a 9x9-inch nonstick baking pan, seam-side down. Let it rise for about 1 hour, or until it comes above the pan rim. Brush the top with the beaten egg white and sprinkle with the sesame seeds. Bake for about 50 minutes, or until the loaf rises another 3 inches above the rim of the pan and is golden brown. When done, cool on a rack. Slice when completely cool.

5. To lower the fat content, replace the olive oil with applesauce or a mashed banana.

Calories: 311. Sodium: 28.84 mg. Protein: 8.639 g. Carbohydrate: 56.1 g. Fiber: 1.94 g. Cholesterol: 26.5 mg. Calcium: 36.7 mg. Iron: 7.462 mg. Potassium: 131 mg. Total Fat: 6.6 g; Saturated fat: 1.3 g. Monounsaturated fat: 3.6 g. Polyunsaturated fat: 1 g.

Yeast Breads

Bread-Making without Salt

You **can** make bread without using salt. Salt, although serving as a leavening agent that controls and slows the rising time, is used (heavily in commercial bread products) mostly as a preservative. Because our recipes contain no salt, the breads will not have as long a shelf life as commercial breads, nor will they be as airy. Bread made from most of our recipes will last about a week in a resealable plastic bag in your refrigerator, but storing them in a freezer is best. You can thaw them in a microwave if you have one, using the "defrost" button, or by letting them stand out for about a half hour or more. You must follow the recipes exactly, however. Any deviation or alteration may well cause the recipe to fail. The use of salt substitutes will neither enhance the life of bread nor help with leavening. ("Salt substitutes" can also be very high in sodium.)

Fat in bread, contributed mostly by oil, butter, shortening, or margarine, is used to help prevent moisture loss. You can leave the fat out of our recipes if your health demands it. We have already cut it in half in our recipes, but you know what you can and cannot eat better than we do.

Using whole eggs in bread runs up the sodium, fat, and cholesterol levels. They are used in many sandwich and toast breads to help keep the crust tender and the bread texture lighter. Rye bread is a good example of where eggs might be used. We have limited our use of whole eggs to very few bread recipes, but recommend that you add the egg white by itself if you want a softer crust or a finer texture. Egg whites have no cholesterol or fat but add about 55 mg of sodium per egg per recipe.

Sugar is used in bread making to "sweeten" the bread and to help give the yeast a kick. We use some, but not what most would use. We have tested all our recipes without sugar and if your diet demands bread without sugar, our recipes will work for you just as well. You may leave out the oil and the sugar with any of our recipes if your health demands require it.

Dough is mixed well in bread machines. When kneading by

hand, it is therefore crucial to be very thorough, since kneading helps develop the gluten, which improves the bread's texture. If you don't have a bread machine, you can use the same recipes and knead the dough by hand, although this isn't always successful, since unsalted breads require "even" kneading. For best results, knead such recipes on a slightly floured bread board for at least 20 minutes, working in as much flour as you can while doing so. Let the dough rise for one hour in a warm place, then roll it over, pressing down gently (some say punch it, but that's not a good way to work with bread), form it in lightly greased baking pans (loaf, baguette, sourdough) or on cookie sheets, and let it rise again. (When it's too cold to let the dough sit out in the kitchen, heat your oven to about 100°F, turn the heat off, and let the dough rise in the warm oven with the door closed.

The correct amount of water per recipe is as important as the correct amount of yeast. However, bread machines, different altitudes, oven temperatures, and other factors may cause your first attempt to produce a loaf of bread (or rolls) that rise too high or not high enough. A general rule of thumb for altitude is: For every 1,000 feet above sea level, subtract about 5 minutes baking time. Bread machines may have to be adjusted by selecting shorter cycles. We recommend in most of our recipes using the bread machine to knead, and your oven to do the baking. That works best with unsalted breads. It's the only way to bake unsalted, no-sugar, no-oil breads with consistent success.

If you bake in a bread machine or in the oven, and the top of your loaf falls or the loaf contains large holes, reduce the water by 1 to 2 tablespoons next time—usually that will solve the problem. If the loaf doesn't rise high enough, or if it's "like a rock," then add 1 to 2 tablespoons water. If it still doesn't rise enough, add another ½ teaspoon yeast. You can usually add up to 3 teaspoons of yeast without causing the kind of failure due to too much yeast (in unsalted breads).

When making bread "by hand," add a pinch of sugar to the water when dissolving the yeast to give the yeast a jumpstart, unless a condition like diabetes prevents this addition.

If your yeast doesn't show any signs of life, like bubbling a few minutes after it is dissolved, discard it and start the process over again with fresh, room-temperature yeast. If your yeast isn't behaving, it may be that it was left out of the refrigerator after being opened. Once opened, always store in the refrigerator.

In most of our recipes we recommend flour that is billed as "best for bread" or "best for bread machines." Check to make sure your local brand or a national brand you use lists sodium at 0 to 6 mg per cup. Some flours add salt, especially "self-rising" flours and some "cake" flours. You do not want to use those. All-purpose flour without sodium is also a good flour to use since it too contains gluten, but do not use it in recipes like pizza, bagels, or waffles. Gluten provides the elastic framework that traps the bubbles of gas created by the yeast when the dough is mixed and kneaded. Gluten also helps to create the texture associated with breads; if no gluten is present, your bread will have a dense texture.

Generally, yeast dough requires at least one rising in a bread machine. However, we find that two risings help make a better bread when we let the machine do the kneading and then bake the bread in the oven. Remember, when placed in the oven for cooking, it may in some cases rise a bit more, but usually not enough to notice.

After kneading, either you or your machine will form the dough into a ball. Cover it and stand it in a warm, not hot, place until it doubles in size. You or your machine will "punch it down" after that, shape it into buns, bread, or whatever the recipe calls for, and let it rise again prior to baking.

Diabetics and those with renal failure may leave both the sugar and the oil, butter, or other fat called for out of your bread. For more flavor, try using apple juice or orange juice for the liquid, or add minced garlic or chopped onions (depending on the kind of bread you're making).

BREAD MACHINES

We recommend that you use a bread machine to make unsalted bread. Follow the manufacturer's directions for combining ingredients, but if no instructions are given, put the warmed liquid ingredients in first. All ingredients except the liquids should be at the same room temperature, the liquid ingredient should be a bit higher, about 120°F to 130°F for bread machines. (Hand-kneaded bread only requires water of about 90°F to 115°F.) We also suggest warming the bread pan with hot water.

I have used many bread machines and learned that most of them work adequately, but a few work better than others. I recommend that you check some of the consumer rating companies to determine which machine you may want to purchase. I have found that most machines will wear out after two years of steady bread making—except for the Salton machine: Breadman TR810. I have also found that the machines that sell for around $100 to $150 are generally the better bread makers. You need not pay more than that, and I also recommend that you not purchase one whose regular price is below $100.

I strongly recommend the Breadman Model TR810 ($129 at www.salton.com, about $149 in most stores). After much experience, this model has proved to be durable, with an excellent consistency for making great unsalted bread. The company also backs up their machine's warranty with a quick response directly from the factory. In any case, make sure the machine you purchase has a dough cycle.

We use Red Star or Fleischmann's Bread Machine Yeast for bread machine recipes, although most any brand will do. Packaged active dry yeast also works in bread machines just as well as bread machine yeast. *Never use rapid rise yeast or compressed yeast in your bread machine.* Buy the yeast in jars, it will prove cheaper for you and easier to measure quantities needed per recipe.

You can make cinnamon rolls, burger buns, French bread, baguettes, dinner rolls, sandwich bread, and other yeast products, including pizza dough, without salt, and always without much sodium. For instance, our **Sandwich Buns,** used for hamburgers, sandwiches, or just for toast if you like, have less than 2 mg sodium while a commercial bun has about 600 mg. Many of our sliced bread recipes have only 1 mg sodium per slice. Compare that to the commercial bakeries with more than 200 mg per slice of both white and whole wheat bread each. With so much sodium cut from your diet without much effort, you can see the advantages of making your own bread.

Tip: You can still bake your favorite cornbread or cake recipes that call for baking powder by exchanging standard baking powder for Featherweight Baking Powder. Featherweight has 2 mg sodium per teaspoon compared to other brands whose sodium count goes as high as 480 mg per teaspoon. If your local grocer doesn't carry it, ask him to order it in. It comes from Hain (previously from the Estee Company). Also check with your local health food store, or in some cases, your chain drugstore. It's also available at www.healthyheartmarket.com (1-888/685-5988).

Visit www.megaheart.com for further Q&A concerning bread making and bread machines. Preorder the book now for first edition delivery at Amazon.com.

❖ Sourdough Starter ❖

MAKES 1 STARTER   SODIUM PER RECIPE: 3.2 MG
This works with all our sourdough recipes.

1 cup water (0 mg)
1 cup unbleached white flour (2.5 mg)
   Healthy pinch of yeast (.7 mg)

1. Combine the ingredients and stir until smooth. Set this mixture aside in a glass or plastic container, covered but not tightly, at room temperature for 5 to 7 days. Make sure the bowl is large enough for the mixture to "grow." You are making a living culture that will bubble. It will also smell a bit unusual. If you live in the Midwest or on the Eastern seaboard, you will probably not be able to create a true San Francisco sourdough. Ambient conditions will alter the sourdough culture, but you'll still get something worth making.

2. Use your starter once a week or remove ½ cup of the mixture, discard it, and replace it with equal amounts of flour and water, stirred together until smooth before adding. This will keep your starter fresh and active. After about 7 days, you will want to store your starter in your refrigerator. Always bring it back to room temperature however before making your bread.

3. After using some of the starter, replace the same amount. For instance, if you use 1 cup starter in a recipe, replace it by mixing together 1 cup flour and 1 cup water. Combine until smooth, then add to the mother starter, and return to refrigerator.

Calories: 459. Sodium: 3.2 mg. Fiber: 3.67 g. Protein: 13.4 g. Carbohydrate: 95.9 g. Cholesterol: 0 mg. Calcium: 19.6 mg. Iron: 14 mg. Potassium: 161.8 mg. Total Fat: 1.3 g; Saturated fat: 0.2 g, Monounsaturated fat: 0.1 g, Polyunsaturated fat: 0.5 g.

Whole Wheat Bread /
❖ Bread Machine Recipe ❖

MAKES 1½-POUND LOAF (16 SLICES)   SODIUM PER RECIPE: 16.8 MG
SODIUM PER SLICE: 1.048 MG
This makes a wonderful sandwich bread and a great morning toast. Commercial whole wheat bread can range between 135 mg to 200 mg of sodium per regular slice and sometimes as high as 400 mg.

1¼ cups water, 105°F to 110°F (0 mg)
 2 tablespoons granulated white sugar (.252 mg)
1½ tablespoons olive oil (trace)

1½ cups Stone Buhr Whole Wheat Great for Bread Flour (9 mg) or other best for bread flour
1⅔ cups unbleached white bread machine flour (4 mg)
2¼ teaspoons bread machine yeast, room temperature (3.5 mg)

1. Add the ingredients to your bread machine in the order listed or in the order your machine instructs. Bake this recipe using your machine's Basic cycle. If you use a timer and let it rest overnight, then make sure the yeast sits on dry flour. Serve as sandwich bread or breakfast toast.

Calories: 102. Sodium: 1.05 mg. Fiber: 1.8 g. Protein: 3 g. Carbohydrate: 19.4 g. Cholesterol: 0 mg. Calcium: 5.998 mg. Iron: 1.72 mg. Potassium: 67.7 mg. Total Fat: 1.6 g; Saturated fat: 0.2 g, Monounsaturated fat: 1 g, Polyunsaturated fat: 0.2 g.

Thanks Don,
I have made several loaves of your no-salt whole wheat bread and will continue to do so. It is important for people like me with heart problems to have a very low sodium diet so we won't retain fluids in our bodies. I do all I can to keep my sodium intake as low as possible to avoid having to have my lungs and or heart area drained.
Bill and Karen Deitemeyer

KNEAD YOUR OWN BASIC
❖ WHITE BREAD / MADE BY HAND ❖

MAKES 36 SLICES   SODIUM PER RECIPE (WATER): 19 MG
SODIUM PER SLICE (WATER): .526 MG

*Sometimes it's enjoyable to make bread by hand—especially if the temperature in your home is right for bread to rise. This white bread recipe has been in our salt-free family for years. It tastes great in the morning toasted with a bit of jam on it and it's especially wonderful for sandwiches, **Dinner Rolls** (page 256), and even, with a touch more sugar, for making delicious* ***Cinnamon Rolls*** *(page 257).*

2 or more tablespoons extra-virgin olive oil (trace)
1 tablespoon active dry yeast (6 mg)
1 cup water, at body temperature (0 mg)
3½ tablespoons granulated sugar (.441 mg)
5 cups best for bread white flour (12.5 mg)

1. You will need two large mixing bowls and one small one. Lightly grease one large bowl with olive oil. In the smaller bowl, soak the yeast in ½ cup of water for about 5 minutes. In the second large bowl, combine the sugar, oil, and rest of water. Add the dissolved yeast to this mixture. Stir in 3 cups of the flour with a wooden spoon and beat until smooth. When smooth, add the rest of the flour gradually, beating or mixing while you do so. When the mixture becomes stiff enough to handle, you are through mixing. Now comes the hard work. Knead the dough until it's elastic. While kneading add the remaining flour. If you feel you need more flour than the recipe calls for, add up to ½ cup, but no more. Now put this dough in the bowl you previously greased. Cover it loosely with waxed paper or a light cloth and let it stand until it doubles in size. The best way to tell if the dough has risen enough is to press your finger into the dough. If the impression stays there, the dough is ready. Punch it down, split it into 2 equal pieces, and let it rest for about 5 minutes.

2. Roll each piece into a rectangle about 9x12 inches. Roll these up into a tight loaf shape. It's best to start with the narrowest end and make sure you roll the 12-inch side, ending with a 9-inch-long roll. Seal the ends by pinching the dough together. Place these rolls in two standard loaf pans, about 9x5 inches, lightly greased and flour dusted, seam-side down. Cover the pans loosely with light cloth or waxed paper until the dough reaches top of pan. This shouldn't take more than 45 minutes.

3. Preheat your oven to 425°F while the dough rises. When the dough is ready, bake the bread for about 25 to 35 minutes. Remove the loaves from the pans right away and cool them on a rack. Don't allow anyone near the bread while it's cooling or you'll have to bake two more loaves right away. Use for toast or sandwiches.

Calories: 76. Sodium: 0.53 mg. Fiber: 0.54 g. Protein: 1.921 g. Carbohydrate: 14.6 g. Cholesterol: 0 mg. Calcium: 2.831 mg. Iron: 1.087 mg. Potassium: 25.3 mg. Total Fat: 0.9 g. Saturated fat: 0.1 g. Monounsaturated fat: 0.6 g. Polyunsaturated fat: 0.1 g.

Apple Kuchen / Bread Machine
❖ Preparation — Oven Baked ❖

SERVES 14   SODIUM PER RECIPE: 245 MG   SODIUM PER SERVING: 17.5 MG
This recipe came to us straight from Germany, from a friend who served in the U.S. Army there. We've lowered the fat and cut the sodium to respectable levels.

¾ **cup nonfat milk, scalded (94.6 mg)**
2 **tablespoons melted unsalted butter (3.124 mg)**
¼ **cup Quick Applesauce (see page 359) (1.912 mg)**
¼ **cup sugar (.5 mg)**
2 **medium eggs, slightly beaten (110.9 mg)**
2¾ **cups unbleached best-for-bread-machine white flour (6.875 mg)**
1 **tablespoon bread machine yeast (6 mg)**

FILLING

- 5 **medium apples (0 mg)**
- ¼ **cup granulated white sugar (.5 mg)**
- ½ **teaspoon ground cinnamon (.303 mg)**
- ½ **cup walnuts, chopped (6 mg)**
- 3 **tablespoons golden raisins (3.48 mg)**
- 2 **tablespoons brown sugar (10.8 mg)**

1. Scald the milk in a saucepan, remove from heat and let butter melt in milk. Then pour into your bread machine pan and add the **Quick Applesauce** (warmed), and the sugar. Add in the beaten eggs and place flour on top of this mixture. Put the yeast in on top of this. Set your bread machine to "Pizza Dough," or "dough" if that's all your machine has. I use a Breadman TR810. You want to have the dough prepared by your machine for only an hour.

2. When dough is ready, remove and place on plate or in a bowl with a light dusting of flour. Cover and chill in the refrigerator for ½ hour. Turn out on a lightly floured board and knead lightly for one minute. Prepare a 9x13-inch baking dish by lightly spray coating it with a spritz of oil.

3. For the filling, preheat the oven to 350°F. Peel and core apples and cut into thin slices. Press apple slices close together into the dough. Combine white sugar, cinnamon, walnuts, and raisins. Sprinkle evenly over apples and exposed dough. Then sprinkle the brown sugar over entire dish lightly. Cover and let rise in your kitchen, about 45 minutes to 1 hour, until dough springs back when touched lightly. Bake for 30 minutes or until apples are done. This wonderful breakfast cake will rise quite high in your oven, so make sure you aren't up against another rack.

Calories: 222. Sodium: 17.5 mg. Protein: 4.902 g. Carbohydrate: 39.8 g. Fiber: 2.56 g. Cholesterol: 31.39 mg. Calcium: 35.5 mg. Iron: 1.7 mg. Potassium: 177.1 mg. Total Fat: 5.4 g; Saturated fat: 1.6 g, Monounsaturated fat: 1.4 g, Polyunsaturated fat: 2 g.

Panettone / Made by Hand—

❉ Not a Bread Machine Recipe ❉

SERVES 24   SODIUM PER RECIPE: 280.8 MG   SODIUM PER SERVING: 11.7 MG

*This glossy fruited Italian bread is generously served to guests.
There are many variations of this recipe, but this is the basic
Italian version from Milan, Italy.**

  2 **tablespoons active dry yeast (12 mg)**
  ½ **cup plus 1 tablespoon lukewarm water, at 105°F to 110°F (0 mg)**
  ½ **cup lukewarm nonfat milk (63.1 mg)**
  ½ **cup plus 1 teaspoon granulated sugar (1 mg)**
  3 **medium eggs (166.3 mg)**
  ¼ **cup unsalted applesauce or Homemade Applesauce (1.912 mg)**
  ¼ **cup extra-virgin olive oil (trace)**
  5 **cups best for bread white flour (12.5 mg)**
  ½ **cup golden raisins (20 mg)**
  ½ **cup candied citron bits (23 mg)**
  2 **tablespoons unsalted roasted pine nuts (.344 mg)**
  2 **teaspoons anise seed (.652 mg)**
  ½ **tablespoon unsalted butter (.781 mg) for greasing bowl and
     baking sheet**

1. For hand kneading, dissolve the yeast in ½ cup lukewarm water in a large bowl for about 5 minutes. Stir in the milk, sugar, 2 of the eggs, the applesauce, oil, and 2½ cups of the flour. Beat with an electric beater at medium speed until creamy. Mix in the fruit, nuts, anise seed, and enough flour to make the dough easy to turn. Turn the dough onto a lightly floured board. Knead until smooth and elastic, about 5 to 8 minutes. Place in a greased bowl and turn so the entire surface is greased. Cover with a light cloth and let stand in a warm place for about 2 hours to allow it to rise.

2. Punch down the dough. Divide it into two pieces. Shape each into a round but slightly flat loaf. Place the loaves in opposite corners of a greased baking sheet. Crisscross a ½-inch-deep cut on the top of each loaf. Let rise until double in bulk—about 1 hour.

3. Preheat the oven to 350°F. Brush the top of the loaves with an egg wash made by combining the remaining egg and the remaining tablespoon of water.

4. Bake the loaves for about 40 to 45 minutes in the preheated oven or until golden brown.

*Calories: 149. Sodium: 11.7 mg. Fiber: 0.99 g. Protein: 4.059 g. Carbohydrate: 25.7 g.
Cholesterol: 23.47 mg. Calcium: 15.2 mg. Iron: 1.763 mg. Potassium: 69.7 mg. Total Fat:
3.3 g; Saturated fat: 0.6 g, Monounsaturated fat: 2 g, Polyunsaturated fat: 0.5 g.*

*This recipe *can* be made in the larger bread machines—just follow the bread machine instructions for adding ingredients.

Christmas Stollen /
❧ Made from Scratch, by Hand ❧

MAKES 2 STOLLEN (SERVES 24)   SODIUM PER RECIPE: 328.2 MG
SODIUM PER SERVING: 13.7 MG

This does take longer to make than the bread machine variety, but it's very popular and worth the effort at least once a year.

¾ cup lukewarm water, 105°F to 110°F (0 mg)
1 tablespoon active dry yeast (6 mg)
½ cup granulated sugar (1 mg)
3 whole eggs (166.3 mg)
1 egg, separated (61.938 mg)
½ cup unsalted butter, softened (12.5 mg)
3½ cups unbleached white flour (8.75 mg)
½ cup unsalted chopped almonds (7.59 mg)
¼ cup candied citron bits (24.6 mg)
1 tablespoon fresh lemon zest, grated (.36 mg)
¼ cup golden raisins (4.95 mg)
¼ cup candied cherries bits (24.6 mg)
¼ cup currants (2.88 mg)
An additional ⅓ cup soft unsalted butter (8.24 mg)
1 tablespoon water (0 mg)
¼ cup blanched unsalted almond halves (3.795 mg)
For decoration extra citron and cherry halves

1. Heat a large mixing bowl with lukewarm water, empty, and dissolve yeast in ¾ cup lukewarm water. Add the sugar, eggs, egg yolk, ½ cup unsalted butter, and 1½ cups of the flour. With an electric beater, beat these ingredients together at slow speed for about ½ minute. Scrape the bowl constantly while blending. Beat for another 10 minutes at medium speed, scraping the bowl occasionally. Stir in the remaining flour, almonds, citron, lemon, raisins, and cherries. Stir in half of the currants, keeping the balance for decoration. Scrape the batter from the sides of the bowl. Cover, let the dough rise in a warm place until double in bulk. This may take 1½ to 2 hours. Stir down the batter with 25 beating strokes. Cover the bowl tightly with plastic wrap and refrigerate for at least 8 hours.

2. Turn the dough onto a well-floured board and coat with flour. Divide the dough in half, pressing each half into an oval of about 7x10 inches. Brush each with 3 tablespoons of the remaining butter. Fold the dough lengthwise in half. Press the edges firmly together and put the dough on a greased baking sheet. Beat the reserved egg white slightly, and add 1 tablespoon water, then brush this mixture over the stollen. Let the dough rise in a warm place until double in bulk, about 1 hour.

3. Meanwhile preheat the oven to 375°F.

4. Bake the stollen for about 20 to 25 minutes or until golden brown in the preheated oven. Frost with glaze. Decorate with almond halves and pieces of citron, cherry halves, and the remaining currants. Serve hot or reheated.

Calories: 190. Sodium: 13.68 mg. Fiber: 1.41 g. Protein: 3.923 g. Carbohydrate: 22.7 g
Cholesterol: 49.42 mg. Calcium: 23.9 mg. Iron: 1.551 mg. Potassium: 103.3 mg. Total Fat:
9.6 g; Saturated fat: 4.4 g, Monounsaturated fat: 3.6 g, Polyunsaturated fat: 0.9 g.

ORANGE REFRIGERATOR ROLLS /
❖ MADE BY HAND ❖

MAKES 24 ROLLS   SODIUM PER RECIPE: 250.2 MG
SODIUM PER SERVING: 10.4 MG

Marlene Winger, creator of this recipe, used to make these for guests and audience members who attended sessions at the Southern California Edison home center, where she worked as a home economist. The recipe is an older, truly tested delight that still holds up as a great low-sodium treat.

2½ teaspoons active dry yeast (3.5 mg)
 ½ cup lukewarm water, at 105°F to 110°F (0 mg)
 ¾ cup plus 1 teaspoon granulated white sugar (1.5 mg)
 1 cup nonfat milk (126.2 mg)
 5 tablespoons unsalted butter, softened (7.8 mg)
 1 egg, well beaten (55.4 mg)
4½ cups sifted unbleached bread flour (11.2 mg)
 ½ cup packed brown sugar (42.9 mg)
   Grated zest of 2 oranges (1 mg)

1. Soak the yeast in lukewarm water with 1 teaspoon of the sugar for about 5 minutes. Scald the milk with 4 tablespoons of the butter and 4 tablespoons of the sugar. Cool. Add the egg and the dissolved yeast and mix thoroughly. Add the flour gradually and beat each addition well. Put the dough in a greased bowl and refrigerate. When the dough is thoroughly chilled, take it out and divide it in half. Roll each piece into an oblong shape about 14 inches by 6 inches. Cover with a generous amount of softened butter. Combine the remaining granulated sugar, the brown sugar, and the grated orange zest and sprinkle ½ the mixture over each piece. Roll the dough up in jelly-roll fashion. Cut each roll into 12 pieces and put them into greased muffin tins. Cover with a light cloth and let stand in a warm place.
2. Preheat the oven to 400°F.
3. When the dough is double in bulk, bake for about 15 minutes. Serve as dinner rolls, warm.

Calories: 165. Sodium: 10.42 mg. Fiber: 0.85 g. Protein: 3.158 g. Carbohydrate: 31.7 g.
Cholesterol: 14.45 mg. Calcium: 24.3 mg. Iron: 1.442 mg. Potassium: 70 mg. Total Fat:
2.8 g; Saturated fat: 1.6 g, Monounsaturated fat: 0.8 g, Polyunsaturated fat: 0.2 g.

❧ OATMEAL BREAD / MADE BY HAND ❧

MAKES 1 LOAF (14 SLICES)   SODIUM PER RECIPE: 54.3 MG
SODIUM PER SLICE: 3.88 MG

    1 tablespoon unsalted butter, softened (1.56 mg)
 1½ cups boiling water (0 mg)
  ¾ cup rolled oats (3 mg)
  ¼ cup light molasses (30.3 mg)
    3 tablespoons extra-virgin olive oil (trace)
    2 teaspoons active dry yeast (3.96 mg)
  ¼ cup lukewarm water, 105°F to 115°F (0 mg)
    2 cups best for bread whole wheat flour* (12 mg)
    2 cups best for bread white flour (5 mg)

1. Grease a 9x5x3-inch pan. In a medium bowl pour the boiling water over the oats. Add the molasses and oil, stirring to mix well. Cool.

2. Sprinkle the yeast over the warm water in a large bowl and stir to dissolve. Stir in the oatmeal mixture, and gradually add both flours. Cover with a towel. Let the dough rise until doubled in bulk, about 30 to 60 minutes. (It should be at or near room temperature, or between 75°F to 95°F.) Stir with a wooden spoon and give the batter 25 vigorous strokes. Spread the dough evenly in a loaf pan, using a buttered spatula to smooth the top. Let it rise for another ½ hour.

3. While it is rising, preheat the oven to 425°F.

4. Bake the bread for 30 to 40 minutes.

5. It is best eaten when warm out of the oven, but it makes great toast and French toast for breakfast.

Calories: 182. Sodium: 3.88 mg. Fiber: 3.31 g. Protein: 5.14 g. Carbohydrate: 33 g. Cholesterol: 0 mg. Calcium: 24.3 mg. Iron: 3.221 mg. Potassium: 210.4 mg. Total Fat: 3.8 g; Saturated fat: 0.5 g, Monounsaturated fat: 2.3 g, Polyunsaturated fat: 0.6 g.

*In the western states, Stone Buhr Whole Wheat labs show only 5 mg per cup for "best for bread" whole wheat. Other bread flour brands will also work. Stone Buhr flour comes from an area where the wheat is recognized as the world's best for nutrients and baking.

Basic White Bread /

❈ Bread Machine Recipe ❈

MAKES 1 LOAF (14 SLICES)   SODIUM PER RECIPE: 13.5 MG
SODIUM PER SLICE: .965 MG

Basic white bread recipes have served for generations as the basis for new bread recipes. It's amazing that the recipes can be so different, and yet produce pretty much the same bread. You may want to experiment with this one; add some honey or even grated orange zest for flavor and vitamins. This recipe makes a great sandwich bread, but like most non-salt, low-sodium breads, it will spoil within 5 days if not stored in an airtight bag.
So, eat up and enjoy.

> 1 cup plus 1 tablespoon lukewarm water, at 105°F to 110°F (0 mg)
> 3 cups best for bread flour (7.5 mg)
> 2 tablespoons Quick Applesauce (.954 mg)
> 2 tablespoons granulated sugar (.252 mg)
> 2½ teaspoons bread machine yeast (4.8 mg)

1. Put all the ingredients into your bread machine per the manufacturer's instructions. I have found it best to put all the bread machine ingredients into my West Bend, let them sit there for 1 or 2 hours to "rest," and then continue the rest of the process. I use the timer to accomplish this effectively. The bread always seems to rise a little higher when I do. You can substitute 2 tablespoons of honey (1.68 mg) for the sugar if you wish.

Calories: 108. Sodium: 0.96 mg. Fiber: 0.89 g. Protein: 3.034 g. Carbohydrate: 23 g. Cholesterol: 0 mg. Calcium: 4.566 mg. Iron: 1.937 mg. Potassium: 43.8 mg. Total Fat: 0.3 g; Saturated fat: 0 g, Monounsaturated fat: 0 g, Polyunsaturated fat: 0.1 g.

Sourdough Whole Wheat Bread /
❖ Bread Machine Recipe ❖

MAKES 1½-POUND LOAF (16 SLICES)   SODIUM PER RECIPE: 27.7 MG
SODIUM PER SLICE: 1.728 MG

This is a bread I make often. If you plan to bake it in the early morning, then let the ingredients sit in your bread machine overnight. That ensures that all the ingredients will be at room temperature. The loaf will rise so well it will push against the lid of your machine.

¾ cup water, at room temperature (0 mg)
1½ cups best for bread white flour (3.75 mg)
1½ cups best for bread whole wheat flour* (9 mg)
2 tablespoons light brown sugar (10.8 mg)
1½ tablespoons extra-virgin olive oil (trace)
1½ cups Sourdough Starter, page 234 (.171 mg)
2 teaspoons active dry yeast (3.96 mg)

1. Add the water to your machine's bread pan first. Then add the flours, the sugar, oil, and **Sourdough Starter.** Add the yeast last, placing it on dry flour. Bake at Basic or White Bread the first time you make this. If you have settings for Light, Medium, and Dark Crust, choose Medium. If bread needs longer cooking time, next bake session choose setting that selects 10 minutes more baking. Serve as toast or for sandwiches.

Calories: 101. Sodium: 1.73 mg. Fiber: 1.81 g. Protein: 2.986 g. Carbohydrate: 19.3 g. Cholesterol: 0 mg. Calcium: 7.434 mg. Iron: 1.522 mg. Potassium: 74.5 mg. Total Fat: 1.6 g; Saturated fat: 0.2 g, Monounsaturated fat: 1 g, Polyunsaturated fat: 0.2 g.

*If you live in the West I recommend Stone Buhr Best for Bread Whole Wheat, which has only 2.5 mg sodium per cup and is milled from the finest Montana wheat.

Don's Healthy Orange Bread / Bread Machine

❋ Recipe for Dough Preparation ❋

MAKES 12 TO 18 BUN-SIZED ROLLS   SODIUM PER RECIPE: 24.4 MG   SODIUM PER ROLL (12 ROLLS): 2.029 MG   SODIUM PER ROLL (18 ROLLS): 1.353 MG

I like to experiment. You may want to alter some of the recipes in this book, but this one you have to try as is. If you want to change the flavor or experiment with your own concoction, please wait until you've tasted the original and then feel free to make your own adjustments. I first tried this when our nutritionist daughter taught us about bioflavinoids. They are best obtained by eating the inside of an orange peel, the stuff most people throw away. One way, of course, is to scrape the bottom side of the peel along your teeth and chew the white stuff off. Another is to make this bread and enjoy your bioflavinoids with a good loganberry jam or some honey. You can also try adding grated orange peel in other bread recipes. If you add no more than ¼ cup of grated orange peel to any of my recipes it shouldn't affect the baking.

    Nonstick olive oil spray (trace)
1¾ **cups orange juice fortified with calcium, heated to about 105°F (4.353 mg)**
  5 **cups bread machine white flour (12.5 mg)**
  1 **teaspoon granulated sugar (.252 mg)**
  2 **tablespoons extra-virgin olive oil (trace)**
    The whole grated peel of 1 large orange (.72 mg)
  1 **full tablespoon bread machine yeast (6 mg)**
  1 **teaspoon unsalted butter for tops of buns (.515 mg)**

1. Spray the side of your bread machine container with light coating of nonstick olive oil spray. Warm the orange juice to about 110°F. Put the orange juice into the bread machine first. Add the flour, then add the sugar, setting it on top of the flour in one corner. Cater-corner to that, put in the olive oil. In your food processor, put the peel of 1 large orange (or 2 medium oranges) and chop it (but do not liquefy it). Add the orange peel to the mixture over the olive oil. Set the yeast on top of the sugar. All ingredients should be at "warm room temperature," but not hot, as in summer heat.

2. Set your machine to the Dough cycle. Let the mixture rest in the machine for about 10 minutes, then turn the machine on.

3. While the dough is being prepared in the machine, put 2 cookie sheets in the oven. Turn the oven on to about 100°F for about 1 or 2 minutes, then turn off the heat but leave the pans in the oven with the door closed.

4. When the dough is ready, roll it out onto a floured board. Cut the dough in half with a sharp knife. Press out (with your hands) one of the halves until it is about ½ inch thick. Cut it into 6 or 9 equal portions. Make elongated or round buns or roll the dough out into dinner rolls. Place these on one of the warmed cookie sheets. Cover with a very light cloth and set in the oven, which should still be slightly warm. Repeat with the other half of the bread dough on the second cookie sheet. Let the dough rise in the oven for about 45 minutes.

5. Carefully remove the pans from the oven and set them down gently on the countertop. You don't want to bump these. Turn the oven up to 425°F and, when ready, bake each sheet of buns for about 6 minutes. Remove the cookie sheets from the oven, rub the top of each bun with a pat of unsalted butter, letting it melt gently into the dough. The buns should have risen to about 1½ to 2 inches thick with a nice fluffy interior.

Based on 12 rolls. Calories: 241.6. Sodium: 2.029 mg. Fiber: 1.9 g. Protein: 6.04 g. Carbohydrate: 46.6 g. Cholesterol: 0 mg. Calcium: 55.6 mg. Iron: 2.645 mg. Potassium: 148.9 mg. Total Fat: 3.149 g; Saturated fat: .591 g, Monounsaturated fat: 1.825 g, Polyunsaturated fat: .421 g.

Experimental Oatmeal Bread with Cinnamon and Orange /

❖ Bake in the Bread Machine Recipe ❖

MAKES 1 LOAF (16 SLICES)   SODIUM PER RECIPE: 26.5 MG
SODIUM PER SLICE: 1.658 MG

I've tried a lot of different bread recipes during my experimentation and development period. This one I like as is, but you can continue to play with it, maybe make it more for your own taste. Add more orange or less, more or less cinnamon. Take out the raisins if you don't like them, or exchange the sweeter golden raisins for the black. Substitute honey for the sugar, even put in a half cup of grated coconut.

   1 cup water (0 mg)
1²⁄₃ cups best for bread white flour (4.15 mg)
   ¾ cup best for bread whole wheat (4.5 mg)
   ¾ cup raw or rolled oats (2.34 mg)
   ½ cup golden raisins, packed (9.9 mg)
   2 teaspoons ground cinnamon (1.21 mg)
   3 tablespoons grated orange peel (.54 mg)
   3 tablespoons light olive oil (trace)
   3 tablespoons granulated sugar (.378 mg)
2¾ teaspoons (1 packet) bread machine yeast (3.5 mg)

1. Add all the ingredients per your machine manufacturer's instructions, or as listed here, beginning with the water. As with all my bread machine breads, I suggest loading the bread machine and allowing the ingredients to "rest" for 1 to 2 hours before starting the cycle. This step is not necessary if all your ingredients are already at equal room temperatures. Set your machine on Basic White, or its equivalent.

2. When done, remove and cool before serving.

Calories: 145. Sodium: 1.66 mg. Fiber: 2.39 g. Protein: 3.716 g. Carbohydrate: 26 g. Cholesterol: 0 mg. Calcium: 16.2 mg. Iron: 1.96 mg. Potassium: 119.1 mg. Total Fat: 3.3 g; Saturated fat: 0.5 g, Monounsaturated fat: 2.1 g, Polyunsaturated fat: 0.5 g.

PEANUT BUTTER BREAD WITH BANANA/
❖ BAKE IN THE BREAD MACHINE RECIPE ❖

MAKES 1 LARGE LOAF (APPROXIMATELY 16 SLICES)
SODIUM PER RECIPE: 96.6 MG   SODIUM PER SLICE: 6.03 MG

I justify my passion for peanut butter by telling my wife it provides potassium, but that's only an excuse.

1½ **cups whole wheat flour (9 mg)**
1½ **cups best for bread white flour (3.75 mg)**
  1 **cup Sourdough Starter, page 234 (.144 mg)**
  2 **ripe medium bananas, mashed (2.36 mg)**
  ½ **cup unsalted peanut butter (21.9 mg)**
  1 **egg (55.4 mg)**
  4 **tablespoons granulated sugar (.5 mg)**
2½ **teaspoons bread machine yeast (3.5 mg)**

1. If you prefer egg substitutes you can simply replace the egg with 3½ tablespoons low-sodium egg substitute.

2. Place all ingredients in your bread machine, set for medium or large loaf, and bake on the shorter Basic Whole Wheat cycle. When done, cool and serve in slices.

Calories: 161. Sodium: 6.04 mg. Fiber: 2.62 g. Protein: 5.477 g. Carbohydrate: 25.7 g. Cholesterol: 11.69 mg. Calcium: 11.2 mg. Iron: 1.32 mg. Potassium: 183 mg. Total Fat: 4.8 g; Saturated fat: 1 g, Monounsaturated fat: 2.1 g, Polyunsaturated fat: 1.3 g.

Italian Milano /

❈ BAKE IN THE BREAD MACHINE RECIPE ❈

MAKES 1 LOAF (15 SLICES)   SODIUM PER RECIPE: 12.3 MG
SODIUM PER SLICE: .823 MG

*I brought this recipe back from Milan, Italy, where they do use salt
in the recipe but don't use honey or sugar. The Italians love bread.
They use it as a "carrier" of other food. This bread is used to
"carry" such delights as prosciutto (which is now out of our diets
because of its high sodium count), tomatoes, and cheeses. Actually,
what we in the low-sodium world can do is use it for a fresh bread
luncheon sandwich on the day it's baked. Because it has no salt,
after a day or two the only way you'll be able to eat it is to lightly
toast it for breakfast or make a special sandwich with a mix of
light olive oil and crushed garlic cloves. You brush the mix onto a
slice of bread, add a slice each of tomato and onion, if you like,
then top that with ½-ounce Alpine Lace Low Sodium Swiss cheese.
Put the sandwich into a toaster oven, and toast until the cheese
melts. My mother often served us that for lunch when we were
growing up and we really liked it.*

¾ **cup plus 1 tablespoon water (0 mg)**
3 **cups unbleached white flour (7.5 mg)**
¾ **cup Sourdough Starter, page 234 (trace)**
1 **tablespoon unsalted applesauce (.477 mg)**
2 **tablespoons granulated sugar (.252 mg)**
2 **teaspoons bread machine yeast (3.96 mg)**

1. Add all the ingredients to your bread machine pan as per your manufacturer's recommendations. Set the machine to Basic White cycle or its
equivalent. Or, if you wish, combine the ingredients in the order listed,
starting with the water. Remember to replenish your **Sourdough Starter**
with equal amounts of water and flour. If you make the dough by hand
and bake it in your oven, shape as a sourdough loaf and bake it at 400°F
for about 15 minutes. When done, remove and cool. Use as dinner bread,
in sandwiches, for French toast, or turkey stuffing.

*Calories: 101. Sodium: 0.82 mg. Fiber: 0.81 g. Protein: 2.829 g. Carbohydrate: 21.5 g.
Cholesterol: 0 mg. Calcium: 4.209 mg. Iron: 1.697 mg. Potassium: 38.5 mg. Total Fat: 0.3 g;
Saturated fat: 0 g, Monounsaturated fat: 0 g, Polyunsaturated fat: 0.1 g.*

CRUSTY FRENCH BREAD (BAGUETTE) / BREAD MACHINE DOUGH PREPARATION—

❈ OVEN-BAKED ❈

MAKES 1 LOAF (16 SLICES)   SODIUM PER RECIPE: 11.7 MG
SODIUM PER SLICE: .728 MG

I ate my first baguette in Papeete, Tahiti, when I was shooting a motion picture for television. We were diving near the coral reefs, filming underwater. The day was exceptionally hot. My white skin was rapidly turning lobster red even though I had kept on a T-shirt while diving. After about 6 hours, I crawled back into the outrigger manned by Rene Tupanno, a native Tahitian with a French name.

I was starving. He handed me a baguette, delivered fresh that morning. I chomped down on that loaf of bread and ate the whole thing myself. Later, while filming in Paris, I saw baguettes being delivered fresh every morning. This recipe is very much like those French ones, but it has no salt and is extremely low in sodium. It's a great accompaniment for soup.

2½ teaspoons bread machine yeast (4.8 mg)
2½ cups bread machine flour (6.25 mg)
1 cup water (0 mg)
½ teaspoon crushed garlic (.238 mg)
1 tablespoon Albers Yellow Cornmeal* (.365 mg)

1. Put the yeast, flour, water, and garlic into your bread machine pan as per your manufacturer's instructions. Set on Dough cycle.
2. When the dough is ready, remove and roll it into a single ball. Press hard when rolling so that you get rid of all air bubbles. Put it on a lightly greased sheet for rising. Cover with a clean light cloth (I use kitchen towels) and let rise for about 45 minutes. If you are in a cold climate and your kitchen is colder than "room temperature," heat your oven to "warm" for no more than 1 minute. Let the heat settle in the stove to near body temperature, then slide in your cookie sheet and close the door. Dough should double in size and be ready for shaping in about 45 minutes. To make sure it's ready, press down lightly with a finger and release. If the indent remains, the dough is ready. Remove it from the stove.
3. Roll the dough into a log about 12 inches long. If making a round loaf, shape it that way instead. Sprinkle a cookie sheet with the cornmeal. Place the loaf on the cornmeal. Let rise again, covered with a light cloth, for about 30 minutes.
4. Preheat the oven to 375°F.

*Or use polenta, or yellow whole grain corn flour.

5. When dough has doubled, spray or brush on gently some cold water. Slit the top diagonally several times with very sharp knife. Bake for 25 to 30 minutes, spraying with water once or twice more. Serve hot. Break apart by hand or slice.

Calories: 75. Sodium: 0.73 mg. Fiber: 0.72 g. Protein: 2.285 g. Carbohydrate: 15.5 g. Cholesterol: 0 mg. Calcium: 3.504 mg. Iron: 1.518 mg. Potassium: 34.7 mg. Total Fat: 0.2 g; Saturated fat: 0 g, Monounsaturated fat: 0 g, Polyunsaturated fat: 0.1 g.

❈ CORNBREAD / BREAD MACHINE RECIPE ❈

MAKES A 1-POUND LOAF   SODIUM PER RECIPE: 87.9 MG
SODIUM PER SERVING: 5.49 MG

Here's a recipe developed over the years by our family and adapted to the bread machine. It contains no salt or baking powder, and only a little sodium, mostly from the egg. Like many of our baked goods, we've cut the fat by exchanging the oil or butter for unsalted applesauce. Serve this right out of the bread machine and eat it all. It will keep for 1 day in an airtight bag.

  1 **cup water (0 mg)**
  ¾ **cup golden raisins or currants (13 mg)**
  ¼ **cup Quick Applesauce (1.912 g)**
  1 **medium egg (55.4 mg)**
1½ **cups plus 2 tablespoons best for bread machine flour (4 mg)**
  ½ **cup granulated sugar (1 mg)**
  1 **cup yellow cornmeal (5.85 mg)**
  3 **tablespoons grated orange zest (.54 mg)**
  1 **tablespoon bread machine dry yeast (6 mg)**

1. Combine all the ingredients in your bread machine pan in the order recommended by the manufacturer or in the order listed above, omitting the raisins. Yeast should be on a dry spot in the basket. Add raisins or currants during the Raisin cycle, generally when the buzzer goes off during the kneading period, or halfway through the kneading process. Serve fresh and hot. Honey is great with cornbread.

Calories: 128. Sodium: 5.49 mg. Fiber: 1.92 g. Protein: 2.692 g. Carbohydrate: 28.3 g. Cholesterol: 11.69 mg. Calcium: 9.607 mg. Iron: 1.595 mg. Potassium: 110.9 mg. Total Fat: 0.8 g; Saturated fat: 0.2 g, Monounsaturated fat: 0.2 g, Polyunsaturated Fat: 0.2 g.

Raisin Bread with Cinnamon /
❈ Bread Machine Recipe ❈

MAKES 2 LOAVES (24 SLICES)   SODIUM PER RECIPE: 41.5 MG
SODIUM PER SLICE: 1.731 MG

5 cups best for bread flour (12.5 mg)
1¾ cups plus 1 tablespoon water (0 mg)
4 tablespoons granulated sugar (.504 mg)
1 tablespoon ground cinnamon (2 mg)
2 tablespoons unsalted applesauce (.954 mg)
1 tablespoon bread machine yeast (6 mg)
1 packed cup raisins (19.8 mg)
¼ teaspoon unsalted butter (trace)

1. Combine all the ingredients except the raisins in your bread machine pan as per the manufacturer's directions. Set the bread machine on the Dough cycle. If you have an older machine, help the dough and water mix with a rubber scraper for the first few minutes. (You won't have to do this with the newer more powerful machines.) Lift the dough from each of the four sides alternately until the machine can knead it without your help. When the mixture has formed a ball, close your machine and allow it to continue on its own. When your machine reaches the Raisin cycle, add them.

2. When the dough is done, break or cut it into 2 pieces. Roll both out on a floured board and put them in greased loaf pans. Cover with a light cloth and let rise at room temperature. The dough should rise to near the top of the pans.

3. Preheat the oven to 425°F. Bake for about 20 minutes. Remove the loaves from the pans and let them set on a rack to cool. You may rub unsalted butter over the tops when removing them from the oven, to flavor the loaves and make them a bit softer. When cool, slice the loaves and freeze those slices you don't use the day you bake it. It will keep in the freezer for up to a full month.

Calories: 127. Sodium: 1.73 mg. Fiber: 1.25 g. Protein: 3.116 g. Carbohydrate: 28.1 g. Cholesterol: 0 mg. Calcium: 11.1 mg. Iron: 2.131 mg. Potassium: 91.8 mg. Total Fat: 0.3 g; Saturated fat: 0.1 g, Monounsaturated fat: 0 g, Polyunsaturated fat: 0.1 g.

Pita Bread / Bread Machine Preparation
❀ or Hand Kneading—Oven Baking ❀

MAKES 12 (6-INCH) PITA   SODIUM PER RECIPE: 22.3 MG
SODIUM PER SERVING: 1.856 MG

*This is easier to put together than it first appears. Use this Middle Eastern recipe for making terrific noontime sandwiches. Fill the pita with **Tabouli** or your favorite mix of lettuce, tomatoes, avocados, etc. Best if baked on tiles or stones, but a heavy-duty nonstick baking sheet will also work.*

1½ cups warm water (0 mg)
 1 cup best for bread whole wheat flour (6 mg)
2½ cups white unbleached flour (6.25 mg)
 2 cloves garlic, minced (1 mg)
 1 tablespoon extra-virgin olive oil (trace)
1½ tablespoons bread machine yeast (9 mg)
  Olive oil for oiling bowl (trace)

1. Combine all the ingredients in your bread machine pan as per the man-ufacturer's directions or in the order listed above. Set the machine on the Dough cycle. When the dough is ready, rub a bit of olive oil in a clean bowl, put the dough in the bowl, turning to coat, and cover tightly with plastic wrap. Let the dough rise in a warm place until doubled in bulk. This should take about 1½ hours. After rising, place the dough on a floured surface, roll it into a log about 12 to 14 inches long. Cut the log into 12 sections and roll each section into a tennis-ball-size ball. With each ball, stretch the dough with your hands, pull it over gently into the center and continue until the ball is smaller and tighter. Pinch the ends together each time. As each ball is completed, put it on a floured surface with the others and cover with a light kitchen towel. These should rest for at least 10 minutes.

2. After this "rising" period, flatten each ball with a rolling pin into the size pita you want, generally about 6 inches diameter. Rolling these out will take pressure. Keep plenty of flour on the breadboard so the dough doesn't stick to it or the rolling pin.

3. Preheat the oven to 500°F. Place each pita-shaped disk on a warm cookie pan sprinkled with Albers or other ungerminated corn flour or very-low-sodium cornmeal. Don't let the pitas touch one another. If you cannot get them all on your cookie sheet, leave the remainder on a board to be baked in a later batch or batches. Let the pitas rest in a warm room under a light cloth for about 20 to 30 minutes.

4. Slip cookie sheet into the preheated oven when ready. Close the oven door quickly and bake for 2 to 3 minutes. Check through the window or slightly break open the oven door after 1 minute to see if disks have ballooned up. When they do, continue baking for another 2 minutes, then remove the pita one at a time with a spatula or paddle. Cool on a flat surface (not a rack) while you bake the remaining disks. They will deflate while cooling. To use, break open while warm and stuff with sandwich filling. Refrigerate the remainder in sealed zipper-type bags or freeze for future use.

Calories: 144. Sodium: 1.86 mg. Fiber: 2.25 g. Protein: 4.666 g. Carbohydrate: 27.9 g. Cholesterol: 0 mg. Calcium: 9.173 mg. Iron: 5.858 mg. Potassium: 100.4 mg. Total Fat: 1.6 g. Saturated fat: 0.2 g. Monounsaturated fat: 0.9 g. Polyunsaturated fat: 0.3 g.

SOURDOUGH BAGUETTES / BREAD MACHINE PREPARATION OR HAND KNEADING—
❧ OVEN BAKING ❧

MAKES 2 LOAVES (16 SLICES)   SODIUM PER RECIPE: 10.2 MG
SODIUM PER SLICE: .636 MG

This is a hybrid of the standard French baguette. It was designed specifically for no-salt, low-sodium tastes. It uses sourdough instead of salt or garlic or any other flavor.

2½ **teaspoons bread machine yeast (3.5 mg)**
2½ **cups bread machine flour (6.25 mg)**
 ½ **cup Sourdough Starter, page 234 (trace)**
 ½ **cup plus 1 tablespoon water (0 mg)**
 1 **tablespoon yellow cornmeal (.365 mg)**
   Optional flavorings to add include rosemary or minced onions

1. Put all the ingredients except the cornmeal into your bread machine pan as per the manufacturer's instructions. Set the bread machine on the Dough cycle and start. When the dough is ready, remove it and prepare it for the type of bread you want—that is, a single round or elongated loaf or 2 smaller loaves. If 2 loaves are desired, cut the dough in half and shape it into short elongated loaves or 2 smaller round loaves. For a larger elongated loaf, simply roll out the dough by hand and put it on a nonstick cooking sheet sprinkled with the cornmeal.
2. The dough should double in size after "resting," so leave room for this. Cover with a clean cloth (I use kitchen towels) and let it rise for about 45 minutes. If you live in a cold climate and your kitchen is colder than normal "room temperature," simply place the dough in the oven after you have heated it to "warm" for no more than 1 minute. Let the heat settle in stove, then slide your cookie sheet in and close the door. It cannot be hot in the oven, only "room temperature." The dough should be ready in

about 45 minutes. To make sure, press down lightly on the dough with a finger and release. If the indent remains, the dough is ready.

3. Preheat the oven to 375°F.

4. When dough has doubled in bulk, spritz or gently brush on cold water. Slit the top diagonally several times with a sharp knife. Bake for 20 to 25 minutes, spritzing with water once or twice more. Serve hot.

TIP: If your bread machine struggles with the kneading process, help it along with a rubber spatula until the ball that is formed readily turns. If the dough becomes too sticky for your machine, add flour a bit at a time while turning with a spatula. Eventually the machine will take over and not struggle after that.

Note: This can be a difficult recipe to succeed with, but it's worth trying. The bread will taste delicious because of the fresh sourdough. Everything you put into this one must be at the same room temperature, including the **Sourdough Starter.** Kneading by hand offers better success than by machine, although the machine will make the dough for you. When slicing, use a very sharp, wet knife and don't press down on the risen dough. Slice across the top without pressing down. A sharp bread knife with serrated edges works best.

Calories: 75. Sodium: 0.64 mg. Fiber: 0.68 g. Protein: 2.232 g. Carbohydrate: 15.5 g. Cholesterol: 0 mg. Calcium: 3.264 mg. Iron: 1.255 mg. Potassium: 31.3 mg. Total Fat: 0.2 g; Saturated fat: 0 g, Monounsaturated fat: 0 g, Polyunsaturated fat: 0.1 g.

SAN FRANCISCO SOURDOUGH LOAF / BREAD
❖ MACHINE PREPARATION—OVEN BAKING ❖

MAKES 1 LOAF (15 SLICES)   SODIUM PER RECIPE: 11.8 MG
SODIUM PER SLICE: .787 MG

If there's one item I miss the most among the variety of breads we eat, it's that large round loaf of San Francisco sourdough. So, to replace that very-high-sodium version—about 500 mg a slice—I created this recipe. What's great about this version is that the sodium level is very low and yet the bread tastes very much like the original. Make the dough in your bread machine or knead it by hand.

¾ **cup plus 1 tablespoon water (0 mg)**
3 **cups unbleached white flour (7.5 mg)**
¾ **cup Sourdough Starter, page 234 (trace)**
1 **tablespoon extra-virgin olive oil (trace)**
2 **tablespoons granulated sugar (.252 mg)**
2 **teaspoons bread machine yeast (3.96 mg)**
2 **tablespoons Albers Yellow Cornmeal (trace)**

1. Put all the ingredients except for the cornmeal into your bread machine pan as per the manufacturer's instructions. Set the machine on the Dough cycle and start. When the dough is done, take it out (it will be sticky and moist), and knead it on a floured board for a few moments. Roll it into a ball and set it on a greased cooking sheet. Let rise at room temperature, or at around 100°F in the oven.

2. After it rises, punch it down, knead it a few times, then shape it into a small round loaf. Sprinkle most of the cornmeal on the greased cooking sheet. Set the loaf atop the cornmeal. With a wet knife, slit the top diagonally several times. Sprinkle the balance of the cornmeal over the top. Let rise again.

3. Preheat the oven to 400°F.

4. After about 30 to 45 minutes, bake the loaf for 12 to 15 minutes. Adjust the time if using a convection oven. Remember to replenish your **Sourdough Starter** with equal amounts of water and flour. Serve hot and stand back.

Calories: 114. Sodium: 0.79 mg. Fiber: 0.93 g. Protein: 2.944 g. Carbohydrate: 22.5 g. Cholesterol: 0 mg. Calcium: 4.144 mg. Iron: 1.946 mg. Potassium: 37.7 mg. Total Fat: 1.2 g; Saturated fat: 0.2 g, Monounsaturated fat: 0.7 g, Polyunsaturated fat: 0.2 g.

Monkey Bread / Bread Machine
❖ Preparation—Oven Baking ❖

MAKES 12 SERVINGS   SODIUM PER RECIPE: 201.5 MG
SODIUM PER SERVING: 16.8 MG

Who hasn't had monkey bread? Some call it "pull-apart," some refer to it as glazed cinnamon bread or even cinnamon rolls. This recipe works well with your bread machine, but if you like to hand-knead your dough, you can do that, too. I suggest preparing this in a bread machine since we aren't using salt and a bread machine kneads evenly without overdoing it. If you hand-knead it, substitute regular active dry yeast for the bread machine yeast.

THE DOUGH
½ cup plus 1 tablespoon water (4.2 mg)
1⅛ cups best for bread white flour (2.18 mg)
1⅛ cups best for bread whole wheat flour (6.75 mg)
3 tablespoons granulated sugar (.378 mg)
2 tablespoons extra-virgin olive oil (trace)
2 medium eggs (110.9 mg)
1¾ teaspoons bread machine yeast (4.2 mg)

THE GLAZE
7 tablespoons unsalted butter (10.9 mg)
¾ cup brown sugar (64.3 mg)
2 teaspoons ground cinnamon (0 mg)

1. Add the dough ingredients in the order your bread machine manufacturer suggests or as listed above. Set your bread machine on the Dough cycle. When the cycle ends, remove the dough, set it on a breadboard, and cover it with a light cloth. While the dough is resting and rising, grease a standard size (10-inch) loaf pan with 2 tablespoons of unsalted butter from the glaze ingredients. Use a glass loaf pan if available.

2. Also sprinkle and shake a few tablespoons of the brown sugar around the loaf pan after you've greased it. Mix the balance of the brown sugar with the cinnamon. Melt the rest of the butter.

3. Split the dough into a dozen balls. Roll each ball in the melted butter, then roll in the sugar-cinnamon mix. Put the balls of dough into the loaf pan about an inch apart. When the bottom of the pan is covered, build the others on top of that. If you have any cinnamon-butter mixture left after you've completed this process, brush or pour a bit of it onto the top layer. Cover the loaf pan and put it in a warm spot (72°F to 90°F) for about ½ hour.

4. Preheat the oven to 350°F.

5. When the dough is ready, bake it for about 25 minutes. When done, remove the bread from the pan quickly. I doubt it'll ever get cold, because you're going to have a tough time holding the family back from eating all of it while it's hot.

Calories: 238. Sodium: 16.79 mg. Fiber: 2.04 g. Protein: 4.021 g. Carbohydrate: 34.3 g. Cholesterol: 49.3 mg. Calcium: 28 mg. Iron: 1.634 mg. Potassium: 132.7 mg. Total Fat: 10.1 g; Saturated fat: 4.8 g, Monounsaturated fat: 3.9 g, Polyunsaturated fat: 0.7 g.

BREAKFAST ROLLS / BREAD MACHINE
❖ PREPARATION—OVEN BAKING ❖

MAKES 24 ROLLS (1 PER SERVING)   SODIUM PER RECIPE: 25.9 MG
SODIUM PER ROLL: 1.08 MG
Make baked glaze like bread-donuts with 3-inch rings. Incredible.
(Can halve this recipe.)

THE ROLLS
5 cups unbleached bread machine flour (12.5 mg)
1¾ cups orange juice fortified with calcium (4.353 mg)
2 tablespoons grated orange zest (.36 mg)
3½ tablespoons granulated sugar (.411 mg)
2 tablespoons extra-virgin olive oil (trace)
1 tablespoon bread machine yeast (6 mg)

THE GLAZE
1 cup confectioners' sugar (1.2 mg)
3 tablespoons orange juice fortified with calcium (.498 mg)
1 tablespoon fresh grated orange zest (.18 mg)
1 teaspoon vanilla extract (.378 mg)

1. To make the Rolls, combine the roll ingredients in the bread machine pan as per the manufacturer's directions. Set the machine on the Dough cycle. After the dough is ready, roll it out with a rolling pin until it is about ¼ to ⅜ inch or more thick. Cut it into 2-inch or 3-inch circles, or cut it into 3-inch triangles. Place the rolls or circles on a greased cooking sheet. If you made triangles, spread a level tablespoon of orange marmalade on the dough and roll up into crescent rolls. You can also make 3-inch and 2-inch circle combinations. Put 1 tablespoon marmalade on a 3-inch circle, top with a 2-inch circle, and seal using a fork. Or, cut 3-inch circles and cut a 1-inch circle out of each. These make great-tasting baked glazed donuts. Let the dough rise under a light cloth for 1 hour at room temperature.

2. Preheat the oven to 425 °F.

3. Bake for 8 minutes.

4. To make the glaze, combine the sugar, juice, zest, and vanilla and brush the mixture generously on the hot rolls right out of the oven. Serve hot or cooled. If you store them in the freezer or refrigerator, refresh them in the microwave before serving.

Calories: 143. Sodium: 1.08 mg. Fiber: 0.93 g. Protein: 3.03 g. Carbohydrate: 29.3 g. Cholesterol: 0 mg. Calcium: 30 mg. Iron: 1.326 mg. Potassium: 78.2 mg. Total Fat: 1.4 g; Saturated fat: 0.2 g, Monounsaturated fat: 0.9 g, Polyunsaturated fat: 0.2 g.

DINNER ROLLS / BREAD MACHINE
❈ PREPARATION — OVEN BAKING ❈

MAKES 24 ROLLS (1 PER SERVING)   SODIUM PER RECIPE: 24.9 MG
SODIUM PER ROLL: 1 MG
Can also be kneaded by hand.

5 cups unbleached bread flour (12.5 mg)
1½ cups tepid water, about 100°F (0 mg)
4 cloves garlic, minced (2 mg)
1 medium onion, diced (3.3 mg)
¼ cup orange juice fortified with calcium, at 105°F to 110°F (.662 mg)
3 tablespoons granulated sugar (.378 mg)
2 tablespoons extra-virgin olive oil (trace)
1 tablespoon bread machine yeast (6 mg)
   Unsalted butter for brushing the tops of baked rolls (.781 mg)

1. Combine all the ingredients in your bread machine pan as per the manufacturer's directions. Set the machine on the Dough cycle. After the dough is ready, cut it in half and roll out each half into a thin rectangle. Slice the rectangle into 24 triangles, roll them up, crescent-roll style, and put them on a greased cookie sheet. You can also roll them into balls and put them into greased biscuit pans. Let the rolls rise under a light cloth for 1 hour.

2. Preheat the oven to 425°F.

3. Bake the rolls for 8 minutes. While hot, brush a dash of unsalted butter over the tops of the rolls.

Calories: 116. Sodium: 1.04 mg. Fiber: 0.91 g. Protein: 2.984 g. Carbohydrate: 22.5 g. Cholesterol: 0 mg. Calcium: 9.204 mg. Iron: 1.818 mg. Potassium: 52 mg. Total Fat: 1.4 g; Saturated fat: 0.2 g, Monounsaturated fat: 0.9 g, Polyunsaturated fat: 0.2 g.

CINNAMON ROLLS / BREAD MACHINE
❖ PREPARATION — OVEN BAKING ❖

MAKES 14 ROLLS (1 PER SERVING)   SODIUM PER RECIPE: 64.9 MG
SODIUM PER ROLL: 4.636 MG

These are the best cinnamon rolls we've ever eaten. Even though they have no salt, and very little sodium, everyone in the family will want them, along with the recipe.

THE DOUGH

1¼ cups water (0 mg)
2 tablespoons Quick Applesauce, page 359 (.956 mg)
2 tablespoons granulated sugar (.25 mg)
3 cups best for bread white flour (7.5 mg)
2¼ teaspoons bread machine yeast (4.5 mg)

THE FILLING

4 tablespoons Homemade Applesauce, page 360, or other unsalted applesauce (.956 mg)
1 tablespoon orange juice fortified with calcium (.398 mg)
2 level tablespoons ground cinnamon (3.58 mg)
¾ cup seedless raisins (14.8 mg)
6 tablespoons brown sugar (28.3 mg)
3 tablespoons chopped unsalted pecans or walnuts (.2 mg)

THE GLAZE

1 cup confectioners' sugar (1.2 mg)
3 tablespoons orange juice fortified with calcium (.585 mg)
2 tablespoons finely grated orange zest (.36 mg)
¼ teaspoon vanilla extract (trace)

1. Put the dough ingredients in the bread machine pan and set the machine on the Dough cycle. Lightly grease the bread machine pan, even if it's the nonstick type. The finished dough will be sticky to the touch. Put it on a lightly floured breadboard and knead it lightly until the stickiness is gone.

2. To prepare the filling, combine the applesauce, juice, cinnamon, raisins, sugar, and nuts.

3. Preheat the oven to 350°F.

4. When the dough is ready, roll it out into a rectangular shape about the size of a standard breadboard. Spread the filling evenly on top. Roll the dough into log shape, then slice it into 14 to 18 equal pieces and place them in a lightly greased baking dish about 1½ inches deep. Put the pieces about ¼ to ½ inch apart until the dish is full. After the rolls rise they should touch each other. After putting them in the preheated oven, they will rise a bit more. Bake at 350°F for 20 minutes in a standard oven, 325°F for about 20 to 25 minutes in a convection oven.

5. To make the glaze, combine the sugar, juice, zest, and vanilla until thick. Spread this over the baked buns as soon as you pull them from the oven. Serve hot.

Calories: 207. Sodium: 4.64 mg. Fiber: 2.03 g. Protein: 3.797 g. Carbohydrate: 46.2 g. Cholesterol: 0 mg. Calcium: 28.4 mg. Iron: 4.933 mg. Potassium: 149.5 mg. Total Fat: 1.3 g; Saturated fat: 0.1 g, Monounsaturated fat: 0.3 g, Polyunsaturated fat: 0.8 g.

SANDWICH BUNS / BREAD MACHINE

❧ PREPARATION — OVEN BAKING ❧

MAKES 14 BUNS SODIUM PER RECIPE: 27 MG SODIUM PER BUN: 1.926 MG

This recipe works well in a bread machine, which is how I make the dough, or you can mix it and knead it by hand if you prefer.

  5 **cups best for bread flour (12.5 mg)**
1¾ **cups plus 1 tablespoon water (0 mg)**
  2 **tablespoons granulated sugar (.25 mg)**
  2 **tablespoons Homemade Applesauce, page 360, or other**
      unsalted applesauce (.954 mg)
  1 **tablespoon bread machine yeast (6 mg)**
  1 **large onion, diced (3.3 mg)**

1. Lightly grease the bread machine pan, even if it's nonstick. The dough will be sticky when done. Combine all the ingredients in the bread machine pan as per the manufacturer's directions. Set the machine on the Dough cycle. For the first 1 to 2 minutes, use a rubber spatula to get the flour and water to mix, lifting the dough with a rubber scraper from each of the four sides alternately until the machine can knead it without your help. When it has formed a ball, close the machine and allow it to continue on its own.

2. After the dough is ready, cut it in half and press out with your hands on a lightly floured board until it measures about ½ to ¾ inch thick and is rectangular. Make sure it is rolled out enough to allow you to cut off 6 to 8 pieces to make buns. You can slice perfectly shaped sandwich rolls (long shape) or hamburger buns (round shape). You can form them with your hands or let the longer buns rise as is. To make larger buns, simply cut fewer pieces (don't forget to adjust the nutrient values per bun). This recipe will also make 18 smaller buns (about store size); remember the nutrient values per bun will decrease.

3. Preheat the oven to 425°F.

4. Put the buns on a lightly greased cookie sheet. Roll out and cut the second half of the dough the same way (or make different-sized buns) and put them on another baking sheet. Cover the buns with a light cloth and set it aside at room temperature to rise. When the buns have doubled in size, bake for about 8 to 10 minutes. Remove the buns from the cookie sheet and set them on a rack to cool.

Calories: 178. Sodium: 1.93 mg. Fiber: 1.67 g. Protein: 5.252 g. Carbohydrate: 37.5 g. Cholesterol: 0 mg. Calcium: 9.287 mg. Iron: 3.334 mg. Potassium: 90 mg. Total Fat: 0.5 g; Saturated fat: 0.1 g, Monounsaturated fat: 0.1 g, Polyunsaturated fat: 0.2 g.

Don's Favorite Sticky Buns / Bread
❈ Machine Preparation—Oven Baking ❈

Makes 12 buns   Sodium per Recipe: 182.7 mg
Sodium per Bun: 15.1 mg

Before my diagnosis of congestive heart failure, I used to love to meet my wife at a local boulangerie for a cup of espresso and a sticky bun. We both worked and the lunch sessions were a special treat. Needless to say, heart failure ended those meetings: sodium for the buns exceeded 1,000 mg each. Not to be daunted by a blip in my lifestyle, I developed this recipe. They have only 14.5 mg per bun. Sticky buns come in many varieties, but mostly they are sticky with a brown sugar, syrup, butter, and pecan coating. The dough can be "elastic," solid, sugary, not sugary, but always delicious.

THE DOUGH

1¼ cups water (0 mg)

  2 tablespoons Quick Applesauce, page 359, or other unsalted applesauce (.956 mg)

  2 tablespoons granulated sugar (.252 mg)

  3 cups best for bread white flour (7.5 mg)

2¼ teaspoons bread machine yeast (5.1 mg)

THE STICKY PART

  ⅓ cup firmly packed light brown sugar (28.3 mg)

  ⅓ cup light corn syrup (131 mg)

3 tablespoons unsalted butter, softened (4.686 mg)
1 cup unsalted pecan pieces or halves (1.08 mg)

THE FILLING
2 tablespoons unsalted butter (3.124 mg)
½ cup unsalted pecans or dates, chopped (.595 mg)
¼ teaspoon ground cinnamon (0 mg)

1. Combine the dough ingredients (all at room temperature) in the bread machine pan as per the manufacturer's instructions. Set the machine on the Dough cycle.
2. To make the sticky part, heat the brown sugar, corn syrup, and butter in a saucepan until the sugar dissolves, stirring often. Pour the mixture into a lightly greased 13x9-inch nonstick baking dish or pan. Arrange the pecans evenly on the bottom.
3. When dough is done and ready for filling, roll it out on a breadboard into a rectangular, ½- to ¾-inch shape. Melt the butter and brush it on the dough. Sprinkle on the cinnamon and the chopped pecans or dates, spreading the filling evenly. Beginning at short end of the dough, roll it up jelly-roll fashion. Pinch the seam to seal it and then cut the roll into 12 pieces. Place these in a prepared baking dish with the cut sides up. Place the pieces close together but not quite touching. Cover lightly and let rise for about 45 minutes to 1 hour at room temperature. After they rise they should push against each other. They will rise a bit more when put in the oven.
4. Preheat the oven to 350°F and bake for about 20 minutes, or until just golden brown.
5. Invert the buns onto a serving tray. Serve immediately or freeze for later use.

Calories: 310. Sodium: 15.23 mg. Fiber: 2.14 g. Protein: 4.692 g. Carbohydrate: 42.2 g. Cholesterol: 12.95 mg. Calcium: 17.8 mg. Iron: 2.88 mg. Potassium: 129.9 mg. Total Fat: 14.6 g; Saturated fat: 3.8 g. Monounsaturated fat: 7.3 g, Polyunsaturated fat: 2.6 g.

CINNAMON RAISIN BAGELS / BREAD MACHINE
✶ PREPARATION — OVEN BAKING ✶

MAKES 10 BAGELS (1 PER SERVING)   SODIUM PER RECIPE: 19.9 MG
SODIUM PER BAGEL: 1.99 MG

These are great for breakfast or as a snack during the day. For a low-sodium diet do not add the cream cheese. You may top with jam, but these bagels are delicious without anything added.

1 cup water (0 mg)
2 cups bread machine flour (5 mg)
1 teaspoon ground cinnamon (.606 mg)
1½ teaspoons sugar (trace)

2½ teaspoons bread machine yeast (3.5 mg)
½ cup seedless raisins (9.9 mg)
1 tablespoon any honey (.84 mg)

1. Combine the water, flour, cinnamon, sugar, and yeast in the order listed, making sure the yeast is in a dry area. If you want these bagels for breakfast, set your timer for the dough to be ready about 1 hour before mealtime. (If your bread machine has a Raisin cycle, you may add them then. If you use a timer, add them after the Dough cycle is completed.)
2. When the dough is ready, remove it and put it on a floured board. Cut it into 10 even pieces—or 8 if you prefer larger bagels. Roll it out into 6- to 8-inch strips. (I make 8-inch strips.) Crease each piece lengthwise and insert a row of raisins as though planting corn. Crimp the dough shut and roll it until smooth. Form a circle by bringing dough around and overlapping it about 1 inch. Pinch it tightly. Place the circle on a lightly greased pan or plate for rising. Continue until you finish making all the bagels. Or, you can shape the dough into breadsticks.
3. Let the dough rise under a light cloth for 45 minutes. When it is ready, bring 2 to 3 quarts of water to a boil in a large pan. Add the honey to the water. (This will help give your bagels a shiny outer layer.)
4. Preheat oven to 375°F.
5. Lower bagel rings into the boiling water, and as soon as rings rise to top of water (this will happen quickly), remove them and put them on a lightly greased cookie sheet. When the bagels are ready for baking, put them into the oven for about 20 minutes. If you don't eat all of them at the first serving, freeze the rest for future use. Without salt, these bagels will not remain fresh for more than a day, unless frozen in a zipper-type freezer bag.

Calories: 127. Sodium: 1.99 mg. Fiber: 1.28 g. Protein: 3.132 g. Carbohydrate: 28.4 g. Cholesterol: 0 mg. Calcium: 11.2 mg. Iron: 2.345 mg. Potassium: 105 mg. Total Fat: 0.3 g; Saturated fat: 0.1 g, Monounsaturated fat: 0 g, Polyunsaturated fat: 0.1 g.

PIZZA DOUGH—THIN CRUST / BREAD
✺ MACHINE PREPARATION—OVEN BAKING ✺

MAKES 10 SLICES EXTRA LARGE PIZZA   *SODIUM PER RECIPE: 8.629 MG*
SODIUM PER SLICE: .863 MG
The nutrient values given are for the entire pizza crust. To estimate your sodium intake, divide the total by the number of slices you cut.

2¼ cups best for bread machine flour (5.625 mg)
¾ cup plus 1 tablespoon lukewarm water (0 mg)
2 teaspoons extra-virgin olive oil (trace)
1½ teaspoons bread machine yeast (3 mg)

1. Put the flour, water, oil, and yeast in the bread machine pan, which you have lightly greased. Set the machine on the Dough cycle. When done, remove the dough and roll it out on a lightly floured board until it is the size of your pizza pan. Transfer it to the pizza pan, cover with a light cloth, and rest for 20 to 30 minutes. (I use a pizza pan that has holes in the bottom of it like a sieve; it is great for ensuring that the pizza dough bakes enough so it is not soggy when done.) Roll the dough edges or flute them, whichever you prefer. Prick the surface slightly with a fork.

2. Preheat the oven to 500°F. Bake the pie with your toppings for about 10 minutes. Check Pizza recipe for added nutrient values.

Per slice. Calories: 112. Sodium: 0.86 mg. Protein: 3.135 g. Carbohydrate: 21.7 g. Fiber: 0.89 g. Cholesterol: 0 mg. Calcium: 4.604 mg. Iron: 2.008 mg. Potassium: 42.1 mg. Total Fat: 1.2 g; Saturated fat: 0.2 g, Monounsaturated fat: 0.7 g, Polyunsaturated fat: 0.7 g.

THICK PIZZA DOUGH / BREAD MACHINE
❖ PREPARATION—OVEN BAKED ❖

MAKES 2 EXTRA-LARGE (10 SLICE) PIZZA CRUST
SODIUM PER RECIPE: 19 MG   SODIUM PER PIZZA SLICE: .948 MG
The nutrient values listed are for the entire pizza crust. To estimate your sodium intake, divide the total by the number of slices you cut.

  5 cups best for bread flour (12.5 mg)
1²/₃ cups lukewarm water (0 mg)
3½ tablespoons sugar (.441 mg)
  2 tablespoons extra-virgin olive oil (trace)
  1 tablespoon bread machine yeast (6 mg)

1. Put the flour, water, sugar, oil, and yeast in the bread machine pan, which you have lightly greased. Set the machine on the Dough cycle. When the dough is done, transfer the dough to a floured board, make a ball, and slice it in half. Roll each half out until it is ½- to ¾-inch thick. Place each on a pizza sheet and curl up the outer edges to make a thick ridge around the circumference. Cover the prepared sheets with a light cloth and let set for about 20 minutes at room temperature.

2. Preheat the oven to 500°F.

3. Spread **Very-Low-Sodium Pizza Topping** (page 132) on the dough and bake for 8 to 10 minutes. Serve hot.

4. Crust is cooked with pizza ingredients from our **Very-Low-Sodium Pizza** (page 132). When crust is filled with pizza ingredients, bake at 500°F for 8 to 10 minutes on a perforated pizza pan.

Crust values only per slice: Calories: 136. Sodium: 0.95 mg. Protein: 3.458 g. Carbohydrate: 26.3 g. Fiber: 0.97 g. Cholesterol: 0 mg. Calcium: 5.096 mg. Iron: 2.156 mg. Potassium: 45.5 mg. Total Fat: 1.7 g; Saturated fat: 0.2 g, Monounsaturated fat: 1 g, Polyunsaturated fat: 0.2 g.

SANDWICHES

❖ ❖ ❖ ❖ ❖ ❖ ❖ ❖

❖ DON'S VERY BEST LUNCHEON SANDWICH ❖

MAKES 1 SANDWICH   SODIUM PER SANDWICH: 33.8 MG

I probably eat more of these than any other, whether at home or on a picnic. And what could be healthier?

2 slices of Sourdough Whole Wheat Bread, page 243 (2.094 mg), or 1 Sandwich Bun, page 258 (1.926 mg)
½ ounce Alpine Lace Low Sodium Swiss (17.5 mg)
1 tablespoon Hain Stone Ground No Salt Added Mustard (3.3 mg)
4 thin slices cucumber (.56 mg)
1 thin slice red onion (.27 mg)
¼ small tomato, sliced (4.05 mg)
1 leaf romaine lettuce, washed (.8 mg)
¼ California avocado (5.19 mg) (optional)

1. Toast the bread lightly in an oven toaster with Swiss on 1 piece. Spread mustard on 1 slice. Top with the cucumber, onion, tomato, and lettuce. Spread the avocado on the other slice of bread. Put the 2 slices together, cut the sandwich in half, and enjoy it with a sodium-free drink of water, orange juice, or tea. A great lunch. For a treat, have 1 **Becky's Oatmeal Cookie** (page 338) or 1 **Don's Classic Oatmeal Cookie** (page 338).

Calories: 329. Sodium: 33.76 mg. Fiber: 6.75 g. Protein: 12.1 g. Carbobydrate: 46 g. Cholesterol: 10 mg. Calcium: 40.8 mg. Iron: 4.318 mg. Potassium: 594.1 mg. Total Fat: 12.2 g; Saturated fat: 3.3 g, Monounsaturated fat: 5.3 g, Polyunsaturated fat: 1.3 g.

⊛ HAMBURGER ⊛

MAKES 1 BURGER   SODIUM PER BURGER: 84.2 MG

I love hamburgers. So, even though I had to lower my sodium to "below the line," I figured out how to make one I could enjoy anytime I wanted. The fat content has also been reduced.

4 **medium mushrooms, diced (2.88 mg)**
1 **slice red onion, diced (1.1 mg)**
3 **ounces any lean ground beef (55.9 mg)**
1 **Sandwich Bun, page 258 (1.927 mg)**
1 **slice medium tomato (1.8 mg)**
½ **ounce Alpine Lace Low Sodium Swiss (17.5 mg)**
1 **teaspoon Hain Stone Ground Honey Mustard (3.3 mg)**
1 **leaf romaine lettuce, washed (8 mg)**

1. Combine the mushrooms and onion with the meat. Cook the hamburger in a nonstick pan. Toast the bun's inner sides only. Lay the cheese on the bun top and let it melt. Spread the mustard on the bun bottom. You can add a dollop of Hunt's low-sodium ketchup if you like (<5 mg per tablespoon). Place the meat against the melted cheese when the meat is done. Top with lettuce and tomato and serve. Delicious.

Calories: 451. Sodium: 84.25 mg. Fiber: 2.99 g. Protein: 27.3 g. Carbohydrate: 42.7 g. Cholesterol: 68.48 mg. Calcium: 36.6 mg. Iron: 6.088 mg. Potassium: 676 mg. Total Fat: 18.7 g; Saturated fat: 7.9 g, Monounsaturated fat: 6.4 g, Polyunsaturated fat: 1 g.

⊛ BARBECUED CHEESEBURGER ⊛

MAKES 1 CHEESEBURGER   SODIUM PER SERVING: 67.5 MG

It's not often that we can enjoy something with a fast-food image and do it with very little sodium. This cheeseburger recipe may seem basic but it's not. Since we all enjoy hamburgers so much, this low-sodium version is an important contribution to this book. Use lean hamburger meat to help keep the fat content as low as possible. (Most ordinary hamburgers have more than 1,000 mg sodium each.)

2 **slices avocado (2.6 mg)**
   Splash of lemon juice (trace)
1 **Sandwich Bun, page 258 (1.927 mg)**
2 **medium slices tomato (3.6 mg)**
1 **slice red onion (.27 mg)**
1 **lettuce leaf of your choice (2 mg)**
1 **ounce mushrooms, sliced (.92 mg)**
1 **teaspoon Hain Stone Ground No Salt Added Mustard (3.3 mg)***

2 ounces very lean ground round, shaped into a burger (37.4 mg)
½ ounce Alpine Lace Low Sodium Swiss (17.5 mg)† or ½ ounce
    Tillamook Low-Sodium Cheddar (27.5 mg)

1. Mash the avocado lightly with a splash of lemon juice. Spread the avocado on the bottom half of the bun and top with the tomato, onion, and lettuce. Sauté the mushrooms either over the stove or in a pan over barbecue flames. Lay the mushrooms on top of the lettuce. Spread the mustard on the top half of the bun. Barbecue the burger over hot coals until the juice sizzles at the top. Turn and complete the grilling. (If you use a nonstick fry pan instead, do not add oil or butter.) After the burger is turned, lay the cheese on top and then cover with the bun top. When cheese has melted down enough, remove the burger from the heat. Top with the bottom half of the bun and serve.

2. If you like mayonnaise on your burger, use 1 teaspoon of **Homemade Mayonnaise Substitute** (page 306), omitting the dill, or choose Hain Sodium-Free Mayonnaise. However, you'll probably find that this hamburger doesn't need mayo or ketchup—we find it juicy enough as it is. (No-salt-added ketchup is available at most grocery stores, should you want it.)

Calories: 417. Sodium: 67.53 mg. Fiber: 3.61 g. Protein: 21.6 g. Carbohydrate: 43.1 g. Cholesterol: 49.12 mg. Calcium: 33.1 mg. Iron: 5.18 mg. Potassium: 576.1 mg. Total Fat: 17.5 g; Saturated fat: 6 mg, Monounsaturated fat: 6.9 g, Polyunsaturated fat: 1.1 g.

❀ TURKEY BURGER ❀

MAKES 1 BURGER   SODIUM PER BURGER: 133.7 MG

 1 Sandwich Bun, page 258 (1.927 mg)
½ ounce Alpine Lace Low Sodium Swiss (17.5 mg)
 3-ounce portion of lean ground turkey or lean ground beef
    (80.4 mg)
¼ medium onion, thinly sliced (.1 mg)
 4 medium mushrooms, sliced (2.8 mg)
 1 tablespoon extra-virgin olive oil (trace)
 1 tablespoon Hain Stone Ground Honey Mustard or Grey
    Poupon Honey Mustard (10 mg)
 1 leaf romaine lettuce, washed (.8 mg)
¼ cup whole cranberry sauce (20 mg)

*If the Hain brand is not available, substitute Grey Poupon Honey Mustard or East Shore Honey Mustard. I also like Mendocino Honey Mustard. If you like a hotter mustard instead of a sweet, use one of the unsalted Dijon mustards such as Featherweight (0 mg), East Shore (0 mg), or Life All Natural (<2 mg).
†The Alpine Lace Low Sodium Swiss that is sold over the deli counter is lower in sodium than that sold in packages.

1. Toast the bun, melting the cheese against the toasted side of the bun top. Grill the turkey burger well. Lightly sauté the onions and mushrooms together in olive oil. Put the mushrooms and onions on top of the melted cheese. Spread the mustard over the bun bottom, then top with the lettuce. Put the turkey patty on top of the lettuce, then the cranberry sauce on top of the turkey patty. Now put the sandwich together and serve.

Calories: 609. Sodium: 133.67 mg. Fiber: 3.46 g. Protein: 27 g. Carbohydrate: 69.4 g. Cholesterol: 77.55 mg. Calcium: 43.6 mg. Iron: 5.617 mg. Potassium: 608.1 mg. Total Fat: 25.5 g; Saturated fat: 5.9 g, Monounsaturated fat: 12.7 g, Polyunsaturated fat: 3.2 g.

TIP: If you grate half a zucchini into the turkey, you won't taste it, but it makes the burger nice and moist.

❧ SOYBURGERS ❧

**MAKES 4 BURGERS SODIUM PER RECIPE: 203.9 MG
SODIUM PER BURGER: 51 MG**
This recipe is from my sister, who is a vegetarian and also eats a low-sodium diet. Prepare this burger mixture the day before you want it.

> 1 cup soy beans (25.2 mg)
> 1 stalk celery, sliced thin (35 mg)
> 1 cup cooked brown rice (7.6 mg)*
> ½ cup whole wheat flour (3 mg)
> 2 medium eggs, beaten (110.9 mg)
> ½ cup sautéed mushrooms (1.4 mg)
> ¼ cup sautéed broccoli (4.8 mg)
> 1 medium onion, chopped and sautéed (3.3 mg)
> 2 teaspoons chopped green onion or other onion (4.8 mg)
> ½ teaspoon sweet basil (.24 mg)
> 2 tablespoons extra-virgin olive oil (trace)
> 4 Sandwich Buns, page 258 (7.706 mg)
> 1 ounce Alpine Lace Low Sodium Swiss (35 mg) or Low-Sodium Tillamook Cheddar (55 mg)

1. Soak the soy beans overnight. Boil them for 3 hours with the celery. Mash the soy beans when done. Combine them with the rice, flour, eggs, mushrooms, broccoli, onions, and basil, and form the mixture into 4 patties. In a medium-hot nonstick skillet warm the olive oil. Cook the patties in the pan just as you would with a turkey burger or hamburger. Top with cheese. You may also add lentils and walnuts to this recipe.

Calories: 596. Sodium: 50.98 mg. Fiber: 7.99 g. Protein: 22 g. Carbohydrate: 93.5 g. Cholesterol: 98.5 mg. Calcium: 129.5 mg. Iron: 6.631 mg. Potassium: 663.9 mg. Total Fat: 15.5 g; Saturated fat: 3.3 g, Monounsaturated fat: 6.9 g, Polyunsaturated fat: 3 g.

*Most of the calories come from the rice; cook it in unsalted water.

❂ Mom's Mystery Burgers ❂

MAKES 12 MYSTERY BURGERS   SODIUM PER RECIPE: 332.1 MG
SODIUM PER BURGER: 27.7 MG

My mother took an old Italian recipe for calzones *and created*
these. She called her concoction "Mystery burgers."
I became a hero to my fellow Marines when I stood in as mess
officer in Okinawa. I got the cooks to use the night's leftovers
to come up with mystery burgers like these for
lunch. They were a big hit.
I've left out some of the high-fat content Mother used and much of
the sodium, but these are good hot or cold and can be reheated
safely in the microwave.

THE DOUGH
   Sandwich Buns, page 258 (27 mg)

1. Make the **Sandwich Buns** according to the recipe. Prepare the other ingredients while dough is in the bread machine so they are ready for the next step. When dough is ready, press it on a slightly floured board with your hands outward, as though making a pizza shell. if your breadboard is too small, cut the dough in half before pressing it out and work on the halves separately. The dough should be about ¼- to ⅜-inch thick when ready. Cut it into 12 pieces double-sandwich-size. You're going to fold them over and pinch them shut.

THE FILLING
1. Take some license here. Use any leftovers—meatballs, chicken pieces, vegetables. Kids love these with peanut butter and jam. When cooked, you can store them in the refrigerator for up to a day, or freeze them for a much longer period. Below is just one suggested sandwich recipe. The general process is the same, whatever ingredients you use.

   2 **tablespoons extra-virgin olive oil (trace)**
   1 **onion, chopped (3.3 mg)**
   ½ **pound mushrooms, sliced (8 mg)**
   1 **pound cooked meat, beef, pork, fowl, chopped or sliced thin**
       (298.3 mg)*
   2 **teaspoons of your choice of flavoring, such as coriander, basil,**
       paprika, thyme (depends on meat or vegetables) (1 mg)
   12 **Sandwich Buns, page 258 (27 mg)**

*Based on 17% lean ground beef; 7% lean ground beef is lower in fat and sodium.

1. In the olive oil sauté the vegetables (and meat if not yet cooked). Stir in the spices or seasonings. You may add pepper if you like it, but no salt.

2. When ready, brush or spread the mixture over half of each square of dough and fold. Sometimes I seal the mixture into a whole piece and lay another over it which makes 6 larger sandwiches that you can cut in half to serve. To do this, pinch the two stuffed pieces together all around. Place these on a lightly greased pan and let them rise for about 60 minutes at room temperature (about 70°F to 80°F). When ready, bake in a preheated 425°F oven for about 8 to 10 minutes, until done.

Calories: 294. Sodium: 27.68 mg. Fiber: 2.02 g. Protein: 12.7 g. Carbohydrate: 39.1 g. Cholesterol: 25.99 mg. Calcium: 14.5 mg. Iron: 4.288 mg. Potassium: 268.1 mg. Total Fat: 9.3 g; Saturated fat: 3 g, Monounsaturated fat: 4.5 g, Polyunsaturated fat: 0.7 g.

❖ BASIC TACO ❖

MAKES 8 TACOS   SODIUM PER RECIPE: 306.4 MG   SODIUM PER TACO: 38.3 MG

Many taco recipes made it into this book. Essentially, you can make up your own. Just remember to stick with low-sodium, low-fat foods and you'll enjoy them without guilt. Because of the high sodium count of flour tortillas, use only the corn type. Check the tortilla packages to make sure the sodium content is zero (0 mg sodium—even the stated 0 mg packages have 2 to 3 mg sodium per tortilla). These packages may also be labeled "Unsalted." If you make your own tortillas, omit the salt and don't use baking soda or powder.

¾ **pound lean beef brisket (244.8 mg)**
2 **cups cooked potatoes (18 mg)**
1 **medium onion, diced (3.3 mg)**
4 **cloves garlic, minced (2 mg)**
1 **teaspoon oregano (trace)**
½ **teaspoon dry mint leaves (trace)**
8 **unsalted white or sweet corn taco shells (15.6 mg)**
3 **tablespoons extra-virgin olive oil (trace)**
8 **romaine or iceberg lettuce inner leaves (6.4 mg)**
Frontier Mexican seasoning to taste* (0 mg)

1. Boil the brisket and grind it in a food processor or food mill. Dice and mash the cooked potatoes with the garlic, oregano, Frontier Mexican seasoning and mint. Cook this mixture with the brisket in a nonstick pan until

*Available mail-order from www.healthyheartmarket.com or by calling 1-888/753-0310.

thick. Fry the corn tortillas quickly in hot oil and fold over, setting them on paper towels to drain. Place 1 lettuce leaf in the well of each taco shell and spoon in the meat-potato mixture and then the diced onions. You may add Tabasco (30 mg teaspoon) or Featherweight Chili Sauce (10 mg per tablespoon) or **Chili Sauce** (page 173) (2 mg per tablespoon). Featherweight Chili Sauce is available at your local health food store.

Calories: 273. Sodium: 38.3 mg. Fiber: 2.63 g. Protein: 15.3 g. Carbohydrate: 22.8 g. Cholesterol: 2.46 mg. Calcium: 39.3 mg. Iron: 2.197 mg. Potassium: 510.4 mg. Total Fat: 13.6 g; Saturated fat: 1.3 g, Monounsaturated fat: 4.9 g, Polyunsaturated fat: 1.6 g.

❄ CONTEMPORARY TACO ❄

MAKES 8 TACOS   SODIUM PER RECIPE: 525.7 MG   SODIUM PER TACO: 65.7 MG

1 **pound ground beef, pork, or chicken pieces (299.4 mg)***
2 **cloves garlic, minced (1 mg)**
1 **teaspoon dried oregano (trace)**
  Frontier Mexican seasoning to taste† (0 mg)
8 **medium unsalted corn taco shells (15.6 mg)**
2 **ounces grated Tillamook Low Sodium Cheddar (165 mg)**
3 **tablespoons extra-virgin olive oil (trace)**
  Tabasco sauce to taste (22 mg)
2 **medium tomatoes, diced (22 mg)**
1 **medium onion, diced (3.3 mg)**
2 **cups finely chopped romaine (8.9 mg)‡**
½ **California avocado, sliced (10.4 mg)**

1. Cook the meat in a nonstick pan, stirring often to keep it loose. Mix in the garlic, oregano, and seasoning while cooking. Fry the taco shells in a nonstick frypan. Fold and set on paper towels to drain. Put the cooked meat into shell first, then a sprinkle of grated cheese. Quickly fry tortilla shells in pan with olive oil. Rest cooked tortilla on paper towels to draw out the oil. Layer in the tomatoes, onion, and lettuce. Next top with the avocado slices and serve.

Calories: 301. Sodium: 65.71 mg. Fiber: 1.97 g. Protein: 15 g. Carbohydrate: 12.3 g. Cholesterol: 48.5 mg. Calcium: 43.7 mg. Potassium: 394.4 mg. Total Fat: 21.6 g; Saturated fat: 7.2 g, Monounsaturated fat: 9.1 g, Polyunsaturated fat: 2 g.

*Based on 17% lean ground beef. Pork and chicken are slightly lower in sodium count.
†Available mail-order from www.healthyheartmarket.com or by calling 1-800/753-0310.
‡If you are using iceberg lettuce instead, the sodium count is 16 mg.

❈ TURKEY TACO ❈

1 **pound lean chopped turkey, formed into 8 burgers (319.8 mg)***
1 **tablespoon extra-virgin olive oil (trace)**
   Frontier Mexican seasoning to taste† (trace)
3 **cloves garlic, minced (1.5 mg)**
8 **unsalted white or sweet corn taco shells (15.6 mg)**
4 **ounces grated Alpine Lace Low Sodium Swiss (140 mg)**
1 **medium onion, diced (3.3 mg)**
2 **medium tomatoes, diced (22 mg)**
1 **small head iceberg lettuce, chopped (29.2 mg)**
8 **teaspoons any reduced-fat low-sodium cultured sour cream
   (15.8 mg)**
1 **California avocado, sliced (21 mg)**

1. Cook the turkey burgers loosely in a nonstick frypan with the oil and seasonings. Mix in the garlic. Cook the taco shells (corn tortillas) and set them aside to drain over dry paper towels. To make the tacos, set the burger into the shell first followed by sprinkles of cheese, onion, and tomatoes, then lettuce, sour cream, and avocado slices.

Calories: 247. Sodium: 71.01 mg. Fiber: 3.21 g. Protein: 13.9 g. Carbohydrate: 13.6 g. Cholesterol: 45.47 mg. Calcium: 60.3 mg. Iron: 1.512 mg. Potassium: 424.1 mg. Total Fat: 15.7 g. Saturated fat: 4.6 g. Monounsaturated fat: 6.3 g. Polyunsaturated fat: 2.7 g.

❈ TOFU TACO ❈

*A high-protein low-sodium cancer-fighting taco that tastes
surprisingly delicious and is very easy to make.*

1 **California avocado, sliced (20.8 mg)**
1 **medium tomato, diced (11 mg)**
1 **medium onion, diced (3.3 mg)**
½ **head romaine lettuce, shredded (4.5 mg)**
2 **ounces Alpine Lace Low Sodium Swiss, shredded (70 mg)**
4 **ounces mushrooms, sliced (2.8 mg)**
1 **teaspoon granulated sugar (.8 mg)**
2 **tablespoons Del Monte No Salt Added Tomato sauce (10 mg)**

*Yield is 11.3 ounces after cooking.
†Available mail-order from www.healthyheartmarket.com or by calling 1-800/753-0310.

2 **teaspoons Tabasco sauce (44 mg)**
2 **tablespoons lemon juice (.3 mg)**
8 **no-salt-added corn tortillas* (15.6 mg)**
1 **tablespoon extra-virgin olive oil (trace)**
8 **ounces tofu† (11 mg)**
2 **tablespoons cornstarch or flour (1.4 mg)**
2 **cloves garlic, minced (1 mg)**
   Frontier Mexican seasoning to taste‡ (trace)

1. Arrange the prepared avocado, tomato, onion, lettuce, cheese, and mushrooms in a ring around a serving dish. Combine the sugar, tomato sauce, Tabasco, and lemon juice and set aside. In a nonstick skillet, fry the tortillas quickly in oil, turning once. Remove them and fold them into taco shapes, setting the shells on paper towels, open-side down. Let them drain for a few minutes. Slice the tofu into lengthwise strips as you would meat. Roll the strips in flour or cornstarch and minced garlic. Heat the oil in a nonstick skillet set over medium heat. Raise the heat to high and fry the tofu for about 3 minutes on each side, until golden brown. Remove and set aside. Brush or pour the tomato sauce mixture over the tofu and add seasoning. Let the diners make their own tacos.

Calories: 173. Sodium: 24.48 mg. Fiber: 2.79 g. Protein: 4.567 g. Carbohydrate: 17.3 g. Cholesterol: 5 mg. Calcium: 49.8 mg. Iron: 1.096 mg. Potassium: 310.7 mg. Total Fat: 10.3 g; Saturated fat: 2.3 g, Monounsaturated fat: 4.9 g, Polyunsaturated fat: 1.9 g.

*If La Hacienda brand is not available, look for no-salt-added corn tortillas that list sodium as 0 mg. The flour tortillas are all too high for low-sodium diets.
†Low-sodium tofu is available in most areas and is preferred for your diet.
‡Available mail-order from www.healthyheartmarket.com or by calling 1-800/753-0310.

❈ Tony's Tacos ❈

SERVES 8   SODIUM PER RECIPE: 467.2 MG   SODIUM PER TACO: 58.4 MG

While I was growing up my father owned a 160-acre ranch in southern California's hot Coachella Valley desert. Really hot. Gnats, mosquitos, snakes, and heat, heat, heat. It's where the best melons, dates, and alfalfa were grown and still are. The ranch was taken care of by Frank Rodriguez and his family. One of his boys, Tony, made a mean taco that I have adapted here. Simple to make, it works for lunch or dinner. By the way, Tony used blackbird meat. Our corn crop always attracted thousands of blackbirds and yep, guess what.

- **2 ounces tofu (1.8 mg)**
- **2 ounces plain yogurt (21.5 mg)**
- **1 tablespoon lemon juice (.15 mg)**
- **8 corn tortillas without sodium (15.6 mg)**
- **1 pound chicken, turkey, or lean ground beef cooked (298.3 mg)***
- **3 tablespoons extra virgin olive oil (trace)**
- **4 ounces no salt added tomato sauce (20 mg)†**
- **1 teaspoon sugar (trace)**
- **1 California avocado, sliced (21 mg)**
- **2 ounces low sodium Alpine Lacer Swiss cheese, shredded (70 mg)**
- **2 teaspoons Tabasco sauce (2.75 mg)**
- **1 onion, finely chopped (3.3 mg)**
- **4 ounces mushrooms, chopped (3.68 mg)**
- **2 cloves garlic, minced (1 mg)**
- **½ head romaine, shredded (8.96 mg)**

1. Mix lemon juice, tofu, and yogurt together using a fork or spoon and set aside in the refrigerator.

2. Shred romaine and cheese and set aside in refrigerator.

3. Heat 1 tablespoon of olive oil in nonstick skillet. Cook meat until nearly done over medium to medium high heat. Add garlic, onion, Tabasco, mushrooms, sugar, and tomato sauce and cook for another 5 minutes, stirring frequently. Allow to simmer at very low heat while you fry the tortillas.

4. To fry tortillas, heat a nonstick frying pan or griddle with 2 tablespoons of olive oil over medium high heat. Lower tortillas into hot oil and quickly

---

*Based on 17% lean ground beef. You may also use meat strips if you like. See Tofu Taco to try a vegetarian taco.

†A product called Finast has only 10 mg sodium. The recipe is based on using either Hunt's no salt added or S&W no salt added tomato sauce.

fry them, turning them as soon as bubbles appear in the tortilla. Lift out, fold for tacos, and place on absorbent paper towels on a dish edges down, fold up. Let oil drip into towel.

When drained, serve hot with meat mixture, cheese sprinkled on meat, romaine on top of that, and the sliced avocado on the romaine. On top of all that, lay a dollop of the yogurt tofu mix. If tofu is not available or you would prefer, add a teaspoon of sour cream instead. Tell your guests that you'll give them a dollar if they can eat these without dripping them on their plates or your tablecloth. You won't lose a nickel.

Serve with fresh fruit, corn on the cob, or refried beans. See Index for low sodium Refried Beans.

Calories: 319. Sodium: 58.4 mg. Fiber: 2.83 g. Cholesterol: 44.22 mg. Calcium: 51.8 mg. Iron: 2.074 mg. Potassium: 450.9 mg. Total Fat: 23.1 g; Saturated fat: 6.6 g, Monounsaturated fat: 11.5 g, Polyunsaturated fat: 2.4 g.

❖ QUICK TACOS WITH OR WITHOUT MEAT ❖

MAKES 2 TACOS SODIUM PER RECIPE: 56.4 MG SODIUM PER TACO: 28.2 MG
I make these from leftovers, especially from a sauté mix I use as a side dish for main courses.

VEGETABLE SAUTÉ
   2 tablespoons extra-virgin olive oil (trace)
   1 onion, sliced (3.3 mg)
   ½ pound mushrooms, sliced (7.366 mg)
   ¼ medium sweet red pepper, chopped (.5 mg)
   ½ stalk broccoli, chopped (2.97 mg)
   ½ cup sliced green beans (3.3 mg)

TACO
   2 unsalted corn taco shells (3.9 mg)
   Spritz of olive oil (trace)
   1 ounce Alpine Lace Low Sodium, shredded Swiss (35 mg) or
     shredded Tillamook Low-Sodium Cheddar (55 mg)

1. If using meat in your tacos, cook it first and set it aside. Make sure you account for the nutrient values in your finished dish.
2. If using leftover sautéed vegetables, place them on a microwave-safe dish and heat for 2 minutes until very hot. Remove the dish and set it aside.
3. If you are going to sauté fresh vegetables, heat the oil in a large wok or frying pan with sides, and sauté the onions and mushrooms first. When mushrooms begin to turn, add the peppers, broccoli, and green beans and continue cooking for about 2 to 3 minutes, then set it aside.
4. Lay the tortilla shells in a microwave-safe dish and spritz lightly with oil. Microwave on full power for 30 seconds. When the taco shells bubble

slightly, add the sautéed vegetables (and meat, if you are using it) to the shells and then layer half the cheese over each shell. Heat in the microwave for another 20 seconds. Fold over and serve hot.

Calories: 235. Sodium: 28.21 mg. Fiber: 4.86 g. Protein: 8.294 g. Carbohydrate: 33.3 g. Cholesterol: 10 mg. Calcium: 63.1 mg. Iron: 1.992 mg. Potassium: 551.7 mg. Total Fat: 7.2 g; Saturated fat: 2.6 g, Monounsaturated fat: 1.7 g, Polyunsaturated fat: 1.4 g.

❈ BURRITO DELUXE ❈

MAKES 1 BURRITO   SODIUM PER RECIPE: 70.5 MG

The burritos that my friends often have as lunch are loaded with cheese, sour cream, and lots of sodium in the refried beans that are generally cooked in high-saturated fat. All this is usually served in a tortilla shell heavily sprinkled with salt. If you're healthy, that's okay once in a while. If you have heart disease, it's not a good idea. But here's a way to cook up your own burrito.

1   **no-salt-added corn tortilla (2.75 mg)**
1   **serving Refried Beans, page 158 (18.5 mg)**
¼   **cup lettuce, shredded (7.29 mg)**
1   **medium tomato, diced (11.1 mg)**
1   **serving Homemade Tomato Salsa, page 307 (3.361 mg)**
½   **ounce Tillamook Low-sodium Cheddar, shredded (27.5 mg)**

1. Heat the tortilla, then put the refried beans on top and spread. Next layer on the lettuce and diced tomato, then spread the salsa on top. Sprinkle the Cheddar on top and heat in a medium oven until the cheese is nearly melted. Roll up and devour.

Calories: 475. Sodium: 70.51 mg. Fiber: 21.68 g. Protein: 21.8 g. Carbohydrate: 70.3 g. Cholesterol: 12.5 mg. Calcium: 183.7 mg. Iron: 6.128 mg. Potassium: 1,534 mg. Total Fat: 14.2 g; Saturated fat: 4.3 g, Monounsaturated fat: 5.5 g, Polyunsaturated fat: 1.5 g.

❈ PITA SANDWICH ❈

MAKES 2 SANDWICHES   SODIUM PER RECIPE: 23.9 MG
SODIUM PER SANDWICH: 12 MG

This recipe suggests adding hummus, but if you prefer ground meat or leftover diced and cooked chicken that works, too.

2   **homemade Pita Bread, page 251 (3.5 mg)**
1   **cup shredded lettuce (4.48 mg)**
½   **tomato, diced (5.5 mg)**
½   **peeled cucumber, diced (2.01 mg)**

¼ **red onion, diced (.825 mg), or 1 green onion, diced**
2 **tablespoons Hummus, page 142 (7.37 mg)**
2 **tablespoons Oil and Vinegar Dressing, page 209 (.16 mg)**

1. Stuff each warmed **Pita Bread** with half the lettuce, tomato, cucumber, onion, and hummus. Spritz the ingredients with the **Oil and Vinegar Dressing**—or you can also use homemade **Ranch-Style Dressing** (page 211).

Calories: 276. Sodium: 11.96 mg. Fiber: 5.83 g. Protein: 9.007 g. Carbohydrate: 41.5 g. Cholesterol: 0 mg. Calcium: 107.4 mg. Iron: 8.427 mg. Potassium: 488 mg. Total Fat: 9.3 g; Saturated fat: 1.3 g, Monounsaturated fat: 4.9 g, Polyunsaturated fat: .4 g.

HUMMUS SANDWICH /
❖ WITH WHOLE WHEAT OR PITA BREAD ❖

MAKES 1 SANDWICH   SODIUM PER SANDWICH: 23.9 MG
Easy to make, healthy, and very good flavors.

2 **slices of homemade Whole Wheat Bread, page 234 (1 mg), or**
   1 Pita Bread, page 251 (1.7 mg)*
1 **tablespoon East Shore Sweet & Tangy Mustard (10 mg)**
4 **thin slices cucumber (.56 mg)**
1 **thin slice red onion (.27 mg)**
¼ **small tomato, sliced (2.767 mg)**
1 **leaf romaine or favorite lettuce, washed (.8 mg)**
2 **heaping tablespoons Hummus, page 142 (7.37 mg)**

1. Toast the bread lightly or heat the pita. Spread the mustard on 1 slice (for 1 side). Lay the cucumber, onion, tomatoes, and lettuce atop it. Spread the **Hummus** on the other slice (or side). Press the sandwich together, then slice in half and enjoy with a sodium-free drink of water, orange juice, or tea. Great lunch. Top it all off with a treat of one **Oatmeal Cookie** (page 338) or **Oatmeal Coconut Cookie** (page 340).

Calories: 370. Sodium: 23.86 mg. Fiber: 8.83 g. Protein: 14.1 g. Carbohydrate: 59.5 g. Cholesterol: 0 mg. Calcium: 177.4 mg. Iron: 7.668 mg. Potassium: 561.7 mg. Total Fat: 10.3 g; Saturated fat: 1.3 g, Monounsaturated fat: 3.3 g, Polyunsaturated fat: 4 g.

*You may also substitute 1 **Sandwich Bun** (page 258).

❖ CHICKEN SANDWICH ❖

MAKES 1 SANDWICH   SODIUM PER SANDWICH: 21.4 MG

1 **Sandwich Bun, page 258 (2.169 mg)**
1 **tablespoon Hain Unsalted Real Mayonnaise or Homemade Substitute Mayonnaise, page 306 (7.64 mg)**
1 **teaspoon East Shore, Grey Poupon, or Mendocino honey mustard (3.3 mg)**
½ **ounce Alpine Lace Low Sodium Swiss (17.5 mg)**
2 **slices (2 ounces) cooked chicken breast meat, chilled (38.3 mg)**
1 **leaf romaine (or favorite) lettuce (.8 mg)**
1 **slice medium-sized tomato (1.8 mg)**
1 **thin slice red onion (trace)**
Pepper or unsalted seasoning blend to taste (trace)

1. Slice the bun in half and toast the insides only. Spread the mayonnaise and mustard on the bottom bun. Add the cheese to the top bun half and melt. Layer the chicken, lettuce, tomato, and onion on the bottom bun. Add seasoning to taste. Press the sandwich together and enjoy.

Calories: 321 g. Sodium: 71.35 mg. Protein: 24.2 g. Carbohydrate: 40.5 g. Fiber: 2.25 g. Cholesterol: 47.72 mg. Calcium: 54.3 mg. Potassium: 351.7 mg. Total Fat: 6.3 g; Saturated fat: 3.3 g, Monounsaturated fat: 0.7 g, Polyunsaturated fat: 0.5 g.

❖ DEVILED EGG SANDWICH ❖

MAKES 4 LARGE SANDWICHES   SODIUM PER RECIPE: 353.5 MG
SODIUM PER SERVING: 88.4 MG

*If you are permitted eggs occasionally, here's a sandwich that you'll like. Use your own homemade **Sandwich Buns** * or **Whole Wheat Bread.** Shape the buns into hero sandwich shapes or round rolls.*

4 **Sandwich Buns page 258 (5.994 mg); or 8 slices Whole Wheat Bread page 234 (4.189 mg); or 8 slices Italian Milano Bread, page 247 (3.291 mg)**
6 **hard-cooked medium eggs, diced (332.6 mg)**
1 **clove garlic, minced (.5 mg)**
½ **teaspoon dry mustard (0 mg)**

*The recipe nutrient data is based on using **Sandwich Buns.**
†Or similar low-sodium product, such as "soybean oil, no-salt mayonnaise." You may also substitute 3 tablespoons vinegar for the mayo. I suggest making our **Homemade Mayonnaise Substitute** (page 306).

¼ **teaspoon black pepper (trace)**
3 **tablespoons Hain Unsalted Real Mayonnaise† (12.4 mg)**

1. Combine the eggs with the garlic, mustard, pepper, and mayonnaise. Chill in the refrigerator for at least 1 hour but preferably for 2. Spread the deviled egg mixture on fresh homemade bread or buns.

Calories: 353. Sodium: 88.38 mg. Fiber: 1.72 g. Protein: 13.7 g. Carbohydrate: 39 g. Cholesterol: 286.61 mg. Calcium: 46 mg. Iron: 4.402 mg. Potassium: 179.4 mg. Total Fat: 15.4 g; Saturated fat: 3.4 g, Monounsaturated fat: 5 g, Polyunsaturated fat: 5 g.

❖ LIGHT SANDWICH ❖

MAKES 2 SANDWICHES   SODIUM PER RECIPE: 58.3 MG
SODIUM PER SANDWICH: 29.1 MG
On a hot summer day, this is perfect.

2 **Sandwich Buns, page 258 (3.853 mg)**
1 **ounce Alpine Lace Swiss, sliced (35 mg)**
1 **tablespoon Hain Stone Ground or Grey Poupon Honey**
    Mustard* (10 mg)
½ **tomato, thinly sliced (5.5 mg)**
2 **thin slices red onion (2 mg)**
2 **inner leaves romaine lettuce (1.6 mg)**

1. Slice the buns in half and lightly toast the insides only. Add half the cheese to each top bun and melt. Spread the mustard on the lower bun. Add the tomato and onion slices on top of the mustard-coated bun half. Top with the lettuce and serve. (If you have a piece of leftover chicken or turkey, slip it into the sandwich (add 18 mg per ounce), and enjoy.)

Calories: 253. Sodium: 29.13 mg. Fiber: 2.86 g. Protein: 10.6 g. Carbohydrate: 43 g. Cholesterol: 10 mg. Calcium: 34.5 mg. Iron: 3.666 mg. Potassium: 246.9 mg. Total Fat: 4.2 g; Saturated fat: 2.1 g, Monounsaturated fat: 0.1 g, Polyunsaturated fat: 0.3 g.

*I personally use Mendocino Honey Mustard. If you like a hotter mustard instead of a sweet one, use one of the unsalted Dijon mustards such as Featherweight (trace), Hain Stone Ground No Salt Added (10 mg), or Life All Natural (<2 mg).

VEGETABLES

❖ ❖ ❖ ❖ ❖ ❖ ❖ ❖

❖ STEAMED BROCCOLI ❖

SERVES 4   SODIUM PER RECIPE: 40.8 MG   SODIUM PER SERVING: 10.2 MG
Buy broccoli florets if you can. If you prefer broccoli with stems, remember the stem itself is high in nutrients and delicious when steamed properly.

1 large spear of broccoli with triple heads or 8 ounces florets (40.8 mg)
1 tablespoon lemon juice (.15 mg)

1. If using the stalk, peel it with a knife, then slice it into 1-inch pieces. Steam the stems first, then add the florets. Spritz with lemon juice when done. Serve plain and hot.

Calories: 11. Sodium: 10.19 mg. Fiber: 0 g. Protein: 1.125 g. Carbohydrate: 1.978 g. Cholesterol: 0 mg. Calcium: 18.1 mg. Iron: .332 mg. Potassium: 122.7 mg. Total Fat: 0.1 g; Saturated fat: 0 g, Monounsaturated fat: 0 g, Polyunsaturated fat: 0.1 g.

❖ STEAMED ASPARAGUS ❖

SERVES 4   SODIUM PER RECIPE: 6.55 MG   SODIUM PER SERVING: 1.638 MG
Fresh asparagus from California arrives in the spring and throughout the summer. It's loaded with great nutrients and is easy to prepare.

16 large asparagus spears (6.4 mg)
1 tablespoon lemon juice (.15 mg)

1. Clean the asparagus spears, then grab the middle and bottom and snap them until they break at a naturally weak spot. Throw away the bottom portion. Set tops into the steamer and bring to a boil in unsalted water with only lemon juice added. When the asparagus just softens, remove and serve. You'll want it crisp and fresh tasting.

Calories: 19. Sodium: 1.64 mg. Fiber: 1.69 g. Protein: 1.838 g. Carbohydrate: 3.956 g. Cholesterol: 0 mg. Calcium: 17.1 mg. Iron: .697 mg. Potassium: 223.1 mg. Total Fat: 0.2 g; Saturated fat: 0 g, Monounsaturated fat: 0 g, Polyunsaturated fat: 0.1 g.

❊ CORN CAKES ❊

SERVES 4   SODIUM PER RECIPE: 170.2 MG   SODIUM PER SERVING: 42.6 MG

  2 **cups fresh sweet corn kernels (46.2 mg)**
  ⅓ **cup red bell pepper, finely diced (.607 mg)**
  ¼ **cup green onion (scallions), diced (4 mg)**
  ¼ **cup minced fresh cilantro leaves (6.21 mg)**
  ½ **cup seasoned homemade bread crumbs* (2.169 mg)**
  ⅛ **teaspoon freshly ground black pepper (.104 mg)**
  2 **medium eggs (110.9 mg)**
  ¼ **cup extra-virgin olive oil (trace)**

1. Combine all the ingredients except the oil and mix thoroughly. Divide the mixture into 4 equal portions. Divide each portion in half and make a small patty from each piece, pressing down between your hands to firm up the cake. Heat the oil in a large skillet over medium-high heat. Brown each cake lightly on both sides. Serve immediately or transfer to a baking dish, cover with foil, and keep warm in a 200°F oven for up to 30 minutes.

Calories: 280. Sodium: 42.55 mg. Fiber: 2.96 g. Protein: 7.004 g. Carbohydrate: 26.8 g. Cholesterol: 93.5 mg. Calcium: 22.4 mg. Iron: 1.933 mg. Potassium: 306.5 mg. Total Fat: 17.4 g; Saturated fat: 2.7 g, Monounsaturated fat: 11.5 g, Polyunsaturated fat: 2 g.

❊ BARBECUED CORN EARS ❊

SERVES 1   SODIUM PER SERVING: 21.9 MG

  ½ **teaspoon melted unsalted butter (.195 mg)**
  ½ **clove garlic, mashed (.255 mg)**
  1 **large fresh ear of corn—white corn is juiciest, husked (21.4 mg)**

1. Melt the butter, add the garlic, and then spread the mixture with a brush across the corn. Wrap the corn tightly in heavy-duty aluminum foil. Barbecue it directly over hot coals, or if cooking with convection heat (lid closed, coals set to the side), set it over an area where coals are not placed. If you are not cooking meats over the convection area, you can set the corn on the grill over coals, but check it every 5 minutes, turning it at the same time.

Calories: 138. Sodium: 21.9 mg. Fiber: 3.89 g. Protein: 4.715 g. Carbohydrate: 27.7 g. Cholesterol: 3.89 mg. Calcium: 5.992 mg. Iron: .772 mg. Potassium: 392.6 mg. Total Fat: 3.1 g; Saturated fat: 1.2 g, Monounsaturated fat: 0.9 g, Polyunsaturated fat: 0.9 g.

*Use bread from **Sandwich Buns** (page 258) or one of the **French Bread** (page 248) recipes, let it dry or toast it first.

Asian Stir-Fry Eggplant/
Vegetarian-Style
❖ or Add Meat of Choice ❖

MAKES 4 SERVINGS   SODIUM PER RECIPE: 35.48 MG
SODIUM PER SERVING: 8.87 MG

*Each year our small town has an "Eggplant Festival," where
everyone brings their own creations, which are then featured
along with other eggplant dishes. When a friend in Hong Kong
discovered this, he sent us this recipe via E-mail. We've tried it
more than once and it's been great each time. We think you'll like
it too. You can cook it in a wok or nonstick frying pan with high
sides. You can also add sautéed chicken, beef, or pork to the recipe,
but if you do, remember to add the sodium count to your
daily total. Estimate that to be approximately 18 mg sodium
per ounce of meat.*

  1   **medium to large eggplant (13.7 mg)**
     Cold water for soaking eggplant (0 mg)
  1   **green pepper (2.38 mg)**
  1   **red pepper (2.38 mg)**
  4   **green beans (1.65 mg)**
10   **medium mushrooms (9.2 mg)**
  8   **snowpeas (1 mg)**
¼   **cup pineapple juice* (.625 mg)**
  2   **teaspoons granulated sugar (trace)**
  2   **tablespoons extra-virgin olive oil (trace)**
  5   **cloves garlic, minced (2.65 mg)**
  1   **teaspoon finely grated gingerroot† (.26 mg)**
  4   **ounces crushed pineapple, packed in water, drained (1.23 mg)**
  2   **teaspoons sesame oil (0 mg)**
¼   **teaspoon Frontier oriental seasoning (trace)**

1. Pare the eggplant and cut it into quarters. Use the entire eggplant. Slice
the quarters into bite-size pieces about 2 inches in length and a ½ inch or
more wide by ½-inch thick. Let these pieces stand for about ½ hour in
cold water.
2. While the eggplant is soaking, slice both peppers into 1-inch strips and
cut the green beans diagonally into 1-inch lengths. Cut the mushrooms

---

*Use the juice from the can of crushed pineapple or use bottled juice or juice concentrate.
†You may use ground ginger if gingerroot is not available.

into ½-inch slices and combine with the beans, whole snowpeas, and peppers. Mix the pineapple juice with sugar.

3. Drain the water from eggplant (don't keep the water) and pat dry with paper towels.

4. Heat a frying pan or wok until very hot. Add the oil and tilt the pan or wok so that all sides are oiled. Add the eggplant, garlic, and gingerroot. Stir-fry this for 1 minute, then add the mushroom vegetable mix and any chunks of cooked meat you may want to use. Stir-fry this mixture for another 2 to 3 minutes. Add the pineapple juice mixture, crushed pineapple, sesame oil, and seasoning and continue to stir-fry for another minute.

5. It's delicious.

Calories: 178. Sodium: 8.87 mg. Protein: 3.692 g. Carbohydrate: 23 g. Fiber: 5.38 g. Cholesterol: 0 mg. Calcium: 36.6 mg. Iron: 1.801 mg. Potassium: 675 mg. Total Fat: 9.6 g; Saturated fat: 1.3 g, Monounsaturated fat: 5.9 g, Polyunsaturated fat: 1.8 g.

❖ JULY FOURTH GREEN BEANS ❖

SERVES 4   SODIUM PER RECIPE: 43.5 MG   SODIUM PER SERVING: 10.9 MG
A chilled colorful side dish for a warm summer lunch or dinner.

  ¼ **cup chopped fresh basil (.424 mg)**
  2 **garlic cloves, minced (1 mg)**
  1 **tablespoon lemon juice (.15 mg)**
  ⅛ **tablespoon dry mustard (trace)**
  1 **tablespoon honey (.84 mg)**
  ¼ **teaspoon ground black pepper (.231 mg)**
  ½ **cup extra-virgin olive oil (trace)**
  1 **cup cider or red wine vinegar (2.4 mg)**
  ¼ **cup blanched fresh green beans (1.65 mg)**
  3 **each, bell peppers, seeded and sliced into ¼-inch strips: red**
     (7.14 mg), yellow (11.2 mg), orange (11.2 mg)
  ½ **cup slivered almonds, lightly coated with sugar and baked in a**
     325°F oven until golden brown (7.25 mg)

1. In a medium bowl, combine the basil, garlic, lemon juice, mustard, honey, and pepper. Add the olive oil while whisking vigorously. Add the vinegar, beans, peppers, and almonds and toss to coat well. Cover and refrigerate for 1 hour. Serve hot with meat dishes or cool and cut into veggie salad.

Calories: 476. Sodium: 10.87 mg. Fiber: 5.83 g. Protein: 7.655 g. Carbohydrate: 36.1 g. Cholesterol: 0 mg. Calcium: 98 mg. Iron: 3.066 mg. Potassium: 987.9 mg. Total Fat: 37.4 g; Saturated fat: 4.6 g, Monounsaturated fat: 26.1 g, Polyunsaturated fat: 4.4 g.

❖ MUSHROOM SAUTÉ ❖

SERVES 4   SODIUM PER RECIPE: 22 MG   SODIUM PER SERVING: 5.507 MG
A great side dish for steaks, burgers, salads, and even wonderful as a lunchtime snack.

⅓ **cup pecan pieces (.284 mg)**
1 **pound assorted fresh mushrooms (14.7 mg)**
3 **cloves garlic, minced (1.5 mg)**
2 **tablespoons extra-virgin olive oil (trace)**
⅛ **cup white wine or nonalcoholic wine, or Welch's white grape juice if you are forbidden alcohol (1 mg)**
   Black pepper to taste (trace)
2 **tablespoons chopped fresh parsley (4.256 mg)**
1 **teaspoon minced fresh rosemary (.182 mg)**

1. Lightly toast the pecans in a 350°F oven. Remove the lower end of stems of the mushrooms (if larger mushrooms used such as portabella, crimini, porcini). Slice the remainder of the caps and stems thin. In a skillet combine the garlic, oil, and wine and sauté for 3 minutes over medium heat. Add the mushrooms, sauté for 4 to 5 minutes, stirring occasionally. Season with black pepper to taste. Add the parsley and rosemary, stir and sauté for an additional 2 minutes.

Calories: 136. Sodium: 5.51 mg. Fiber: 1.9 g. Protein: 2.702 g. Carbohydrate: 6.821 g. Cholesterol: 0 mg. Calcium: 14.7 mg. Iron: 1.509 mg. Potassium: 390.4 mg. Total Fat: 11.8 g; Saturated fat: 1.3 g, Monounsaturated fat: 7.8 g, Polyunsaturated fat: 1.9 g.

PARSNIPS AND CARROTS
❖ WITH SESAME SEEDS ❖

SERVES 4   SODIUM PER RECIPE: 89.5 MG   SODIUM PER SERVING: 22.4 MG

1½ **cups parsnips, peeled, cut into ¾-inch chunks (20 mg)**
1½ **cups carrots, peeled and cut into ¾-inch chunks (64.1 mg)**
1 **tablespoon sesame seeds (.99 mg)**
2 **teaspoon extra-virgin olive oil (0 mg)**
2 **tablespoons pure maple syrup* (3.6 mg)**
   Juice of 1 orange (.86 mg)

1. Steam the parsnips and carrots together until barely done. Toast the sesame seeds in a medium-sized skillet set over a medium flame. When

*Do not use imitation syrups like Log Cabin, Aunt Jemima's, etc. These are too high in sodium.

they begin to turn color slightly, add the oil, maple syrup, and orange juice. Stir in the carrots and parsnips. Turn heat up to medium-high and cook, stirring with increasing frequency until the liquid is reduced to a glaze.

Calories: 126. Sodium: 22.36 mg. Fiber: 4.12 g. Protein: 1.619 g. Carbohydrate: 23.1 g. Cholesterol: 0 mg. Calcium: 61.3 mg. Iron: 1.022 mg. Potassium: 408.7 mg. Total Fat: 3.6 g: Saturated fat: 0.5 g, Monounsaturated fat: 2.1 g, Polyunsaturated fat: 0.8 g.

❧ STUFFED PEPPERS IN A CROCK-POT ❧

SERVES 7   SODIUM PER RECIPE: 665.1 MG   SODIUM PER SERVING: 95 MG
Easy to prepare.

7 small green peppers (10.4 mg)
1 pound ground chuck (303.9 mg)
 10-ounce package unsalted frozen corn, defrosted (8.52 mg)
 8-ounce can Hunt's No Salt Added Tomato Sauce (70 mg)
¼ teaspoon Mrs. Dash Lemon & Herb blend (trace)
4 cloves garlic, minced (2 mg)
¼ teaspoon ground pepper (trace)
6 ounces shredded Alpine Lace Low Sodium Swiss (210 mg)
½ teaspoon any Worcestershire sauce (39 mg)
¼ cup chopped onion (1.2 mg)
2 tablespoons Contadina No Salt Added Tomato Paste (20 mg)
¼ teaspoon granulated sugar (trace)

1. Wash the peppers, cut the tops off and seed them. Drain well. Brown the meat in a nonstick pan and set it aside. In a mixing bowl, combine the corn, tomato sauce, herbs, garlic, pepper, cheese, Worcestershire and onions and mix well. Stuff the peppers two-thirds full. Pour 3 tablespoons water into the Crock-Pot. Arrange the stuffed peppers on top. Mix the sugar and tomato paste together, then pour the mixture over the top of the peppers. Cover and cook on low for 6 to 8 hours or on high for 3 to 4 hours. Serve hot with a salad and freshly made unsalted **Sourdough Bread** (page 243) or toasted **Sandwich Buns** (page 258).

Calories: 253. Sodium: 95.01 mg. Fiber: 3.09 g. Protein: 23 g. Carbohydrate: 20.1 g. Cholesterol: 56.02 mg. Calcium: 38.3 mg. Iron: 2.75 mg. Potassium: 476.1 mg. Total Fat: 10.1 g: Saturated fat: 5.3 g, Monounsaturated fat: 1.9 g, Polyunsaturated fat: 0.5 g.

✦ BAKED POTATO SLICES ✦

SERVES 8   SODIUM PER RECIPE: 52 MG   SODIUM PER SERVING: 6.494 MG

8 large red potatoes (or substitute white new potatoes), cut in half (43.9 mg)
1 teaspoon dried oregano (.22 mg)
1 tablespoon or more fresh rosemary to taste (.442 mg)
2 tablespoons extra-virgin olive oil (trace)
½ pound mushrooms, sliced (7.36 mg)

1. Preheat the oven to 425°F.
2. In a flat Pyrex baking dish layer the potatoes and drizzle oil across them. Sprinkle with dried oregano and fresh or dried rosemary. Bake in the preheated oven for about 35 to 45 minutes, stirring every 10 to 15 minutes. Serve with lamb, chicken, or ribs.

Calories: 109. Sodium: 6.49 mg. Fiber: 1.85 g. Protein: 2.402 g. Carbohydrate: 17.7 g. Cholesterol: 0 mg. Calcium: 11.2 mg. Iron: 1.09 mg. Potassium: 586.5 mg. Total Fat: 3.6 g: Saturated fat: 0.5 g, Monounsaturated fat: 2.5 g, Polyunsaturated fat: 0.4 g.

✦ BECK'S SPUD CITY ✦

SERVES 2   SODIUM PER RECIPE: 106.7 MG   SODIUM PER SERVING: 53.3 MG
This one comes from my sister's river rafting trips.

2 large russet potatoes (22.1 mg)
3 broccoli florets (8.9 mg)
3 sliced carrots, or use the smaller prepeeled, precut carrots (64.1 mg)
2 tablespoons canola oil (trace)
½ teaspoon dried thyme (.3 mg)
½ teaspoon dried marjoram (.2 mg)
½ teaspoon dried oregano (.1 mg)
½ teaspoon dried basil (.2 mg)
1 onion, diced (3.3 mg)
½ pound mushrooms, sliced (7.36 mg)

1. Bake potatoes and steam the broccoli and sliced carrots. Heat the oil in a nonstick fry pan and add the thyme, marjoram, oregano, and basil. Try using only half the oil in order to cut down on the fats. Add the onion and sauté until it becomes translucent. Add the mushrooms and sauté until cooked. When the baked potatoes are done, slice each down the middle and put steamed veggies on top and smother with onions and mushrooms.
2. Low-sodium sour cream is an optional accompaniment. Trader Joe's has a mozzarella with low sodium that you may grate (1 or 2 ounces) and add

to this dish. If you prefer Swiss cheese, use ½ ounce of Alpine Lace Low Sodium Swiss per potato. Alpine Lace also has Low Sodium Cheddar and Low Sodium Jack cheese.

Calories: 356. Sodium: 53.34 mg. Protein: 7.946 g. Carbohydrate: 53 g. Fiber: 8.77 g. Cholesterol: 0 mg. Calcium: 84 mg. Iron: 4.183 mg. Potassium: 1798 mg. Total Fat: 14.5 g; Saturated fat: 2 g, Monounsaturated fat: 10 g, Polyunsaturated fat: 1.5 g.

❖ ROSEMARY ROASTED NEW POTATOES ❖

SERVES 4   SODIUM PER RECIPE: 30.9 MG   SODIUM PER SERVING: 7.737 MG
These work great as an addition to a roast beef or
roasted lamb dinner.

    1 **pound small new or red potatoes, scrubbed (29.3 mg)**
    2 **cloves garlic, minced (1 mg)**
1½ **tablespoons extra-virgin olive oil (trace)**
    1 **teaspoon rosemary, crumbled (.5 mg)**
       Black pepper to taste (trace)

1. Preheat the oven to 400°F.
2. In a bowl combine the potatoes, garlic, oil, rosemary, and pepper to taste. Mix to coat the potatoes, then transfer to a roasting pan. Roast for about 45 minutes, or until golden brown and cooked through.

Calories: 144. Sodium: 7.74 mg. Fiber: 2.12 g. Protein: 2.638 g. Carbohydrate: 22.6 g. Cholesterol: 0 mg. Calcium: 15.2 mg. Iron: 1.067 mg. Potassium: 671.7 mg. Total Fat: 5.2 g; Saturated fat: 0.7 g, Monounsaturated fat: 3.7 g, Polyunsaturated fat: 0.5 g.

❖ WILD RICE PILAF ❖

SERVES 6   SODIUM PER RECIPE: 141.7 MG   SODIUM PER SERVING: 23.6 MG

    4 **tablespoons (½ stick) unsalted butter (1.562 mg)**
    2 **tablespoons extra-virgin olive oil (trace)**
    1 **medium onion, chopped (3.3 mg)**
    2 **celery stalks, diced (69.6 mg)**
    1 **large carrot, diced (25.2 mg)**
  ½ **cup slivered unsalted dry-roasted almonds (7.59 mg)**
    1 **cup wild rice (11.2 mg)**
    1 **cup brown rice (7.6 mg)**
    2 **cups chopped fresh mushrooms (5.6 mg)**
    2 **cups chicken broth made by combining 2 teaspoons Herb-ox**
       Low Sodium Chicken Broth (10 mg) with 2 cups water (0 mg)

1. Preheat the oven to 350°F.

2. In a large skillet, melt the butter with the oil over medium-high heat and sauté the onion, celery, carrots, and almonds next for 2 to 3 minutes. Add the wild and brown rice and the mushrooms, then sauté for an additional 4 minutes. Transfer the contents of the skillet to a casserole dish, stir in the broth. Cover and bake in the oven for 1 hour.

Calories: 358. Sodium: 23.61 mg. Fiber: 5.5 g. Protein: 9.125 g. Carbohydrate: 51.9 g. Cholesterol: 5.18 mg. Calcium: 62.5 mg. Iron: 1.994 mg. Potassium: 480 mg. Total Fat: 13.7 g: Saturated fat: 2.6 g, Monounsaturated fat: 8.1 g, Polyunsaturated fat: 2.2 g.

❖ HASH BROWNS ❖

SERVES 1   SODIUM PER SERVING: 18.1 MG

You can eat unsalted frozen hash browns without guilt. Serve along with your omelet or egg, or even as your main course if you follow this recipe.

1¼ cups Ore-Ida frozen unsalted Country Style Hash Browns (15 mg)
½ onion, diced (2 mg)
1 clove garlic, minced (.5 mg)
¼ green pepper, diced (.5 mg)
1 tablespoon olive oil (trace)

1. In a nonstick skillet combine all the ingredients and stir-fry over high heat for about 5 minutes, stirring frequently. Serve hot.

Calories: 238. Sodium: 18.11 mg. Protein: 3.23 g. Carbohydrate: 25.9 g. Fiber: 3.92 g. Cholesterol: 0 mg. Calcium: 20.4 mg. Iron: 379 mg. Potassium: 496.4 mg. Total Fat: 13.7 g; Saturated fat: 1.9 g, Monounsaturated fat: 10 g, Polyunsaturated fat: 1.2 g.

❖ CHARLOTTE'S POTATOES ❖

SERVES 8   SODIUM PER RECIPE: 52 MG   SODIUM PER SERVING: 6.494 MG

8 large red potatoes, cut in half* (43.9 mg)
1 teaspoon oregano (.22 mg)
1 tablespoon fresh rosemary† (.442 mg)
2 tablespoons extra virgin olive oil (trace)
8 ounces mushrooms, sliced (7.36 mg)

1. Place potatoes in flat Pyrex baking dish and drizzle extra virgin olive oil across them. Sprinkle with dried or fresh oregano and rosemary. Bake at 425°F degrees, stirring every 10 to 15 minutes. Bake about 35 to 45 minutes.

Calories: 109. Sodium: 6.49 mg. Protein: 2.402 g. Carbohydrate: 17.7 g. Dietary Fiber: 1.85 g. Total Sugars: 0 g. Cholesterol: 0 mg. Calcium: 11.2 mg. Potassium: 586.5 mg. Total Fat: 3.6 g; Saturated fat: 0.5 g, Monounsaturated fat: 2.5 g, Polyunsaturated fat: 0.4 g. Vitamin K: 2.39 mcg.

*Or use white new potatoes.

†If you like rosemary, use more. Same with the oregano.

✺ ORIGINAL OVEN-ROASTED FRENCH FRIES ✺

SERVES 4   SODIUM PER RECIPE: 29.3 MG   SODIUM PER SERVING: 7.32 MG

Low on fat and with very little sodium, I first made these fries for the family in the early sixties. They've been popular ever since.

4 medium or large russet potatoes—or you may substitute yams or sweet potatoes (29.3 mg)
Extra-virgin olive oil (trace)
Spice mix such as Frontier barbecue seasoning or another of your choice (trace)

1. Preheat the oven to 450°F.
2. Scrub the potatoes clean but do not peel them. Slice them lengthwise, then set on sides and slice again so that you have strips of potato about ½ inch wide by ⅛ or ¼ inch thick. Lightly oil a large baking sheet and lay strips down flat alongside each other but not touching. Place the baking sheet in the oven and bake for 20 minutes on one side. Lower the heat to 350°F, flip the fries over, and bake for another 5 to 10 minutes. You can make a lot of these, then bag them in a zipper-type bag and freeze them for a long time. When ready to use, pull out those you want, heat them at 450°F for 10 minutes, and voilà! Serve hot sprinkled with a spice mix and/or "no-salt-added" tomato ketchup.

Calories: 98. Sodium: 7.32 mg. Fiber: 1.95 g. Protein: 2.525 g. Carbohydrate: 21.9 g. Cholesterol: 0 mg. Calcium: 8.54 mg. Iron: .928 mg. Potassium: 662.5 mg. Total Fat: 0.3 g; Saturated fat: 0.1 g, Monounsaturated fat: 0.1 g, Polyunsaturated fat: 0.1 g.

✺ GARLIC MASHED POTATOES ✺

SERVES 6   SODIUM PER RECIPE: 107.9 MG   SODIUM PER SERVING: 18 MG

A very popular recipe from Silver Sage Caterers in northern California. I have modified it for low-sodium diets.

3 cloves garlic (1.53 mg)
3 pounds baking potatoes, peeled and quartered (65.9 mg)
2 tablespoons extra-virgin olive oil (trace)
⅓ cup regular sour cream (40.5 mg)
Pepper to taste (trace)

1. Roast the garlic cloves in a 350°F oven until softened and lightly browned, then mash into a coarse paste. Put the potatoes in a stockpot, cover with water and boil, covered, for about 20 minutes until the potatoes are cooked. Remove the stockpot from the heat. Drain potatoes in a colander, return them to the pot and mash. Add the oil, sour cream, garlic, and pepper to taste and continue to mash until light and fluffy. Serve hot.

Calories: 214. Sodium: 17.99 mg. Fiber: 2.96 g. Protein: 4.285 g. Carbohydrate: 34 g. Cholesterol: 5.62 mg. Calcium: 30.3 mg. Iron: 1.446 mg. Potassium: 1018 mg. Total Fat: 7.3 g; Saturated fat: 2.3 g, Monounsaturated fat: 4.1 g, Polyunsaturated fat: 0.6 g.

RED POTATOES WITH ROSEMARY

❖ AND SPINACH ❖

SERVES 8   SODIUM PER RECIPE: 295.9 MG   SODIUM PER SERVING: 37 MG

My favorite. I first had this dish in a restaurant in Burbank, California, while I was working on sitcoms and other shows during the seventies. The restaurant was called Hampton's. As far as I know it's still there.

THE POTATOES
- **2 pounds red potatoes (65.9 mg)**
- **2 tablespoons extra-virgin olive oil (trace)**
- **2 tablespoons fresh chopped rosemary (.884 mg)**
- **Pepper or ground cloves to taste (trace)**

THE SPINACH
- **10-ounce cello bag fresh spinach (224.4 mg)**
- **3 cloves garlic, minced (1.5 mg)**
- **1 tablespoon grated low-sodium Parmesan* (3.15 mg)**

1. Scrub potatoes clean, but do not peel or skin. Wash the spinach well and pat dry or use a salad spinner. Dice potatoes into 1-inch or slightly larger pieces. Boil them in unseasoned water for about 10 minutes, or until slightly tender. Drain and cool to room temperature or cover and refrigerate overnight. (You may continue with them when cooled to room temperature or use them the following day.)

2. Heat the olive oil in a large nonstick sauté pan set over high heat. Add the potatoes and sauté until they are crisp and slightly browned. Add the rosemary and pepper and stir. Now add the spinach, garlic, and sauté until it begins to wilt. Sprinkle on the Parmesan and cook for another 2 minutes. Serve hot.

Calories: 151. Sodium: 36.98 mg. Fiber: 3.24 g. Protein: 4.203 g. Carbohydrate: 26.4 g. Cholesterol: 0.4 mg. Calcium: 56.8 mg. Iron: 2.075 mg. Potassium: 951.5 mg. Total Fat: 3.9 g. Saturated fat: 0.6 g. Monounsaturated fat: 2.6 g. Polyunsaturated fat: 0.4 g.

*Low-sodium Parmesan is available at most health food stores, some supermarkets, and specialty sources like Trader Joe's. If you can't find low-sodium Parmesan, you can substitute 1 tablespoon regular grated Parmesan, but you have to add 90 mg sodium to the recipe total.

◆ SCALLOPED POTATOES ◆

SERVES 4   SODIUM PER RECIPE: 155.8 MG   SODIUM PER SERVING: 39 MG
This recipe is from Pete Eiden, a heart transplant candidate who started www.healthyheartmarket.com to help other heart patients find low-sodium products.

⅓ **cup finely chopped onion (1.5 mg)**
4 **cloves garlic, minced (2 mg)**
2 **tablespoons unsalted butter (3.1 mg)**
2 **tablespoons unbleached flour (.312 mg)**
⅛ **teaspoon ground pepper (.115 mg)**
1 **cup nonfat milk (126.2 mg)**
½ **teaspoon dried tarragon (.5 mg)**
3 **medium russet potatoes, peeled and sliced (22 mg)**
   Optional: 2 boneless skinless chicken breast halves or 4 thin pork chops

1. Preheat the oven to 350°F.
2. To make the white sauce, sauté the onion and garlic in the butter until the onion turns translucent. Stir in the flour and pepper. Add the milk and stir. Cook, stirring constantly, until the sauce is thick and bubbles appear. Remove from the heat and set aside.
3. Place half the sliced potatoes in a greased casserole (9x9 inches or 9x13 inches). Cover with half the sauce. Layer the rest of the potatoes on top and cover with the rest of white sauce. Bake, covered, in the oven for 35 minutes. Uncover and bake for an additional 30 minutes, or until the potatoes are tender.
4. You may add 4 thin pork chops or 2 boneless, skinless chicken breast halves on top before cooking. If adding chicken, add ½ teaspoon coriander to the recipe while making the white sauce. If adding pork, calculate the additional sodium count by multiplying 20 mg per ounce of meat. Let stand for 5 minutes and serve hot.

Calories: 169. Sodium: 38.95 mg. Fiber: 1.9 g. Protein: 4.843 g. Carbohydrate: 24.7 g. Cholesterol: 16.64 mg. Calcium: 94.9 mg. Iron: 1.076 mg. Potassium: 643.9 mg. Total Fat: 6.1 g; Saturated fat: 3.7 g, Monounsaturated fat: 1.7 g, Polyunsaturated fat: 0.3 g.

With chicken added. Calories: 234. Sodium: 77.3 mg. Protein: 18.5 g. Carbohydrate: 24.7 g. Fiber: 1.9 g. Cholesterol: 50.86 mg. Calcium: 101.4 mg. Iron: 1.501 mg. Potassium: 794.4 mg. Total Fat: 6.8 g; Saturated fat: 3.9 g, Monounsaturated fat: 1.9 g, Polyunsaturated fat: 0.5 g.

With pork added. Calories: 300. Sodium: 80.8 mg. Protein: 25.1 g. Carbohydrate: 24.7 g. Fiber: 1.9 g. Cholesterol: 67.79 mg. Calcium: 114.4 mg. Iron: 1.783 mg. Potassium: 1035 mg. Total Fat: 11 g; Saturated fat: 5.4 g, Monounsaturated fat: 3.9 g, Polyunsaturated fat: 0.8 g.

❧ STEAMED SPINACH ❧

SERVES 4   SODIUM PER RECIPE: 48.6 MG   SODIUM PER SERVING: 12.1 MG
*Steam your spinach instead of boiling it, to retain flavors
and nutrients.*

2 **cups packed raw spinach, washed and dried (47.4 mg)**
1 **tablespoon lemon juice (.15 mg)**
2 **cloves garlic, minced (1.02 mg)**

1. Place the spinach in a steamer. Sprinkle the lemon juice on top and spread the garlic over all. Steam until soft but not overcooked. Serve hot.

Calories: 6. Sodium: 12.14 mg. Carbohydrate: 1.345 g. Fiber: 0.45 g. Protein: .539 g. Cholesterol: 0 mg. Calcium: 17.8 mg. Iron: .433 mg. Potassium: 94.4 mg. Total Fat: 0.1 g: Saturated fat: 0 g, Monounsaturated fat: 0 g, Polyunsaturated fat: 0 g.

❧ SPINACH WITH MUSHROOMS AND ONIONS ❧

SERVES 6   SODIUM PER RECIPE: 237.4 MG   SODIUM PER SERVING: 39.6 MG
*Niçoise this is not. But spinach is high in beta-carotene, vitamin C,
and iron, which remain necessary to our diets. This recipe is basic
but it is included here because it is so compatible with our
many low-sodium entrées.*

2 **tablespoons extra-virgin olive oil (trace)**
2 **cloves garlic, minced (2 mg)**
¼ **white or yellow onion, diced (.8 mg)**
¾ **pound mushrooms, sliced thin (11 mg)**
10 **ounces spinach* (224.4 mg)**
1 **tablespoon lemon juice (.15 mg)**
   Pepper to taste (trace)

1. Heat the oil in a nonstick pan. Sauté the garlic, onions, and mushrooms, stirring constantly for about 3 to 4 minutes. Add the spinach, cover, and steam.† Stir in the lemon juice, pepper, and sauté for another 2 minutes, uncovered. Add pepper to taste and serve.

Calories: 66. Sodium: 39.57 mg. Fiber: 1.95 g. Protein: 2.443 g. Carbohydrate: 4.748 g. Cholesterol: 0 mg. Calcium: 52.1 mg. Iron: 1.903 mg. Potassium: 448.8 mg. Total Fat: 4.9 g: Saturated fat: 0.7 g, Monounsaturated fat: 3.3 g, Polyunsaturated fat: 0.5 g.

*Use a 10-ounce cello package of fresh spinach and prepare as directed. If using fresh loose spinach, clean it and cut off the stems.
†You may also steam the spinach in a steamer. To do so, place spinach in the steaming tray, then top with the sautéed mushrooms and onions and steam until the spinach is just wilted. Transfer mixture to a nonstick skillet.

❈ BANANA SQUASH ❈

SERVES 4   SODIUM PER RECIPE: 48 MG   SODIUM PER SERVING: 12 MG
*Available in spring, summer, and fall, this squash also stores well
through the winter.*

   1-pound banana squash, halved (44.7 mg)
 1 tablespoon unsalted butter (1.562 mg)
 1 tablespoon brown sugar (1.794 mg)

1. Preheat the oven to 400°F.
2. Wash the squash and put it in a baking pan or on a baking sheet. Bake
for 30 minutes. In a small pan, melt the butter until soft and mix it with the
brown sugar. Brush the mixture on the squash, then continue baking until
the squash is fork-tender. Serve hot with entrée.

*Calories: 94. Sodium: 12 mg. Fiber: 0 g. Protein: 3.22 g. Carbohydrate: 15 g. Cholesterol:
7.77 mg. Calcium: 24.1 mg. Iron: .666 mg. Potassium: 515.3 mg. Total Fat: 3.7 g; Saturated
fat: 2 g, Monounsaturated fat: 0.9 g, Polyunsaturated fat: 0.4 g.*

❈ BUTTERNUT DELIGHT ❈

SERVES 4   SODIUM PER RECIPE: 18.5 MG   SODIUM PER SERVING: 4.632 MG
*Another winter special. Butternuts are generally yellow or beige
colored, shaped like pears, and are heavier than they appear.*

 2 large butternut squash (16.8 mg*)
 1 tablespoon extra-virgin olive oil (trace)
   Pepper to taste (trace) and sodium free herb seasoning to taste
   (trace)
 2 tablespoons honey (1.68 mg)
   Optional: slivered almonds, chopped pecans (.284 mg per
   ounce), or chopped walnuts for garnish (.284 mg per ounce)

1. Preheat the oven to 350°F.
2. Cut the squash in half end to end. Clean out the seeds and slice the
squash into ¾-inch to 1-inch rings. Brush the rings with the oil and put
them on a nonstick baking sheet. Season to taste with pepper and herb
seasoning substitute. Bake for about 15 to 20 minutes, or until slightly soft.

*The sodium total is based on 1 pound baked or 2 cups cubed squash.

Turn the squash over and sprinkle with the honey. Continue baking for another 20 minutes, or until fork-tender.

Calories: 109. Sodium: 4.63 mg. Carbohydrate: 20.9 g. Fiber: 0.03 g. Protein: 1.084 g. Cholesterol: 0 mg. Calcium: 51.1 mg. Iron: .799 mg. Potassium: 375.4 mg. Total Fat: 3.5 g. Saturated fat: 0.5 g, Monounsaturated fat: 2.5 g, Polyunsaturated fat: 0.3 g.

❈ STEAMED SUMMER SQUASH ❈

SERVES 2   SODIUM PER RECIPE: 16.242 MG   SODIUM PER SERVING: 8.121 MG

4 medium summer squash (15.7 mg)
1 garlic clove, minced (.51 mg)
1 teaspoon lemon juice (trace)

1. Clean and strip the stems off the squash. Fill the steamer with water and add the garlic and lemon juice. Put the squash in the steamer tray and steam until barely soft. You can cut the squash into slices before steaming or you can steam them whole. Serve hot.

Calories: 41. Sodium: 4.06 mg. Carbohydrate: 8.881 g. Fiber: 3.74 g. Protein: 2.365 g. Cholesterol: 0 mg. Calcium: 40.6 mg. Iron: .915 mg. Potassium: 386.7 mg. Total Fat: 0.4 g. Saturated fat: 0.1 g, Monounsaturated fat: 0 g, Polyunsaturated fat: 0.2 g.

WINTER SQUASH /
(ALSO TABLEQUEEN SQUASH,
❈ ACORN SQUASH) ❈

SERVES 4   SODIUM PER RECIPE: 35.3 MG   SODIUM PER SERVING: 8.821 MG

It's called "Winter squash" because its harvest season is winter through spring. This delicious squash stores well for a long time and it's easy to prepare.

2 large winter squash (25.9 mg)
2 tablespoons unpacked brown sugar (7.02 mg)
1 tablespoon honey (.84 mg)
1 tablespoon unsalted butter or margarine (1.5 mg)

1. Preheat the oven to 400°F.
2. Slice across the stem and top to make flat surface but don't break into the heart of the squash. Halve the squash crosswise—that is, not stem to top. Now you have two halves that will stand up on your baking sheet without rolling over. Clean the heart of the squash with a spoon, taking out the seeds. Place the squash pieces on a lightly greased baking sheet.

3. Combine the sugar, honey, and butter or margarine. Put ¼ of the mixture into each squash half. Bake in the oven for about 30 to 40 minutes, or until the squash is fork-tender.

Calories: 145. Sodium: 8.82 mg. Carbohydrate: 31.2 g. Protein: 1.77 g. Fiber: 3.24 g. Cholesterol: 7.77 mg. Calcium: 76.1 mg. Iron: 1.622 mg. Potassium: 767 mg. Total Fat: 3.1 g; Saturated fat: 1.8 g, Monounsaturated fat: 0.8 g, Polyunsaturated fat: 0.2 g.

❧ GRILLED ZUCCHINI ❧

SERVES 4   SODIUM PER RECIPE: 19.4 MG   SODIUM PER SERVING: 4.845 MG
The Sporting Chef, Scott Leysath, serves this tasty zucchini with many of his wild game feasts. It's also great with standard fare, like Italian dishes, steaks, or barbecued ribs.

2 large zucchini (8 mg)

1. Slice the zucchini lengthwise in strips about ⅛ inch thick or even thinner if you like. Lay the strips across hot stovetop burners or the barbecue grill. Singe the zucchini on each side. If barbecuing, lay on the grill over the coals until they show grill burns, then turn and char on the other side. These don't take long, so stay with them. Serve hot. Pepper or favorite spice to taste (trace).

Calories: 23. Sodium: 4.85 mg. Carbohydrate: 4.684 g. Protein: 1.873g. Fiber: 1.94 g. Cholesterol: 0 mg. Calcium: 24.2 mg. Iron: .678 mg. Potassium: 400.5 mg. Total Fat: 0.2 g; Saturated fat: 0 g, Monounsaturated fat: 0 g, Polyunsaturated fat: 0.1 g.

❧ "SALTING" A TOMATO HERB MIX ❧

SODIUM PER BATCH: 7.409 MG   SODIUM PER "PINCH": .185 MG
Herb mixes allow you to "salt" that tomato, boiled egg, or corn on the cob.

1 teaspoon finely ground celery seed (3.2 mg)
1 tablespoon dried savory (1.062 mg)
4 teaspoons dried basil (1.917 mg)
½ tablespoon dried marjoram (.655 mg)
½ tablespoon dried thyme (.383 mg)
2½ teaspoons sage (.192 mg)

1. Combine the herbs and grind them in a mortar and pestle or in a dish with the blunt end of a plastic kitchen tool. Store the mixture in a small bottle (one that previously held spices is good). If you want more punch, add paprika or crushed dried onion granules. Never add any bottled seasoning with the word "salt" in it, like "celery salt," "garlic salt," etc. These are high in sodium. This mix is good for seasoning stews, soups, eggs, meats, pizza, burgers, tomatoes, etc.

Calories: 1. Sodium: 0.19 mg. Carbobydrate: .232 g. Fiber: 0.15 g. Protein: 0.45 g. Cholesterol: 0 mg. Calcium: 7.663 mg. Iron: .174 mg. Potassium: 7.596 mg. Total Fat: 0 g; Saturated fat: 0 g, Monounsaturated fat: 0 g, Polyunsaturated fat: 0 g.

❖ WHITE BEANS ❖

SERVES 4   SODIUM PER RECIPE: 55.6 MG   SODIUM PER SERVING: 13.9 MG
A slow-baked side dish that complements any entrée but goes especially well with poultry and pork. Also great as a lunchtime meal with a side salad.

1 cup dried white kidney beans (44.2 mg)
2 tablespoons fresh sage (.44 mg) or 2 teaspoons dried (.154 mg)
**2 cups chicken broth made by combining Herb-ox Low Sodium
    Chicken Broth (10 mg) with 2 cups water (0 mg)**
2 cups cold water (0 mg)
2 garlic cloves (1 mg)
1 tablespoon extra-virgin olive oil (trace)
Pepper to taste (trace)

1. In a large bowl, cover the beans with cold water. Cover the bowl with a lid or plate and allow to stand overnight. (If you don't have time, you can quick-soak the beans by bringing them to a boil in a large pan of water. Remove the pan from the heat and let stand for 2 hours. Drain the beans, rinse, then cook in fresh water until tender.)
2. Preheat the oven to 375°F.
3. If you use fresh sage, chop it into thin shreds. In a large skillet, bring the stock and the 2 cups cold water to a boil. Add the beans, the sage, and garlic, the return to a boil for 10 minutes. Place the beans and cooking liquid in a casserole, cover, and bake for 40 minutes to 1 hour, or until the beans are tender and most of the liquid has been absorbed. (If too much liquid remains after 1 hour of baking, remove the lid and bake for another 10 minutes.) Remove from oven, splash with oil and pepper and stir well. Serve hot.

Calories: 193. Sodium: 13.91 mg. Carbobydrate: 29.7 g. Protein: 11 g. Fiber: 11.89 g. Cholesterol: 0 mg. Calcium: 85 mg. Iron: 8.092 mg. Potassium: 663.5 mg. Total Fat: 3.9 g; Saturated fat: 0.6 g, Monounsaturated fat: 2.5 g, Polyunsaturated fat: 0.5 g.

❧ VEGETARIAN RATATOUILLE ❧

SERVES 4   SODIUM PER RECIPE: 118.8 MG   SODIUM PER SERVING: 29.7 MG

*We always enjoyed our mother's ratatouille, but it never tasted
quite the same twice. One ingredient remained consistent,
however: eggplant. Always the eggplant. Still, with ratatouille (we
pronounced it rat-a-tooey) you can exchange items, add items, or
leave some out. It's a vegetable dish that lends itself easily to
leftovers and you can even add meat if you like. This one is
meatless and very low in sodium.*

16-ounce can Del Monte, S&W, or other no-salt-added stewed
   tomatoes or crushed or diced tomatoes (60 mg)
3 tablespoons extra-virgin olive oil (trace)
2 large onions, chopped (9 mg)
3 cloves garlic, crushed or finely chopped (1.53 mg)
1 medium green pepper, diced (2.38 mg)
1 sweet red pepper, diced (2.38 mg)
4 zucchini (23.5 mg)
1 eggplant, pared and diced (13.7 mg)
16 ounces frozen, unsalted peas (20 mg)
1 teaspoon dried oregano (.22 mg)
1 teaspoon dried sweet basil (.48 mg)
1 teaspoon dried thyme (.76 mg)
½ teaspoon dried tarragon (.5 mg)
   Pepper to taste (trace)
2 tablespoons chopped fresh parsley (4.26 mg)

1. Drain the juice from the canned tomatoes. In a roaster pan or Dutch
oven, heat 2 tablespoons of the oil over medium heat. Add the onions and
garlic. Sauté, stirring for about 5 to 8 minutes—you want this mixture to be
golden color when done. Add the peppers and continue to sauté for another 6 to 8 minutes. Remove the pan from the heat and using a slotted
spoon (to drain any liquid) transfer the vegetables to a glass bowl.
2. Return the roaster pan to the stove. Sauté the zucchini next, stirring
constantly for about 8 minutes or until just soft. Add this to the glass bowl.
Heat the rest of the olive oil in the roaster pan. Add the diced eggplant and
sauté, stirring constantly, for about 5 to 6 minutes or until the eggplant has
slightly softened.
3. Return the vegetables in the glass bowl to the roaster pan along with
the peas, dried herbs, and tomatoes. Cover and simmer over low heat for
about 30 minutes, or until the vegetables are soft. Sprinkle the chopped
parsley on top. Serve hot or at room temperature.

*Calories: 221. Sodium: 29.71 mg. Protein: 5.712 g. Carbohydrate: 26.7 g. Fiber: 8.76 g.
Cholesterol: 0 mg. Calcium: 86.8 mg. Iron: 2.582 mg. Potassium: 1085 mg. Total Fat: 11 g.
Saturated fat: 1.5 g. Monounsaturated fat: 7.5 g. Polyunsaturated fat: 1.2 g.*

❖ BARBECUED VEGETABLES ❖

SERVES 4   SODIUM PER RECIPE: 47.9 MG   SODIUM PER SERVING: 12 MG

Grilled or barbecued, here's a way to cook and serve vegetables everyone will love.

  2 **large zucchini (19.4 mg)**
  1 **large red bell pepper (3.28 mg)**
  1 **large green bell pepper (3.28 mg)**
  2 **large onions (9 mg)**
  2 **summer squash (12.9 mg)**

1. Cut the zucchini lengthwise into strips about ⅛ inch thick. Clean out the bell peppers and slice them lengthwise into 1-inch-wide strips. Slice the onion into large rings. Cut the squash into strips. Put all the vegetables on a barbecue grill (or in an oven griller under the broiler element) and cook until grill marks appear. Turn once so that both sides are cooked. Serve hot.

Calories: 106. Sodium: 11.97 mg. Carbohydrate: 23.5 g. Protein: 5.379 g. Fiber: 7.91 g. Cholesterol: 0 mg. Calcium: 78.9 mg. Iron: 1.963 mg. Potassium: 978.3 mg. Total Fat: 0.8 g; Saturated fat: 0.2 g, Monounsaturated fat: 0.1 g, Polyunsaturated fat: 0.4 g.

❖ VEGETABLE SAUTÉ ❖

SERVES 4   SODIUM PER RECIPE: 36 MG   SODIUM PER SERVING: 9 MG

Use this recipe as a side dish for meats, or the centerpiece of a vegetarian meal; try including a baked potato. Serve with bread, taco shells, or by itself. You can add ground beef, sliced or ground chicken or pork.

  2 **tablespoons extra-virgin olive oil (0 mg)**
  ½ **pound mushrooms, sliced in half (7.36 mg)**
  1 **medium onion, thinly sliced (3.3 mg)**
  ¼ **red bell pepper, cut into strips (.82 mg)**
  ¼ **green bell pepper, cut into strips (.82 mg)**
  ½ **broccoli spear, chopped (20.4 mg)**
  ½ **cup sliced green (string) beans (3.3 mg)**

1. In a large wok or frying pan with sides, add the oil and tilt to cover the bottom of the pan. Sauté the mushrooms and onions over medium-high heat. When the mushrooms and onions begin to turn color, add the peppers, broccoli, onions, and beans. Continue cooking for about 2 to 3 minutes. Serve hot atop baked potatoes, rice, barbecued steaks, burgers, or oven roasts.

Calories: 97. Sodium: 9 mg. Carbohydrate: 7.801 g. Protein: 2.276 g. Fiber: 1.68 g. Cholesterol: 0 mg. Calcium: 23.8 mg. Iron: 1.06 mg. Potassium: 339.7 mg. Total Fat: 7.1 g; Saturated fat: 1 g, Monounsaturated fat: 5 g, Polyunsaturated fat: 0.7 g.

❖ STEAMED VEGETABLES ❖

SERVES 4   SODIUM PER RECIPE: 68.7 MG   SODIUM PER SERVING: 17.2 MG

12 medium asparagus spears (3.84 mg)
 1 medium yellow crookneck squash (1.3 mg)
 2 cups broccoli florets* (38.3 mg)
 1 large carrot (25.2 mg)
    Pepper or unsalted seasoning blend to taste (trace)

1. Break the asparagus spears at the point where they naturally snap off. Keep the top half and discard the bottoms (or save them for vegetable broth). Break the spear tops into two pieces and set them aside. Cut the squash lengthwise, then slice it into medium-thin slices and set it aside. Break up the broccoli florets and set them aside. Slice the carrot lengthwise, then cut it into bite-size pieces and set them in a steamer. Begin by steaming the carrots first. After 2 to 3 minutes, add the other vegetables and continue to steam for 2 minutes. Season to taste and serve hot with roast beef, pork tenderloin, or baked chicken.

Calories: 32. Sodium: 17.18 mg. Carbohydrate: 6.537 g. Protein: 2.493 g. Fiber: 1.86 g. Cholesterol: 0 mg. Calcium: 35.5 mg. Iron: .905 mg. Potassium: 339.3 mg. Total Fat: 0.3 g; Saturated fat: 0.1 g, Monounsaturated fat: 0 g, Polyunsaturated fat: 0.1 g.

❖ STEAMED ZUCCHINI ❖

SERVES 4   SODIUM PER RECIPE: 5.284 MG   SODIUM PER SERVING: 1.321 MG

Probably the easiest vegetable to cook, and one of the best, zucchini is a great source of vitamin C. It not only tastes great, it makes a colorful side dish for fish, pork, and chicken or as part of a vegetarian plate.

2 large zucchini (1 mg)
1 medium yellow or red onion (3.3 mg)
1 clove garlic, minced (.5 mg)
   Juice of 1 lemon (.47 mg)
   Pepper to taste (trace)

1. Clean the zucchini and cut them into thin slices. Slice the onion thin and quarter it. Using a steamer, put the zucchini and onion pieces in the basket and steam for about 4 minutes. Remove, spritz with lemon juice, add the garlic, and season to taste with pepper. Serve hot.

Calories: 16. Sodium: 1.32 mg. Carbohydrate: 3.9 g. Protein: .631 g. Fiber: 0.65 g. Cholesterol: 0 mg. Calcium: 9.469 mg. Iron: .147 mg. Potassium: 97.8 mg. Total Fat: 0.1 g; Saturated fat: 0 g, Monounsaturated fat: 0 g, Polyunsaturated fat: 0 g.

*If you use a standard broccoli bunch, then skin the stems, chop them, and use them, too. You'll find them delicious as well as full of nutrients.

❋ VEGETABLE STIR-FRY ❋

SERVES 4   SODIUM PER RECIPE: 242.3 MG   SODIUM PER SERVING: 57.3 MG
*This is a relatively easy meal to "toss" together. Served atop
rice, it's delicious.*

1 cup medium-grain white rice (1.95 mg)
1 cup chicken broth made by combining 1 teaspoon Herb-ox
   Low Sodium Chicken Broth (5 mg) and 1 cup water (0 mg)
2 chicken boneless, skinless breast halves, diced (optional)
   (153.4 mg)
2 tablespoons extra-virgin olive oil (trace)
¼ medium red pepper, diced (.595 mg)
1 8 ounce can water chestnuts, sliced (8.4 mg)
1 8 ounce can bamboo shoots, sliced (18.3 mg)
2 medium carrots, diced (42.7 mg)
1 medium zucchini, thinly sliced (5.88 mg)
1 cup fresh snow peas (2.52 mg)
1 8 ounce can crushed pineapple in water or heavy syrup
   (2.46 mg)
1 teaspoon curry powder (1.04 mg)

1. Cook the rice per package instructions, using the Herb-ox Low Sodium broth. No salt is necessary. In a nonstick pan, stir-fry the chicken first in the oil. (To cut the fat by 25 percent, use only 1 tablespoon of the oil). Add the remaining vegetables, pineapple juice or syrup, and curry. When done, serve over the hot rice. Use the remaining juice in the pan as a "sauce" to pour over the rice.

Calories: 358. Sodium: 57.27 mg. Protein: 19.1 g. Carbohydrate: 51.4 g. Fiber: 4.05 g. Cholesterol: 34.22 mg. Calcium: 44.2 mg. Iron: 3.824 mg. Potassium: 550.7 mg. Total Fat: 8.2 g; Saturated fat: 1.3 g, Monounsaturated fat: 5.3 g, Polyunsaturated fat: 1 g.

❋ VEGETABLE STEW ❋

SERVES 6   SODIUM PER RECIPE: 223.7 MG   SODIUM PER SERVING: 37.3 MG
*My wife makes the most eclectic stews. They never seem to be the
same, but every one of them is delicious. This particular stew was
assembled from leftovers in the refrigerator. So, when you've got a
refrigerator full of vegetables you need to do something with, try
this mix. And, remember, you can add or subtract whatever you
want. If you're using a Crock-Pot, just combine all the ingredients
and cook on the lowest setting.*

4 cloves garlic, crushed (2 mg)
2 large red potatoes (14 mg)

2 tablespoons extra-virgin olive oil for sautéing (trace)
1 large stalk celery, thinly sliced (55.7 mg)
1 stalk broccoli, sliced (30.8 mg)
2 carrots, thinly sliced (50.4 mg)
½ cup red wine* (5.15 mg)
2 medium zucchini, sliced and diced (5.88 mg)
3 tablespoons Contadina Natural Tomato Paste or another
   no-salt-added brand (30 mg)
6 ounces mushrooms, sliced (5.52 mg)
3 tablespoons light molasses (22.2 mg)
1 teaspoon dill weed (2 mg)
   Pepper to taste

1. Sauté the onions, garlic, and potatoes in oil in a stew pot. When the potatoes are tender, add the celery, broccoli, and carrots along with the wine. Steam until all the vegetables begin to soften. Add the zucchini, tomato paste, mushrooms, molasses, and dill. Cover and simmer over low heat for 20 to 30 minutes. Pepper to taste.
2. (You may add other vegetables to the recipe——diced eggplant, yellow squash, summer squash, and so forth.)

Calories: 147. Sodium: 37.29 mg. Carbohydrate: 22 g. Protein: 3.215 g. Fiber: 2.48 g. Cholesterol: 0 mg. Calcium: 54.4 mg. Iron: 2.43 mg. Potassium: 515.2 mg. Total Fat: 4.8 g; Saturated fat: 0.7 g, Monounsaturated fat: 3.3 g, Polyunsaturated fat: 0.5 g.

❧ VEGETABLE DELIGHT ❧

SERVES 2   SODIUM PER RECIPE: 19.6 MG   SODIUM PER SERVING: 9.78 MG
Serve this delight with chicken, pork, or pasta. It's easy to prepare and is loaded with vitamins and great flavors. Add whatever spices you like to the mix or eat it as presented here.

1 large Roma tomato (11 mg)
1 crookneck yellow squash (2.6 mg)
4 large mushrooms (3.68 mg)
½ medium red onion (1.65 mg)
1 clove garlic (.5 mg)
1 tablespoon extra-virgin olive oil (trace)
   Dash of pepper (trace)

1. Dice the tomato. Slice the squash lengthwise into ⅛-inch-thick pieces. Slice the mushrooms into thin pieces. Cut the onion into 6 sections. Crush the garlic. Sauté the onions, garlic, and mushrooms in a nonstick pan

*Only use table wine because cooking wine is very high in sodium.

coated with oil. Add the tomato, squash, and pepper. Sauté for about 5 minutes over medium heat. Serve hot as side to entrée.

Calories: 109. Sodium: 9.78 mg. Carbohydrate: 10.5 g. Fiber: 3 g. Protein: 2.515 g. Cholesterol: 0 mg. Calcium: 27.5 mg. Iron: 1.285 mg. Potassium: 494.3 mg. Total Fat: 7.4 g; Saturated fat: 1 g, Monounsaturated fat: 5 g, Polyunsaturated fat: 0.8 g.

❈ YAMS WITH SAUCE ❈

SERVES 12   SODIUM PER RECIPE: 115.2 MG   SODIUM PER SERVING: 9.603 MG
From Mae DiMarco comes this low-sodium, lower-than-usual fat, and flavorful dish. Add it to your repertoire.

8 yams (40.5 ounces) (72 mg)
2 tablespoons extra-virgin olive oil (trace)
1 cup brown sugar, not packed (56.6 mg)
½ teaspoon ground cinnamon (.303 mg)
½ cup orange juice fortified with calcium (1.244 mg)
1 cup crushed pineapple packed in water (drain water) (2.46 mg)
½ cup 100% pure Canadian or Vermont maple syrup (14.2 mg)*

1. Clean and scrape the yams. Cut them into ½- to ¾-inch slices and arrange them in one layer on the bottom of 2 lightly oiled oven baking dishes measuring about 9x12 inches with sides of 1½ to 2 inches. In a medium pan set over medium heat, combine the sugar, cinnamon, juice, pineapple, and maple syrup and mix until smooth. Pour the sauce over the yams in the baking dish. If you are using a standard oven, bake for about 50 minutes at 400°F. If you are using a convection oven, bake for 35 to 40 minutes at 400°F. Serve hot.

Calories: 136. Sodium: 9.6 mg. Protein: .736 g. Carbohydrate: 33.9 g. Fiber: 1.77 g. Cholesterol: 0 mg. Calcium: 42.2 mg. Iron: .72 mg. Potassium: 420.8 mg. Total Fat: 0.1 g; Saturated fat: 0 g, Monounsaturated fat: 0 g, Polyunsaturated fat: 0 g.

*Do not use Log Cabin or other commercial pancake syrups. They are not made from pure maple syrup and are high in sodium.

RELISHES AND PICKLES

❖ ❖ ❖ ❖ ❖ ❖ ❖ ❖

◆ NO-SALT DILL PICKLES ◆

MAKES 1 QUART JAR   SODIUM PER JAR: 42.1 MG
SODIUM PER PICKLE: 6.016 MG*

The basis for this recipe came to us from "Maddjak" Davis in cyberspace. You can adapt it to your own tastes by adding other vegetables, such as cauliflower, cabbage, or Brussels sprouts. You can also heat it in the microwave before refrigerating to help the cucumbers absorb the flavors more quickly.

5 to 7 medium pickling cucumbers, sliced into quarters or any
   size you want, or 7 small whole cucumbers (28.1 mg)
1 cup water (0 mg)
½ cup white distilled vinegar (2.4 mg)
1 small onion, minced (2 mg)
6 cloves garlic, finely minced or grated (3.06 mg)
2 tablespoons ground dill seed (2.607 mg)
1 teaspoon celery seed (3.2 mg)
1 tablespoon whole pickling spice (3 mg)
2 teaspoons whole mustard seed (.3 mg)
2 teaspoons dried sage (.154 mg)

1. Put the slices or small whole cucumbers into a wide-mouth quart jar with a lid. Combine the water, vinegar, onion, garlic, dill seed, celery seed, pickling spice, mustard seed, and sage. Pour the marinade over the cucumbers in the jar. Fill the jars to within ½ inch of the top with the liquid. Seal the jar and set it in the refrigerator for 2 or 3 days, then serve. You'll love these.

Calories: 49. Sodium: 6.02 mg. Protein: 2.035 g. Carbohydrate: 10.5 g. Fiber: 2.29 g. Cholesterol: 0 mg. Calcium: 78.8 mg. Iron: 2.335 mg. Potassium: 394.9 mg. Total Fat: 1 g; Saturated fat: 0.1 g, Monounsaturated fat: 0.4 g, Polyunsaturated fat: 0.2 g.

*The sodium count is based on 7 cucumber pickles per jar. The juice makes a good marinade for fish, by the way.

❖ CHERRY CHUTNEY ❖

MAKES APPROXIMATELY 4 CUPS   SODIUM PER RECIPE: 117.7 MG
SODIUM PER CUP: 29.4 MG   SODIUM PER TABLESPOON: 1.839 MG
*A great accompaniment for chicken, turkey, and
pork—and game birds.*

2½ pounds pitted cherries, fresh (15 mg) or frozen (5 mg)
 1 cup diced yellow onion (4.8 mg)
 2 tablespoons fresh ginger, minced (1.5 mg) or ¾ tablespoon
    ground ginger (1.315 mg)
 3 garlic cloves, minced (1.5 mg)
1½ cups granulated sugar (trace)
 2 teaspoons mustard seeds (.3 mg)
⅛ teaspoon ground cinnamon (trace)
¼ teaspoon celery seed (.8 mg)
¼ teaspoon dried red pepper flakes (.25 mg)
⅛ teaspoon ground allspice (.18 mg)
½ teaspoon coriander (.3 mg)
1½ cups white wine vinegar (3.6 mg) or genuine brewed rice
    vinegar (3.6 mg)
¼ cup light corn syrup (99.2 mg)

1. Put all of the ingredients except the vinegar and corn syrup into a heavy
saucepan. Bring the mixture to a boil. Cook until reduced to a thick consistency, stirring often. Mix together the vinegar and corn syrup and add
to the chutney mixture. Boil it down to a syrupy consistency, then remove
it from the heat let it cool. The chutney will slightly thicken as it cools.
Store in refrigerator.

*Nutrient values per cup. Calories: 290. Sodium: 29.43 mg. Protein: 4.196 g. Carbohydrate:
70.4 g. Fiber: 5.18 g. Cholesterol: 0 mg. Calcium: 32.4 mg. Iron: .985 mg. Potassium: 193 mg.
Total Fat: 3.1 g; Saturated fat: 0.7 g, Monounsaturated fat: 0.4 g, Polyunsaturated fat: 0.1 g.*

*Nutrient values per tablespoon. Calories: 18. Sodium: 1.84 mg. Carbohydrate: 4.397 g.
Fiber: 0.32 g. Protein: .262 g. Cholesterol: 0 mg. Calcium: 2.023 mg. Iron: .062 mg. Potassium: 12.1 mg. Total Fat: 0.2 g; Saturated fat: 0 g, Monounsaturated fat: 0 g, Polyunsaturated fat: 0 g.*

❖ MOM'S MANGO CHUTNEY ❖

MAKES 5 PINTS   SODIUM PER RECIPE: 348.4 MG   SODIUM PER PINT: 69.7 MG
SODIUM PER CUP: 34.8 MG   SODIUM PER TABLESPOON: 2.177 MG

 1 pint cider vinegar (4.8 mg)
3½ cups loosely packed brown sugar (197.9 mg)
 2 medium-sized onions, chopped (6.6 mg)
 1 lemon, thinly sliced (3.24 mg)

1 teaspoon minced garlic (.476 mg)
1½ cup seedless raisins or currants (26.1 mg)
¼ teaspoon cayenne pepper (.135 mg)
2 teaspoons ground cinnamon (1.211 mg)
¾ teaspoon allspice (1.097 mg)
1 tablespoon mustard seed (.51 mg)
4 ounces crystallized ginger, thinly sliced (15.7 mg)
6 tomatoes, peeled and cut into eighths (66.4 mg)
1 green bell pepper, chopped (2.38 mg)
6 whole cloves (5 mg)
¼ teaspoon ground nutmeg (trace)
6 medium apples, peeled, cored, and sliced (0 mg)
4 large mangoes, peeled and sliced (16.6 mg)

1. In a large kettle, combine all the ingredients except the apples and mangoes. Cook for 1 hour, or until the liquid is clear and syrupy. Add the apples and mangoes; continue cooking until the fruit is tender. Fill hot sterilized canning jars, leaving ½ inch head space. Seal. Process the jars for 10 minutes in a steamer. Store the jars in a cool place. Once a jar is opened, store it in the refrigerator for up to 2 weeks.

Nutrient values per cup. Calories: 411. Sodium: 34.84 mg. Carbohydrate: 106.3 g. Fiber: 7.34 g. Protein: 2.953 g. Cholesterol: 0 mg. Calcium: 103.1 mg. Iron: 2.863 mg. Potassium: 912.6 mg. Total Fat: 1.5 g; Saturated fat: 0.3 g, Monounsaturated fat: 0.4 g, Polyunsaturated fat: 0.4 g.

Nutrient values per tablespoon. Calories: 26. Sodium: 2.18 mg. Carbohydrate: 6.646 g. Fiber: 0.46 g. Protein: .185 g. Cholesterol: 0 mg. Calcium: 6.446 mg. Iron: .179 mg. Potassium: 57 mg. Total Fat: 0.1 g; Saturated fat: 0 g, Monounsaturated fat: 0 g, Polyunsaturated fat: 0 g.

❈ OCEAN SPRAY® CRANBERRY SAUCE ❈

MAKES ABOUT 2¼ CUPS   SODIUM PER RECIPE: 4.85 MG
SODIUM PER ¼ CUP: .539 MG

The nice thing about this recipe is that because cranberries have their own unique flavor, salt has never been required to make a great sauce. Every canned cranberry sauce has no salt added to it. This recipe is straight off a package of Ocean Spray® cranberries. Nutrient values here are directly from USDA figures.

1 cup granulated white sugar (2 mg)
1 cup water (0 mg)
12-ounce package Ocean Spray® fresh or frozen cranberries (2.85 mg)

1. In a saucepan mix the sugar and water and stir to dissolve the sugar. Bring to a boil, add the cranberries, then return to a boil and reduce the heat. Boil gently for 10 minutes, stirring occasionally. Remove from the heat and cool completely at room temperature. Refrigerate until ready to use.

Calories: 102. Sodium: 0.54 mg. Carbohydrate: 26.2 g. Fiber: 1.33 g. Protein: .123 g. Cholesterol: 0 mg. Calcium: 2.439 mg. Iron: .966 mg. Potassium: 22.9 mg. Total Fat: 0.1 g; Saturated fat: 0 g, Monounsaturated fat: 0 g, Polyunsaturated fat: 0 g.

✸ EGGPLANT RELISH ✸

SERVES 4   SODIUM PER RECIPE: 41.8 MG   SODIUM PER SERVING: 10.4 MG
A Middle Eastern favorite.

- 1 **eggplant (16.4 mg)**
- 1 **medium red pepper (2.38 mg)**
- 1 **garlic clove, minced (.5 mg)**
- 1 **tablespoon chopped cilantro (2.5 mg)**
- 2 **teaspoons balsamic vinegar (trace)**
- ¼ **teaspoon Lawry's salt-free lemon pepper (19.3 mg)**

1. Put the eggplant and red pepper on a rack in your broiler pan about 2 to 3 inches from the heat. Broil for about 8 minutes, or until the skin blisters, turning occasionally. Transfer the vegetables to a plate lined with paper, then cover the vegetables with paper towel or wax paper and let cool. Remove the skins from the eggplant and the seeds and veins from the pepper, then finely chop both vegetables. Combine the eggplant, pepper, garlic, cilantro, vinegar, and lemon pepper. Serve with beef, pork, or chicken. Heat the relish in a pan over medium heat for about 5 minutes before spooning it onto cooked meat.

Calories: 47. Sodium: 10.44 mg. Carbohydrate: 11 g. Fiber: 4.09 g. Protein: 1.801 g. Cholesterol: 0 mg. Calcium: 16.3 mg. Iron: .577 mg. Potassium: 365.8 mg. Total Fat: 0.3 g; Saturated fat: 0.1 g, Monounsaturated fat: 0 g, Polyunsaturated fat: 0.1 g.

✸ SALSA SUPREME ✸

MAKES 1 GALLON   SODIUM PER RECIPE: 135.8 MG
SODIUM PER CUP: 8.49 MG   SODIUM PER TABLESPOON: .531 MG
We've adapted this recipe that came to us from "Maddjack" Davis to help lower the sodium of the original.

- 6 **softball-sized tomatoes (98.3 mg)**
- 3 **softball-sized onions (13.5 mg)**
- 1 **head garlic (9.18 mg)**
- 8 **fresh jalapeño or habanero peppers to taste, prepared as per the recipe for Anaheim Chilies, page 308 (1.12 mg)**
- 2 **tablespoons no-salt dill pickle with juice (1.504 mg)**
  (Use the juice from No-Salt Dill Pickles, page 301)

**1 to 3 Anaheim Chilies or other chili peppers prepared the
   same way (9.45 mg)**
1 tablespoon red pepper flakes* (1.59 mg)
¼ cup lemon juice (1.22 mg)
4 or 5 drops of liquid smoke† (0 mg)

1. Grind the vegetables in your salsa maker or use a food processor. The pieces of tomato and onion should be twice the size of the rest of the vegetables but never larger than ¼-inch chunks. Using a wooden spoon, mix all the ingredients together and refrigerate for 2 or 3 days. This recipe is fine for marinating white fish, red snapper, or chicken and pork.

Note: If you want a thicker salsa you can add a can of Contadina Natural Tomato Paste with an equal amount of lemon juice. Add 102 mg sodium to the recipe total for this addition.

Nutrient values per cup. Calories: 839. Sodium: 8.49 mg. Fiber: Carbohydrate: 8.932 g. 1.81 g. Protein: 1.485 g. Cholesterol: 0 mg. Calcium: 19.6 mg. Iron: .641 mg. Potassium: 275.2 mg. Total Fat: 0.4 g; Saturated fat: 0.1 g, Monounsaturated fat: 0.1 g, Polyunsaturated fat: 0.2 g.

Nutrient values per tablespoon. Calories: 2. Sodium: 0.53 mg. Carbohydrate: .558 g. Fiber: 0.11 g. Protein: 0.93 g. Cholesterol: 0 mg. Calcium: 1.226 mg. Iron: .04 mg. Potassium: 17.2 mg. Total Fat: 0 g; Saturated fat: 0 g, Monounsaturated fat: 0 g, Polyunsaturated fat: 0 g.

---

*The original recipe called for 1 tablespoon Tabasco sauce. To cut the higher sodium, I've replaced the Tabasco with red pepper flakes, cayenne, or white pepper. Go easy at first. Taste as you add this seasoning until it's just the way you like it.
†If liquid smoke is not available in your area, replace it with ⅛ teaspoon chili powder, cumin, or curry.

❈ Mango Salsa ❈

MAKES 32 TABLESPOONS   SODIUM PER RECIPE: 18 MG
SODIUM PER TABLESPOON: .562 MG
Serve with pork, chicken, white-fleshed fish.

1½ **cups mango, peeled and diced into ½-inch cubes (4.95 mg)**
⅓ **cup finely diced red bell pepper (.983 mg)**
2 **tablespoons finely diced red onion (.6 mg)**
¼ **cup chopped fresh cilantro (6.21 mg)**
¼ **teaspoon chili flakes (.135 mg)**
¼ **cup diced green onions (scallions), white part only (4 mg)**
Dash of cumin (.352 mg)
Dash of Tabasco (.375 mg)
Juice of 1 lime (.38 mg)

1. Combine the above ingredients and refrigerate for 1 hour before serving.

Calories: 205. Sodium: 17.99 mg. Protein: 2.891 g. Carbohydrate: 53.1 g. Fiber: 7.05 g. Cholesterol: 0 mg. Calcium: 65 mg. Iron: 1.347 mg. Potassium: 694.9 mg. Total Fat: 1.1 g; Saturated fat: 0.2 g, Monounsaturated fat: 0.3 g, Polyunsaturated fat: 0.3 g.

❈ Homemade Mayonnaise Substitute* ❈

MAKES 1 CUP   SODIUM PER RECIPE: 118.5 MG
SODIUM PER TABLESPOON: 7.404 MG
Use this recipe when you make potato salad or many of the other
salads that require mayonnaise. Dill is optional, but it's very tasty.
You may also add minced garlic when you use it
for making potato salad.

½ **cup light sour cream (61.3 mg)**
⅓ **cup plain yogurt (56.8 mg)**
1 **teaspoon dried dill or 1 tablespoon chopped fresh dill (.415 mg)**

1. Mix the ingredients together and chill for 10 minutes. Serve cold as a dressing for salads.

Per Tablespoon. Calories: 19. Sodium: 7.4 mg. Protein: .513 g. Carbohydrate: .735 g. Fiber: 0.03 g. Cholesterol: 3.5 mg. Calcium: 19.6 mg. Iron: .03 mg. Potassium: 23.7 mg. Total Fat: 1.6 g; Saturated fat: 1 g, Monounsaturated fat: 0.5 g, Polyunsaturated fat: 0.1 g.

*Hain makes a terrific Mayonnaise Substitute. You can order it at www.healthy heartmarket.com or by calling Healthy Heart at 1-800/753-0310, or check your local market.

❖ HOMEMADE TOMATO SALSA ❖

MAKES ½ PINT   SODIUM PER RECIPE: 26.9 MG
SODIUM PER TABLESPOON: .84 MG

For a low-sodium treat, and a great addition to everything from egg-white omelets to burgers, sandwiches, and unsalted chip dipping, try this tangy salsa.

2 small tomatoes (22 mg)
1 small onion (2.1 mg)
¼ large green pepper (.5 mg)
3 cloves garlic (1.5 mg)
2 tablespoon fresh-squeezed lemon juice (.3 mg)
Pepper to taste (0 mg)

1. Clean the tomatoes, onion, and pepper and dice them. Transfer the vegetables to a salsa maker* and follow the manufacturer's instructions. Store the salsa in a sealed jar in the refrigerator or use it immediately. You may double the recipe and add other vegetables to taste, such as cucumbers, zucchini, carrots, etc.

Nutrient values per ½ pint. Calories: 110. Sodium: 26.89 mg. Protein: 3.954 g. Carbohydrate: 25.7 g. Fiber: 5.01 g. Cholesterol: 0 mg. Calcium: 48.4 mg. Iron: 1.61 mg. Potassium: 801.9 mg. Total Fat: 1.047 g; Saturated fat: 0.1 g, Monounsaturated fat: 0.1 g, Polyunsaturated fat: 0.4 g.

Nutrient values per tablespoon. Calories: 3. Sodium: 0.84 mg. Protein: 124 g. Carbohydrate: .802 g. Fiber: 0.16 g. Cholesterol: 0 mg. Calcium: 1.512 mg. Iron: .05 mg. Potassium: 25.1 mg. Total Fat: 0 g; Saturated fat: 0 g, Monounsaturated fat: 0 g, Polyunsaturated fat: 0 g.

*You can purchase a manual salsa maker at most houseware stores or departments in major department stores. A good salsa maker is one called "Salsa Master" and may be found by writing to R. Foster Enterprises, 11711 Coley River Creek, #8, Fountain Valley, CA 92708. I also use a Braun handheld mixer with an attachment that works well.

❈ AVOCADO SALSA ❈

MAKES 2 CUPS   SODIUM PER RECIPE: 69.7 MG
SODIUM PER SERVING: 8.714 MG

Here's another great sauce for white-fleshed fish. This one was created by our home economist, Marlene Winger.

   2 **medium to large ripe avocados (41.5 mg)**
   1 **tablespoon fresh lemon juice (.15 mg)**
1½ **cups fresh tomatoes, peeled, seeded, and diced (24.3 mg), or substitute Hunt's No Salt Added Peeled Tomatoes (46.8 mg)**
   2 **tablespoons chopped green onion (scallions) (2 mg)**
   2 **tablespoons chopped red onion (.6 mg)**
   2 **tablespoons red wine vinegar (.3 mg)**
   2 **tablespoons extra-virgin olive oil (trace)**
   1 **teaspoon sesame seed oil (0 mg)**
      Pinch of black pepper (trace)
   1 **clove garlic, minced (.51 mg)**
   2 **prepared Anaheim Chilies (below) minced (.28 mg)**

1. Peel and dice the avocados. Sprinkle with lemon juice to keep them from turning color. Combine the remaining ingredients in a salsa maker or a medium-sized bowl. Add the avocados and mix together. (You may also put the avocado in the salsa maker, but it will become puréed and will lose its texture.) Serve with white-fleshed fish or pork. Serve immediately; may store in refrigerator for a few hours.

Calories: 123. Sodium: 8.71 mg. Protein: 1.337 g. Carbohydrate: 5.607 g. Fiber: 2.69 g. Cholesterol: 0 mg. Calcium: 9.516 mg. Iron: .761 mg. Potassium: 372.6 mg. Total Fat: 11.6 g; Saturated fat: 1.7 g, Monounsaturated fat: 7.6 g, Polyunsaturated fat: 1.5 g.

❈ ROASTING ANAHEIM CHILIES ❈

Roast Anaheim or Pasilla chilies in your oven broiler, or over a gas flame, until the chili skins bubble or appear to bubble off. Plunge the chilies into a bowl of ice water and then peel off the skins. (You may, if you wish, also cook the chilies over a hot barbecue grill or directly on your stovetop burners until they turn black; then dip them into ice water and peel.)

Jams, Jellies, and Preserves

❖ ❖ ❖ ❖ ❖ ❖ ❖ ❖

❖ Hints for making berry jam ❖

Bottle Sterilization

Before making your jam, prepare your bottles. Clean the jars (regular canning jars). Place the jars top (mouth) down on a cookie sheet and bake at 350°F for 15 minutes. Allow them to cool until no longer hot to the touch. Keep each jar mouth-down until the moment of filling. This form of sterilization is better than boiling.

Lid Sterilization

You should grip the lids only at the edges. Make sure that neither your fingers nor sugar make contact with the rubber seal on the lid.

The Berries

If you freeze your berries before using them, thaw them before making jam. They will be softer and juicier and are less likely to burn.

Sugar

If you like a full sugar load in your jam, then our berry recipe is not the one for you. But, remember, you can sugar to taste and still keep it low. Begin with the minimum amount of sugar and lemon juice or acid. You can always add more later.

PECTIN

Some berries actually don't need any pectin, But adding at least 1 tablespoon of pectin shouldn't affect the flavor. Wild berries contain more pectin than domestic berries.

ACID

Generally, raspberries don't need added acid. However, you may find it necessary to add lemon juice or citric acid to strawberries, blackberries, and loganberries. Wild gooseberries have enough acid but domestic ones don't.

FOAMING

If your jam foams in the pot, add a few drops of olive oil or butter—not too much, though, or your jam may develop a slightly rancid flavor after several months.

BUBBLES, TEMPERATURES, BOILING POINTS

To prevent bubbles from forming in the jam during bath processing, make sure the water temperature does not rise above 190°F.

❈ BEST BERRY JAM ❈

MAKES 6 (8-OUNCE) JARS   SODIUM PER RECIPE: 28.1 MG
SODIUM PER JAR: 4.679 MG   SODIUM PER TABLESPOON: .292 MG

Domestic and wild blackberries, loganberries, ollalieberries, gooseberries, and fresh strawberries, raspberries, blueberries, and other berry fruits can be turned into delicious jams and jellies for your toasted zero-sodium bread, special waffles, and even for sorbet topping. It's easy to make jam, so why not give it a try?

> 3 **pounds berries* (3 mg)**
> ½ **cup water (0 mg)**
> 1 **level tablespoon pectin† (24 mg)**
> 2 **cups granulated sugar (4 mg)‡**
> 1½ **teaspoons freshly squeezed lemon juice or citric acid (trace)**

1. Combine the berries and water in a large stainless-steel pot. Heat over high or medium-high heat. Stir often and don't let the fruit burn.

2. In a bowl mix together the pectin and ½ cup of the sugar. When the fruit is hot (reading 180°F to 190°F on a candy thermometer), gently sprinkle in the pectin mixture while stirring. Continue to heat while adding the pectin. Bring this mixture to a simmer (195°F to 200°F), and stir while it simmers for 2 minutes.

3. Turn off the heat. Add the balance of the sugar while stirring. Add the lemon juice (or citric acid if you use it). Check the taste and adjust the sugar and acid as necessary.

4. The addition of the sugar should cool the jam to the filling temperature of about 160°F to 170°F. Do not allow the jam to cool below 160°F while in the pot. You may have to apply low heat to hold the jam at that temperature during filling.

5. Skim off any foam before filling sterile jars with the jam. Cap each one immediately after it's filled. I like to process my jam in a bottle steamer I picked up in a small kitchen store in Jackson, California. It's made by Back To Basics and is probably available in your area. I process the jam for 10

---

*Wild gooseberries, unlike cultivated gooseberries, will have to be cooked into a jelly. Wild blackberries come with thorns and stickers in the mix, and often the seeds are too "seedy," and the berries must be converted to a jelly. To make jelly, boil the berries in very little water until soft, even broken down. Reserve the water (which is now a juice). Strain the berries through cheesecloth into a bowl. Strain the reserved liquid into the same bowl. Then strain the water/juice in the pot. Use the liquid to make jelly.

†Use either apple pectin or Pomona's Pectin. If you do not want to use pectin, then cook jam down slowly, until it is thick enough to barely slip off a spoon. You can use a slice of apple if you don't need much pectin.

‡Or use ¼ cup less or more depending on your taste and the amount of sugar in the fruit.

minutes at full steam. This helps ensure that the lids are sealed tightly and that all bacteria are killed. Processing also helps extend shelf life.

6. However, low-sugar jams have a shorter shelf life than standard recipe jams. If possible, you will want to store unopened jars in the refrigerator or at least in a cool area on your shelves. Opened jars must be refrigerated. The typical shelf life for jams is 8 months for unopened refrigerated jars, 4 months for unopened nonrefrigerated jars. Homemade low-sugar jams will last 1 month opened in a refrigerator and only about 3 days opened and kept at room temperature.

Nutrient values per tablespoon. Calories: 33. Sodium: 0.58 mg. Protein: .001 g. Carbohydrate: 8.564 g. Fiber: 0.02 g. Cholesterol: 0 mg. Calcium: .112 mg. Iron: .095 mg. Potassium: .378 mg. Total Fat: 0 g, Saturated fat: 0 g, Monounsaturated fat: 0 g, Polyunsaturated fat: 0 g.

❖ QUICK STRAWBERRY JAM ❖

*MAKES 2½ PINTS   SODIUM PER RECIPE: 14.9 MG   SODIUM PER CUP: 2.988 MG
SODIUM PER TABLESPOON: .187 MG*
One quart of berries equals one month of tasty goodness.

> **4 cups cleaned and stemmed fresh strawberries (6.64 mg)**
> **4 cups granulated sugar* (8 mg)**
> **2 tablespoons freshly squeezed lemon juice (3 mg)**

1. Place the strawberries in a heavy cooking pot (about 10 to 12 inches). Mash a few of the berries to get some juice into the pot. Cover the berries with the sugar. Stir this mixture gently over low heat with a wooden spoon. (Never make jam with a metal spoon.) When it begins to juice, raise the heat to medium or moderate and stop stirring. When the mixture begins to boil, continue for only 15 minutes.† Allow it to cook during this time without disturbance, except that you may, if you wish, slowly scrape the bottom of the pan with your wooden spoon to make sure it isn't sticking. When done, slide the pot off the heat. Let the mixture cool for a few moments, then sprinkle it with the lemon juice. After a few minutes, stir the berries gently. Spoon the mixture into sterile pint-sized jars and seal. To double the recipe, double the quantity of each item. Store in cool place. After opening, store in refrigerator. Can use as heated sauce on vanilla ice cream or as jam for toast or sandwich.

Nutrient values per tablespoon. Calories: 41. Sodium: 0.19 mg. Protein: 0.52 g. Carbohydrate: 10.6 g. Fiber: 0.19 g. Cholesterol: 0 mg. Calcium: 1.288 mg. Iron: .038 mg. Potassium: 14.4 mg. Total Fat: 0 g; Saturated fat: 0 g, Monounsaturated fat: 0 g, Polyunsaturated fat: 0 g.

*You may reduce the sugar to 3 cups if you prefer or if the berries are very ripe.
†Boil for 1 or 2 additional minutes if the berries are very ripe.

❊ BLUEBERRY JAM ❊

MAKES 2 PINTS   SODIUM PER RECIPE: 41 MG
SODIUM PER PINT: 20.5 MG   SODIUM PER TABLESPOON: .64 MG

If you grow your own blueberries, pick them when they are still red. Red berries make an incredible jam, not unlike lingonberries. The following recipe works well with ripe or unripe berries.

4 cups trimmed fresh blueberries (34.8 mg)
1½ cups water (0 mg)
3 cups granulated sugar—or 4 cups if using red berries (6 mg)
1 tablespoon lemon juice (.15 mg)

1. Put the berries in a heavy cooking pot. Mash the bottom layer and add the water, then cook over medium heat. Simmer until the berries are nearly tender. Add the sugar and lemon juice and cook while stirring over low heat until a drop of the jam from your wooden spoon barely falls to a plate and remains there without moving. Pack the jam in sterilized jars, then seal and steam-process to ensure long shelf life. See hints for making berry jams on pages 309–310.

Calories: 41. Sodium: .64 mg. Carbohydrate: 10.7 g. Fiber: .25 g. Protein: .062 g. Cholesterol: 0 mg. Calcium: .654 mg. Iron: .084 mg. Potassium: 8.544 mg. Total Fat: 0 g; Saturated fat: 0 g, Monounsaturated fat: 0 g, Polyunsaturated fat: 0 g.

❊ DON'S ORANGE MARMALADE ❊

MAKES 8 PINTS   SODIUM PER RECIPE: 18.5 MG   SODIUM PER PINT: 2.31 MG
SODIUM PER TABLESPOON: TRACE

I use lemons, grapefruit, and oranges in this one. Some may find it bitter, but to me it's "tangy." If you like the idea of the multiple fruits, but don't want a tangy bite to your marmalade, add about 3 additional cups of sugar.

6 Valencia or thin-skin navel oranges (0 mg)
2 thin-skinned lemons (6.48 mg)
2 medium thin-skinned grapefruit (0 mg)
2 cups water (0 mg)
6 cups granulated sugar (12 mg)

1. Cut each piece of fruit into ½-inch slices. Clean out the seeds and cut off the end pieces. Cut the orange and lemon slices into quarters. Cut the grapefruit slices into eighths. Using a large cooking pot (6 to 12 quarts), combine the fruit and water. Bring to a boil, then cover and simmer until the peel is fork-tender. This should take about 25 minutes after it comes to a boil. Stir gently occasionally during the boiling. Add the sugar and stir until it dissolves. Increase heat to medium-high and cook uncovered. Stir often while mixture thickens. Boil for about 25 to 30 minutes or until the jell point is reached. Cover and let stand at room temperature for about 18 hours or more. After this period, bring the marmalade to a rapid boil and pour into 8 pint-sized jars. Steam process for 10 minutes to guarantee seal. Store in a cool place. After opening, store in the refrigerator. Can be used as warmed sauce for chicken or ice cream topping.

Calories: 20. Sodium: 0.07 mg. Fiber: 0.11 g. Protein: .05 g. Carbohydrate: 5.258 g. Cholesterol: 0 mg. Calcium: 1.907 mg. Iron: .076 mg. Potassium: 8.873 mg. Total Fat: 0 g; Saturated fat: 0 g, Monounsaturated fat: 0 g, Polyunsaturated fat: 0 g.

❈ QUICK ORANGE MARMALADE ❈

**MAKES 4 PINTS   SODIUM PER RECIPE: 18.5 MG   SODIUM PER PINT: 4.62 MG
SODIUM PER TABLESPOON: .144 MG**

It seems that I've been making marmalade all my life. It's still my favorite fruit spread on morning toast. This recipe is a low-sugar recipe I've developed to my taste. If you like it sweeter, add an additional 2 to 3 cups of sugar.

> 3 **large Valencia oranges (0 mg)**
> 2 **large lemons (6.48 mg)**
> 10 **cups water (0 mg)**
> 6 **cups granulated sugar (12 mg)**

1. Wash the oranges well and remove all blemishes and stems. Valencias make the best marmalade, but I have used navels when Valencias weren't available. (If substituting navels, peel and slice the peelings into ⅛-inch-wide strips. Make sure to keep the white pulp intact.)
2. Peel 1 of the Valencias by cutting through the peel from the top to the bottom in ¼-inch bands. Remove these and slice them top to bottom to make them about ⅛ inch or less long. Quarter the peeled orange along with the other 2 oranges. Put them into a large pot with water and let them soak overnight in the refrigerator or in the kitchen if it is cool. When ready to cook, remove the fruit from the water and cut it into small shreds, the consistency of what you'd like your marmalade to be. Return it to the water where it soaked overnight and boil for 1 hour. Then add the sugar and boil the marmalade until the juice forms a jellylike substance. Spoon the mixture into sterilized jars and seal. Steam for 10 minutes in a steamer to ensure long shelf life.

Calories: 38. Sodium: 0.14 mg. Carbohydrate: 9.883 g. Fiber: 0.15 g. Protein: .05 g. Cholesterol: 0 mg. Calcium: 2.258 mg. Iron: .708 mg. Potassium: 7.711 mg. Total Fat: 0 g; Saturated fat: 0 g, Monounsaturated fat: 0 g, Polyunsaturated fat: 0 g.

PIES AND PASTRY

❖ ❖ ❖ ❖ ❖ ❖ ❖

❖ ONE-CRUST PIE SHELL ❖

MAKES 1 PIE CRUST   SODIUM PER RECIPE: 15.2 MG
SODIUM PER SLICE (⅛ CRUST): 1.92 MG

*This is my wife's recipe for a single-crust pie. We especially like it when used with her low-sodium **Lemon Meringue Pie** (page 317).*

1 cup unbleached white flour (2.5 mg)
1 tablespoon lemon juice (.15 mg)
2 teaspoons granulated sugar (trace)
½ cup (1 stick) unsalted butter (12.5 mg)
3 to 4 tablespoons cold water (0 mg)

1. Combine the flour, lemon juice, and sugar in a mixing bowl. Cut in the shortening with a pastry blender or with two knives until the mixture is the consistency of coarse cornmeal or small peas. Sprinkle in the cold water, 1 tablespoon at a time, tossing and stirring with a fork. Each time, add the water to the driest part of the mixture. The dough should be moist enough to hold together when pressed gently with a fork, but it should never get sticky. Shape the dough into a smooth ball with your hands and roll it out by hand or with a rolling pin. You may want to refrigerate it for about 30 minutes in order to manage it better. This recipe makes enough crust for one 8-inch to 9-inch pie shell.

Nutrient values for the whole shell. Calories: 1,305. Sodium: 5.22 mg. Carbohydrate: 105.1 g. Protein: 13.9 g. Fiber: 3.43 g. Cholesterol: 248.45 mg. Calcium: 46.6 mg. Iron: 7.991 mg. Potassium: 182 mg. Total Fat: 93.3 g; Saturated fat: 57.5 g, Monounsaturated fat: 26.7 g, Polyunsaturated fat: 3.9 g.

Nutrient values per slice, based on 8 slices. Calories: 163. Sodium: 1.9 mg. Carbohydrate: 13.1 g. Fiber: 0.43 g. Protein: 1.742 g. Cholesterol: 31.06 mg. Calcium: 5.82 mg. Iron: .999 mg. Potassium: 22.8 mg. Total Fat: 11.7 g; Saturated fat: 7.2 g, Monounsaturated fat: 3.3 g, Polyunsaturated fat: 0.5 g.

❖ TWO-CRUST PIE SHELL ❖

MAKES 2 PIE CRUSTS   SODIUM PER RECIPE: 24.2 MG
SODIUM PER SLICE (⅛ CRUST): 3 MG

  2 cups best for bread flour (5 mg)
  **¾ cup (1½ sticks) unsalted butter, at room temperature (about
    70°F) (18.7 mg)**
  ½ cup lukewarm water (0 mg)
  1 tablespoon granulated sugar (trace)
  2 tablespoons lemon juice (.3 mg)

1. In a medium or large bowl, combine the flour and butter. Stir in the water with a fork and mix until all is combined. If the dough becomes too sticky add a bit more flour. Roll the dough into a ball with your hands until it seems just right. Set it in the refrigerator while preparing your pie filling. If you want a prebaked shell, bake it at 425°F for about 10 minutes.

2. Roll out half the dough on your floured board until the crust will fit into the pie pan. Use a glass pie pan, not a metal one. Roll crust around the roller, lay it over the pan, and unroll it to fit. Crimp the edges.

3. If you want a prebaked shell, bake it at 425°F for about 10 minutes. Otherwise, pour the pie filling into the shell until it is brimming at the edges. If it's for a 2-crust pie, roll top layer on and crimp edges. Cut slits in top. (If there is any filling left over along with crust dough, you can roll out the remaining shell dough and make smaller tarts.) Sprinkle any topping called for over the top of the pie. Roll out the second crust, crimp edges around pie, and bake according to the recipe's instructions.

Nutrient values for the whole 2-crust shell. Calories: 2,203. Sodium: 24.2 mg. Carbohydrate: 210.2 g. Fiber: 6.87 g. Protein: 27.4 g. Cholesterol: 372.68 mg. Calcium: 79.8 mg. Iron: 15.9 mg. Potassium: 349.3 mg. Total Fat: 140.5 g; Saturated fat: 86.3 g, Monounsaturated fat: 40.1 g, Polyunsaturated fat: 6.2 g.

Nutrient values per slice, based on 8 double-crust slices. Calories: 275. Sodium: 3.02 mg. Carbohydrate: 26.3 g. Fiber: 0.86 g. Protein: 3.423 g. Cholesterol: 46.58 mg. Calcium: 9.972 mg. Iron: 1.986 mg. Potassium: 43.7 mg. Total Fat: 17.6 g; Saturated fat: 10.8 g, Monounsaturated fat: 5 g, Polyunsaturated fat: 0.8 g.

❖ LEMON MERINGUE PIE ❖

SERVES 8   SODIUM PER RECIPE: 276.6 MG   SODIUM PER SERVING: 34.6 MG

*This one is my wife, Maureen's, own recipes for a delicious low-sodium dessert. Most of the sodium in this recipe
comes from the eggs.*

THE PIE
   1 baked 9-inch One-Crust Pie Shell, page 315 (15.2 mg)
1½ cups granulated sugar (1 mg)
1½ cups water (0 mg)
 ½ cup cornstarch (5.76 mg) combined with ⅓ cup water (0 mg)
   4 medium egg yolks—save the whites for the meringue (28.6 mg)
 ½ cup freshly squeezed lemon juice (1.22 mg)
   3 tablespoons unsalted butter (4.686 mg)
   1 teaspoon grated lemon zest (.12 mg)

THE MERINGUE TOPPING
   4 egg whites (219.1 mg)
 ¼ teaspoon cream of tartar (.39 mg)
   3 tablespoons granulated sugar (.378 mg)
 ½ teaspoon vanilla extract (.189 mg)

1. Combine the sugar and water in a saucepan. Heat to boiling while stirring.
Combine the cornstarch with the ⅓ cup water and mix into a smooth paste.
Add the boiling mixture gradually to the cornstarch mixture, stirring constantly. Cook this mixture until thick and clear. Remove from heat and let rest.
2. Combine the egg yolks and lemon juice. Stir this into the thickened corn-
starch/sugar mixture. Return the pan to the stove and cook, stirring constantly, until the mixture bubbles. Remove from the heat and stir in the butter
and lemon zest. Cover the pan and let it cool until the mixture is lukewarm.
3. To make the meringue, first preheat the oven to 350°F.
4. Whip the egg whites until they are frothy. Add the cream of tartar and
whip until the whites become stiff enough to form pointed tops. Make
sure you don't overwhip them or they will be dry. Beat in the sugar about
1 teaspoon or less at a time. Do not overbeat since that will prevent the
whites from building up. Beat in the vanilla extract.
5. Pour the filling into the cooled pie shell. Place the meringue on top and
spread it evenly and lightly over the top until it reaches the crust of the
pie. Work the meringue gently but make peaks when you do. Bake at
325°F for about 15 minutes, or until lightly browned. Cool for at least 1
hour before serving. Cut with a wet knife to make even slices without
"dragging" meringue through the next slice.

*Calories: 341.4. Sodium: 34.6 mg. Carbohydrate: 39.4 g. Fiber: 0.59 g. Protein: 5.017 g.
Cholesterol: 149.04 mg. Calcium: 21.2 mg. Iron: 2.364 mg. Potassium: 91.6 mg. Total Fat:
18.5 g; Saturated fat: 10.7 g, Monounsaturated fat: 5.6 g, Polyunsaturated fat: 1 g.*

❖ Pecan Pie ❖

SERVES 8   SODIUM PER RECIPE: 330.7 MG   SODIUM PER SERVING: 41.3 MG
*This easy recipe has been around for years. I'm not sure where it came from, but it's been a favorite of mine for more than fifty years. We squeezed the sodium down as low as we could yet maintained all the flavor. Also try **Walter's Pecan Pie**, which follows this recipe.*

  2 **eggs (110.9 mg)**
  ⅔ **cup granulated sugar (1.32 mg)**
  ½ **cup light corn syrup (198.4 mg)**
  2 **tablespoons unsalted butter (3.124 mg)**
  1 **teaspoon vanilla extract (.378 mg)**
  1 **cup fresh unsalted pecans (1.08 mg)**
  1 **unbaked 8- or 9-inch One-Crust Pie Shell, page 315 (15.2 mg)**
18 **unsalted pecan halves (.27 mg)**

1. Preheat the oven to 425°F.
2. Put the eggs, sugar, corn syrup, butter, and vanilla in blender and mix well. Add the cup of pecans and pulse until the nuts are coarsely chopped. Pour this mixture into the prepared pie shell. Arrange the pecan halves on top to cover. Bake the pie in the preheated 425°F oven for 15 minutes, reduce the heat to 350°F and continue baking for approximately 30 minutes, until the top is slightly browned. Serve hot or cold. The pie will freeze well.

Calories: 441. Sodium: 41.34 mg. Carbohydrate: 48.6 g. Protein: 4.454 g. Fiber: 1.71 g. Cholesterol: 85.58 mg. Calcium: 19 mg. Iron: 1.543 mg. Potassium: 105.1 mg. Total Fat: 27.1 g; Saturated fat: 10.2 g, Monounsaturated fat: 11.7 g, Polyunsaturated fat: 3.6 g.

❖ Walter's Pecan Pie ❖

SERVES 8   SODIUM PER RECIPE: 389.2 MG   SODIUM PER SERVING: 48.7 MG
Not just another pecan pie, this one comes straight to us from a dear friend who owns thousands of acres of pecan trees in Georgia. (Just imagine how many pecans that is!) This is not an adaptation, but the real thing.

1 **cup granulated sugar (2 mg)**
½ **cup light corn syrup (198.4 mg)**
¼ **cup (½ stick) unsalted butter, melted (6.242 mg)**
3 **medium eggs, well beaten (180 mg)**
1 **cup fresh unsalted pecans (.992 mg)**
1 **unbaked 9-inch One-Crust Pie Shell, page 315 (15.2 mg)**

1. Preheat the oven to 375°F.

2. Combine the sugar, corn syrup, and melted butter in a mixing bowl. Add the well-beaten eggs and the pecans to the mixture, stirring until well blended. Pour the filling into the uncooked pie shell. Bake for 45 minutes. Cool before serving.

Calories: 475. Sodium: 48.65 mg. Carbohydrate: 56.8 g. Protein: 4.851 g. Fiber: 1.58 g. Cholesterol: 116.71 mg. Calcium: 20.8 mg. Iron: 1.544 mg. Potassium: 91.8 mg. Total Fat: 27.1 g; Saturated fat: 11.9 g, Monounsaturated fat: 10.6 g, Polyunsaturated fat: 2.9 g.

◄► STRAWBERRY PIE ◄►

MAKES 1 DOUBLE-CRUST 9-INCH PIE   SERVES 8   SODIUM PER RECIPE: 31.9 MG
SODIUM PER SERVING: 3.897 MG

We get wildly excited every year when the fresh strawberries arrive. Strawberries make wonderful jams, cookies, and pies. Of course, they are also great in salads, on cereal, and when dipped in chocolate. But strawberry pie is probably our favorite strawberry indulgence.

Pastry for a 9-inch Two-Crust Pie Shell, page 316 (24 mg)
1 cup fresh whole strawberries (1.44 mg)
1 cup water (0 mg)
4 tablespoons granulated sugar (.5 mg)
2½ tablespoons quick-cooking tapioca (.237 mg)
1½ tablespoons cornstarch (1 mg)
3 cups fresh strawberries sliced in half (4.56 mg)
1 teaspoon lemon juice (trace)

1. Preheat the oven to 425°F.

2. Crush the whole berries and combine them with the water. Heat the mixture over medium heat in a medium saucepan, stirring frequently. Add the sugar, tapicoa, and cornstarch. (Add cornstarch very slowly so that it doesn't form lumps.) Raise the heat and cook until the mixture thickens, but do not bring it to a boil. When done, set it aside to cool. After cooling, add the berries and lemon juice. Pour this filling into your pastry-lined 9-inch pie pan. Roll the top crust over the pie and bake on the oven's lowest rack for 30 minutes, or until nicely browned. Serve warm with ice cream scoop (45 mg) or chill and serve cold.

Note: If substituting frozen strawberries, cut the sugar by 1 tablespoon.

Calories: 331. Sodium: 3.99 mg. Carbohydrate: 39.8 g. Protein: 3.893 g. Fiber: 2.63 g. Cholesterol: 46.58 mg. Calcium: 21.2 mg. Iron: 2.328 mg. Potassium: 169.4 mg. Total Fat: 17.8 g; Saturated fat: 10.8 g, Monounsaturated fat: 5.1 g, Polyunsaturated fat: 0.9 g.

✦ STRAWBERRY GLACÉ PIE ✦

SERVES 8   SODIUM PER RECIPE: 28 MG   SODIUM PER SERVING: 3.5 MG
A wonderful summer treat, this pie recipe has passed the test of time.

1 unbaked 9-inch One-Crust Pie Shell, page 315 (15.2 mg)
  6 cups fresh strawberries (8.64 mg)
  1 cup granulated sugar (2 mg)
  3 tablespoons cornstarch (2.16 mg)
 ½ cup water (0 mg)
    Commercial nonfat whipped cream for garnish (trace)

1. Preheat the oven to 425°F and bake the pie shell for 10 minutes.
2. Clean and stem the berries. Mash enough berries to make 1 cup. Combine the sugar and cornstarch in a saucepan. Gradually stir in the water and the crushed strawberries. Cook over medium heat, stirring constantly, until the mixture comes to a boil; then cook, stirring, for 1 minute. Allow the mixture to cool.
3. Put the remaining whole berries in the pie shell, reserving a few large choice ones for garnish. Pour the cooked mixture over the berries and chill for at least 2 hours. Serve with commercial nonfat whipped cream that has 0 mg sodium. Garnish with the reserved whole berries.

Calories: 304. Sodium: 3.5 mg. Carbohydrate: 48.4 g. Protein: 2.408 g. Fiber: 2.94 g. Cholesterol: 31.06 mg. Calcium: 21.2 mg. Iron: 1.939 mg. Potassium: 202.6 mg. Total Fat: 12.1 g; Saturated fat: 7.2 g, Monounsaturated fat: 3.4 g, Polyunsaturated fat: 0.7 g.

✦ DON'S PUMPKIN PIE ✦

SERVES 10   SODIUM PER RECIPE: 439 MG   SODIUM PER SERVING: 43.9 MG
We don't have to give up eating the main Thanksgiving dessert just because of sodium. Here's a version everyone can enjoy.

  1 unbaked 9-inch One-Crust Pie Shell, page 315 (15.2 mg)
1¼ cups canned pumpkin (do not use pumpkin pie mix) (15 mg)
 ¾ cup granulated sugar (1.5 mg)
 ¼ teaspoon ground ginger (.15 mg)
1½ teaspoons ground cinnamon (.9 mg)
  1 teaspoon unbleached flour (trace)
  2 medium eggs, lightly beaten (110.9 mg)
  1 cup evaporated milk (294.4 mg)
  2 tablespoons water (0 mg)
 ½ teaspoon vanilla extract (.19 mg)
    Nondairy whipped cream from can (trace)

1. Preheat the oven to 400°F.

2. Combine the pumpkin, sugar, ginger, cinnamon, and flour in a mixing bowl. Add the lightly beaten eggs and mix well. Beat in the evaporated milk, water, and vanilla. Pour the mixture into the prepared unbaked pie shell. Bake it in the preheated oven for 45 to 50 minutes, or until a knife inserted near the center comes out clean. (In a convection oven, bake at same temperature for about 30 to 35 minutes.) Top with sodium-free commercial whipped topping or use a teaspoon of honey. Enjoy.

3. To make two pies, double the recipe.

Calories: 235. Sodium: 43.86 mg. Carbohydrate: 31.5 g. Protein: 4.806 g. Fiber: 1.43 g. Cholesterol: 63.17 mg. Calcium: 95.5 mg. Iron: 1.784 mg. Potassium: 180 mg. Total Fat: 10.4 g; Saturated fat: 6.1 g, Monounsaturated fat: 3 g, Polyunsaturated fat: 0.5 g.

❈ FRENCH APPLE PIE ❈

SERVES 8   SODIUM PER RECIPE: 78.7 MG   SODIUM PER SERVING: 9.835 MG

While working in Paris one year I often had lunch at a Basque restaurant across the street from Jacques Cousteau's film lab. Basques are of an unknown origin, but lived primarily in the Spain/France area of the Pyrenees. The owners of this restaurant must have had the French influence because their apple pie was indeed a "French Apple Pie" with an absurdly delicious topping. It was similar to my own apple pie but mine has absolutely no salt and very little sodium.

PIE INGREDIENTS
     1 unbaked 8- or 9-inch One-Crust Pie Shell, page 315 (15.2 mg)
    10 medium Golden Delicious apples (trace)
    ¼ to ½ cup water (0 mg)
    ½ cup granulated sugar (1 mg)
     2 teaspoons ground cinnamon (3.581 mg)
    ¾ teaspoon ground nutmeg (.284 mg)
     1 tablespoon cornstarch (.72 mg)

TOPPING INGREDIENTS
     1 cup flour (2.5 mg)
    ½ cup packed brown sugar (42.9 mg)
    ½ cup unsalted butter (12.5 mg)

1. Core and slice the apples. Put them in a pot with the water and bring it to a boil over moderate heat, stirring occasionally. When the apples have slightly softened, remove from the heat. Drain half the liquid and pour the apples into a mixing bowl. Add the sugar, cinnamon, nutmeg, and the cornstarch. Stir until it is completely combined. You may add a bit more cinnamon if you desire.

2. To make the topping, cut the butter into thin slices. Combine the butter, flour, and sugar in a medium bowl and mix with an eggbeater until it's either a crumbly or loose mixture. Set it aside. Sprinkle the topping over the top of the pie, using it all.

3. Bake the pie on a cookie sheet in a preheated standard oven at 350°F for 40 minutes, or in a fan-driven convection oven at 375°F for 40 to 45 minutes. Serve hot or cold.

Calories: 533. Sodium: 9.83 mg. Carbohydrate: 78.1 g. Protein: 3.84 g. Fiber: 6.49 g. Cholesterol: 62.09 mg. Calcium: 56.7 mg. Iron: 2.986 mg. Potassium: 298.7 mg. Total Fat: 24.1 g; Saturated fat: 14.5 g, Monounsaturated fat: 6.7 g, Polyunsaturated fat: .2 g.

❧ MARGE'S APPLE PIE ❧

SERVES 8   SODIUM PER RECIPE: 115.2 MG (INCLUDES THE TOPPING)
SODIUM PER SERVING: 14.4 MG

There are more than 4,000 shades of green. I believe there are also more than 4,000 apple pie recipes. This one comes from my sister. It has a nice tangy flavor.

THE PIE AND FILLING
    1 **unbaked 10-inch One-Crust Pie Shell, page 315 (15.2 mg)**
    8 **medium Golden Delicious apples, sliced (trace)**
1¾ **cups water (0 mg)**
    6 **tablespoons granulated sugar (.756 mg)**
    3 **tablespoons packed brown sugar (16.1 mg)**
 ⅛ **teaspoon ground nutmeg (trace)**
 ¾ **teaspoon ground cinnamon (.454 mg)**
    2 **tablespoons grated orange zest (.36 mg)**
    1 **tablespoon lemon juice (.15 mg)**
    4 **tablespoons raisins—optional (4.35 mg)**
    2 **tablespoons cornstarch (1.44 mg)**

DUTCH TOPPING
 ⅓ **teaspoon vanilla extract (.125 mg)**
 ½ **cup (1 stick) unsalted butter, softened or almost melted**
        (12.5 mg)
    1 **cup loosely packed brown sugar (56.6 mg)**
 ⅔ **cup granulated sugar (1.32 mg)**
    2 **cups best for bread flour (5 mg)**
    1 **teaspoon ground nutmeg (.356 mg)**
 ¾ **teaspoon ground cinnamon (.454 mg)**

1. Bring the apple slices to a near boil in 1½ cups of the water. Simmer for 4 minutes, then add the white and brown sugars, nutmeg, and cinnamon along with the grated orange zest and the lemon juice. Bring back to a near boil and then simmer over medium heat for about 5 minutes. Add the raisins just before finishing. Adjust the time so that the apples don't get too mushy. Mix the cornstarch with the remaining water and add it to the apple mixture at this time. Continue to cook, stirring occasionally, until the mixture thickens slightly. Pour this mixture into your pie shell.

2. To make the Dutch topping, combine the vanilla and softened or almost melted butter. Next combine the sugars, flour, nutmeg, and cinnamon and then mix them with the butter mixture. The topping should be dry or only slightly damp, but it shouldn't be wet.

3. Preheat the oven to 350°F.

4. Use the Dutch crumb topping to cover the entire pie well. Bake in the preheated oven for 50 minutes, or until the crumb topping has browned. This recipe is for a 10-inch pie. If you make a 9-inch pie, use the balance of your pie mixture and crust in smaller apple turnovers you can bake in your toaster oven while the pie is baking. Then adjust the nutrient values to suit.

5. Serve hot. Add slice of low-sodium Tillamook Cheddar (28 mg) or a ½ cup vanilla ice cream (45 mg).

Calories: 674. Sodium: 14.4 mg. Carbohydrate: 113.1 g. Protein: 5.568 g. Fiber: 5.66 g. Cholesterol: 62.11 mg. Calcium: 54.3 mg. Iron: 5.221 mg. Potassium: 342.8 mg. Total Fat: 24.1 g; Saturated fat: 14.6 g, Monounsaturated fat: 6.7 g, Polyunsaturated fat: 1.2 g.

❧ MARLENE'S APPLE PIE ❧

SERVES 8   SODIUM PER RECIPE: 65.36 MG   SODIUM PER SERVING: 8.17 MG

1 unbaked 9-inch Two-Crust Pie Shell, page 316 (24 mg)
6 large apples, unpeeled—favorites include Granny Smith,
    Golden Delicious, or Macintosh (trace)
1 tablespoon fresh lemon juice (trace)
½ teaspoon grated lemon zest (.36 mg)
½ cup unpacked brown sugar (28.3 mg)
1 tablespoon cornstarch diluted in water per instructions
    on the box (.7 mg)
1½ teaspoons ground cinnamon (1 mg)
¼ teaspoon ground nutmeg (trace)
¼ teaspoon ground cloves (1.25 mg)
⅛ teaspoon ground ginger (trace)
1 tablespoon unsalted butter (1.5 mg)
1 teaspoon granulated sugar (trace)
    Dash of ground cinnamon (trace)
1 tablespoon nonfat milk (7.8 mg)

1. Preheat the oven to 450°F.

2. Core and thinly slice the apples. Toss with the lemon juice and grated zest. Mix in the brown sugar, cornstarch, and spices. Toss with the apples to coat.

3. Fill the bottom 9-inch pie shell with the apple mixture. Dot the top with cut-up pieces of butter. Roll the remaining dough into a round large enough to cover the top of the apples. Roll the crust over the rolling pin, then transfer it and unroll it over the pie filling carefully. Crimp the edges of the crusts together. Make slits in the top crust to vent. Mix the granulated sugar with a dash of cinnamon and brush the top of crust with the tablespoon of milk and sprinkle lightly with cinnamon sugar.

4. Bake at 450°F for 10 minutes. Reduce heat to 375°F and bake for an additional 20 to 30 minutes. To prevent blackened or burned edge crust, cut 1-inch strips of aluminum foil, link them together, and lightly grease. Wrap this longer strip around the pie for the first 20 minutes. Remove for the last 20 minutes and continue to bake. Serve hot or cool.

Calories: 417. Sodium: 8.17 mg. Carbohydrate: 59.5 g. Protein: 3.854 g. Fiber: 5.52 g. Cholesterol: 50.5 mg. Calcium: 38.6 mg. Iron: 2.635 mg. Potassium: 268.5 mg. Total Fat: 19.6 g; Saturated fat: 11.8 g, Monounsaturated fat: 5.5 g, Polyunsaturated fat: 1 g.

◈ BLACK BOTTOM PIE ◈

SERVES 8   SODIUM PER RECIPE: 413.6 MG   SODIUM PER SERVING: 51.7 MG

A rich chocolate dessert worth making at least once a year.

1 unbaked 9-inch One-Crust Pie Shell, page 315 (15.2 mg)
½ cup plus ⅓ cup granulated sugar (1.66 mg)
2 tablespoons cornstarch (1.4 mg)
2 medium eggs, separated (110.9 mg)
2 cups nonfat or 1% milk (252.4 mg)
2 tablespoons unflavored gelatin (27.4 mg)
3 tablespoons water (0 mg)
2 teaspoons rum extract flavoring (trace)
1 ounce unsweetened chocolate, melted (3.9 mg)
⅓ teaspoon cream of tartar (.5 mg)
Commercial zero-sodium canned whipped cream for garnish (3.9 mg)
Grated chocolate shavings for garnish (.3 mg)

1. Bake the pie shell according to the recipe directions on page 315.

2. Combine ½ cup of the sugar and the cornstarch in a saucepan. Stir in the egg yolks and milk, then cook over medium heat, stirring constantly, until the mixture comes to a boil. Reserve 1 cup of the custard mixture and set it aside.

3. Soften the gelatin in the cold water. Stir this into the remaining hot custard mixture. Next stir in the rum flavoring. Place the pan in a bowl of ice water, stirring occasionally until the mixture mounds slightly when dropped from a spoon. Combine the chocolate and reserved custard mixture. Pour this mixture into the baked pie shell:

4. Beat the egg whites and cream of tartar until foamy. Beat in the remaining ⅓ cup sugar 1 tablespoon at a time and continue beating until stiff and glossy. Don't underbeat the whites. Fold the remaining custard mixture into the meringue. Spread this on the chocolate mixture. Chill for at least 3 hours or until set. Garnish with whipped cream. It's also nice to sprinkle grated chocolate on top.

Calories: 313.5. Sodium: 51.7 mg. Carbohydrate: 39.9 g. Protein: 7.072 g. Fiber: 0.79 g. Cholesterol: 63.13 mg. Calcium: 90.6 mg. Iron: 1.702 mg. Potassium: 188.2 mg. Total Fat: 11.9 g; Saturated fat: 7 g, Monounsaturated fat: 3.6 g, Polyunsaturated fat: 0.6 g.

❖ SWEET POTATO PIE ❖

SERVES 8   SODIUM PER RECIPE: 206 MG   SODIUM PER SERVING: 25.8 MG

Thought you'd never be able to have sweet potato pie again? Well, this may change your mind. Here's a low-sodium version of that popular dessert. If you've never had sweet potato pie, try it once. You'll discover a whole new taste treat.

4 medium sweet potatoes or yams—about 1½ pounds (67.6 mg)
1 unbaked 9-inch Two-Crust Pie Shell, page 316 (24 mg)
1 cup light brown sugar (56.6 mg)
½ teaspoon ground cinnamon (.606 mg)
⅛ teaspoon ground nutmeg (trace)
½ teaspoon ground ginger (.292 mg)
6 tablespoons unsalted butter, cut into bits (.292 mg)
½ cup light cream or whole milk (47.5 mg)

1. Boil the potatoes until half-cooked, about 15 to 25 minutes. Peel and slice them thinly.
2. Preheat the oven to 425°F.
3. Mix the sugar and the cinnamon, nutmeg, and ginger together. Place a layer of sweet potatoes in the unbaked pie shell. Sprinkle the first layer with some of the sugar/spice mixture and dot with a little butter. Add the rest of the sweet potatoes in similar layers until completed, sprinkling each layer with the sugar/spice mixture. Top with all the cream (or milk). Transfer the top crust and cover the potato mixture completely, then flute the edges of the pastry and cut vents. Bake in the preheated 425°F oven for 30 to 40 minutes. If the potatoes are not tender, continue to bake at 350°F until done. Serve hot.

Calories: 511. Sodium: 25.75 mg. Carbohydrate: 60.6 g. Protein: 5.015 g. Fiber: 2.99 g. Cholesterol: 79.81 mg. Calcium: 60.3 mg. Iron: 2.861 mg. Potassium: 263 mg. Total Fat: 29.3 g; Saturated fat: 18 g, Monounsaturated fat: 8.4 g, Polyunsaturated fat: 1.3 g.

❊ SWEET POTATO PUREE PIE ❊

SERVES 8   SODIUM PER RECIPE: 444.9 MG   SODIUM PER SERVING: 55.6 MG

Try this one—it's great. If it doesn't taste like pumpkin pie, I'll eat the other seven slices.

1 unbaked 9-inch One-Crust Pie Shell, page 315 (15.2 mg)
1¼ cups boiled, mashed sweet potatoes (21.6 mg)
¾ cup granulated sugar (1.5 mg)
¼ teaspoon ground ginger (.146 mg)
1½ teaspoons ground cinnamon (.908 mg)
1 teaspoon unbleached flour (trace)
2 medium eggs, lightly beaten (110.9 mg)
1 cup evaporated milk (294.4 mg) or substitute whole milk (147.2 mg)
2 tablespoons water (0 mg)
½ teaspoon vanilla extract (.189 mg)
Commercial zero-sodium canned whip cream for garnish (trace) or 1 teaspoon honey for garnish (3.9 mg)

1. Preheat the oven to 400°F.

2. Combine the potatoes, sugar, ginger, cinnamon, and flour in a mixing bowl. Add the lightly beaten eggs and mix well. Mix in the milk, water, and vanilla. Pour this mixture into the unbaked pie shell. Bake in the preheated oven for 45 to 50 minutes, or until a knife inserted near the center comes out clean. Garnish with whipped cream or a teaspoon of honey. Serve hot or warm. To make 2 pies, double the recipe.

Calories: 302. Sodium: 55.61 mg. Carbohydrate: 41.3 g. Protein: 5.93 g. Fiber: 1.3 g. Cholesterol: 78.96 mg. Calcium: 114 mg. Iron: 1.695 mg. Potassium: 188.6 mg. Total Fat: 12.9 g; Saturated fat: 7.6 g, Monounsaturated fat: 3.8 g, Polyunsaturated fat: 0.7 g.

OATMEAL PIE /

❖ A LOW-FAT, LOW-SODIUM TREAT ❖

SERVES 8   SODIUM PER RECIPE: 347.10 MG   SODIUM PER SERVING: 43.4 MG

I first made this pie years ago after visiting my friend Walter in Georgia. Walter owned a ten-thousand-acre pecan farm. We ate pecans until they came out of our ears. He suggested to me that I could concoct a pie without pecans that would taste just like pecans if I just put in the same other ingredients. So, I used one of my favorite recipes and developed this "quick pecan" pie. It sure tastes like a pecan pie, but it uses oats instead of pecans and brings with it a great many nutrients. I've lowered the fat, too.

¼ cup unsalted applesauce (1.912 mg) or Homemade
   Applesauce, page 360 (trace)
½ cup granulated sugar (1 mg)
½ teaspoon ground cinnamon (.303 mg)
½ teaspoon ground cloves (2.55 mg)
½ cup light corn syrup (198.4 mg)
½ cup loosely packed light brown sugar (28.3 mg)
2 tablespoons water (0 mg)
2 eggs (110.9 mg)
1 cup oats* (3.76 mg)

1. Cream together the butter and sugars in a saucepan over low heat. Stir in corn syrup. Remove from heat put into mixing bowl. Add eggs one at a time, stirring after each until blended. Stir in the oats. Pour into pie shell and bake in 350°F oven for about an hour or until knife inserted in center of pie comes out clean.

Calories: 192. Sodium: 43.39 mg. Carbohydrate: 46.7 g. Protein: 3.434 g. Fiber: 2.03 g. Cholesterol: 46.75 mg. Calcium: 23.6 mg. Iron: 1.204 mg. Potassium: 119.3 mg. Total Fat: 2 g; Saturated fat: 0.5 g, Monounsaturated fat: 0.7 g, Polyunsaturated fat: 0.5 g.

*Buy rolled, raw, or Quaker Oats. Make sure that the ones you buy are plain oats with no salt added.

Cakes, Cookies, Bars, and Frostings

❖ ❖ ❖ ❖ ❖ ❖ ❖ ❖

❖ Apple Cake ❖

SERVES 12   SODIUM PER RECIPE: 252.9 MG   SODIUM PER SERVING: 21.1 MG

APPLE MIXTURE
- ¼ cup granulated sugar (.5 mg)
- 3 medium to large apples, peeled, cored, and sliced (0 mg)
- 2 teaspoons ground cinnamon (1.211 mg)

BATTER
- 2½ cups granulated sugar (5 mg)
- 3 cups unbleached flour (7.5 mg)
- 1 cup canola oil* (trace)
- 4 medium eggs (221.8 mg)
- 2½ teaspoons vanilla extract (.945 mg)
- 1 tablespoon Featherweight Baking Powder (13.5 mg)
- ½ cup orange juice (1.244 mg)
- 1 cup walnut halves or pieces (1.25 mg)

1. Preheat the oven to 350°F.

2. Combine the apple mixture ingredients in a bowl. Beat the batter ingredients together in another bowl until smooth. Pour half the batter into a greased tube or Bundt pan, add the apple mixture evenly, and top off with the rest of the batter. Bake for 1½ to 1¾ hours. Serve warm or cool.

Calories: 567. Sodium: 21.08 mg. Carbohydrate: 78.5 g. Protein: 7.749 g. Fiber: 2.55 g. Cholesterol: 62.33 mg. Calcium: 92.3 mg. Iron: 2.33 mg. Potassium: 295.5 mg. Total Fat: 26 g. Saturated fat: 2.2 g, Monounsaturated fat: 12.6 g, Polyunsaturated fat: 9.7 g.

*Try using 1 cup unsalted applesauce (commercial or **Homemade**) instead, to help cut the fat and punch up the flavor. If you do, add an additional teaspoon of ground cinnamon. You can also use olive oil instead of canola oil or use half oil and half unsalted applesauce.

✦ APPLESAUCE CAKE ✦

MAKES 1 CAKE (16 SLICES) SODIUM PER RECIPE: 247.9 MG
SODIUM PER SLICE: 15.5 MG

*Fresh applesauce, made from any seasonal apples, will help make this a very tasty dessert. If you do not want to make **Homemade Applesauce** (page 360), make sure you buy an unsalted applesauce.*

2 cups granulated sugar (4 mg)
3 medium eggs (166.3 mg)
2 cups best for bread flour (5 mg)
2 teaspoons ground cinnamon (1.211 mg)
2 teaspoons Featherweight Baking Powder (9 mg)
2 teaspoons vanilla extract (.756 mg)
3½ cups unsalted applesauce (26.8 mg)
2 cups seedless golden raisins, soaked—optional (34.8 mg)

1. Preheat the oven to 350°F.
2. Mix all the ingredients together in a large bowl. Pour the batter into a greased and floured 13x9-inch pan. Bake in the preheated oven for 50 to 55 minutes. Serve it hot or cold. Right out of the oven it's incredibly delicious—so good, in fact, that it doesn't need frosting. However, if you like frosting, make a simple confectioners' sugar frosting like the one below and spread it on the cake when it comes hot from the oven.

Calories: 266. Sodium: 15.49 mg. Protein: 3.371 g. Carbobydrate: 63.1 g. Fiber: 1.99 g. Cholesterol: 35.06 mg. Calcium: 49.1 mg. Iron: 1.54 mg. Potassium: 261.8 mg. Total Fat: 1.2 g; Saturated fat: 0.3 g, Monounsaturated fat: 0.3 g, Polyunsaturated fat: 0.2 g.

✦ ORANGE ZEST FROSTING ✦

MAKES 1 CUP (FOR 16 PORTIONS) SODIUM PER RECIPE: 1.862 MG
SODIUM PER PORTION: .116 MG

1 cup confectioners' sugar (1.2 mg)
1 teaspoon vanilla extract (.378 mg)
1 or 2 tablespoons fresh orange juice (.284 mg)
2 to 3 tablespoons grated orange zest (.36 mg)

1. For the frosting, mix the sugar, vanilla, and zest with the orange juice. Spread the mixture on the hot cake. Serve warm.

Calories: 34. Sodium: 0.12 mg. Protein: .091 g. Carbobydrate: 8.579 g. Fiber: 0.19 g. Cholesterol: 0 mg. Calcium: 3.324 mg. Iron: .015 mg. Potassium: 17.6 mg. Total Fat: 0 g; Saturated fat: 0 g, Monounsaturated fat: 0 g, Polyunsaturated fat: 0 g.

❈ CARROT CAKE ❈

MAKES 1 CAKE (15 SLICES)   SODIUM PER RECIPE: 298.8 MG
SODIUM PER SLICE: 19.9 MG

This cake is proof that you can enjoy the best of the best. A standard carrot cake recipe will have about 5,700 mg sodium or nearly 475 mg per serving—compare this recipe, which has 298.8 mg total, or 19.9 mg per serving. We've also cut the fat down from about 29 g per piece to under 7 g. This cake is so good, that it really doesn't need frosting, but we've included one in case you want to serve one.

CARROT CAKE

1½ cups Homemade Applesauce, page 360, or unsalted applesauce (11.5 mg)
 2 cups granulated sugar (4 mg)
 3 eggs (166.3 mg)
 2 cups best for bread flour (5 mg)
 2 teaspoons ground cinnamon (1.211 mg)
 2 teaspoons Featherweight Baking Powder (9 mg)
 2 teaspoons vanilla extract (.756 mg)
 2 cups shredded carrots (77 mg)
 1 cup chopped walnuts (optional) (1.25 mg)
 1 cup loosely packed seedless golden raisins, soaked (17.4 mg)
½ cup crushed pineapple packed in water, drained (1.23 mg)*

LEMON SAUCE FROSTING†

 1 tablespoon cornstarch (.72 mg)
½ cup granulated sugar (1 mg)
  The grated zest of 1 lemon (.36 mg)
¾ cup water (0 mg)
 2 tablespoons fresh lemon juice from the above lemon (.47 mg)
 1 tablespoon unsalted butter (1.562 mg)

1. Preheat the oven to 350°F.

2. Mix the cake ingredients together in a large bowl. Pour the batter into a greased and flour-dusted 13x9-inch pan. Bake for 50 to 55 minutes. Serve hot or cold.

3. If desired, for a frosting, try this lemon sauce, served hot. Use only enough for the amount of cake you plan to serve. You can freeze the rest of the cake for future use. To prepare the frosting, combine the cornstarch,

---

*Some pineapple is higher in sodium than others. We recommend using canned Dole chunks, drained, crushed in your food processor with the shredder blade.
†You may also substitute **Lemon Cake Frosting** (page 336).

sugar, zest, and water in a saucepan set over medium heat. Cook and stir until thick. Remove the pan from the heat and then stir in the lemon juice and butter before serving. You may freeze the frosting for future use.

Calories: 324. Sodium: 19.92 mg. Protein: 5.434 g. Carbohydrate: 63.5 g. Fiber: 2.31 g. Cholesterol: 39.47 mg. Calcium: 56.6 mg. Iron: 2.152 mg. Potassium: 293.2 mg. Total Fat: 6.7 g; Saturated fat: 1.1 g, Monounsaturated fat: 1.6 g, Polyunsaturated fat: 3.4 g.

Thanks so much for all the sample recipes that you sent us. I have already tried the carrot cake! Boy, was it yummy! We had company for dinner Thursday night and I served it for dessert. Everyone loved it even without icing! It is certainly a "make again and again" recipe! Thanks.
Kay and Jerry Heller

❖ NO-SUGAR-ADDED CARROT CAKE ❖

MAKES 1 CAKE (15 SLICES)   SODIUM PER RECIPE: 347 MG
SODIUM PER SLICE: 23.1 MG

*This cake was created at the suggestion of Colleen Jarecki, who dropped by our website and asked for a sugarless dessert. This is an adaptation of the previous **Carrot Cake** recipe, which has been in our family for years. Moist, tasty, you won't miss the sugar.*

1½ cups Homemade Applesauce,* page 360 (431 mg)
1½ cups unsweetened apple juice concentrate (11.2 mg)
 4 egg whites, well beaten (219.1 mg)
 1 cup best for bread flour (2.5 mg)
 1 cup whole wheat flour (6 mg)
 2 teaspoons ground cinnamon (1.211 mg)
 2 teaspoons Featherweight Baking Powder (9 mg)
 2 teaspoons vanilla extract (.756 mg)
 2 cups shredded carrots (77 mg)
 1 cup chopped walnuts (1.25 mg)
 1 cup golden seedless raisins, soaked (17.4 mg)
 ½ cup crushed pineapple packed in water, drained (1.23 mg)†

1. Preheat the oven to 350°F.
2. Mix the ingredients together in a large bowl. Pour the batter into a greased and floured 13x9-inch pan. Bake in the oven for 40 to 50 minutes.

*Optional—you may substitute canola oil instead. If you do, add 11.9 g fat to your total fat count.
†Some pineapple is higher in sodium content. We recommend canned Dole chunks, drained, crushed in your food processor with the shredder blade.

Insert a knife or toothpick into the center of the cake and when it comes out clean, your cake is done. Serve hot or cold. It does not need a topping when fresh and warm, but you could spread the top with low-fat cream cheese if you choose. Watch out for the additional sodium, however.

Calories: 176. Sodium: 23.14 mg. Carbohydrate: 29.3 g. Protein: 5.469 g. Fiber: 3 g. Cholesterol: 0 mg. Calcium: 55.1 mg. Iron: 1.56 mg. Potassium: 338.4 mg. Total Fat: 5.1 g; Saturated fat: 0.4 g, Monounsaturated fat: 1.1 g, Polyunsaturated fat: 3.3 g.

❖ PRUNE CAKE ❖

MAKES 1 CAKE (15 SLICES)   SODIUM PER RECIPE: 319.5 MG
SODIUM PER SLICE: 21.3 MG

Ever since my youth, this has been my cake of choice for my birthday. With a light chocolate frosting, it can be fantastic.

1½ **cups granulated sugar (3 mg)**
2½ **cups white flour (6.25 mg)**
 1 **teaspoon Featherweight Baking Powder (4.5 mg)**
½ **teaspoon ground cloves (2.55 mg)**
 1 **cup extra light virgin olive oil (trace)**
 3 **whole eggs (166.3 mg)**
 1 **cup cooked pitted prunes (6.8 mg)**
 1 **cup low-fat buttermilk (130 mg)***

1. Preheat the oven to 325°F.
2. Sift the sugar, flour, baking powder, and cloves together in a large mixing bowl. Make a well in center and add the oil, eggs, prunes, and buttermilk. Beat with a spoon until well blended. Bake in a 10x13-inch Pyrex cake pan for 45 minutes, or until the center springs back to the touch. The cake may be served plain or frosted in the pan. For a layer cake, bake the cake in two 9-inch pans. Icing for **Easy Chocolate Cake** (page 333) is excellent for a large cake or **Lemon Cake Frosting** (page 336) for a layer cake.

Using olive oil. Calories: 324. Sodium: 21.3 mg. Protein: 4.152 mg. Carbohydrate: 44 g. Fiber: 1.4 g. Cholesterol: 39.07 mg. Calcium: 28.3 mg. Iron: 3.76 mg. Potassium: 152.2 mg. Total Fat: 15.9 g; Saturated fat: 2.5 g, Monounsaturated fat: 11 g, Polyunsaturated fat: 1.4 g.

Using canola oil. Calories: 325. Sodium: 21.29 mg. Protein: 4.152 g. Carbohydrate: 44 g. Fiber: 1.4 g. Cholesterol: 39.07 mg. Calcium: 47.5 mg. Iron: 3.706 mg. Potassium: 152.2 mg. Total Fat: 16 g; Saturated fat: 1.5 g, Monounsaturated fat: 9 g, Polyunsaturated fat: 4.5 g.

*Our figure is based on using Knudsen Buttermilk. Make sure your buttermilk container lists 130 mg or less for sodium. If you can find it, there is "low-sodium buttermilk"; its sodium count is only 6 mg per cup.

❖ EASY CHOCOLATE CAKE ❖

SERVES 12   SODIUM PER RECIPE: 16.1 MG   SODIUM PER SLICE, NO ICING:
1.345 MG   SODIUM PER SLICE WITH ICING BELOW: 8.239 MG

1½ cups unbleached white flour (3.75 mg)
  1 cup granulated sugar (0 mg)
  3 tablespoons Hershey's cocoa (3.402 mg)
1½ teaspoons Featherweight Baking Powder (3 mg)
  1 tablespoon white vinegar (.15 mg)
  6 tablespoons canola oil (trace)
  1 teaspoon Cook's powdered vanilla (.378 mg)
  1 cup water (0 mg)

1. Preheat oven to 350°F.
2. Combine all ingredients in a medium-sized mixing bowl. Stir together with a wooden spoon until just mixed. Pour into a very lightly greased and floured 8-inch square Pyrex or 9-inch layer pan. Bake for 30 to 35 minutes. Test with a toothpick or knife. Let cook for about two minutes, then spread topping on.

Calories: 186. Sodium: 1.34 mg. Fiber: 0.84 g. Protein: 1.859 g. Carbohydrate: 29.7 g. Cholesterol: 0 mg. Calcium: 31.2 mg. Iron: 1.696 mg. Potassium: 115.8 mg. Total Fat: 7.1 g; Saturated fat: 1 g, Monounsaturated fat: 5 g, Polyunsaturated fat: 0.6 g.

❖ ICING FOR EASY CHOCOLATE CAKE ❖

MAKES 1 CUP (12 SERVINGS)   SODIUM PER RECIPE: 82.7 MG
SODIUM PER SERVING: 6.849 MG

  4 squares semisweet cooking chocolate (4 mg)
½ cup (1 stick) unsalted butter (12.5 mg)
½ cup nonfat milk (63.1 mg)
  1 pound confectioners' sugar (2.4 mg)
  2 teaspoons vanilla extract (.7 mg)

1. Melt the chocolate and butter in a saucepan over low heat. In a bowl, mix the milk and sugar until smooth. Stir it into the chocolate mixture and add vanilla. Beat with a wooden spoon until thick. Spread on cake when cake is cool.

Calories: 196. Sodium: 6.85 mg. Protein: 1.096 mg. Carbohydrate: 25.9 g. Fiber: 0.17 g. Cholesterol: 20.89 mg. Iron: .365 mg. Potassium: 59.5 mg. Total Fat: 10.7 g; Saturated fat: 6.6 g, Monounsaturated fat: 3.3 g, Polyunsaturated fat: 0.4 g.

❖ STRAWBERRY SHORTCAKE ❖

MAKES 1 SHORTCAKE (8 SERVINGS)   SODIUM PER RECIPE: 203.6 MG
SODIUM PER SERVING: 25.5 MG

Here's another great low-sodium recipe developed
by Marge Gentry.

THE SHORTCAKE
- 3 cups unbleached flour (7.5 mg)
- 3½ teaspoons Featherweight Baking Powder (15.8 mg)
- ½ cup granulated sugar (1 mg)
- ½ cup (1 stick) softened butter (trace)
- 1 cup nonfat milk (126.2 mg)

THE TOPPING
- 1 quart strawberries (5.76 mg)
- ½ cup granulated sugar (1 mg)
- ½ cup confectioners' sugar (1.2 mg)
- ¼ cup (½ stick) unsalted butter (6.242 mg)
- ½ cup whipped cream or regular or canned dairy whipped cream (39 mg)

1. First wash and hull the strawberries for the topping and then slice for eating. In a bowl, combine them with ½ cup granulated sugar. Stir gently. Let sit for about 15 minutes. Do not pour out the juices that develop.

2. Preheat the oven to 450°F.

3. To make the shortcake, mix the flour, baking powder, and sugar in a large bowl. Pour in canola while stirring, until the mixture resembles cornmeal. Add the milk and stir lightly with a wooden spoon or fork until just blended. Turn the dough out onto a lightly floured surface. Knead by hand for about 20 turns. Divide the dough in half. Put each half in a greased and flour-dusted 8x11-inch 2-layer pan, or, for a more textured biscuit, pat both halves into 8-inch rounds on a lightly greased and floured cookie sheet. Now bake the shortcake for 20 minutes.

4. While baking, finish the topping. Blend the confectioners' sugar and butter in a small bowl until smooth. When the shortcake biscuits are done, cool them and split them in half. Spread the bottom layers with the butter mixture and half the strawberries and whipped cream. Top with the remaining biscuit layer, strawberries, and cream. Serve immediately.

Calories: 541. Sodium: 25.45 mg. Protein: 6.508 g. Carbohydrate: 83.7 g. Fiber: 2.97 g.
Cholesterol: 18.93 mg. Calcium: 155.5 mg. Iron: 2.677 mg. Potassium: 449.5 mg. Total Fat:
21 g; Saturated fat: 5.2 g, Monounsaturated fat: 10 g, Polyunsaturated fat: 4.6 g.

❀ HUGUENOT TORTE ❀

MAKES 1 CAKE (9 SERVINGS)* SODIUM PER RECIPE: 124.9 MG
SODIUM PER SERVING: 13.9 MG

Peggy Shultz created this many, many years ago.

2 medium eggs (110.9 mg)
1 cup granulated sugar (2 mg)
1 teaspoon vanilla extract (.378 mg)
⅔ cup white unbleached flour (1.65 mg)
2 teaspoons Featherweight Baking Powder (9 mg)
1 cup pared and chopped apple (0 mg)
1 cup chopped unsalted pecans (.992 mg)
  Zero-sodium canned whipped cream or low-sodium sorbet for
  garnish (add 2 mg per serving)

1. Preheat the oven to 350°F.
2. Beat the eggs. Gradually add the sugar and vanilla. In a separate bowl, sift together the flour and baking powder. Fold the dry ingredients into the wet ingredients. Add the apples and nuts. Pour the batter into a greased 8x8-inch pan and bake in the preheated oven for 35 to 40 minutes. Cut the cake into squares. Serve with canned whipped cream or low-sodium sorbet.

Calories: 216. Sodium: 13.88 mg. Protein: 27.6 g. Carbohydrate: 308 g. Fiber: 1.63 g. Cholesterol: 41.56 mg. Calcium: 59.3 mg. Iron: .933 mg. Potassium: 189.8 mg. Total Fat: 8.2 g; Saturated fat: 0.9 g, Monounsaturated fat: 4.8 g, Polyunsaturated fat: 1.9 g.

❀ APPLE CRISP ❀

SERVES 12 SODIUM PER RECIPE: 72 MG SODIUM PER SERVING: 5.998 MG

A favorite around our house for many years. A good way to use apples that may have been sitting around too long to eat out of hand.

10 medium-sized apples (trace)
3 tablespoons fresh lemon juice (.45 mg)
1½ cups old-fashioned rolled oats (5.64 mg)
1 cup loosely packed brown sugar (56.6 mg)
¾ cup unbleached white flour (1.875 mg)
4 tablespoons (½ stick) unsalted butter (6.248 mg)
2 teaspoons ground cinnamon (1.211 mg)
  Frozen sorbet or plain yogurt (optional)

*You can cut the slices smaller and make 12 servings. Adjust the sodium count to suit.

1. Preheat the oven to 375°F.

2. You can use green or red apples, and not necessarily "cooking" apples. Slice the unpeeled apples. Toss the apples with the lemon juice and place them in an ungreased 9x13-inch pan. Mix the remaining ingredients and sprinkle the mixture evenly over the apples. Bake for 30 minutes. Serve with frozen sorbet if desired. Add 2 mg sodium per serving.

Calories: 207. Sodium: 6 mg. Carbohydrate: 43.7 g. Protein: 3.128 g. Fiber: 5.35 g. Cholesterol: 10.36 mg. Calcium: 32.4 mg. Iron: 1.591 mg. Potassium: 256.7 mg. Total Fat: 5.2 g; Saturated fat: 2.6 g, Monounsaturated fat: 1.4 g, Polyunsaturated fat: 0.6 g.

❧ DON'S SWEET CHOCOLATE MIX ❧

MAKES 3 CUPS   SODIUM PER CUP: 14.2 MG
SODIUM PER TABLESPOON: .887 MG

- 1 cup cocoa powder (16.3 mg)—not cocoa mix
- 1 cup ground semisweet (not milk chocolate) chocolate (24 mg)
- 2 cups granulated sugar (2 mg)
- 2 teaspoons powdered vanilla (.252 mg)

1. Mix the ingredients together in a food processor. Store what you don't use for future use. Can be used for brownies, cakes, or you can make a delicious hot chocolate drink using 2 or 3 tablespoons per cup warm non-fat milk.

Nutrition facts per Tablespoon. Calories: 44.2. Sodium: 0.89 mg. Carbohydrate: .836 g. Protein: .524 g. Fiber: 0.73 g. Cholesterol: 0 mg. Calcium: 3.452 mg. Iron: .447 mg. Potassium: 47.9 mg. Total Fat: 1.9 g; Saturated fat: 1.39 g, Monounsaturated fat: .62 g, Polyunsaturated fat: .124 g.

❧ LEMON CAKE FROSTING ❧

MAKES ENOUGH FROSTING FOR ONE 9x13-INCH CAKE (15 SERVINGS)
SODIUM PER RECIPE: 17.7 MG
SODIUM PER SERVING (BASED ON 15-SERVINGS): 1.178 MG

Great for carrot cakes, prune cakes, and other single-layer cakes. It is based on the C&H "Buttercream Frosting" recipe found on a box of C&H confectioners' sugar.

- 2 teaspoons vanilla extract (.756 mg)
- ¼ cup grated or finely chopped lemon zest (1.44 mg)
- ¼ cup fresh lemon juice (.6 mg)
- 2 cups confectioners' sugar (2.4 mg)
- ½ cup (1 stick) unsalted butter, softened (12.5 mg)

1. Combine all the ingredients and beat with an electric beater or heavy spoon until smooth. If it becomes too stiff, beat in a few more drops of lemon juice. Apply to cake and then chill.

Calories: 120. Sodium: 1.18 mg. Carbohydrate: 16.6 g. Protein: .104 g. Fiber: 0.19 g. Cholesterol: 16.55 mg. Calcium: 4.422 mg. Iron: .036 mg. Potassium: 10.6 mg. Total Fat: 6.2 g; Saturated fat: 3.8 g, Monounsaturated fat: 1.8 g, Polyunsaturated fat: 0.2 g.

SAUCE OF FROZEN RASPBERRIES
❈ WITH CANTALOUPE ❈

SERVES 4*   *SODIUM PER RECIPE: 54.5 MG*   *SODIUM PER SERVING: 13.6 MG*
Fresh raspberries may improve recipe somewhat—but not enough to justify waiting until raspberry season. Frozen berries are generally just as tasty as fresh berries. This sauce can also serve as a base for roasted game or lean pork.

10-to 12-ounce package frozen raspberries (2.84 mg)
2 teaspoons fresh lemon juice (.3 mg)
2 tablespoons honey (1.68 mg)
1 medium whole cantaloupe, sliced (49.7 mg)
Sprig of mint or thin slice of orange for garnish

1. Using a food processor or blender, purée all but a handful of raspberries until smooth. Strain this through a fine sieve or cheesecloth. Add the lemon juice and honey and mix together. Spread a quarter of the purée in each of 4 serving dishes. Place sliced cantaloupe on each plate and serve. Garnish with a sprig of mint or a thinly sliced orange piece. (When using the sauce to accompany the meats, spread it on the plate in the same manner and lay the cooked meat on top just before serving.)

Calories: 155. Sodium: 13.62 mg. Protein: 1.771 g. Carbohydrate: 39.4 g. Fiber: 4.28 g. Cholesterol: 0 mg. Calcium: 27 mg. Iron: .798 mg. Potassium: 522.1 mg. Total Fat: 0.5 g; Saturated fat: 0.1 g, Monounsaturated fat: 0 g, Polyunsaturated fat: 0.2 g.

*You can also use this as a cake topping. There's enough to cover a cake that serves 12. The sodium count for that use is 4.898 per serving.

❧ BECKY'S OATMEAL COOKIES ❧

MAKES 24 COOKIES   SODIUM PER RECIPE: 162.7 MG
SODIUM PER COOKIE: 6.779 MG
Oatmeal cookies usually are either good or not so good.
These are great.

- ½ cup (1 stick) unsalted butter (12.5 mg)
- ¾ cup packed brown sugar (64.3 mg)
- 1 medium egg, lightly beaten (55.4 mg)
- 1½ teaspoons vanilla extract (.567 mg)
- 1 cup whole wheat best for bread flour (6 mg)
- ¾ teaspoon Featherweight Baking Powder (3.375 mg)
- ½ cup toasted wheat germ (2.26 mg)
- ¾ cup rolled oats (2.43 mg)
- ¾ cup packed raisins (14.8 mg)
- ¾ cup chopped walnuts (.938 mg)

1. Preheat the oven to 375°F.
2. Cream the butter and sugar. Add the egg and vanilla and beat well. Stir the flour, baking powder, wheat germ, and rolled oats together in a bowl using a fork. Blend the mixture with the remaining ingredients and the butter/sugar mix, adding 1 tablespoon or more water if necessary to hold the dough together. Make 24 cookies by dropping spoonfuls of dough on cookie sheets. Press down to shape cookies slightly. Bake for 10 to 12 minutes until brown.

Calories: 34. Sodium: 0.12 mg. Carbohydrate: 17.9 g. Protein: 3.162 g. Fiber: 0.19 g. Cholesterol: 0 mg. Calcium: 3.324 mg. Iron: .015 mg. Potassium: 17.6 mg. Total Fat: 0 g; Saturated fat: 0 g, Monounsaturated fat: 0 g, Polyunsaturated fat: 0 g.

❧ DON'S CLASSIC OATMEAL COOKIES ❧

MAKES 24 2-INCH COOKIES OR 15 4-INCH COOKIES
SODIUM PER RECIPE: 241.9 MG   SODIUM PER 3-INCH COOKIE: 10.1 MG
SODIUM PER 4-INCH COOKIE: 16.1 MG
This one will delight your sodium-eating friends.
It's easy to make, too.

- ¾ cup canned, sweetened low-sodium coconut (11.5 mg)—or substitute same amount of unsalted flaked coconut (11.5 mg)
- 2 cups quick or regular rolled oats (6.48 mg)
- 1½ cups loosely packed brown sugar (84.8 mg)
- ¾ cup unbleached white flour (2.5 mg)
- 1 teaspoon ground cinnamon (.6 mg)
- ⅓ teaspoon ground cloves (1.7 mg)
- 2 tablepoons granulated white sugar (2.5 mg)

1 **medium banana (1.18 mg)**
1 **medium egg (55.4 mg)**
2 **teaspoons vanilla extract (.75 mg)**
1 **cup loosely packed seedless black raisins (17.4 mg)**
¼ **cup semisweet chocolate chips (4.8 mg)**
¼ **cup dry unsalted roasted cashew, walnut, pecan, or peanut bits (5.48 mg)**
¼ **cup Homemade Applesauce, page 360 (.6 mg)**

1. Preheat the oven to 325°F.

2. The ideal way to make these cookies is to put the coconut and 1 cup of the oats into food processor first, and, using the metal cutting blade, shred them to a finer chop (not dustlike, however). Then add the brown sugar, flour, cinnamon, cloves, granulated sugar, and mix with the same blade for 1 minute. Remove the mixture from the container and put it into a large mixing bowl. Next slice the banana thinly into the bowl. Then add the other cup of oats and the egg and the vanilla. Combine with a handheld mixer. Then stir in the raisins, chips, and nuts with a wooden spoon. (If it doesn't turn into a manageable dough, add ¼ cup **Homemade Applesauce**.)

3. Drop the dough by spoonfuls onto a cookie sheet that has been finely dusted with cornmeal. (Greasing the cookie sheet will cause the cookie bottoms to turn black.) Press down to shape each cookie because of the absence of baking soda and salt. Bake for 13 minutes at 325°F. Cool on a rack. Makes 2 dozen 2-inch cookies or 1 dozen 4-inch cookies.

4. If you don't have a food processor, mix all the ingredients together with a hand mixer and a wooden spoon and bake for the same time at the same temperature. You may also add more cinnamon and ginger to taste. Make the first batch, taste, and adjust if desired.

Calories: 167. Sodium: 10.08 mg. Carbohydrate: 34.7 g. Protein: 2.495 g. Fiber: 1.85 g. Cholesterol: 7.79 mg. Calcium: 33.4 mg. Iron: 1.235 mg. Potassium: 201.2 mg. Total Fat: 2.7 g; Saturated fat: 1.3 g, Monounsaturated fat: 0.8 g, Polyunsaturated fat: 0.4 g.

✪ WAY GOOD OATMEAL COOKIES ✪

MAKES 36 2-INCH COOKIES   SODIUM PER RECIPE: 274.8 MG
SODIUM PER COOKIE: 7.633 MG

*This recipe came to us from Santa Barbara. The cookies have more
saturated fat than Don's Classic Oatmeal Cookies, but they also
bring a different oatmeal cookie flavor.*

¾ **cup honey (10.2 mg)**
3 **medium eggs (166.3 mg)**
¾ **cup olive oil (trace)**
4½ **cups rolled oats (14.6 mg)**
¼ **cup nonfat milk (31.5 mg)**
1¼ **cups wheat germ (17.2 mg)**
¾ **cup canned sweetened coconut flakes (11.5 mg)**
⅔ **cup chopped walnuts (.825 mg)**
⅔ **cup raisins or chopped dates (19.8 mg)**
1½ **teaspoons ground cinnamon (2.686 mg)**

1. Preheat the oven to 350°F.

2. Warm the honey to about 100°F. Beat the eggs with the oil. Combine
the eggs and honey and whip until smooth. In another larger bowl, combine the remaining ingredients. Next add the wet ingredients and quickly
mix it all together. When it is thoroughly combined, let the mixture stand
for 20 minutes, covered. Portion the batter out into ¼-cup blobs and
squash each to ½ inch thick on a cookie sheet that has been dusted with
cornmeal. (You can grease the sheet if you prefer, but that will tend to
blacken the bottom of the cookies.) Bake in the preheated oven for 15
minutes. Cool on a wire rack.

*Calories: 156. Sodium: 7.63 mg. Carbohydrate: 19.6 g. Protein: 3.852 g. Fiber: 2.14 g. Cho-
lesterol: 15.61 mg. Calcium: 18.4 mg. Iron: 1.079 mg. Potassium: 135 mg. Total Fat: 7.7 g:
Saturated fat: 1.4 g, Monounsaturated fat: 4 g, Polyunsaturated fat: 1.8 g.*

✪ DATE BARS ✪

MAKES 24 COOKIES   SODIUM PER RECIPE: 34.8 MG
SODIUM PER COOKIE: 1.45 MG

*Next to Date Shakes, these bars were my favorite date treats.
Careful, though, because they're high in calories.*

¼ **cup (½ stick) unsalted butter (6.2 mg)**
¼ **cup unsalted, sweetened applesauce (1.912 mg)**
¾ **cup honey (10.2 mg)**
2⅓ **cups oat or white flour or combination of both (5.8 mg)**
2½ **cups rolled or multigrain oats (6 mg)**

2½ cups chopped pitted dates (13.3 mg)
   1 cup water (0 mg)
   2 tablespoons granulated sugar (.252 mg)
   ½ cup finely chopped walnuts, optional (.24 mg)
   1 teaspoon ground cinnamon (.6 mg)
   1 teaspoon vanilla extract (.4 mg)

1. Preheat the oven to 400°F (or 375°F for a convection oven).
2. Mix together the butter, applesauce, and honey. Combine the flours and add them to the wet mixture, then add the oats. Mix it all together using a wooden spoon or your hands. Pat two-thirds of this mixture thinly onto the bottom of a greased (oiled) 8x12-inch pan.
3. Combine the dates, honey, water, and sugar and cook over medium to medium low heat for about 10 minutes, stirring constantly until it thickens, then add the walnuts and stir. Pour or scrape this mixture evenly onto the prepared crust. Crumble the reserved crust mixture on top of dates and pat lightly to spread evenly. Bake for 35 minutes in the preheated oven (or for 25 minutes in a convection oven). Cut into bar cookies while warm.

Calories: 204. Sodium: 1.45 mg. Cholesterol: 5.18 mg. Protein: 4.889 g. Carbohydrate: 31.8 g. Fiber: 3.27 g. Calcium: 12.5 mg. Iron: 1.408 mg. Potassium: 171.1 mg. Total Fat: 7.7 g; Saturated fat: 1.6 g, Monounsaturated fat: 0.6 g, Polyunsaturated fat: 0.2 g.

❋ CHOCOHOLIC COOKIES ❋

MAKES 60 COOKIES   SODIUM PER RECIPE: 694.4 MG
SODIUM PER COOKIE: 11.6 MG

Just because we can't eat much sodium, we don't have to forego a good cookie now and then. Make these, then freeze some for later use as a treat. This recipe was created by my daughter, Kathleen.

     12-ounce package semisweet chocolate chips (48 mg)
   ¼ cup unsalted butter* (6.242 mg)
1½ cup sweetened condensed milk (388.6 mg)
   1 teaspoon + ½ teaspoon vanilla extract (.378 + .185 mg)
   2 level cups best for bread flour (5 mg)
   ½ cup finely chopped black walnuts (.625 mg)
  60 Hershey's Hugs candies, unwrapped (246 mg)
   1 teaspoon canola oil (trace)

1. Preheat the oven to 350°F.
2. Put 10 ounces of the chocolate chips into a double boiler with the butter and slowly melt them. Add 1 cup of the condensed milk and 1 tea-

*You may substitute unsalted applesauce for the butter in order to cut down on the saturated fat.

spoon of the vanilla. In a large bowl mix together the flour and nuts. Stir the chocolate mixture into the flour and nuts until well blended. For each cookie, put a Hershey's Hugs candy on 1 tablespoon of flattened dough and pinch the dough around the candy to seal it. Put the cookies on a lightly greased cookie sheet about 1 inch apart. Bake for 7 minutes in the preheated oven. Cool on a wire rack.

3. Melt the remaining 2 ounces of semisweet chocolate with the remaining ½ teaspoon vanilla (or substitute 2 ounces white chocolate). Mix in the oil. Drizzle the chocolate over the cooled cookies.

4. Enjoy. Then jog for 10 miles.

Calories: 101. Sodium: 11.58 mg. Carbohydrate: 12.6 g. Protein: 1.641 g. Fiber: 0.5 g. Cholesterol: 4.9 mg. Calcium: 27.5 mg. Iron: .506 mg. Potassium: 68.3 mg. Total Fat: 5 g; Saturated fat: 2.7 g, Monounsaturated fat: 1.5 g, Polyunsaturated fat: 0.7 g.

❖ RAISIN CRUNCH COOKIES ❖

MAKES 60 COOKIES   SODIUM PER RECIPE: 76.6 MG
SODIUM PER COOKIE: 1.277 MG

This is one of the better salt-free, eggless cookies. This recipe came to us from our river rafting friends.

 1 cup (packed) seedless raisins (19.8 mg)
 1 cup commercial unsalted applesauce (2.65 mg) or Homemade
    Applesauce,* page 360 (.379 mg)
 1 tablespoon vanilla extract (1.17 mg)
 1 cup pure honey (13.6 mg)
 3½ cups unsalted sunflower seeds (13.4 mg)
 3½ cups whole wheat flour (21 mg)

1. Preheat the oven to 350°F.

2. Soak the raisins for about 10 minutes in lukewarm water. Drain and mix together with the applesauce, vanilla, honey, and sunflower seeds. When the mixture becomes manageable, slowly add the flour and continue mixing. You might need an additional ½ cup of sunflower seeds and an additional ½ cup of flour. When the dough is not too sticky to handle, make small cookie balls, put them on a greased cookie sheet, and press down lightly with fork to flatten and shape. Bake in the preheated oven for 12 to 15 minutes. Cool on a wire rack before serving.

Calories: 97. Sodium: 1.28 mg. Carbohydrate: 14.6 g. Fiber: 1.86 g. Protein: 2.52 g. Cholesterol: 0 mg. Calcium: 9.597 mg. Iron: .643 mg. Potassium: 118.2 mg. Total Fat: 3.9 g; Saturated fat: 0.4 g, Monounsaturated fat: 0.7 g, Polyunsaturated fat: 2.5 g.

*For moister, crunchier cookies, use ½ cup olive oil and ½ cup applesauce instead.

◈ ANISE COOKIES WITH ALMONDS ◈

MAKES 36 TO 48 COOKIES   SODIUM PER RECIPE: 249.9 MG
SODIUM PER COOKIE: 6.941 MG (BASED ON 36 COOKIES)

A delicious treat from Mae DiMarco.

1¼ cups granulated sugar (2.5 mg)
 4 medium eggs (221.8 mg)
 ½ cup extra-virgin olive oil or canola oil (trace)
 2 teaspoons lemon juice (trace)
 3 cups unbleached flour (7.5 mg)
 1 tablespoon Featherweight Baking Powder (13.5 mg)
1½ teaspoons vanilla extract (.567 mg)
1½ teaspoons anise extract (.567 mg)
 1 teaspoon grated lemon zest (.12 mg)

1. Preheat the oven to 325°F.

2. Combine and lightly beat the sugar, eggs, oil, and lemon juice in a mixing bowl. Combine the flour, baking powder, vanilla, anise, and lemon zest and add to the egg mixture, lightly beating as you do so. Roll the dough out on a floured board and cut 2-inch round cookies. Put them on a lightly greased cookie sheet and top each with an almond. Bake in the preheated oven for about 10 to 12 minutes (longer for crisper cookies). Cook before serving.

Calories: 105. Sodium: 6.94 mg. Carbohydrate: 15.4 g. Fiber: 0.43 g. Protein: 1.846 g. Cholesterol: 20.78 mg. Calcium: 24.9 mg. Iron: .64 mg. Potassium: 67.4 mg. Total Fat: 4.1 g; Saturated fat: 0.6 g, Monounsaturated fat: 2.7 g, Polyunsaturated fat: 0.5 g.

◈ NOT-TOO-SWEET PEANUT BUTTER COOKIES ◈

MAKES 36 COOKIES   SODIUM PER RECIPE: 148.4 MG
SODIUM PER COOKIE: 4.12 MG

We use no sugar but some honey to sweeten these. The peanut butter makes up for the difference. Use only unsalted peanut butter—two good brands are Adams and Laura Scudder's.

⅔ cup canola oil (trace)
1⅔ cups unsalted peanut butter (72.8 mg)
1¾ cups honey (23.7 mg)
 2 teaspoons vanilla extract (.756 mg)
 4 cups whole wheat flour (24 mg)
1½ teaspoons Featherweight Baking Powder (3 mg)
 ¾ cup chopped unsalted peanuts (24.1 mg)

1. Preheat the oven to 350°F.

2. In a mixing bowl, blend together the oil, peanut butter, honey, and vanilla. Add the flour, baking powder, and peanuts and mix well with an electric mixer at high speed. Drop the dough by the spoonful onto a very lightly greased cookie sheet. Press each one with a fork, making crisscross tong marks across the top. Bake in the preheated oven for 10 to 12 minutes. Cool on a wire rack.

Calories: 220. Sodium: 4.12 mg. Carbohydrate: 26.1 g. Fiber: 2.65 g. Protein: 5.671 g. Cholesterol: 0 mg. Calcium: 13.3 mg. Iron: .925 mg. Potassium: 165.1 mg. Total Fat: 11.8 g: Saturated fat: 1.8 g, Monounsaturated fat: 6 g, Polyunsaturated fat: 3.5 g.

❈ CHOCOLATE CHIP APPLESAUCE COOKIES ❈

MAKES 30 3-INCH COOKIES   SODIUM PER RECIPE: 316.8 MG
SODIUM PER COOKIE: 10.6 MG

This recipe will surprise your doubting friends and your family, too. Salt-free as well as free of baking soda or baking powder, the ingredients are essentially healthy, and the calories lower than in most cookie recipes.

¼ **cup (½ stick) unsalted butter, softened (6.424 mg)**
¾ **cup commercial unsalted applesauce or Homemade Applesauce, page 360 (5.738 mg)**
½ **cup granulated sugar (1 mg)**
1½ **cups firmly packed brown sugar (128.7 mg)**
2 **medium eggs (110.9 mg)**
1 **teaspoon vanilla extract (.378 mg)**
1½ **cups best for bread flour* (3.75 mg)**
2 **teaspoons ground cinnamon (1.211 mg)**
3 **cups raw oats—you can use unsalted processed oats (11.3 mg)**
1 **packed cup golden raisins (19.8 mg)**
1 **cup semisweet mini-chocolate chips (19 mg)**
1 **cup Planters unsalted peanuts—optional (8.76 mg)**

1. Preheat the oven to 350°F.

2. Beat together the butter, applesauce, and sugars until creamy. Add the eggs and vanilla, then mix well. Add the flour and cinnamon and mix well. Next stir in the oats, raisins, chocolate chips, and optional peanuts and mix until well combined. On an ungreased heavy cookie sheet, form round cookies. I use a small-mouth canning jar lid as a cookie cutter by placing it screw-side down and pressing the dough into it on the cookie sheet, then lifting it off. Your cookies will not expand during cooking since there

*Stone Buhr or other best for bread flour works best for these cookies.

is no baking soda or salt in the dough, so the shape you make is what you'll get.

3. Bake in the preheated oven 10 to 12 minutes. These cookies will not brown deeply and you don't want to overcook them. Cool on a wire rack. You can make bar cookies instead, but then the baking time will be longer, about 30 minutes or so.

TIP: When purchasing flour for your bread making, make sure you don't buy self-rising flour or flour with sodium levels in the nutrient list. Most flour manufacturers now have a "best for bread," or a "bread machine" flour. Make sure to buy unbleached white flour, too.

Calories: 196. Sodium: 10.56 mg. Protein: 4.253 g. Carbohydrate: 35.5 g. Fiber: 2.73 g. Cholesterol: 16.61 mg. Calcium: 27.2 mg. Iron: 1.526 mg. Potassium: 201 mg. Total Fat: 6.7 g; Saturated fat: 2.6 g, Monounsaturated fat: 2.6 g, Polyunsaturated fat: 1.2 g.

❖ CAROB CHIP COOKIES ❖

MAKES 48 COOKIES   SODIUM PER RECIPE: 329 MG
SODIUM PER COOKIE: 6.855 MG
A sweet cookie much like the classic chocolate chip kind.

  1 cup (2 sticks) unsalted butter, softened (25 mg)
  1 cup pure honey (13.6 mg)
  1 cup fresh coconut, grated or shredded (15.4 mg)
  1 cup carob chips (261.2 mg)
1½ cups rolled oats (4.86 mg)
1½ cups whole wheat flour (9 mg)

1. Preheat the oven to 350°F.
2. Combine all the ingredients in a large mixing bowl and stir until the dough is firm. Drop the mixture by spoonfuls onto a greased cookie sheet. Bake in the preheated oven for 8 to 10 minutes. Cool on a wire rack.
3. If desired, you may also add ½ cup semisweet chocolate chips, but remember to add 12 mg sodium to the recipe title.

Calories: 104. Sodium: 6.86 mg. Carbohydrate: 12.7 g. Fiber: 1.04 g. Protein: 1.499 g. Cholesterol: 10.53 mg. Calcium: 20.9 mg. Iron: .374 mg. Potassium: 66.6 mg. Total Fat: 5.8 g; Saturated fat: 3.2 g, Monounsaturated fat: 1.9 g, Polyunsaturated fat: 0.4 g.

❖ DANNY BOY'S CHOCOLATE CHIP COOKIE ❖

MAKES 40 COOKIES   SODIUM PER RECIPE: 229.2 MG
SODIUM PER COOKIE: 5.73 MG

*Here's a recipe that will impress your friends. Danny Boy's is a
cookie company started and operated by my son and his wife, Kim.
That's a job you don't want. Up at 2 A.M., a metaphoric ton of
dough, scooping, baking, and then selling them. Why do all that
when you can make this adaptation to their wonderful recipe?
With their permission, of course. Chewy, sweet, but with very low
sodium. Watch out, though, anything this good has
to be high in calories.*

1 **cup brown sugar (56.6 mg)**
¾ **cup granulated sugar (1.5 mg)**
1 **cup Quick Applesauce, page 359 (.86 mg)**
1 **teaspoon Cook's powdered vanilla (3.78 mg)**
1 **large egg (63 mg)**
3 **cups best for bread flour (7.5 mg)**
1 **cup semisweet mini-chocolate chips (19 mg)**
1 **cup seedless raisins (20 mg)**

1. Preheat the oven to 350°F.

2. Combine the sugar, applesauce, and vanilla in a large mixing bowl. Add
the eggs and mix well with a handheld electric beater. Add the flour and
mix until creamy. Add the chips and raisins and mix with a wooden spoon
until well combined. Drop the dough by the spoonful onto an ungreased
cookie sheet and press down to shape the cookies. Remember, there is no
baking soda or salt, so they won't "sit down" nor will they spread out without your help. Bake in the preheated oven for about 12 to 14 minutes.
Cool on a wire rack.

*Calories: 121. Sodium: 5.73 mg. Protein: 1.8 g. Carbohydrate: 23.9 g. Fiber: 0.86 g. Choles-
terol: 0.62 mg. Calcium: 10.1 mg. Iron: .772 mg. Potassium: 76.9 mg. Total Fat: 2.5 g; Saturated fat: 1.2 g, Monounsaturated fat: 0.5 g, Polyunsaturated fat: 0.1 g.*

*Using butter instead of applesauce: Calories: 142. Sodium: 6.52 mg. Fiber: 0.57 g. Protein:
1.612 g. Carbohydrate: 20.4 g. Cholesterol: 23.05 mg. Calcium: 10.6 mg. Iron: .787 mg.
Potassium: 73.1 mg. Total Fat: 6.1 g; Saturated fat: 3.7 g, Monounsaturated fat: 1.8,
Polyunsaturated fat: 0.4 g.*

> *"Your Danny Boy cookies are great. Don't change a thing!! We defi-
> nitely don't feel deprived when we can make a cookie this good.
> Can't wait to try other recipes!! My thirteen-year-old son and his
> friends said they were really, really good!"*
> —*Nancy Szatkowski <slpyhead56@aol.com>*

❧ MACAROONS ❧

MAKES 24 MACAROONS   SODIUM PER RECIPE: 105.3 MG
SODIUM PER MACAROON: 4.386 MG

¼ cup (½ stick) unsalted butter, softened (6.242 mg)
½ cup honey (6.78 mg)
1 medium egg (55.4 mg)
2 cups canned, sweetened coconut, flaked (30.8 mg)
1 cup whole wheat flour (6 mg)

1. Preheat the oven to 350°F.
2. Cream the butter first, then add the honey and mix them together. Beat in the egg; next stir in the coconut and flour and beat until the batter is smooth. Drop the dough by the spoonful onto a greased cookie sheet. Bake in the preheated oven for 10 to 12 minutes, or until the bottoms of the macaroons turn a golden brown (not dark, but light). Cool on a wire rack.
3. Optional additions to this recipe include 1 teaspoon almond extract (0 mg) or 1 teaspoon ground cinnamon (.606 mg). To give the macaroons a light chocolate flavor, add 1 tablespoon carob powder (16.32 mg) or ½ cup semisweet chocolate chips (12 mg).

Calories: 87. Sodium: 4.39 mg. Carbohydrate: 12.1 g. Fiber: 0.91 g. Protein: 1.17 g. Cholesterol: 12.97 mg. Calcium: 4.476 mg. Iron: .372 mg. Potassium: 47.5 mg. Total Fat: 4.2 g: Saturated fat: 3.1 g, Monounsaturated fat: 0.7 g, Polyunsaturated fat: 0.2 g.

❧ GINGERSNAPS ❧

MAKES 24 SNAPS   SODIUM PER RECIPE: 87.5 MG
SODIUM PER SNAP: 3.645 MG

This recipe is from Louise Santana, whose gingersnaps are the best ever. You can make them with olive oil, canola oil, or unsalted butter, or a combination of any of them. Remember, because there is no salt or baking soda in the recipe, the cookies will bake in the shape you've established by pressing them down on the cookie sheet.

1 cup granulated sugar (2 mg) + 1 tablespoon for rolling the balls (.126 mg)
¾ cups (1½ sticks) unsalted butter, softened (18.7 mg)
2 teaspoons light molasses (2.442 mg)
1 medium egg (55.4 mg)
2 cups best for bread white flour (5 mg)
1 teaspoon ground ginger (.584 mg)
1 teaspoon ground cinnamon (.606 mg)
½ teaspoon ground cloves (2.55 mg)

1. Preheat the oven to 350°F.

2. Mix all the ingredients (except the extra sugar) together with a wooden spoon. Form the dough into walnut-size balls (they'll be crumbly) and roll them in the extra granulated sugar. Drop the dough balls on a very lightly greased pan, pressing them down, and bake for 12 to 15 minutes in the preheated oven. Cool on a wire rack.

Calories: 127. Sodium: 3.65 mg. Carbohydrate: 17.2 g. Fiber: 0.36 g. Protein: 1.379 g. Cholesterol: 23.32 mg. Calcium: 6.327 mg. Iron: .588 mg. Potassium: 21.4 mg. Total Fat: 6.1 g; Saturated fat: 3.7 g, Monounsaturated fat: 1.7 g, Polyunsaturated fat: 0.3 g.

❋ BISCOTTI ❋

MAKES 20 COOKIES   SODIUM PER RECIPE: 236 MG
SODIUM PER COOKIE: 11.8 MG

*Here's a crisp cookie from Mother's Italian kitchen. The big plus is that they are very low in sodium. Try the **Anise Biscotti** recipe, too. Each has its own flavor, but both are delicious treats.*

2½ **cups unbleached flour (6.25 mg)**
1¼ **cups granulated sugar (2.5 mg)**
 ½ **cup Zante currants (5.76 mg)**
 2 **large egg whites (109.6 mg)**
 2 **medium to large eggs (110.9 mg)**
 1 **tablespoon extra-virgin olive oil (trace)**
 1 **tablespoon water (0 mg)**
 1 **teaspoon anise seeds (.326 mg)**
 2 **teaspoons anise or vanilla extract (.756 mg)**

1. Preheat the oven to 350°F.

2. Combine the flour, sugar, and currants in a medium mixing bowl. In another, smaller bowl, beat the egg whites until fluffy. Then beat the whole eggs, oil, water, anise seeds, and anise or vanilla extract together. Using a rubber scraper (spatula), stir the egg mixture and the stiff egg whites into the dry ingredients until a dough is formed. You may have to use your hands to knead it once or twice to get the dough to form.

3. Lightly coat a baking pan with vegetable oil or cooking spray. With the rubber scraper, move the dough onto the pan. Using the scraper (moistened with water), shape the dough into a log about 15 inches by 3 inches but flat on the bottom, with a slight biscotti cookie shape on the top. Bake the cookies for 30 to 35 minutes in the preheated oven. Remove the biscotti from the oven. The log will be flatter now. Cut it diagonally and crosswise into ¾-inch slices. Place the slices upright on a clean baking sheet, and continue to bake for 15 minutes, or until lightly crisp. Remove and put the biscotti on a wire rack to cool.

4. Variations of biscotti cookies can be made. These include chocolate, nuts and spices, raisins, and even cappuccino. For chocolate biscotti, e.g, replace the anise seeds with ½ cup semisweet chocolate chips (10 mg). For cappuccino, use a single shot of latte in place of 1 tablespoon water.

Calories: 131. Sodium: 11.8 mg. Carbohydrate: 27.3 g. Fiber: 0.68 g. Protein: 2.681 g. Cholesterol: 18.7 mg. Calcium: 8.646 mg. Iron: .981 mg. Potassium: 61.3 mg. Total Fat: 1.3 g; Saturated fat: 0.3 g, Monounsaturated fat: 0.7 g, Polyunsaturated fat: 0.2 g.

❧ ANISE BISCOTTI ❧

MAKES 30 COOKIES   SODIUM PER RECIPE: 352.5 MG
SODIUM PER COOKIE: 11.7 MG

This version of biscotti was served at our house for many years. It has been modified to lower the sodium count as much as possible. Note the absence of butter in this version. It is easy to prepare and extras can be frozen for future use.

- **3 cups best for bread flour (7.5 mg)**
- **1 tablespoon Featherweight Baking Powder (6 mg)**
- **5 egg whites (273.9 mg) and 5 egg yolks (35.7 mg)**
- **1 cup granulated sugar (2 mg)**
- **1 tablespoon anise extract (1.17 mg)**
- **1 cup toasted unsalted almonds (18.7 mg)**

1. Preheat oven to 375°F.

2. Grease 2 baking sheets with light spray of canola oil from spray can. Sift the flour with the baking powder and set it aside. In a large chilled bowl, beat the egg whites until soft peaks form. Sprinkle the sugar over the whites and continue beating until the mixture is stiff. Fold in the egg yolks and anise extract, blending well. Sprinkle the flour mixture gradually over the egg mixture, folding well after each addition. Add the almonds and fold until just combined.

3. Pour the batter and form a 3x14¾-inch rectangle on each baking sheet. Bake in the preheated oven until a cake tester inserted in center comes out clean—about 30 minutes. Remove the pans from the oven and cool for 15 minutes or so. Cut slices across the rectangle 1 inch thick. Place the slices on their sides on an ungreased baking sheet and toast at 400°F until lightly browned on both sides—about 8 to 10 minutes. Can be served immediately or frozen for future use.

Calories: 119. Sodium: 11.75 mg. Carbohydrate: 17.9 g. Fiber: 0.98 g. Protein: 3.497 g. Cholesterol: 35.44 mg. Calcium: 43.8 mg. Iron: 1.004 mg. Potassium: 119 mg. Total Fat: 3.9 g; Saturated fat: 0.6 g, Monounsaturated fat: 2.2 g, Polyunsaturated fat: 0.8 g.

❖ PEANUT BUTTER CRUNCH BARS ❖

MAKES ABOUT 30 BARS   SODIUM PER RECIPE: 187.8 MG
SODIUM PER BAR: 6.261 MG

The sodium count is low but the flavor rating is high. These are crunchy bite-size bars about 2 inches square.

1¼ **cups honey (17 mg)**
2 **teaspoons vanilla extract (.756 mg)**
¾ **cup unsalted peanut butter (32.9 mg)***
1¼ **cups rolled oats (4.05 mg)**
1 **cup chopped unsalted cashews (21.9 mg)**
1 **cup wheat germ (13.8 mg)**
6 **cups sesame seeds (95 mg)**
⅝ **cup hulled unsalted sunflower seeds (2.412 mg)**

1. Preheat the oven to 350°F.
2. Cream together the honey, vanilla, and peanut butter in a large mixing bowl. Combine the oats, cashews, wheat germ, sesame seeds, and the sunflower seeds and add to the peanut butter mixture, working it well with a wooden spoon or your wet hands. Flatten the mixture to a uniform thickness in an oiled 8x14-inch pan. The dough will be stiff and hard to manage, so this will take a few minutes. Bake in the preheated oven for about 20 to 25 minutes. Cool and serve warm or cold.

Calories: 317. Sodium: 6.26 mg. Carbohydrate: 26 g. Fiber: 5.12 g. Protein: 9.363 mg. Cholesterol: 0 mg. Calcium: 291 mg. Iron: 5.207 mg. Potassium: 270.7 mg. Total Fat: 21.8 g; Saturated fat: 3.3 g. Monounsaturated fat: 8.6 g. Polyunsaturated fat: 8.8 g.

❖ LOGANBERRY SHORTBREAD BARS ❖

MAKES 24 BARS   SODIUM PER RECIPE: 152.7 MG   SODIUM PER BAR: 6.363 MG

This recipe has been in our family for many years. The first version is attributed to our oldest daughter. We have "refined" it down to a minimum-sodium treat that everyone in your family will enjoy. You may substitute any of your favorite berry preserves, including lingonberry, gooseberry, and the more available raspberry, blackberry, or strawberry for the loganberry. You may also substitute fresh apricot preserves, dates, or, if you prefer, mincemeat for the berry preserves.

*The sodium count is based on using Hollywood, Laura Scudder's, or Adam's Unsalted Peanut Butter. Some unsalted peanut butters may have sodium, so be sure to check the Nutrition Facts on the label before purchasing.

THE COOKIE CRUST
½ cup (1 stick) unsalted butter, softened (12.5 mg)
½ cup confectioners' sugar (.6 mg)
   The yolk of 1 large egg (7.138 mg)
½ teaspoon vanilla extract (.189 mg)
¾ teaspoon ground cinnamon (.454 mg)
1½ cups white best for bread flour (3.75 mg)

THE TOPPING
1 cup loganberry preserves (128 mg)
¾ cup finely chopped unsalted walnuts (trace)

1. Preheat the oven to 350°F.
2. Line a 9x2x13-inch baking pan with baker's parchment or aluminum foil, leaving a few inches of the foil or paper extending beyond the short side of the pan. Spray lightly with olive or canola oil.
3. In a large bowl, using an electric mixer, beat the butter, sugar, egg yolk, vanilla, and cinnamon until fluffy. With the mixer on low speed, beat in the flour to form moist crumbs. Spread the crumbs over the bottom of your prepared pan and press to form an even layer. Bake for about 16 to 20 minutes until set. Remove the pan and cool on a wire rack while you prepare the topping.
4. Spread the preserves over the crust, then top with the chopped nuts. Bake for 15 minutes, or until the walnuts are toasted. Let the cookies cool in the pan, preferably on a wire rack, for about 15 to 20 minutes.
5. When ready, lift the bars out of the pan by pulling up on the overlapping foil or paper and transferring the mixture to your cutting board. Cut the baked piece lengthwise into 6 long strips. When completed, cut each strip into 8 bars.

Calories: 129. Sodium: 6.36 mg. Carbohydrate: 17.5 g. Fiber: 0.57 g. Protein: 1.922 g. Cholesterol: 19.21 mg. Calcium: 6.815 mg. Iron: .489 mg. Potassium: 21 mg. Total Fat: 6.2 g; Saturated fat: 2.6 g, Monounsaturated fat: 1.2 g, Polyunsaturated fat: 0.2 g.

❖ SESAME CRUNCH BARS ❖

MAKES 18 BARS   SODIUM PER RECIPE: 88.4 MG   SODIUM PER BAR: 4.91 MG

½ cup unsalted or no-salt-added peanut butter (21.9 mg)
½ cup honey (6.78 mg)
2 cups unsalted sesame seeds (31.7 mg)
1 cup hulled unsalted sunflower seeds (3.84 mg)
1 cup chopped unsalted peanuts or cashews (8.76 mg)
1 cup canned sweetened flaked coconut (15.4 mg)

1. Preheat the oven to 350°F.

2. Combine the peanut butter and honey in a mixing bowl. Add the remaining ingredients and mix all together. Press the dough into a lightly greased and floured 11x7-inch pan. Bake in the preheated oven for 10 to 15 minutes, or until the edges turn brown. Cut the baked cookie into 3 pieces lengthwise, then cut each strip into 6 bars. Do this while the cookie is still warm. Allow the bars to cool before removing them from the pan.

Calories: 271. Sodium: 4.91 mg. Protein: 8.11 g. Carbohydrate: 18.1 g. Fiber: 3.96 g. Cholesterol: 0 mg. Calcium: 169.2 mg. Iron: 3.032 mg. Potassium: 255.4 mg. Total Fat: 20.5 g; Saturated fat: 4 g, Monounsaturated fat: 7.5 g, Polyunsaturated fat: 8.1 g.

Apple Bars / or Apricot, Peach,
❈ or Date Bars ❈

Makes 24 bars   Sodium per Recipe: Apple (57.5 mg)
Apricot (96.5 mg)   Date (101 mg)   Sodium per Bar: Apple   (2.397 mg)
Apricot (4.022 mg)   Date (4.207 mg)
Use any of the above fruits to make delicious low-sodium cookies, but serve them only to your guests, as they have a few calories in them.

THE CRUST
  1 **cup softened unsalted butter (25 mg)**
  ½ **cup honey (6.78 mg)**
1¾ **cups bread flour (4.375 mg)**
  ½ **cup low-fat soy flour (7.92 mg)**
  3 **cups rolled oats (9.72 mg)**
  2 **teaspoons unsalted sesame seeds or 2 tablespoons hulled
       unsalted sunflower seeds (1.98 mg)**

THE FILLING
  **(Mix together only one set of ingredients for your chosen
     filling)**

APPLE
2½ **pounds cored, peeled, and finely chopped apples (0 mg)**
  1 **tablespoon ground cinnamon (1.791 mg)**

DATE
3½ **cups pitted dates (soaked for ½ hour) (18.7 mg)***
1¼ **cups seedless raisins (24.8 mg)**
  1 **tablespoon ground cinnamon (1.791 mg)**

*The sodium count is for fresh dates. Some packaged dates, like Dromedary or Dole, list a sodium content of zero.

APRICOT

> 3 **cups dried apricots (39 mg)**
> 1 **tablespoon ground cinnamon (1.791 mg)**

1. Preheat the oven to 350°F.
2. Spread the chosen filling over the bottom crust. Press the rest of the crust on top of the filling. Bake in the preheated oven for about 20 to 30 minutes until golden. Cut the baked cookie dough into 24 pieces and cool on a rack.

Nutrition Facts for Apple Bars. Calories: 194. Sodium: 2.4 mg. Carbohydrate: 26.1 g. Fiber: 2.72 g. Protein: 3.727 g. Cholesterol: 20.7 mg. Calcium: 26 mg. Iron: 1.283 mg. Potassium: 144 mg. Total Fat: 9 g; Saturated fat: 5 g, Monounsaturated fat: 2.6 g, Polyunsaturated fat: 0.8 g.

Nutrition Facts for Date Bars. Calories: 271. Sodium: 4.21 mg. Carbohydrate: 46.6 g. Fiber: 4.05 g. Protein: 4.463 g. Cholesterol: 20.7 mg. Calcium: 36.4 mg. Iron: 1.672 mg. Potassium: 336.7 mg. Total Fat: 9.1 g; Saturated fat: 5 g, Monounsaturated fat: 2.6 g, Polyunsaturated fat: 0.8 g.

Nutrition Facts for Apricot Bars. Calories: 212. Sodium: 4.02 mg. Carbohydrate: 30.7 g. Fiber: 3.23 g. Protein: 4.253 g. Cholesterol: 20.7 mg. Calcium: 30.8 mg. Iron: 1.984 mg. Potassium: 327.3 mg. Total Fat: 9 g; Saturated fat: 5 g, Monounsaturated fat: 2.6 g, Polyunsaturated fat: 0.8 g.

❈ APRICOT BARS ❈

MAKES 24 LARGE BARS   SODIUM PER RECIPE: 72.7 MG
SODIUM PER BAR: 3.031 MG

Orange juice adds another flavor to these delicious bar cookies.

> 1 **cup orange juice fortified with calcium (2.488 mg)**
> 1 **cup loosely packed dried apricots (13 mg)**
> ½ **cup softened unsalted butter (12.5 mg)**
> ½ **cup honey (6.78 mg)**
> 1½ **cups rolled oats (4.86 mg)**
> 1 **cup whole wheat best for bread flour (2.5 mg)**
> ½ **cup wheat germ (2.26 mg)**
> 1 **teaspoon ground cinnamon (.606 mg)**
> 1 **cup raisins, partly cut up (17.4 mg)**
> ⅔ **cup toasted unsalted almond meal (10.4 mg)**

1. Preheat the oven to 350°F.
2. Bring the orange juice to a boil in a saucepan. Add the dried apricots and bring to a boil again. Turn off the heat. Cover the pan and let the apricots absorb juice until they are tender enough to cut easily with a table knife, but not really soft.
3. Meanwhile, combine the honey and butter in a mixing bowl. In another bowl stir the oats, flour, wheat germ, and cinnamon together. Drain the apricots and add the juice to the honey/oil mixture. Chop the apricots

coarsely and add them to the dry ingredients along with the raisins and almond meal. Combine the wet and dry ingredients and press the mixture into an oiled 9x13-inch baking dish. Bake in the preheated oven for about 30 minutes. Keep an eye on them, though, because cookies made with honey brown quickly. Allow the pan to cool before cutting the rectangle into 2 dozen large squares (cut lengthwise into 3 strips and then cut each strip into 8 pieces).

Calories: 165. Sodium: 3.03 mg. Fiber: 2.28 g. Protein: 3.441 g. Carbohydrate: 24.4 g. Cholesterol: 10.35 mg. Calcium: 35.2 mg. Iron: 1.298 mg. Potassium: 220.2 mg. Total Fat: 7 g; Saturated fat: 2.7 g, Monounsaturated fat: 2.9 g, Polyunsaturated fat: 1 g.

❧ ENERGY BARS ❧

MAKES 24 BARS   SODIUM PER RECIPE: 103.8 MG
SODIUM PER BAR: 4.325 MG

These beat the commercial varieties, which have higher sodium and cause you to drink a lot of water with them. You can freeze these energy bars for later use also. Keep some on hand and eat when you feel that midmorning or midafternoon pang of hunger. You can find the ingredients for this recipe at a Trader Joe's, if there is one in your area, or visit www.traderjoes.com

¾ **cup chopped dried apricots (9.75 mg)**
¾ **cup chopped dried dates (4.005 mg)**
½ **cup chopped dried figs (10.9 mg)**
½ **cup chopped dried apples or pears (.425 mg)**
½ **cup roasted unsalted pine nuts (pignolia)* (2.72 mg)**
½ **cup unsalted rolled oats (1.62 mg)**
½ **cup whole wheat flour (3 mg)**
1 **large egg, beaten (63 mg)**
¼ **cup apple juice fortified with calcium (4.335 mg)**
1 **ounce semisweet chocolate chips (4 mg)**

1. Preheat the oven to 325°F.
2. Line a jelly-roll pan with cooking parchment. In a food processor, combine the dried fruits until finely chopped. Stir in the pine nuts, oats, and flour and mix well. Stir in the egg and apple juice. Turn the batter into the pan and bake in the preheated oven for about 25 to 30 minutes. Let it cool in the pan. When cooled, set the rectangle on the cutting board and slice it into bars (cut it lengthwise into 3 strips and each strip into 8 pieces). Melt the semisweet chocolate (the double boiler is best for this) and brush

*Pinion pine nuts have 160 mg sodium per ½ cup, pignolia have only 8 mg. We suggest using the pignolia type from China.

the mixture on the bars. When cooled and the chocolate is set, serve. Store extras in the freezer in zipper-lock-type bags for future use.

Calories: 81. Sodium: 4.33 mg. Carbohydrate: 14.9 g. Fiber: 2.1 g. Protein: 1.998 g. Cholesterol: 8.85 mg. Calcium: 16.6 mg. Iron: .879 mg. Potassium: 172.6 mg. Total Fat: 2.2 g; Saturated fat: 0.5 g, Monounsaturated fat: 0.8 g, Polyunsaturated fat: 0.8 g.

❖ "LEGAL" BROWNIES ❖

MAKES 18 BROWNIES   SODIUM PER RECIPE: 200.4 MG
SODIUM PER BROWNIE: 11.1 MG

Okay, so we're on a low-sodium diet. Nobody said we couldn't have a treat now and then—and this brownie is a real treat. Make sure you use only Featherweight Baking Powder. We use our own **Homemade Applesauce** *instead of butter to help lower the fat content. If you're not worried about saturated fats, you can use unsalted butter instead, but try them this way first. The taste will surprise you. This recipe uses about 800 mg sodium less than standard brownies. The flavor remains, but the guilt is gone.*

¾ cup Homemade Applesauce, page 360, or unsalted commercial applesauce (3.825 mg)
1⅓ cups granulated sugar (3.5 mg)
3 medium eggs (166.3 mg)
1 teaspoon vanilla extract (.378 mg)
¾ cup unbleached flour (1.875 mg)
⅔ cup cocoa powder (alkali) (10.8 mg)
¾ teaspoon Featherweight Baking Powder (3.375 mg)
⅓ cup chopped walnuts (.413 mg)
8 ounces (1⅓ cups) semisweet chocolate chips (8 mg)

1. Preheat the oven to 350°F.
2. In a mixing bowl, beat the applesauce and sugar together until creamy or fluffy. Add the eggs and vanilla and combine. Set the mixture aside. Combine the flour, baking powder, and cocoa and blend this into the applesauce/sugar mixture. Fold in the walnuts and chocolate chips. Spread the batter into a greased 9x13-inch pan. Bake in the preheated oven for 25 minutes. Remove the pan and let it cool. Cut into 18 squares when cooled.

Calories: 195. Sodium: 11.13 mg. Protein: 3.491 g. Carbohydrate: 35 g. Fiber: 1.55 g. Cholesterol: 31.17 mg. Calcium: 23.8 mg. Iron: 1.418 mg. Potassium: 185.4 mg. Total Fat: 6.5 g; Saturated fat: 3 g, Monounsaturated fat: 2.1 g, Polyunsaturated fat: 1.2 g.

◈ DON'S SPECIAL BROWNIES ◈

MAKES 18 BROWNIES   SODIUM PER RECIPE: 142 MG
SODIUM PER PIECE: 7.888 MG

When we tried to develop a very-low-sodium brownie recipe, we tested many commercial products but ended up using our own mix. You can add more chocolate chips or use fewer if you like (adjust the sodium count to suit). This recipe cuts the fat and sodium levels to way below those of commercial brownies. The flavor of the salt is gone, but everyone seems to really enjoy them—the proof is in the eating!

  2 **medium eggs, lightly beaten (110.9 mg)**
  ¾ **cups granulated sugar (1.5 mg)**
  1 **teaspoon vanilla extract (.378 mg)**
  ½ **cup Homemade Applesauce, page 360, (1.89 mg), or commercial unsalted applesauce (3.825 mg)**
  ¾ **cup Don's Sweet Chocolate Mix, page 336 (3.528 mg)**
  ⅔ **cup best for bread white flour (1.65 mg)**
  ¼ **teaspoon Featherweight Baking Powder (1.125 mg)**
  ½ **cup chopped walnuts (.625 mg)**
  ¾ **cup (6 ounce package) semisweet chocolate chips (18.5 mg)**

1. Preheat oven to 350°F.

2. In a mixing bowl, combine the eggs with the sugar and vanilla. Add the applesauce and stir to combine. Sift the **Chocolate Mix** with the flour and baking powder. Slowly add and stir the dry ingredients into the egg mixture. Finally add the walnuts and chips. Spread this batter in a greased or nonstick 9x9-inch square pan. Bake in the preheated oven for 25 to 30 minutes. (Or on the bottom rack of a convection oven for about 27 minutes.) When done, cool, then cut the square lengthwise into 4 strips and crosswise into 4 pieces, making 16 brownies.

Calories: 138. Sodium: 7.89 mg. Fiber: 1.1 g. Protein: 2.451 g. Carbohydrate: 21.4 g. Cholesterol: 20.78 mg. Calcium: 12.3 mg. Iron: .817 mg. Potassium: 85.6 mg. Total Fat: 5.7 g; Saturated fat: 2.2 g, Monounsaturated fat: 1.7 g, Polyunsaturated fat: 1.5 g.

✦ Aunt Mildred's Cookies ✦

Makes 24 cookies   Sodium per Recipe: 157.1 mg
Sodium per Cookie: 6.548 mg

Aunt Mildred was the greatest character I have ever known. Born in the late 1800s, she became a lawyer during a period when women just didn't do that sort of thing. She was a sophisticated lady, a tough woman who rode alone down the side of a Sierra mountain on horseback to have her baby in Fresno, California. Her husband was an engineer who worked above Yosemite. She was always "up," never pessimistic about a thing. We loved visiting Aunt Mildred for her stories, her love, and her incredible meals. This recipe is directly from her kitchen, and one we looked forward to every visit.

½ cup (1 stick) unsalted butter, softened (12.5 mg)
1 packed cup brown sugar (85.8 mg)
1 medium egg, lightly beaten (55.4 mg)
1 cup best for bread flour (2.5 mg)
½ cup broken unsalted pecan pieces (.54 mg)
1 teaspoon Cook's powdered vanilla (.378 mg)

1. Preheat the oven to 325°F.
2. Cream the butter and sugar together in a mixing bowl. Stir in the rest of the ingredients. Drop the batter by teaspoonful on a greased cookie sheet. Bake in the preheated oven for 12 to 15 minutes. Cool on a wire rack.
3. You may add chocolate chips to this recipe but remember to adjust the sodium count if you do so—1 cup chips = 20 mg sodium.

Calories: 106. Sodium: 6.55 mg. Carbohydrate: 13.4 g. Fiber: 0.31 g. Protein: .982 g. Cholesterol: 18.14 mg. Calcium: 11.4 mg. Iron: .499 mg. Potassium: 49.8 mg. Total Fat: 5.6 g; Saturated fat: 2.6 g, Monounsaturated fat: 2.1 g, Polyunsaturated fat: 0.6 g.

Fruit, Desserts, and Treats

❖ ❖ ❖ ❖ ❖ ❖ ❖ ❖ ❖

❖ Baked Apples ❖

SERVES 6   SODIUM PER RECIPE: 14 MG   SODIUM PER SERVING: 2.338 MG

  6 medium apples, cored, (6 mg)
½ cup seedless raisins (8.7 mg)
  3 tablespoons best for bread flour (.468 mg)
⅓ cup granulated sugar (.66 mg)
½ teaspoon ground cinnamon (.303 mg)
1½ tablespoons unsalted butter, softened (4.686 mg)
¼ cup chopped walnuts (.312 mg)
½ cup water (0 mg)
½ cup orange juice fortified with calcium (1.244 mg)

1. Preheat the oven to 375°F.
2. Arrange the apples in a greased baking dish. Fill the centers with raisins. Combine the flour, sugar, cinnamon, and butter and mix until crumbly. Add the walnuts and sprinkle the mixture over the apples. Pour the water and orange juice around the apples. Bake in the preheated oven for 1 hour, basting every 15 minutes. Serve with honey (½ cup = 6.78 mg sodium), if desired, or zero-milligram-sodium canned whipped cream.

Calories: 241. Sodium: 2.34 mg. Carbohydrate: 47.6 g. Fiber: 4.72 g. Protein: 2.501 mg. Cholesterol: 7.77 mg. Calcium: 47.6 mg. Iron: 1.613 mg. Potassium: 322.4 mg. Total Fat: 6.4 g. Saturated Fat: 2.1 g. Monounsaturated fat: 1.5 g. Polyunsaturated fat: 2.2 g.

❖ Don's Very Best Baked Apples ❖

SERVES 4   SODIUM PER RECIPE: 15.2 MG   SODIUM PER SERVING: 3.789 MG

  4 large baking apples, or other suitable apples (0 mg)
½ cup chopped unsalted pecans (.6 mg)
¼ teaspoon ground cinnamon (.15 mg)
⅓ cup golden raisins (5.7 mg)
½ cup chopped dried apricots (6.5 mg)
    The grated zest and juice of 1 lemon (.36 mg)
  1 tablespoon unsalted butter (1.5 mg)
  1 tablespoon honey (.84 mg)

1. Preheat the oven to 350°F.

2. Wash the apples well and core them. In a medium-sized bowl, combine the pecans, cinnamon, raisins, apricots, and grated lemon zest (hold the lemon juice for later use). After making tiny slits in the skin around the circumference of the apples (to release steam), put them into an oven-safe baking dish—or, if you have large enough glass muffin (Pyrex-type) cups, place them in individual cups. Fill the cored cavities with the raisin/apricot mixture and pour some lemon juice over the mixture in each apple. Top each apple with a dab of unsalted butter and a spot of honey. Bake in the preheated oven for about 30 to 35 minutes. Serve hot.

Calories: 335.9. Sodium: 3.789 mg. Protein: 2.626 g. Carbohydrate: 59.7 g. Fiber: 8.16 g. Cholesterol: 7.77 mg. Calcium: 33.4 mg. Iron: 1.454 mg. Potassium: 563.7 mg. Total Fat: 13 g; Saturated Fat: 2.69 g, Monounsaturated fat: .899 g, Polyunsaturated fat: .362 g.

❈ QUICK APPLESAUCE ❈

MAKES 4 CUPS   SODIUM PER RECIPE: 3.41 MG   SODIUM PER CUP: .86 MG
If you don't eat up all your fresh apples, and they begin to look a bit tired, this recipe will save them them and create a wonderful side dish.

 5 to 10 medium apples (trace)
 ½ cup water (0 mg)
 1 tablespoon lemon juice (.15 mg)
 ½ cup sugar (1 mg)
 ½ tablespoon ground cinnamon (.591 mg)

1. Core the apples. Slice each into eight pieces. Combine the water, lemon juice, and apple chunks in a cooking pot. Bring to a quick boil, stirring often. Reduce the heat to medium-high and continue light boiling, stirring occasionally. When the apples soften and appear to be ready to sauce, add the sugar and cinnamon and stir often for about 5 minutes. Remove the pot from the heat and let it stand for 5 minutes, covered. Serve it hot or cold.

Calories: 262. Sodium: 0.44 mg. Fiber: 7.77 g. Protein: .56 g. Carbohydrate: 67.8 g. Cholesterol: 0 mg. Calcium: 26.7 mg. Iron: .726 mg. Potassium: 325.4 mg. Total Fat: 1 g; Saturated fat: 0.2 g, Monounsaturated fat: 0 g, Polyunsaturated fat: 0.3 g.

Homemade Applesauce /
❈ Canning Instructions ❈

MAKES 7 QUARTS   SODIUM PER RECIPE: 22 MG
SODIUM PER QUART: 3.423 MG   SERVING PER CUP: .856 MG

This recipe is for canning 7 quarts applesauce at a time. You can buy apples in 20- and 40-pound lugs. This recipe calls for about 10 pounds, or 60 to 80 apples.

60 apples* (trace)—almost any variety of apple will suffice
4 to 6 cups water† (0 mg)
½ cup fresh lemon juice (1.22 mg)
3 cups sugar‡ (4 mg)
2 to 3 level tablespoons ground cinnamon (3.58 mg)

1. In a very large cooking pot (at least 12 quarts), add 4 to 6 cups water, depending on the apple type you chose. Add the lemon juice.

2. Core all the apples and cut them in half. Using the slicing blade of a food processor, or by hand, slice the unpeeled apples to about ⅛ inch thickness. Add these slices to the pot until they reach about 2 to 3 inches to the top. Bring the mixture to a rapid boil, stirring occasionally, then turn down the heat and let the apples simmer, stirring often. When apples are soft and about ready to "sauce," stir in the sugar and cinnamon. Stir steadily for about 5 minutes while the sugar "cooks."

3. Reduce the heat to the lowest setting and scoop the sauce into 7 quart jars. Clean off any sauce or sugar that has dropped on the top edges of the jars. Seal them tightly with new lids and process in a canning steamer for 10 minutes. (If you don't have a canning steamer, which you can find at most houseware stores, put the jars on a rack in a deep pot, cover with water, and bring to a boil, then boil for 2 to 3 minutes.) Remove the jars from the heat and let cool. The processing ensures that your seal will last for at least 1 year.

Per cup. Calories: 232. Sodium: 0.31 mg. Fiber: 8.27 g. Protein: .597 g. Carbohydrate: 60.1 g. Cholesterol: 0 mg. Calcium: 27.1 mg. Iron: 2.442 mg. Potassium: 348.2 mg. Total Fat: 1.1 g; Saturated fat: 0.2 g, Monounsaturated fat: 0 g, Polyunsaturated fat: 0.3 g.

*If using tart apples, add slightly more sugar. It may make more or less sauce, based on apple size.

†You may have to add more water if your apples are the dry type. If using a variety like Delicious, 4 cups should suffice; if using McIntosh, Granny Smith, or other tart or dry apples, begin with 5 cups.

‡Taste before canning. You may want to add more or less of these ingredients.

❧ CARAMELIZED APPLES ❧

MAKES 2 CUPS SODIUM PER RECIPE: 9.208 MG
SODIUM PER TABLESPOON: .288 MG

Not just a side dish but a great sauce, too. Use this with ice cream, omelets, or as a topping on our low-sodium pancakes and waffles. It goes with salads as well.

5 medium-size apples* (trace)
4 tablespoons unsalted butter (6.248 mg)
½ cup granulated sugar (1 mg)
¼ cup apple juice† (1.86 mg)
   Pinch of nutmeg (trace)
   Pinch of cinnamon (trace)

1. Peel and core the apples and then cut them into ½-inch slices. In a non-stick skillet measuring 10 inches or more, melt the butter over medium heat. Stir in the sugar. Cook, stirring, until the syrup turns a light caramel brown. Add the apples and continue to cook, turning the slices over until they are all well coated with caramel and begin to put out juices. Continue cooking for about 10 minutes, until the fruit is tender and the liquid has evaporated. The fruit should appear glossy and translucent. Stir in the apple juice, sprinkle mixture with nutmeg and cinnamon, and remove the skillet from the heat. The apples may be refrigerated for 5 to 10 days.

Calories: 39. Sodium: 0.29 mg. Carbohydrate: 6.647 g. Fiber: 0.59 g. Protein: 0.58 g. Cholesterol: 3.89 mg. Calcium: 2.194 mg. Iron: 0.54 mg. Potassium: 27. mg. Total Fat: 1.5 g: Saturated fat: 0.9 g, Monounsaturated fat: 0.4 g, Polyunsaturated fat: 0.1 g.

❧ STRAWBERRY DELIGHT ❧

SERVES 4 SODIUM PER RECIPE: 147.9 MG SODIUM PER SERVING: 37 MG

Don't turn your nose up at this recipe. It produces an exciting flavor.

1 cup fresh or frozen medium to large strawberries (1.44 mg)
3 teaspoons balsamic vinegar (.45 mg)
4 teaspoons granulated sugar (.168 mg)
4 (⅓-cup size) scoops light vanilla ice cream (145.9 mg)‡

*Use tart apples. If none are available, you may use sweeter apples, but cut the sugar quantity in half.
†If apple juice is not available, use 3 tablespoons water combined with 1 tablespoon lemon juice.
‡Select ice cream according to the sodium count per ½ cup. Breyer's is an example of an ice cream with only 25 mg per ½ cup.

1. Cut half the strawberries into three pieces each, the remaining ones in half. Combine the strawberries, the sugar, and the vinegar in a mixing bowl and allow to macerate. Put a scoop of ice cream into 4 sherbet dishes and layer the strawberries and sauce over each serving. Serve immediately.

Calories: 88. Sodium: 36.98 mg. Carbohydrate: 17.1 g. Protein: 1.85 g. Fiber: 0.83 g. Cholesterol: 6.01 mg. Calcium: 65.4 mg. Iron: .25 mg. Potassium: 161.6 mg. Total Fat: 2 g; Saturated fat: 1.1 g, Monounsaturated fat: 0.5 g, Polyunsaturated fat: 0.1 g.

❈ PEARS WITH RED WINE ❈

SERVES 4   SODIUM PER RECIPE: 24.6 MG   SODIUM PER SERVING: 6.155 MG

½ **cup granulated sugar (1 mg)**
½ **cup water (0 mg)**
1 **stick cinnamon (1.79 mg)**
½ **cup sweet red wine (5.15 mg)**
2 **large pears, peeled (0 mg)**
4 **tablespoons canned whipped cream (15.6 mg)**
4 **strawberries (1.08 mg)**

1. Combine the sugar, water, cinnamon stick, and wine and boil for about 15 minutes, stirring frequently. Peel, core, and cut pears in half and simmer in the sauce for 15 minutes. Serve in sherbet glasses with commercial zero-sodium canned whipped cream and a fresh berry on top.

Note: Before using alcoholic beverages to cook with or serve, check with your doctor.

Calories: 197. Sodium: 6.16 mg. Protein: .786 g. Carbohydrate: 44.8 g. Fiber: 4.05 g. Cholesterol: 2.28 mg. Calcium: 41.5 mg. Iron: 2.138 mg. Potassium: 217.7 mg. Total Fat: 1.2 g; Saturated fat: 0.5 g, Monounsaturated fat: 0.3 g, Polyunsaturated fat: 0.2 g, Alcohol: 7%.

❈ FRESH BERRIES ❈

SERVES 6   SODIUM PER RECIPE: 15.3 MG   SODIUM PER SERVING: 2.544 MG

Berries are one of Mother Nature's most refreshing snacks—all natural, full of vitamins, and very, very health as well as tasty.

2 **cups fresh strawberries (3.32 mg)**
1 **cup fresh raspberries (0 mg)**
1 **cup fresh blueberries (8.7 mg)**
1 **cup small Thompson seedless grapes (3.2 mg)**
1 **teaspoon granulated sugar (trace)**

1. Clean the berries, halve the strawberries and grapes, then combine. Sprinkle a light coat of sugar over the top. Stir once or twice. Serve chilled in individual sherbet glasses.

Calories: 62. Sodium: 2.54 mg. Carbohydrate: 15.1 g. Fiber: 3.59 g, Protein: .862 g. Cholesterol: 0 mg. Calcium: 16.6 mg. Iron: .438 mg. Potassium: 193.9 mg. Total Fat: 0.6 g; Saturated fat: 0.1 g, Monounsaturated fat: 0.1 g, Polyunsaturated fat: 0.3 g.

❧ BAKED FRUIT ❧

SERVES 4   SODIUM PER RECIPE: 25.9 MG   SODIUM PER SERVING: 6.478 MG

Baked fruit is a popular European and Middle Eastern dish. It makes a great dessert for a lamb or roast beef dinner.

½ **teaspoon ground cinnamon (.303 mg)**
1½ **pounds ripe peaches, sliced (0 mg)**
½ **pound apples, cored, sliced (trace)**
½ **pound ripe or dried pears, sliced (0 mg)**
¼ **pound dried figs, chopped (21.9 mg)**
½ **cup apple cider (3.72 mg)**

1. Preheat the oven to 375°
2. Combine the cinnamon with the fruits and put fruit mixture and juice into a 2-quart baking dish or a nonstick roaster. Bake, covered, for 45 minutes. Serve warm as a dessert or a side dish, or as a sauce over **Blinis** (page 215), **Pancakes à la Popover** (page 216), or **Whole Wheat Pancakes** (page 213).

Calories: 382. Sodium: 6.48 mg. Carbohydrate: 98 g. Protein: 3.734 g. Fiber: 16.81 g. Cholesterol: 0 mg. Calcium: 111.8 mg. Iron: 2.132 mg. Potassium: 1,097 mg. Total Fat: 1.8 g; Saturated fat: 0.2 g, Monounsaturated fat: 0.3 g, Polyunsaturated fat: 0.6 g.

❧ FRUIT COMPOTE ❧

SERVES 8   SODIUM PER RECIPE: 66.2 MG   SODIUM PER SERVING: 8.279 MG

You can experiment with this recipe to suit your taste. The suggested dried fruits make it possible to prepare this compote at any time of year.

1 **cup dried peaches, halved (11.2 mg)**
1 **cup whole pitted prunes (6.8 mg)**
⅓ **cup dried pears (3.564 mg)**
1 **cup dried apricots (13 mg)**
½ **packed cup golden raisins (9.9 mg)**
½ **stick cinnamon (1.791 mg)**
2 **whole cloves (5 mg)**
2 **cups apple cider (14.9 mg)**

1. Combine all the ingredients in a large pot. Simmer, covered, over medium heat for about 1 hour. Remove cinnamon and cloves after cooking. Serve warm on **Blinis** (page 215), or **Whole Wheat Pancakes** (page 213), or **Pancakes à la Popover** (page 216).

Calories: 220. Sodium: 8.28 mg. Carbohydrate: 57.1 g. Fiber: 6.19 g. Protein: 2.444 g. Cholesterol: 0 mg. Calcium: 48.2 mg. Iron: 3.019 g. Potassium: 778.9 mg. Total Fat: 0.6 g; Saturated fat: 0.1 g, Monounsaturated fat: 0.2 g, Polyunsaturated fat: 0.2 g.

❈ COMPOTE WITH APRICOTS AND PEARS ❈

SERVES 4   SODIUM PER RECIPE: 17.4 MG   SODIUM PER SERVING: 4.356 MG
*This dish is very low in sodium and very high in delicate fruit
aroma and flavors. Serve with cookies or yogurt or simply by itself.*

1⅓ **cups orange juice fortified with calcium* (3.234 mg)**
   The juice and grated zest of 1 lemon (8.3 mg)
  2 **tablespoons honey (1.68 mg)**
  2 **tablespoons vanilla extract (2.34 mg)**
  1 **teaspoon ground cloves (5 mg)**
  8 **fresh apricots, seeded and halved (2.8 mg)**
  2 **firm but ripe D'Anjou pears,† quartered (trace)**
  2 **tablespoons dried or fresh currants (1.44 mg)**

1. Combine the orange juice, lemon juice and zest, honey, vanilla, and
cloves in a saucepan and bring it to a boil. Reduce the heat and simmer
for 5 minutes uncovered. Add the apricots and pears and bring the mixture to a boil. Lower the heat, cover, and simmer for 5 to 8 minutes, or
until the fruit is slightly tender. Add the currants, remove the pan from the
heat, and cool to room temperature in the syrup before serving.

*Calories: 188. Sodium: 4.36 mg. Carbohydrate: 43.4 g. Protein: 2.171 g. Fiber: 4.55 g. Cho-
lesterol: 0 mg. Calcium: 128.3 mg. Iron: .926 mg. Potassium: 542.5 mg. Total Fat: 0.8 g: Saturated fat: 0.1 g, Monounsaturated fat: 0.2 g, Polyunsaturated fat: 0.2 g.*

❈ MIXED FRUIT COMPOTE ❈

SERVES 6   SODIUM PER RECIPE: 71.1 MG   SODIUM PER SERVING: 11.8 MG
This is a great dinner dessert and also a terrific side dish.

  2 **cups orange juice fortified with calcium (4.975 mg)**
 ⅓ **cup honey (4.475 mg)**
  2 **teaspoons finely grated orange zest (.12 mg)**
  2 **teaspoons finely grated lemon zest (.24 mg)**
1½ **tablespoons fresh lemon juice (.225 mg)**
   Pinch of ground cloves (.255 mg)
   Pinch of nutmeg (trace)
 12 **ounces mixed dried fruit: pitted prunes, apricots, pears,
    peaches, figs, apples (57 mg)**
 ⅓ **cup dried currants (3.802 mg)**

1. Combine first the orange juice, honey, orange and lemon zest, lemon
juice, cloves, and nutmeg in a saucepan and bring it to a boil over medium

*Or use store-bought fresh not-from-concentrate "homemade-style" orange juice.
†You may substitute Bartlett pears.

heat. Reduce the heat and simmer for 5 minutes. Add the dried fruits and currants and simmer covered for another 15 to 20 minutes, or until the fruit is soft. Transfer the fruit and its syrup to a serving bowl and allow it to cool to room temperature before serving.

Calories: 247. Sodium: 11.84 mg. Carbohydrates: 64.6 g. Protein: 2.276 g. Fiber: 5.02 g. Cholesterol: 0 mg. Calcium: 130.8 mg. Iron: 1.863 mg. Potassium: 665.1 mg. Total Fat: 0.3 g; Saturated fat: 0 g, Monounsaturated fat: 0.1 g, Polyunsaturated fat: 0.1 g.

❖ DRIED PEACH COMPOTE ❖

SERVES 6 SODIUM PER RECIPE: 34.5 MG SODIUM PER SERVING: 5.746 MG
When fresh fruit isn't available, here's another compote to come to the rescue.

2½ **cups orange juice fortified with calcium (6.219 mg)—or you may substitute an equal amount of apple cider or juice (18.6 mg)**
⅓ **cup honey (4.475 mg)**
2 **teaspoons grated orange zest (.12 mg)**
2 **teaspoons grated lemon zest (.24 mg)**
1 **teaspoon almond extract (0 mg)**
10 **ounces dried peaches, halved, or dried apricots (17.9 mg)**
⅓ **cup slivered unsalted almonds, toasted (5 mg)**
1½ **teaspoons chopped fresh mint (.496 mg)**

1. Combine the orange juice, honey, orange and lemon zest, and almond extract in a saucepan and bring it to a boil over medium heat. Reduce the heat and simmer for 5 minutes. Add the peaches or apricots to the syrup, partially cover, and simmer for an additional 25 minutes. Transfer the mixture to a serving bowl and allow the fruit to cool to room temperature in the syrup. Add the almonds and sprinkle with mint before serving.

Calories: 251. Sodium: 5.75 mg. Carbohydrate: 54.9 g. Protein: 3.57 g. Fiber: 4.95 g. Cholesterol: 0 mg. Calcium: 162.6 mg. Iron: 18.9 mg. Potassium: 694 mg. Total Fat: 4.3 g; Saturated fat: 0.4 g, Monounsaturated fat: 2.7 g, Polyunsaturated fat: 1 g.

❖ BRUNCH COMPOTE ❖

SERVES 8   SODIUM PER RECIPE: 13.4 MG   SODIUM PER SERVING: 1.68 MG

*If you prefer brunch to breakfast, try this compote with **Biscotti**. It can be made with fresh or frozen berries.*

1 cup blueberries (8.7 mg)*
1 cup raspberries (trace)†
1 cup black currants (2.24 mg)
1 cup strawberries, halved (1.5 mg)‡
⅓ cup granulated sugar (.66 mg)
1½ tablespoons fresh lemon juice (.2 mg)
½ tablespoon water (0 mg)
¼ teaspoon vanilla extract (trace)

1. Combine all the ingredients in a large saucepan and gently stir over low heat until the sugar dissolves. Remove from the heat and allow to cool. Pour the compote into a glass bowl and chill. Serve with **Biscotti** (page 348).

Calories: 65. Sodium: 1.68 mg. Protein: .584 g. Carbohydrate: 16.3 g. Fiber: 1.98 g. Cholesterol: 0 mg. Calcium: 15.1 mg. Iron: .537 mg. Potassium: 120 mg. Total Fat: 0.3 g; Saturated fat: 0 g, Monounsaturated fat: 0 g, Polyunsaturated fat: 0.1 g.

❖ ALICE'S PECAN PRALINES ❖

MAKES 18 PRALINES   SODIUM PER RECIPE: 116.8 MG
SODIUM PER PRALINE: 6.487 MG

These are low in sodium but a bit high in calories. Unfortunately, they are absolutely delicious, so save them for special occasions.

2 cups granulated sugar (4 mg)
1 cup lightly packed brown sugar (85.8 mg)
1 tablespoon light Karo syrup (24.2 mg)
1½ cups water (0 mg)
1 teaspoon vanilla extract (.378 mg)
2 cups unsalted pecan pieces (2.38 mg)

1. In a saucepan, heat the sugars, Karo syrup, water, and vanilla until the mixture reaches the soft-ball stage (238°F on a candy thermometer or until ½ teaspoonful or so forms a soft ball when dropped in cold water). Remove the pan from the heat. Stir in the pecan pieces. Stir for 1 minute.

*Fresh blueberries have 10 mg sodium per cup; frozen berries have 2 mg.
†Fresh raspberries have only a trace of sodium; frozen berries have 2 mg per cup.
‡Fresh strawberries have 2 mg sodium per cup; frozen have 4 mg.

Drop by the spoonful on a lightly greased sheet to make 2-inch patties. Store in sealed bags or containers in cool place.

Calories: 224. Sodium: 6.49 mg. Carbohydrate: 37.4 g. Fiber: 1 g. Protein: 1.025 g. Cholesterol: 0 mg. Calcium: 15.4 mg. Iron: 1.196 mg. Potassium: 95 mg. Total Fat: 8.9 g; Saturated fat: 0.7 g, Monounsaturated fat: 5.6 g, Polyunsaturated fat: 2.2 g.

❈ GLAZED WALNUTS ❈

MAKES APPROXIMATELY 90 *WALNUT HALVES*   *SODIUM PER RECIPE:* 110.1 *MG*
ESTIMATED SODIUM PER WALNUT HALF:* 1.223 *MG

½ **cup granulated sugar (1 mg)**
1 **unpacked cup brown sugar (56.6 mg)**
½ **cup low-fat sour cream (49 mg)**
1 **teaspoon vanilla extract (.378 mg)**
2½ **cups unsalted, shelled walnut halves (3.125 mg)**

1. In a saucepan, heat the sugars and sour cream until the mixture reaches the soft-ball stage (238°F on a candy thermometer or until ½ teaspoon or so forms a soft ball when dropped in cold water). Add the vanilla and beat until thickened. Add the walnuts, stir, and spread on a lightly greased platter or cookie sheet to cool. Separate the walnut halves if necessary after cooling. Serve hot or cold. Great for salads, ice cream, or snacks.

Calories: 33. Sodium: 1.22 mg. Carbohydrate: 3.161 g. Fiber: 0.17 g. Protein: .885 g. Cholesterol: 0.52 mg. Calcium: 4.803 mg. Iron: .139 mg. Potassium: 25.6 mg. Total Fat: 2.1 g; Saturated fat: 0.2 g, Monounsaturated fat: 0.5 g, Polyunsaturated fat: 1.3 g.

❈ ALMOND ROCA ❈

MAKES 16 PIECES   *SODIUM PER RECIPE:* 85.7 *MG*
SODIUM PER SERVING:* 5.359 *MG

Our daughter, Maria, teaches Spanish in a northern California high school. While earning her degree at UC Davis, she spent six months in Spain immersed in her new language. She was also immersed in some fairly fine eating. This recipe came to us from Spain, where almonds and almond roca are very popular.

¾ **cups unsalted butter (18.7 mg)**
2 **cups granulated sugar (4 mg)**
2 **cups (generous) whole unsalted, roasted, or blanched almonds (30.4 mg)**
8 **ounces Nestlé's semisweet chocolate chips (32 mg)**
2 **tablespoons ground almonds (to sprinkle) (.66 mg)**

1. Melt butter over medium heat. Add sugar. Stir constantly. Bring to boil and cook 5 minutes at slightly reduced heat.

2. Keep stirring. Add almonds. Stir constantly. Bring to boil again and cook an additional 8 minutes.

3. Pour onto cookie sheet, spread out evenly, and immediately sprinkle chocolate chips over toffee mixture, distributing them evenly. They should melt. Sprinkle ground almonds evenly. Cool, then crack with knife into bite-size pieces of your choice.

Calories: 351. Sodium: 5.36 mg. Fiber: 2.91 g. Protein: 3.469 g. Carbohydrate: 38.1 g. Cholesterol: 23.29 mg. Calcium: 57.5 mg. Iron: 1.20 mg. Potassium: 188.5 mg. Total Fat: 21.7 g; Saturated fat: 8.7 g, Monounsaturated fat: 9.5 g, Polyunsaturated fat: 6 g.

❖ DATE SHAKE ❖

MAKES 3 (8-OUNCE) SERVINGS   SODIUM PER RECIPE: 89.6 MG
SODIUM PER SERVING: 29.9 MG

As a youngster, I spent a lot of my time in California's date country. The great thing about dates is you can use them anywhere you use other fruit. On your cereal, in cakes and muffins, and in a milk shake. Date Shakes were our favorite. But today, with ice cream being a bit too laden with saturated fat (and sodium), I use a recipe from a date company in Thermal, California (with their permission).

12 **chopped pitted dates (2.988 mg)**
½ **banana (.59 mg)**
½ **cup low-fat plain yogurt (86 mg)**
⅛ **teaspoon vanilla extract (trace)**
 2 **cups shaved ice (0 mg)**

1. Put all the ingredients, including the ice, in a blender jar and mix until smooth. Serve cold.

Calories: 136. Sodium: 29.87 mg. Carbohydrate: 31.9 g. Protein: 3 g. Fiber: 2.96 g. Cholesterol: 2.49 mg. Calcium: 86.4 mg. Iron: 5.809 mg. Potassium: 390.1 mg. Total Fat: 0.9 g; Saturated fat: 0.5 g, Monounsaturated fat: 0.2 g, Polyunsaturated fat: 0 g.

❖ PAPA'S LEMON ICE ❖

SERVES 4   SODIUM PER RECIPE: .768 MG   SODIUM PER SERVING: .192 MG

An old family tradition in Mae DeMarco's family for a hot day is this simple, sodium-free treat that satisfies any thirst. The ingredient amounts are suggestions. Mix your own to suit your personal tastes.

4 **cups water (0 mg)**
4 **teaspoons granulated sugar (.168 mg)**
4 **tablespoons fresh lemon juice (.6 mg)**

1. Combine the ingredients, adjusting the sugar and lemon to taste. Put the mixture into an ice cream maker and process until frozen.

Calories: 20. Sodium: 0.19 mg. Carbohydrate: 5.49 g. Protein: .057 g. Fiber: 0.06 g. Cholesterol: 0 mg. Calcium: 1.092 mg. Iron: 8.008 mg. Potassium: 18.7 mg. Total Fat: 0 g; Saturated fat: 0 g, Monounsaturated fat: 0 g, Polyunsaturated fat: 0 g.

❈ CARROT STICKS ❈

MAKES 4 SERVINGS   SODIUM PER RECIPE: 85.4 MG
SODIUM PER SERVING: 21.4 MG

I like to leave a bowl of these in the refrigerator and will often reach in and grab a few to help quell hunger. Try it yourself.

- **4 medium carrots (85.4 mg)**
- **1 cup ice cubes (0 mg)**
- **¼ cup cold water (0 mg)**

1. Clean, peel, and slice the carrots lengthwise into sticks. Set them in a flat container with water and ice cubes and store covered, in the refrigerator. Eat anytime.

Calories: 26. Sodium: 21.35 mg. Carbohydrate: 6.185 g. Fiber: 1.83 g. Protein: .628 g. Cholesterol: 0 mg. Calcium: 16.5 mg. Iron: .305 mg. Potassium: 197 mg. Total Fat: 0.1 g; Saturated fat: 0 g, Monounsaturated fat: 0 g, Polyunsaturated fat: 0 g.

❈ DON'S TRAIL MIX ❈

MAKES 1 QUART   SODIUM PER RECIPE: 79.8 MG
SODIUM PER ¼ CUP: 4.98 MG

Sometimes this snack was all I would take with me on a trip by horseback. I once made such a trip into the Sierra Nevadas—it took two weeks and all I had with me to eat was a saddlebag full of homemade trail mix. You can add dried fruit. I left it out here, putting in only high-energy foods that have plenty of iron and potassium. Make a large batch and store it in vacuum-sealed jars. (You can vacuum-seal canning jars with a FoodSaver sealer.)

- **1 packed cup golden raisins (19.4 mg)**
- **1 cup Craisins or Cranlings (sweetened dried cranberries) (9 mg)**
- **1 cup dry-roasted chopped unsalted cashews (21.9 mg)**
- **1 cup black raisins (19.8 mg)**
- **½ cup semisweet chocolate chips (9.24 mg)**

1. Mix all the ingredients together and store the mixture in a large quart jar. Keep ½ cup for immediate use. A tight lid will hold this fresh in the refrigerator for a few months. If you have children who would enjoy this snack, and they aren't worried about sodium, you can make a batch for them with mini-marshmallows.

Calories: 161. Sodium: 4.98 mg. Carbohydrate: 28.7 g. Protein: 2.213 g. Fiber: 1.77 g. Cholesterol: 0 mg. Calcium: 16.1 mg. Iron: 1.077 mg. Potassium: 221.9 mg. Total Fat: 5.6 g; Saturated fat: 1.7 g, Monounsaturated fat: 2.9 g, Polyunsaturated fat: 0.7 g.

SAMPLE FOUR-WEEK MENU PLANNER
AND
HOLIDAY MENUS

The following menu planning guide has been designed to demonstrate how easy the recipes in this book can be used for a healthy, balanced, low-sodium diet. Each day provides between 1,800 and 2,500 calories, with 22 to 30 percent of the calories from fat, about 1,000 milligrams of calcium, and no more than 500 milligrams of sodium.

By using this guide you will be able to figure out your sodium count and that of most other nutrients for the day. You will be able to tell when you can have that extra serving of fruit or dessert, as well as when to cut back.

Please keep in mind when using this guide that the menus do not take into consideration fluid or other dietary restrictions, such as protein or carbohydrate, that your physician may have prescribed for your specific medical condition. The caloric content of the suggested menus may be high for some heart patients. However, by developing menus in the 2,000-calorie range, we are considering the high-end need of some people while maintaining the sodium count under the most stringent of restrictions—500 milligrams per day. Butter has been listed as an optional item on seven of the following menus. For patients who have been advised to omit butter from their diet because of its saturated fat content, please heed your physician or dietitian's recommendation. The suggested menus may certainly be adjusted to fit your personal caloric need.

As with most restricted diets, supplementing with a multivitamin may be necessary. However, be sure to consult your physician regarding the use of any dietary supplements, including multivitamins.

Note: Recipe items in boldface in this menu planner are based on recipes in this book. The sodium counts in this menu planner are listed by whole day and by individual item.

The above has been created by Jeannie M. Gazzaniga, Ph.D., R.D. Dr. Gazzaniga recently directed the University of California San Francisco and California Department of Health Services' Cardiovascular Disease Outreach Resources and Epidemiology Program. She has a masters in human nutrition and doctorate in epidemiology. Her research has focused on heart disease and stroke. She has taught college-level nutrition courses and worked as a clinical dietitian focusing on special diets for people with heart disease, renal disease, cancer, and diabetes. Dr. Gazzaniga has been an active member of the American Dietetic Association for fourteen years and is the daughter of this book's proud author.

DAY 1

Breakfast

2 **Sourdough Belgian Waffles**, page 218 (38.8 mg)
3 tablespoons natural maple syrup (5.4 mg)
1 tablespoon unsalted butter (optional) (1.562 mg)
½ medium banana (.59 mg)
  8-ounce glass orange juice fortified with calcium (2.488 mg)

Midmorning Snack

1 medium apple (trace)

Lunch

1 **Hummus Sandwich**, page 275 (23.9 mg)
1 **Carrot Stick**, page 369 (21.4 mg)
½ cup nonfat milk (63.1 mg)

Midafternoon Snack

1 ounce unsalted sunflower seeds (.213 mg)
¾ cup nonfat yogurt with fruit (98.7 mg)

Dinner

1 serving **Chicken and Vegetables**, page 109 (122.7 mg)
1 serving **Mixed Green Salad,** page 185, with **Oil and Vinegar Dressing**, page 209 (4.772 mg)
1 **Dinner Roll**, page 256 (1 mg)

Dessert

1 **Baked Apple**, page 358 (2.279 mg)

Calories: 2,345. Sodium: 385.9 mg. Carbohydrate: 383.8 g. Fiber: 37.9 g. Protein: 82.6 g. Cholesterol: 217.7 mg. Calcium: 1257 mg. Iron: 27.9 mg. Potassium: 6,092 mg. Total Fat: 59.6 g; Saturated fat: 14.9 g, Monounsaturated fat: 21.8 g, Polyunsaturated fat: 16.7 g.

DAY 2

Breakfast

1 serving **Spoon-Size Shredded Wheat** (1 cup orange juice, ¾ cup
nonfat milk, ¾ cup Spoon Size Shredded Wheat, 1 small banana)
(100.4 mg)

Midmorning Snack

1 medium pear (trace)
1 slice **Whole Wheat Toast**, page 234 (1 mg)
1 tablespoon unsalted butter (optional) (1.562 mg)

Lunch

1 **Tony's Taco**, page 272 (58.4 mg)
1 serving **Mixed Green Salad**, page 185, with **Oil and Vinegar
    Dressing**, page 209 (4.772 mg)
½ cup **Rice Pilaf**, page 134 (11.7 mg)
1 cup grapes (1.84 mg)

Midafternoon Snack

1 apple, with skin (trace)
¾ cup nonfat yogurt with fruit (98.7 mg)

Dinner

1 serving **Don's Quick and Easy Chicken Casserole**, page 93 (95 mg)
1 serving **Steamed Broccoli**, page 278 (10.2 mg)
1 **Dinner Roll**, page 256 (1 mg)

Dessert

1 slice **Walter's Pecan Pie**, page 318 (48.7 mg)

*Calories: 2,297. Sodium: 443.06 mg. Carbohydrate: 348.6 g. Fiber: 28.49 g. Protein: 82.8 g.
Cholesterol: 262.73 mg. Calcium: 1,011 mg. Iron: 13.3 mg. Potassium: 3,817 mg. Total Fat:
72 g; Saturated fat: 27.8 g, Monounsaturated fat: 29.1 g, Polyunsaturated fat: 7.5 g.*

Day 3

Breakfast

- 1 serving **Egg White Omelet**, page 130 (91.5 mg)
- 1 slice **Pear Coffee Cake**, page 226 (17.9 mg)
  8-ounce glass orange juice fortified with calcium (2.488 mg)

Midmorning Snack

- 1 apple (trace)
- 1 **Oat Bran and Jam Muffin**, page 220 (20.6 mg)

Lunch

- 1 serving **Herb Patties** made with beef, page 91 (78 mg)
- 1 **Sandwich Bun**, page 258 (1.927 mg)
- 1 serving **Carrot Salad**, page 189 (23.7 mg)
  8-ounce glass orange juice fortified with calcium (2.488 mg)

Midafternoon Snack

- ½ cup **Papa's Lemon Ice**, page 368 (.192 mg)
- ½ cup **Fresh Berries**, page 362 (2.544 mg)

Dinner

- 1 serving **Pork Tenderloin Chili Verde**, page 83 (110.3 mg)
- 1 serving **Couscous**, page 141 (26 mg)
- 1 serving **Vegetable Sauté**, page 296 (8.999 mg)

Calories: 2,202. Sodium: 386.19 mg. Carbohydrate: 298.6 g. Fiber: 30.22 g. Protein: 98.3 g. Cholesterol: 370.97 mg. Calcium: 951.7 mg. Iron: 25.1 mg. Potassium: 4,498 mg. Total Fat: 76.6 g; Saturated fat: 20.3 g, Monounsaturated fat: 29.9 g, Polyunsaturated fat: 9.5 g.

Day 4

Breakfast

1 cup **Applesauce Oatmeal**, page 165 (9.434 mg)
½ cup nonfat milk (63.1 mg)
   8-ounce glass orange juice fortified with calcium (2.488 mg)
1 slice **Whole Wheat Toast**, page 234 (1.047 mg)
1 tablespoon **Quick Orange Marmalade**, page 314 (.144 mg)

Midmorning Snack

1 cup seedless grapes (1.84 mg)

Lunch

1 **Don's Very Best Luncheon Sandwich**, page 263 (33.8 mg)
1 ounce unsalted potato chips (2.268 mg)
   8-ounce glass orange juice fortified with calcium (2.488 mg)

Midafternoon Snack

1 medium apple (trace)
1 tablespoon unsalted peanut butter (2.72 mg)

Dinner

1 serving **Scampi in Wine**, page 126 (29.5 mg)
1 cup or less **Basmati Pilaf**, page 135 (2.049 mg)
1 serving **Steamed Vegetables**, page 297 (17.2 mg)
1 slice **Roasted Garlic Toast**, page 35 (2.662 mg)

Dessert

1 **Danny Boy's Chocolate Chip Cookie** made with applesauce, page
   346 (5.731 mg)
1 cup nonfat milk (126.2 mg)

*Calories: 2,217. Sodium: 302.47 mg. Carbohydrate: 363.6 g. Fiber: 28.43 g. Protein: 64 g.
Cholesterol: 72.08 mg. Calcium: 1,290 mg. Iron: 28.4 mg. Potassium: 4,203 mg. Total Fat:
62.9 g; Saturated fat: 17.8 g, Monounsaturated fat: 26.5 g, Polyunsaturated fat: 12.3 g.*

DAY 5

Breakfast

1 serving **Scrambled Eggs with Peppers and Mushrooms**, page 127
   (99.1 mg)
1 slice **Whole Wheat Toast**, page 234 (1.047 mg)
1 tablespoon **Quick Strawberry Jam**, page 312 (.187 mg)
8-ounce glass orange juice fortified with calcium (2.488 mg)

Midmorning Snack

1 cup sliced melon (20.4 mg)

Lunch

1 cup **Lentil and More Soup**, page 55 (26.8 mg)
1 **Pita Bread**, page 251 (1.771 mg)
1 cup nonfat milk (126.2 mg)
1 serving **Carrot Sticks**, page 369 (21.4 mg)

Midafternoon Snack

1 **Oat Bran and Jam Muffin**, page 220 (20.6 mg)
1 cup seedless grapes (1.84 mg)

Dinner

2 **Turkey Tacos**, page 270 (142 mg)
½ cup **Refried Beans**, page 158 (18.5 mg)
1 serving **Chopped Vegetable**, page 185 (11.4 mg)

*Calories: 2,217. Sodium: 493.8 mg. Carbohydrate: 313 g. Fiber: 63.3 g. Protein: 99.6 g.
Cholesterol: 461 mg. Calcium: 1,154 mg. Iron: 42.1 mg. Potassium: 5,781 mg. Total Fat:
73.8 g; Saturated fat: 19.6 g, Monounsaturated fat: 34.5 g, Polyunsaturated fat: 11 g.*

DAY 6

Breakfast

1 serving **Fresh Fruit Salad**, page 204 (13.1 mg)
½ cup nonfat fruit-flavored yogurt (71 mg)
2 slices **Whole Wheat Toast**, page 234 (2.094 mg)
2 tablespoons **Quick Strawberry Jam**, page 312 (.373 mg)

Midmorning Snack

1 **Lemon and Currant Scone**, page 225 (12.3 mg)
1 cup nonfat milk (126.2 mg)

Lunch

1 **Dill Chicken Summer Salad**, page 196 (113.1 mg)
2 slices **Crusty French Baguette**, page 248 (1.456 mg)
1 cup orange juice fortified with calcium (2.488 mg)
1 medium apple (0 mg)

Midafternoon Snack

1 serving **Carrot Sticks**, page 369 (21.4 mg)

Dinner

1 serving **Hamburger with Bun**, page 264 (84.2 mg)
1 serving **Original Oven-Roasted French Fries**, page 287 (7.32 mg)
1 serving **Steamed Broccoli**, page 278 (20.4 mg)

Dessert

1 **Peanut Butter Crunch Bar**, page 350 (6.261 mg)

Calories: 2,226. Sodium: 471.72 mg. Protein: 97.2 g. Carbohydrate: 352.5 g. Fiber: 31.58 g. Cholesterol: 182.83 mg. Calcium: 1,363 mg. Potassium: 4,841 mg. Total Fat: 54.7 g; Saturated fat: 17.5 g, Monounsaturated fat: 17.7 g, Polyunsaturated fat: 11.8 g.

Day 7

Breakfast

1 serving **Spoon-Size Shredded Wheat** (1 cup orange juice, ¾ cup nonfat milk, ¾ cup Spoon Size Shredded Wheat, with ½ cup blueberries) (104.5 mg)

Midmorning Snack

1 slice **Whole Wheat Toast**, page 234 (1.047 mg)
1 banana (1 mg)

Lunch

1 **Hamburger**, page 264 (84.2 mg)
1 serving **Pasta Salad**, page 203 (9.806 mg)
1 serving **Steamed Summer Squash**, page 292 (8.121 mg)

Midafternoon Snack

2 **Anise Cookies**, page 343 (13.9 mg)
1 cup nonfat milk (126.2 mg)

Dinner

1 serving **Baked Red Snapper**, page 118 (60 mg)
½ cup **Wild Rice Pilaf**, page 285 (11.8 mg)
1 serving **Steamed Vegetables**, page 297 (17.2 mg)
1 **Dinner Roll**, page 256 (1 mg)
1 tablespoon unsalted butter (optional) (1.562 mg)

Calories: 2,122. Sodium: 488.73 mg. Carbohydrate: 315 g. Fiber: 30.64 g. Protein: 110 g. Cholesterol: 201.29 mg. Calcium: 1,217 mg. Iron: 19.1 mg. Potassium: 5,341 mg. Total Fat: 52.9 g. Saturated fat: 13.3 g. Monounsaturated fat: 24.3 g. Polyunsaturated fat: 8.4 g.

DAY 8

Breakfast

1 serving **Apple Omelet**, page 128 (101.1 mg)
1 slice **Whole Wheat Toast**, page 234 (1.048 mg)
1 tablespoon **Quick Orange Marmalade**, page 314 (.144 mg)
   8-ounce glass orange juice fortified with calcium (2.488 mg)

Midmorning Snack

1 fresh sliced apple (trace)

Lunch

1 **Don's Very Best Luncheon Sandwich**, page 263 (33.8 mg)
   8-ounce glass orange juice fortified with calcium (2.488 mg)
1 **Loganberry Shortbread Bar**, page 350 (6.363 mg)

Midafternoon Snack

1 serving **Vegetable Delight**, page 299 (9.777 mg)

Dinner

1 cup **Broccoli Soup**, page 46 (73.8 mg)
1 serving **Roasted Chicken with Grilled Red Bell Pepper Sauce**,
      page 96 (81.2 mg)
1 serving **Charlotte's Potatoes**, page 286 (6.494 mg)
½ cup unsalted peas cooked in unsalted water (3.625 mg)

Dessert

1 serving **Baked Fruit**, page 363 (2.339 mg)

Calories: 1,846. Sodium: 324.6 mg. Carbohydrate: 279.8 g. Fiber: 31.54 g. Protein: 78.4 g. Cholesterol: 403.31 mg. Calcium: 1,046 mg. Iron: 19.3 mg. Potassium: 4,319 mg. Total Fat: 53.4 g; Saturated fat: 15.7 g, Monounsaturated fat: 20.5 g, Polyunsaturated fat: 8 g.

Day 9

Breakfast

3 **Becky's Oatmeal Pancakes**, page 213 (60.3 mg)
1 cup **Fruit Compote**, page 363 (8.279 mg)
1 cup nonfat milk (126.2 mg)

Midmorning Snack

1 slice **Don's Healthy Orange Bread**, toasted, page 244 (1.99 mg)
1 tablespoon **Quick Orange Marmalade**, page 314 (.144 mg)

Lunch

1 serving **Grilled Chicken Salad**, page 198 (101.1 mg)
1 slice **Cornbread**, page 249 (5.491 mg)
8-ounce glass orange juice fortified with calcium (2.488 mg)

Midafternoon Snack

1 medium apple (trace)

Dinner

1 serving **Spanish Cod**, page 124 (69.5 mg)
1 serving **Chopped Vegetable**, page 185 (11.4 mg)
1 **Dinner Roll**, page 256 (1 mg)
1 tablespoon **Quick Orange Marmalade**, page 314 (.144 mg)

Dessert

1 serving **Applesauce Cake**, page 329 (15.5 mg)

Calories: 2,469. Sodium: 404.02 mg. Protein: 92.6 g. Carbohydrate: 443.5 g. Fiber: 39.54 g. Cholesterol: 237.47 mg. Calcium: 1,193 mg. Potassium: 5,024 mg. Total Fat: 46.6 g; Saturated fat: 7.2 g, Monounsaturated fat: 28.1 g, Polyunsaturated fat: 6.8 g.

DAY 10

Breakfast

1 serving **Potato and Egg Frittata**, page 131 (72.5 mg)
2 slices **Whole Wheat Toast**, page 234 (2.095 mg)
2 tablespoons **Quick Strawberrry Jam**, page 312 (.373 mg)
  8-ounce glass orange juice fortified with calcium (2.488 mg)

Midmorning Snack

1 orange, peeled and cut into sections (1.4 mg)
¾ cup fruit-flavored nonfat yogurt (98.7 mg)

Lunch

1 serving **River Guide Black-Eyed Pea Salad**, page 196 (42 mg)
2 slices **Sourdough Baguette**, page 252 (1.272 mg)
  8-ounce glass orange juice fortified with calcium (2.488 mg)

Midafternoon Snack

1 serving **Date Shake**, page 368 (29.9 mg)

Dinner

1 serving **Chicken Curry**, page 110 (84.9 mg)
½ cup **Basmati Pilaf**, page 135 (2.048 mg)
½ cup **Spinach with Mushrooms and Onions**, page 290 (39.6 mg)

Calories: 2,184. Sodium: 379.79 mg. Carbohydrate: 331.9 g. Fiber: 27.67 g. Protein: 76 g. Cholesterol: 268.84 mg. Calcium: 1,306 mg. Iron: 29.7 mg. Potassium: 4,509 mg. Total Fat: 67.3 g; Saturated fat: 12 g, Monounsaturated fat: 42.2 g, Polyunsaturated fat: 7.1 g.

Day 11

Breakfast

1 serving **Spoon-Size Shredded Wheat** (1 cup orange juice, ¾ cup
nonfat milk, ¾ cup Spoon Size Shredded Wheat, 1 small banana)
(100.4 mg)

Midmorning Snack

¼ cup **Don's Trail Mix**, page 369 (4.985 mg)

Lunch

1 serving **Turkey Salad**, page 199 (46.4 mg)
1 **Dinner Roll**, page 256 (1.036 mg)
1 cup nonfat milk (126.2 mg)

Midafternoon Snack

1 cup **Fresh Fruit Salad**, page 204 (13.1 mg)

Dinner

2 slices **Very-Low-Sodium Pizza**, page 132 (53.9 mg)
1 serving **Mixed Green Salad**, page 185, with **Oil and Vinegar
Dressing**, page 209 (10.6 mg)

Dessert

½ cup Citrus Sorbet (available in most grocery stores) (8 mg)

*Calories: 2,149. Sodium: 364.64 mg. Carbohydrate: 337.7 g. Fiber: 29.56 g. Protein: 64.9 g.
Cholesterol: 48.02 mg. Calcium: 1,023 mg. Iron: 15.3 mg. Potassium: 4,554 mg. Total Fat:
67.8 g; Saturated fat: 10.9 g, Monounsaturated fat: 44.7 g, Polyunsaturated fat: 7.7 g.*

DAY 12

Breakfast

1 cup sliced cantaloupe (14 mg)
2 slices **Whole Wheat Toast**, page 234 (2.095 mg)
1 tablespoon unsalted butter (optional) (1.562 mg)
1 tablespoon **Quick Strawberry Jam**, page 312 (.187 mg)
8-ounce glass orange juice fortified with calcium (2.488 mg)

Midmorning Snack

1 cup seedless grapes (3.2 mg)

Lunch

1 **Soyburger** with **Sandwich Bun**, pages 266 and 258 (51 mg)
1 serving **Carrot Salad**, page 189 (34.3 mg)
½ cup nonfat milk (63.1 mg)

Midafternoon Snack

¾ cup nonfat fruit-flavored yogurt (98.7 mg)

Dinner

1 serving **Chicken Enchiladas**, page 112 (132 mg)
1 serving **Mixed Green Salad**, page 185, with **Oil and Vinegar Dressing**, page 209 (10.6 mg)
1 serving **Rice Pilaf**, page 134 (11.74 mg)

Dessert

¾ cup sliced fresh strawberries (1.14 mg)

Calories: 2,312. Sodium: 431.2 mg. Carbohydrate: 349.9 g. Fiber: 31.3 g. Protein: 82.5 g. Cholesterol: 1,98.9 mg. Calcium: 1,188 mg. Iron: 17.4 mg. Potassium: 4,274 mg. Total Fat: 74 g; Saturated fat: 20.9 g, Monounsaturated fat: 33.2 g, Polyunsaturated fat: 11.1 g.

DAY 13

Breakfast

2 slices **French Toast**, page 219 (59.8 mg)
1 cup **Fruit Compote**, page 363 (8.279 mg)
2 tablespoons real maple syrup (3.6 mg)

Midmorning Snack

8-ounce glass orange juice fortified with calcium (2.488 mg)

Lunch

1 **Chicken Sandwich**, page 276 (63.9 mg)
1 portion **Mixed Green Salad**, page 185, with **Oil and Vinegar Dressing**, page 209 (10.6 mg)
1 cup nonfat milk (126.2 mg)

Midafternoon Snack

1 ounce unsalted pistachios (1.701 mg)

Dinner

1 serving **Becky's Stuffed Mushrooms**, page 41 (13.4 mg)
1 serving **Pappy's Beef Kabobs with Peppers**, page 70 (74 mg)
1 serving **Scalloped Potatoes**, page 289 (39 mg)
1 serving **Steamed Broccoli**, page 278 (20.4 mg)

Dessert

1 slice **No-Sugar-Added Carrot Cake**, page 331 (23.1 mg)

Calories: 2,338. Sodium: 446.31 mg. Carbohydrate: 312.6 g. Fiber: 25.97 g. Protein: 93.6 g. Cholesterol: 264.85 mg. Calcium: 1,054 mg. Iron: 23.1 mg. Potassium: 4,941 mg. Total Fat: 85.9 g; Saturated fat: 17.9 g, Monounsaturated fat: 40 g, Polyunsaturated fat: 10.6 g.

DAY 14

Breakfast

1 **Don's Omelet**, page 129 (72.5 mg)
1 serving **Hash Browns**, page 286 (18.1 mg)
8-ounce glass orange juice fortified with calcium (2.488 mg)

Midmorning Snack

1 **Cranberry Whole Wheat Muffin**, page 222 (25 mg)

Lunch

1 serving **Sweet Pepper Salad**, page 191 (17.2 mg)
1 **Pita Bread**, page 251 (1.771 mg)

Midafternoon Snack

1 slice **Don's Healthy Orange Bread**, page 244, toasted (0.612 mg)
8-ounce glass orange juice fortified with calcium (2.488 mg)

Dinner

1 serving **Mushroom Soup**, page 52 (11.6 mg)
1 serving **Roasted Chicken with Grilled Red Bell Pepper Sauce**,
page 96 (81.2 mg)
1 serving **Spinach with Mushrooms and Onions**, page 290
(39.6 mg)
1 **Dinner Roll**, page 256 (1.036 mg)

Dessert

1 portion **Baked Apples**, page 358 (2.339 mg)

Calories: 2,035. Sodium: 275.84 mg. Carbohydrate: 290 g. Fiber: 27.11 g. Protein: 68.3 g. Cholesterol: 302.66 mg. Calcium: 934.1 mg. Iron: 20.2 mg. Potassium: 4,327 mg. Total Fat: 74.5 g. Saturated fat: 12.8 g. Monounsaturated fat: 43 g. Polyunsaturated fat: 12.2 g.

Day 15

Breakfast

1 **Egg** (medium), poached, without salt (55.5 mg)
1 serving **Hash Browns**, page 286 (18.1 mg)
8-ounce glass orange juice fortified with calcium (2.488 mg)
1 slice **Whole Wheat Toast**, page 234 (1.048 mg)
1 tablespoon **Best Berry Jam**, page 311 (.292 mg)

Midmorning Snack

1 cup sliced melon (20.4 mg)

Lunch

1 **Light Sandwich**, page 277 (29.1 mg)
1 ounce unsalted potato chips (2.268 mg)
1 cup seedless grapes (3.2 mg)
8-ounce glass orange juice fortified with calcium (2.488 mg)

Midafternoon Snack

½ cup **Fresh Berries**, page 362 (4 mg)
½ cup Citrus Sorbet (available in most grocery stores) (8 mg)

Dinner

1 serving **Raspberry Lamb**, page 88 (70.3 mg)
1 serving **Charlotte's Potatoes**, page 286 (6.494 mg)
1 serving **Mixed Green Salad**, page 185, with **Oil and Vinegar
Dressing**, page 209 (10.6 mg)

Dessert

1 serving **Baked Fruit**, page 363 (6.48 mg)

*Calories: 2,368. Sodium: 240.31 mg. Carbohydrate: 412.4 g. Fiber: 41.85 g. Protein: 65.8 g.
Cholesterol: 269.58 mg. Calcium: 914.2 mg. Iron: 18 mg. Potassium: 5,561 mg. Total Fat:
61.2 g; Saturated fat: 13.7 g, Monounsaturated fat: 31.3 g, Polyunsaturated fat: 9.4 g.*

DAY 16

THE DAY'S SODIUM COUNT: 360.61 MG

Breakfast

1 serving **Pear Coffee Cake**, page 226 (18.2 mg)
1 serving **Egg-White Omelet**, page 130 (91.5 mg)
  8-ounce glass orange juice fortified with calcium (2.488 mg)

Midmorning Snack

1 medium banana (1.18 mg)

Lunch

2 **Tofu Tacos**, page 270 (49 mg)
1 medium orange, cut in wedges (1.4 mg)
1 cup nonfat milk (126.2 mg)

Midafternoon Snack

1 serving **Carrot Sticks**, page 369 (21.4 mg)
  8-ounce glass orange juice fortified with calcium (2.488 mg)

Dinner

1 serving **Pasta with Balsamic Onion and Sun-Dried Tomatoes**,
    page 148 (27.4 mg)
1 serving **Quick Mixed Green Salad**, page 185 (6.985 mg)
2 tablespoons **Balsamic Vinaigrette**, page 209 (.581 mg)
1 slice **Crusty French Bread**, page 248 (.728 mg)

Dessert

1 **"Legal" Brownie,** page 355 (11.1 mg)

Calories: 2,274. Sodium: 362.01 mg. Carbohydrate: 360.4 g. Fiber: 26.36 g. Protein: 58.8 g. Cholesterol: 167.48 mg. Calcium: 1,261 mg. Iron: 17.7 mg. Potassium: 4,145 mg. Total Fat: 74.6 g; Saturated fat: 15.1 g, Monounsaturated fat: 42.7 g, Polyunsaturated fat: 10.2 g.

Day 17

Breakfast

2 **Cornmeal Crêpes**, page 214 (64.4 mg)
1 serving **Fruit Compote,** page 363 (8.279 mg)
½ cup nonfat milk (63.1 mg)

Midmorning Snack

8-ounce glass orange juice fortified with calcium (2.488 mg)
1 serving **Don's Trail Mix**, page 369 (4.985 mg)

Lunch

1 serving **Mom's Mystery Burger**, page 267 (27.7 mg)
1 serving **Original Oven-Roasted French Fries**, page 287 (7.32 mg)

Midafternoon Snack

¾ cup nonfat yogurt (98.7 mg)
1 pear (0 mg)

Dinner

1 serving **Vegetarian Ratatouille**, page 295 (29.7 mg)
1 serving **Quick Mixed Green Salad**, page 185 (6.985 mg)
1 serving **Mustard Salad Dressing**, page 211 (.763 mg)
2 slices **Sourdough Baguette**, page 252 (1.272 mg)
1 tablespoon unsalted butter (optional) (1.562 mg)

Calories: 1,930. Sodium: 315.7 mg. Carbohydrate: 300.4 g. Fiber: 24.38 g. Protein: 53.9 g. Cholesterol: 144.1 mg. Calcium: 1,011 mg. Iron: 26 mg. Potassium: 4,305 mg. Total Fat: 66.4 g; Saturated fat: 13 g, Monounsaturated fat: 40.2 g, Polyunsaturated fat: 8.1 g.

DAY 18

Breakfast

---

1 serving **Pancake à la Popover**, page 216 (63.4 mg)
½ cup sliced bananas (1.125 mg)
½ cup **Fresh Berries**, page 362 (2.54 mg)
3 tablespoons natural maple syrup (5.4 mg)
8-ounce glass orange juice fortified with calcium (2.488 mg)

Midmorning Snack

¾ cup nonfat yogurt (98.7 mg)

Lunch

---

5 squares **Pizza Snacks**, page 39 (2.432 mg)
1 portion **Mixed Green Salad**, page 185, with **Oil and Vinegar Dressing**, page 209 (10.6 mg)
8-ounce glass orange juice fortified with calcium (2.488 mg)

Midafternoon Snack

---

1 medium apple (0 mg)

Dinner

---

1 serving **Peppercorn Kabobs**, page 71 (58.7 mg)
1 serving **Scalloped Potatoes**, page 289 (39 mg)
1 serving **Steamed Vegetables,** page 297 (17.2 mg)

Dessert

---

1 serving **Pears with Red Wine**, page 362 (1.985 mg)

Calories: 2,214. Sodium: 306 mg. Carbohydrate: 367.1 g. Fiber: 24.89 g. Protein: 59 g. Cholesterol: 110.33 mg. Calcium: 1,269 mg. Iron: 16.6 mg. Potassium: 4,409 mg. Total Fat: 62.3 g; Saturated fat: 10 g, Monounsaturated fat: 24 g, Polyunsaturated fat: 4.5 g.

DAY 19

Breakfast

1 serving **Spoon-Size Shredded Wheat**, (1 cup orange juice, ¾ cup nonfat milk, ¾ cup Spoon Size Shredded Wheat, 1 small banana) (100.4 mg)

Midmorning Snack

1 **Orange Banana Muffin**, page 222 (1.807 mg)
1 cup nonfat milk (126.2 mg)

Lunch

4 slices **Marinated Beef Strips**, page 37 (67 mg)
1 serving **Vegetable Sauté**, page 296 (8.999 mg)
½ cup **Basmati Pilaf**, page 135 (2.049 mg)

Midafternoon Snack

8-ounce glass orange juice fortified with calcium (2.488 mg)
1 ounce unsalted peanuts (about 20 nuts) (2.19 mg)

Dinner

4 ounces **Poached Salmon Steak with Dill Sauce**, page 121 (62.9 mg)
1 serving **Risotto Milanese**, page 137 (4.071 mg)
1 serving **Steamed Asparagus**, page 278 (4 mg)

Calories: 2,195. Sodium: 385.19 mg. Carbohydrate: 295.3 g. Fiber: 19.41 g. Protein: 93.3 g. Cholesterol: 76.27 mg. Calcium: 1,338 mg. Iron: 23.4 mg. Potassium: 4,354 mg. Total Fat: 75.2 g; Saturated fat: 21 g, Monounsaturated fat: 27.9 g, Polyunsaturated fat: 12.7 g.

DAY 20

Breakfast

1 **Oat Bran and Jam Muffin**, page 220 (20.8 mg)
1 serving **Brunch Compote**, page 366 (2 mg)
1 cup nonfat milk (126.2 mg)

Midmorning Snack

1 **Date Shake**, page 368 (29.9 mg)

Lunch

1 serving **Kung Pao Tofu**, page 162 (26 mg)
2 tablespoons **Mom's Mango Chutney**, page 302 (4.355 mg)
1 serving **Fried Rice**, page 138 (37.9 mg)
1 serving **Steamed Broccoli**, page 278 (20.4 mg)

Midafternoon Snack

1 serving **Vegetable Delight**, page 299 (9.777 mg)
8-ounce glass orange juice fortified with calcium (2.488 mg)

Dinner

1 serving **Incredible Chicken**, page 98 (91.7 mg)
2 slices **Roasted Garlic Toast**, page 35 (5.324 mg)
1 serving **Spinach with Mushrooms and Onions**, page 290 (39.6 mg)

Calories: 2,249. Sodium: 414.16 mg. Carbohydrate: 305.7 g. Fiber: 26.24 g. Protein: 99.2 g. Cholesterol: 190 mg. Calcium: 1,070 mg. Iron: 24.4 mg. Potassium: 3,971 mg. Total Fat: 80.4 g; Saturated fat: 16.3 g, Monounsaturated fat: 40.9 g, Polyunsaturated fat: 9.9 g.

DAY 21

THE DAY'S SODIUM COUNT: 356.3 MG

Breakfast

1 serving **Whole Wheat Waffle**, page 217 (34.5 mg)
3 tablespoons real maple syrup (5.4 mg)
1 tablespoon unsalted butter (optional) (1.5 mg)
  8-ounce glass orange juice fortified with calcium (2.488 mg)

Midmorning Snack

1 banana (1.18 mg)

Lunch

1 serving **Baba Ganouj**, page 38 (6.04 mg)
1 **Sandwich Bun**, page 258 (1.297 mg)
1 serving **Snake River Carrot Salad**, page 190 (68 mg)
  8-ounce glass orange juice fortified with calcium (2.488 mg)

Midafternoon Snack

1 serving **Afternoon Salad Snack**, page 209 (43.6 mg)

Dinner

1 serving **Hot Barbecued Country Pork Ribs**, page 84 (105.7 mg)
1 serving **Picnic Potato Salad**, page 195 (19.7 mg)
1 **Barbecued Corn Ear**, page 279 (21.9 mg)
1 serving **Grilled Zucchini**, page 293 (4.845 mg)

Dessert

1 serving **Strawberry Delight**, page 361 (37 mg)

Calories: 2,063. Sodium: 356.34 mg. Carbohydrate: 340.7 g. Fiber: 27.88 g. Protein: 66.4 g. Cholesterol: 187.44 mg. Calcium: 1,348 mg. Iron: 25 mg. Potassium: 4,683 mg. Total Fat: 60.5 g; Saturated fat: 19.3 g, Monounsaturated fat: 26.4 g, Polyunsaturated fat: 9.9 g.

DAY 22

Breakfast

¾ cup nonfat yogurt (98.7 mg)
½ cup **Fresh Berries**, page 362 (2.544 mg)
2 slices **Whole Wheat Toast**, page 234 (2.095 mg)
2 tablespoons **Quick Strawberry Jam**, page 312 (.373 mg)

Midmorning Snack

1 **Lemon and Currant Scone**, page 225 (11.9 mg)

Lunch

1 **Chicken Sandwich**, page 276 (63.9 mg)
1 ounce unsalted potato chips (2.268 mg)
1 serving **Carrot Sticks**, page 369 (21.4 mg)

Midafternoon Snack

1 medium apple (trace)
8-ounce glass orange juice fortified with calcium (2.488 mg)

Dinner

1 serving **Easy Pork Chop Casserole**, page 86 (117 mg)
½ cup **Steamed Spinach**, page 290 (12.1 mg)
1 **Dinner Roll**, page 256 (1.036 mg)

Dessert

1 serving **Black Bottom Pie**, page 324 (41.3 mg)

Calories: 2,157. Sodium: 377.22 mg. Carbohydrate: 334.6 g. Fiber: 23.56 g. Protein: 83.7 g. Cholesterol: 212.32 mg. Calcium: 985.6 mg. Iron: 15.1 mg. Potassium: 3,305 mg. Total Fat: 57.5 g; Saturated fat: 20 g, Monounsaturated fat: 15.6 g, Polyunsaturated fat: 6.8 g.

DAY 23

Breakfast

1 cup **Applesauce Oatmeal**, page 165 (9.434 mg)
½ cup nonfat milk (63.1 mg)
    8-ounce glass orange juice fortified with calcium (2.488 mg)

Midmorning Snack

2 slices **Whole Wheat Toast**, page 234 (2.095 mg)
2 tablespoons **Quick Strawberry Jam**, page 312 (0.373 mg)

Lunch

1 **Deviled Egg Sandwich**, page 276 (88.4 mg)
1 serving **Carrot Sticks**, page 369 (21.4 mg)
    8-ounce glass orange juice fortified with calcium (2.488 mg)

Midafternoon Snack

1 tomato, sliced (11.1 mg)
2 tablespoons **Balsamic Vinaigrette Dressing**, page 209 (.581 mg)

Dinner

1 serving **Pasta**, page 143 (7.4 mg)
1 serving **Homemade Marinara Sauce**, page 146 (22.7 mg)
1 serving **Mixed Green Salad**, page 185, with **Oil and Vinegar
    Dressing**, page 209 (10.6 mg)
1 **Dinner Roll**, page 256 (1 mg)

Calories: 2,168. Sodium: 241.82 mg. Fiber: 24.7 g. Total Sugars: 28.3 g. Cholesterol:
291.44 mg. Calcium: 1,070 mg. Potassium: 3,575 mg. Total Fat: 70.3 g; Saturated Fat:
11.6 g, Monounsaturated fat: 41.1 g, Polyunsaturated fat: 11.5 g.

DAY 24

Breakfast

1 serving **Don's Omelet**, page 129 (73 mg)
2 slices **Whole Wheat Toast**, page 234 (2 mg)
2 tablespoons **Best Berry Jam**, page 311 (.585 mg)
   8-ounce glass orange juice fortified with calcium (2.488 mg)

Midmorning Snack

1 slice **Sour Cream Coffee Cake**, page 224 (18.2 mg)
1 cup nonfat milk (126.2 mg)

Lunch

1 serving **Sweet Pepper Salad**, page 191 (17.2 mg)
1 slice **Cornbread**, page 249 (5.498 mg)
1 tablespoon honey (.84 mg)
   8-ounce glass orange juice fortified with calcium (2.488 mg)

Midafternoon Snack

1 serving **Fresh Fruit Salad**, page 204 (2 mg)

Dinner

1 serving **Meat and Rice Casserole**, page 81 (64.1 mg)
1 serving **Aunt Dee Dee's Favorite Persimmon Salad**, page 206
   (1.537 mg)
1 serving **Steamed Zucchini**, page 297 (1.321 mg)

Calories: 2,134. Sodium: 349.72 mg. Carbohydrate: 364.4 g. Fiber: 27.92 g. Protein: 61 g. Cholesterol: 284.38 mg. Calcium: 1,190 mg. Iron: 16 mg. Potassium: 4,230 mg. Total Fat: 56.8 g; Saturated fat: 11.2 g, Monounsaturated fat: 31 g, Polyunsaturated fat: 9 g.

DAY 25

Breakfast

1 serving **Spoon-Size Shredded Wheat**, (1 cup orange juice, ¾ cup nonfat milk, ¾ cup Spoon Size Shredded Wheat, 1 small banana) (100.4 mg)

Midmorning Snack

1 **Breakfast Roll**, page 255 (1.08 mg)
8-ounce glass orange juice fortified with calcium (2.488 mg)

Lunch

1 serving **Okra Soup with Wild Rice**, page 56 (60.8 mg)
1 serving **Chopped Vegetable**, page 185 (11.4 mg)

Midafternoon Snack

1 **Date Shake**, page 368 (29.9 mg)

Dinner

1 serving **Roasted Chicken with Grilled Red Bell Pepper Sauce**, page 96 (81.2 mg)
1 serving **Garlic Mashed Potatoes**, page 287 (18 mg)
1 serving **Steamed Asparagus**, page 278 (1.637 mg)

Dessert

1 **Apple Crisp,** page 335 (5.998 mg)

Calories: 1,882. Sodium: 310.29 mg. Carbohydrate: 303.2 g. Fiber: 33.86 g. Protein: 82.2 g. Cholesterol: 149.02 mg. Calcium: 947.3 mg. Iron: 19.6 mg. Potassium: 5,230 mg. Total Fat: 47.6 g; Saturated fat: 15.4 g, Monounsaturated fat: 22.7 g, Polyunsaturated fat: 5.2 g.

Day 26

Breakfast

1 **Cinnamon Raisin Bagel**, page 260 (1.991 mg)
2 tablespoons **Quick Strawberry Jam**, page 312 (.373 mg)
1 cup nonfat milk (126.2 mg)
1 cup cubed cantaloupe (14 mg)

Midmorning Snack

8-ounce glass orange juice fortified with calcium (2.488 mg)

Lunch

1 serving **Quick Nachos**, page 42 (17.8 mg)
1 serving **Burrito Deluxe**, page 274 (70.5 mg)
1 cup nonfat milk (126.2 mg)

Midafternoon Snack

1 serving **Vegetable Platter with Herb Dip**, page 38 (21 mg)

Dinner

1 serving **Pasta**, page 143 (7.4 mg)
1 serving **Sun-Dried Tomato Pesto**, page 145 (6.6 mg)
1 slice **Roasted Garlic Toast**, page 35 (2.662 mg)
1 serving **Mixed Green Salad**, page 185, with **Oil and Vinegar Dressing**, page 209 (10.6 mg)

Dessert

½ cup Citrus Sorbet (available in most grocery stores) (8 mg)

Calories: 2,053. Sodium: 415.79 mg. Fiber: 33.21 g. Total Sugars: 25.3 g. Cholesterol: 42.04 mg. Calcium: 1,318 mg. Potassium: 4,447 mg. Total Fat: 68.6 g; Saturated fat: 15.8 g. Monounsaturated fat: 37.9 g, Polyunsaturated fat: 8 g.

DAY 27

Breakfast

3 **Becky's Oatmeal Pancakes**, page 213 (60.3 mg)
1 cup **Fruit Compote**, page 363 (8.279 mg)
1 cup nonfat milk (126.2 mg)
1 tablespoon unsalted butter (optional) (1.562 mg)

Midmorning Snack

¼ cup **Don's Trail Mix**, page 369 (4.985 mg)

Lunch

1 serving **Leon's Pita Salad**, page 192 (22.1 mg)
1 medium apple, sliced (0 mg)
8-ounce glass orange juice fortified with calcium (2.488 mg)

Midafternoon Snack

1 ounce unsalted pretzels (80.9 mg)
8-ounce glass orange juice fortified with calcium (2.488 mg)

Dinner

1 serving **Herb-Roasted Wild Turkey**, page 110 (74.4 mg)
1 serving **Cherry Chutney**, page 302 (29.4 mg)
1 serving **Yams with Sauce**, page 300 (9.603 mg)
1 serving **Steamed Summer Squash**, page 292 (8.12 mg)
1 **Dinner Roll**, page 256 (1.036 mg)

Calories: 2,262. Sodium: 432.38 mg. Fiber: 38.09 g. Total Sugars: 57.4 g. Cholesterol: 199.71 mg. Calcium: 1,394 mg. Potassium: 5,292 mg. Total Fat: 55.6 g. Saturated fat: 17.1 g. Monounsaturated fat: 24.4 g. Polyunsaturated fat: 7 g.

DAY 28

Breakfast

1 serving **Spoon-Size Shredded Wheat** (1 cup orange juice, ¾ cup
nonfat milk, ¾ cup Spoon Size Shredded Wheat, 1 small banana)
(100.4 mg)

Midmorning Snack

1 cups seedless grapes (3.2 mg)

Lunch

1 serving **Picha's Thai Salad**, page 193 (14 mg)
1 **Pita Bread** (to make a sandwich with the Thai Salad), page 251
(1.771 mg)
8-ounce glass orange juice fortified with calcium (2.488 mg)

Midafternoon Snack

1 **Gingersnap**, page 347 (3.645 mg)
8-ounce glass orange juice fortified with calcium (2.488 mg)

Dinner

1 serving **"Beef Wellington,"** page 77 (110.5 mg)
1 serving **Mixed Green Salad**, page 185, with **Balsamic Vinaigrette
Dressing**, page 209 (11.8 mg)
½ cup frozen unsalted green peas, boiled in unsalted water (69.6 mg)

Dessert

½ cup Citrus Sorbet (available in most grocery stores) (8 mg)

Calories: 1,973. Sodium: 327.85 mg. Carbohydrate: 324.4 g. Fiber: 21.73 g. Protein: 57.6 g.
Cholesterol: 113.83 mg. Calcium: 1,419 mg. Iron: 16.1 mg. Potassium: 4,116 mg. Total Fat:
58.1 g; Saturated fat: 10.4 g, Monounsaturated fat: 23.6 g, Polyunsaturated fat: 7.8 g.

HOLIDAY MENUS

❖ ❖ ❖ ❖ ❖ ❖ ❖ ❖

The holidays are generally associated with traditional meals at our house. I suspect this is true at yours, too. Use the following guidelines to devise your own menus.

LABOR DAY

It's fall, and summer foods are giving way to winter foods. Fire up the barbecue and enjoy the change of weather and diet.

SODIUM PER SINGLE MEAL: 193.23 MG.

Salad

1 serving **San Francisco Fisherman's Wharf Salad**, page 207 (62 mg)

Entrée

1 serving **Barbecued Lemon Chicken**, page 105 (73.8 mg)
1 **Barbecued Corn Ear**, page 279 (21.9 mg)
1 serving **Banana Squash**, page 291 (12 mg)
1 **Dinner Roll**, page 256 (1.036 mg)

Dessert

1 **Don's Special Brownie**, page 356 (7.8 mg)
1 serving **Raspberry Sauce**, page 180 (14.7 mg)

Calories: 1,170. Sodium: 182.11 mg. Carbohydrate: 160.6 g. Fiber: 11.27 g. Protein: 48 g. Cholesterol: 117.65 mg. Calcium: 213.9 mg. Iron: 8.117 mg. Potassium: 2,152 mg. Total Fat: 42 g; Saturated fat: 11.2 g, Monounsaturated fat: 22 g, Polyunsaturated fat: 5.9 g.

THANKSGIVING DINNER

The total sodium count for a Thanksgiving dinner could skyrocket if you're not careful. Here is a suggested menu based on what I serve for Thanksgiving. Of course, Thanksgiving dinner at your house may include different foods. The following is only a guide for you to use to ensure that your sodium count for the day remains within your target range.

SODIUM PER SINGLE MEAL: 133.7 MG

Salad

1 serving **Cranberry Raisin Salad**, page 208 (8.405 mg)

Entrée

3 ounces fresh turkey breast meat, no skin* (54.5 mg)
1 serving **Yams with Sauce**, page 300 (9.603 mg)
½ cup unsalted green peas, boiled in unsalted water (3.625 mg)
½ cup **Cranberry Sauce**, page 303 (1.077 mg)
1 **Dinner Roll**, page 256 (1.036 mg)

Dessert

1 slice **Don's Pumpkin Pie**, page 320 (43.9 mg)
3 tablespoons pressurized whipped cream† (11.7 mg)

Calories: 1,017. Sodium: 133.7 mg. Carbohydrate: 174.4 g. Fiber: 16.42 g. Protein: 42.6 g. Cholesterol: 138.83 mg. Calcium: 272.1 mg. Iron: 9.768 mg. Potassium: 1,693 mg. Total Fat: 18.8 g; Saturated fat: 8.4 g, Monounsaturated fat: 7.2 g, Polyunsaturated fat: 1.7 g.

*Packaged and frozen turkeys are often supplemented with salt, salted butter, or even MSG. Read packaging label carefully before buying other than a fresh bird.
†Many canned whipped cream products offer low fat and low sodium.

CHRISTMAS SUPPER WITH BEEF WELLINGTON

Holiday meals with traditional fare often can prove difficult to plan if you must restrict your intake of sodium or fats or sugars. Sodium and fats are the toughest since most holiday chefs pour on the salt via boiled vegetables, meat seasoning, butter, sauces, etc. To get around that, I developed this Christmas supper that satisfies my "lust" for a great meal on Christmas Day and still satisfies the tastebuds of guests. I excluded a dinner roll, which often requires butter, since the "bread" is here in the form of Yorkshire Pudding, which is part of the Beef Wellington.

SODIUM PER SINGLE MEAL: 156.42 MG

Salad

1 serving **Aunt Dee Dee's Favorite Persimmon Salad**, page 206 (1.537 mg)

Entrée

1 serving **"Beef Wellington,"** page 77 (117.9 mg)
1 serving **Charlotte's Potatoes**, page 286 (6.494 mg)
1 serving **Steamed Broccoli**, page 278 (20.4 mg)
½ cup raw green peas, or unsalted frozen green peas, cooked in unsalted butter (3.625 mg)

Dessert

1 serving **Huguenot Torte**, page 335 (13.9 mg)

Calories: 953. Sodium: 156.42 mg. Carbohydrate: 123.9 g. Fiber: 17.04 g. Protein: 36.6 g. Cholesterol: 128.75 mg. Calcium: 262.3 mg. Iron: 7.284 mg. Potassium: 1,906 mg. Total Fat: 38.3 g. Saturated fat: 3.6 g. Monounsaturated fat: 14.5 g. Polyunsaturated fat: 5.3 g.

EASTER SUPPER

Ham is generally loaded with sodium and therefore it is nearly impossible to serve it for Easter dinner. I love leg of lamb and so I have replaced the Easter ham with the more succulent lamb.

SODIUM PER SINGLE MEAL: 150.2 MG

Salad

1 serving **Mandarin-Avocado Salad**, page 205 (9.392 mg)

Entrée

4 ounces **Barbecued Butterflied Leg of Lamb**, page 89 (92.8 mg), served with mint jelly (0 mg)

1 serving **Red Potatoes with Rosemary and Spinach**, page 288 (37 mg)

½ cup fresh green peas or unsalted frozen green peas boiled in unsalted water (3.625 mg)

1 **Dinner Roll**, page 256 (1.036 mg)

1 tablespoon **Quick Strawberry Jam**, page 312 (.187 mg)

Dessert

1 slice **French Apple Pie**, page 321 (9.835 mg)

Calories: 1,151. Sodium: 150.23 mg. Carbohydrate: 152.7 g. Fiber: 15.29 g. Protein: 44.4 g. Cholesterol: 159.35 mg. Calcium: 176.4 mg. Iron: 11 mg. Potassium: 2,291 mg. Total Fat: 43.5 g; Saturated fat: 18.8 g, Monounsaturated fat: 17.6 g, Polyunsaturated fat: 3.4 g.

MOTHER'S DAY

No joke! Take Mom out to dinner tonight. Here's what you do step by step:

Let Mom know you're taking her out. When you clear that hurdle, ask her where she'd "love" to go for dinner—we're talking a nice restaurant, now.

Once that is established, call the restaurant and ask if they'll prepare a no-salt, low-sodium meal for whomever needs it, you or Mom or someone else in your party. Make sure they understand that by no sodium you don't want food cooked in butter, with baking soda, baking powder, or sulfites (some restaurants will put sulfites on lettuce to keep it fresh). You want no MSG or packaged foods (like bread). And then ask them if you can bring your own bread (if you want bread with dinner). Most restaurants will gladly accommodate you.

Once in the restaurant, make sure the waiter/waitress understands you called ahead. Then make sure again the kitchen understands what sodium is. Some chefs believe that sea salt, for instance, isn't salt, so, remember to double-check. Then enjoy. We do it often, and it's worth the effort.

MEMORIAL DAY AFTERNOON PICNIC

This is often a holiday when families travel to favorite weekend havens because the weather has changed from spring to summer. Picnics and outdoor barbecues come alive again. Our favorite Memorial Day outing usually involves potato salad, chilled baked chicken legs, and fresh corn on the cob.

SODIUM PER SINGLE MEAL: 203 MG

Salad

1 serving **River Guide Black-Eyed Pea Salad**, page 196 (42 mg)

Entrée

2 **Baked Chicken Legs**, page 101 (111.4 mg)
1 cup diced cantaloupe or other melon (14.4 mg)
1 serving **Picnic Potato Salad**, page 195 (19.7 mg)

Dessert

1 serving **Applesauce Cake**, page 329 (15.5 mg)

Calories: 1,186. Sodium: 203.01 mg. Carbohydrate: 137.6 g. Fiber: 13.97 g. Protein: 39.4 g. Cholesterol: 130.54 mg. Calcium: 220 mg. Iron: 7.347 mg. Potassium: 2,105 mg. Total Fat: 57 g; Saturated fat: 8.6 g, Monounsaturated fat: 37.9 g, Polyunsaturated fat: 6.4 g.

FATHER'S DAY

Father's Day is a time for a "macho" meal. You can adapt this menu to use beef, chicken, fish, or just burgers. But if Dad likes pork roast or ribs, this is worth the effort.

SODIUM PER SINGLE MEAL: 157.4 MG

Salad

1 serving **Cranberry Raisin Salad**, page 208 (8.405 mg)

Entrée

1 serving **Pork Roast Barbecue with Don's Barbecue Sauce**, page 82 (107.6 mg)
1 serving **Barbecued Corn Ear**, page 279 (21.9 mg)
1 serving **Homemade Applesauce**, page 360 (.854 mg)

Dessert

1 serving **Carrot Cake**, page 330 (18.7 mg)

Calories: 1,270. Sodium: 157.38 mg. Carbohydrate: 238.8 g. Fiber: 24.26 g. Protein: 46.6 g. Cholesterol: 139.17 mg. Calcium: 233.9 mg. Iron: 8.761 mg. Potassium: 2,635 mg. Total Fat: 31.4 g; Saturated fat: 5.1 g, Monounsaturated fat: 9.1 g, Polyunsaturated fat: 5.1 g.

FOURTH OF JULY

Independence Day brings memories of corn on the cob, hot dogs, hamburgers, barbecued chicken legs, fruit salads, ice-cold watermelon, and picnics with friends and families. If yours is an outing with barbecued hamburgers in mind, take along your own sandwich buns, beef, and salt-free herbs and spices for your burger, corn, and/or salad.

SODIUM PER SINGLE MEAL: 121.6 MG

Salad

1 serving **Fresh Fruit Salad**, page 204 (13.1 mg)

Entrée

1 serving **Barbecued Cheeseburger**, page 264 (67.5 mg)
    (includes **Sandwich Bun**, page 258)
1 serving **Barbecued Corn Ear**, page 279 (21.9 mg)
1 serving **July Fourth Green Beans**, page 281 (10.9 mg)

Dessert

1 serving **Marlene's Apple Pie**, page 323 (8.17 mg)

Calories: 1,659. Sodium: 121.59 mg. Carbohydrate: 217.2 g. Fiber: 23.92 g. Protein: 41.4 g. Cholesterol: 103.51 mg. Calcium: 217.4 mg. Iron: 12.6 mg. Potassium: 3,175 mg. Total Fat: 79.6 g; Saturated fat: 24.4 g, Monounsaturated fat: 39.6 g, Polyunsaturated fat: g.

WEIGHTS, MEASUREMENTS, AND VOLUME CONVERSION

	USA	Europe
Flour	1/4 cup	30 gm.
	1/2 cup	60 gm.
	1 cup	125 gm.
Sugar or Butter	1/4 cup	60 gm.
	1/2 cup	125 gm.
	1 cup	250 gm.
Liquids	1/4 cup	5 cl.
	1/2 cup	1.25 dl.
	3/4 cup	1.8 dl.
	1 cup	2.5 dl.
	4 cups (1 quart)	1 liter

STANDARD MEASURING DEVICES FOR COOKING

UNITS	US EQUIVALENT	METRIC EQUIVALENT
cup, liquid	8 ounces, liquid	237 ml.
quart, dry (US)	2 pints, dry	500 gm.
quart, liquid (US)	2 pints, liquid	948 ml.
tablespoon, liquid	3 teaspoons	15 ml.
teaspoon, liquid	1/3 tablespoon	5 ml.
tablespoon, dry	3 teaspoons	12 gm.
teaspoon, dry	1/3 tablespoon	4 gm.

INDEX